FROM
METAPHYSICS
TO MIDRASH

Indiana Studies in Biblical Literature
Herbert Marks, general editor

FROM METAPHYSICS TO MIDRASH

Myth, History, and the Interpretation of Scripture in Lurianic Kabbala

S H A U L   M A G I D

INDIANA UNIVERSITY PRESS
Bloomington and Indianapolis

This book is a publication of

Indiana University Press
601 North Morton Street
Bloomington, IN 47404-3797 USA

http://iupress.indiana.edu

Telephone orders 800-842-6796
Fax orders   812-855-7931
Orders by e-mail iuporder@indiana.edu

The paper used in this publication meets the minimum requirements of
American National Standard for Information Sciences—Permanence of Paper
for Printed Library Materials, ANSI Z39.48-1984.

Manufactured in the United States of America

Library of Congress Cataloging-in-Publication Data

Magid, Shaul, date
From metaphysics to midrash : myth, history, and the
interpretation of Scripture in Lurianic Kabbala / Shaul Magid.
p. cm. — (Indiana studies in biblical literature)
Includes bibliographical references and index.
ISBN 978-0-253-35088-6 (cl : alk. paper) 1. Luria, Isaac ben Solomon,
1534–1572. 2. Cabala—History. 3. Bible. O.T. Pentateuch—Criticism,
interpretation, etc, Jewish. 4. Metaphysics. 5. Other (Philosophy)
6. Tsefat (Israel)—Religion—16th century. I. Title.
BM525.L835M34 2008
222'.1068092—dc22
          2007040650

1 2 3 4 5 13 12 11 10 09 08

To Dovid Din, in memoriam

. . . to exaggerate the essential and leave the obvious vague.
Vincent van Gogh

A divine voice (*bat kol*) declared, "Concealed matters went forth
from within Me."

יצתה בת קול ואמרה ממני יצאו כבושים
Babylonian Talmud Sotah 10b

CONTENTS

ACKNOWLEDGMENTS

The prehistory of this book began in 1982 in the Mekor Barukh neighborhood of Jerusalem. It was there, at Yeshivat ha-Hayyim ve ha-Shalom, that I began attending the afternoon seminars or *shiurim* in Lurianic Kabbala (*kitvei ARI*) by the renowned Jerusalem kabbalist Ha-Rav Mordechai Attia. During the three years I studied with Rav Attia I gained preliminary access to the complex world of Lurianic Kabbala and its literature according to the tradition he received from his grandfather and Ha-Rav Mordechai Sharabi of Beit El. I am eternally grateful to Rav Attia for the breadth and depth of his knowledge and, as important, his generosity of spirit. During that period Shabbatei Teicher was a true friend, teacher, and guide and thus deserves recognition.

The history of this book began with an essay I published on Lurianic Kabbala and the Garden of Eden that appeared in *AJS Review* in 1996. It was then that I began to think seriously about a larger project on Lurianic Kabbala and the interpretation of Scripture. There are many people who deserve thanks and recognition from the years this book took shape. A few chapters were written during a sabbatical year in Paris where I was fortunate to have made the acquaintance of Paul Fenton. Moshe Mykoff remains a cherished *havruta*, even from afar. His journey remains inspiring. Menahem Kallus has been generous with his knowledge of the Lurianic tradition and its sources and the many conversations with him are greatly appreciated. Elliot Wolfson has been supportive throughout and was always willing to offer advice and suggestions from his deep knowledge of Kabbala and philosophy. His succinct comments on chapter 4 were particularly instructive. Ben Sommer's corrections and comments on the biblical portion of my survey of Lurianic myth saved me from some embarrassing errors. For the past three years Nathaniel Berman has been a steady study partner in Kabbala (and beyond) and has enriched my own understanding of the Zohar and its commentaries. Zalman Schachter-Shalomi has been a true teacher and friend. His trust and support are greatly cherished.

Many have commented on drafts of chapters or have simply been a part of the larger intellectual and spiritual process that resulted in this book. They are: Daniel Abrams, Aryeh Cohen, Alan Cooper, James Diamond, Jason Fickel, Lawrence Fine, Talya Fishman, Yehuda Gellman, Pinhas Giller, Aubrey Glazer, Gloria Greenfield, Joel Hecker, Shai Held, Boaz Huss, Moshe Idel, Zvi Ish-Shalom, Martin Kavka, Kathryn Lofton,

Yehuda Mirsky, David Novak, Peter Ochs, Andrea and Steve Peskoff, Or Rose, Miryam Segal, Eliezer Shore, Ely Stillman, and Yossi Turner.

I came to Indiana University in the middle of this project. The Religion Department and Borns Jewish Studies Program at IU have been rich intellectual homes and have given me the opportunity to see this through to completion. In particular I would like to thank David Brakke, Constance Furey, David Haberman, Richard Miller, Michael Morgan, Jeffrey Veidlinger, Mary Jo Weaver, and Steven Weitzman. Many thanks to Herb Marks, editor of the series on biblical interpretation at Indiana University Press and professor of Comparative Literature at IU for seeing this project for what it was and for his meticulous critique and comments, particularly on chapter 5. Thanks to Janet Rabinowitch and Dee Mortensen of IU Press, to Joyce Rappaport for her copyediting, and to Hila Ratzabi, again, for the index.

To my partner Nancy Levene for always pushing me to places unknown and for going there with me. To my adult children Yehuda, Chisda, and Miriam, for finding their own way and for our cherished Kinneret, for helping us find ours. This book is dedicated to Dovid Din (d. 1985), may his memory be a blessing, a unique figure whose short but intense life touched many more people than he even knew. To me he was a friend, a teacher, a guide, a fellow traveler, someone who feared nothing of the spirit. Like masters of a previous era, he wrote almost nothing yet his words and his presence still resonate more than twenty years after his death. Sometimes I think he was born too late, sometimes I think he was born too early. In any case, without him I would be a completely different person. This is my belated gift to him.

ABBREVIATIONS

AdY	Adam Yashar. Jerusalem: Yeshivat Ahavat Shalom, 1994.
EH	*ʿEtz Hayyim.* Jerusalem: Makor Hayyim, n.d.
EHD	*Etz ha-Daʿat Tov.* Jerusalem: Wagshal, 1985.
LiT	*Likkutei Torah.* Vilna, 1880.
MeS	*Mevo Shearim.* Jerusalem: Gross Brothers, n.d.
OT	*ʿOlat Tamid.* Jerusalem: Yeshivat Ahavat Shalom, 1997.
OzH	*ʿOzrot Hayyim.* Jerusalem: Yeshivat ha-Hayyim ve ha-Shalom, n.d.
PEH	*Pri ʿEtz Hayyim.* Jerusalem: Makor Hayyim, n.d.
SeD	*Sefer ha-Derushim.* Jerusalem: Yeshivat Ahavat Shalom, 1996.
SeL	*Sefer ha-Likkutim.* Jerusalem: Lifshitz Brothers, 1913.
SeG	*Sefer ha-Gilgulim.* Jerusalem, 1903.
ShG	*Shaʿar ha-Gilgulim* with Bnei Aaron. Jerusalem, 1990.
SeK	*Sefer ha-Kavvanot.* Jerusalem: Yeshivat Ahavat Shalom, 2004.
ShK	*Shaʿar ha-Kavvanot.* Jerusalem: Makor Hayyim, n.d.
ShKY	*Shaʿar ha-Kavvanot ha-Yashan.* Jerusalem: Ahavat Shalom Institute, 2004.
ShH	*Shaʿar ha-Hakdamot.* Jerusalem, 1901.
ShM	*Shaʿar ha-Mitzvot.* Jerusalem, n.d.
ShMH	*Shaʿar Mamrei Hazal.* Jerusalem, 1985.
ShMR	*Shaʿar Mamrei Rashbi.* Jerusalem, 1985.
ShP	*Shaʿar ha-Pesukim.* Jerusalem: Lifshitz Brothers, 1913.
ShRK	*Shaʿar Ruah ha-Kodesh.* Jerusalem: Yeshivat ha-Hayyim ve ha-Shalom, n.d.
ZHR	*Zohar ha-Rakiya.* Jerusalem: Yeshivat Shaʿar ha-Shamayim.
Gen.	Genesis
Ex.	Exodus
Lev.	Leviticus
Num.	Numbers
Deut.	Deuteronomy
Josh.	Joshua
I Sam.	First Samuel
II Sam.	Second Samuel
I Kgs.	First Kings
II Kgs.	Second Kings
Isa.	Isaiah

Jer.   Jeremiah
Ezek.   Ezekiel
Ps.   Psalms
Lam.   Lamentations
Eccles.   Ecclesiastes
Dan.   Daniel
b.T.   Babylonian Talmud
p.T.   Palestinian Talmud

From Metaphysics to Midrash

INTRODUCTION
Kabbala, New Historicism, and the
Question of Boundaries

Freedom is only present where there is no other for me that
is not myself.
—Hegel, *The Encyclopedia of the Philosophical Sciences*

From heresy to deviation to degeneration to syncretism, the
notion of the different which claims to be the same or, pro-
jected internally, the disguised difference within, has produced a rich vocabulary of denial and estrangement. For in
each case, a theory of difference, when applied to the proximate "other," is but another way of phrasing a theory of
"self."
—Jonathan Z. Smith, "Differential Equations:
On Constructing the Other"

This is a book about the nexus between Kabbala (in particular Lurianic
Kabbala) and the interpretation of Scripture. More than that, it is a book
that views scriptural interpretation as literature, a series of texts that
emerge from the reading of other texts but that also stand alone as a testament to how a particular community understands itself, its station in
history, and its legacy through the lens of its literary canon. It also argues
that textual traditions are not only produced *by* or *from* history but, in
fact, produce history themselves—that the mythic world of Lurianic Kabbala is both a response to, and a construction of, the historical reality in
which it lived; furthermore, its canonical status influences the way future
generations understand their own historical station. If the textual tradition becomes canonical (as Lurianic Kabbala certainly does) the "his-

tory" it produces often becomes normative and the underlying historical circumstances that produced that history are often effaced by the powerful myth that constructs its own "historical" trajectory.

The historicity of Lurianic Kabbala as canonical is well-documented, as are its metaphysical assumptions and influences. What interests me is, first, to explore the exegetical imagination of this tradition and the affiliations between metaphysics and that imagination. My second aim is to examine factors that enabled these texts to work—that is, to learn the nature of their "connection" to Scripture, and to understand how Scripture worked for them to create a historical reality refracted through the biblical narrative.

If the Hebrew Bible is the unquestioned canon of Judaism (a canon that is, of course, re-created and "rewritten" constantly), then all subsequent "canons" will need the Bible to refract and reflect their own specific agendas. But the Bible is much more than a *text* for these traditional communities: it is the lens through which one fashions oneself, how one sees, and does not see, God, and is a template that enables one to decipher the real from the illusory.

I begin with the assumption of canonical layers—the Hebrew Bible and Lurianic Kabbala—each with its own force and influence. In between, of course, is the whole of classical Judaism from the rabbis and their intellectual descendants, the Zohar and subsequent Kabbala, Jewish philosophy, pietism, Musar literature, and so on. This book will examine a specific moment in the unfolding and ever-changing canonicity of the Bible in Judaism, viewing that moment in context but, more importantly, examining how the literature produced from (and in response to) that moment often challenges, subverts, and sometimes undermines what precedes it for reasons that are rooted in particular communal identities.

What were these texts (the Lurianic interpretation of Scripture) connected to that enabled them to succeed, to convince, and to prosper? Why should we be interested in this particular exegetical trajectory? Part of the answer lies in the particular nexus of Judaism, Christianity, and Islam in sixteenth-century Safed that informed and may have partially driven this exegetical approach. While this nexus was quite fleeting (lasting no more than thirty or forty years), the influence of Lurianic Kabbala was and remains widespread.[1] Moreover, we are witnessing a new nexus of these three traditions, quite different from theirs (modernity separates us from them) but containing enough similarities to constitute a "contemporary concern." I aspire, then, to function as a critic—a concerned reader who reads the past with a curiosity about the way it produces the present and can help us understand the present anew. Reading historically is thus never reading solely about the past—it is (also) about reading and (re)creating the present. I assume that the past's own rendering of its own past essentially does the same thing.[2]

Much has been written on the nature and history of Jewish biblical exegesis.[3] Much less work has been done on the nature and agenda of kabbalistic interpretation of Scripture, especially after the Middle Ages.[4] I make a distinction here between kabbalistic hermeneutics more generally and the more focused enterprise of scriptural commentary. The first concerns the way kabbalists read and interpret all texts (including the Bible); the second is how kabbalists, as biblical exegetes, offer new readings of biblical narratives through the lens of their metaphysical and cosmological systems. What is at stake here is not simply how kabbalists interpret Scripture as an intellectual or spiritual exercise, but (also) how this interpretation functions as a critical tool to address issues and events in their contemporary world.[5] This requires, even necessitates, creating the Bible in one's own image.[6]

This book is about the interpretation of Scripture filtered through the lens of an intricate metaphysical system developed by the Jewish mystic and metaphysician Isaac Luria (d. 1572) and his circle. It offers an alternative reading of this literature liberated from the tendency to view it solely within its internal metaphysics and logic. Treating Lurianic exegetical writings as imaginative and fictive literature, I explore how this "literature" may be working out contemporary issues and in so doing, may be revaluing canonical literature and tradition.[7] In particular, I argue, Lurianic exegesis presents a mythic way of envisioning the relationship between Judaism and its surrounding culture(s), thinning the more opaque and ostensibly irreconcilable walls separating Jew and Gentile, man and woman, true religion and false religion, rationalism and mysticism, the human and the divine. This is not to say that Lurianic Kabbala is progressive in any conventional sense. It is not. It is only to say that the context in which it developed, especially in its formative period in sixteenth-century Safed, enabled its authors, or perhaps compelled them, to re-evaluate the dualistic universe that pervaded earlier Kabbala. More to the point, deconstructing the metaphysical dualism in Lurianic teaching in my view reflects a social reality that may have in some instances necessitated, and in others merely allowed for, viewing the world in a different way.

Throughout this book I argue that it is not only that Luria and his circle were responding to cultural and religious changes through their writings (this is an obvious point made by other scholars reading earlier Jewish literature).[8] Rather, it is that their exegetical agenda offers a revaluation of Scripture driven by the local nexus of the three religions and their relationship in the historiosophic unfolding of redemption. Luria's stature as an inspired reader of Scripture and the authority that emerged around that claim makes his rereading of the Bible canonical. This is also informed by his historical station living a generation after the expulsion, a time that witnessed a sharp demographic shift eastward resulting in the first systematic re-population of Erez Israel by Jews since late antiquity. Luria and his circle viewed their own station in history through the Bible, reifying it to conform to its messianic agenda.[9]

The phenomenon of rewriting the Bible through strong reading raises questions about particularity and universality, a dichotomy that challenges ancient Israelite religion and later Judaism from their inception. Substantiating the claim that Lurianic reading represents a moment of religious transformation—that is, how Lurianic Judaism (and it is, in some sense "a" Judaism) defines the "other," in particular the Christian and Muslim—requires an attentiveness to the philosophical, hermeneutical, and historical–cultural dimensions of Lurianic thinking. While there are some seminal studies on the literary overlaps between Jewish, Christian, and Islamic writing, little has been written that addresses how cultural influences may have influenced and infiltrated the thought processes of Lurianic thinking or Kabbala more generally.[10]

These encounters and connections will be examined from three distinct but interrelated perspectives: the philosophical, the hermeneutical, and the historical. From a philosophical perspective, this book explores the issue of exclusion and inclusion as concomitant with particularism and universalism. Judaism's notion of the covenant, beginning in the Hebrew Bible, is constructed to separate Israel from all other nations, viewing them as a distinct entity, uniquely "chosen among the nations."[11] This uniqueness quickly, and all too easily, lends itself to a doctrine of exclusivity whereby Israel defines itself, in part, by who they are not, producing the "other" who is often maligned as spiritually (and in Kabbala, ontologically) inferior and deficient. Yet from the outset there is a tension in that orientation emerging most prominently in the Hebrew Prophets. Some scholars argue that the utopianism and latent universalism implicit in some prophetic teachings undermines the more particularistic doctrine of the Pentateuch (and later the rabbis), while others claim it complements such claims. Nevertheless, it would seem that Kabbala's metaphysical and ontological rendering of classical Judaism solidifies the exclusivist doctrine of separation and distinction. Often this is the case. However, I argue that in Lurianic Kabbala ontology is turned against itself because one of its basic premises is that all things contain their opposite; consequently, all otherness is only a temporary instantiation of the self. Thus the liminal nature of Lurianic metaphysics lends itself to complicate the exclusivist doctrine of religion (separating Jew and gentile) and gender (separating, by essentializing, the masculine from the feminine).

The hermeneutical perspective reads Lurianic Kabbala simultaneously as exegesis and literature. That is, it looks at the way Lurianic metaphysics emerges out of Scripture, and then uses its metaphysics as a grid to reread Scripture. In some ways I argue that Lurianic exegesis resembles what Michael Fishbane (describing Buber's *Moses*) calls "hermeneutical transference," "the projection of one's life agenda onto the text."[12] While Lurianic Kabbala is not known for its scriptural exegesis (for example, there is scant scriptural exegesis in *ʿEtz Hayyim*, arguably the foundational text in the Lurianic corpus), numerous exegetical texts, often viewed as subsidiary to the metaphysical or ritually oriented texts, exists. I argue that these exegetical texts are doing more than simply applying Lurianic cosmology to verses in Scripture. Rather, they revalue Scripture itself through the lens of a metascriptural system of *sephirot* and *parzufim* (which, of course, is loosely structured around the biblical narrative). In this sense, these exegetical texts are not ancillary to the metaphysical literature but, in fact, may be the engine that drives the entire project. By means of reconstructing Judaism through a revaluation of Scripture, Lurianic Kabbala offers its most potent and longlasting critique of tradition.

The historical perspective of this book is "New Historicist" in orientation. I am reading Lurianic Kabbala as literature, suggesting that it both reflects and constructs historical narratives.[13] The interpretations of biblical narratives in this literature can be viewed as windows to view communal dilemmas and struggles, and to regard its cosmology a reification of new social conditions.[14] Moreover, this exegetical literature evaluates anew Judaism's understanding of itself and the "other" that confronts it. Here I assume an exegetical construction whereby a text both reflects the reader and the imaginative desires of what the reader wants to be read into the text.[15] Lurianic metaphysics, built from Scripture, also serves to reimagine Scripture in its own image in a way that addresses the dilemmas of its local culture and context.

As mentioned above, my underlying assumption is that sixteenthcentury Safed (at least until the second third of that century) was a distinctive nexus between Judaism, Christianity, and Islam.[16] The Islamic context was the newly founded Ottoman Empire, beginning in 1516, that was progressive and unusually tolerant of its Jewish citizenry. The Christian context was embodied in conversos, mostly Portuguese, who migrated to Safed in the early part of the century in order to reenter a Judaism they were forced, or chose, to abandon in Iberia. The Jewish context is the fact that at this time Safed served as one of the centers of Jewish scholarship. During the short span of about fifty years, Safed produced the *Shulkhan Arukh* (Code of Jewish Law) by Joseph Karo which would become the standard legal code in modern Judaism; the kabbalistic writings of Moses Cordovero whose *Pardes Rimonim* was an unmatched collection and reevaluation of medieval Kabbala; and the creative teachings of Isaac Luria, whose influence intellectually, liturgically, and ritually influenced the Sabbatean heresy in the seventeenth century, the Italian Renaissance, early modern Christian Kabbala, Lithuanian spirituality, Hasidism, and contemporary Jewry. It is not my intention to enter into the scholarly debate about the impact of Lurianic teaching more generally but simply to point out that sixteenth-century Safed provided a distinctive cultural, literary, and historical moment not often seen in the history of Jewish literature that had a profound impact on Jewish life and letters for centuries to come.

My premise is that the Islamic and Christian (via conversos) contexts of sixteenth-century Safed influenced Lurianic teaching. This is not to say that Luria or his disciples were overtly influenced by Islamic or Christian religion or sociality (although I do make certain claims in that direction) nor that Lurianic Kabbala is a direct response to contemporary Islam and Christianity (although I also make certain claims in that direction). I prefer to see the Lurianic relationship to these two cultures–religions as fluid and multivalent. That is, I suggest that some of the major themes in Luria's rendering of Scripture are concerned with ideas directly relevant to both Christianity and Islam, and Israel's relationship to those systems and communities; I maintain that this attention is not accidental. The challenges that both Christianity and Islam posed to the Jews in sixteenth-century Safed were not lost on the Lurianic circle.[17]

The five main instances of "otherness" explored in this book are: (1) sin, (2) conversion, (3) gender, (4) Gentile prophecy (that is, the status of Gentile religion as a prophetic tradition), and (5) incarnation, traversing the ostensibly opaque barrier separating the human and the divine. In each of these cases, Lurianic exegesis exhibits resonances of either Christianity or Islam without ever mentioning either religious tradition or culture. In constructing a new Judaism in light of the cultural and theological challenges in the presence of both "others," Lurianic Kabbala absorbs and transforms the others into itself, refashioning them as a part of its dialectical and redemptive metaphysical worldview.

A Brief Statement on Method

On the question of historical method, any close reader of these texts can justifiably contest the above claim by pointing out that Lurianic Kabbala seems utterly uninterested in the realia of material existence. Yet we know the mystics in question were very active members of their society and many took on rabbinical and advisory functions in their communities. My assumption, therefore, is that their metaphysical writings, while void of any blatant reference to local issues and controversies were, in fact, the occasion (often through the traditional mode of scriptural exegesis) to reconstruct tradition (sometimes radically) in response to the challenges that they faced, in particular, the challenge of the returning conversos.

This interpretive challenge is not new in Kabbala. It is appropriate here to mention the cautionary words of Ronald Keiner on this question regarding the Zohar:

> When does a textual homily become a statement of contemporary affairs? When does a symbolic discussion of Ishmael's role in the *sephirotic* world also serve as a comment on the theosophic role of the Ishmaelities, i.e. the Muslims, and their faith? We cannot always know, but at the same time it would be imprudent to assume that all discussions of the biblical Ishmael, even when transformed into a *sephirotic* symbol, necessarily impart a judgment concerning the world of Islam. It would seem we are confronted with a situation in which the sum of the whole is greater than the constituent parts.[18]

Keiner is certainly correct that we must be careful to avoid the "McCarthy factor," seeing what we want to see in every textual nuance or inference, or, even more broadly, to make what appears to us to be obvious connections between exegetical or *sephirotic* references and the context in which they are made. Having said that, this care should not prevent us from examining the abundance of what may seem like circumstantial evidence (which is all we will ever have since these authors rarely tell us what they thought about their world in any explicit way).[19] I suggest that these exegetical or metaphysical comments may have social import and, more importantly, that the exegetical enterprise is a way of reenvisioning canonical literature so that these social changes can be integrated into tradition.[20] Moreover, we also need to consider to what extent these references may be inadvertently responding to current, and often changing, attitudes toward the "other."

In this regard I have greatly benefited from the work of Stephen Greenblatt and the New Historicists. Navigating the complex relationship between literature and the construction of the social world, Greenblatt notes "the complex circulation between the social dimension of an aesthetic strategy and the aesthetic dimension of a social strategy."[21] I argue that Lurianic exegesis is a fictional and thus aesthetic comment on the so-

cial reality of Safed, one that compels the reader to think carefully about
the relationship between "the social presence to the world *of* the literary
text and the social presence of the world *in* the literary text."[22]

I argue that the Lurianic exegesis of Scripture is not merely "commentary" in the classical sense but constitutes an independent body of
literature distinct from its more well-known metaphysic literature. The
myth and alternate narrative it propagates has brought me close to the
assumption that historical context often plays a crucial role in literature that oftentimes does not mention contemporary events or phenomena and that this literature is not merely reacting but, in fact, is
producing that context. This is not merely to say that context "matters"
in order to understand a text (this is a fundamental principle of classical historicism)[23] but that the fictional narrative of the text depicts and,
in many cases, creates, the historical context. In this sense, Lurianic
Kabbala, particularly its exegetical texts, illustrates a "cultural poetics,"
showing that texts often create a prism simultaneously refracting *realia*
and constructing an idealized vision of what the author would like the
real to be.[24] On this point, Louis Montrose argues that "to speak of the
social production of 'literature' or of any particular text is to signify not
only that it is socially produced but also that it is socially productive—
that it is the product of work and that it performs work in the process of
being written, enacted, or read."[25] It is not sufficient to say that kabbalistic texts reify reality—rather, it is the reified metaphysical realm, as a
fictionalization of the narrative of the Bible that creates the social reality the kabbalists seek to depict.[26]

In most instances, there is no "smoking gun" or "hard evidence."
The critic must depend on an understanding of literature and culture
that, in fact, can never be empirically proven but only surmised via a
close reading of opaque and suggestive texts.[27] "Literary texts [and here
I would include exegetical texts, S.M.] may indeed not be particular responses to unique moments; they may not refer directly to the world;
they may not offer 'proof' of anything at all."[28] This is the case if, as historians, we are looking, and even believe in, a "great story" waiting to
unfold. If we are more skeptical about grand narratives or at least our
ability to discover them, these texts can help us unravel the complex
ways their authors envisioned a historical moment and fashioned their
own identity in the fictional drama they created.[29]

It must be noted that New Historicism is primarily a literary and not
a historical or historicist movement. It uses historical context primarily
as a tool to decipher literature; it does not use literature to make objec-
tive historical claims.[30] The texts that will serve as the foundation of
this book show what Louis Montrose called "a reciprocal concern with

the historicity of texts and the textuality of history," even though it is exegesis and metaphysics and not historical writing per se that are its author's main concern.[31] My interest and focus is less about the role Christianity (via the conversos) and Islam (via the Ottoman Empire) played in the Safed community (a more formal historical question) and more about the ways in which these "others" may have been a vehicle for fashioning new identities, perhaps proto-messianic identities, in the imagination of Luria's circle. That is, I seek to determine how the "other" becomes less other in preparation for a moment when the "other" is effaced altogether. In this way, I am arguing that Lurianism is re-inventing prophetic utopianism (and universalism) from its own ontology of exclusion.

There are, nonetheless, some crucial hard facts that underlie my analysis. The fact that the problem of returning conversos was an issue in sixteenth-century Safed is undeniable, as scholars such as Abraham David indicate.[32] The fact that the conversos present us with an interesting and problematic community is generally accepted. What I am doing is linking the historical fact with a particular literary trope as it appears in Lurianic exegesis and am suggesting how one may have informed the other.

The question of returning conversos raises the question of conversion more generally.[33] More specifically, it introduces the problem of (un)conversion, or reacceptance without conversion, of an ambiguous and marginal community that also raised the question as to the status of the non-Jewish religion from which they were returning. The conversos are a community of Jews who carry with them some dimension of "Judaism" yet are, or may not be, fully Jews.[34] Some come with theological training that stands in stark opposition to Judaism, and the extent to which this training can be erased is a live issue in these decades. The force behind the case for the absorption of these communities in both Vital and Luria is that the converts' rejudaization serves as a prerequisite for the completion of the covenant that failed in the Sinai desert and subsequently created a new opportunity for the final redemption. Lurianic texts explicitly claim in numerous places that their generation is the generation of the desert and thus they must re-play the desert narrative and, this time, get it right.[35] In fact, in some cases it seems that the continued marginalization of these communities, even as such exclusion is maintained for the sake of protecting the covenant, prevents the fulfillment of Israel's covenantal responsibility. Thus the doctrine of strict separation of the Jew from the Gentile indicative of traditional Judaism throughout history is problematized by the communities (the ʿerev rav or mixed multitude in Exodus and the conversos) that are neither Jew nor Gentile—or, both Jew and Gentile.

Reversion and inversion, making boundaries transversable, seeing the same in the "other" and redeeming the "other" for the sake of the (collective) self all play a central role in the way Luria and his disciples reenvision the scriptural narrative. Esotericism in this case is not only revealing the concealed but undermining the revealed, exhibiting how seemingly transgressive behavior has redemptive import and how the "enemy" as enemy is also part of the unfinished self in need of completion.

Chapter Synopses

This book is divided into five chapters, each chapter addressing the issues as they are refracted through one of the five books of the Pentateuch. The texts examined are largely, albeit not exclusively, drawn from a body of Lurianic material that focuses on scriptural exegesis.

The chapter on Genesis discusses original sin, asking whether Christian doctrines (in this case original sin) had seeped into a kabbalistic system being read by (and sometimes written by), among others, ex-conversos. While a Jewish notion of original sin (or in the Zohar primordial sin) is extant in many kabbalistic texts, in Luria this idea becomes a prominent, perhaps even a dominant, trope having an influence on metaphysics, cosmogony, cosmology, and biblical interpretation. Does the claim that Israel, as descendants of Adam, are tainted by original sin, have an impact on equalizing the status of Jew and Gentile? Are human beings born corrupted? The Christian doctrine of original sin as it matures in Augustine and his school erases any distinction between Jew and Gentile, arguing that all are corrupted and can only overcome that state through belief in the uncorrupted Son of God. While Luria surely does not erase the distinction between Jew and Gentile, we can still ask the following question: if both are subject to original sin, is the difference between them one of degree or one of kind? Founded on the audacious claim that only Jews are created "in the image of God" and are progeny of Adam and Eve, Luria presents us with a doctrine of original sin that makes an ontological distinction between Jew and Gentile and yet opens up the possibility of their convergence by means of his theory of soul construction. Luria's position in *Sefer ha-Gilgulim* and *Sha'ar ha-Gilgulim* is that a Gentile can have a Jewish soul and a Jew can have a Gentile one. This introduces permeability regarding the biological and spiritual distinction between Jew and Gentile, the self and the "other." This plays itself out in Luria's metaphysical system and the way it informs his biology and physiology in interesting and provocative ways.

The chapter on Exodus focuses on the *'erev rav* (mixed multitude) as depicted in Hayyim Vital's pre-Lurianic *Etz ha-Daʿat Tov,* and then continues analyzing material that Vital and others wrote in light of Lurianic teaching. While the ʿerev rav and the conversos (at least those who chose to return to Judaism) are essentially different constituencies, the former being Egyptians who "convert" (or desire to convert) to the Israelite religion,[36] the latter being Jews who convert "out of Judaism" and later desire to return, there are interesting parallels between them that serve as the foundation of Vital's exegetical correlation.[37] For example, in *Etz ha-Daʿat Tov* Vital (basing himself on earlier sources) claims that the ʿerev rav, while not Israelites, are also not considered part of the other nations. Reading this back into the biblical narrative, the Bible's world is no longer simply divided into Israelites and non-Israelites but also contains a community of non-Israelites who, having experienced revelation, also have a stake in the Israelite covenant. They have an attenuated knowledge of Sinai and a close relationship to Moses who, reared as an Egyptian, continues to be their advocate.[38] Thus they are a kind of liminal community, neither Jew nor Gentile.[39] Many conversos, especially those who remained in southern Europe, were viewed by some Jews in a similar light. Although ostensibly Christian, many claimed their conversion (or their parents' or grandparents' conversion) was not volitional and thus they maintained, especially those who emigrated from the Iberian Peninsula and settled in Jewish communities, that they were still Jewish and should be accorded full membership in the community.[40] Did they need to convert?[41] Should they be allowed to return? This was the dilemma of sixteenth-century Jewry, especially in the Holy Land.[42] Many conversos held Jewish beliefs and customs, even though they did not know their meaning, content, or context, but practiced a kind of unarticulated clandestine Judaism while externally adhering to Christianity.[43] Moreover, many of their Jewish practices, while externally rabbinic, were based on Christian principles. For example, the ex-converso Isaac Cardoso interpreted circumcision as a compensation for original sin, a belief that has no basis in the conventional Jewish understanding of circumcision.[44]

As a correlate to the experience of unarticulated inclusion, Vital claims that the ʿerev rav experienced God's "voice" (*kol*) at Sinai but did not hear His "words" (*dibur*).[45] Thus they were not commanded but heard God nonetheless. Not only were they witnesses to revelation (they were present at Sinai) but they too were changed by revelation. As a result they were, in some sense, also unarticulated Israelites; they had a claim to and a stake in the covenant while not being fully a part of it. They experienced God's presence; that is, their understanding of God and their relationship to God changed through revelation, but by not hearing God's words, they had no direct commandment and thus no direction as to how to live according to that experience. These and other parallels make for a correlation between the *ʿerev rav* and the conversos, an association I argue Vital esoterically creates in order to support the claims of the conversos who desired once again to become Jews. And, more strongly, he felt that the reabsorption of this deviant community is a necessary part of the messianic drama.

The chapter on Leviticus relates this permeability of self and other to the question of gender construction as viewed through the lens of male homosexuality. If, as Luria suggests, gender is not solely biologically determined because males can contain female souls and vice versa, what impact does this have on the gender construction of traditional Judaism in wide terms, and for sexual desire and behavior in particular? I argue that Luria's discussion of this matter points to a pre-Freudian notion of the innate bisexuality of all humans (perhaps influenced by literature extant in Islam), that undermines the natural law theory of sexuality common in traditional Jewish circles (a theory adopted from medieval Christianity). In this chapter I argue that this subtle shift in orientation interestingly reflects similar sentiments in Ottoman Islam in the sixteenth century where male homosexuality was forbidden but tacitly tolerated.

The chapter on Numbers discusses the status of non-Israelite prophecy in the Lurianic system with reference to the biblical episode of Balaam (Num. 22:1–25:9). The chapter again brings together exegetical and philosophical perspectives to explore the boundaries of exclusivity and inclusion, and particularism and universalism. Relegated by the rabbis and then by the Zohar to the status of villain and sorcerer, Balaam makes a comeback in the Lurianic tradition. He is refashioned as simultaneously a prophet rooted in the demonic, and a non-Israelite prophet who desires, and ultimately succeeds, in returning to Israel. As constructed by the rabbis and the Zohar, Balaam challenges the exclusivist nature of the covenant by ordering Balak to build seven altars, representing the seventy nations. Subsuming Balaam into Moses/Israel thus subsumes the universal into the particular, transforming the latter into something new. In some sense, Luria presents a different kind of Balaam—a figure who, though demonic, also exhibits a spiritual bond with Moses and speaks of a pure desire to be reunited with a lost part of himself.

The final chapter, on Deuteronomy, turns to the doctrine of incarnation and ethics, a fundamental dogma of Christianity and an idea that plays on the margins of some mystical schools in Judaism throughout history. The notion of incarnation more generally has a complex history in Judaism, beginning in pre-Christian intertestamental literature. Readers of Jewish literature rarely use the term *incarnation,* preferring less value-laden (and less Christian) terms such as *embodiment* or *divine indwelling.*[46]

In this chapter, I argue that Lurianic texts suggest a notion of divine embodiment that traverses its normative boundary of "indwelling" and enters into incarnational thinking. The zoharic idea that "God, Israel, and Torah are one" takes on a hyperliteral meaning in the Lurianic teaching. The Lurianic texts under discussion do not conform to the particular Christian formulation of incarnation, the one-time and mysterious incarnation of God into the body of Jesus Christ, but fall into a wider definition whereby the boundaries separating the human and the divine become so thin that they all but disappear. In my analysis of this material I draw heavily from the Eastern Orthodox notion of incarnation and *theosis* in the teachings of Gregory of Palamas and Nicholas Cabasilas, as that tradition focuses most heavily on the centrality of the incarnation of the worshiper through the sacraments. This is not to argue for any direct historical influence on Lurianic Kabbala from Eastern Orthodoxy as much as to view incarnational thinking as evident in Lurianic thinking,

This study explores whether Lurianic Kabbala more generally and Lurianic exegesis in particular are influenced by the challenges of returning conversos, many of whom had been raised with the idea of incarnation. Again, this is not to suggest Luria and his circle read Christian literature; they likely did not, at least not in any systematic way. However, the canon of Jewish tradition available to the Lurianic circle contains ample material about divine embodiment and indwelling that would enable them to engage in "incarnational thinking" without employing Christian teachings. Using their creative exegetical talents and the particular social context in which they lived, I ask whether we can draw any connections between the classical notion of divine embodiment and a Lurianic mutation into the realm of the incarnational.[47]

The premise of this book is that Lurianic Kabbala, a kabbalistic school that transformed subsequent Jewish mysticism in modernity, is also a literary creation that exhibits strong readings of its historical circumstances as well as strong rereadings or misreadings of the literary canon. The historical circumstances of which I speak are not only, as Gershom Scholem argued, historiosophic (that is, concerned with the nexus between history and theology) but also local. I also attempt to shift the focus of the study of Kabbala more generally and Lurianic Kabbala in particular from its metaphysical and cosmological frame to an exegetical and hermeneutical one. Finally, I argue (along with others) that the dichotomous and dualistic framework of kabbalistic metaphysics, especially in the early modern period, undergoes a significant, albeit subtle, shift away from dualism and toward a more dialectical model. In this sense, Kabbala seems to be deconstructing itself, driven partially by its messianic agenda and the consequent need to thin the boundaries between self and other.

Did the challenges posed by a tolerant Islam and a New Christian community seeking refuge in the Jewish community contribute to the Lurianic mission of absorbing the "other," thereby creating the fertile soil for redemption's final disclosure? If so, this was not accomplished primarily through metaphysical speculation but through scriptural exegesis, translating the here-and-now into the mythic world of the Bible giving substance to the biblical narrative by discovering it anew in the lives of its readers.

THE LURIANIC MYTH
A Playbill

ספר אילן הגדול
סימן י״א

א״ה כאן התחיל עוד הפעם לסדר עולם האצילות וסדר עמידתן עם הכ״ב צינורות שהם סוד השפעות
שבהספירות מספירה לספירה ולעליהם מורים הקוים שבכאן (והם כ״ב כנגד כ״ב אותיות) עיין ביאור הגר״א על
ספר יצירה פ״ה מ״ב. ובפרדס שער הצינורות.

א״ה בסימן הזה נרשם באילן הנדפס עוד שלושה קוים המורים על הצינורות ג״כ שבכל ע״ס, והיינו השלושה קוים הם מחכמה לבינה,
ומחסד לגבורה ומנצח להוד, וכן הוא צריך להיות שם צינורות רק לא נרשמו הצינורות בפירוש מטעם שגם המעיין יבין מדעתו.
[אמנ״ה גם דע שבהכ״י מהר״ק ז״ל נמצאו קוים שמורים על הצינורות מכל ע״ס אבא לכל ע״ס אימא היינו מבינה דאבא לחכמה
דאימא, וכן מכל ע״ס יש״ס לתבונה ומע״ס דז״א לע״ס דלאה, אמנם כאן הוא כמו בהנדפס מקודם].

רישא דלא אתיידע
כתרא [דא״א]
מוחא [דא״א]
דא לגו מן דא

[בכ״י פרצוף אבא] עשר ספירות אבא   עשר ספירות אימא [בכ״י פרצוף אימא]

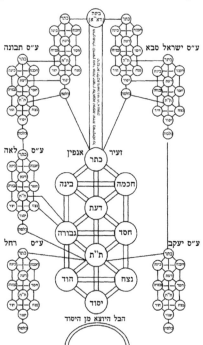

ע״ס ישראל סבא

ע״ס תבונה

צינור מחכמה לבינה,
צינור מחסד לגבורה,
צינור מנצח להוד, [בכ״י
צינור מבינה לחכמה]
בכ״י צינור מדעת אבא
לדעת דאימא, בכ״י צינור
מגבורה לחסד, בכ״י צינור
מת״ת לתפארת, בכ״י
צינור מהוד לנצח, בכ״י
צינור מיסוד אבא ליסוד
אימא, וכן ממלכות, וכן
בכל ספירות הפרצופים
וכו״ל, צינור מחכמה
לבינה צינור מחסד
לגבורה צינור מנצח להוד
צינור לבינה צינור להוד
צינור לגבורה צינור
מחכמה לבינה ג״כ צינור
מחסד לגבורה ג״כ צינור
מנצח להוד ג״כ

לאה   ע״ס   אנפין   זעיר

ע״ס ישראל סבא

ע״ס יעקב

רחל   ע״ס

ע״ס יעקב

כתר
חכמה
דעת
חסד
ת״ת
נצח
הוד
יסוד

בינה
גבורה

הבל היוצא מן היסוד

קרקע עולם האצילות להדום רגלי כל הי״ב פרצופים, ומשם יפרד והיה לשלושה עולמות בריאה יצירה עשיה, זה למטה
מזה ואדון יחיד מתיחד ומושל על כולם, יה צבאות יהדורין, המושל על עולם הבריאה

Figure 1. From Hayyim Vital, *ʿOzrot Hayyim*
(Jerusalem: Makor Hayyim, n.d.)

אוצרות חיים

שער העיגולים דרוש א"ק

מליאות אדם קדמון לכל הקדומים הנז' כזוהר ובתי' ואחריו
נמשך סדר כל המדרגות כולם. דע כי כזה התגלל נמצא (ס"א
נאצל). זה האדם הנק' קדמון לכל הקדומים כנז' יש בו מליאות
עשר ספירות והס ממלאות את כל החלל הזה. ואחרכה תחילת
יצאו עשר ספירותיו בדרך עיגולים אלו בתוך אלו ואח"כ בתוך
העיגולים נמשך דרך קו היושר לייר אדם אחד בעשר ספירות באורך
כל העיגולים הנז' כליור זה

הכל היה כל המליאות אור פשוט ונק' אין סו"ף
ולא היה שם שום חלל ושום אויר פנוי. אלא הכל היה אור הא"ס
וכשעלה ברצונו הפשוט להאציל הנאצלים לסיבה נודעת והיא
להקרא רחום וחנון ד) וכיוולא כי אם אין בעולם מי שיקבל רחמיו
ממנו איך יקרא רחום וכן עד"ז בכל הכנויים ואו למטה ה)
עלמני בהמצא האור שלו א) בנקודת המרכז האמצעית שבו ושם
נמצא עלמו אל הצדדין והסביבות ונשאר חלל ב) בנקצעא עגול ב)
היה למצלוס הראשון של המאציל עולס האצילות וכל העולמות
נתונים תוך החלל הזה. ואור הא"ס מקיפו בשוה מכל צדדיו.

ואין אנו עוסקים
כלל בעיגולים רק
בבחי' היושר
בלבד. ולהלן נבאר
מליאות העיגולים
ויהושר מה עניינים
והנה על ידי למצוס
הזה הנז' כאשר
נעשה האדם הנז'
היה כ"ו בבחי' שלמות
ועלים כי למצוס
האור גרם עשיית
והויית הכלים כמו
שנבאר לק מן
בעזרת האל ואין

לנו רשות לדבר יותר במקוס נבוה זה והמשכיל יבין ראשית דבר
מאחריתו כאשר נבאר בע"ה בדרושים אחרים כבאהי לפנינו
האמנס אינו כלי ממש אלא שבעד לך האור שבתוכו נק' כלי אמנס
הוא זך ובהיר בתכלית הבהירות והדקות והזיכוך. והנה האדם
קדמון הזה הוא מבהיר מן הקלף העליון עד קלה התתחתון. (פי'
ולא עד בכלל) בכל חלל האצילות הנז'. וכזה האדם נכללין כל
העולמות כמו שנבאר לקמן בע"ה והנה בכ' פנימיותו ועלמיותו
של האדם הזה אין אנו יכולים להשיג כלל אמנם נתמשכת
גדול מאד לכן לא היו יכולים לקבל אלא באמלעותו זה האדם
קדמון ואפילו מזה האדם קדמון עלמו אין מליאות לקבלו
אלא אחר יציאת חולה לי דרך הנקבים והחלונות שבו שהם
האזנים והעינים והחוטס והפה ובמו שנבאר למטה בעזרת האל:

שער מנת"א פ' א'

פ"א ונבאר עתה עניינים. דע כי אין מליאות לייר קומת

אדם בשולם שלא יהיה בו בללות ד' בחינות
אלו אשר כוללים כל האצילות וכל העולמות ואלו הס שם
ע"ב ס"ג מ"ה ב"ן. ושם ע"ב כזה יו"ד ה"י וי"ו ה"י ושם ס"ג כזה יו"ד ה"י וא"ו ה"י
ואל"ף כזה יו"ד ה"א וא"ו ה"א ושם
מ"ה כזה יו"ד ה"א וא"ו ה"א. ושם
ב"ן כזה יו"ד ה"ה ו"ו ה"ה. והנה אלו ארבע שריו"ת
הנחלקות בארבעה מילויין האלו הס בחינה א) שטעמי שם ע"ב
בחינת

Is the Bible myth or "history"? Is Kabbala myth or symbol? More generally, is Judaism founded on myth and, if so, what does a Jewish myth look like? These questions lie at the root of any serious engagement with classical Jewish texts and more so with kabbalistic sources that are wed to a notion of understanding this world as a reflection of the cosmic realm. Like other mystical systems, Kabbala posits that the empirical world we live in is accompanied by another nonempirical dimension—created yet not corporeal, divine yet not fully God. This noncorporeal dimension does not only exist outside this world in some transcendent universe but also occupies the very world we live in. The kabbalistic fraternity examined in this study refers to this noncorporeal world as the world of the *sephirot* (cosmic spheres). These *sephirot* (ten in number but divided into many subgroups) both affect us and are affected by us. They affect us because the cosmic realm serves as an intermediary between our world and the undifferentiated God (known by our kabbalists as *eyn sof*—without end). There is very little the kabbalists have to say about *eyn sof* since this God, as ineffable, has no real relation to us nor do we have any relationship to it. In this sense, some kabbalistic theology is not far from the neo-Aristotelian "negative theology" popular among many medieval philosophers. However, whereas negative theologians leave it at that, kabbalists posit a divine-yet-created cosmic realm with which we have an intimate, and reciprocal, relationship. This realm is the primary focus of their attention. The cosmos is affected by us because the kabbalists understand the covenantal theology of the Hebrew Bible in literal or even hyperliteral terms. That is, they hold that human action affects God, not God as *eyn sof* (who, as infinite, is beyond human influence) but the dimension of God that is "created" or the world of *sephirot*. To act in accordance with divine command results in the reparation (*tikkun*) of the cosmic realm damaged by the initial rupture of the creative act.

The *sephirot* serve as catalysts filtering divine effluence as it moves from the *eyn sof* to the material world. The kabbalists of the Lurianic School hold that creation was, in a sense, a failure. That is, the "divine intention" of creation was to produce a corporeal space that could absorb the unmitigated flow of divine energy that would very quickly result in the reabsorption of creation into the undifferentiated God. Things worked out quite differently. The failure of creation is exhibited in the two central parts of the creation myth in Lurianic Kabbala; *zimzum* (divine contraction) and *shevirat ha-kelim* (the rupture of the vessels) about which I will have more to say below. For our kabbalists, the fallen state of creation is not solely due to the sin of Adam and Eve. The origin of failure, exile, and sin, is the fractured process of creation itself. The sin of Adam and Eve is, in some sense a mirror of the fallen world they occupied. According to this school, the sin was not only predictable but also perhaps inevitable. While our world is the consequence of this failed creation process (in Lurianic Kabbala our world is, by definition, exilic) the damage also exists in the cosmic realm (the world of the *sephirot*). As disjointed or uncoupled (the natural state of the *sephirot* is to be in perennial heterosexual union or *yihud tamidi*) the *sephirot* cannot serve as conduits for an even descent of divine effluence into the world. This disunity results in a world (our world) dominated by the powers of the demonic. This is the basis of Lurianic theodicy. This dark vision of existence is tempered by the notion that the human being (in Lurianic Kabbala this is largely limited to the male Jew) is created in the "image of God" (*zelem elohim;* Gen. 1:26) and has the unique ability to restructure the broken cosmos through the performance of mitzvot. This enables divine light to descend and diffuse the dominion of the demonic. The restructuring or reparation (*tikkun*) of the cosmic realm is brought about through the performance of commandments (mitzvot) especially enhanced by the intricate contemplative techniques.

This cosmic/divine realm of *sephirot* in Lurianic Kabbala, sometimes called the Godhead by scholars, is not a precept the adept accepts on faith or reasoned argument but is posited as a "real" object of intense focus and concentration that can be experienced through meditative techniques. Thus kabbalistic cosmology is often accompanied by a practice manifest as contemplative techniques accompanying rituals whereby the mystic deploys these principles toward experiential ends. The adept is expected to devote their life to the deep study and practice of the *sephirotic* system as explained in Lurianic literature.

Gershom Scholem (1897–1982), founder of modern Kabbala studies, argued that Kabbala emerged in the Middle Ages as a rejection of what he understood as the rabbinic demythologizing of the Bible in its creation of law as the central motif of Jewish thinking and practice. On this reading Kabbala sought to reinvigorate the genealogy of what many scholars in Scholem's generation viewed as the "Jewish" mythology of the Hebrew Bible, the ur-text of Ancient Israelite religion that would later morph into Judaism. The talmudist David Halivni suggests that midrash (the rabbinic method of reading Scripture) is, in part, a response to the distance the sages felt between themselves and the Bible—a distance created by time, circumstance, religious sentiment, and necessity (the cultic religion of the Bible simply became irrelevant for the sages in late antiquity). According to Halivni Rabbinic Judaism sought to revive the Bible through midrashic reading but also transform it from a largely mythic guide to a text whose centerpiece is the law. Among other things, he argues, this resulted in undermining the Bible's mythic foundations and worldview. From Halivni's perspective, the rabbinic sages wanted their audience to focus more on the text (*their* reading of the text) than on God, more on obedience than on *cultus*. They were uninterested in contemplating the life of the divine as an end in itself and wanted to redirect Jews away from mystical gnosis and toward a religious life of daily obligations. For the talmudic sages, mysticism and myth, on Halivni's reading, were largely relegated to what Max Kiddushin called "normal mysticism" experienced primarily through the act of prayer. This is not to say there weren't Jews in late antiquity who continued in the mystical and mythic world of the Bible. There surely were and these figures are studied by Scholem and later scholars of Jewish mysticism. It is to say, rather, that what *became* Rabbinic Judaism through the redaction and reception of the two Talmuds (Babylonian and Palestinian) presents us with a Judaism that is not dominated by myth but the adherence to law.

This generalized view of the rabbis as myth-destroyers has been duly criticized by scholars of both Talmud and Midrash. Most recently, Michael Fishbane, in his work on rabbinic midrash and myth, has meticulously shown that the homiletical traditions (midrash) of the rabbis not only kept myth alive but, in fact, deepened biblical myth by embellishing it and extending it to include new vistas of imaginative thinking. The rabbis were, in fact, mythmakers in Fishbane's view. On this reading Scholem's schematic assessment distinguishing the Hebrew Bible from Rabbinic Judaism is in need of correction and has been, in fact, reexamined by contemporary scholars of Jewish mysticism. That said, for our limited purposes it may be useful to dwell on the rabbinic–kabbalistic dichotomy posed by Halivni and Scholem, with all its caveats, as a heuristic tool to sketch the context of Lurianic teaching.

One way rabbinic law nullifies or perhaps reconfigures the myth that informs at least some of the Hebrew Bible is by separating law and practice from cosmic events. That is, by distinguishing law as *nomos* and forcefully arguing that law as *nomos* is the proper—in fact, only—way to properly understand the Bible. By constructing the law from biblical verses and viewing the Bible as primarily *teaching* law, the rabbis contribute to demythologizing the biblical narrative even as Fishbane argues correctly the same rabbis also embellish and expand the biblical myth in other ways (and create myths of their own). In the rabbinic imagination, the Bible does not tell us who or what God *is* as much as about what God requires from us. The law commemorates the past (memory functions as a central motif of biblical law) and saves historic events from erasure through the legal obligation of performance as remembrance. Alternatively, in a (biblical) religion based primarily on myth, historical events are always lived again and again through the

cosmos where the past always reverberates in the present. For the rabbis, religious practice carves a distinct realm for the past that, while
connected to the present, is not identical to it.

Kabbala has its own myth based loosely on the Bible. It does not bring
biblical myth back to life (that would be impossible), but it uses biblical
myth as a template for its own metaphysical constructions (that is, constructing the world of the *sephirot*). It also does not directly undermine the
legal demythologizing of the Bible. That would be overtly heretical. What
it offers is a revised myth based on the Bible (and the rabbis!) incorporat-
ing the rabbinic legal tradition that, according to Halivni, arose to sub-
vert myth! That is, Kabbala saves the law by mythologizing it and, in doing
so, transforms the law (which replaced sacrament) back into a kind of
noncultic sacrament. The sacrament now is no longer geographical (the
Temple) but cosmic (the *sephirot*). Kabbala's elaborate web of "reasons for
the commandments" (*ta'amei ha-mitzvot*) is essentially a resacramentation
of rabbinic law. This is all to say that what Kabbala does through its myth
is transform the anthropomorphic God of the Bible into cosmology and
make the largely inaccessible God of the rabbis "real," proximate, and
palpable while still leaving the transcendent ineffable dimension of God
(*eyn sof*) intact. This allows the practitioner to enter into the life and body
of God (as one enters the cosmos through knowledge, gnosis, and "legal"
practice accompanied by contemplative techniques), making kabbalistic
Judaism a new kind of postbiblical sacramental religion by absorbing the
law into a newfangled mythic reformulation of the Bible. Kabbala's myth
tells us much more about God (that is, the created divinity of the *sephirot*)
than the Bible. It discloses the secret life of God by putting God (or the
godhead) under an X-ray exposing the inner workings of the divine body,
a body that is, as Elliot Wolfson suggests, an example of "incorporeal
corporeality."

Myths almost always have a pragmatic foundation—they do important
cultural work. Most Jewish myths subsequent to the Bible are founded on
three covenantal principles the first two of which are explicit in the Pentateuch and the third (at most) implicit: God as creator, God as revealer, and
God as redeemer. Covenant stands on these three pillars and demands
human devotion as a response. Postrabbinic, kabbalistic myth includes the
law of the *cultus* of human devotion, the law that not only answers the divine command but alters the mythic realm of the *sephirot*.

The Lurianic myth is one of the grandest in the history of Kabbala
and perhaps in the history of Judaism after the Bible. It begins with an
imaginative cosmogony (thus preceding Gen. 1:1 which begins with creation) and concludes with redemption as the culmination or fulfillment
of creation, the reabsorption of the corporeal into the undifferentiated

God as *eyn sof.* Luria's myth is triadic, containing *zimzum* (divine contraction), *shevirat ha-kelim* (divine rupture), and *tikkun* (reparation). *Zimzum*
appears to be Luria's alternative to the more common Neoplatonic theory
of emanation from the "one to the many" that dominates earlier Kabbala.
While *zimzum* does have precedent in Kabbala before Luria, only Luria
makes it the exclusive act of cosmogony. While there are numerous versions of the cosmogonic myth among Luria's many disciples I will forego
the scholarly debates and simply map out the basic contours of the story.

 Zimzum suggests that an outward emanation of the divine must be
preceded by a receding of the divine within itself, a voluntary act of self-
limitation that "creates" a vacuum known in Lurianic nomenclature (adopted from the Zohar) as *tehiru.* This divine vacuum was not actually void
of God (that would be metaphysically impossible) but rather contained a
diminished state of God that could accommodate something outside itself. There is a lively post-Lurianic debate about whether *zimzum* should
be viewed literally (that God is absent in the *tehiru*) or metaphorically
(that God is merely concealed in the *tehiru*) but this is not directly relevant
to this introduction. In any case, this realm of diminished divinity later
becomes the source of divine judgment (*dinim*) and contributes to the
formation of the demonic. Intermingled with this force of judgment are
remnants of divinity that had contracted, now in a weaker state, known in
Lurianic nomenclature as *reshimu* (remnant). The doctrine of *zimzum* posits a decentering of God as a prelude to the creation process. God is present and absent in creation, suggesting a kind of monotheistic pantheism
where the presence of God as transcendent (*eyn sof*) is beyond human
comprehension and the presence of God in the world is concealed but
can be disclosed through mystical gnosis.

 Luria's myth posits a process of emanation immediately following *zimzum* (time, of course, had not been created yet so this is all "as if") where
light from outside the vacuum (*tehiru*) is inserted into it. This light has
two dimensions: one called straight light that descends until the middle
point of the circular space of *tehiru;* and a second called circular light that
fills the vacuum in gradations as it enters into the circle. These two lights
(which are really two dimensions of the same light) become the Cosmic
Man in Lurianic Kabbala known as *adam kadmon* (primordial man; see
figure 2). Primordial man is the form of the initial phase of divine descent into the space "created" by *zimzum.* As the divine light continues to
flow after the formation of primordial man it now emanates out of his (fa-
cial) orifices (eyes, ears, and nose, in some texts the mouth, navel, and
phallus) and descends to construct the lower cosmic realms. Vessels to
contain this emanated light were formed from the remnant of light that
remained after the *zimzum* (the *reshimu*). The failure of creation begins as

the vessels prove too weak to contain this newly emanated divine light and shatter, descending further toward the center of the circle (the farthest point from the circumference). This center point will become the nether-world (the realm of the demonic). As the shards of the vessels descend they carry with them sparks of divine light that were already embedded in the vessels as a result of (1) the fact that the vessels are made of divine light, albeit of a diminished kind; and (2) sparks of light that had already become absorbed in the vessels from the initial stages of emanation. The number of sparks that descend into the center point embedded in the ves-sels number 288. The detailed mapping of the act of rupture, known in Lurianic nomenclature as *olam ha-nekudim* (the world of atomized light taken from Gen. 31:10) is quite a complicated process that need not con-cern us here. What we need to know is that this tragic moment creates the template for creation of our world and those fallen sparks in need of lib-eration are one important focus of Lurianic devotion.

The detailed explanation of reparation (*tikkun*) and reconstruction of the cosmos (known as *olam ha-berudim*, the world of reconstruction) serves as the foundation of the Lurianic myth that is used to interpret Scripture. To retell the myth of reparation in all its labyrinthine details would constitute a separate study far beyond the scope of this brief syn-opsis. Here I intend only to familiarize the reader uninitiated into the Lurianic worldview with certain general dimensions of the myth that will be relevant to the chapters that follow.

After the vessels of creation ruptured due to their inability to contain the divine light that filled them (*shevirat he-kelim*), sparks of that light de-scended into the netherworld. Material existence is thus composed of de-monic materiality that contains hidden sparks of divinity. These sparks need to be liberated as part of the Great Reparation: redemption. The liberation of these sparks accomplishes two things: First, it enables them to return to their divine source above (Luria assumes a common Neopla-tonic principle that things naturally seek to return to their source). Sec-ond, the liberation of the divine sparks robs the demonic of any life force because the demonic or evil, in Luria's imagination, is only sustained by proximity to some form of divinity. The first stage of return is to the womb of the primordial mother (represented as the *sephirah* "mother," *bina* or *ima*) after which the *parzufim*, or clusters of *sephirot* that are formed as part of the reparation, will be emanated a second time. By this time the divine fallen sparks will have been liberated from the demonic, rob-bing the demonic of power and thus removing any threat to the newly formed cosmic realm. The messianic vision for Luria is not wholly clear and has been the subject of numerous studies by contemporary scholars. Some argue that his messianic vision is the culmination of creation and

the nullification of all existence, returning everything back to the undifferentiated God of *eyn sof.* However, this would be an apocalyptic messianic vision quite uncommon in post-rabbinic Judaism. Others suggest
that, more in line with traditional categories, Luria argues for resurrection of the dead and what is a yet unfathomable state of permanent union
of all cosmic forces. The endtime or reabsorption of all back in to the All
will occur in the distant future.

The work of humanity and the (male) Jew in particular, is to reconstruct the broken cosmic "persons" or *parzufim* that took form in the cosmos after the rupture of divinity. *Parzufim* are divine constellations or clusters each made up of ten *sephirot* that are mostly depicted in human form
(mostly as biblical characters). The word *parzuf* literally means "face" but
may better translate as "interface," the nexus where the infinite meets the
finite. It is the root metaphor of the Lurianic system, largely adopted from
the Tikkunei Zohar. *Parzufim* are formed through the process of emanation after the destructive moment of rupture. The broken nature of the
parzufim is illustrated by the fact that they cannot maintain a state of heterosexual coupling (*yihud*) due to the ever-present demonic forces that
seek to suckle from their divinity. The higher three *parzufim* (*arikh anpin*
or long-suffering or patient one, *abba* or primordial father and *ima* or primordial mother) occupy a space that is free from demonic influence. Yet
in order to construct and rectify the lower *parzufim* (*zeir anpin* or impatient
one, Jacob, Rachel, and Leah) *abba* and *ima* must descend into the space
where the demonic has dominion. This idea of "descent for the sake of ascent" (*yerida zarikh aliya*) is a constant trope of Lurianic metaphysics and
post-Lurianic Kabbala more generally.

Parzufim

There are twelve or thirteen clusters of *sephirot* in the Lurianic system
known as *parzufim. Parzufim* constitute a combination of reified forms of
biblical characters mixed with Luria's only mythic interpretations
largely drawing from the Zohar. These *parzufim* are metaphysical actors
that rehearse the biblical drama as a way of creating the proper conditions for divine flow into the material world. Of these twelve or thirteen
only five or six constitute the main stage of the cosmic drama. As mentioned above, the *parzufim* are formed after the rupture of *adam kadmon,*
constructed from the first infusion of divine light into the "empty"
space (*tehiru*) created by *zimzum*. The *parzufim* are generally understood
to be Luria's extension of the more elementary formulations of *sephirotic*
clusters in the Idrot sections of the Zohar (the Great Idra and the

Lesser Idra) and the Tikkunei Zohar. These sections of the Zohar are predictably the most often cited in Lurianic literature. When these gendered *parzufim* are able to unite in sexual union (sexual union being the root metaphor for healthy symmetry), divine effluence descends and the world undergoes a process of *tikkun*. When they are prevented from this union, for various reasons, divine effluence is diminished and the demonic gains dominion over the material and spiritual worlds. The complex topography of this drama will be explored in the body of this study. Here I will map out some of the basic *parzufim* in order to familiarize the reader with this system. For our purposes there are five major *parzufim*, some of which have sub-*parzufim* that will become clear below.

Arikh Anpin (long-suffering or patient one) is the first or highest *parzuf*, the *sephirotic* cluster closest to *eyn sof* and thus the most pristine. It is not overtly gendered but generally is referred to as "male." In some cases *arikh anpin* is identified as *keter*, the highest *sephirah* but Lurianic Kabbala does not seem as concerned with the identification of *keter* and *arikh anpin* as some earlier kabbalistic schools. Its place in the cosmos is beyond the grasp of the demonic and it is thus not susceptible to the effects of human sin. Because it is beyond human influence *arikh anpin* represents a dimension of the created-divine world (the cosmos) that most closely resembles *eyn sof*. In certain cases, human beings, more specifically the righteous illuminati can, via contemplation, reach the lower recesses of *arikh anpin*.

Abba (father) and *ima* (mother) are the *parzufim* that correspond to the *sephirot hokhma* and *bina*. *Abba* and *ima* also occupy a place in the cosmos that is beyond demonic influence but since as cosmic "parents" they are interconnected with *zeir anpin* and *nukva* (the *parzufim* that interact most directly with the corporeal world), they are affected by human sin (as can be seen in the discussion on male homosexuality in chapter 3). One essential difference between *arikh anpin* and *abba* and *ima* is that the latter are mobile. That is, they move from their place in the cosmos (in a state of perpetual heterosexual union not threatened by demonic contamination) and enter into the body of *zeir anpin* (viewed as their "son") in order to construct, nurture, and sustain him. Upon entering into the body of *zeir anpin*, who occupies a realm where the demonic have at least some influence, they must decouple in order to protect their "backs" from contamination as the back is the most vulnerable dimension in the cosmic body. This decoupling simultaneously makes them uniquely vulnerable and diminishes their impact on the lower worlds (since it is heterosexual union that facilitated the downward flow of divine light).

Abba and *ima* are divided into two parts. The upper half of *abba* is called by the generic name *abba* and the bottom half, from *tiferet* of *abba* to *malkhut* of *abba* (each *parzuf* has its own ten *sephirot*), is called *yisrael saba* (Israel the grandfather; see figure 1). The top half of *ima* is referred to as *ima* and the bottom half is called *tevunah* (understanding). Thus *abba* and *ima* are two *parzufim* that are really four. This is important because part of the construction of *zeir anpin* requires the descent of *abba* and *ima* (the bottom half of each, *yisrael saba* and *tevunah*) into the body of *zeir anpin* while the top pairs of each remain in their lofty place. Because *abba* and *ima* dwell above the dominion of the demonic they are generally in a state of constant heterosexual union (*yihud tamidi*). This means that they are continuously delivering divine effluence below (even as this flow may be interrupted by the uncoupling of *zeir anpin* and *nukva*).

Yihud tamidi means that *yesod* of *abba* (his phallus) is always enveloped inside *yesod* of *ima*. As we will see, this changes once the lower portions of *abba* and *ima* descend into the body of *zeir anpin* where they uncouple in *tiferet* of *zeir anpin*. *Yesod* of *ima* stays in *tiferet* of *zeir anpin* while *yesod* of *abba* continues to descend and is exposed (that is, not enveloped in *ima*) from *tiferet* to *yesod* of *zeir anpin*. Since the lower parts of *abba* and *ima* are mobile and descend into the body of *zeir anpin*, they too become susceptible to the demonic. However, in most cases, even when the lower portion of *abba* and *ima* descend and uncouple, their upper halves remain in a state of union above (there are a few cases where this is not true as we will see in the chapter on male–male intercourse). Hence *abba* and *ima* are often in a state of unity and disunity simultaneously (their upper half is in a state of *yihud tamidi* and their bottom half is uncoupled inside the body of *zeir anpin*).

Most of the activity in the Lurianic myth occurs in the realm of four *parzufim: zeir anpin*, Jacob, Rachel, and Leah. As is known, the biblical Jacob has two names, Jacob and Israel (Gen. 32:28; 35:10). The unique quality of Jacob's name-change is that, as opposed to Abraham and Sarah whose names are also changed in Genesis (Gen. 17:5; 17:15), after Jacob becomes Israel he is still sometimes called Jacob throughout the Pentateuch. That is, his more refined and mature identity does not efface his initial identity and birth name. In Luria's reification of this phenomenon there are two distinct *parzufim* that loosely correspond to the biblical figure Jacob/Israel: *zeir anpin*, which loosely corresponds to Israel, and a smaller *parzuf* that stands in front of *zeir anpin* called Jacob (see figure 1). The two female *parzufim* are Jacob/Israel's two wives, Rachel and Leah. These two *parzufim* generally represent the female Eve (the extent to which *zeir anpin* very loosely represents Adam) who is constructed from Adam's rib (Gen. 2:22). Thus, in Lurianic cosmology, Leah and Rachel are constructed from light that emanates out of the back of *zeir anpin* (Leah and Rachel are situated in back of *zeir anpin*).

This light is drawn from different dimensions of *abba* and *ima* who descend into *zeir anpin* also to use *zeir anpin* as a catalyst to filter light into the female Rachel and Leah. *Zeir anpin* thus cannot unite with either Leah or Rachel until they are fully constructed *parzufim* by means of light they receive from him. The biblical notion of the female constructed from the male becomes the foundation of metaphysical (en)gendering in the Lurianic myth. In some sense, then, the female is always an extension of the male and never attains independent status. Constructed from *zeir anpin*, the female (Rachel/Leah/*shekhina*) remains totally dependent on the male.

The descent of *abba* and *ima* into the body of *zeir anpin* is a central topic of Lurianic metaphysics. It serves at least two functions: (1) it serves to construct and repair *zeir anpin* (remember all *parzufim* are created blemished as a result of the rupturing of the vessels in Luria's creation myth); and (2) the lights of *abba* and *ima* emanate out the back of *zeir anpin* and construct the two female consorts Rachel and Leah, enabling *zeir anpin* to engage in sexual union and filter divine effluence into the lower worlds.

The body of *zeir anpin* is divided into four major sections. The first is the head that constitutes the *sephirot hokhma* and *bina* of *zeir anpin*. The next is *daʿat*, which sits on the base of the brain (the brain stem) and filters divine effluence from the upper part of *zeir anpin* to its body. *Daʿat* (which occupies the place where the knot of the head phylactery rests) functions as the "narrows" (*mezarim*) of the cosmic body. It serves two major roles. First, it gathers the male and female effluence from above (from the head of *zeir anpin* and light from *abba* and *ima* that descend into its head) and filters it downward. As a "narrows" it is also the place where the holy and demonic meet. For example, in Lurianic exegesis *daʿat* is the nexus where Moses (who is rooted in *daʿat* of *zeir anpin*) and Pharaoh have a direct confrontation. Moses is from the side of the holiness of *daʿat* and Pharaoh is from the side of demonic in *daʿat*. This is based on the biblical context of Moses and Pharaoh's meeting in Egypt (Exod. 7–11). The Hebrew word for Egypt (*Mizrayim*) comes from the root of narrows (*mezar*). *Daʿat* of *zeir anpin* is also the first place where light emanated out of *zeir anpin* to the head of Leah that stands behind him from his head to his chest cavity (two thirds of *tiferet*).

The next major part of *zeir anpin* begins in *tiferet* or the chest cavity (*hesed* and *gevurah* stand between *daʿat* and *tiferet* of *zeir anpin*). It is here that the light from *daʿat* that filters into *hesed* and *gevurah* (the male and female upper body—shoulders and arms) reaches the body of *zeir anpin* (*tiferet* is the place of the breast *and* the heart). *Tiferet* houses all these lights and prepares them to descend further. *Tiferet* is also the place of Leah's feet and the head of Rachel (visually the *parzuf* Leah is standing on Rachel's head). Finally, it is the place where *abba* and *ima* decouple inside the body of *zeir anpin*. The descent of *ima* generally culminates in *tiferet* of *zeir anpin*, while the descent of *abba* continues to *yesod* (or the genitals) of *zeir anpin*. The reasons for this are complicated and not directly relevant here. It is only important to note that since *ima* functions as mother and sustainer to *zeir anpin*, Leah, and Rachel, her place is the place of the breast (*tiferet*) of *zeir anpin*, the site of maternal sustenance. *Ima's yesod*, or sexual organ, rests in the breast of her son (*zeir anpin*). When *abba* and *ima* reach this point they uncouple, enabling *ima* to function as mother rather than lover.

Biology and physiology play central roles in the Lurianic worldview. Our kabbalists (like the talmudic sages) took note of the fact that when a woman is lactating she generally does not menstruate. The correlation between the whiteness of breast milk and the redness of menstrual blood has a long history in rabbinic literature and plays a central role in the reified physiology of the Zohar. Thus, when *ima* plays the role of sustainer (as a nursing mother for *zeir anpin*) she does not serve as the object of *abba*'s desire. In fact according to the Zohar *ima* (or the *sephirotic* correlate *bina*) is often viewed as male. During sustained sexual union (*yihud tamidi*) outside *zeir anpin*, the light of *abba* (housed in his *yesod* or phallus) is enveloped in the vaginal cavity of *ima*. When they uncouple inside the body of *zeir anpin abba*'s light housed in his *yesod* is exposed as it descends from *tiferet* (the chest cavity) of *zeir anpin* until *yesod* (the phallus) of *zeir anpin*. This newly exposed light of *abba* is more powerful and unadulterated and yet also more vulnerable than it was when it was protected by the *yesod* of *ima*. The implications of this will be developed in various ways throughout this book.

The biblical context of Lurianic metaphysics is never abandoned in its myth. Leah is the "unloved" wife of Jacob (Gen. 29:31) and Rachel is the beloved object of Jacob's desire (Gen. 29:18). Yet Leah is the first wife and the more fertile mother. The sexual relationship with Leah is essential (although not desired), as it produces most of Jacob's progeny (this includes children born from the two maidservants Bilah and Zilpah). Jacob's sexual relationship with Rachel is a pure expression of his love yet only produces two children, Benjamin and Joseph. In the Lurianic imagination, only Rachel is considered *nukva de-zeir anpin* (literally the "hole" or vessel of *zeir anpin*, Jacob's true female consort). When she can unite with him (liturgically this occurs during the daily morning service) the cosmos are in harmony. However, when Jacob as Israel (*zeir anpin*) unites with Leah, it is a time of harshness (*dinim*) that needs to be sweetened. Since Leah is composed of more *dinim* than Rachel, she is a more appropriate partner at a time when harsh judgment (*dinim*) predominates.

As mentioned above, Leah's feet are juxtaposed to the chest cavity of *zeir anpin*, directly above Rachel's head. To unite with *zeir anpin* she must grow to encompass the length of his entire body (in order for their genitals to be aligned) and, in doing so, "exiles" Rachel to a lower realm (to the world of *beriah* below the world of *ʿazilut*) where she is alone or without a partner. This occurs at midnight, the time of mourning for the destruction of the Temple and exile in Lurianic practice. However, when *zeir anpin* unites with Rachel, Leah is not relegated to exile. Rather, Leah lends her divine light to Rachel, who then grows to her full size in preparation for her union with *zeir anpin*. Leah rarely descends below the highest world of *ʿazilut* and thus is never the direct object of the adept's attention. When Rachel unites with Jacob, Rachel and Leah temporarily merge into one *parzuf* sometimes called *nukva de-zeir anpin*. In fact, though, only Rachel is really *zeir anpin*'s true partner. Rachel is also sometimes conflated with the *shekhina* who descends into exile with Israel and, in Lurianic teaching, also serves as the "first wife" (*zivug rishon*) of the righteous ones.

Another dimension of Leah and Rachel that will become relevant in the chapter on Balaam is that Leah's feet are actually embedded in part of Rachel's head. That is, there is overlap and thus inextricable interdependence between the unloved (Leah) who is weaker (Gen. 29:17) because she only has the light of *ima* and *abba* as enveloped within *ima*, and the beloved Rachel (Gen. 29:18) who has the light of *ima* (through Leah) and the full light of *abba* (because she is situated in the bottom half of *zeir anpin* where he is exposed). In general, Leah is more vulnerable to demonic attachment. Yet because Leah's feet are embedded in Rachel's head, Rachel too is vulnerable to the absorption of the demonic and its corrosive influence.

Worlds

Lurianic Kabbala adopts the system of the four worlds from the Zohar and earlier Kabbala. The four worlds include *ʿazilut*, the world of emanation; *beriah*, the world of creation; *yezeriah*, the world of formation; and *asiah*, the world of action or materiality. Each world has its own set of ten *sephirot* and *parzufim*. The general distinction between the worlds is that the highest, *ʿazilut*, is beyond the grasp of demonic influence and the lowest, *asiah*, is quite vulnerable to demonic influence. The other two worlds (*yezeriah* and *beriah*) are within the demonic grasp but not limited by it. The lower world of *asiah* does not represent the material world but still represents cosmic space, albeit the cosmic space that is closest to the corporeal world. This will become relevant in the first chapter on original sin, where Lurianic exegesis speaks of five different Adams from Adam of *ʿazilut* to the Adam of creation. Unless otherwise indicated in most Lurianic texts, when *parzufim* are discussed they usually refer to *parzufim* of the world of *ʿazilut*. For example, when Rachel is exiled at midnight to make space for Leah's coupling with *zeir anpin,* she descends into the world of *beriah* where she is comforted by the righteous who arise at midnight and recite the nocturnal liturgy of mourning (*tikkun hazot*).

Each world is a complete world to itself, reflecting the world above and below. Yet each world has specific characteristics, much of which is directly related to how it is affected or unaffected by the demonic. Generally, the human being has access to the three lower worlds (*beriah, yezeriah,* and *ʿasiah*) but no regular access to the world of *ʿazilut* except, in certain cases and at certain times, when one can have access to or can occupy the dimension of *malkhut* of *ʿazilut* (and sometimes even beyond that). The righteous, however, have freer access to the realm of *ʿazilut* through contemplative prayer, via Lurianic *kavvanot,* and the study and recitation of esoteric doctrine. In many cases there are worldly overlaps where *malkhut* of a higher world is grafted onto *keter* of the lower world. Among other things this suggests a kind of seamlessness, organicity, and circularity between worlds. In the chapter on original sin we will see a long discussion about *malkhuyot*—the lowest dimension of each *sephira*—in a particular world and its relationship to *keter* of the world below.

Hasadim and Gevurot

In the Lurianic system, divine effluence is largely transmitted by means of *hasadim* and *gevurot.* These literally mean "kindness" and "judgment" respectively but, as is often the case in Kabbala, these nouns are transformed into proper nouns to depict signs of the male and female "blood" of the divine body. Each *parzuf* contains five *hasadim* and five *gevurot.* In general the *hasadim* and *gevurot* transmit consciousness (*mohin*) of *daʿat* of *zeir anpin* to the lower body of *zeir anpin.* This idea has precedent in the opaque zoharic work called the Idra Zuta. This "blood" transmits consciousness (*mohin*) from one *parzuf* to another or from one part of one *parzuf* to another. A normal descent would have the *hasadim* descend first in order to sweeten the harsher (female) *gevurot* that follow. These cosmic lights/blood fill the *sephirot* with divinity from higher realms. If they do not descend in proper order (e.g., if the feminine *gevurot* descend before the masculine *hasadim*) or only in parts, the *sephirot* and *parzufim* in question cannot complete the process of reparation (*tikkun*). The reason for the number five seems to be that under optimal circumstances each one of the lower five *sephirot* of any *parzuf* (excluding *yesod* which is viewed as the culmination of the other *sephirot*) of any *parzuf* (*hesed, gevurah, tiferet, nezah, hod*) would have one *hesed* and one *gevurah*. Since optimal circumstances rarely occur due to cosmic dysfunctionality and human sin, in most cases the *hasadim* and *gevurot* are misplaced. Sometimes the *gevurot* descend first without the accompanying *hesed*, thereby blemishing the *sephirot* they occupy. Sometimes certain *hasadim* or *gevurot* get trapped in *tiferet* and cannot descend at all leaving the lower *sephirot* of a *parzuf* without the necessary effluence to sustain them healthily. Sometimes only part of a *hesed* or *gevurah* will descend providing some sustenance but not enough to fully construct the *parzuf* properly. There are many reasons why these *hasadim* and *gevurot* cannot descend or cannot descend fully. These reasons will be explained in their appropriate places later in this study.

Eros and Desire

Another related idea to the *hasadim* and *gevurot* is the notion of masculine and feminine waters (*mayim dekhurin* and *mayim nukvin*). The Lurianic myth is founded on erotic desire. A healthy cosmos is a cosmos in the state of erotic desire leading to sexual union (*yihud*). An unhealthy cosmos is one where the masculine and feminine are uncoupled due to their proximity to the demonic. Erotic desire is aroused through the materialization of female desire (*mayim nukhvin*) which is reciprocated by male desire (*mayim dekhurin*). This appears to be based loosely on Genesis 4:16, *And your urge shall be for your husband.* That is, female desire initiates the erotic encounter. This idea is also the foundation of the necessity of mitzvot as the human arousal of the divine through devotion (in this case the Jewish male plays the female to God's male) resulting in God's (male) response of descending blessing. While this does not play a central role in our texts, it is implied throughout.

Divine Names and Numerology (*Gematriot*)

In chapter 5 on Deuteronomy, the reader will encounter a sustained analysis of Luria's use of divine names and *gematriot* (isopsephism). The use of divine names is another way of explaining the Lurianic myth that is grafted onto the *parzuf* tradition. It is more common among some Lurianic kabbalists and less in others. There are, as is well known, many names attributed to God in the Bible. These names take on important resonance in Lurianic metaphysics. Following Tikkunei Zohar, Luria further complicates matters by suggesting various ways these names can be spelled, written, or pronounced, increasing the potential for tracing divine manifestation. For example, the common name YHVH can be spelled in simple form, YHVH (numerically equaling 26) or in what is known as full form (*milui*) Yud Hay Vav Hay, which yields a higher numerical value. And with that expanded spelling it can be spelled in three forms; with "hays," "alefs," or "yuds." For example, י"ה וי"ו ה"י ד or יוד ה"א וא"ו ה"א or יוד ה"י וי"ו ה"י or יוד ה"ו ו ה"ה. The first spelling equals 72, the second 63, the third 45, and the fourth 52. These four permutations correspond to various dimensions of the godhead and the Hebrew letters that are envisioned as the manifestation of God in the world. Linguistically, the highest (72) corresponds to the musical trop that accompanies the letters in the Masoretic text; the second (63) corresponds to the vowels beneath the letters (Hebrew letters are all consonants); the third (45) corresponds to the crowns on the letters in Hebrew orthography; the fourth (52) to the letters themselves. Of course, each permutation of this divine name also includes all the other categories. In terms of *parzufim*, these four represent the four parzufim *abba* (72), *ima* (63), *zeir anpin* (45), and *nukva* (52) and the four worlds, ʿ*azilut* (72), *beriah* (63), *yezeriah* (45), and ʿ*asiah* (52).

There are various other ways of spelling the tetragramaton (YHVH). Another common method is called building. This is as follows: Y YH YHV YHVH and so on. This can also be combined with the full form or simple form to yield a plethora of names and numerical permutations. The method is not limited to the YHVH but can be used with numerous other names (Elohim, Adonai, El, Shaddai, Ehyh, etc.). There is also a method of combining two divine names, known as *hibur* or "connecting." If we take YHVH and Adonai (ADNY), we can have the following: YAHDVNHY. Each name can also be manifest out of order, as in YHVH, VHYH, HVHY, HYVH, and so on, and this can then be used to make many combinations with other names that are spelled out in similar ways, mixing them in hundreds of combinations. This method of name permutations maximizes the ways in which Lurianic kabbalists delineate divine flow, divine presence, and the ways in which the adept can access the divine realm. Finally, Lurianic kabbalists, especially those interested in applied *kavvanot* of prayer, use the vowels underneath the letters (shifting them around, multiplying them, and altering them) as another way of delineating the particular nature of a divine name. Since the name YHVH is not pronounced, the vowels serve no phonetic function and the adept can use the vowels as orthographic signs to indicate different permutations of the divine name as referring to different *sephirot* or combinations thereof.

The use of these and other name permutations was particularly popular in the eighteenth-century Lurianic kabbalism of the Beit El school led by Shalom Sharabi in Jerusalem and other locals and remains the mainstay among Lurianic contemplative practitioners of prayer (*kavvanot*). It also exists in early Hasidic prayer books. It is relevant in this study largely in the final chapter. The exegetical texts of the Lurianic system do not often apply this letter methodology although *gematriot* are a popular mainstay of the entire system. The final component of the Lurianic system relevant to this study is the use of metempsychosis or *gilgul neshamot*. A detailed analysis is taken up in the book so I will refrain from doing so now.

This brief synopsis in no way does justice to the intricacies of the Lurianic system. I have selected only those elements that are applied in this book in order to familiarize the reader with the topography of Lurianic metaphysics and the generalities of what Lurianic exegetes expect of their readers. They freely use their own myth—based loosely on Scripture—as the template to interpret the biblical myth. As Lurianic metaphysics is a world of symbols and signs it is challenging to explain the system outside of the system's own nomenclature. This is a common method in esoteric traditions to prevent the uninitiated reader from deciphering the code. A detailed elaboration of the myth is never given in one place in order that a full understanding of any part of the system requires a full understanding of the entire system. Whether this is true or not (that is, whether one needs the entire system to understand any part of it) is a contestable point but it does seem to be an underlying premise of Luria's obscurantism. It is arguably the case that all of Lurianic Kabbala is a system of elaborate "introductions," each introduction adding new dimensions to the introduction that preceded it.

In the past two centuries, numerous more sweeping "introductions" that serve as "initiation texts" (*sifrei ezer*) enabling those who do not have access to an oral transmission from teacher to student have appeared. Many of these texts have become primary texts in their own right. This very brief and schematic introduction cannot perform that function. It only lays out the major "players" in Luria's drama and begins to describe part of its "script." As the drama unfolds again and again in the course of Luria's interpretation of Scripture, I hope this playbill will be of use to the reader.

1

GENESIS

"And Adam's Sin Was (Very) Great":
Original Sin in Lurianic Exegesis

The longing for Paradise is man's longing not to be man
—Milan Kundera, *The Unbearable Lightness of Being*

For all die in Adam, and so will be made alive in Christ.
—1 Corinthians 15:22

Adam's sin, the fruits of which we are still consuming in this
world . . . will not be fixed until the coming of the messiah. . . .
—Hayyim Vital, *Sefer ha-Gilgulim*

Original Sin, Christianity/Judaism, and Kabbala

In the history of Jewish interpretation of Scripture, the utility of the book
of Genesis is an ongoing question. The telos of Genesis is arguably the
covenant with Abraham (Gen. 12:2–3), descent of the tribe of Jacob into
Egypt (Gen. 42, 43) culminating in the birth of Moses and the Israelite
people in the opening chapters of Exodus. Genesis describes life before
Sinai and Torah. The canonical exegete Isaac of Troyes (Rashi) begins
his commentary to Genesis by questioning the book's utility, implying
that perhaps it does not serve a primary function in the formation of Judaism.[1] While Genesis teaches very few commandments it nonetheless
has deep universal value. Genesis 1–11 is an extended meditation on the

nature of being human (beginning in Gen. 2–3) and the construction of human community (particularly Gen. 6–11).

This chapter explores the infatuation with Genesis of an insular Jewish mystical fraternity, particularly Genesis 3. It is curious that a fraternity whose interests seem so parochial and Judeocentric should base its entire metaphysical worldview (and subsequent reading of the Bible) on these early universal chapters of Genesis. By examining Luria's understanding of Adam's sin and his use of Genesis as a metaphysical template, I argue that the apparent mystical insularity of the Lurianic fraternity veils a much more complex project of traversing borders, erasing difference and perhaps even undoing opaque boundaries that separate the self (Israel) from the other (the gentile). I submit that Luria's interest, even infatuation, with Adam's sin may point to the pressing social issues of his day— the question of conversion and the converso. How can one be born a Christian (with a Jewish past) and return to one's ancestral tradition? Does the blemish of being born "outside" forever distinguish one from those born "inside"? Or are all humans blemished such that one's particular station in life (born a Christian, born a Jew) does not determine one's ultimate fate? Is there an antidote for Adam's sin or are all human beings, as mirrors of creation, corrupt from their inception?

My contention is that Genesis 3 is crucial for Luria and his disciples because their interests are precisely about the contours of being human, its limitations and possibilities, and not simply about the history of Israel in the conventional sense. Israel is, of course, central in Lurianic teaching (Adam is clearly the Jew and not the gentile) and he generally adopts a negative view of the gentile from earlier kabbalistic traditions.[2] However, his focus on Genesis, even as Adam is construed as Israel, is a noteworthy shift in Lurianic teaching worth exploring. I suggest this is at least partially due to this fraternity living at a time when communal borders were being redrawn and many identities were in flux. The locale of Erez Israel and the not-too-distant expulsion from Spain and Portugal added a strong messianic dimension to this teaching. The repopulation of Erez Israel and the return of many conversos to the Jewish fold may have contributed to the Lurianic exploration of the elasticity of boundaries, making an analysis of the human a desideratum. Adam's sin functions in this kabbalistic tradition simultaneously as the template of cosmogony and the unalterable nature of humanity.

Christianity, beginning with Paul, is similarly invested in the story of the sin, not simply in a reading of Genesis 3 but as a foundation for its religious worldview (Rom. 7–8). Jewish exegesis is not as focused on Adam's sin as is Christian exegesis. Its prototype of sin is the episode of the golden calf (Exod. 32). The curious return to Genesis 3 in Lurianic

Kabbala (preceded in part by the Zohar) will serve as the underlying question of this chapter. What does Genesis 3 do for Lurianic Kabbala that Exodus 32 cannot?

It is often thought that Adam's sin, as the basis for original sin, is the prerequisite of Christianity's claim of salvation through Jesus (who is both human and divine).[3] It is sometimes viewed as a doctrine that takes form after Christianity severed its ties to Judaism and partially defines that very separation. That is, original sin made Christianity both possible and necessary and, at least from the Pauline perspective, made Judaism inefficacious and obsolete. What would eventually become the doctrine of original sin is not explicit in the synoptic gospels; it appears first in Paul's epistles.[4] As doctrine, original sin emerges in late Patristic literature (particularly in Augustine) and becomes more prominent in early medieval Christian attempts to address theological and sacramental issues of the day.[5] The fact that such doctrinal formation was grafted anachronistically onto the Hebrew Bible in general and onto Genesis 3 in particular should come as no surprise.[6] Both Christianity and Rabbinic Judaism readily canonize their own positions in Scripture. The need becomes even more pronounced when the sacred texts cannot easily bear the weight of the doctrine espoused.[7]

In any case, to consider original sin an exclusively Christian phenomenon, as many contemporary Jewish scholars tend to do, is shortsighted.[8] The argument against a doctrine of original sin in Judaism is based on the undeniable fact that many Jewish thinkers, especially from Spain and Italy in the two centuries preceding the Lurianic School, strenuously denied original sin as endemic to Judaism.[9] The polemic against original sin in Judaism is largely the product of medieval Jewish polemicists and modern Jewish apologists, both of whom were and are deeply invested in highlighting the ostensible incompatibility between Judaism and Christianity.[10]

For example, commenting on the lack of original sin in Judaism, Samuel Cohen writes, "For all the artificiality of their methods of Biblical interpretation and for all the tenuousness of their ideas regarding imputed guilt and merit, the rabbis bravely championed the dignity of human nature and consistently upheld the justice of God. . . . Even the more mystic among them, who admit that the 'pollution of the serpent' infected humanity, refuse to consider human nature as hopelessly corrupted."[11] Cohen may be right about the rabbis, if by that he means the later rabbis (really medieval Jewish sages) who canonized the "theology" of Rabbinic Judaism.[12] However, this rejection of inherited sin was not unequivocally accepted by those who viewed themselves in the Jewish "chain of tradition" (*shalshelet ha-mesorah*).[13]

It is my contention that Lurianic exegesis actually brings Judaism and Christianity closer together, perhaps because his mystical fraternity flourished at a time when New Christians were returning to Judaism, thinning the opacity between these two competing religions.[14]

The immigration of conversos from Portugal put Safadean Jewry (most of who were from Muslim countries) in close proximity to Christianity.[15] The extent to which these conversos influenced Jewish intellectual life in Safed is a matter of scholarly debate.[16] Some (especially those who ended up in Safed) had a strong affinity for mysticism before they left Portugal and thus their interest in, and subsequent influence on, Kabbala after becoming Jews cannot not be underestimated.[17] With this in mind I will turn to original sin, its formation in the Lurianic tradition, and its role in constructing a Judaism with permeable boundaries.

In this chapter, I explore two dimensions of original sin in Lurianic Kabbala: the sin of Adam (and Eve), and the sins of Cain and Abel. Both also play prominent roles in Christianity (Abel's sin is not dealt with in Christianity, as we have no biblical indication that he, in fact, sinned). The distinction between Adam and Cain/Abel is crucial. The sin of Adam underlies the entire Lurianic metaphysical scheme that I will examine in detail. The sins of Cain and Abel, though less prominent in Jewish interpretation, play a central role in the nature of the human condition according to Luria. This is exemplified in great detail in the two texts devoted to metempsychosis (*gilgul* and *ʿibbur*), *Shaʿar ha-Gilgulim* and *Sefer Gilgulim*.[18]

Neither the Zohar nor the Lurianic circle use a term that easily translates as "original sin." The common term primordial sin (חטה קדמון) speaks of a cosmic rather than a human phenomenon (although the two can never be severed in Lurianic Kabbala). Primordial sin contains some important similarities to original sin, both in its sexual character and its consequences.[19] Thus I will refer to the Lurianic interpretations of Genesis 3 and terms such as חטה קדמון, the sin of the serpent (חטה הנחש) and the sin of the first Adam (חטה אדם הראשון) as examples of original sin that depart significantly from rabbinic and even zoharic notions of a similar idea, understanding that this terminological translation is not without its difficulties. The underlying conditions of the doctrine of original sin in Christian literature already exist in prerabbinic Jewish texts in ways that make my comparison tenable. Hence the emergence of a doctrine of original sin in Lurianic Kabbala is not necessarily the direct result of its contact with Christianity (through conversos), although that contact may have inspired a reassessment of an older "Jewish" nexus.

The Lurianic doctrine of original sin is based on a Gnostic and cosmocentric interpretation of Genesis 3. This is due to at least three major factors: historical, metaphysical, and socio-psychological. All three categories point in some way to the converso phenomenon, a cultural up-

heaval that had a strong impact on Safedean Judaism in the middle decades of the sixteenth century. The historical factor is the firm belief in
the coming of the eschaton that pervades sixteenth-century Kabbala and
is at least partially a product of a (Christian-inflected) messianism that
many conversos promoted.[20]

The metaphysical factor has to do with the centrality of *zimzum* (divine contraction) in Lurianic cosmogony and the fact that *zimzum* becomes the lens through which the origin of existence is constructed.[21]
Elsewhere I argued that the cosmogonic myth of *zimzum* and *shevirat ha-
kelim* (the rupture of the vessels) can be viewed as an expression of a
kind of divine sin—creation born from and into sin.[22] In that case, original sin serves as a kind of *imitatio dei*, a human extension of God's first
act that creates the material space that Adam and Eve inhabit.[23] The returning conversos, many carrying the weight of sins that were beyond
their control, represent a microcosm of the return of God to His original and pure state before creation, actualized in a second *zimzum*, or
final return, to a pristine and nonmaterial divinity.[24]

Finally, the socio-psychological factor relates to the plight of the conversos' return and the very possibility of salvation (through conversion) by
means of the study and practice of Jewish esotericism. There is a systematic
and carefully crafted theory of conversion underlying much of Lurianic
Kabbala.[25] The metaphysical doctrine of *zimzum* as divine "sin" causes Adam's sin, and sin more generally, to occupy a dominant place in the Lurianic system. It is arguably the case that this entire metaphysical system
emerges from three biblical points of sin: the sin of Adam in Genesis 3, the
sin of Cain in Genesis 4, and the death of the Kings of Edom in Genesis
36:31. Breaking ranks with the conventional notion that Judaism does not
have a doctrine of original sin, exhibited in part by the claim that Judaism
marginalizes Genesis 3, the Lurianic school turns to Genesis 3 as the origin and the reason for the demise of all history as well as its resolution—a
"second" creation that stands between humanity and the end of time.[26]

I will not rehearse the numerous references to Adam's sin in rabbinic literature. Suffice it to say that the rabbis, while considering the
notion of original sin in reading Genesis 3, ultimately marginalized the
Garden of Eden and chose Exodus 32, the episode of the golden calf,
as their archetype for sin.[27] Paul, drawing on pre- and extrarabbinic
apocryphal literature such as 2 Baruch (54:15,19), 1 Enoch, and 4 Ezra
(texts that also seemed to have had at least some influence on rabbinic
renderings of Gen. 3) constructs a notion of original sin not based
solely on an interpretation of Genesis 3 but an adaptation of scattered
verses in the Hebrew Bible such as Psalms 14:3, 51:5, and Job 14:4–5.[28]

Gary Anderson argues in *The Genesis of Perfection* that Adam's sin for

Paul counters the rabbinic archetype of the sin of the golden calf, implying that only Israelites and not humanity in its entirety are in need of
Christ's salvation.[29] For Paul the depravity of humanity through the acts
of Adam and Eve make Christ a universal and not merely a Jewish savior.[30]
As an exclusively Israelite act of sin, the episode of the golden calf understandably resonates more with the rabbis, whose agenda was to use the
Hebrew Bible as a prototype for Jews and not humanity more generally.

Before proceeding to the Lurianic texts, I will comment briefly on
one rabbinic and zoharic treatment of this issue. The passage quoted
below serves as a window into the ways in which the rabbis consider
original sin and subsequently reject it and the way the Zohar rewrites
the very same rabbinic rejection of original sin to bring it into the center of its own metaphysics.[31]

The serpent came upon Eve and inseminated her with poison.[32]
When Israel stood at Sinai, this poison ceased to function. For gentiles (*ʿovdei kokhavim*) who did not stand at Sinai the [serpent's]
poison never ceased to affect them. . . . R. Abba bar Kahane disagrees. Says R. Abba bar Kahane, this poison only affected them
[progenitors of Israel] for three generations in our patriarchs.
Abraham gave birth to Ishmael, Isaac gave birth to Esau, and
Jacob gave birth to the twelve tribes who had no deficiency (*ve-lo
be-hem shum dofi*). (b.T. Shabbat 146b).

When Israel stood before Mount Sinai, the impurity of the
serpent was removed from them so that the evil inclination was
suppressed among them. In consequence, they were able to attach themselves to the Tree of Life . . . When they sinned by wor-
shipping the calf, they descended from their high perch and lost
their illumination. They were thus deprived of their protection
from God and were exposed to the evil serpent as before, and so
brought death into the world (Zohar 1.52a).[33]

The Talmud posits that humanity was polluted through the serpent's
insemination of Eve in the garden (Gen. 3: 1–5, according to b.T. Shabbat
146b).[34] This defiled state continued until Sinai (although Abraham and
his progeny began to overcome it), at which time the Torah served as the
final antidote for the sin.[35] According to the rabbis, the emergence of
Abraham (in Gen. 12 and Sinai in Exod. 19) finally erased the sin of Genesis 3. R. Abba bar Kahane does not want to allow Sinai as prominent a
role here, arguing that the effect of Adam's sin, at least for Israel, actually
ended with Jacob's sons. In short, Israel's purity was a prerequisite for,
and not a consequence of, Sinai. Implied here is that the gentile nations,

not stemming from the patriarchal lineage of Jacob and not having stood at Sinai, forever remain under the spell of Adam's sin.[36] In fact, R. Yohanan makes this quite explicit when he says that those who did not accept the Torah (i.e., gentiles) are not free of Adam's sin.[37] Hence, original sin was both preserved and erased. Paul preserves original sin yet offers Jesus and a resolution in the future through salvation. The rabbis erase original sin through Sinai (or Jacob) offering a this-worldly resolution to Genesis 3; however, that erasure is only available through covenant, that is, to Israel. In the rabbinic mind, this concept is further complicated by a passage that insists the sin of the golden calf (Exod. 32) in effect destroys, or at least problematizes, the ontological impact of Sinai (Exod. 19) by bringing Genesis 3 back into existence.[38] However, Exodus 32 does not erase Exodus 19 entirely. Rather, the golden calf merely brings Adam's sin back into the Israelite experience, modified through the fulfillment of the Torah. To make too much of the apparent ontological bifurcation of humanity (Jew, gentile) in these talmudic passages is, perhaps, presumptuous. It is unclear whether the rabbis understood the consequence of Genesis 3 as ontological or behavioral (a disagreement that stands at the center of the Christian formulation of the doctrine before its canonization, culminating in Pelagius' criticism of Augustine and the latter's vehement response).[39] Even as we have numerous rabbinic passages that seem to argue for the behavioral and not ontological consequence of Adam/Eve's sin, there are others that lean decidedly toward an ontological reading. In fact, Rabbinic Judaism per se may not have a position on this. It is the postrabbinic sages in the Middle Ages, many of whom were invested in the utter incompatibility of Judaism and Christianity (and who claimed the inferiority of the latter) who anachronistically construct a "rabbinic stance" on original sin.

The Zohar, far more invested in the ontic status of humanity and existence more generally, enters this discussion by extending, and bending, this rabbinic trope to say that the sin of the calf brought Israel back to the state before Sinai (and back to the status of the gentiles). The Torah and the covenant remain but are no longer shielded against the pollution of humanity, Jew or gentile, since the sin of the calf in the zoharic (and later Lurianic) imagination replicates the sin of Adam and Eve. As a second instance of creation, revelation, like its predecessor, fails. In this case, the rabbis seem more rigid than the Zohar, in that the Zohar claims that the Israelites are chosen and unique but, via the sin of the calf, share the fate of Adam's sin just as do the gentiles.[40]

The Zohar's revision of the talmudic aggadah subverts the rabbinic attempt to erase original sin for Jews.[41] According to the Zohar, at least as illustrated in this passage, Jews replay the sin of Adam through the sin of the calf. This line of reasoning is made explicit in Luria. Regarding the death of Nadav and Avihu, the sons of Aaron, we read:

If Israel had not sinned with the calf the poison of the serpent would have been permanently erased, as is known. Even though Nadav and Avihu sinned with sacrificial spices (*ketoret*)[42] it would have been sufficient for them to die [a more natural death]. However, since Israel sinned with the calf causing the return of the serpent's poison in the soul of Adam it was thus necessary for them to be burnt and not die without burning. This is why Israel cried at their burning because it was the sin of the calf that caused it.[43]

If Sinai can no longer save the Jew from original sin, what solution does the Zohar posit to liberate the Israelites and later Jews from the human fate? It is the study of the Zohar itself, or the esoteric tradition more generally, that represents both an extension and an overcoming of Sinai and thus is the exclusive path out of human depravity.[44] Exodus 32 made it clear that the Torah (normative Torah and mitzvot) is not a sufficient antidote to Genesis 3. What is required is the esoteric Torah that has the power to prevent Israel from remaining hopelessly embroiled in the cyclical web of Genesis 3.[45]

While this surely points to a notion of original sin, it falls short of Augustine and those who follow him in Christianity. In effect, both the rabbis and the Zohar, at least here, reflect the Christian notion of *peccatum originans* (the event of human sin) and not *peccatum originatum* (the condition of the human being as sinful). It is this distinction, articulated by Augustine, that underwent informal canonization in the councils of Carthage (in 411–418) and Orange (in 529) and formal canonization in the Council of Trent in 1545, on which the entire doctrine of original sin rests. As I will illustrate, the adaptation of *peccatum originatum*, coupled with a particular cosmology (*zimzum*) and theory of the soul's inheritance (*gilgul*) becomes the centerpiece of the Lurianic formulation of a full-blown Jewish doctrine of original sin.

There are at least three elements that underlie Augustine's doctrine of original sin, each of which I think speaks to our Lurianic texts and contexts. The first is guilt, the second salvation, and the third the origin of the soul. It is not inconsequential that Augustine first articulates this doctrine in his most personal work, *Confessions* (5.9.16) and only later in the more oft-cited passages in his theological *City of God*. In *Confessions*, paraphrasing I Corinthians 15:22, *As in Adam all die*, Augustine mentions original sin as a "bond" from which no one can escape. This is set in an existential moment of physical anguish and pain, when he is afraid of dying the death of a convert "carrying with me all the sins I have committed against you." After conversion, one continues to sin as *peccatum originans.* Yet while distinct from *peccatum originatum,* conversion does not erase it. *Peccatum originans* is simply an expression of human failure or concupiscence. This dimension also resonates with Luther's existential rather than purely doctrinal extension of Augustinian doctrine that resulted in the Council of Trent's formal canonization of original sin as doctrine, in 1545.[46]

While both the Talmud and the Zohar may come close to defining original sin it is only with Lurianic Kabbala in the sixteenth century that the concept takes concrete form in Judaism.[47] For Paul and Augustine, original sin justifies the necessity of Christ but, as each comes from outside Christ and enters into Christ through personal conversion (Paul from Pharisaic Judaism to Christ,[48] Augustine from paganism to Christianity), original sin also explains how one can be saved without previous knowledge of salvation. For Augustine, original sin is not simply an idea that solves a dilemma in Christian doctrine as it does, say, for Origen. Rather, it is an idea that makes his own life possible.

Luria and Vital have no converso past nor much knowledge of Christianity but their growing converso audience (who are essentially converts back to Judaism) are likely acutely aware of these issues. "Born into sin," many conversos in sixteenth-century Safed had been given the opportunity to return to Judaism by the kabbalistic community through acts of penance and purification. Some became members of the fraternity.[49] For many conversos, traversing the borders between the mundane (Christianity) and the holy (Judaism) purged them of the sin of the calf, and subsequently of the sin of Adam.[50]

Adam's Sin in Lurianic Exegesis I:
Adam as a Collective Soul of Creation

Most scholarly studies on Lurianic Kabbala have thus far dealt primarily with its metaphysical system (cosmogony and cosmology) and, to a lesser degree with its understanding of mitzvot in general and prayer in particular.[51] While these topics are indeed foundational parts of the fraternity's work, there are also a series of exegetical texts included in the eight-gate compendium redacted by Hayyim Vital and edited by his son Schmuel Vital (known as the *Shemonah Sheʿarim*), and various other Lurianic texts edited by Benjamin ha-Levi, Jacob Zemah, and his student Meir Poppers that have important exegetical components. These exegetical texts employ the metaphysical framework developed in the more systematic texts through which Torah, talmudic literature, and the Zohar should be read.[52] My discussion of Adam and Eve's sin in Genesis 3 will be generated primarily by these exegetical texts, including two devoted to the subject of metempsychosis (*gilgul neshamot*) *Sha'ar ha-Gilgulim* and *Sefer ha-Gilgulim*,[53] The texts under discussion in this chapter include Vital's *Sha'ar ha-Pesukim* and *Sefer Ha-Likkutim, Sha'ar Mamrei Rashbi* and Poppers' (ed.) *Likkutei Torah,* which also includes material reproduced in *Sefer ha-Derushim* of Efrayim Penzari. The larger agenda aims to illustrate the ways in which Lurianic metaphysics serves exegetical ends by exposing a doctrine of original sin that addresses the three historical–cultural concerns mentioned above.

In the Lurianic imagination, the human and the divine are so intertwined that drawing distinctions between them is impossible.[54] Cosmic man and earthly man are mirror images of one another, and it is often not clear which is being discussed in any text.[55] Lurianic Kabbala is not simply a system of causality (the cosmos being the cause, instigated by human sin or mitzvah, and humanity, the effect).[56] The dependency of Lurianic psychology on cosmology, and visa versa, is paramount as the cosmos serve as a reified theater of human desire and failure.[57] As with earlier mystical schools, the Lurianic School takes the biblical notion of humanity being created "in the image of God" very literally, even hyperliterally, suggesting a physiological and even existential correlation between the human and the divine realm.[58]

Perhaps the most fundamental idea necessary for original sin is the notion that Adam represents, or contains, the collective soul of humanity. This is an underlying principle of patristic formations of the doctrine from Clement through Augustine, and it also stands at the center of Luther's Reformation view of original sin.[59] This notion also plays a central role in the Lurianic doctrine of Adam and the fall:

> Behold, after *zeir anpin* and *nukva* descend to their place they turn back to back because it is impossible to stand [face-to-face] because of the strength of the *kelipot.* . . . At that moment they bring forth *the soul of Adam and Eve and in them is included all the souls of creation* [my emphasis].[60]

At least in classical Kabbala from the Zohar until Luria, Adam as the collective soul seems to refer exclusively to the collective soul of Israel.[61] This is also implied strongly in the following passage from *Sha'ar ha-Gilgulim:*

> All souls included in Adam are divided into many different dimensions, into many roots. . . . In the beginning they are divided

into the three fathers (Abraham, Isaac, and Jacob), afterward
into the twelve tribes, afterward into seventy souls [who descended into Egypt] and afterward into many thousands of
smaller roots.[62]

Luria takes this notion one step further and, via a strong and hyperliteral reading of Genesis 2:20 (*And Adam gave names to all the cattle and
to the birds of the sky and to all the wild beasts*), suggests that the soul of
Adam includes the entire creation in that his actions either rectify or
alter creation:

> Know: there are fours types in creation: animals with linguistic ca-
> pability, that is, Adam; animals with no linguistic capability; vege-
> table life; and simple inorganic matter. When the world was or-
> dered, only Adam was complete and the other three categories
> were not. Afterward, through Adam non-linguistic animal life was
> fully ordered, as this is what it means, *And Adam gave names to all the
> cattle and to the birds of the sky and to all the wild beasts*. . . . Afterward,
> when Adam sinned with the Tree of Knowledge, the world was re-
> turned to a state of disorder in all its levels. Even the animals
> sinned and ate of the Tree of Knowledge, as is known.[63]

I have not located any classical source predating Luria that states explicitly that the animals also sinned by eating of the Tree of Knowledge.
We do have a talmudic source asserting that animals sinned in the generation of Noah (b.T. Sanhedrin 108a, cited in Rashi to Genesis 6:12). That
reading has a solid linguistic foundation.[64] Given the biblical narrative, it
would be difficult to see how animals were implicated in Adam's sin unless we assume that the souls of the animal kingdom were, in fact, included in Adam, perhaps as a result of his naming them and "completing
their order." In any event, the sin of the animals has more far-reaching results than just affecting the human species. In fact, the entire creation
has been transformed as a result of the sin. Adam's world was permanently altered in a way that even he cannot rectify.[65] The Zohar's elaborate discussion of how Adam and Eve are transformed, both physically
and phenomenologically, as a result of the sin is extended in Luria to the
entire creation.[66] This collective notion is also connected to time: "In the
beginning [before the sin] Adam embodied all the souls that would be in
the entire six thousand [years of creation]."[67]

There are thus two fundamental notions here that constitute original
sin: (1) that all souls were present at the time the sin was committed;[68]
and (2) that all souls and the world were unalterably affected by the sin.[69]

Vital makes this quite clear when he states, "There is no soul that is not enveloped in some way in the *kelipot*, according to its place and level, from the dimension of its sin, in being part of Adam. This [demonic] garment surrounds it and clings to it all its life."[70] Although we have seen these conditions met in numerous texts, they are made explicit in the following excerpt from *Sefer ha-Gilgulim:*

> Know that when Adam sinned he encompassed within him all souls. Hence there was no human being in the world who was not there at the sin, and does not receive some of the blemish of that sin.[71] After the sin the souls became dispersed to various parts.[72]

What emerges from this rendering of Adam as a repository of all souls, all creation, and all time is that his actions are not only inherited by other humans, a basis of *peccatum originatum,* but even more strongly, that his actions have an impact upon the very environmental context in which he lives. He is not merely limited by his materiality; he is the creator of it:

> Know: Even though it is impossible in this world to rectify all this descent [of worlds resulting from Adam's sin] through acts, one can nevertheless merit full rectification of these blemishes in the future days of the Messiah.[73]

Before we move on to the effect of the sin itself, it is important to see how the creation of Adam and Eve (before the sin) already implies a blemished and imperfectable being. Lurianic tradition posits that the union of the cosmic Adam Kadom and his female consort, Nukva, was tainted and resulted in compromised progeny.[74] The context of this next passage is that after the rupturing of the vessels (*shvirat ha-kelim*) the cosmos were already susceptible to the demonic *kelipot,* and cosmic union in any realm below ʿ*azilut* had to be "back-to-back" (as opposed to the proper "front to front," *panim ʿal panim* union) in order to be protected from these demonic forces.[75] Here we are introduced to the union that begat Adam and Eve, a union that, due to the fragmented state of the cosmos, could not yield its intended results.

> In order to unify properly they [*zeir anpin* and *nukva*] would have to be "face-to-face." This was impossible.[76] If they had done so the *kelipot* would have attached themselves to their backs as long as Adam was not there to [protect them through mitzvot]. What did they do? *Abba* and *ima* passed their *mayim nukvin* ("feminine waters" that activates Eros) to *malkhut* [the lowest cosmic realm]

and rose up to their own place of residence. There they brought with them *zeir anpin* and *nukva* [whose place is below]. In this place the *kelipot* had no jurisdiction.[77] This is where the union of *zeir anpin* and *nukva* took place [face-to-face]. Know that before Adam and Eve came into existence, [the necessary] *mayim nukvin* residing in *malkhut* were not sufficiently pure. That is why they unified in *bina*, borrowing her *mayim nukvin*. The result, however, was that Adam and Eve came out too pure [for the world] and remained attached to their lofty place above [in *bina*]. When *zeir anpin* and *nukva* descended to their rightful place in order to bring [human] souls into the world from the union that produced Adam and Eve, they returned to their state of "back to back." . . . In that state they brought forth the souls of Adam and Eve. This is what we mean when we say the souls of Adam and Eve were produced by means of a "back-to-back" union. If they had been able to unify below in a state of "face to face" [union] they would have produced an Adam and Eve who were perfected and the worlds would have been complete.[78]

This passage speaks of a double birth, one occurring in a place too lofty to achieve its desired results, bringing Adam and Eve into the world, and the second in a diminished state that also made Adam and Eve unable to complete their vocation of bringing human souls into the world. The compromise produced a human species that had a home, but the home was so corrupted that they could not achieve their intended (and commanded) goals. It is true that Adam and Eve's behavior, that is, the sin, deepened their inherent weaknesses and tarnished their own ability to rectify their actions. But given the compromised union that produced them, Adam and Eve were destined to remain in a fallen state. Their sin was, in effect, a natural and necessary extension of their origin.

Adam's Sin in Lurianic Exegesis II:
Adam's Soul, Its Divine Image, and Its Descent

In Lurianic Kabbala, the sin of Adam in the garden has a tripartite quality: (1) *zimzum* (pre-creation divine rupture) and the sin of cosmic man (*adam kadmon*); (2) the sin of *zeir anpin*,[79] and; (3) the sin of Adam and Eve as created beings. The biblical story is predicated on certain conditions set forth before the advent of the story (that is, before creation). What is assumed here is that for Adam and Eve to sin, the world already had to have been corrupted. The condition of imperfection created through *zimzum* and *shevirat ha-kelim* (the shattering of the vessels) is repeated as the "sin" of *adam kadmon* (or at least *adam kadmon*'s demise). *Zeir anpin,* the cosmic correlate of earthy Adam, is the consequence of blemished emanation and thus was already flawed and in need of repair.

Luria reads the term *Elohim* as both describing creation (*In the beginning Elohim created;* Gen. 1:1) and the formation of Adam (*And Elohim said, let us make Adam in our image;* Gen. 1:27):

> Scripture says, *And Elohim said let us make man in our image and likeness* (Gen. 1:27). It is known that when the cause of all causes (*ʿilat ʿal kol ha-ʿilot*) who is called *eyn sof* desired to emanate from God's unified light, the light that immediately went out was called Elohim. This is because the word Elohim refers to *din* (severity) when it is severed from the First Cause (in which it is) concealed and sealed.[80]

The G/god who is created/emanated in order to create in Genesis 1:1 is called Elohim. This Elohim is already alienated from its source (*eyn sof*) and hence is called severity or *din.* Elohim is the dimension of God that creates but is born in need of repair. To be Elohim already means to be imperfect. The creative turn in Luria's reading of these verses is the juxtaposition of Elohim in Genesis 1:1 to Elohim in Genesis 1:27. The realm of divinity that serves as the "image and likeness" from which Adam and Eve are created is a divinity already in a contracted and fragile state. To be created *be-zelem elohim* means to be in the image of an imperfect G/god in need of a repair (*tikkun*) that will only take place at the end-time when Elohim will fold back into *eyn sof.* Adam is created in "the image of *din*" and, as such, is already fallen from birth. His corrupted state, or *peccatum originatum,* is rooted in the very image from which he was created.

This ontic notion of a fallen Adam preceding human action is bolstered by Luria's deployment of the zoharic theory of the three Adams who preceded the creation of the earthly Adam: the Adam of *ʿazilut,* the Adam of *beriah,* and the Adam of *yezeriah.*[81] The fourth, or earthly, Adam (who is a fallen version of the Adam of *ʿasiah*) only appears later in Genesis 2:5, 6, and 7 *when no scrub of the field was yet on earth and no grasses of the field had yet sprouted . . . the Lord God (YHVH Elohim) formed the man [*וייצר יהוה אלוהים את האדם*] from the dust of the earth.*

> This verse refers to Adam of *ʿasiah,* the Adam who was created [or would become] the earthly Adam. Adam of *ʿasiah* was created when the Adam of *yezeriah* was created, as it is written, *the Lord God (YHVH Elohim) formed the Man [*וייצר יהוה אלוהים את האדם*] from the dust of*

*the earth. He blew into his mouth the breath of life (נשמת חיים) at which
point he obtained a nefesh hayya [living soul]. This is the Adam who
sinned before God and destroyed the worlds that would be fixed
in the future, as it is written, This the book of the generations of Adam
(Gen. 5:1). The day Elohim created Adam he made him in the
likeness of Elohim. At first it says, Let us make Adam, 1:26 and then
and Elohim created Adam 1:27, and further, And the Lord God formed
Adam, 2:7, and later, this is the book of the generations of Adam on the
day Elohim created him 5:1. The meaning of all this is the following:
The vessels of divinity descended twice; the first time they descended by themselves due to their inability to contain the great
divine light [referring to shevirat ha-kelim]. The second time they descended as a result of the sin. The third time they [will] descend to
facilitate the final rectification of the worlds. The secret of the first
descent is that they descended by themselves, the second time they
descended via commandment [that is, the transgression of com-
mandment], as it says, And Elohim said, let us make Adam in our image
and by our likeness to hold sway over the fish of the sea . . . [וירדו בדגת הים]
(Gen. 1:26) . . . Afterward comes the tikkun, as it says, This is the
book of the generations of Adam.*[82]

For our purposes, the verses from Genesis cited above connect the first
descent or rupture (*shevirah*), defined as happening "on its own accord,"
and the second descent facilitated by the sin. Yet the first descent creates
the context for, and the inevitability of, the second. On this reading, Adam
was not created perfect or without blemish and corrupted through sin.[83]
Adam—that is, the earthly Adam who is already the fallen Adam of ʿasiah,
was imperfect from his very creation; he was, in a sense, born as the result
of an initial descent and was created in the image of the already alienated
dimension of divinity. It is true that the sin caused further descent into the
realm of the demonic (*kelipot*), making rectification impossible before the
final *tikkun*. But even before that, Adam's very essence, as the image of Elohim, is blemished. After the sin, Adam of ʿasiah becomes the Adam of the
garden, both imperfect and imperfectable. He is a Jewish version of *peccatum originatum*. The sin of Adam is thus predictable, and even inevitable,
due to Adam's corrupt origin.

The Adam of ʿasiah (the third Adam who becomes the fourth through
descent) is not yet human. Yet it is this Adam who sins, and the earthly
Adam is created through that sin, as Vital explains in *Shaʿar Mamrei Rashbi*.

When (the cosmic) Adam was first created he had no portion in
the world of ʿasiah.[84] His body was from *yezeriah*, his soul was from

beriah, and his spirit was from *nukva d'zeir anpin* of *ʿazilut.* The root
of his soul (*neshama de-neshama*) was from *abba* and *ima* . . . When
he sinned he brought about the realm of the profane [נתהווה ביומין
דחול] (that is, the world embedded in the *kelipot*). . . . Adam was
commanded not to eat of the Tree of Knowledge (*Etz ha-Daʿat*) because it was from *ʿasiah* and Adam had no portion in *ʿasiah,* only
in *yezeriah* and above, as we explained. Since he transgressed and
ate of the Tree of Knowledge, which was located in *ʿasiah,* it caused
a blemish in all the worlds. All the worlds descended from their respective original places as follows: *yezeriah* became enveloped
in *ʿasiah* . . . *beriah* became enveloped in *yezeriah,* and *nukva*
of *ʿazilut* descended to *beriah. Zeir anpin* became enveloped in his
nukva. And so it was with all the supernal worlds . . .[85]

Adam sinned by partaking of the *Etz ha-Daʿat* (Gen. 3:6) which in
Luria's reading was in the world of *ʿasiah,*[86] a world in which the cosmic
Adam has no portion. As a result, the entire cosmos shifted downward,
drawing divinity into the realm of the demonic. Thus the birthplace of
the earthly Adam is a world already broken. The complex mapping of the
descent is not at issue here. What is relevant is only the fact that the descent resulted in Adam not only occupying the realm of the demonic
(that is, the earthly plane, albeit when it was still only in potential) but, in
fact, of also being created there. In this case, the biblical narrative is not
demarcating the earthly plane but is describing the cosmic plane that
brought the earthly plane into existence. As a result of Adam being embedded, or reconstituted, there (from cosmic man to earthly man), it is
impossible for him to elevate the fallen material world to its original
place.[87] This is not to say the human cannot elevate certain sparks. In fact,
this is the purpose of mitzvot. It is to say, rather, that being "born" into a
corrupted world limits one's abilities to affect *tikkun* due to the constant
presence of the demonic in the material world. In short, Adam's striving
for sanctification runs antithetical to the natural force that the Adam
of *ʿasiah* brought into existence.

The sin of the not-yet-human Adam of *ʿasiah* creates the condition for
the birth of the earthly Adam. *Shaʿar ha-Likkutim* argues: Before the sin
Adam's body was from *yezeriah* and his soul was from *beriah* (and a small
portion of *malkhut* or *nefesh* of *ʿazilut*). After the sin, his spirit is from *yezeriah,* his soul is from *ʿasiah,* and his body is from the realm of the *kelipot.*
Even though his soul may be noncorporeal, his divine soul is already
tainted and thus unable to maintain any temporary ascendance.

Both Adam of *ʿasiah*'s soul after the sin and the soul of the earthly
Adam are described in Lurianic literature as *halato shel ʿolam* (the best

of the world).[88] The nature of Adam's soul is transformed, reinforcing the notion that transgression radically and irrevocably transformed Adam into something that makes recovery of his pristine prelapsarian past impossible. The transformative nature of the sin—Adam after the sin is simply not the same Adam as before the sin—underlies the entire exegetical agenda of Lurianic interpretations of Genesis 3 and serves as the foundation of a Jewish notion of original sin.[89]

Sha'ar ha-Pesukim delineates three clusters of souls that originally constitute Adam, comprising ten *parzufim*.[90] The highest is called *zihara 'ilah* (the higher illumination) that is not subject to demonic influence and departs from Adam at the time of the sin (or immediately before), not to return until the end of days.[91] This is read back into Genesis as an interpretation of *they perceived that they were naked* (Gen. 3:7).

> When they (Adam and Eve) sinned, the *zihara 'ilah* departed from them, as it is written in Zohar 1.36b (top). *And their eyes were opened and they perceived that they were naked.* And they knew that they lost their *zihara 'ilah*—that it flew from them and departed, and they remained naked of it. This *zihara 'ilah* resided between the walls of the [cosmic] Garden of Eden for three hundred years and was then given to Enoch [Seth's son]. . . .[92] After Adam sinned his garments changed from light ('*ohr*) to skin (*or*). The internal dimension, which is light, was taken by Enoch and Elijah. . . . The external dimension was taken by Nimrod and those like him.[93]

It is significant that the only humans who inherit this *zihara 'ilah*, according to rabbinic and kabbalistic tradition, experience apotheosis—that is, do not die (Enoch and Elijah). In fact, it is precisely this inheritance that enables them to become noncorporeal divine beings.

> The soul of Enoch was from the soul of Adam that he [Adam] gave to him. The dimension that Adam gave him was the *zihara 'ilah*, so he was able to ascend with his body and soul intact unlike the patriarchs. Now you know why Enoch did not die like Adam and all the others. It is because his soul was from the soul of Adam whose place was under the Throne of Glory. This is why he did not die and could never taste the taste of death.[94]

It would appear that Enoch had no portion in Adam's sin. However, we read in *Likkutei Torah*, that "Enoch came and took this [*zihara 'ilah*] which enabled him to dwell with the angels. However, he did not reach the level

of his father [Adam] before he sinned."[95] This suggests, without explanation, that the consequence of the sin was so great that even the dimension
of Adam's soul that departed so as not to be corrupted by the sin was, after
the sin, still tarnished to some degree.[96]

In any event, the soul of Enoch (the *zihara ʿilah*) was immortal, not
having experienced sin, and thus he was able to function in the celestial
world as Luria notes in the same passage. "The reason why God took
Enoch in body and soul is that we know a celestial union (*zivug*) requires
an arousal from below. When there is no arousal from below, the union
can be facilitated by Enoch who is 'from below.'"[97] Mortal humans lack
this prelapsarian Adamic soul and are limited, both physically and spiritually, by the material environment created by Adam's sin.[98]

> The sin of Adam preceded the birth of Cain and Abel. At that
> time, the *zihara ʿilah* departed from Adam, which constituted the
> three higher dimensions of *ʿazilut*. It is this departure that scrip-
> ture intends when it says, *for as soon as you eat of it [the Tree of
> Knowledge] you will die.* (Gen. 2:17). That is, *when you eat of it* the
> three higher portions of your soul rooted in *ʿazilut* will depart.
> We know there is no death more difficult than that.[99]

Death is not a punishment for sin in the conventional sense but a consequence of Adam's sin. Vital writes: "Those that die from the 'kick' of
the serpent (*be-ativ shel ha nahash*), even though they did not sin in their
lifetime, it is due to the blemish of Adam that remains. This is the cause
of their death."[100] Just as Adam creates his environment as a result of
the sin, he also (re)creates the composition of his own soul that will become the inherited souls of his progeny.[101]

The second, lower level of the human soul remains with Adam after
the sin. This portion is also not subject to demonic influence and is
called *halato shel ʿolam*.[102] Before the sin these two levels (*zihara ʿilah* and
halato shel ʿolam) were one. The result of the sin was that the highest and
most pristine level of the human soul departed and ascended upward
so as not to be defiled by the sin. The third level, consisting of the nine
lower *sephirot* of all the *parzufim*, descended downward into the realm of
the demonic. It is this dimension of the soul that will be revived in the
messianic future.[103]

> The difference between the two lower levels of the human soul is
> as follows: All human souls are comprised of the lower two levels.
> The second level is higher because it contains all the remnants
> of the *ketarim* (the highest level of each *sephirah*). Another reason

for its superiority is that the second level never fell into the *kelipot* as a result of the sin while the third level fell in its totality. When souls are born into the world to fix these fallen souls it requires great effort . . . since Adam before the sin embodied souls and light from the world of *ʿazilut* . . . When he sinned those dimensions of his soul departed, except for *nefesh* of *ʿazilut*. Hence when a soul comes into this world, a soul made up of elements from (the worlds of) *beriah, yezeriah,* and *ʿasiah,* it can only recover *nefesh* of *ʿazilut* with great effort but no more . . . With the coming of Messiah ben David all will be rectified. The second level will be completed by containing all ten *sephirot* of each *keter* and once again become one with the first level that departed from Adam immediately before the sin. . . .[104]

The salient point here concerns the extent to which Vital divides the human soul after the sin in a way that separates its highest elements from the soul of any human. *Zihara ʿilah* is part of the composite cosmic soul yet is distinct from the human soul. This speaks to the extent to which Adam and, more importantly, his progeny are irrevocably changed by the sin. The second level (*halato shel ʿolam*) is not totally engulfed in the demonic yet is not pure of the sin either and must engage with the third level that is fully enveloped in the demonic in order to facilitate a future where the first and second level can once again become unified.[105] While this is optimistic in terms of the human ability to separate the human soul from its demonic context, there is also a tacit acknowledgment of the inevitability of sin (cosmic and human) as part of the human condition that cannot simply be erased or effaced through repentance or adherence to the law.[106]

At the end of *Sefer ha-Gilgulim,* Vital addresses the category of repentance and its limited efficacy in the chapter called "Sod Hibuk ha-Kever." It is important to cite a few brief excerpts from this discussion, as scholars have long argued that repentance is the category that proves the absence of original sin in Judaism.

By means of complete repentance (*teshuva shelama*) one can remove the *kelipot* that have become attached to you, even from very grave sins. However, the poisonous *kelipah* that is attached to all souls by means of the sin of Adam is not affected by repentance.[107] Only death can separate this poison. Hence, even though God accepted Adam's repentance, and atoned for his sin, the poisonous *kelipah* that became attached to him can never depart from him except through death. The reason for this is that the sin of Adam is very great. . . . This is true even for those who died from the "kick of the snake" (i.e., without sin): Benjamin, Amram, Ishai, and Caleb, and even Joshua bin Nun who did not sin with the golden calf. Even though they did not sin the poisonous *kelipot* were attached to them because of Adam's sin and it cannot separate itself until death.[108]

Thus repentance (*teshuva*) can do some important work in terms of creating partial distance between the demonic and the human, but is ultimately powerless to cure the damages wrought by Adam's sin. While repentance may suggest a slightly less pessimistic view of original sin than some forms of Christianity (in other ways Luria's doctrine is even darker), Luria is still quite invested in the notion that the consequence of Adam's sin is the very fabric of the human condition.

In part, this is because the dimension of Adam's cosmic soul that departs immediately preceding sin never descends into any human being until (or immediately preceding) the end-time. Adam is the "best of the world" (*halato shel ʿolam*), but the world where he reigns is a world constructed from sin, a world in which sin is integral and inevitable. Human action has a constructive role in the process but salvation and the erasure of Adam's sin are accomplished only via divine fiat.

Soul Inheritance (*Gilgul*), and Original Sin: The Sin of Cain and Abel and the Rise of the Human Condition

The concept of *gilgul* plays a crucial role in understanding Luria's position on Adam's sin as original sin.[109] If all human souls are composites of other souls, and are all rooted in Adam and refracted through his sons Cain, Abel and Seth, then all souls are born into the sins of past souls who await liberation. There is a notion in Lurianic Kabbala that the messianic soul is a "new soul."[110] This idea also appears in Christian readings of the soul of Jesus, which, as divine, was not tainted by Adam's sin.[111] Such a soul would then be more divine than human since human souls are defined precisely as having been tainted by Adam's sin. Such a messianic soul could thus overcome death (mortality being a punishment for the sin). The notion of the messianic soul as one that rectifies Adam's sin and thus overcomes the human condition born from that sin is the basis of the Lurianic doctrine of original sin.[112]

In the context of original sin, *gilgul* implies at least two things: (1) that all souls are inextricably tied to one another and ultimately rooted in Adam; and (2) that most souls return because they cannot complete their purpose in any one lifetime due to their corrupted origins.[113] Human beings are a composite of constantly recycled souls in search of final rectification.[114] If souls of the past were cleansed of sins, no new individuals would be born. The connection between *gilgul* and Adam's sin is an explicit doctrine in Lurianic teaching.

> Behold: Because of the sin of Adam, resulting in the admixture of good and evil, it is necessary for souls to return many times until [their blemishes] are rectified. Each time [that is, each time they descend into a corporeal body] they fix small numbers of sparks.[115]

This may be based on the popular rabbinic idea that redemption will only come when all souls have come into the world, an idea that also contributes to the Lurianic focus on conversion.[116] In fact, if we were not born in sin we would not be born at all—sin is the occasion for the descent of the soul into the world according to the doctrine of *gilgul*.[117]

> Now I will explain yet another dimension of the consequence of the sins of Adam and Cain and Abel. Know that by means of their sins not only is good mixed with evil but good itself is mixed [with other dimensions of good]. That is, sparks of the soul of Adam are mixed with sparks of Cain, and sparks of Cain with Adam.... Therefore one soul can be mixed with various sparks from different souls, from Adam, from Cain, and from Abel.[118]

Here, *gilgul* is not simply about the rectification of the sins of past lives but about the act of separation (*berur*) of the good dimensions of any human soul that resulted from Adam's sin. This concept widens our understanding of *gilgul*, connecting it not only to individual sin but also to the sin that created the human condition. *Gilgul* thus works to rectify that which is beyond any individual act of transgression.

How does *gilgul* function as an exegetical trope in the biblical narrative? How does it point to the human condition as presented in the Hebrew Bible and influence the way readers of the Bible understand the Bible and subsequently themselves? More to the point, how does *gilgul* affirm and even deepen Luria's notion of original sin? This last point requires moving away from Adam's sin and exploring the more delicate and less overt notion of the sins of Cain and Abel, the two sons of Adam who become the real progenitors of Israel and humanity.[119]

In the remaining sections of this chapter I analyze the sins of Cain and Abel in the Lurianic corpus, focusing on the ways they deepen

Luria's doctrine of original sin. This discussion will consist of three sub-sections: (1) the birth and soul construction of Cain and Abel; (2) the sins of Cain and Abel; and (3) the rectification of the sins of Cain and Abel in Moses, the Egyptian taskmaster (Exod. 2:11–16), Jethro, and Moses' wife Zipporah.[120]

The episode of Cain and Abel in Genesis 4:1–17 does not attract much attention in classical Jewish literature.[121] The Zohar does draw the story into other biblical narratives but its discussion is still quite limited. Only in Tikkunei Zohar are the sins of Cain and Abel prominent.[122] In this regard, Luria picks up a thread in Tikkunei Zohar and navigates new territory by making the sins of Cain and Abel a centerpiece of its cosmology and psychology.

The Birth and Soul Construction of Cain and Abel

One of the challenges of ascertaining the soul construction of Cain and Abel is to determine exactly when they were born. In so doing we will be better prepared to explore their relationship to Adam's sin. The Torah places their birth in the opening verses of Genesis 4, immediately following Adam's expulsion from the garden. This would put their *birth* after the sin, but the Bible never tells us of their time of conception. Was it before or after the sin? Shlomo Yizhaki of Troyes (Rashi), citing Genesis Raba, suggests that the verb form "*yada*" (instead of "*ve-yada*") to describe the conception of Cain and Abel, problematizes the plain-sense chronology of the verse, suggesting that Cain and Abel were born before the sin.[123] A similar suggestion is proffered by Avot de-Rebbe Natan, 1, not cited in Rashi. The Zohar 1.36b suggests that the sons are born after the sin, although it does not seem wed to that chronology.[124] Luria essentially agrees with the Zohar's position yet suggests an even stronger reading—that they are born *during* the sin, or, through/in sin.[125] While not in direct opposition to the Zohar, Luria draws the biblical narrative closer to a doctrine of original sin than we have in the Zohar. For Luria, the chronology is crucial because Cain and Abel (and their progeny; i.e., humanity), are the consequence of Adam's sin.

If Adam had not had sex [with Eve] on that day and also had not sinned [by eating of the Tree of Knowledge] but would have waited until Sabbath eve, all the worlds would have been rectified, as we explained regarding the sin of Adam and Eve.[126] But, because he and his wife sinned, taking the advice of the serpent, the serpent came upon Eve and inseminated her with poison (*zuhama*) *before* the union of Adam and Eve [that led to the conception of Cain and Abel].[127] Because of this [or, through this union] Cain and

Abel were born after the union (*zivug*) of Adam and Eve [and the serpent] and were already mixed with good and evil because of the poison that the serpent first placed in her.[128]

Vital acknowledges in the very same text that certain Zohar passages seem to indicate that "first, Adam and Eve were engaged in sexual union (*ʿasukim be-tashmish*) and the serpent saw them and was jealous and afterward placed his poison in her."[129] That is, the sex act may have preceded the serpent's insemination of Eve even as it occurred after "the consumption of the fruit." This implies that while the sin was considered sexual in nature, the eating of the fruit is not simply a metaphor for the sexual act but a prelude to Adam and Eve's premature coupling. While Vital entertains this second possibility in the Zohar, placing Adam's and Eve's sexual encounter before the serpent's insemination of Eve but after the eating of the fruit, he suggests that the first scenario appears more likely.[130] His reason will soon become clear. The mixing of Adam and the serpent's seed inside Eve, making Cain and Abel both human and demonic, is a central component of Luria's understanding of the two brothers. They are sons with two fathers: Adam and the serpent.[131]

A more detailed description of this event is offered in *Shaʿar ha-Pesukim* which points to the deficiencies in both Cain and Abel that contribute to their sinful nature.

In a previous comment[132] we described how the sin of Adam caused a blemish in *zeir anpin* and [the *parzufim* of] Leah and Rachel. . . . Included in these various blemishes we find a blemish in the consciousness (*mohin*) of *daʿat* of *zeir anpin* [whose place is the base of the brain] which descended [as a result of the sin] to the chest cavity (*tiferet*) of *zeir anpin*. There, *daʿat*'s five [male] *hasadim* became ensconced in the body of *zeir anpin* and could not continue to descend [to the remainder of the body of *zeir anpin*]. However, the [five] *gevurot* [of *daʿat*] began to descend, beginning with the three lower ones, finally reaching *nezah, hod,* and *yesod* of *zeir anpin*. The upper two (female) *gevurot* of *daʿat* had no place to descend and thus remained in the *moah* (mind or consciousness) of *daʿat* above [now located in *tiferet* of *zeir anpin*]. Know that Cain and Abel were born after the blemish and sin of Adam at which time the celestial Adam and Eve also were unified and gave birth to the celestial Cain and Abel. . . . It is known that every union requires male stimulus (*mayim dekurin*) which are the five *hasadim* and a female stimulus (*mayim nukvin*) which take the form of the five *gevurot*. In this case [i.e., sinful union] things were reversed. The male seminal drop (*mayim dekurin*) was from the *gevurot* that descended since the *hasadim* remained in *da'at*. Not only that, but there were only three *gevurot* [and not five] that descended. . . .[133]

The descent of *da'at* to *tiferet* (the chest cavity) of *zeir anpin* is a central tenet of the sin of Adam in Lurianic texts, an idea that will become more prominent when we discuss the sin of Cain and Abel. What this particular text explores is how the union itself was irregular in that it was not initiated by the proper admixture of masculine and feminine desire. More to the point, the proper descent of these male and female potencies (*hasadim* and *gevurot*) allows the five male potencies to descend into the body of *zeir anpin* first in order to temper and sweeten the more severe female potencies (*gevurot*) that follow. The premature descent of *da'at* (which contains these ten potencies) to *tiferet* of *zeir anpin* (a place not conducive to a proper filtering of the rest of the body of *zeir anpin* since it lies below its shoulders, representing *hesed* and *gevurah*) was that the *hasadim* were prevented from descending fully (they had no place to go!), resulting in a forced and deficient descent of *gevurot* without being properly tempered by *hasadim*. The outcome of this reversal was that the birth of Cain and Abel was constituted from "unsweetened" severity (*din/gevurah* without the masculine) that became manifest in their sins.[134] While this was more true of Cain than of Abel (supporting the biblical version of the story), even Abel's tempered personality (more *hesed* than *gevurah*) was still rooted in untempered *gevurot* (even his *hesed* was rooted in *gevurah* as opposed to the authentic *hesed* of Seth) and thus was highly susceptible to sin. Given that both Cain and Abel were born after the sin and in some versions from the same seminal emission, Abel could not have avoided sinning even if the Torah does not relate what the sin was.[135]

So far, Luria has basically adopted and extended the assumption in the Zohar that Cain and Abel were born after the sin. While this interpretation renders them postlapsarian and thus ontologically blemished human beings, it does not root their conception in the sin itself. In other texts, however, particularly in a striking text from *Likkutei Torah*, Cain and Abel are conceived in the sin itself, a notion that deepens an already entrenched description of original sin and also explains their own contribution to the downfall of humanity.

After he ate of the Tree of Knowledge, Adam continued to sin, giving birth to demons, as is known. At first he ejaculated (*zera le-vatala*) and afterward, while still in the midst of this evil deed came upon Eve and impregnated her with Cain who was from the first drop of seed. Afterward, from the second drop of seed, Abel was conceived. After that, he continued to ejaculate for 130 years in this manner:[136] There are two [really, three] realms here. The first is the masturbatory seed before Cain's conception, the seed afterward, and then Cain in the middle. When the seed that conceived Cain was emitted, it was mixed with the seed (*zera le-vatala*) that preceded it because these two ejaculations were like one continuous emission (*re-zuf teikef me-zeh le-zeh*). Therefore, the admixture of seed [from the drop of *zera le-vatala* that preceded Adam entering Eve] is part of Cain. Hence, he was born mostly evil (*rubo ra*) with a small portion of good (*u-mi'uto tov*).[137]

This text grafts Genesis 3 onto Genesis 4. The order of the sin narrative is completely effaced in that the act of seminal emission and the conception of Cain and Abel ("*yada*," Gen. 4:1) are identical, or at least consecutive, moments.[138] More than being born after the sin, here Cain and Abel are born *in* or as a result of the sin. They do not merely inherit the sin but essentially *are* the sin! As we will see, this affects their diminished soul construction and foreshadows their sinful behavior and the behavior of their soul progeny: the generation of the flood, of Babel, and of Sodom. Those born from Adam's 130 years of spilled seed culminates in Jacob and his family's descent to Egypt (Jacob being prefigured in Adam) resulting in the generation of Egypt, called "the generation of knowing" (*dor de'ah*) and the birth of Moses (prefigured as Seth).[139]

Before arriving at the culmination of the process, more must be said of Cain and Abel. The above rendering of the biblical narrative is not only found in this one place in the Lurianic corpus. In *Sefer ha-Gilgulim* there is a similar rendition with some minor but noteworthy changes.

When Adam began to emit seed his desire was greatly increased. At that moment he copulated with Eve. From the first drop came Cain, and Abel was born from the second drop. . . .[140]

Sefer ha-Gilgulim suggests that the impetus for the union of Adam and Eve was the increased desire resulting from the act of masturbation, itself a product of eating of the Tree of Knowledge. One could argue from *Sha'ar ha-Pesukim* alone that Adam's turn to Eve in the midst of this act might be construed as a moment of repentance. *Sefer ha-Gilgulim* would seem to put that idea to rest. The desire, and thus sin, that was aroused through the consumption of the fruit was not premature sexual union with Eve but, in fact, masturbation followed by sexual union.[141] Cain and Abel are products of both masturbation and premature copulation.

The demonic souls created through masturbation are considered by Luria to be very lofty—loftier, in fact, than souls born of a union between a man and a woman.[142] One striking example is the prophet Ezekiel, whose soul Luria states is rooted in the drop of semen that was emitted before intercourse with Eve, making him a particularly lofty soul and thus called "*ben Adam*" (a "true" son of Adam, or Adam alone).[143] The elevated status of the souls who are derived from the 130 years is that they are conceived from pure masculinity and are thus purely spiritual.[144] Having no vessel to hold them, they become embedded in the demonic and are thus in need of *tikkun*. Once rectified, however, they are the loftiest souls in creation. As we will see, the generation of Egypt is considered to be the progeny of Adam's spilled seed. The souls of both the Israelites and the *ʿerev rav* (mixed multitude, Exod. 12:38) were conceived during Adam's 130 "years of wasted seed" before the birth of Seth (and subsequently Moses).

The Sins of Cain and Abel

Before discussing the actual sins of Cain and Abel in Lurianic exegesis, we must ascertain who they were. In what part of the cosmic body of *zeir anpin* did they originate, and what soul inheritance did they receive from their father? We find at least two blemishes in Cain and Abel resulting from their birth after or during Adam's sin: one horizontal and the second vertical, the former between Cain and Abel (the foundation of Cain's sin) and the latter internal (the foundation of Abel's sin). *Shaʿar ha-Gilgulim* offers a general description:

> Know: *zeir anpin* has three levels of consciousness (*mohin*): *hokhma* and *bina* and between them, the third consciousness that is called *daʿat* which includes *hasadim* and *gevurot* from the two crowns (*ketarim*). When Adam sinned he caused a descent of the consciousness of *daʿat* to the two shoulders of *zeir anpin*, to the highest third of *tiferet*, which reaches until the chest cavity of *zeir anpin*. There the *hasadim* separated to the right shoulder and the *gevurot* to the left shoulder [of *zeir anpin*]. Cain and Abel were born after the sin of Adam. Cain is constituted by the *gevurot* in the left shoulder after their descent because there they do not shine as they did when they were above in the consciousness of *daʿat* itself. This is a significant deficiency.[145]

The salient point here is the way in which separation produces weakness. This is a fundamental premise of the Lurianic system and points to a neoplatonic perspective it inherits from the Zohar. In general, Luria views the consequence of this sin as one of irreconcilable separa-

tion, *tikkun* being the gradual process toward reunification. The premise here is that separation results in alienation of the male *hasadim* and
female *gevurot*.[146] Cain and Abel are each imbalanced due to the separation of the consciousness of *da'at* as it descends into the (wider) body of
zeir anpin. There is a dimension of homelessness in each son, and they
are destined to clash because each has the portion that the other needs.
The ontological and inalterable deficiency of both sons becomes clearer
as this text continues to describe the horizontal blemish:

> There is another deficiency in Cain. If Cain was located in *da'at*
> [of *zeir anpin*] in his place the external dimension of his *nefesh*
> would be from the bone and flesh of the head [of *zeir anpin*]. We
> know that all souls (*nefashot*) have an internal and external realm,
> the latter of which is its garment. The internal realm, which is
> from the *gevurot* of the consciousness (*moah*) of *da'at*, would be
> justly related to the external realm which is from the bone and
> flesh of the head [of *zeir anpin*] from its left side. However, since
> the consciousness of *da'at* descended [to *tiferet*], we find that the in-
> ternal realm of the soul of Cain is from the *gevurot* of the con-
> sciousness (*moah*) of *da'at* and the external realm is from the left
> shoulder [of *zeir anpin*]. These two dimensions have no relation.[147]

This text delineates the vertical misalignment of Cain's own soul in a
mode similar to the horizontal imbalance delineated in the first part of
the text. Both in relation to his sibling (Cain to Abel and visa versa) and
internal to their own souls, Cain and Abel are born deficient as a result
of being born from the sin. The consequence is profound. "Even
though in this world the human does not have the power (*koah*) to repair these deficiencies, even by good deeds (*ma'asim tovim*), nevertheless if one acts righteously in this world in the future, in the days of the
messiah, these blemishes will be repaired."[148]
    It would seem that there is no inherent structural difference be-
tween Cain and Abel, though in substance Abel contains more *hesed*
and is less precarious (but also, as we will see, has less potential). On
this point Luria presents us with one of his most daring departures
from rabbinic and zoharic tradition. Throughout classical Jewish literature, Cain is viewed as a "lower" soul than his brother (indeed, in the
biblical story Abel appears innocent). This hierarchy is affirmed in the
Zohar.[149] Luria argues that, in fact, in the future (that is, after the final
tikkun) it will become clear that Cain's soul is rooted in a higher source
than Abel's. There are numerous reasons for this and also various consequences. One reason is that, as stated with regard to Ezekiel, Cain is

born from the drops of spilled seed (*zera le-vatala*) of Adam whereas
Abel was not. These drops produce the highest souls because they are
derived from pure masculinity. The problem is that they have no female
vessel and are thus taken by demonic female(s) (Lilith or Na'amah) and
must be recovered through good deeds (mitzvot).[150] Cain is unique in
that he was born from this pure masculinity but has a female vessel
from his conception in Eve's womb. Thus, while the forces of evil may
have more dominion over Cain as he is *gevurah* without *hesed*, once he is
rectified, the elevated stature of his soul will become apparent.

The seemingly counter-intuitive advantage of Cain over Abel stems
from the fact that Cain, rooted in *ima*, actually has more potential because his original state is more revealed:

In this you will understand the advantage of Cain over Abel.
This is because the light of *abba* [the root of Abel] has no way to
pass into *zeir anpin* except from being enveloped in the lights of
ima. Hence, the souls from Abel must be sustained from the
lights of *ima* through the souls of Cain. Understand this
well. . . . The name of *zelem* (TZ'L'M) refers to the *zelem* of *ima*,
which is Cain. Hence the *gematria* (numerical value) of Cain
(160) is equal to the *gematria* of *zelem* (160).[151]

This is Luria's understanding of the first-born status of Cain and is also
his way of exhibiting the radical reversal that *tikkun* creates more generally. Rooted in a higher source, Cain is more fallible and, in fact, fails.
But when rectified, like Ezekiel, the very origin of his fallibility (the
pure masculinity of masturbation) becomes his most important quality.
On this reading, the seventeenth-century Sabbatean reversal of sin and
mitzvah so prominent in the work of Nathan of Gaza and others is not
so far from Luria's own depiction of the end.

The Lurianic circle does not follow the heretical route of their Sabbatean descendants. However, the notion that fallen souls (the conversos?)
may be, in fact, rooted in a higher source and that when they return can
reach a higher level of sanctity is quite suggestive given the sociological
context in which this material was composed. Conversion to the Body of
Israel as a vehicle of return not only reconstructs the cosmic body but also
invigorates it with energy Israel alone could not produce. The conditions
for redemption must include thinning the opacity of metaphysical and sociological barriers and the redrawing of previously conceived boundaries.

To return to our discussion, the sins of Cain and Abel not only repeat original sin but in fact extend it further. The *tikkun* for the sins of
Cain and Abel, which we will examine below, is a partial *tikkun* for orig-

inal sin in the Lurianic imagination. This is another way in which Luria
presents the biblical narrative in Genesis 4 as central; first he projects it
backward to the original sin narrative in Genesis 3 and then forward to
the history of humanity as depicted in the Bible:

> The rabbis teach, "Cain was hanging by a thread and the flood
> came and drowned him."[152] This is the explanation. Cain em-
> bodied all the drops of semen first and last [meaning, before Ad-
> am's union with Eve and afterward, for the next 130 years]. They
> [the products of this seed] were not from [the *yihud*] of *zeir anpin*
> and *nukva* [but from Adam alone]. Cain, who was also from the
> *yihud* [of *zeir anpin* and *nukva*], embodied them, They [the souls
> of the first seed] were also all from his soul root. Cain was obli-
> gated and charged with rectifying all these dimensions. How-
> ever, he did the opposite—he added to the sin. This is the secret
> meaning of the passage that the generation of the flood were de-
> scendants of Cain who all "spilled their seed on the ground,"[153]
> destroying everything in the past by bringing the flood upon
> themselves.[154]

Luria portrays the generation of the flood, the first of the four generations culminating in the generation of Egypt (Flood, Babel, Sodom,
and Egypt), as replaying the garden narrative of masturbatory sin, now
linked not to Adam but to Cain. Cain embodies the consequence of
pure masculinity (he is conceived in the masturbatory act) and his sin,
as we will presently see, is also of a sexual nature.[155]

The Bible relates that Cain's sin was one of fratricide brought about
by jealousy. Cain brings a sacrifice to God that is not accepted and Abel
brings one that is accepted (Gen. 4:3–16). Luria's reading of these passages illustrates his predilection to view the biblical text as a metaphor or
allegory (*mashal*) and then to offer his inner reading of the metaphor
(*nimshal*) to draw out its esoteric meaning.[156] In so doing, he systematically reconstructs the narrative to meet his particular metaphysical and
symbolic needs. The *nimshal* of the metaphor of jealousy is psychologized,
resulting in an act that almost replicates the sin of Adam and sets up the
rectification of this act in Moses killing the Egyptian taskmaster.

There is a popular midrashic motif that Cain and Abel each had a
twin sister. From a plain-sense perspective this is obvious—how else could
they procreate? Since the Bible never tells us if Eve became pregnant
after Cain and Abel, it is easier to suggest that each son was born with a
twin sister who also became his mate. The midrash goes further than
merely solving this "gap" in the narrative. It extends the twin-sister con-

struction, linking it to Cain's jealously of Abel, the source of the first act of murder. His jealously, the midrash posits, is not about the sacrifice (Gen. 4:4–5) but about Abel's extra twin sister–mate who Cain claims the right to possess: "Says Rav Huna about the extra twin that was born with Abel—this one (Cain) says, 'I will take her because I am the first-born.' And this one (Abel) says, 'I will take her because she is born with me.' From this we have the verse, *And Cain arose [to kill his brother]*."[157] This idea comes into play as a central motif in the Lurianic tradition, even though Luria changes the nature of the argument by adding a second twin to Cain, not present in the midrash. Luria's extension and transformation of the midrashic trajectory appears numerous times in the Lurianic corpus, but its most succinct presentation is from *Sefer ha-Gilgulim.*

> Now we will explain the extra [female] twin born with Abel who was the source of Cain's jealousy, consequently killing Abel. First we must explain that it is permissible for a king to marry 18 wives.[158] We have already explained in chapter 26 that Cain was the *zelem* of *yesod* of *abba* and Abel was the *zelem* of *yesod* of *ima*. We also explained there that *nezah, hod, yesod* (NHY) of *abba* is enveloped in NHY of *ima*.[159]

Vital then explains that both *abba* and *ima* have two *malkhuyot* or feminine components.[160] The point is simply to account for the extra feminine (*malkhut*) component in Abel that is absent in Cain, absent because Cain's extra twin emanated outward to become *parzuf* Leah, the first wife of Jacob. It is the extra "sister" of Abel who becomes the object of Cain's jealousy.[161]

In another variant we read, "Since Cain was mixed with *kelipot* he did not have an extra twin because the *kelipot* cannot reach the upper ה, as is known."[162] Luria presents us with an extension of the midrash, creating a scenario whereby Cain's sin is one of sexual jealousy, reflecting a reading of Adam's sin as one of sexual jealously in seeing Eve and the serpent engaged in a sexual encounter. Whereas Cain's sin is, prima facie, one of murder, earlier we examined how Luria connected Cain to the generation of the flood and interpreted the sins of that generation as one of "spilling seed."[163] Cain's sin has thus been transformed to yet another instantiation of misplaced sexual desire, another moment of original sin.

Turning to Abel's sin requires Luria to engage in a more radical form of exegesis since we have no evidence in the Bible that Abel was guilty of any sin. Nor does the rabbinic tradition invent one for Abel.[164] As is the case for all midrashic interpretation, the exegete must first create the space, the condition, and thus the need for his midrashic interpretation.[165] If we assume that Abel was born from the same seminal emission as Cain, as a by-product of original sin, he too must sin. From a purely kabbalistic perspective, if Abel is to play a role in the *tikkun* of Adam's sin by returning via *gilgul* (and not only spiritual impregnation—*ʿibbur*) he must have something to rectify.[166] In fact, as we will see, Abel's role is crucial as he comprises one-third of Moses' soul (M=Moses, Sh=Seth, H=Hevel [Abel]).[167]

In one approach, Abel's sin is explained as one of "gazing" at the *shekhina*, an act that appears to reflect the prohibition Rabbi Akiba warns against in the talmudic description of the four who entered Pardes.[168] There are a few Lurianic texts that describe Abel's act of transgression although no one text ties it back to Adam's sin in any satisfactory way. For example, in *Likkutei Torah* we have an off-handed correlation of Abel's sin to Adam's in the context of Abraham and Isaac and the binding of Isaac:[169]

> Know that Adam and Abel both sinned in that they gazed (*sh'hezizu*). They were both reincarnated in Abraham and both in Isaac. The reason for the reincarnation into Isaac was to rectify Abel's sin and in Abraham to rectify Adam's sin. . . . Isaac was Abel (Hevel) as it is written, *the son born to him* (**B**eno **H**anolad **Lo** = He**V**e**L**) (Gen. 21:3). This sin was rectified by means of the *akedah* (Gen. 22). Hence Isaac was not brought up [to be bound] until he was 37 years old—37 being the numerical equivalent of Abel (He**V**e**L**—H=5, V=2, L=30). Thus it is written, *God will show him the goat* (Gen. 22:8). This is in order to rectify the sin of Abel who sinned with sight. . . .[170]

From this we only know that Abel's sin was like his father's and that both sinned with unwarranted gazing. We are not told of the object of the gaze in either case. Regarding Adam, at least as read into the biblical narrative, it is likely that the gaze refers to his gazing upon Eve and the serpent, a scene that aroused his desire, resulting in wasted seed (*zera le-vatala*). In terms of the object of Abel's gaze, we read the following:

> We can now understand the mishna "Even he sees a skull (*galgolet*) floating on the water" (Avot 2:6). We already know that the sacrifice of Cain was from *ketz ha-yamim* (the end of days), the word *ketz* (KZ) referring to the darkness that covers the face of creation, as is known.[171] And the sacrifice Abel brought was from *ketz ha-yomin*, as is known.[172] Therefore it is written *Abel brought also from it* (*gam hu*) (Gen. 4:4). It should have said, "And Abel brought from the

first of his flock." Why does it add *also from it?* It does so to point out the secret of the matter. That is, that the sacrifice of Abel was also mixed [with the demonic]. What was this admixture? You already know that *ʿarikh anpin* [the skull of cosmic man] contains 370 lights (*nehirin*). Regarding Abel's sacrifice, it is written, *And God paid heed to Abel and his sacrifice (vayesha [ישע] Ha-shem ʾel Hevel . . .)*. At that time, Abel gazed upward to the place of the 370 lights [of *ʿarikh anpin*]. There is a barrier between the 370 lights of the skull [*ʿarikh anpin*] and what lies below it. . . . This is the secret meaning of the rabbinic statement, "Even he sees a skull (*galgolet*) floating on the water." This refers to Abel who gazed upon the 370 lights of the skull of *ʿarikh anpin*.[173]

The 370 lights (*nehirin*) of *ʿarikh anpin* in general refer to the inner union between the head of *ʿarikh anpin* and the *shekhina*, resulting in an overflow producing the lower *parzufim*.[174] This also refers to the *ʿor peneʾal* or "light of the face" of *ʿarikh anpin* (hence the notion of gazing at the face is also implied).[175] The reference to gazing at the *shekhina* is made explicit in *Shaʿar ha-Pesukim:* "Behold, Abel gazed upon the *shekhina*, and so did Isaac as it is written, *And his eyes became weak* (Gen. 27:1). The sages say this was because he gazed at the *shekhina* (Pirkei de-Rebbe Eliezer, 32)."[176] Abel was guilty of gazing beyond where he was permitted—to *ʿarikh anpin*. This is what the text means when it says, "There is a barrier (*masakh*) between the 370 lights of the skull [*ʿarikh anpin*] and what lies below it." The sin of unwarranted gazing is viewed here as being fixed with Moses and the burning bush. "When was Abel's sin of gazing before the *tikkun* rectified? It is with the burning bush, as it is written, *And Moses hid his face because he was afraid to look at God.*"[177]

Up to this point we have a link between Adam's sin and Abel's sin, and various versions of how both involved illicit gazing. However, we have not yet seen a connection, even by inference, between this and the sexual nature of Abel's sin that would link it to original sin. This link appears in *Shaʿar ha-Klalim*, a fairly early redaction of Lurianic material by Vital:

This is the secret of Moses, **M**=Moses, **Sh**=Seth, **H**=Hevel. Abel sinned by gazing at the *shekhina*. This means that Abel wanted to direct the light that emanated out from *yesod* of *abba* that broke through [*parzuf*] Jacob. Abel wanted to return it to the back of Jacob and give it to Rachel [who is situated in the back of Jacob], who is called *shekhina*. This is why he gazed to shoot (*hiziz*) toward the *shekhina*. He wanted to enlighten and *hiziz* the *shekhina* with light that was Jacob's.[178]

At play here is the double entendre of *hiziz* (to gaze) with a more erotic meaning of "to shoot," to "emanate toward" or to "blossom." What is suggested is that Abel, in gazing where his eyes should not have been was trying to turn the emanation of *yesod* of *abba*, a clear reference to seed, from the front of Jacob to his back in order to inseminate the *shekhina* (Rachel).[179] If successful, this would have produced a premature *tikkun*. Abel was prematurely trying to *hiziz* seed (*zera*) to the *shekhina*. The premature sexual encounter more generally lies at the very foundation of Adam's sin, and is rooted in classical rabbinic tradition and more overtly in the Zohar.[180] What is implied here is that Abel's sacrifice, although accepted, was also tainted (*Abel brought also from it [gam hu]*) (Gen. 4:4), the blemish being that it was accompanied by a premature attempt to inseminate the *shekhina* with the seed of *abba* instead of *zeir anpin:* that is, to circumvent the back-to-back status of Jacob (*zeir anpin*) and Rachel (*shekhina*) by turning the light (seed) of *abba* toward her.

But there is more here. Earlier we read that Abel is identified as "*yesod* of *abba*."[181] If so, this attempt to direct the "light" (seed) of *yesod* of *abba* to the *shekhina* is actually Abel trying to inseminate the *shekhina* himself! The term *hiziz* now takes on an even stronger sexual connotation. Through the power of the gaze, Abel ventured where he did not belong and, as a result, caused a blemish in the world that required, as we will presently see, his reincarnation in Moses.

The Tikkun *of the Sins of Cain and Abel and the* End *of the* 130 Years *of Sin*

In the beginning of this chapter, I discussed how, according to Luria, Sinai played a role, however temporary, in rectifying the sin of Adam for Israel. In both the Talmud and the Zohar, the sins of Cain and Abel do not play any role in the Sinai event (in fact, the sins of Cain and Abel do not play a role in talmudic literature whatsoever, and only a nominal role in the Zohar). Given the attention paid to Cain and Abel's sin exhibited here, the reversal to Adam would logically require an initial rectification of their sins to set the stage for the Sinai event that would annul the demonic poison of the serpent, thus elevating Israel to a prelapsarian state.[182] According to the Zohar, the purified state achieved at Sinai did not last long. The sin of Adam was reintroduced into Israel through the sin of the golden calf only to be rectified through salvation or the messianic age. Thus, the Zohar supports at least some notion of original sin.

In Lurianic exegesis, the doctrine of original sin becomes stronger, even central, to its whole worldview. This is exemplified by the sins of Cain and Abel who, as the progeny of Adam, repeat their father's sin further distancing humankind from any possibility of retrieving a prelapsarian state. The biblical narrative in Exodus that leads up to Sinai (Exod. 1–19) is interpreted by the Lurianic school as the rectification of the sins of Cain and Abel in preparation for the Sinai event. The Exodus characters embody the mythic figures of Cain, Abel, and Abel's sister–wife. The Exodus counterparts include Moses, the Egyptian taskmaster (Exod. 2:11), Jethro, and Zipporah. Luria's reading combines a tragic sense of ultimate justice and a typological hermeneutic of prefiguration. His uses metempsychosis (*gilgul*) to envision the first chapters of Exodus (particularly Exod. 2 and 3) as a redramatization, with different results, of Genesis 4. Each Genesis figure, guilty in some way, returns (or part of their soul returns) in the Exodus figures. A drama then ensues whereby the one guilty of sin atones or acts in a way that completes unfinished business.

The deployment of inspiration, or *ruah ha-kodesh*, serves to justify how Moses could commit an act of murder (Exod. 2:12). But this *ruah ha-kodesh* appears to be more intuitive than cognitive. According to Luria Moses senses that he must act in such a way toward the Egyptian taskmaster, but the full ramifications of the act remain concealed.

Before analyzing Luria's portrayal of the early chapters of Exodus, we must first understand why this *tikkun* is appropriate now. That is, why is the generation of Egypt ready for the dramatic redux?[183] The prehistory of Israel, and its first generation in Egypt, are viewed by Luria as necessary stages in the four-part progression of *gilgul* required to complete the *tikkun* of any soul.[184] The sin that initiates the need for *tikkun* is the sin of Adam. The generations are as follows: the generation of the flood, the tower of Babel, Sodom, and finally Egypt.[185] While each generation holds the potential for *tikkun*, each ultimately fails for at least two reasons: first, each continues to sin and extends the original sin of Adam; and second, because the sins of Cain and Abel are not rectified in any of these generations, the possibility for a complete *tikkun* is never realized.

These four generations are viewed as Adam's progeny from his 130 years of wasted seed, *zera l'vatala*, culminating with the birth of Israel as a nation in Egypt. The following citation from *Sha'ar ha-Pesukim* maps out the process that concludes with Israel in Egypt as the final phase of the *tikkun* of Adam's 130 years of wasted seed. What is not yet rectified is the other dimension of Adam's sin, the premature insemination of Eve. That will occur via divine fiat at Sinai.

All of the demons and spirits that were created through the 130 years Adam separated from Eve were lofty and holy souls from the realm of *da'at* that became enmeshed in the demonic (*keli-pot*), requiring many reincarnations in order to purify them. Hence we do not see the emergence of Israel until Jacob. This is because most of those souls [of the 130 years] were in the *kelipot* and were in the process of clarification from generation to generation [until that time]. The *tikkun* did not begin in earnest until Jacob, the chosen of the patriarchs (*bakhir sh be-avot*), who rectified the sin of Adam. Then the *tikkun* begins with his sons who are from this seed (of the 130 years). . . . The beginning of the process of *tikkun* occurred in the *gilgul* of the generation of the flood. Since their origin was from a bitter place, that is, the product of Adam's spilled seed, they rebelled against God. Their sin was one of spilling seed on the earth as it is written, *All flesh corrupted (hishkhit) their ways on the earth* (Gen. 6:12). And also, *And God said, I will blot out all humans* (Gen. 6:7). This refers to the generation of the flood, for they are sons of Adam himself (that is, Adam and not Eve) who spilled seed for 130 years. . . . Afterward, these souls were reincarnated in the generation of separation (or Babel, Gen. 11). They also committed evil like their predecessors, however, not with spilling seed. The Lord came down to see the city and tower *adam* [i.e., the descendants of Adam] built (Gen. 11:4). The Zohar and the sages read this to mean literally "the sons of man," referring to Adam.[186] That is, they were his sons from the 130 years. They were reincarnated a third time in the generation of Sodom, of which we read, *The inhabitants of Sodom were very wicked sinners against God* (Gen. 13:13). This hints that their wickedness was likened to the spilled seed of Adam's [sin].[187] . . . After the reincarnation of these three generations, *Truly God does all these things, two or three times to a man* (Job 33:29) they were reincarnated a fourth time in the children of Israel in Egypt. At that time the *tikkun* began.[188]

This text goes on to explain the tortured nature of Egyptian servitude as the final stage of preparation. The important point is that the generation originating as the product of Adam's spilled seed in the garden is no longer required to undergo collective *gilgul* but can complete any necessary rectification while in Egypt. There is another important dimension to this generation that we will speak about in the next chapter: the *ʿerev rav* who are also from the source of Adam's sin but were not quite as prepared as Israel for the covenant.[189] Part of Israel's work or, more precisely Moses' work (Israel is merely an extension of Moses, according to Luria),[190] is to facilitate the preparation of these *ʿerev rav* to exit Egypt with Israel and be a part of the Sinai experience. In fact, Luria implies that the main purpose of Israel being in Egypt (since they were already rectified themselves through Jacob) was to gather these *ʿerev rav*.[191]

From Luria's perspective, the second crucial component here is the return of Cain and Abel who are not fully rooted in the seed of the 130 years but whose sins play an important role in the fall of humankind. The souls of the 130 years, now ready for redemption, must wait for the rectification of the sins of Cain and Abel in order to move forward. The birth of Moses (who is both Abel and Seth) is a sign of the final phase of the *tikkun* of the 130 years and the beginning of its final rectification. "Know that Moses is in the realm of Adam. . . . Adam sat for 130 years and did not have sex with Eve and afterward she gave birth to Seth. So Yoheved was 130 years old when Moses was born. During these 130 years Adam, who was evil (*ra*), brought forth demons and spirits, who were rectified through the servitude in Egypt. Afterward Moses was born, who was good (*tov*), as it is written, *she saw he was good (tov)* (Gen. 2:2)."[192]

The correlation between Moses–Abel and Moses–Seth (who was born 130 years after Cain and Abel's sin and thus represents Adam's *tikkun*) is replete in Lurianic exegesis.[193] One of the more succinct versions of this narrative can be found in *Sefer ha-Gilgulim:*

Now we will expand our explanation of the *gilgulim* of Cain. Behold, the Egyptian taskmaster (*'ish mizri*) who Moses killed (Exod. 2:11) inherited the *nefesh* of Cain from the side of evil. Moses held the *nefesh* of Abel from the side of good. Just as Cain killed Abel and took his twin sister, so the Egyptian (*mizri*) beat a Hebrew (*'ish ivri*) after taking his [the Hebrew's] wife, Shelomit bat Divri.[194] This is why it is written, *He saw an Egyptian beating a Hebrew, from his brother.*[195] What does *from his brother* mean? If he was an Israelite, let him just say Hebrew (*'ish ivri*). If you will say he was related to Moses, this cannot be because he [the Hebrew] was from the tribe of Dan, and Moses was a Levite.[196] Rather, Moses [who is Abel] saw with inspiration (*ruah ha-kodesh*) that the Egyptian who was beating the Hebrew was *from his brother* that is, from Cain . . . Cain was reincarnated to fix his blemish and [Moses saw that] he was, in fact, extending it [by beating the Hebrew because he, the Egyptian, had raped his wife]. Therefore, he killed him.[197]

The alteration of the modifying noun "from his brother" (*me-ehav*) to describe the Egyptian and not the Hebrew is a classic example of the rabbinic intolerance for superfluous language in scripture (even as the rabbis seem to ignore this particular instance). However, instead of using the extra word to justify Moses' action as an act of compassion toward "his brother" suggested in midrash, Luria turns the modifying noun to apply to the Egyptian, making the Egyptian Moses' brother thereby justifying Moses' murderous act.[198] Yet while this liberates the good side of Cain, which immediately attaches itself to Jethro, it also is a violent act that requires punishment. Hence the rectification of the sin of Cain that readies Israel for redemption is not fulfilled. The stain of Cain's original sin remains.

> After Moses killed him, a part of Moses' soul departed and attached itself to the soul of Jethro, who was from Cain. At that moment, Jethro converted. . . . However, Moses was punished for this act, as we will explain. We read, *if anyone kills Cain, sevenfold vengeance shall be taken on him* (Gen. 4:15).[199] The vengeance that God will take on Cain's death will be through Moses, who has seven names, as the rabbis teach. He killed the Egyptian, who was a *gilgul* of Cain.[200]

The end of this passage suggests something quite provocative. Moses' death, while usually viewed as retribution for his hitting the stone in the desert, is actually punishment for killing the Egyptian (Cain), a transgression of God's word in Genesis 4:15 even as the act was necessary for the exodus! While the evil side of Cain is diminished (it actually becomes part of Balaam, Moses' counterprophet) it can only be done through an act of murder that extends the blemish of Cain's sin! The second fall (Exod. 32 and the episode of the golden calf) is prefigured in Moses' murderous act coupled with his claim, correct in principle, that Israel's purpose in Egypt was to redeem the ʿerev rav.[201]

The completion of Moses' pre-exodus vocation was to marry Zipporah, the daughter of Jethro (now the rectified Cain). Of course, this could never have happened had Moses not killed the Egyptian and fled to Midian where Jethro lived. Luria suggests that by marrying Zipporah, Moses was remarrying the lost twin sister whom Cain stole from Abel. The correlation between Zipporah and Abel's twin is explicit in several Lurianic texts:

> Jethro was the final completion of the *tikkun* because he returned the extra twin sister that Cain took from Abel and gave her to Moses, who is Abel. Jethro gave his daughter Zipporah [to Moses], who was that extra twin. Jethro was Cain, as he had seven names, as it is known.[202] Moses, who was Abel, also had seven names.[203] Therefore, Moses and Jethro embody *sevenfold* (Gen. 4:15); they were seven and seven. At that moment, Cain *rose up* and was rectified. Now, [that is after Moses' *tikkun*] the language of *And Cain rose up* (*va-yakum Kayin*) refers to raising up (*kima*) and *tikkun*.[204]

The rectification of Cain's sin is complete through the marriage of Moses to Zipporah. Moses now returns to Egypt to redeem Israel and complete the final *tikkun* of Adam's sin. Yet, as we will see, this cannot occur because in order to prepare Israel for redemption and to rectify the soul of Cain, Moses has to kill Cain (the Egyptian) and suffer the consequences.[205]

Moses and the Second Fall: The Return of Original Sin

Luria's rendition of the story of the exodus and Sinai is not only a story of failure but a story whose failure is prefigured from the beginning. Moses fixes Cain's sin, thus diminishing the unredeemable evil in Cain's soul, and does as much as possible to erase Adam's sin as well. There are two events, however—one collective and one individual—that illustrate the impossibility of overcoming original sin: the golden calf (Exod. 32), and Moses' sin with the rock in the desert (Num. 20:8–11). I suggest that these events do not erase the *tikkun* accomplished, but that the *tikkun* itself was corrupted. That is, Adam's sin, as inherited, cannot be overcome except by divine fiat. The episode of the golden calf will be discussed at length in the next chapter. Here I want to discuss Moses' sin in the desert as replicating Adam's sin, thereby erasing his pre-Exodus *tikkun* making original sin a permanent part of Israel's condition.

First, Luria is interested in the way the golden calf affects Moses' soul. Since Moses is the individual incarnation of collective Israel, his potential is directly affected by the collective.

> *But God was wrathful with me on your account* (Deut. 3:26). You already know that Moses contains the realms of smallness (*katnut*) and expansion (*gadlut*), as is the case with all souls. . . .[206] The secret is as follows: God gives wisdom to the leaders of the generation (*parnasei ha-dor*) according to the merit of the generation. When Israel sinned with the calf, Moses returned to an embryonic state (*'ibbur*) and lost the levels of enlightenment he had achieved previously. What remained was only an embryonic remnant, and thus he returned to a state of smallness. The *'ibbur* [gestation] of *zeir anpin* is in the womb of the supernal *ima*, and so it is written **V**=*veyitavor*, **Y**=*YHVH*, **L**=*le-ma'ankhem* (Deut. 3:26).[207] Moses returned to the name of YHVH who is *ima* and gestated there once again. Hence the verse contains the letters YVL (*yuval*) because *ima* is called *yuval*, which is the fiftieth (Jubilee) year.[208] Just as [their] sins caused *zeir anpin* to reenter a state of *'ibbur*, so it is with the leader of the generation.[209]

Here we see that Moses blames Israel for his own loss, a logical extension of Luria's assumption that Moses embodies the collective soul of Israel so that their sin equally corrupts him. The plain-sense meaning of God's anger toward Moses is taken to mean a separation between God and Moses, one that erases his previous accomplishments (i.e., reaching the state of *gadlut*). While Moses may have achieved a quasi prelapsarian state by rectifying Cain's sin, his experience at the burning bush and the theophany at Sinai, he now returns to a fallen state, inevitably destined to repeat Adam's failure. In fact, this is exactly how Luria understands Moses' sin of hitting the rock.

> Regarding the rock that Moses struck (Num. 20:11) we have already explained that the rock is Rachel. Therefore, the rock was not given to the generation of the desert, only to the future generation that will enter Erez Israel.[210] This is explained in the secret of the generation of the desert. We explained there that Moses' intention was to turn Rachel, face-to-face with *zeir anpin*, even when the generation of the desert was still alive. We also explained the secret of Moses in this act. . . . Moses wanted to take the lights emanating from *yesod* of *abba*, which emanate out from the front of *zeir anpin* and turn them to *zeir anpin*'s back, to Rachel. This would facilitate the complete *tikkun* of Rachel by the means of these lights. The staff would be the catalyst for this. This is why Moses struck the rock, just as a man would strike something with his staff in order to push it back, so Moses struck [the rock] with his staff opposite *zeir anpin* to push the lights [of *yesod* of *abba*] to Rachel, who stands in back of *zeir anpin*, which is called *sela* (rock). The numerical value of *sela* is 161 [30=ל, 60=ס, 70=ע, plus 1 represented by the word itself] and is manifest in the name *ehyeh*, spelled with *yudim*, which Rachel embodies as all of her essence is from *yesod* of *bina*, which is also 161. The sin in all this is that Rachel was not able to receive those lights by means of Moses' striking them backward. Rather, she could only receive them if she and *zeir anpin* were face-to-face, whereby she could receive them without any act of striking.[211]

Here Luria reads the act of striking the rock as identical to the way he understands Cain's sin as replicating Adam's. This correlation, until now only implied, is finally made explicit:

> The sin of Moses with the rock is exactly (*mamash*) like the sin of Adam when he laid with Eve before Shabbat, which caused the

union to take place between *yesod de-katnut* (a *yesod* not fully formed) and the *shekhina*. *Yesod de-katnut* is also called *nahash* (serpent). This is also the meaning of the sin involving the serpent coming upon Eve. [And] it is identical to the striking of the rock, the rock being Rachel and the staff being *yesod de-katnut*.[212]

Moses fails, partly because he is pulled down by Israel via the golden calf and partly, perhaps, because his own *tikkun* (killing the Egyptian) corrupted him. He was able to get Israel to Sinai but not fully overcome Adam's sin and end human history. In Luria's imagination, Moses the redeemer becomes Adam the sinner, as he must. For this kabbalistic school, Adam's sin is not simply a moment in the biblical rendition of human history but permeates the entire biblical understanding of the human condition, a condition that human beings simply cannot overcome.

Conclusion

Returning to my initial claim about the possible historical context of original sin in mid-sixteenth-century Safed, in this chapter I explored the curious fact that the sin of Adam moves from the periphery in much of classical Jewish exegesis to the center of Lurianic thinking. I suggest that the theme of sin more generally, usually rooted in Exodus 32, now returns to Genesis 3. My initial intuitions led me to explore Christian readings of Genesis 3 and 4 and Exodus 32. Through this study I came to realize that Luria was, in some way, following a Christian interpretive trajectory. This chapter explored this trajectory and some possible reasons underlying this unexplained shift of emphasis from Exodus 32 to Genesis 3–4.

We know that some conversos who chose to immigrate to Safed found kabbalistic fraternities a welcome community. We know a few kabbalists in the sixteenth and seventeenth centuries (Solomon Molkho, Jacob Zemah, Abraham Herrera, and perhaps Judah Albotini) were in fact conversos.[213] What we do not know is the extent to which these conversos may have influenced kabbalistic doctrine in this period. We also do not know whether our kabbalists catered, perhaps unwittingly, to the concerns of their converso constituents or viewed their return as a sign of redemption that was then reified into their metaphysics and subsequently used as a template for their scriptural exegesis.[214]

In this chapter, I suggested that the Lurianic doctrine of original sin did, in fact, accommodate to the converso phenomenon, and perhaps was influenced by it. The converso burdened with the weight of sin from birth can see himself as a mirror of the cosmos. And his soul, blemished beyond repair like all others, may in fact be rooted in the highest realms of the cosmic world.

To some extent this claim is best contrasted with a similar claim that comes to the opposite conclusion. In an article about Jewish critiques of original sin, Joel Rembaum suggests that the converso phenomenon lies behind the polemics against its existence in Judaism. He states, "Jewish criticism of the doctrine of original sin [helped] stem the tide of apostasy and help[ed] the relapsed conversos to return to Judaism. . . ."[215] While I would agree that the converso plight might be operative here, my reading of Lurianic Kabbala yields the opposite conclusion. It may be the converso phenomenon, a community born into sin and looking for liberation, that, in effect, brought original sin into the very center of kabbalistic discourse. Perhaps the Lurianic system and, as others have argued, Kabbala more generally, provides an esoteric nexus between Judaism and Christianity that subverts the classical arguments about their incompatibility.[216]

The Lurianic material examined in this chapter provides us with is a rereading of the entire Bible and history through the lens of Genesis 3 and 4, precisely following what Paul did for early Christianity as it was separating itself from Judaism. While Luria does not give us a savior who, having overcome death, can help us overcome original sin, he provides a model whereby the inherited sin of Adam can only be overcome by salvation (i.e., messiah) via divine fiat. Sinai, Torah, and even Moses cannot cleanse the poison of the serpent from Israel. The transmigration of souls (*gilgul*) is a hermeneutic tool to procure the rectification of human failing, but that rectification never erases, nor *can* it erase, the human stain Adam bequeathed to his progeny.

2

EXODUS

The "Other" Israel: The ʿErev Rav
(Mixed Multitude) as Conversos

Where there is no narrative, there is no history.
—Benedicto Croce

History is a claustrophobic modern novel, [Amos Oz] implies, whose characters refuse to be wholly heroes or victims,
and whose conflict will not reach a resolution but, at best, an
uncomfortable accommodation.
—Gershom Gorenberg, *The Accidental Empire*

Sometimes legends make reality, and become more important than the facts.
—Salman Rushdie, *Midnight's Children*

The historian's function must be to understand myths that
people live by, because these myths have often a tenuous link
to reality, though they are placed within reality.
—George Mosse, *Nazism: A Historical and
Comparative Analysis of National Socialism*

It is probably safe to say that among groupings of people in
every society are always some that distinguish people who are
my people, or are more my people, from people who are not
so much my people.
—Robert Redfield, *The Primitive World
and Its Transformations*

This chapter focuses on the depiction of the biblical ʿerev rav ("mixed
multitude," Exod. 12:38) in Hayyim Vital's ʿEtz ha-Daʿat Tov (EDT) an
early commentary to the Torah written before his discipleship with Luria.
I argue that Vital's idiosyncratic depiction of the ʿerev rav in this early
work may be a mirror of the conversos who were immigrating or had recently immigrated to Safed during the first third of the sixteenth century
in hopes of being reabsorbed into the Jewish community. Vital's portrayal
of the ʿerev rav as simultaneously problematic for the Israelites yet ulti-

mately necessary for redemption uses them to make a case for reabsorb-
ing the conversos back into the Jewish community at a time when the
hope of redemption was heightened.

As is the case with most kabbalistic and exegetical works, EDT does
not mention the conversos or any contemporary issue. My assertion,
therefore, is based on a literary reading of the text within a particular
context coupled with Vital's own likely relationship to the converso
community in Safed. This ostensible leap linking textuality and history,
or what Walter Cohen calls, "[a] commitment to arbitrary connected-
ness,"[1] is based on three factors, two literary and one methodological.
The first is that the ʿerev rav appear in Vital's text in peculiar places.
One would expect to find them in the episode of the golden calf and
the rebellion of the riffraff (asafsuf) in the Book of Numbers (where
they play a role in rabbinic literature). However, in EDT, the ʿerev rav
appear prominently at revelation (Exod. 19–21) and throughout the
desert narrative. In fact, in EDT the ʿerev rav surface throughout most
of the last four books of the Pentateuch. This leads me to conjecture
that they have a special role to play in Vital's imagination even as that
role is never made explicit in Vital's text. While the conversos are never
explicitly linked to the ʿerev rav, Vital relates that Luria told him that
his generation was the generation of the ʿerev rav and thus he had a special obligation to bring them to Torah.[2]

Second, the depiction of the ʿerev rav in EDT presents a counter-narra-
tive to the way they are treated in classical Jewish and zoharic literature.
There is an explicit attempt here to vindicate them, making their case by
speaking in their voice, expounding on the intimacy between them and
Moses that is mentioned but never developed in midrashic literature. More
generally, Robert Bonfil suggests that the use of the Bible as the basis of
"historical writing" is quite common in the sixteenth century, yet Bonfil focuses on those formally writing of "history" and not on the writing of history under the guise of scriptural interpretation.[3] Here I argue that biblical exegesis and homiletics can also serve as a vehicle to communicate the
author's vision of history, revealing what he would like history to be, and
reading those aspirations back into canonical texts.[4] Thus, my focus is on
literature (here biblical exegesis) as history, and not on the writing of history per se.

I argue that the construction of the ʿerev rav in Vital's EDT is a fictional
and hence an aesthetic comment on the social reality of the converso immigration to Safed, a demographic change that was deemed significant
for these messianic-minded mystics. My interest is less on the formal historical question of the role the conversos played in the Safed community,
and more on about the ways in which the conversos, via the ʿerev rav, may

have been a mirror used to fashion new identities, perhaps proto-messianic identities, in the imagination of Vital.

At issue here is the nature of conversion in general, and more specifically, on the problem of (un)conversion, or reacceptance without conversion, of an ambiguous and marginal community. Both the ʿ*erev rav* and the conversos are indistinct communities—both carry with them some dimension of "Judaism": the ʿ*erev rav* through witnessing revelation at Sinai yet being excluded from the covenant, and the conversos by being descendants of Jews and maintaining some remnants of the Jewish religion but being considered "Christian" by most Jews. Yet both are not fully Israelites/Jews.[5] The force behind the case for absorption of these communities in Vital is that their rejudaization serves as a prerequisite for the completion of the covenant that failed in the Sinai desert. It is the continued marginalization of both communities, even as such exclusion is done for the sake of protecting the covenant, that prevents the fulfillment of Israel's covenantal responsibility.

Safed in the Sixteenth Century: Transition and Innovation

Erez Israel in the sixteenth century was a place of intense transition and innovation.[6] The massive demographic changes in the late fifteenth and early sixteenth centuries, resulting from the Spanish and Portuguese expulsions and various inquisitions on the Iberian Peninsula, coupled with the Ottoman conquest of the Holy Land in 1516, created a new community of Jews in two major population centers, Jerusalem and Safed, the latter being a small hamlet in the central Galilee.[7] Due to two major factors, the first economic[8] and the second eschatological, Safed became a center of Jewish life and letters in Erez Israel during the first two thirds of this century.[9]

Historians of rabbinic activity in Safed have documented the extent to which these rabbinical courts were engaged in important political and cultural decisions that touched the lives of many Jews, both inside and outside the communities in Erez Israel.[10] On the surface it appears that the mystics in Safed were less interested in or at least less engaged with the *realia* of their world, focusing more on collecting and organizing previous kabbalistic material (Cordovero), translating kabbalistic metaphysics into devotional literature (Elijah da Vidas, Eliezer Azikri, and Moshe Alshekh), or constructing new metaphysical systems built on the classical kabbalistic tradition (Luria and his school). The mystical texts of this period rarely mention specific events, contemporary issues, or communal crises.[11] Our knowledge of how these figures viewed their world comes from letters and a few court documents that contain the names of some mystics who also functioned as legal experts.

Yet given the tumultuous events of that era, the significance of what was at stake, and the tight-knit nature of the Safed community at that time, it is hard to imagine that these mystics were not deeply invested in and opinionated about contemporary matters and that they did not feel obliged in some way to record their opinions for posterity.[12] I argue that Vital used his exegetical skills in EDT to convey his position on one such vexing issue under the guise of his metaphysical or, in this case, kabbalistic–exegetical writings.[13]

In his youth, Vital was a disciple of Moses Cordovero (1522–1570), Jacob Berab (ca. 1474–1541), and Moshe Alshekh (d. after 1593). After Cordovero's death (or, according to some, immediately preceding it), Vital became the most eminent disciple of Rabbi Isaac Luria, whose kabbalistic teachings Vital recorded and which were later disseminated by Vital's son Samuel.

Before moving from Cordovero to Luria, Vital began work on an extensive commentary to the Torah entitled *'Etz ha-Da'at Tov* (The Tree of the Good) that remained in manuscript until 1871. This work shows strong influences from the Zohar, as well as Cordovero and many others, although it is a work clearly intended for non-initiates rarely entering into detailed kabbalistic discussions.[14] In fact, it is one example of an exegetical work accessible to nonkabbalists, framed in the worldview of classical Kabbala, and intended, perhaps, to widen the circle of kabbalistic influence. In this regard, this work stands very much in line with ideas of Vital's early teacher Moses Cordovero. However, unlike Cordovero's popular works, all of which are systematic in structure, EDT is a work of commentary using Kabbala in the more widely read genre of scriptural exegesis.[15] While Vital does not reject outright the canonical rendering of the *'erev rav* (most prominently in the Zohar) as evil, dangerous, and even demonic, he creatively twists rabbinic and post-rabbinic readings so that the *'erev rav*'s making of the golden calf is partially justifiable, at least from their perspective and the perspective of Moses. And, more importantly, he views the relationship between the *'erev rav* and Moses, a relationship already documented in rabbinic literature, as paramount in understanding the plight of the *'erev rav* whom he aptly calls *'am shel Moshe* (Moses' people).[16]

The Conversos as Ba'alei Teshuva?

The Jews of Safed in the middle decades of the sixteenth century witnessed an immigration of converso Jews, mostly from Portugal, who arrived in Safed (less so in Jerusalem) between 1525 and 1555.[17] Much of this immigration was the result of the forced conversion and subsequent expulsion of Portugal's Jews in 1497 by King Manuel, the renewed threat of an inquisition against judaizing conversos in Portugal in 1531, the tribunals of the Holy Office in 1536 and the autos-da-fé in 1540.[18] By the middle decades of the sixteenth century it was Portuguese and not Spanish Jews who constituted the majority of conversos in Erez Israel.[19] Their choice of Safed had to do with its economic viability, but for at least some conversos it likely also had to do with their belief in the impending redemption.[20] There was a popular tradition, rooted in the Zohar and part of civil religion for many Jews from Mediterranean lands, especially after 1516, that the messiah will not come from Jerusalem but from Galilee.[21] For those so inclined, Safed's appeal was due to a popular belief that conversos immigrated to Safed as a place where they could shed their Christian identity and become reabsorbed into the Jewish community.[22]

As noted, the status of returning conversos in Europe and the Mediterranean was a complex issue in the sixteenth century. By mid-century we are dealing with individuals who were in most cases born "Christian" and had little or no memory of their Jewish past. The question of their Jewishness was a hotly debated issue. For example, the sixteenth-century jurist Jacob ibn Habib supported the position, advocated earlier by Rashi and others, that an apostate retains his or her Jewish status but denies that status to the children of apostates who were conceived outside the parameters of the covenanted community.[23] Accordingly, while it may have been relatively easy for conversos themselves to be reabsorbed into the Jewish community without formal conversion, their progeny would have a much harder time doing so.[24] In some way this may have only strengthened the resolve of some conversos to immigrate to Erez Israel, where they hoped they would have a more sympathetic ear and more readily be accepted back into the Jewish fold.[25]

In his numerous studies on the history of Safed in the sixteenth century, Abraham David traces the lives of conversos in Safed and Jerusalem during these decades.[26] While we only know of a few kabbalists in Erez Israel who were conversos during these decades (e.g., Solomon Molkho a generation earlier, and Jacob Zemah and Judah Albotini who worked in Jerusalem in the seventeenth century)[27] there seems to have been close relationships between converso communities and Safadean mystics during this period.[28] David argues that the Portuguese Jewish communities in Safed during these decades were mostly of converso origin.[29] There was also a popular pietistic "Ba'al Teshuva Society," the members of which practiced acts of severe penitence. While this society, of which we know little, surely included nonconversos who simply opted for a life of piety and asceticism, it likely included some ex-conversos who used the society as a way of publicly displaying their desire to abandon Christianity.[30] Moses Cordovero, a leading kabbalist during the middle decades of that century and of Portuguese origin, was the head of the Portuguese synagogue during the 1520s, precisely at the time many conversos were arriving in Safed.[31] More significant for our purposes is that fact that the young Hayyim Vital, then a student of Cordovero as well as the halakhist Jacob Berab, studied with Cordovero during those years. While we do not know the details of Vital's relationship to the conversos of that community, it is likely that he was acutely aware of their plight and sympathetic to their cause. Aside from his relationship to Cordovero, he also studied with Moshe Alsekh who also expressed a quite tolerant attitude toward the plight of the returning conversos.[32]

Vital would not have been alone in making a case for the returning conversos. We have more explicit evidence that leading figures in Safed made their feelings known on this issue. For example, the kabbalist and author of the Sabbath hymn "Lekha Dodi," Shlomo Alkabetz composed a prayer for the many new immigrants to Erez Israel that included mention of the conversos in a positive light.[33] Moreover, scholars have argued that one of the reasons for the failed attempt to reinstate "official ordination" (*semikha*) and the establishment of a Sanhedrin in Safed was to resolve the converso crisis.[34] In short, the issue of conversos was one issue among many in Safadean Jewry from the 1520s until the late 1570s, at which time the Jewish community in Safed began a steady decline.[35] Given evidence that, as a disciple of Cordovero, Vital had a relationship with the Portuguese synagogue, and the fact that Vital also served as a rabbinic decisor (he was one of the few who received rabbinical ordination from Jacob Berab) and a believer in the impending redemption, it is at least plausible that he viewed the conversos as playing a significant role in the redemptive process. This plausibility is strengthened by his idiosyncratic and controversial depiction of the *'erev rav* as "returning converts" in the biblical narrative.

It is striking that neither Cordovero nor Luria (at least as documented by his disciples) overtly confront the converso crisis in their written work. In Luria's case this is more understandable. He only arrived in Safed in 1570, long after the *semikha* controversy and the mass immigration of the conversos (ending around 1555). Cordovero, with whom he briefly studied, was no longer the head of the Portuguese synagogue and his connection to that community may have ended. Immigrating from Egypt, where he grew up, born of an Egyptian mother and European father, Luria was likely not personally affected by this event.

For Vital, however, the situation was very different for at least three reasons. First, in studying with Cordovero while he was heading the

Portuguese synagogue, he must have had close relationships with conversos. Second, as a recipient of ordination from Jacob Berab and thus personally involved in the *semikha* controversy, he was certainly aware of the legal debates regarding this issue. Finally, even though his family came directly from Italy, Vital always felt a close allegiance to Spanish Jewry, its inhabitants and its kabbalistic tradition. In a text written after Vital became a student of Luria, and long after the converso controversy, Vital makes this sentiment clear:

> My master [Luria] told me that I am obligated to facilitate merit for those transgressors more than other people. This is because all the transgressors in this generation are likened to the *ʿerev rav* who are mostly, or perhaps totally, from the [soul] root of Cain. They mixed his good sparks with evil ones, resulting in a majority of evil sparks. Therefore, I am obligated to rectify them because they [the transgressors or *ʿerev rav*] share the source of my soul.[36]

It is not surprising, then, that Vital could have found a way to incorporate his sympathy for the plight of the conversos into his commentary on the Pentateuch. Although the *ʿerev rav* were an obvious choice as they constituted a marginal community wanting to become part of Ancient Israel, Vital's political–exegetical agenda had to overcome considerable hurdles in order to make the *ʿerev rav* something other than a demonic force trying to destroy Israel internally. Zoharic sources connecting the *ʿerev rav* to the serpent in the Garden of Eden, making their evil absolute, had to be reread in light of Vital's more positive assessment. His exegetical creativity and willingness to confront and revise canonical doctrine regarding the *ʿerev rav* illustrates the way in which the notion of mystics as apolitical may be shortsighted.[37]

The 'Mixed Multitude' in Classical Midrash: Scapegoats or Converts?

The mixed multitude, or *ʿerev rav*, are only mentioned once in Tanakh. Describing the Israelites' confiscation of silver and gold objects before leaving Egypt, the text tell us that *The Israelites journeyed from Raʿamses to Succoth, about six hundred thousand men on foot, aside from children. Moreover a mixed multitude (ʿerev rav) went up with them, with very much livestock, both flocks and herds* (Exod. 12:37–38). There is no mention of the *ʿerev rav* again, and the Torah gives us no indication that they were a negative influence on Israel. The discussion of the *ʿerev rav* in early midrashic literature is very scant. Shlomo ben Isaac of Troyes (Rashi, 1040–1105), cites

Mekhilta d'Rebbe Shimon bar Yohai, stating that these *ʿerev rav* were "converts" (*gerim*).[38] The *ʿerev rav* as "converts" is problematized when the Midrash transforms them into inciters, later to become demonic forces in Kabbala.[39] In later aggadic midrashim, there is a tension between the *ʿerev rav* as (good) converts and even people of great talent, and people who would eventually facilitate the downfall of Israel in the desert. For example, in Exodus Raba we read (on Exod. 12) that "all those that did not want Israel to be redeemed died with the first born. . . ."[40] Hence, those that went out with Israel (i.e., the *ʿerev rav*) were those who believed in the Israelite message. Later in the same midrash we read that the *ʿerev rav* were "rich, some were wise, and very talented."[41] In short, Exodus Raba, while it does not openly refute that the *ʿerev rav* were behind the episode of the golden calf and other Israelite rebellions, stays close to the Torah text in refraining from viewing the *ʿerev rav* as definitive in the desert narrative.

The move that enables the rabbis to view the *ʿerev rav* as a perennial internal threat to Israel comes to fruition by connecting them to the riffraff (*asafsuf*) in Numbers 11:4. *The riffraff in their midst felt a gluttonous craving; and then the Israelites wept and said "If only we had meat to eat!"*[42] The identity of the riffraff with the *ʿerev rav,* while almost unequivocal in the medieval tradition, is not so in the midrashic tradition. Midrash Tanhuma, a late midrashic collection, still records a rabbinic disagreement about the identity of these "riffraff." "*The riffraff in their midst felt a gluttonous craving.* Who are these riffraff? Rabbi Shmuel bar Nahmani and Rabbi Nehemiah [weigh in]. One says these are the converts (*gerim*) who went out with the Israelites from Egypt, as it says, *a mixed multitude (ʿerev rav) went up with them.* One says that they were the Sanhedrin, as it says *Gather to me seventy men . . .*" (Num. 11:17).[43] Identifying the riffraff as the *ʿerev rav* enables later exegetes to simply equate the *ʿerev rav* with all the failures of the Israelites in the desert, most prominently the sin of the golden calf. A telling example of this can be found in the classical commentaries to Numbers 11:4. Both Rashi and Abraham ibn Ezra simply state, without mentioning the disagreement recorded in the midrash, that the riffraff were "the *ʿerev rav.*"[44] This extends the *ʿerev rav* from a group of Egyptians who the Torah views quite benignly—perhaps even necessary given their wealth—to a troubling thorn in the side of Israel, and finally to inciters of the golden calf episode. However, even in their most damning depictions, the *ʿerev rav* are referred to as "converts," an appellation that will play a prominent role in Vital's reading of the desert narrative and will serve, as I shall argue, as the key linguistic link to conversos.[45]

The rabbinic myth that moves the *ʿerev rav* from a benign appendage of Israel to a troubling thorn is constructed as a disagreement between

Moses and God as to the fate of those Egyptians who desire to be part of the exodus. The myth is placed as the backdrop to God's communicating that the people willingly built the calf (or had Aaron build it for them). Moses asks God to allow the ʿerev rav to leave Egypt with Israel. God initially denies this request, warning Moses that they will eventually bring down the nation. But Moses is insistent, claiming they will enhance God's standing in the world. God reluctantly concedes. This mythic conversation returns numerous times in rabbinic interpretation, most commonly cited in God's command to Moses to descend the mountain in the calf episode as "your people" are transgressing (Exod. 32):

> *Your people have transgressed.* It doesn't say "people" but "your people." God said to Moses, "Your people (i.e., the ʿerev rav not Israel, who are described as My people) made the calf. I already told you, *When Pharaoh does not heed you, I will lay my hand upon Egypt and deliver My ranks, My people the Israelites, from the land of Egypt with extraordinary chastisements* (Exod. 7:4). You were the one who caused me to accept the ʿerev rav by saying "it will be good to receive penitents." I responded "but see what they will do in the future, they will make the calf, they will be idolaters, and cause the nation to sin with them. . . ."[46]

This text accomplishes a few important things. First, it claims the ʿerev rav are the cause of Israel's sin, although it does not lift all responsibility from the Israelites. Moreover, it distances the ʿerev rav from God who, as the myth teaches, did not want them to leave Egypt with "his people." Moreover, it makes an important distinction between "God's people" Israel, and "Moses' people," the ʿerev rav. Calling the ʿerev rav "his people" ties them very tightly to Moses and serves as a foundation for the more audacious claim by Vital that the ʿerev rav are "Moses' people (ʿam shel Moshe)."[47] The juxtapositions suggested in this midrash become important in what I consider Vital's reading of the ʿerev rav as conversos, both in terms of God's distance from them and in terms of Moses, who represents the prototype of the messiah who feels his mission is not complete until he successfully absorbs them into Israel, even at the expense of his own life and mission.[48]

While the midrashic tradition uses the ʿerev rav as scapegoats in the episode of the calf, it does not resolve the ambiguity as to the nature of the ʿerev rav in general. That is, the Midrash generally stays close to the Torah's initial depiction of the ʿerev rav as simply a community of Egyptians, many of who sincerely desired to become part of Israel's covenant with God. The important link between the ʿerev rav and the riffraff is left as an unresolved disagreement between two rabbinic sages, albeit one that all but disappears in classical medieval commentaries. In Kabbala, first in Gerona and then more prominently in the Zohar, the ʿerev rav turn into a demonic force set out to destroy Israel. They become correlates to other evil characters, such as the serpent in the Garden of Eden, Esau, and Amalek. They thus lose any of the benign characteristics they have in the Torah and Midrash.[49]

The ʿErev Rav in the Zohar: Temporary or Absolute Evil?

While the Zohar generally follows the midrashic depiction of the ʿerev rav's culpability in the sin of the golden calf, it extends this position to view the ʿerev rav as the embodiment of spiritual defilement that needs to be erased before the advent of the messianic era.[50] Exegetically, this is accomplished by arguing that whenever the Torah uses the word *people* (ʿam) without any identification (i.e., the people of Israel, the House of Jacob), it is referring to the ʿerev rav.[51] This hermeneutic of substitution enables the Zohar to reread the desert narrative as a description of two distinct peoples in the desert: Israel and the ʿerev rav. The ʿerev rav are more present and highly influential in many biblical episodes, albeit negative ones, and do not disappear, as they do in the Bible, after the exodus. This hermeneutic of substitution creates a more inclusive and expansive role for the ʿerev rav in the biblical drama.[52] This is spelled out in numerous ways:

> If the ʿerev rav had not bound themselves to Israel they would not have done that deed [the golden calf] and all those Israelites who died would not have perished, and all that happened to Israel would not have happened. . . . That deed was the cause of everything; it caused death, it caused the subjection to other nations, it caused the destruction of the first tablets, it caused the death of many thousands of Israelites. All of this was due to the existence of the ʿerev rav.[53]

The ʿerev rav become more than simply a malicious bunch of outcasts who seek refuge in the community of Israel during the exodus. They are even more evil than the rebels who incite the sin of the golden calf. In the Zohar they are rooted in the very bowels of impurity from the story of creation, and their fate is inextricable linked to the messianic age.

"The son of David [i.e., the messiah] will not come until all the souls will be born [in bodies]."[54] At that time renewal [hithadshut]

will come to the world. Then the ⁽*erev rav* will be erased [*mitavrin*]
from the world. Then it will be said to Israel and Moses that all will
have their proper soul mates and both Adam and Eve will be
naked [⁽*arumim*]; they will not be ashamed since licentiousness
[⁽*ervah*] will be erased from the world. ⁽*Ervah* (ERVA) is the ⁽*erev*
rav (ERV-RV) who brought exile into the world, the ⁽*erev rav* in
particular! It is said about the ⁽*erev rav, and the serpent was the shrewd-
est (⁽arum) of all the wild beasts God had made* (Gen. 3:1). He was
shrewd for evil purposes more than *all the wild beasts*, who are the
idolatrous nations of the world. The ⁽*erev rav* are the children of
the serpent in the garden, they are surely the poison that the serpent placed inside Eve.[55] Cain, who came from this poison, killed
his brother Abel (*be-sh'gam hu basar*).[56] This refers to Abel. And this
also refers to Moses, and they (the ⁽*erev rav*) also killed Moses. This
was Cain, who was the firstborn of Adam.[57]

This passage extends the ⁽*erev rav* backward to the serpent, the original inciter of human sin. It views them as undermining the proper sexuality required to assure that all souls are incarnated, a rabbinic prerequisite for the coming of the messiah. Moreover, it ties them to Moses in a
curious way. Since the poison of the serpent becomes a dominant part of
the soul of Cain, Moses (as a *gilgul* of, among others, Abel)[58] becomes the
hapless victim of the ⁽*erev rav*, the very people he tried to save. Perhaps
the reason that the ⁽*erev rav* are worse than the idolatrous nations is that
they are so close to Israel. For example, the Zohar envisions Moses and
the ⁽*erev rav* as brothers (Cain and Abel) whose reconciliation is of paramount and redemptive importance.[59] Their connection to the Israelites is
not just that they leave Egypt with them. They have a profound recognition of God in having experienced the theophany at Sinai. They are not
like the other nations, yet they carry the seductive trait of the serpent
and, as a result, become the correlate of the serpent in the Zohar's rendering of Sinai as a replay of the Garden of Eden.

There is, however, an interesting caveat in the Zohar's demonization
of the ⁽*erev rav*. In one of its more extensive discussions on the topic, the
Zohar speculates as to the exact makeup of this anonymous community.
It claims that the ⁽*erev rav* were not simply Egyptians who recognized the
merits of Israel's mission, a description suggested in the Midrash, but the
very magicians and sorcerers who tested Moses in his trials with Pharaoh.[60] The ⁽*erev rav* were, in a sense, turncoats from Pharaoh's inner circle who understood the implications of God's intervention in the episode
of the Ten Plagues. Their aristocratic background makes Moses' advocacy for them more understandable.

On this reading, the ʿ*erev rav* did not partake of the manna in the desert yet did experience revelation.[61] They argued that they should be included "as one people" with Israel, prompting a response from Aaron, "God forbid that these people should be like one with the Holy Nation. This nation shall not absorb this other people. Rather it is appropriate that they should remain separate until Moses returns."[62] When Moses disappears, their status is diminished. However, Aaron is savvy enough to refrain from judgment until Moses returns. This phrase "until Moses returns" illustrates the Zohar's earlier statement that the ʿ*erev rav* will be "erased" in the future. That is, when Moses returns (both from Sinai and in the messianic future), the problem of the ʿ*erev rav* will be resolved. While resolution can surely mean subjugation, eradication, or destruction, I think the Zohar has something else in mind.[63] While Moses' resolution is never made explicit, in another passage a more textured possibility is presented. Discussing the rabbinic passage "there will be no converts in the messianic era,"[64] a rabbinic dictum that is quite significant in Kabbala's dialectical rendering of the necessity and mistrust of conversion and converts, the Zohar explores the notion of conversion and its relationship to the end of days:[65]

> Israel is like a dove, running from the eagle, which is the bird of the nations. At this time [i.e., the beginning of redemption] the eagle [from the side of holiness] will be aroused and spread its wings over the multitude of nations, Esau, Ishmael, the Amalekites, and the evil mixed multitude of Israel [ʿ*arbuvia bish de-Yisrael*].[66] And this [holy] eagle will devour them. And no remnant of them will remain, in order to fulfill what is said, *The Lord alone did guide them, no alien god at His side* (Deut. 32:12). From that moment onward converts will not be accepted, as the sages taught, "converts are not accepted in the days of the Messiah" (b.T. Yebamot 24b). God will arouse a ruthless leader (*hayye de-adam*) to rule over those gentiles that remain in order to fulfill the verse, *For the nation or the kingdom that does not serve you shall perish; such nations shall be destroyed* (Isa. 60:12). And to fulfill what it says concerning Israel, *They shall rule over the fish of the sea* . . . (Gen. 1:26) and *The fear and the dread of you shall be upon all the beasts of the earth* . . . (Gen. 9:2)[67]

There are five types of produce; they are wheat, barley, spelt, goat grass, and oats.[68] They are likened to Israel, as it says; *Israel is holy to God, the first fruits of His harvest* (Jer. 2:3). When Israel is in exile they are fragmented until the [edible] food is properly separated from its straw. That is, until it becomes clear that the

Israelites among the *ʿerev rav* become separated.[69] That is, those [*ʿerev rav* who are really Israelites] who are already separated from the straw. . . . At the time when the Israel is cleansed from the straw, the name of God will descend upon them. And then they will be called "the firstborn of Israel."[70]

In the initial section of this passage the *ʿerev rav* are lumped together with the other nations. However, there are two substantive distinctions: First, they are spoken of as a distinct and separate entity; and second, they are called the *ʿerev rav* of Israel, denoting a proximity and even relationship to Israel that the other nations simply do not have.[71] Here the *ʿerev rav* are viewed as one group who will be dominated by Israel in the future. The second section puts the *ʿerev rav* under a microscope while ignoring the other nations completely. Using the rabbinic categories of produce requiring tithes, the Zohar reveals a different quality to the *ʿerev rav*, a quality that requires a more careful analysis. Here the *ʿerev rav* are made up of two distinct groups, those not from Israel and those originally from Israel who, for some reason, have become part of this marginal community. It is not wholly clear what is meant by "the Israelites in the *ʿerev rav*," but it is certainly plausible to suggest that the Zohar holds that a percentage of the *ʿerev rav* descended from Israelites who assimilated into Egyptian society, the exodus presenting itself as an opportunity for them to return to their ancestral heritage. Given the predominance of such a phenomenon in the history of Israel, it is not surprising that this would be reified back into the biblical myth. If this is so, Vital's implicit correlation of the *ʿerev rav* and the conversos is rooted in this one strain of zoharic interpretation.[72] This reading would also make Moses' advocacy of the *ʿerev rav* more understandable as he too had such an assimilated experience. The clarification of this dual nature of the *ʿerev rav* (the fallen Israelite and the Egyptian convert) is understood as necessary for Israel to become "God's firstborn" or God's chosen people. That is, what Israel needed to accomplish in the exodus is at least twofold: first, to attract the fallen Israelites who are now living as Egyptians back to the Israelite nation;[73] second, largely according to Lurianic Kabbala, to redeem all the "Jewish" souls who had been born into non-Israelite bodies. That is, to attract converts who, as souls, are really Jews. In the Lurianic scheme, conversion, in either direction, is always a construct of redemption because it holds the possibility of liberating lost remnants of Israel scattered among the nations. Unconversion as return is a second phase of that process.

In the second part of this passage, the first section is revised. It is not simply that the *ʿerev rav* are to be destroyed or are to come under Israel's dominion like the gentiles. Rather, their erasure comes about by rending the veil that separates those who are truly Israelites and those who are of the nations. Here exile denotes the alienation of Israelites from the nation of Israel, and redemption requires the reunion of that lost community. Hence, the demonic view of the ʿerev rav in the Zohar requires some nuance.[74] While the group may be demonic, they also hold the lost remnant of Israel in need of liberation. It is the clarification of the ʿerev rav and not the domination of the gentiles that holds redemption at bay.

The dual nature of the ʿerev rav suggested here lends itself to Vital's correlation of the ʿerev rav and the conversos, even though, to my knowledge, Vital never cites this passage.[75] Using the Zohar's reading, the Israelites included in the ʿerev rav could easily be likened to the New Christians in sixteenth-century Erez Israel, once overt and now covert Jews. As we will presently see, this fleeting allusion in the Zohar, intentionally or not, becomes the foundation of Vital's reading of the entire desert narrative in the Bible.

Vital's ʿErev Rav at Sinai: Witnesses without a Voice

Even though the ʿerev rav were demonized in the classical tradition and were often made into scapegoats for Israel's sins, they did constitute a middle category between Israelites and non-Israelites. And they shared that liminal status with Moses, which enabled certain midrashic strands to affirm his sympathy for their plight. Moses was the insider who was (also) an outsider; in a parallel situation, the ʿerev rav are outsiders who are (also, having witnessed Sinai) insiders. A similar, although not identical, case can be made for the conversos. The ambiguity of both these communities, one imagined, the other "real," created space for Vital's rendering of the ʿerev rav as witnesses without a voice, also making a case for the returning conversos as a necessary part of messianic history.

One of the more curious lacunae in the tradition's depiction of the ʿerev rav is the fact that very few sources before Vital describe the experience of revelation from their perspective. We know from the Torah that the ʿerev rav left Egypt and from the midrash that when they were at Sinai they drew Israel into worshiping the golden calf immediately after the revelation at Sinai.[76] What we do not know is what they actually experienced *at* Sinai and the consequences of that experience, both in terms of their own self-perception and in terms of their status among the Israelites. This is paramount, as it is the key to the all-important distinction between the ʿerev rav and the "other nations," none of whom had any firsthand experience of revelation.

These preliminary questions are not invented by Vital but seem to be

implied in Moses Nahmanides' rendering of the history of the ʿ*erev rav*
and the exodus from Egypt.[77] Interpreting the biblical commandment for
strangers (*gerim*) to offer paschal sacrifices, Nahmanides comments:

> The converts that went out of Egypt with Israel, the ʿ*erev rav*, sac-
> rificed a paschal lamb even though they were not [directly] part
> of the miracle. However, those that would convert later, in the
> desert of Erez Israel, would not be obligated in the paschal lamb
> because neither they nor their ancestors had any connection to
> the miracle. Therefore, the verse had to come and command
> those future converts.[78]

What is striking here is the extent to which Nahmanides ties Israel to
the ʿ*erev rav* even as he maintains a formal legal distinction. Even though
they were not part of Israel, they celebrated the exodus with Passover in
the same manner as the children of Israel.

This is the starting point of Vital's treatment of the subject as a way of
constructing a category that is both non-Israelite and *not* non-Israelite. If
we define being an Israelite not simply genealogically but also as a by-
product of the experience of revelation, the ʿ*erev rav* must have some stake
in the Israelite mission, even as it may be of an inferior nature. This is especially true if we accept the *Mekhilta de-Rabbi Shimon bar Yohai*'s reading
of the ʿ*erev rav* as "converts" (*gerim*), a reading canonized by Rashi. This
category of neither–nor, making the ʿ*erev rav* a category of "excluded insiders," reflects a similar sentiment about the conversos in the sixteenth
century.[79] Their genealogical Jewishness notwithstanding, many were
raised as Christians holding onto unarticulated remnants of their Jewish
past.[80] The ʿ*erev rav* could not be excluded because they experienced
Sinai, yet they could not be fully included because, according to most interpretations, they were not Israelites. The conversos could not be excluded because of their Jewish genealogy, yet they could not be fully, or
easily, included, because of their Christian beliefs and practices.[81] It is
this symmetry of "excluded insiders," a label that defines both of these
communities, that informs Vital's peculiar yet quite illuminating interpretation of the ʿ*erev rav*.

Vital begins his analysis of revelation by stating that Sinai is the defining moment separating Israel from the nations:

> Since I loved you more than all the nations; *behold you alone saw*
> (Exod. 20:18) *that I spoke to you from the heavens*—[to you] and not
> to them.[82] Therefore, it is fitting for you *not to make a likeness of me*
> (Exod. 20:19). If the nations mistakenly commit acts of idolatry

it is because they did not hear my voice on Mount Sinai and did
not apprehend the truth of my mitzvot.[83]

At first blush, this is quite conventional. God loves Israel and thus reveals Himself to them, commanding them to fulfill His mitzvot. However, the biblical phrase, with Vital's revision *you alone saw* is problematized when Vital suggests that it was not only Israel who saw God (or,
saw the voices) but also the ʿ*erev rav.* Placing such importance on Sinai,
Vital sets up a distinction between "the nations" and the ʿ*erev rav* who
indeed did experience Sinai, albeit differently from Israel:

> *And all the people witnessed the thunder and the lightening* (Exod.
> 20:15). . . . Know that God took Israel out of Egypt. This is not
> the case with the ʿ*erev rav,* who were taken out by Moses, as it
> says, *who you took out of the Land of Egypt* (Exod. 32:7). It does not
> say "I [God] took them [the ʿ*erev rav*] out." Therefore the ʿ*erev*
> *rav* are called "Moses' people." . . . They are no worse than the
> other nations; in fact, they are better since they came [out] in
> order to convert, as we will explain.[84]

By including the ʿ*erev rav* in the Sinai experience, a point obvious yet
overlooked by the classical sources, Vital sets them apart from the nations. Moreover, their desire to "convert" (or return) while still in Egypt
puts them in much closer proximity to the Israelites, making them Israel's "proximate other."[85] It is, perhaps, this very desire that enables them
to merit being present at Sinai. However, so as not to collapse the Israelites and the ʿ*erev rav,* something that the traditional sources simply
could not tolerate, Vital must distinguish between these two groups
who both *saw the voices* at Sinai. He does this by creating a hierarchy of
experience in the Sinai event, one that has profound consequences for
both parties yet also leaves open the possibility of traversing at least
some of those barriers:

> Only the congregation of Jacob heard divine speech articulated with
> letters. Thus it says: *God spoke to the entire community* (Deut. 5:19) to ex-
> clude the community of the ʿ*erev rav,* as the Zohar teaches on the
> verse: *And Moses gathered together the entire community of Israel* (Num.
> 20:10).[86] Thus it says: *I am the Lord your God who took you out of the Land*
> *of Egypt* (Exod. 20:2). This is not the case with the ʿ*erev rav* who were
> taken out by Moses. There are thus three categories of peoples: (1)
> the entire world (meaning the nations); (2) the ʿ*erev rav;* and (3) Is-
> rael alone. We are not dealing here [at Sinai] with "the entire world"

because they are on the lowest level. [However] we must describe the ʿerev rav, who are called "people" (ʿam stam) [in the Torah].[87] Only Israel heard *I am the Lord your God*. The ʿerev rav did not hear God's articulated speech but they did *see the voices . . . on the morning of the third day* (Exod. 19:11). . . . Since they saw the voices and the raging fire with their very eyes they knew (yadʿu) and apprehended (hekiru) that it was God, as a consuming fire, who was speaking, and not Moses. . . . As a result they acquired another kind of faith.[88] By experiencing the voices it became clear to them that God was speaking. However, it was still possible [from their perspective] that God was speaking from heaven.[89]

By using a model of substitution (substituting "people" for ʿerev rav), a trope initially deployed by the Zohar to identify the ʿerev rav in purely negative terms, Vital is able to describe the ʿerev rav's experience at Sinai as an attenuated revelation, but a revelation nonetheless. Moreover, this experience changed them in a positive way even though it also made them realize the extent to which they were unwanted by God. Without hearing God's words (only his voice) they apprehended that God was indeed speaking and that something, albeit something they could not hear, was being transmitted to Israel. God's unarticulated voice was, in one sense, a voice of rebuke and in another sense, a voice of inclusion. By *seeing the voices*—that is, by experiencing God directly— they were forever bound to Israel (and God), surely as outsiders in terms of God's direct relationship to Israel but also as inside the covenant. Vital uses this feeling of exclusionary inclusion as the basis for the ʿerev rav's motive in making the golden calf and using it as an intermediary between them and God.[90]

The negative realization of the ʿerev rav at Sinai—that they did not have the same status as Israel—is viewed by Vital as the seed of their demise and the root of their rebellious behavior. It is also used to justify their fear and dissatisfaction. Throughout the desert narrative, their constant attempt to derail Israel's commitment can be viewed as an attempt to show God that they are no worse than Israel and should ultimately merit equal status (even though they willingly acknowledge their diminished status at Sinai). Vital's depiction evokes sympathy for the ʿerev rav in that their sincere desire to become "one people" with Israel is consistently challenged by God even as they appear committed to the Israelite vision.[91] I would suggest that Vital, while using the ʿerev rav to vindicate the conversos, also uses the same narrative to warn them of the dangers of their own position in their plight to reenter Israel. As we will see, this becomes more explicit in his reading of the golden calf:

In all this the *ʿerev rav* understood that God gave the Torah to Israel. However, as *the people saw* (*ve-yar'e ha-ʿam*) they had yet another vision in their mind's eye (*be-eynei ha-sekhel*). That is, they
knew that God did not want to speak to them. . . . As a result,
their faith wavered (*naʿum emunatam*), as the Zohar teaches on
the verse *Egypt's idols will tremble (ve-naʿu) before him* (Isa. 19:1).[92] In
the beginning they wanted to become one nation with Israel.
Now, *they stood from afar,* with distant hearts from Israel, as the
verse says, *Peace, peace, to the far and the near* (Isa. 57:19). It is like
one who distances his heart and sins. It was also that they separated and distanced themselves [from the experience] in fear of
being consumed by the great fire. Thus they said to Moses, "We
do not, God forbid, disbelieve!" This is because it [revelation]
had already become certain for them (*nitʿamet lahem*). They said,
We acknowledge the truth of God and his Torah, and we also
know that we are not fit like Israel to receive it. Yet we are also
not, God forbid, equal to the other nations because we have converted. Therefore, we must have a higher status even if it is not
on the level of Israel, *for you speak to us* (Exod. 20:16) and we
heard. For this reason we should have a higher status from all
the other nations. That is, we received the Torah through you
[Moses], as it says *speak to us* (Exod. 20:17) and do not speak to
the other nations . . . We know [we cannot hear like Israel] because we are not on that level, *lest we perish* (Exod. 20:16).[93]

Vital rereads the Sinai episode as affecting two communities on two different levels. To my knowledge, no other commentator who uses the Zohar's hermeneutic of substitution employs it to describe two positive ex-
periences at Sinai. The striking consequence of this two-tiered rendering
of Sinai is that Israel, via Sinai, actually grows less dependent on Moses
(since they hear God's command directly) and the *ʿerev rav* become more
dependent on Moses because he becomes the necessary catalyst for them
to articulate God's word. In fact, Sinai liberates Israel from Moses and inextricably ties him to the *ʿerev rav,* a point that will become relevant in justifying why the *ʿerev rav* instigated the golden calf.

 If we apply the Zohar's hermeneutic of substitution and replace
Moses in the exodus narrative with the messiah or messianic age (something already explicit in the Zohar and Lurianic Kabbala), we can reread Vital's rendition to suggest that the *ʿerev rav,* or the conversos, are
a marginalized community destined to remain so until the moment, or
generation, before redemption. Given the messianic hope so rampant
in the sixteenth century, particularly among conversos, this substitution

is quite telling.[94] When the redemption is at hand, the ʿ*erev rav* or conversos must be absorbed back into Israel to complete the final *tikkun*. Both communities need Moses (or, messiah) to justify their case or, to paraphrase the Zohar cited above, "the problem of the ʿ*erev rav* will be resolved when Moses returns."[95]

On Vital's reading, the ʿ*erev rav* were marginalized because they had revelation but no Torah, not unlike many conversos who knew they were Jews but had little knowledge or no context to express that identity. Both communities were not Israelites and not fully non-Israelites.[96] The analogy, of course, is not clean. The conversos were once full Jews whose Jewishness was severely compromised, if not erased, due either to forced or volitional conversion. The ʿ*erev rav* are Egyptians, even as the Zohar suggests and as I think as Vital holds, that many (perhaps like Moses) may have been fallen Israelites. They desire to come back but carry with them the baggage of another culture, religion, and identity, all of which are problematic and embodied in the talmudic dictum "converts are like sores to Israel." Since the final fulfillment of the covenant, just as its inception, requires *the entire people* (*kol ha-ʿam*) (Exod. 19:11), including the ʿ*erev rav*, these fallen Israelites or fallen Jews must be returned. What the Sinai narrative does for Vital is articulate the model and frame of the impending redemption. Redemption did not occur in the desert because of Israel's sins, largely caused by the ʿ*erev rav*. However, this does not mean that the ʿ*erev rav*, or their modern-day correlates (the conversos) need to be denied access to the covenant. Rather, the future redemption will replay the desert narrative, enabling the contemporary ʿ*erev rav* to successfully become absorbed into Israel (or, as the Zohar suggests, that the Israelites among them will be separated and thus liberated).[97] In order to make this work, Vital must also incorporate the ʿ*erev rav* as inciters into his more inclusive narrative, focusing on two main episodes; the golden calf and the Israelite (or ʿ*erev rav-ian*) rebellion for meat in the desert (Num. 11).

The Golden Calf: Justifiable Worship Corrupted?

The episode of the golden calf is the place where the ʿ*erev rav* appear in their most brazen glory in most post-biblical sources. While Israel is guilty of worshiping the calf and is thus rightfully punished, most medieval exegetes, basing themselves on classical midrash, argue that the ʿ*erev rav* incite the Israelites to sin and thus prove God's warning to Moses against allowing the ʿ*erev rav* to join Israel in the exodus (stated only in midrash). In fact, the midrashic tradition includes mention of the golden calf in God's mythic conversation with Moses while still in

Egypt.[98] What the classical sources fail to discuss, and what medieval exegetes largely ignore, is why the ʿerev rav would do such a thing. That is, what prompted them to draw Israel to sin, and what did they hope to accomplish? In the Zohar and most subsequent kabbalistic literature influenced by the Zohar, this question becomes moot because the ʿerev rav are likened to the serpent in the Garden of Eden and to Amalek.[99] So demonized, the ʿerev rav simply act according to their determined role and nature. No rationalization is necessary.

Vital is not satisfied either with the midrashic silence on the matter or with the Zohar's essentializing treatment of ʿerev rav as unredeemable evil. Instead, he implies that the ʿerev rav's incitement must be based on their experience at Sinai and must be understood in light of their perennial desire to become "one people" with Israel. Existing in a state of the excluded insider wanting to shed its marginal status, the ʿerev rav act out in order to convince both God and Israel that they are no worse than Israel and thus should be fully included in the covenant. By pulling Israel momentarily *out* of the covenant, exhibiting their fallibility, the ʿerev rav seek to justify their own fallibility and argue for their inclusion *in* the covenant.

Based on this reading, I argue that the episode of the golden calf serves Vital simultaneously as a justification of ritual and doctrinal sin (i.e., Christianity, not to erase the culpability of the golden calf but to understand the underlying condition of its emergence) and as a warning to the conversos who desire to reenter Israel. While the ʿerev rav's case is justified in the episode at Sinai, the episode of the golden calf justifies the ambivalence of those Jews who are reluctant to simply allow these New Christians to return, without any preconditions, to their Jewish roots. For the conversos to succeed in their quest of reintegration, they must avoid the failure of their biblical avatars by understanding the ways in which their fears and feelings of inferiority, however justified, can never become a tool to entrap Israel.[100] Paradoxically, it is the excluded insiders (the ʿerev rav/conversos) who carry the weight of redemption. By shedding their status of exclusion and through an acknowledgment by Israel of their covenantal importance, the ʿerev rav enable the final stage of exile to come to a close. Vital's reading of these stories comes alive in his belief in the impending redemption and his messianic role in the process.[101]

One of the more curious dimensions of EDT is that the ʿerev rav do not simply play a marginal part of the golden calf episode but are its central characters. In fact, according to Vital, the episode of the golden calf and, in some way, the Bible's telling of the theophany at Sinai more generally, are really not predominantly, or at least exclusively, about Israel, but about the ʿerev rav, their relationship to Moses, and their fear of losing him.

Vital begins by challenging the conventional wisdom of the entire episode of the golden calf. This story begins with the verse, *When the people
saw that Moses was so long in coming down from the mountain, the people gathered against Aaron* (Exod. 32:1). Commentators not bound by the Zohar's
hermeneutic of substitution ("people" = ʿ*erev rav*) understand this as a reference to Israel who feared losing Moses and being abandoned in the
desert. The Zohar reads this verse as referring to the ʿ*erev rav* yet it has no
inclination to understand their fear since the ʿ*erev rav* are viewed simply
as the demonic.[102] While accepting the Zohar's assumption Vital rejects
its basic premise:

> *When the people saw that Moses was so long in coming down from the
> mountain* (Exod. 32.1). We must understand this according to the
> Zohar when it says that "people" (*stam* ʿ*am*) refers to the ʿ*erev rav*.
> That is, even though Israel also saw that Moses was delayed, they
> thought that he was delayed for some unknown reason. More-
> over, even if they would have surmised that he died [on the
> mountain, they should not have cared]. They already heard the
> voice of God in the Ten Commandments and they already en-
> tered into a covenant and oath with God. This covenant would
> not have collapsed with Moses' death. Behold, God is alive for-
> ever and his Torah is forever. However, we [that is, the ʿ*erev rav*][103]
> have not heard God directly on Mount Sinai . . . "and [they knew
> that] God wanted to reject them. It was only Moses who accepted
> them against God's wishes. . . . Therefore, the people [the ʿ*erev
> rav*] were afraid, even if he would not be dead . . . when they saw
> that he was delayed. The ʿ*erev rav*, who did not receive the Torah,
> immediately approached Aaron and said *Come make us a god [elo-
> him] who shall go before us* . . . (Exod. 32:1) because Aaron was a
> partner with Moses in taking them out."[104]

Vital bases himself on the Zohar in order to establish this entire episode
about the ʿ*erev rav;* he then rejects, or brackets, the Zohar's demonization
of the ʿ*erev rav*. The ʿ*erev rav*'s dependence on Moses is paramount, for
without Moses as their advocate they feared they would be vulnerable to
the wrath of God who never accepted them. Thus they approached
Aaron, whom, as the brother of Moses, they believed would be supportive
of their plight. They asked him to create an intermediary to protect them
from God until Moses returned. It appears that more than simply a substitute for Moses, the calf was also intended to be a substitute for the
Cloud of Glory from which they were excluded. That is, without Moses
they were left unprotected and disconnected from their experience at

Sinai. Moreover, the calf was used as a tool to challenge their inferior status and as part of an attempt for them to extricate themselves from their
marginality. Vital continues:

> [The ʿerev rav] argued to Aaron, "We voluntarily and without co-
> ercion converted. God did not have to ask us by saying *If you heed
> my voice.* Given that, we should also have the name of YHVH pro-
> tect us just as it protects Israel with the Cloud of Glory. We
> should also be included in this, as it says, the convert (or
> stranger, *ger*) and the citizen (the Israelite) should have one
> Torah."[105] Behold, God and his court (*bet din*), that is, the name
> of YHVH and *Elohim,* both protect Israel.[106] However, [now, hav-
> ing lost Moses, their *elohim*] we don't even have *Elohim* that pro-
> tects all the other nations. Therefore, we want to make an *elohim*
> ourselves just as God and his court are physically manifest in the
> Pillar of Fire and Cloud of Glory. . . . Even though we do not
> merit God's [YHVH] direct protection, at least give us some in-
> dication that he desires us.[107] This is not for the purpose of idola-
> try; God forbid, we only desire the living God. The calf is a like-
> ness [of the divine] like the Tabernacle, and the cherubim with
> human faces, *where I [God] will dwell.* . . . Therefore, the reason
> [for the calf] is that when Moses was here (*kayam*) he protected
> us like a merciful father. He was, for us, like an *elohim.*[108]

Vital deepens his case, justifying the ʿerev rav's claim for wanting the
calf by arguing that their status as volitional converts should merit their
divine protection in light of their *elohim*'s (Moses') disappearance. They
also make an argument of equivalence between the physical manifestations of divinity in the calf with the ritual objects commanded by God.
Moreover, Vital argues that the ʿerev rav, only hearing the voice of God
and not his words, did not hear the commandment against making divine images. Therefore, for them, the making of the calf cannot be
deemed transgressive. On this reading, the ʿerev rav were justified in
their action to build the calf, making sense of Aaron's strange acquies-
cence to their demands. As we will see, even the worship of the calf, if
done properly, would not have been transgressive for the ʿerev rav, because their experience at Sinai required an intermediary: first Moses
and now the calf. That is, as long as an absolute distinction exists between the intermediary and God—"This is not for the purpose of idolatry; God forbid, we only desire the living God"—their actions would not
have brought about their demise.[109]

According to Vital, the episode turns sour when the ʿerev rav take this opportunity to use the calf in an attempt to equalize their status with Israel. In doing so, they bring Israel into their world of excluded inclusion. As a result, they are further marginalized. In an attempt to rend the veil of their exclusion, they undermine their status of inclusion. Although the specific frame of this turn is the fact that Israel is led by YHVH and *Elohim* and the *ʿerev rav* are only led only by *Elohim* (manifest as *elohim*/Moses), the larger context has to do with Vital's discussion of two types of heresy. Both heretical views are resolved for Israel at Sinai, while only one is resolved for the *ʿerev rav*.

There are two kinds of heresy. The first is to say, God forbid, that there is no God. The second is that there is a God, but there are two independent realms of the divine, one in heaven and one on earth.[110] Both of these notions were refuted by God when he said, *And you know today* (Deut. 11:2), *in the heavens above and the earth below* (Deut. 4:39). . . . The reason for all these verses[111] is to remove from Israel's heart these [two heretical] notions. If God would have spoken to them [only] from the heavens or [only] below on Sinai they would have acknowledged that there is a God but they may still have thought there are two divine powers, God forbid. Now that the verses attest to God being from the heavens (*shamayim*) to the earth on Sinai, they knew there is one God in the heaven and on earth.

Therefore, do not err like the *ʿerev rav* who acknowledged God's existence, as it says, *so that God will not speak [directly] to us* (Exod. 20:16). However, they were never sure about the second notion of two divine powers. That is why they said, regarding the golden calf, *Come make us an elohim that shall go before us on the way, for that man Moses who brought us from the land of Egypt* (Exod. 32:1) he led us in the land. Make for us an *elohim* in the form of Moses for the God (*Elohim*) in the heavens will not (or may not) lead us in the land. . . . The reason for their mistake was that they stood at a distance from Sinai and did not experience *face to face I spoke to them* (Deut. 5:4). But you Israel, who have seen [Me], you should not make the mistake to think that there are two powers. That is why I commanded you, *Do not make an image*, that is, do not make anything that will be viewed as sharing my power.[112]

Earlier we saw how Vital had the *ʿerev rav* argue that, given their conversion status, they deserved to be protected at least by *Elohim*, if not YHVH. Here, Vital widens the lens to suggest that the *ʿerev rav*'s unarticulated revelatory experience had at least two consequences: first, not having heard the command against making images of the divine, a command that requires the experiential understanding of one God in heaven and on earth, they are not culpable for making the calf. Second, having not experienced the fullness of revelation, they were still vulnerable to the heresy of "two powers in heaven." This vulnerability itself does not make them culpable and, as mentioned, if they worshiped the calf while maintaining an absolute distinction between the calf, as an *elohim*, and God, it would have not been tragic. However, since they also apprehended the unique experience of Israel at Sinai—that is, Israel's direct contact with God (YHVH)—their attempt to draw Israel into worship of *Elohim/elohim* was a manifestation of this second type of heresy and thus an egregious sin for both communities. They should have simply worshiped the calf and patiently waited for Moses to return. According to Vital, the sin of the *ʿerev rav* was that they made an oath to Moses before he ascended Sinai, stating that they would not draw Israel into their acts of worship.[113] Thus their action was a sin against Moses who was their covenantal partner and catalyst to God. When the *ʿerev rav*, pointing to the calf, said to Israel, *This is your God, O Israel, who brought you out of the land of Egypt* (Exod. 32.3) they sinned, not because the calf as an *elohim* was wrong for them, but because they incited Israel to think it was *Elohim* alone, and not YHVH who took Israel out of Egypt. Once Israel worships *Elohim* through any *elohim*, they refute their unique status and relationship to God as YHVH and, by extension, diminish their experience at Sinai to the experience of the *ʿerev rav*.[114]

The Heresy of Mediation and "Counter-History": The Golden Calf as Jesus?

According to Vital, for the *ʿerev rav*, and perhaps also the conversos, to become reabsorbed into Israel they must abandon their experiential basis of worship and their theological suppositions of mediation and adopt Israel's stance of unmediated worship, even as that stance does not reflect their own theological sensibilities. It may not have been simply the eschatological underpinnings of Kabbala that attracted these returning Jews. Since many maintained their Jewish identity but worshiped God as if they were Christians (serving God through the mediation of Jesus or Christian doctrine), Kabbala, with its doctrine of the *sephirot*, may have served as a form of legitimate mediation, one that could more readily be adopted by those who already believed in mediation as a legitimate form of worship.[115]

If, as I suggest, Vital constructs the golden calf as representing medi-

ated worship and as a biblical mirror to Christianity, it is an interesting inversion of the way in which this episode has been used in Jewish–Christian
polemics in the Middle Ages and constitutes an example of what Amos
Funkenstein calls "counter-history."[116] As scholars have long argued, much
of Jewish medieval exegesis on the episode of the golden calf, especially in
medieval Christendom, is in response to the Christian use of this narrative to undermine Jewish claims of election.[117] The Christian position is
based on the Book of Acts 7. In the culmination of Stephen's speech (Acts
7:35–53), Stephen uses Israel's rebellion against Moses and God in Exodus
32 as the precursor to their rejection of Jesus ("as your fathers did so do
you"; verse 51).[118] In subsequent Christian literature, the calf episode was
used against contemporary Jews, and conversion was presented as a way of
overcoming "the sins of the fathers" and completing the Israelite mission
derailed by the sin of the golden calf.[119] To become a Christian means to
take oneself out of the damned state of the sin of the golden calf. More
strongly, theologians such as Augustine "allegorized the punishment of
the Israelites into an eternal damnation" basing himself on Israel's sin of
the golden calf.[120] While Jewish exegetes acknowledge the tragedy of the
sin and go quite far in holding Israel accountable, they could not leave this
Christian challenge unanswered and thus construct various ways showing
that Israel's guilt is either diminished or their sin forgiven.[121]

The entire Christian interpretation is founded on an assumption that
makes perfect sense from the scriptural text, that it was Israel who made
and worshiped the calf. The rabbinic and later medieval use of the *ʿerev
rav*, and their claims that the worship of the calf did not constitute idolatry, problematizes this reading somewhat, although it does not erase it
completely because most medieval Jewish exegetes still maintain that Israel did sin in some way even as they may have been seduced into doing
so by non-Israelites.[122]

Vital's reading offers another approach, one that reverses the guilt yet
maintains that conversion or more precisely unconversion (now from
Christianity back to Judaism), is the answer.[123] It must be acknowledged
that we have little reliable evidence about Vital's knowledge of Christianity. While his family was originally from Italy, Vital lived his entire adult
life in Muslim contexts (Safed, Jerusalem, Damascus). He likely had relationships with conversos, but we do not know the level of Christianity that
he absorbed from them, especially since those immigrating to Safed were
doing their best to shed their Christian origins. Hence, the notion of mediated worship and its links to Christianity may very well be quite thin
and are informed more by popular notions of Christianity than by any
educated position.

According to Vital, the Israelites were not central players in this epi-

sode but were only guilty by not protesting that the ʿ*erev rav* tried to se-
duce them. The sin of the calf, and the extent to which it was a sin of
idolatry, was twofold: first, it was the result of the ʿ*erev rav*'s use of mediation (the calf as *elohim*) to worship *in order to* gain favor with God
(YHVH); and second, it was their ultimate failure to maintain the necessary distinction between the object of mediation and the object of
true worship.[124] While Vital acknowledges that, given their attenuated
experience at Sinai, mediation was a potentially viable form of worship
for the ʿ*erev rav*, their sin lies primarily, if not exclusively, in attempting
to draw Israel into such mediated worship. Israel, which had no need
for mediation, is therefore forbidden to partake in it. This approach
draws a distinction between Israel and the nations (including the ʿ*erev
rav*) on the prohibition of idolatry.[125] By making the sinners the ʿ*erev rav*
and the sin of mediated worship gone awry, Vital presents us with a
counter-history that turns the tables on the medieval Christian use of
this narrative to curse the Jews.[126]

   On this reading, the sin of the golden calf was an expression of corrupted monotheism based on the precarious nature of mediated worship, which was at least one way medieval Jews defined Christianity.
This definition, however, in some ways softens the harder edge equating Christianity with idolatry, thus making the "sins" of the conversos
less egregious and more redeemable. Vital utilizes various strands of
medieval exegesis to arrive at this new position, one that supports his
more pressing goals. First, for him the ʿ*erev rav*, not the Israelites, are
the primary sinners in this episode. Second, the sin was not a sin of
idolatry proper but one of mistaken monotheism.[127] Third, by defining
the sin as a corrupt form of otherwise legitimate worship, at least for
non-Israelites, Vital simultaneously accuses Christianity of being corrupt while opening the possibility for New Christians (conversos) to be
welcomed back into Israel because, as Christians, they were not idolaters. This last point now needs to be fleshed out in greater detail.

   The question of mediated worship, its legitimacy, and its limits,
stands at the center of Vital's reading of the golden calf episode.[128] The
question, then, is not about idolatry per se but about the qualified legitimacy of mediation for the ʿ*erev rav* and the limits of mediation for Israel. The second heresy mentioned above (the belief in "two powers") is
a potential outgrowth of mediation. That is, at least for non-Israelites
who did not experience God as YHVH at revelation, when the use of an
object as a vehicle for worship of the one God turns into an independent divine force (even if that divine force is still born out of the one
God, or Father), the legitimate practice of mediation is effaced by the
prohibition of idolatry. This does not seem to have been an issue with

the *ʿerev rav* and the golden calf. Vital insists on numerous occasions that the *ʿerev rav* never intended the calf to be a substitute for God (YHVH), but that they only viewed it as an *elohim* to protect them in the desert.[129] The *ʿerev rav* were, in Vital's reading, adamant monotheists before and after the calf episode. However, their desire to create equity with Israel drew them to worship the calf in a way that not only crossed the line for Israel, but also made their own worship transgressive.

It is known that the *ʿerev rav* wanted to be included under the protection of the *shekhina*. If they were rejected and returned to their past ways, it would constitute a desecration of the divine name (*hilul ha-Shem*) to the world and would be the kind of sin for which there is no atonement. . . . It would also dissuade many thousands of converts in generations to come. It must be seen that [in this context] the sin of the golden calf was quite nominal [*kal ma'od*] according to how they viewed it. They intended it for the sake of heaven.[130]

The turn of the calf from legitimate mediation to transgression occurs as a result of the *ʿerev rav* witnessing what they deemed was the miraculous nature of the calf's construction:

And Aaron said to them, "Take off your gold rings that are on the ears of your wives, your sons and your daughters, and bring them to me." And all the people took off the gold rings that were in their ears and brought them to Aaron (Exod. 32.2–3). Since they [the *ʿerev rav*] saw that this was successful, they took off more and more and then said, *This is your God, O Israel, who brought you out of the land of Egypt* (Exod. 32.4). That is, the name of YHVH is not yours alone. We are all equal together. Therefore you should also serve the calf, as you too want to be its beneficiaries. This is supported by the [midrash] that states that the "the calf formed itself, rose and said *I am the Lord your God.*" Behold the name of *Elohim* is directing you and all the more so us who do not have YHVH to protect us.[131]

Interpreting the fact that the calf "formed itself" as a sign of the power of the *Elohim* (the divine) in *elohim* (the calf), the *ʿerev rav* immediately turned to Israel and tempted them into a devotion of mediation.[132] This act of seduction, done to create equity between the *ʿerev rav* and Israel resulted in the transgression that forced Moses down from the mountain (Exod. 32:7) and his smashing of the tablets (Exod. 32:19). Vital notes that the calf and even the construction of the calf as an intermediary to

God would not have been such a heavy sin for the ⁽erev rav. "Moreover, if the ⁽erev rav would have said, 'this is *our* God,' it would not have been such a grave sin because the divine name *Elohim* is their protector. However, they also said to Israel, 'this is *your* God,' which is not true. It is YHVH who goes before them day and night."[133] The ⁽erev rav did sin, claims Vital, because the calf was used as an object of worship and not merely an intermediary. "The second day they [the ⁽erev rav] worshiped the calf and sacrificed to it. This is really idolatry but thus far it was only they who were guilty."[134] Moreover, by seducing Israel to sin (although Vital maintains that Israel's only sin was refraining from protest) the ⁽erev rav lost whatever merit they might have had, or achieved, as a result of their unique status.

Vital's reading does much more than simply view the ⁽erev rav as inciters to Israelite sin. The entire episode is really about them and their tortured relationship to Moses and the God of Sinai. One linguistic reason for the focus on the ⁽erev rav here is that the generic term *people* (the Zohar's substitute for ⁽erev rav) occurs frequently in this chapter of Exodus. More substantively, the whole notion of the golden calf presents a perfect opportunity for Vital to discuss mediated worship esoterically, an idea quite prominent among many New Christians returning to Judaism.[135] I would suggest further that the calf here serves as a biblical mirror of Jesus (not as messiah but as intermediary), who, under certain conditions, may be legitimate for non-Israelites but not for Israel.[136] Vital reads this episode to note the precarious nature of mediated worship, and how it can, without intent, become idolatry. He also notes that such worship is perhaps necessary for a people who had no experience or, in the case of the ⁽erev rav, had an attenuated experience of revelation and thus no direct link to God as YHVH. God as *Elohim* can, at times, tolerate, and even necessitate, *elohims*.

The disdain many Jews had about returning conversos was similar to the hatred many Christians held toward the conversos whom they suspected of "judaizing" and thus defiling the pure Christian faith.[137] Both Jews and Christians thought the conversos would bring with them doctrinal and practical remnants of their sordid past. Writing about the suspicion of Christians toward conversos in Spain, Yosef Hayyim Yerushalmi puts this very succinctly: "The traditional mistrust of the Jew as an outsider now gave way to an even more alarming fear of the converso as an insider."[138] This status of double persecution resonates with certain midrashic readings of the ⁽erev rav. For example, there is a notion that Pharaoh openly despised them and redeemed Israel in part to purge Egypt of the ⁽erev rav.

Many conversos left Spain and Portugal because of the inquisitions that followed the expulsion. And at least some Jews were skeptical that the conversos could abandon their Christian past and become full Jews once again.[139] Vital describes the episode of the golden calf as a story about and for conversos; the *ʿerev rav* mirror their liminal status, rejected by Pharaoh for recognizing the God of Israel and rejected by Israel for not descending from their patriarchal lineage.

They hold a twofold claim to the covenant: (1) that they willingly converted in Egypt; and (2) they experienced God at Sinai. I argue that Vital reconstructs this narrative as founded on the assumption that the conversos should be given full status as Jews if they can overcome the fate of the *ʿerev rav;* that is, if they can accept the fact that they can no longer practice mediated worship of any kind. Giving this up would not be easy, as it was not easy for the *ʿerev rav,* not because of habit or lack of will but because many of the second- or third-generation conversos had no articulated connection to Judaism. They were like the *ʿerev rav* who only heard God's voice but not his words.

Yet, like the *ʿerev rav* (or at least the *ʿerev rav* who were fallen Israelites) they would not accept the status of convert, which in a sense would have made it easier for both communities. The challenge of the *ʿerev rav* or the conversos was that as Jews (or as inheritors of Sinai), they adopted mediated worship, and as Jews they had to abandon it.[140] It is one thing to serve God through an intermediary, one that is idolatry from the perspective of medieval Judaism, and then abandon it to become a Jew. It is quite another to hold oneself a Jew and engage in mediated worship and then completely abandon it while continuing to be a Jew. Yet in some sense this is what the conversos were being asked to do. Vital maintains that this rejection of mediated worship by the Jew qua Jew is a required part of the redemptive process.[141] On this reading, Moses may have brought the *ʿerev rav* out of Egypt because he knew some were Israelites and he knew that those Israelites, and others who would later convert, had to become part of Israel. Perhaps Vital held that those conversos who were returning needed a biblical model, both to justify their claims of legitimacy and to warn them of their perilous spiritual journey. In EDT he gives them a biblical frame of reference.

Reconstructing the Soul of the Messiah:
The *ʿErev Rav* as the Soul of Moses

Earlier I suggested that the midrashic description of Moses' relationship to the *ʿerev rav* is expanded in the kabbalistic tradition to something more than Moses' sympathy or compassion. Using the hermeneutic tool of reincarnation (*torat ha-gilgul*), the Kabbala, especially in the sixteenth century, ties together biblical characters and later rabbinic and contemporary figures, envisioning one complex web of soul inheritances as a tool to explain the lives of classical Jewish personalities. *Gilgul* is a fascinating hermeneutical trope for many reasons.[142] Vital uses its doctrine, here and later in *'Etz Hayyim*, to justify Moses' strange and unexplained bond to a group of individuals whom God argues has no place in His covenant. In EDT, *gilgul* extends beyond an exegetical trope and becomes a source for cultural critique. Living at a time of heightened messianic fever, Vital uses the biblical Moses as an image of the messiah and the *'erev rav* as the lost remnant of Moses' (i.e., the messiah's) soul in need of reconstruction before redemption can unfold.[143] The connection between Moses and the *'erev rav* is based on the fact that they are both part of the same fallen soul from Adam. The compassion Moses has for them is a result of seeing them as a lost part of himself. Asking the question as to why Moses would have protested against God's warning not to take the *'erev rav*, Vital writes:

> Without a doubt Moses did not invest his life and mission (*moser nafsho*) in the *'erev rav* for no reason. More specifically, he died and was buried outside the land because of them, as the Zohar teaches . . . on the verse, *And his grave was set among the wicked* (Isaiah 53:9).[144] The explanation to this is based on what is commonly known. Due to Adam's sin, all the souls [that came from him] were mixed with both good and evil. The evil that was mixed in/with Moses' soul were [the souls] of the *'erev rav*, "the chaff and husk of my pure and good soul," as we explained on the verse, *If you would deal thus with me, kill me, rather, I beg you, and let me see no more of my wretchedness* (Num. 11:15).[145] The *'erev rav* are the evil part of Moses' soul. That is why he tried so hard to bring them back [lit., to fix them]. . . . Israel is a part (or portion) of God, as it says, *For the Lord's portion is his people* (Deut. 32.9).[146] Therefore God Himself takes them out [of Egypt]. However, the *'erev rav* who are not yet fixed, and are thus likened to husks, are still under the provanance of the name *Elohim*. . . . Just as the name *Elohim* took them out, Moses took them out in order to fix himself because they were his husks.[147]

The connection between Moses and the *'erev rav* is now fully exposed as the struggle for Moses to reunite the lost remnants of his soul in order to fulfill his role as the archetypal Jewish leader—the messiah. Leaving them behind, even though God said they will sin and cause Israel to sin, would have made his entire mission futile because Moses himself would never have fully left Egypt.[148] It is for this reason that Vital suggests that

Moses felt more responsibility for the *ʿerev rav* then he did for the Israel-ites.[149] The notion of the messiah being a Marrano (or converso) became quite common in Sabbatean doctrine a century later. Abraham Miguel Cardoso (1627–1706), himself a convert, writes, "In the future Messiah the King will don the garments of a Marrano, and on account of that the Jews will not recognize him."[150] There is also a hint of this, albeit only by implication, in Vital's *Shaʿar ha-Gilgulim*. Discussing the phenomenon that lofty souls, such as those of Abraham and King David, can only by-pass the *kelipot* by being born through sin, he describes this concept as common for the messianic lineage (as in David, Ruth, Judah, and Tamar) and "the souls of converts."[151] In any case, once the soul link is made be-tween the *ʿerev rav* and Moses, Moses' own identity as converso becomes plausible, a notion that is not so far from that found in the medieval com-mentaries, although none would dare go so far as to say this explicitly.

The use of the verse *For the Lord's portion (helko) is His people* is quite in-teresting here. The term *helek* or *helko* in the biblical verse implies "por-tion," yet more literally (or hyperliterally) means "part of." I suggest that Vital is subtly turning the term toward its more literal meaning in order to argue that the *ʿerev rav* are "part of" Moses. In doing so, however, he is also implying that the *Israelites* are "part of" God, more precisely, part of YHVH. This reading distances Moses from the Israelites in the following way: If the *ʿerev rav* are part of Moses or *Elohim* and not part of YHVH and the Israelites are part of YHVH, then at least part of Moses must not be a part of YHVH. Or, perhaps Moses' status as a fallen Jew, having grown up in Pharaoh's house and not having experienced the servitude that cleansed the Israelites from their "extraneous husks," required him to re-construct his own soul by taking the evil in himself (the *ʿerev rav*) and bringing it into the covenant. Thus, the fear of losing Moses on the moun-tain was, for the *ʿerev rav* but not for Israel, a fear of losing their only chance of reunification with their good portion. The narrative of the *ʿerev rav* now becomes the inner struggle of Moses, who needs them to com-plete himself.

This notion of the *ʿerev rav* as Moses is taken up again in *ʿEtz Hayyim*. Now working totally within the labyrinthine world of Lurianic meta-physics, Vital expands his brief remarks in EDT.

> I will now explain the two diagonal lines that represent the two sides of the generation of the desert (*dor midbar*) in the first line that is closest to *zeir anpin*. Behold, there are two lines on the two sides of Jacob[152] on the outside. The one on the right is the *ʿerev rav*. They converted because their souls came from the right side. This is what is meant that the *ʿerev rav* are the sparks of Moses' soul, in the verse,

Go down for your people have sinned (Exod. 23:7). This is also the reason Moses tried so hard on their behalf. He desperately wanted to fix them, as we mentioned elsewhere. The light from the left of Jacob is Esau, his brother. Because Esau is from the left he/they did not convert. . . . The reason Moses tried so hard to convert the ʿerev rav was because they were the sparks [of his soul]. . . . The generation of the desert embodied the realm of *Daʿat* (knowledge) from the side of the primordial father (*abba*) that is within *zeir anpin*, which is called the upper *daʿat*.[153] The ʿerev rav were also rooted in that place, as was mentioned. Hence the numerical value of ʿerev rav is also *daʿat* (400).[154]

The Lurianic context of this passage is not directly relevant for our present discussion. For our purposes, what is important is that the ʿerev rav, far from having the demonic valence in the Zohar, have a place that is higher than Esau's (i.e., the nations) and are inextricably connected to Moses. The verse, *Go down for your people have sinned* no longer speaks about God's direction to Moses to descend the mountain but rather about the diminishing of Moses' soul as a result of the ʿerev rav (and by extension, him) sinning. The sin results in the partial failure of his mission in that he and some of *them* must die in the desert. By extension, had they not sinned, Moses would have successfully reconstructed his own soul, entered Israel with the Israelites (now including the ʿerev rav), and been their messiah.

Yet Moses' mission with the ʿerev rav was not a total loss. In fact, Vital implies that Moses sacrificed his life and the completion of his mission in order that some of the ʿerev rav could re-enter Israel. Commenting on one of the rebellions against Moses in the desert (Num. 21), Vital suggests that one purpose of God's retribution was to erase finally and forever many of the ʿerev rav who did not merit remaining with Israel:

> *The Lord sent serpents against the people. They bit the people and many of the people (ʿam rav mi-Yisrael) died* (Num. 21:6).[155] It should have written "many people" or "many Israelites died." However, the intent of the passage was to state that all of the ʿerev rav, who were ʿam rav [a multitude], died and were cut away from Israel, leaving Israel alone. . . . At that time, Israel was cleansed from all its husks, like pure silver, and could enter the land without any strangers in their midst. As to the ʿerev rav, the time was not ripe for their fixing.[156]

This all sounds quite conventional. However, Vital continues by saying as follows:

At that time some of the *ʿerev rav* who merited *tikkun* apprehended their sin and confessed their transgression, saying, *we
sinned by speaking against the Lord (YHVH) and against you* (Num.
21:7). However, all those that were not fit died [in the desert].
Those that were fixed [as a result of their confession] recognized
that their sin was not only against the name *Elohim*, but also rose
to the name YHVH who sent the serpents. Thus it says, *by speaking against the Lord (YHVH)* and not "by speaking against *Elohim*,"
as it does earlier, *And the people spoke out against Elohim and against
Moses* (Num. 21:5). Now they saw that YHVH wanted to kill them
because they incited Israel to sin [with the golden calf]. However, they knew that they sinned against you (YHVH). That is,
they said, "Your intention, God, was always for our well being in
order to fix us because we are mixed with the poison of the serpent who inseminated Eve. . . ."[157] When God saw that the
remaining *ʿerev rav* confessed and repented it became clear to
him that their time for *tikkun* had arrived. Then he said to Moses,
Make a seraph (serpent) and mount it on a standard (Num. 21:8).
Make it for your benefit. This is because the *ʿerev rav* who remain
are part of your soul. Since they are now fixed, they have become
a great benefit to you.[158]

The destruction of the *ʿerev rav* is thus not their total annihilation but,
as the Zohar passage above suggests, represents the separation of the
Israelites within the *ʿerev rav* who repent and were saved.

Behold, after the remaining *ʿerev rav* repented and were fixed
God wanted to include them under the provenance of the *shekhina*, taking part in all the miracles that happened to Israel, allowing them to drink the holy water from the fountain [of
Miriam] . . . the fountain about which God said to Moses, *Assem-
ble the people that I may give them water* (Num. 21:16). That is, I will
also give them water. As I said, from this time onward the fountain was also for the *ʿerev rav*. In terms of Israel, the fountain [i.e.,
Miriam's well] already followed them from the time Miriam
died. This moment marks a new miracle, that is, that the fountain gave forth even more water to serve the *ʿerev rav*. Therefore,
and at that time, *Israel sang this song* (Num. 21:17).[159]

While Vital never explicitly states here, or anywhere in his corpus, that
these penitents were fallen Israelites who were part of the *ʿerev rav*, there
are numerous factors that suggest the plausibility of such a reading. First,

the notion of the ʿ*erev rav* as containing fallen Israelites is already suggested, albeit by implication, in the Zohar. Second, according to Vital,
the ʿ*erev rav* who remained were the transformed part of Moses' soul, at
least implying their Israelite roots (or, Moses' non-Israelite roots).[160]
Third, the Lurianic tradition argues that the entire purpose of the exile
in Egypt was to gather the fallen souls who were trapped in Egypt and
bring them under God's provenance.[161] Finally, Vital's rendering of *the
song of Israel* that immediately follows the integration of the remaining ʿ*erev
rav* implies that this moment marked a state of completion in Israel that
would allow them to fulfill the final leg of their journey to Erez Israel.
The irony of this reading is that both Moses and the ʿ*erev rav* (at least
those who did not merit absorption into Israel) die in the desert. The
consequence of this is that Israel's mission is not complete, that the messianic soul of Moses is not fully reconstructed and must wait for another
moment in history to occur. Is it possible that Vital viewed this biblical
moment being played out in the immigration of the conversos to Erez Israel in order to reenter the provenance of the *shekhina* after a lapse of foreign worship and identity using the ʿ*erev rav* in his EDT as the tool to convey this position to his readers. The messianic pretensions of Vital (and
his teacher Luria) are well known.[162] Sixteenth-century Safed as a replay
of the Sinai desert has the conversos playing the role of the ʿ*erev rav* and
Vital, as their advocate, the role of Moses.

Conclusion

Regarding Kabbala more generally, Vital states, "[it] reveals one hand-
breadth and conceals one thousand."[163] Yet Kabbala's self-conscious esotericism may not only be about the opacity of its presentation but also
about the way it conceals its cultural and political agenda behind the
guise of an apparently "holy indifferent" metaphysics. The extent to
which one can wed these texts to their contexts and interpret them in
that light is one important dimension of scholarship albeit arguably not
its final goal. Here I have suggested how Vital, especially in his scriptural
exegesis, may exhibit his deep engagement in his contemporary world,
showing that his local context may be decisive in disclosing some of the
subtextual apparatus of the teachings. This assumes that kabbalists were
not divorced from or disinterested in their communities but, like jurists,
were involved and engaged in their surroundings, using their exegetical
skill to reinvent the world through their own imaginative lens.

It is largely uncontested that the effects of the Spanish and Portuguese expulsions created much more than a demographic shift in Jew-

ish population centers.[164] The expulsions also created a crisis of identity for many Jews who, as New Christians, were now confronted with opportunities to revert to their Jewish roots beyond the influence of the Iberian monarchs.[165] Not trusted by Christian Europe and resented by many Jews, many of these individuals had to make a choice, even as both options were fraught with danger and possible rejection.[166]

This new reality that began in the early part of the sixteenth century, brought about by events both related and unrelated to the Jewish community, presented an interesting paradigm that required new thinking on the complex notion of conversion and apostasy in Jewish literature. The rabbis express disdain, suspicion and, at best, a sober optimism about converts. In the Jewish mystical tradition, especially later Kabbala, conversion is complicated by the notion of traveling (*ʿibbur*) and reincarnated souls, resulting in the possibility of Jewish souls in non-Jewish bodies and vice versa.

Yet there is more here than simply exhibiting a link between literature and history. This presentation also has cultural and metaphysical implications. The distinctions between self and other, Jew and gentile, the opacity of borders and the hierarchy of categories, real and imagined, are put into question. Conventional distinctions are reexamined by refracting reality back through the lens of the end-time, even before its appearance. Perhaps later Kabbala's most innovative contribution to Jewish thought is the way it constructs and then navigates the permeability of boundaries, liminal space where one thing becomes another, where the Jew can be both Jew and non-Jew, or, through the doctrine of *ʿibbur* (soul impregnation) first Jew and then non-Jew and then Jew again, where the soul can easily traverse biological and gender boundaries. Understandably, the converso phenomenon presented a particular problem for Jews in this period, but for the kabbalists it was also an opportunity precisely because the converso claimed to be Jewish while living as a non-Jew. For one who practiced Christianity yet maintained a surreptitious Jewish identity, conversion was not really available or required; yet conversos were identified as those who "crossed over" and then "crossed back." They became the embodiment of Kabbala's liminal metaphysical universe. In this chapter I have chosen to label them, along with *ʿerev rav*, "excluded insiders" who had some claim, but not a full claim, to the covenant.

The phenomenon of converso immigration to Safed in the first third of the sixteenth century likely made an impression on the young Vital and could easily have led to a renewed hope in the possibility of completing what was unfinished in the Sinai desert of Exodus. Very much aligned with kabbalistic dialects more generally, Vital's depiction of the *ʿerev rav* raises an issue that points to an important dimension of Kabbala's subtle revision (and subversion) of Jewish traditionalism. Redemption now depended on the excluded insiders, the apostates who absorbed the doctrines and practices of a religious civilization that tirelessly oppressed Israel (Egypt and Christendom).[167] More strongly, Vital suggests that this obscure biblical community called the *ʿerev rav*, whom he calls "Moses' people," is, in actuality, the lost remnants of Moses' (and the messiah's) own soul! To be redeemed is to thin the opacity separating the self and the "proximate other." It is not necessarily to make them one but rather to see the self as in need of the "other" to fulfill its own destiny. On this reading, it is heresy reversed, and not piety maintained, that inaugurates the final fulfillment of the covenant of Sinai.[168]

3

LEVITICUS

The Sin of Becoming a Woman:
Male Homosexuality and the Castration Complex

"He was a man?"
"Yes, a sweet boy."
"And was he a woman?"
"Yes."
"God has not made such things."
"God has made everything."
—Jeanette Winterson, *Art and Lies*

For I maintain that not only are you made [by it] into a
woman, but you also cease to be a man; yet neither are you
changed into that nature, nor do you retain the one you had.
—John Chrysostom, "Epistle on Romans" 4.2–3

The feminine (*nekava*) is rooted (*ʿikara*) in the masculine
and the masculine is rooted in the feminine. It is only in
their formation (*ubʾzuratam*) that they differ.
—Shneur Zalman of Liady, "Homily on the Wedding,"
Sefer Tefillah mʾKol ha-Shana

Foucault is not trying to beat classical philologists at their own
games, nor does he propose to make historical exegesis irrelevant; rather, he is trying to do something that traditional
scholars do not do—something that helps arrange and place
insights culled from philology in a new and different light.
—David Halperin, *One Hundred Years of Homosexuality*

Any attempt to delineate, explore, or analyze transgressive sexual practices in the kabbalistic tradition is fraught with seemingly insurmountable difficulties.[1] As a pietistic tradition deeply invested in the normative
legal tradition, kabbalists will never (or, at least rarely) disregard prohibitions or erase transgressions. Theologically, and in practice, their commitment to the rabbinic construction of commandments is concrete and
unassailable. However, a closer look at the kabbalistic worldview, espe-

cially through a hermeneutical lens, yields a more complex picture. As is well known and well documented, theosophic Kabbala is a highly eroticized metaphysical system, and kabbalists, while overtly practitioners of normative law (*Halakha*) were often covertly antagonistic to the normative construction of that legal system in nonmystical Judaism.[2] Thus, while the kabbalists overtly followed the law, often in a supererogatory and hypernomian fashion, they did not always conform to the underlying principles of the normal rabbinic legal tradition.[3] Writing about the symmetry between Shabbetai Zvi and the anonymous kabbalistic work, *Sefer ha-Kaneh*, Gershom Scholem noted, "it [Kaneh] reveals the same combination of pious devotion and mystical reverence for the *Halakha* with veiled but sometimes very radical criticism of its precepts."[4] I think the same can be said, albeit in a more veiled and less overt fashion, about some Lurianic material.

In many cases, this motif surfaces in the unique reasons given for biblical or rabbinic prohibitions in the Kabbala (*taʿamei ha-mitzvot*).[5] Given the pious behavior of kabbalistic fraternities, it is easy to be persuaded that *taʿamei ha-mitzvot* does not affect the very foundations of the law as practiced. However, I argue that this is not the case, that is, that the descriptions given in the Lurianic tradition as to what happens (both cosmically and materially) when a commandment is transgressed, influences how these communities viewed any particular mitzvah or prohibition.

This chapter is devoted to an exploration of one biblical prohibition, that of male–male intercourse, or penal penetration (*mishkav zakhur*, or *mishkavei isha*), a prohibition that we know was consistently transgressed throughout (Jewish) history yet curiously received little attention (until the latter part of the twentieth century).[6] The brief but quite detailed and provocative discussion in the Lurianic corpus about *mishkav zakhur* will be viewed through the lenses of earlier positions on this matter (biblical and rabbinic) coupled with a contextual analysis of the attitude toward male homosexuality in the Ottoman Empire in the sixteenth century and how that may have served as the backdrop for the Lurianic attention to this prohibition.

As is well known, the Lurianic tradition in sixteenth-century Safed (and later in Italy, Jerusalem, and Damascus) viewed itself as an interpretation and extension of the Zohar. It was invested in the enterprise of *taʿamei ha-mitzvot*, an elaborate reification of commandments that served as the building blocks delineating the flow of divine effluence into this world. Whereas the Zohar also engages in this interpretive exercise, the prohibition of *mishkav zakhur* (or male–male sex) in Leviticus 18:22 and 20:13 is curiously scant in zoharic literature. In Lurianic material, however, it appears in numerous texts, describing the cosmic ef-

fect of this transgression and the requirements for rectifying the cosmic damages caused by such a sin.[7] The Ottoman context is surely a
factor here. In two recent articles, Yaron ben Na'eh and Ruth Lamdan
carefully illustrate the existence and tepid tolerance of male homosexuality in the Ottoman Empire, suggesting that Islam's stance on the
matter, while prohibitive, is far less intolerant than that of late and post-
medieval Christianity in terms of allowing controlled homosexual behavior to exist in its communities.[8] This less stringent attitude toward
male homosexuality (surely not acceptance of the practice but more of
a "don't ask, don't tell" policy) pushed the rabbis in Islamic countries
into a difficult position. While maintaining a commitment to this prohibition as confirmed unequivocally in rabbinic and post-rabbinic literature, they nevertheless were aware that male homosexual practices
were quietly tolerated in the surrounding environment and that Jews
were not immune to that influence.

The existence of male homosexual activity among sixteenth-century
Jews in the empire was explicitly, albeit briefly, mentioned by Hayyim
Vital in his mystical diary, *Sefer Hizyonot*.[9] While this brief comment gives
us little to work with, it does anecdotally corroborate the more descriptive
material in Islamic literature regarding the prevalence of homosexuality
at this time. Therefore, it is not coincidental that we find the appearance
of elaborate kabbalistic discussions of *mishkav zakhur* in this sixteenth-
century Ottoman environment, particularly in the school of Isaac Luria,
who was raised in the exclusively Islamic culture of early sixteenth-century Egypt. Given the transgressive and clandestine nature of homosexual behavior in premodern society, we can never fully reconstruct the
regularity of male homosexuality among Jews in sixteenth-century Safed
and Jerusalem.

Yet we do have some documentary evidence of how religious authorities deal with such behavior, including rabbinic edicts curbing male
adolescent freedom (that is, requiring that all adolescents be chaper-
oned by an adult married male). This is even codified in Joseph Karo's
Shulkhan Arukh, also the product of mid sixteenth-century Safed.[10] And
we have the record of an odd edict prohibiting the residence of single
males in Jerusalem and its environs. These and other materials point to
the fact that the phenomenon was, if not rampant, then surely not uncommon among Jews.[11]

I argue that Luria's treatment of this issue, one that the Zohar all
but ignores, emerges at least in part from the Islamic context and serves
as a metaphysical response to a social reality that accompanies the legal
decrees of his colleagues. However, as I will illustrate, Luria and Vital's
analysis of *mishkav zakhur* is quite suggestive, both in its curiously non-

judgmental appraisal of the act and its implicit acknowledgment of the natural inclination for such sexual practices, at least among men (as far as I know, Luria does not deal with female homosexual practices).[12] These two points, both of which depart from conventional understandings of *mishkav zakhur* in nonmystical rabbinic and post-rabbinic Judaism are aligned with Muslim attitudes toward male homosexuality in these centuries and environs.

Before moving to either Luria or his cultural context (i.e., Ottoman Islam) I will review some recent work of scholars who have written on homosexuality in the Hebrew Bible, the ancient world more generally, and Rabbinic Judaism. This will give texture to Luria's analysis, which is, of course, informed by both biblical interpretation and, more precisely, by rabbinic analysis. My point here is not to contribute anything new to the discussion of this prohibition in classical Judaism but to show how Luria alters the general tenor of *mishkav zakhur* in his kabbalistic analysis. Next, I will turn more carefully to the Islamic context and will exhibit how Muslim society, both before and during the Ottoman Empire, dealt with the clear prohibition of homosexuality in the Quran, Hadith, and Sha'aria literature, coupled with the continued existence of homoerotic artistic imagery and behavior among Muslims. With Luria's intellectual (i.e., rabbinic and zoharic) context in full view and his historical context more clear, I will turn to the Lurianic texts themselves in an attempt to show where his reading simultaneously retains the prohibition yet undermines its traditional rendering.

Partners in Crime? Male–Male Intercourse in the Hebrew Bible

Much has been written about the prohibition of male–male intercourse in the Hebrew Bible. The verses themselves are quite limited, and limiting, and the language not at all uniform. In Judaism, discussions about these matters largely take place around two verses in Leviticus 18:22 and 20:13, where the terms denoting male–male sex are introduced. (Given its general antipathy for the cultic and legal traditions of the Hebrew Bible, by contrast Christianity, in the New Testament and beyond, pays closer attention to the Sodom story in Genesis 19.)[13] Even though one strain of the classical Jewish tradition interprets the sin of Sodom as a male homosexual act,[14] in general Jewish exegetes focus on the Leviticus verses, which are more unambiguous and leave little for interpretation (or so it seems).[15] While this prohibition is conventionally, and erroneously, called the prohibition against "homosexuality," many scholars of the classical tradition (including the Bible and rabbinic literature) limit the biblical prohibition to one specific act—male–male intercourse—which, while surely one part of homosexual Eros, is not identical to it.[16]

Saul Olyan's position on this matter is a good place to begin.[17] Olyan first clarifies the two basic terms used in the Hebrew Bible that describe male–male sexuality, *mishkav zakhur* and *mishkavei isha*, in an attempt to determine how and why these terms refer to male–male intercourse, defining them respectively as "male penetration" and "vaginal receptivity."[18] Olyan argues that the terminology, and thus the prohibition, is always and only about the act of penetration without any indication as to why this act is prohibited. Moreover, he argues, and here his case is contested by Jerome Walsh, the Bible's prohibition illustrates a divergence from Greek and Roman depictions of the identical act.

For our purposes, Olyan makes three essential points. First, that the prohibition is only defined as the act of a male having intercourse with another male via anal penetration.[19] He argues that there is some fluidity in the culpability of the act in the Bible. Leviticus 18:22 only holds the penetrator responsible, whereas Leviticus 20:13 extends the liability to the penetrated partner as well.[20] He suggests that this discrepancy reflects a progressive attitude of the biblical authors, one that also, as we shall see, attests to a divergence between them and members of other ancient Mediterranean cultures. Olyan expresses this point as follows:

> However, a rhetoric of inclusivity permeates much of H's (Holiness Code) material, particularly in the discourse sections following the laws; there is one law for all, for the native born as well as for the resident alien (Lev. 24:22) . . . On this one may compare both the Holiness Source and the evidence from the classical world; in both contexts, receptivity is associated with femininity and feminization. In Leviticus 18:22 and 20:13, as in MAL A 20 the receptive partner was not originally punished, though in the biblical context there is no evidence to suggest that the penetrator used coercion.[21]

Second, he acknowledges that the Bible gives no indication, explicitly or by implication, as to the reason for this prohibition. This challenges anyone who reads into these biblical prohibitions any notion of natural law or moral theory.[22] This subject becomes more relevant in rabbinical literature, as we will see, but the Bible is silent on the matter.

Finally, Olyan makes a connection between this prohibition and the defiling of the land of Israel.[23] Following Mary Douglas, Olyan suggests that the prohibition is part of a larger list of prohibitions connected to the defilement of the holiness of the land of Israel. Given that the Lurianic fraternity was living and working in the land of Israel and took their geographical location quite seriously, it is worth considering the possible connection between the resurgence of interest in *mishkav zakhur* in sixteenth-century Safed, the resettlement of the land, and the messianic implications inherent therein.

Olyan argues that Ancient Israelite society sets itself apart from its surrounding cultures by initially making the penetrator, alone, culpable and only later extending accountability to both partners.[24] He claims that the authors of the Hebrew Bible distinguish themselves from other societies for whom the act was disapproving because it feminized the passive partner. In other Mediterranean cultures (e.g., Greece and Rome), the transgression of male–male intercourse was based on subjecting oneself to feminization, which is identified with receptivity. In Israel, according to Olyan, initially it was only the insertive, and not the receptive, partner who was guilty, thus raising the question as to the origin of this prohibition. Olyan basically agrees with Bigger and Douglas that the Levitical prohibition is not about gender per se but, as Jerome Walsh puts it in his critique of Olyan, "[that] the purity of the land of Israel is threatened by any act that mixes two separate, potentially defiling bodily fluids in the same receptacle; human and animal semen (Lev. 18:23, 20:15–16), semen and menstrual blood (Lev. 18:20, 20:10), the semen of two different men (Lev. 18:20, 20:10)."[25] Olyan's analysis yields the following results: "Did Israelites abhor male couplings, as has been generally assumed up to the present? Certainly the evidence of the Hebrew Bible is insufficient to support this view. . . . Though the males' origin of the proscription is opaque, in the final form of H [the Holiness Code] they cannot be separated from purity-related concerns."[26]

Walsh questions Olyan's conclusions by reading the passages in Leviticus to hold the receptive partner initially culpable in Leviticus 18, the latter verse (Lev. 20:13) adding the culpability of both partners. If correct, this position would imply an initial external parity between Ancient Israelite religion and its surrounding cultures, where the partner who submits to being feminized is the one held accountable.[27] Only in the latter redaction of the prohibition (Lev. 20:13) do the biblical authors distinguish themselves from their neighbors. Given this analysis, Walsh suggests a gendered interpretation of the prohibition, one that mirrors surrounding cultures with a unique biblical twist. Following Thomas Thurston and Daniel Boyarin, Walsh suggests that the prohibition was about "the inviolability of gender dimorphism."[28] That is, the negative effect of a male voluntarily being treated as a woman (both Olyan and Walsh deny these passages are talking about male–male rape). This can only apply to the receptive partner, as the penetrating partner is acting in full accordance with his sexual role. It is only later that the Bible holds the penetrator also responsible.

Walsh suggests that the later redaction "strives to differentiate between Israelite practice and that of 'Egypt' and 'the nation that was before you' (18:3, 24–28) and thereby protects the holiness of Israel from the *to'evah* [abomination] of confusion with other nations."[29] According to Olyan, the *to'evah* is the boundary crossing of the penetrating partner in using, or treating, a man as a woman. The receptive partner is "'feminized' and not deserving of punishment."[30] For Walsh, however, the *to'evah* represents the incongruity between Israel and the other nations. Thus, the later passage distinguishes Israel from the nations extending culpability to the penetrator; both are guilty of boundary crossing (the penetrating partner being the accessory). This legal precedent separates God's holy people from all other nations.[31]

In sum, Olyan and Walsh disagree on where the Bible begins and where it ends. This difference will inform the rabbinic understanding of the prohibition and subsequently our Lurianic texts that view gender dimorphism as more than metaphoric or cultural—they view it both materially and metaphysically.

"Cross-Dressing" and Playing the Woman: Male–Male Intercourse in Rabbinic Culture

By the time the biblical prohibition in Leviticus is read by the rabbis in late Antiquity, the prohibition of male–male intercourse applied to both parties (apparently equally). Yet, as Michael Satlow notes, "Palestinian rabbis focused nearly all of their discourse on homoeroticism on the penetrated male."[32] While the underlying reason for the prohibition is far from obvious, Satlow argues that rabbinic culture generally reflected Roman and Greek society whereby the free male citizen who allowed himself to be penetrated was "looked upon with loathing."[33] In these cultures, the prohibition of being penetrated was connected to both status and political power. While Satlow acknowledges that the rabbinic proscription is not limited to the question of status, and even concludes that "rabbinic sources rarely explicitly link gender and political discourses,"[34] he implies that the general ethos of rabbinic host cultures colored the rabbinic reading of the biblical narrative, at least regarding the penetrated partner. Moreover, and this Satlow does not mention, it is worth considering, in light of John Boswell's thesis regarding early Christianity, the extent to which prejudices against these transgressors, especially among readers of the rabbis, are extensions of non-Jewish attitudes and not endemic to rabbinic tradition.[35]

In an essay published in 1995, Daniel Boyarin analyzes this prohibition of male–male intercourse in rabbinic culture from a slightly different perspective.[36] Boyarin's concern is not so much to trace the parallel trajectories of rabbinic and Hellenistic society but to examine the extent to which rabbinic literature confirms Michel Foucault's assertion that sexuality was not a category prior to modernity.[37] Boyarin uses the rabbinic understanding of the biblical prohibition coupled with the rabbinic extension to include female homoerotic practice (not mentioned in the Hebrew Bible) as a way of challenging the contemporary conflation of (the anachronistic terminology) *homosexual* or *homosexuality* with the biblical and rabbinic prohibition against male–male intercourse.

While Satlow and Boyarin agree on some basic principles of rabbinic attitudes on this issue, they fundamentally disagree on the underlying nature of the prohibition in rabbinic culture. Satlow extends the parallel between rabbinic and Hellenistic society quite far, viewing the rabbinic focus on the penetrated partner as paramount. He claims that the rabbinic imagination largely distinguishes between the image in the rabbinic imagination of the "lascivious over-sexed Gentile" and the more modest and controlled Jewish male who limits his sexual appetite.[38] Acknowledging that, for the rabbis, same-sex attraction is commonplace and even natural, Satlow suggests that the prohibition of the penetrator in the rabbis is really a prohibition against hedonism and more generally advocates the pious practice of remaining within "God-given bounds."[39]

Whereas Satlow acknowledges that "no evidence suggests that the rabbis defined people by the gender or the object of their sexual desire," he does not go nearly as far as Boyarin in discussing the ramifications of this claim. Boyarin connects the rabbinic rendering of the prohibition back to its biblical context (at least as posited by Olyan, Walsh, and Thomas Thurston)[40] by making male–male intercourse a transgression of border crossing or, with Douglas, of a "mixing of kinds." Here, I suggest, penetration of a male also constituted a consignment of him to the class of females, but, rather than a degradation of status, this constituted a sort of mixing of kinds, a generally taboo occurrence in Hebrew culture.[41] The prohibition is likened metaphorically to cross-dressing, and in fact, is aligned with the actual prohibition against cross-dressing in the Hebrew Bible (Deut. 22:5).[42] Boyarin rejects the notion that the rabbis were mirroring the Roman concern with status and citizenship.[43] In a sense, he suggests that the rabbis did not really depart very far from the biblical text. That is, they were more engaged in exegesis than eisegesis. Moreover, the rabbis update and deepen the biblical position, which, he argues, is one that is "pre-gendered" or "pre-sexed" by affirming the viability of anal intercourse as a heterosexual practice and by distinguishing between female homoeroticism and male–male intercourse.[44] The latter case is used by Boyarin to illustrate that the issue has nothing to do with gender or same-sex acts per se but simply that a male being penetrated is a case of gender dimorphism that mirrors other nonsexual prohibitions in the Bible.

Satlow, Boyarin, Olyan, and Walsh, while disagreeing on substantive matters, all agree that the issue in the Bible and with the rabbis is not about "homosexuality" in any contemporary sense but about the prohibition of one particular act. And, they all agree, to one extent or another, that the Israelite and later Jewish attitudes about this "act" are influenced by the surrounding culture, absorbing and Judaizing its valuation. Even Boyarin, who argues that the rabbis are more influenced by the Bible than by the contemporary Hellenistic ethos, agrees that one cannot fully comprehend rabbinic attitudes toward homosexuality without understanding the Roman and Greek context. While it is not new, especially in biblical scholarship, this cultural-comparative approach to the rabbinic treatment of the issue yields some interesting results. The rabbis were far more expansive than the Bible in their rendering of this transgression and gave us a better sense of the values underlying their abhorrence of the male–male sex act. While they did not overtly cite Hellenistic influence, the link between sexual practices and morality points the reader of rabbinic literature in that direction. In terms of the biblical community, we simply do not have the answers. For our limited purposes, the question must now be asked: in what respect are these early rabbinic texts and attitudes relevant to the sixteenth-century kabbalistic approach, specifically in Safed? I will suggest three areas of convergence.

First, the distinction between the homosexual act and homoeroticism more generally will play a role in the Lurianic texts under discussion.[45] I will show that the Lurianic approach is not wed absolutely to the act but also to the desire for the act. As we will see, homoerotic desire alters the physical makeup of the passive partner to make him a woman (that is, to actualize his already inherent femininity) and make him a sexual partner for the male.[46] It is the desire that initiates the cosmic (and material) shift that enables the act of male–male intercourse to take place. Moreover, I will argue that the Lurianic kabbalists, very much in tune with their Ottoman brethren, did not view homoerotic desire to be unnatural in any way. Natural law theory on this issue, first appearing in Philo and Josephus (drawing from Hellenistic critics of the male–male sex act) and then in Paul and subsequent Jewish and Christian literature, is not the focus of our kabbalistic tradition.[47] So, while Luria extends the prohibition to homoeroticism (or the desire for male–male intercourse) more generally, he also tacitly acknowledges that this desire is not unnatural, only forbidden.

As we will see, his reasons will have to do with his understanding of the dimorphic nature of the human being. That is, it is not unnatural for a male to desire another male because the other male is, by constitution, also potentially a female. His desire for the "male" is really his desire for the female that is contained within him. Thus, not far from Freud, all sexual desire is heterosexual desire of the male toward the female, even as it may sometimes manifest as desire for the male.[48]

Second, whereas in the Bible and the rabbis the feminization of the receptive partner is both shameful and indicative of "a mixing of kinds," the kabbalistic material views homoerotic desire as *causing* and not only "performing" gender transformation. It is not the receptive partner acting as, or being treated as, a woman but actually *becoming* a woman—this becoming is not only the consequence of the act but the very condition that makes the act possible. Moreover, becoming a woman (which is the actualization of already innate potential) both requires and causes cosmic transgendering that results in disunity (i.e., the uncoupling of heterosexual partners) and inappropriate heterosexual union (*yihud*) that produces cosmic disarray. As we will see, Luria maintains that a man, as male, simply cannot be penetrated. Hence the possibility of man becoming *nekava/nukva* (a penetratable, or literally, holed, creature) means that he must become a she, not simply cross-dressing or acting "as a she" which is still external, but temporarily transgendered. And, as we will see, the transgendering of the male receptive partner also causes the transgendering of the female inside him (*ima* as heterosexual partner to *abba*) into a male (*ima* as a male nursing being).

Third, Olyan's suggestion that the prohibition may have been connected to other prohibitions dealing with defiling the land will be considered in relation to the Lurianic fraternity's place in the land of Israel and its attempt, in other ways, to make the soil of the land fertile for messianic redemption.[49] Though it was not the driving factor underlying Lurianic attention to this prohibition, the land and its purification play a role more generally in Luria's metaphysical project. Readying the land for redemption was certainly a goal of the Lurianic fraternity.[50] This metaphysical framework, coupled with the prohibition against homosexual practices under the category of transgressions that "defile the land," is a connection worth exploring.

Transgression and Tolerated Practice:
The Islamic and Ottoman Context

The question as to the influence of the Islamic and, more specifically, Ottoman context on Lurianic teaching is a desideratum in scholarship in this period.[51] Luria spent most of his life in Egypt and only a small portion in Ottoman-ruled Erez Israel (Palestine).[52] However, many of his disciples, Vital in particular, spent most of their lives in the empire after it conquered the land of Israel in 1516.[53] In chapter 2, I discussed the influence of Spanish and Portuguese (i.e., converso) Jewry on the spiritual renaissance in Safed in the sixteenth century. But this largely parochial and internal dynamic must also be understood within the influence of Safed's host culture, a culture that was undergoing a rapid period of modernization and liberalization. I argue here that the linguistic, cultural, and theological context of Islam and the empire is relevant to Luria's treatment of the prohibition of male–male intercourse and contributes to the query as to why this transgression, almost ignored in the Zohar (Luria's primary textual focus), is now a topic ripe for metaphysical analysis.[54]

There is no debate as to the prohibitive nature of male–male sex in the sacred texts of Islam—the Quran, the Hadith, Shari'a and Akhbar.[55] There are seven references in the Quran to the "people of Lot" (the Sodomites), and the sin of Sodom is considered to be one of a (homo)sexual nature.[56] While there is no uniform legal position in the Shari'a (Islamic legal traditions) on this transgression, all positions consider the homosexual act to be illegal even as the severity of the punishment (*hadd*) varies widely.[57] While the illegality of such an act is without question in Islamic law, the more pertinent question is the extent to which Islamic cultures and the Ottoman Empire in particular tolerated male homosexual practices and the extent to which male homosexuality was a part of Jewish culture existing under Islam in that period.[58] It is precisely this tolerated deviance that may point to a renewed interest in this behavior in Judaism. Stephen O. Murray argues that same-sex activity was always a part of Islamic culture, reflected in the pervasive homoerotic imagery in Islamic poetry, the plethora of Arabic terms for homosexual relations,[59] the use of young (beardless) boys as cupbearers in palaces, and even the spiritual practice of *nazr* (gazing at young boys) to arouse love of the creator, among Sufis.[60] Khalid Duran notes that homosexuality in Muslim society was often tolerated as long as it did not become a public nuisance—that is, the homosexual was expected to curtail any overt homosexual behavior or manner in the public square.[61]

When we move from the strict legal prohibition of male–male intercourse in Islam to homoeroticism more generally, Islam's tolerance and extensive use of male homoerotic imagery far exceeds that of both Judaism and Christianity.[62] As Everett K. Rowson puts it, "Islamic law condemned homosexual activity, not homosexual sentiment."[63] Moreover, a highly consistent trope in Islamic literature is the naturalness of male–male attraction. Justifications for the prohibition, even among the stringent Hanbilite legalists, never employ the "against nature" argument that we see in late Antique Hellenistic Judaism and more pervasively in medieval Christianity.[64] Nor is homosexual practice considered licentious, immoral, or abnormal. Rowson is most succinct when he says, "as was clearly the case from the ninth century on . . . men's attraction to boys was considered as natural as their attraction to women."[65] The naturalness of same sex attraction enabled Islamic poets, many of whom were also legalists, to compose love poetry using the male youth as a metaphor for all kinds of sensual and erotic desires, including the desire for the beardless boy, the Islamic form of pederasty, the love of boys common in ancient Greek society. In many instances, the homoerotic love expressed in these poems goes unconsummated but in some instances the poet goes even further, making explicit reference to the consummation of the forbidden act. As we will now see, this trope appears both in Christianity and Judaism and flourished among Jews in the Middle Ages, in both secular and religious poetry, living under the banner of Islam.

It is well known that Jews living in the Islamic *ʾumma* were widely influenced by all dimensions of Islamic life. The concept of ʿArabiyya, Arabic language and culture, and its impact on Jews and Judaism, are discussed at length by Norman Roth in his essay "Jewish ʿArabiyya and the Renaissance of Hebrew in Spain."[66] Jews not only learned philosophy through Arabic translations, but also learned theology, poetic meter, science, and the systemization and codification of religious law (*fique*). Given the pervasive cultural diffusion of scholarly methods, theories, and ideas, there is little reason to assume that Jews were not also influenced by Islamic popular culture, "ethical" norms, and behaviors including sexual practices, proclivities, and tolerances, as part of the larger ʿArabiyya ethos.[67] And, it is reasonable to assume that these popular influences made their way into the more elite circles of Jewish rabbis and mystics.

The obvious place to begin is the realm of poetry. The great scholar of medieval Hebrew poetry, Hayyim Shirmann, first pointed out the prominence of the boy, or ephebe, as a metaphoric motif in medieval Hebrew poetry.[68] The initial reaction against Shirmann has, in many ways, come full circle. His early detractors empathically denied that Jews, many of whom were great rabbinic figures, could have written about "young boys" in such an erotic fashion.[69] Of late, scholars are claiming that Shirmann, who acknowledged this phenomenon yet denied that it reflected any normative homosexual activity among the writers or their readership, did not go far enough. For example, while admitting that medieval Hebrew poetry was far more sober and less explicit than its Muslim counterpart, Norman Roth points to some responsa literature that indicates homosexual activity indeed was not absent in Jewish society in the Middle Ages.[70] Roth's essay, constructed as a respectful critique of Shirmann, is devoted largely to Hebrew *sevi* ("gazelle") poetry—poems that speak of the love of boys using the metaphor of the young deer. Scholars until Shirmann, and many after, maintained that the masculine *sevi* is really a synonym for the female *seviah,* and that the poems are about heterosexuals and not homosexual Eros. Shirmann, and later Roth, illustrate how this notion is linguistically problematic. Based on my understanding of Roth's theory of ʿArabiyya, we can assume that Jews, like Muslims, lived in a world where male–male homosexual activity was present, even as it was, in both traditions, forbidden. Moreover, this activity was not closeted but was a part of the popular culture that filtered into more elitist expressions of love. As Yom Tov Assis notes, "Despite the fact that family affairs and sexual relations could be an area almost entirely controlled by Jewish law and traditions, sexual behavior among the Jews was much influenced by the standards which prevailed in the society at large. Virtually all sexual practices found among Spanish Jews have their parallels in non-Jewish society."[71] In many ways, this seems obvious. However, the history of prohibited practices in Judaism, especially those that have been linked to immorality and acts "against nature," have often been (intentionally) written out of Jewish history under the assumption that Jews, especially those of the elite classes, simply did not directly relate to, and surely did not engage in, such behavior.[72] And, when references to such behavior do appear, they are explained away as aberrations rather than norms. I am not arguing that male–male sex was prominent among Jews in sixteenth-century Erez Israel, although rabbinic documentation at least suggests it was common enough to merit special attention among community leaders. Rather, I simply want to highlight the extent to which the Lurianic fraternity was living and working in an environment, both Muslim and Jewish, in which homoeroticism and homosexual practices were not absent or even rare, even as male–male sex remained prohibited. We do not know if the Lurianic kabbalists, including Luria himself, read widely in Arabic love poetry and we do not know how they interpreted Jewish medieval love poetry, if they indeed read it at all. What we do know is that homoeroticism was a feature of the culture in which this fraternity lived and worked. The link between homoerotic aesthetics (poetry) and homosexual practices (*mishkav zakhur*) is not assumed to be obvious and requires further exploration.

Shirmann's claim that we have no explicit indication from medieval Jewish literature, other than poetry, that Jews engaged in these practices cannot be maintained when we move to the Ottoman Empire in the sixteenth century (a period that neither he nor Roth deal with in their essays on the subject).[73] In this context we have many texts—rabbinic edicts, letters, responsum, and the like, that clearly indicate that male–male homosexuality was an issue and, in certain areas, was viewed as a real problem that required rabbinic intervention. It is precisely here that we encounter the Lurianic fraternity and its brief and provocative discussions on *mishkav zakhur.* While poetry remained an important literary genre in sixteenth-century Erez Israel, with Luria himself engaging in poetic flourishes,[74] it no longer had the prominence it did in medieval Spain.[75] Yet, as scholars of Kabbala have duly noted, the poetic imagination also served kabbalistic metaphysics.[76] Homoeroticism was certainly a literary trope in the Kabbala of the Middle Ages, as Elliot Wolfson has shown.[77] With Luria, however, the poetic homoeroticism of the Zohar is now coupled with a practical discussion about male–male intercourse, a discussion that fuses homoerotic metaphysics with homosexual behavior. This fusion only strengthens what Lawrence Fine concludes about the Lurianist's engagement with the mundane and what Roth writes about the Hebrew poets of Spain. "In our time it is often popularly assumed that the poet is somehow sheltered from the world and lives in a kind of aesthetic paradise of his or her own. The medieval poet of Spain, however, was totally involved in the life and problems of the community."[78]

The two most useful essays on this topic are Yaron Ben-Na'eh's "*Mishkav Zakhur* in the Jewish Community in the Ottoman Empire," and Ruth Lamdan's "Deviations from Normative Ethical Practice in the Jewish Communities of Erez Israel and Egypt in the Sixteenth Century." In these essays, Ben-Na'eh and Lamdan explore the sociosexual norms in sixteenth-century Jewish Mediterranean culture, focusing on the existence of and reaction to male homosexual practices. I will briefly review some of the salient points in both of these essays in order to concretize my claim that our kabbalistic community was living in an interesting nexus between Islamic and Jewish culture that included male homosexuality as a norm and, as such, saw it as a "problem" important enough to merit the attention of the rabbinic elite.

Lamdan suggests that post-expulsion Mediterranean Jewry was a community rife with "deviant" behavior of all kinds. The expulsion and its aftermath resulted in a fractured family structure, separating families from their children and resulting in the formation of new communities made up of males and females (many adolescent) who were severed from their familial ties.[79] This was surely the case in Safed.[80] One result of this weakened communal structure was the freedom to deviate from accepted behavioral norms and the difficulty that rabbinic authorities had in enforcing its restrictions. The situation became so dire that the sages in Safed set up a "committee to clarify transgressions" (*va'adat berrurei averot*), organized to enforce laws of modesty (*zeniut*).[81] This indicates that the rabbis saw their situation as one in need of drastic, even draconian, measures. One oft-cited source is Joseph Karo's decision to counter previous precedents and forbid two males from being alone together (in a state of *yihud*) because of the culture "of our time." If, as others argue, homosexual behavior was not a "major problem" for the sages because it was not common practice among Jews, why would Karo, not known for his stringent views, need to reject previous opinions and explicitly justify such actions within his historical and cultural context?[82]

Lamdan suggests a more sociological reason for the strict pieties of the mystics in Safed, many of which are documented in Meir Benayahu's *Toldot ha-Ari*. It is commonplace to assume that the severe asceticism of the Safed kabbalists primarily stemmed from their religious outlook coupled with a belief in the impending redemption.[83] Lamdan suggests that it may (also) have been in reaction to the permissive environment in which they lived. That is, their turn to hypernomian behaviors and attitudes may have partially been a way to gain control of a populace that was living in an ethical free fall.[84] Hence, the mystics decreed certain severe restrictions on male–female encounters, encouraged children to marry young, and perhaps used kabbalistic metaphysics describing in gory detail the cosmic ramifications of immodest behavior, as a deterrent to the larger community.[85]

Lamdan's analysis may contribute toward an understanding of the curious treatment of the male homosexual act in Luria's corpus. That is, living in a community in desperate need of a justification for these behavioral prohibitions, Luria confronted the issue as a practical and not merely a metaphysical matter. Instead of dwelling on the more subtle and ethereal realm of homoeroticism (which he also did) he, or Vital, addressed the very practical issue of *mishkav zakhur*—what it is, what it does, and how one undoes its cosmic consequences. As we will see, in doing so Luria exhibits a unique vision of gender that may contribute to the burgeoning literature on this topic.

As discussed earlier, homosexual behavior was not uncommon in classical Muslim society and became even more commonplace in the Ottoman Empire.[86] For Jews in the Ottoman Empire, the phenomenon of 'Arabiyya occupied a wide cultural sphere, including behavioral norms. As Lamdan argues, this may partially have been the result of dislocation and the severing of family ties that was so common among exiles from Iberia.[87] The recorded instances of homosexual behavior among Jews also increased (whether this indicates an increased frequency of such behavior or just an increase in recorded instances is impossible to determine). Rabbinic edicts against young males congregating and the prohibition of single males living in the confines of Jerusalem attest to the fact that the fear of homosexual behavior was not marginal.[88]

Given the work of scholars such as Assis and Roth, this should not be any surprise. Jews were living in a society where homosexual behavior was illegal (and religiously forbidden) yet was practiced and, to a great extent, tolerated. Jewish values reflected the culture's values, and even as rabbinic authorities tried to deter this activity it continued nonetheless. For our limited purposes, the fact that (1) homosexual behavior in sixteenth-century Ottoman Erez Israel was not uncommon; and (2) according to Boyarin, the rabbinic depictions of this behavior do not indicate that it is not different than any other transgression, will fit nicely into our analysis of the Lurianic interpretation of *mishkav zakhur*. As I argued in the previous chapter regarding the ʿerev rav, the Torah serves the Lurianic fraternity as a template from which to engage with contemporary issues and matters of communal concern. Luria's transition from classical homoeroticism to behavioral homosexuality illustrates this point quite well. In the following sections, I will offer a reading of Luria's discussion of *mishkav zakhur* and its implications in the more general discussion of gender theory and religion.

Mishkav Zakhur and the "Plasticity of Sex": Lurianic Kabbala and Gender Dimorphism

In the previous sections, I presented the classical Jewish literary and historical context of the biblical prohibition of *mishkav zakhur*, suggesting that Lurianic attention to this transgression can be understood in light of the influence of Muslim culture on Jewish thought and practice in sixteenth-century Ottoman Erez Israel. I will now turn to Luria's treatment of the issue, arguing that he illustrates a creative, and somewhat subversive, rendering of male–male homosexual behavior. I will view his discussion through the lens of some contemporary theories of the en/gendering and de/gendering of males and females and the ways in which homosexual practices, as performing gender, complicate this process. I argue that Luria's comments on *mishkav zakhur* are an example of what Judith Butler calls the "plasticity of sex," albeit in a culture that lived solidly within a tradition where such plasticity was, or at least seemed, anathema.[89] More directly relevant to our historical period, it has been duly noted that in sixteenth-century Europe, the Ottoman Empire, and the Levant, gender ambiguity or "playing with gender" was common in many cultures.[90] Without making any direct claims of cultural influence, the plasticity of gender in Lurianic Kabbala is in concert with similar phenomena in other traditional societies.

While Luria's discourse exists solely, or at last primarily, in the realm of cosmic tropes and metaphysical constructs that never overtly translate into bodies as such, as a reader I am taking the liberty to view his reified universe as a reflection of how he or his disciples may have responded to a phenomenon that was very much a part of their everyday lives. I am taking this license in part from Hayyim Vital's uncharacteristic comment that frames Luria's discussion about *mishkav zakhur*. In the printed edition of *Shaʿar ha-Yihudim*,[91] Vital introduces the discussion of *mishkav zakhur* with the following words: "Our master (Luria) gave advice to three men in the matter of male–male relations (*haʿbah ʿal zakhar*). I do not know, however, if the advice he gave each one applies to all of them."[92] This anecdotal reference offers two insights. First, its personal nature suggests that he was referring to an actual case—that real homosexual behavior was the impetus for the question, giving the metaphysical discussion a certain real-world concrete foundation. Second, Luria's response seems to put no value judgment on the questioner. In this sense it reflects Boyarin's assessment of rabbinic attitudes discussed earlier. The transgression is treated as any other and the penances enumerated at the end of the passage, while quite strict, are not substantively different from other seemingly less egregious sins.[93] While the context of this preface can never be reconstructed, the seeming ease of the discussion, void of any moral indignation, is consistent with its Ottoman context.[94]

I will briefly map the general construct of the cosmic male, known as *zeir anpin*, in Lurianic metaphysics as a prelude to how this male is transformed via homosexual desire.[95] To reiterate, my premise in this analysis is that Luria's metaphysical "cosmic male" (*zeir anpin*) is a correlate to the real world of human males. Hence, I view Luria's metaphysics as groundwork for his psychology. The generic male is constructed out of a combination of masculine and feminine effluence that descends from his primordial "parents," the *parzufim* of *sephirotic* clusters *abba* and *ima*, also known in more generic *sephirotic* language as *hokhma* and *bina*, although these two pairs are not always identical. These cosmic personas are actually metaphors for spiritual lights, and the actualization of these *parzufim* is always described using the imagery of light. The consciousness of *zeir anpin* emerges from elements of both parents as they descend into the male body (the female body is later constructed out of the male, based on Genesis 2:22). The delineation of these lights is complex and I will only focus here on the parts that are relevant to the topic. The emanation of *abba* descends into the body of the male (*zeir anpin*), extending until its *yesod* or the place of its sexual organ. The light of *yesod* of *abba* is thus aligned with the *yesod* of *zeir anpin*.[96] *Ima's* effusion, however, descends into *zeir anpin* only until the chest cavity, or two-thirds of *tiferet* of *zeir anpin*. There are remnants of her light that descend further downward (known as *hasadim megulim* or disclosed grace), which is one reason why the Zohar calls *ima* or *bina* male, but her *yesod* remains above in *tiferet* of *zeir anpin*.[97] Disclosed grace (*hasadim megulim*) is an essential part of the male construction, as we will see, and is blemished as a result of male–male coitus. In that state, that is, inside *zeir anpin*, *ima* takes on a male valence because she functions as a mother for her child, motherhood defined in the Zohar as male because it is a posture of giving and not one of receptivity.

This descent of *abba* and *ima* into *zeir anpin* only occurs in the bottom half of each (called *yisroel saba* and *tevunah* respectively). The upper halves of *abba* and *ima* remain outside *zeir anpin* and exist in a state of perpetual heterosexual union (known as *yihud tamidi*), described in the Zohar as "going out and existing as one."[98] Inside *zeir anpin*, however, *abba* and *ima* are not in a unitive state as each one's *yesod* occupies a different place in the constructed male body (*ima* in the chest cavity and *abba* in *yesod* of *zeir anpin*). This is important because a union of *abba* and *ima* inside *zeir anpin* would have two destructive consequences. First, by making *ima* receptive (that is, a sexual partner for *abba*), it would destroy her "maleness" as mother. Second, since *zeir anpin* occupies a cosmic place that is accessible to the demonic (the bottom section of ʿ*azilut* and all the worlds below), a union of *abba* and *ima* in that place would endanger cosmic harmony by enabling the demonic to benefit. As I will presently show, homosexual/homoerotic desire and consummation changes the positioning of these parts in ways that create a disharmony in need of repair. It is worth noting here that homosexual activity is not unique in causing a dysfunction of the cosmos. All transgressions cause cosmic reshuffling that require repair. I am arguing, however, that what occurs as a result of *mishkav zakhur* tells us something interesting about Luria's sexual ethos more generally.

I am reading the Lurianic phrase describing *mishkav zakhur*, "*bitul zeir anpin legamre*"—"the total nullification of the generic male" as an act of castration.[99] The interpretation of this phrase as castration is more apparent in a later variant of this text in Vital's *Shaʿar ha-Kelalim*. In that variant, we read the following: "in that moment, as it were, [*zeir anpin*] is nullified completely, because it is not able to withstand the forceful descent of those lights [*abba* and *ima*]."[100] Moses Zakuto, commenting on this formulation, asks the question, "Why is this so? We know that there are remnants of the lights of *bina* [*ima*] that descend into *zeir anpin* until *hod* and it does not cause such nullification." Zakuto answers, "It is different here because that light [the light of *ima*] is enveloped in the light of *nezah*, *hod, yesod* of *abba* and enters slowly . . . whereas here, the sin [of *mishkav zakhur*] causes the descent of *abba* and *ima* is one fell swoop (*bebat ehat*) without any garments. This causes the nullification."[101] *Shaʿar ha-Kelalim*'s contribution here, coupled with Zakuto's explanation, is that the *bitul* (nullification) of *zeir anpin*, the stripping of its masculinity, is a violent act, severing *yesod* of *zeir anpin* from its body. The quick and unmediated descent of light from above causes this rupture or severance, similar to the rupturing of the vessels (*shevirat ha-kelim*) at creation and at the sin of Adam. The connection of this rupture to creation is implied when Vital states in *Shaʿar ha-Kelalim*, "the nullification, as it were, of *zeir anpin* is like the death of [the king] Bela son of Beor" (referring to Gen. 36:33).[102] The violence implied in this act of nullification here leads me to conjecture that it can indeed be likened to an act of castration. The correlation between Adam's sin and the feminization of the male due to *mishkav zakhur* is supported by another text from *Sefer ha-Gilgulim:*

> *Daʾat* of *zeir anpin* descended between the two shoulders of *zeir anpin* [as a result of the sin] which was a wide space. Hence, the *gevurot*, which were below the *hasadim*, descended first and spread out in the body of *zeir anpin*. As a result, there was no room for the *hasadim* to descend and be absorbed in *zeir anpin*. *Zeir anpin* thus lost his potency (*tashash kokho*) like a woman (*kenekava*) because he received the [feminine] *gevurot* in place of the [masculine] *hasadim*.[103]

The upshot here is that the sin of Adam results in the descent of feminine and not masculine energy into the male *zeir anpin*, thus robbing him of his male potency and essentially making him a woman while he retained the biological characteristics of a man. The connection is made even more explicit in the following text from the earliest Lurianic recension of Efrayim Penzari's *Sefer ha-Drushim:*

> There is yet another blemish Adam caused by means of his sin that was not mentioned earlier. [By means of the sin] the male was turned into a female because the five *gevurot* (female) descended [into *zeir anpin*] first into the six positions as would be the case for a female.[104]

The story, however, is far more complex. The "plasticity of sex" here does not limit castration to the male but, in line with Jacques Lacan's discussion in his essay "The Meaning of the Phallus," also points to the castration of the female or mother inside the male body.[105] The phallus, as Freud taught, is not an object or a fantasy but a signifier; in kabbalistic terms it is the signification of potency, a force that gives, sustains, and perpetuates life. Lacan's description of Freud is helpful here:

> For the phallus is a signifier, a signifier whose function in the intrasubjective economy of analysis might lift the veil from that which it served in the mysteries. For it is to this signified that it is given to designate as a whole the effect of their being a signified, inasmuch as it conditions any such effect by its presence as signifier.[106]

The phallus should not be viewed as a fantasy, an object, or an organ. Rather, it metaphorically points to something, and can disclose something latent in "the signified." In this sense, the phallus, as *yesod*, has no gender per se but, in some manner, creates and transmorphs gender. The material phallus (that is, the male organ) of the penetrative male partner discloses (and thus transforms) something in the signified, that is, receptive partner. It is this disclosure that creates cosmic disorder by de- and regendering the male and female within the penetrative partner.

I will now turn directly to the texts in question to exhibit this plasticity of sex and the way in which Luria's reification of the male homosexual act points to an amoral depiction of this prohibition. I will focus on three Lurianic texts: Hayyim Vital's discussion in *Shaʿar ha-Yehudim*, supplemented with small sections from *Shaʿar Ruah ha-Kodesh* and *Shaʿar ha-Kelalim* that contain essentially the same discussion in abbreviated form with some moderate variations.

The discussion ensues in an attempt to make sense of a rabbinic dictum explaining *mishkav zakhur* in b.T. Nedarim fol. 50a:

> Ben Eleasa, a very wealthy man, was Rebbi's son-in-law, and he was invited to the wedding of R. Shimon ben Rebbi. Bar Kappara asked Rebbi, "what is meant by *toevah* [referring to the term for abomination as a punishment for *mishkav zakhur* in Lev. 20:13]?" [After being challenged by Rebbi to offer his own interpretation], Ben Eleasa replied, "Let your housewife come and fill me a cup." She came and did so, upon which Ben Eleasa said to Rebbi, "Arise and dance for me that I may tell you [the answer]." Thus says the divine law: *toevah toʿeh attah bah* (you were mistaken in what you did to her [i.e., your wife] that is, by abandoning her and copulating with him).

Luria asks: Shouldn't it say "you were mistaken in him (*bo*)," that is, you mistook a man for a woman. He continues:

This is how such a discrepancy can be explained: It is known that [part of the cosmic potencies] *abba* and *ima* [in fact, the lower half of each] exist inside of *zeir anpin* in the realm of his consciousness (lit., brains, or *mohin*). The dimensions of *abba* and *ima* that dwell inside *zeir anpin* are in their lower three *sephirot*, i.e., *nezah, hod* and *yesod* [of each]. *Yesod* of *ima* [representing her genitalia] reaches to the chest of *zeir anpin* [*tiferet* of *zeir anpin*]. When a male comes upon another male [who, as a male, is likened to *zeir anpin* and thus cannot be the recipient of intercourse], what happens is that this act causes *yesod* of *ima* (now residing in the chest cavity of *zeir anpin*) to descend until *yesod* of *zeir anpin*. The general effect of a male coming upon a male is the descent of the *yesod* of *ima* [to the *yesod* of *zeir anpin*, which is not her place; in short, she is embodied in the phallus]. This man [the active partner] thinks that he is having intercourse with another man (*zeir anpin*) but he is mistaken, for "he mistakes him [*bo*] for her [*bah*] (*yesod* of *ima*)." This is because there is no possibility of intercourse with a male. What happens is that *ima* descends with *abba* and they cohabit there in *yesod* of *zeir anpin*. This is the *to'evah* (abomination); that is, he mistakes *zeir anpin* for *ima*. He does not know that his partner is (already) really "her" (*ima*).[107]

This text points to a number of issues touched on in very different ways by Freud and Lacan through the lens of Judith Butler. The active partner, in trying to do what cannot be done (that is, have intercourse with a male)[108] castrates the passive partner by engendering the passive partner's *yesod* [the phallus] with the *yesod* of *ima*, thus "feminizing" the *yesod* of *zeir anpin* so that he can participate in this act of intercourse. In *Sha'ar Rush ha-Kodesh* (16a) the language is even stronger: "the *yesod* of *ima* descends until it embodies the *yesod* of *zeir anpin* itself (שהיסוד שלה יורד עד תוך היסוד שבו עצמו)." It continues, "You think he is a man but he is [really] a woman enveloped in a man. You are not having intercourse with a man but with a woman" 16b) (ואן אתה שוכב בזכר אלא בנוקבה). What is implied here is that one is doing so, in fact, because he has made the man a woman through desire.

As Butler notes in *Bodies that Matter,* the fear of castration already implies that the phallus is detachable, or in our case, transferable.[109] Since cosmic identity is so focused on gender in the Lurianic system, the liminality of gender is not uncommon. In this case, however, we are not talking about the transmorphing of one gender to another. Rather, we mean a double castration, the de/gendering and re/gendering of cosmic tropes in which the male phallus is nullified by being occupied by the female and the female phallus, the mother's breast, is nullified by occupying the space of the male phallus. Moreover, the de/gendering that emerges from *mishkav zakhur* is not simply the feminizing of the passive partner, an idea that has precedent in Hellenistic and premodern nonmystical Jewish literature. Here the feminine that takes on the castrated phallus of *zeir anpin* undergoes gender transformation in two distinct ways: first, her descent into *yesod* of *zeir anpin* results in the castration of her maternal male quality (embodied in the Zohar's rendering of the verse "*a mother who cares for her children*"; Deut. 21:6), resulting in her becoming female inside *yesod* of *zeir anpin*, both an object of desire for the male and a receptive partner to *abba*. Second, where she should be female—that is, her upper half who is in a state of heterosexual *yihud* with *abba* outside *zeir anpin*, now must descend into the body of *zeir anpin* and thus becomes male.[110] Through homosexual desire, femaleness is simultaneously constructed and effaced. Moreover, her femininity as the partner of *abba* is rendered useless because *yesod* of *zeir anpin* is susceptible to the demonic and is thus in an inappropriate place for the copulation of *abba* and *ima*.[111]

Most interesting is that this de/gendering, or castration, is not done as a result of the act but, apparently, in response to the desire to act, supporting Lacan's position that sex is that which marks the body prior to the mark. Desire creates its object by marking the body before the act. On this reading, the cosmic damage is not done by the male becoming female (which translates as the cultural damage in the rabbinic construction) but by the engendered femaleness of *ima*, making her a partner for her heterosexual partner *abba* in a place where such a union is dangerous. Moreover, it results in the descent of her upper half into *zeir anpin*, thus forfeiting the perpetual union of *abba* and *ima* above and thereby destroying any constructive female role in this metaphysical system.

In the words of Butler, "the body is marked by sex but the body is marked prior to that mark, for it is the first mark that prepares the body for the second one."[112] The first mark here is desire, the result of which is the de/gendering of *zeir anpin* as a male and subsequent en/gendering of *zeir anpin* as a female, accomplished by displacing the female *ima* from her place in his *tiferet* to his *yesod*. This enables the homosexual act to occur. The displacement of *ima*, forcing her to occupy *yesod* of *zeir anpin* (sharing this space with her heterosexual partner, *abba*) also castrates her as mother, making her female (where she should be male), and thus making intercourse with a male, who is now a female, possible. Butler puts it this way: "the sexed integrity of the body is paradoxically achieved through the identification with its reduction into symbolized synecdoche ('having' or 'being' the phallus)."[113] It is not that he is feminized through the act—rather, in this system, he becomes female through the desire of the active partner, for it is only the female who can be the recipient of intercourse. This act of double castration results in a tenuousness of gender that re-marks both bodies within the body of the male. The male desire for the male transforms the male to female in order to enable the desire to be consummated. In order for this to occur, *ima* as male, that is, as mother, is (re) feminized by castrating her maternity, making her phallus, that is, her breasts, nonfunctional.

Vital writes further in the same text, "You already know that the descent of *nezah, hod,* and *yesod* of *ima* into [*tiferet*] of *zeir anpin* is the secret of the verse, *the mother who hovers over her fledglings* (Deut. 21:6)." That is, the lower half of *ima* in *zeir anpin* is male because she is mother. As such, inside *zeir anpin* she does not copulate with her male partner, *abba,* who occupies *yesod* of *zeir anpin.* What occurs as a result of homoerotic desire is the de/gendering or castrating of the female as "mother" and the en/gendering of the mother in the phallus of the male (*zeir anpin*), resulting not in her becoming male but in her becoming female (which is now disguised as male in *yesod* of *zeir anpin*) and the object of desire for the active homosexual partner. That is, the active partner mistakenly thinks that the passive partner is really female, *ima.* Hence, *toeh bah:* he mistook a female (*ima*) for a male (*zeir anpin*). In fact, the desire results in the castration of *zeir anpin* (the passive partner) which makes him, her but in doing so also makes *ima,* who was male, into a female. What takes place is a double castration and gender transference, making the male, female and the male part of the female (as mother), female and thus an object of male desire. The phallus of *tiferet* (the breast) is severed and her femaleness is now concealed in the phallus of *yesod.* The desire of the active partner creates the object of his desire. In doing so, cosmic damage ensues. Vital continues:

> When a male comes upon a male it causes the descent of *abba* and *ima* to *yesod* of *zeir anpin* (actually *abba* is already there) where they engage in *yihud.* This is the secret meaning of the Zohar when it says, "*Bina* is called the masculine world because she ends in the masculine realm (i.e., the phallus of *zeir anpin*)."[114] This means the following: Her *yesod* is concealed in *zeir anpin* reaching until the middle of his chest (*tiferet*). From there, a trace of her *yesod* (which are the five *hasadim*) descends until the *yesod* of *zeir anpin.* This is where they rest. This is what the Zohar means when it says, "the end of *bina* is masculine." This is why she is called masculine. This is also the meaning of "he mistook her (*toeh bah*)" b. Talmud Nedarim 50a. When you see her, you think she is male but she is really female. This is because she is

concealed in the male (*yesod* of *zeir anpin*). When a man lies with a male he is, in reality, lying with a female![115]

The force of the law in our case, dealing with the prohibition of male–male intercourse, is not a prohibition against the consummation of pure male–male desire, which Luria maintains is impossible, but a consummation of misdirected heterosexual desire, the object being the female concealed in the male that, via that desire, castrates him and makes her female where she should be male. The very existence of male sexual desire requires, for Luria, a feminine object; that is, the trace of the *yesod* of *ima* that exists in *zeir anpin*'s *yesod* (as mentioned above). To what, then, does the mistake (*to'eh*) refer? Luria can be read to suggest that the desire for male homosexual relations is not unnatural but, in fact, quite natural in that it still means a desire for the female who is disguised in the male. This assumes, of course, that for Luria "natural" desire is still heterosexual. However, given that males have the trace (or more) of the feminine, an expression of that "natural" desire can also materialize through desire for the male.

In the conclusion of this chapter I will suggest how this notion of desire contributes to a theory of gender that lies between the essentialist and constructivist models. Here I just want to point out that this Lurianic interpretation complements the Islamic context that, while prohibiting homosexuality does not, like much of Christianity, argue that homosexual desire is abnormal or unnatural. That is, male homosexuality is forbidden even though it may be a natural (i.e., heterosexual) expression of human desire. This may point to the tepid tolerance of deviance in Islamic societies that seemed to prevail in those centuries. In a similar vein, following Freud and Lacan, Butler notes that "'gender' appears to be secured through the depositing of nonheterosexual identifications in the domain of the culturally [I would add here in our context cosmically] impossible, the domain of the imaginary . . . which is rendered illegitimate through the force of the law."[116] In a kind of Foucauldean twist, homosexuality, for both Luria and Butler, is not unnatural desire but prohibitive natural desire. "The domain of the imaginary" for Butler is similar, although surely not identical, to Luria's interpretation of the talmudic rendering of *'to 'eva* as *to'eh ʿatah bah*.

The notion of disguise here—that she is concealed in him, or he appears as she, is an interesting instance of cosmic drag that supports Butler's theory of the "plasticity of sex." Butler states, "Gender is neither a purely psychic truth, conceived as 'internal' and 'hidden' nor is it reducible to a surface appearance; on the contrary, its undecidability is to be traced as the play between psyche and appearance. Further, this will be a 'play' regulated by heterosexist constraints though not, for that reason, fully reducible to them."[117] As I understand it, there is a strong undecidability in Luria's construction of gender here: a male body with a female trace, a female who is male (*ima* in *zeir anpin*) yet retains her femaleness elsewhere (outside *zeir anpin*). Yet she is castrated of her maleness (the breast) through the desire of the male for another male. Becoming female ruins her disguise—that is, her trace in *yesod* of *zeir anpin*—and thus reveals herself as an object of male desire. More urgently, this downward movement (from *tiferet* to *yesod*) effaces her original femaleness (through the necessary descent of her upper half into *zeir anpin*, hence becoming "male"). The consequences of this progression are as follows: (1) the possibility of perpetual heterosexuality between *abba* and *ima* above is destroyed; and (2) the destabilization of concealment that takes place in *zeir anpin* (she is concealed in him) and the consequential destruction of the whole workings of gender transference and the implied plasticity of desire. One might say that Luria champions the notion of the plasticity of desire, or at least affirms its existence, viewing the abstinence of some desires as necessary for the performance of others. Butler refers to this as "the 'play' that is regulated by heterosexist constraints."

Butler also argues that the dichotomy of essentialist versus constructivist models of gender is, at best, limited. Essentialism, she argues, is problematic even on its own terms.[118] On the constructivist position, she says that the theory of the performance of gender always functions to reiterate norms that exist outside it. While one may understandably posit that Kabbala promotes an essentialist model of gender, Elliot Wolfson has shown that gender in the Zohar and beyond is far more complex than the essentialism we find in rabbinic and other medieval Judaisms.[119] Here I attempt to show that the essentialist model, one where sex is precultural and rooted in what Butler calls a "metaphysical site," does not dominate Lurianic thinking. Yet the constructivist notion that gender is created purely through performativity could never bear the weight of kabbalistic metaphysics. Performativity plays a central role, as Butler argues, yet it is one that is constrained by metaphysical norms. However, rather than setting the limits of performativity, these metaphysical constraints "impel and sustain performativity."[120] That is, the "plasticity of sex" here is the result of desire and human performance.

The desire to act and the performance of that desire creates, constructs, and transforms gender. This act of transference functions in a male body that is already bisexualized. The essentialism is maintained here precisely because Luria holds that human males, like their cosmic counterpart *zeir anpin*, ultimately contain both genders.[121] Castration and re-membering, or transmorphing and transexualizing the male body through performativity are not purely constructivist exercises but a play *within* the essentialist notion of the male body, a body that by definition contains both male and female and can, given another's desire, function as either. The consequence of this act, as explained, is the castration of *ima* as male, that is, as mother, and the engendering of the upper *ima* as male as she descends into the male body of *zeir anpin*.

On this reading, the prohibitive status of *mishkav zakhur* is the way in which it problematizes heterosexuality in two ways. First, it forces the upper halves of *abba* and *ima* to descend into the body of the male (*zeir anpin*) and uncouple because she becomes a man (that is, a mother), thus interrupting the divine flow resulting from that union. Second, it causes a dangerous heterosexual union of the lower half of *ima* and *abba* inside *yesod* of *zeir anpin*, exposing them to the demonic that occupies that space. What I find fascinating, however, is not the way in which this reading reinforces the transgressive nature of the act, as it surely does, but the way it destabilizes and undermines the ways in which this act, and its accompanying desire, has been viewed in Judaism as unnatural, immoral, and culturally destructive. Charles Mopsik argued in his posthumous *Le sexe des âmes* that this kabbalistic approach to the question (particularly regarding the liminality of soul incarnation) opens up new possibilities for erasing the prohibition.[122] While I am not as optimistic as Mopsik (although I support his hope), I do think it presents a new model of the prohibition that avoids the conflation of gender politics and morality so pervasive in the contemporary discussion about this issue.

"The Plasticity of Sex," Mishkav Zakhur, and Metempsychosis (Gilgul)

The metaphysical discussion in the above cited texts is reiterated in the frame of metempsychosis or *gilgul* in *Sha'ar ha-Gilgulim* and *Sefer ha-Gilgulim*. While the concept of *gilgul* (transmigration of souls or reincarnation) exists in both kabbalistic and nonkabbalistic literature from the Middle Ages, first appearing in the ninth century in Sa'adia's Gaon's rejection of the idea,[123] in Lurianic Kabbala it becomes a central tenet and foundational part of its metaphysics.[124] The notion of soul migration and soul impregnation (*'ibbur*) is directly relevant to Luria's construction of gender and his theory about the "plasticity of sex" via the transgression of *mishkav zakhur*. Moreover, as we will see, it provides us with another instance in which these cosmic notions are embedded in a historical setting. To begin, Luria's entire cosmology is founded on a gendered notion of existence; it is thus no surprise that he believed souls, like bodies, are engen-

dered. In the following text from *Sha'ar ha-Gilgulim*, Vital relates a Lurianic teaching regarding the engendering of souls and its implications:

> Behold, one of the four hundred questions that Doag and Ahitofel
> asked the "tower suspended in the air" (*migdal pore'ah b'avir*)[125] re-
> lates to the following: Know that the trait of *gilgul* applies to men
> (*ha-zekharim*) and not to women (*nekavot*). This is the secret of the
> verse, *One generation (dor) goes, another comes, but the earth (ha'arez) re-*
> *mains the same forever* (Eccles. 1:4). *One generation (dor) goes, another*
> *comes;* this refers to men who transmigrate (*mitgalgalim*). *But the*
> *earth (ha'arez)*, these are women who are called "earth" (*arez*), as is
> known, *remains*, that is, they do not return through *gilgul.*[126] There
> is also another reason. Men, because they engage in the mitzvah
> of Talmud Torah, do not enter into Gehenna, because the light of
> Gehenna has no power over them.[127] . . . However, women, who do
> not engage in Torah, can enter Gehenna in order to become puri-
> fied from their sins and thus do not need *gilgul.*[128]

The limitation of *gilgul* to men here is intriguing. *Gilgul*, among other
things, is a process of purification from the sins of past lives, an alternative to the more anguished purification of Gehenna.[129] Male souls, due to
their relationship to the study of Torah as commandment, are exempt, in
principle, from the fires of Gehenna since they are able to purge their
sins through *gilgul.*[130] This raises the following question: If only male souls
are reincarnated, then women are either new souls never before descended into the world (a very exalted and limited category called "*nesh-*
amot hadashot"),[131] or are composites of parts of male souls who become
manifest in women's bodies, which will become relevant later on. Vital
suggests a third possibility:

> Even though female souls are not reincarnated, they sometimes
> enter [into a body, presumably female] through impregnation[132]
> with the sparks of new female souls of women. It is also possible
> that after they enter into the soul of a woman, if that woman
> gives birth to a daughter, that female soul that came through im-
> pregnation can be fully reincarnated in the daughter.[133]

According to this text, a female soul can only achieve the status of reincarnation (*gilgul gamur*) through her mother. The ability to achieve
such a status requires the temporary state of impregnation in the mother
which must always serve a specific purpose. Below is the specification of
that purpose.

Also know that sometimes a man (male soul) can be reincarnated in a female body because of a particular sin like *mishkav zakhur*.[134] In this case, this male soul that is reincarnated in a female body [results in] her barrenness because she has no "feminine waters" to rise up and receive the seminal drop from the "masculine waters."[135] The only way she can become pregnant and give birth is by another female soul entering into her through temporary "impregnation (*ʿibbur*)." By joining with her [another female soul in a female body] . . . she can give birth. However, she can never give birth to sons for two reasons. First, because it is written, *When a woman "emits semen" (tazria) and gives birth to a male* (Lev. 12:2), but here the woman is a male like her husband and thus cannot bear sons, only daughters![136] The second reason is because the soul of the woman that entered her [via *ʿibbur*] did so only temporarily in order to help her give birth. When the woman gives birth, the impregnated soul no longer has any purpose being there. At the time of birth that soul enters into the child. Hence the child will always be female and not male . . . We thus see that all women who have male souls can only bear daughters. And, the daughter she bears has the soul of the [female] soul that entered her via *ʿibbur* to help her give birth [thus achieving the state of *gilgul*]. In certain very rare cases, it is possible that at the time of birth, the female soul that entered through *ʿibbur* will depart, enabling a male soul to enter the child [thus producing a boy].[137]

There is much to say about the rich blend of biology and soul construction. However, given that my concerns are quite narrow, I will highlight only those elements that directly relate to the question at hand. First is the notion that there is not necessarily a correlation between the soul gender and body gender. More importantly, Luria argues, by implication, that gender is simply not only a biological category. There is nothing innovative in this, as such an idea has precedent in other cultures throughout history.[138] Luria never weighs in on whether one's gender is determined by body or soul, but here it appears that the body is determinate (the female with the male soul is called "the woman"; in a later text he implies the opposite). Yet the gender is limited by the soul within. The inability of a woman to bear children in one case and bear sons in another is not an insignificant blemish in traditional societies. The barren woman, a topic quite important in the Bible, is explained in this text as a woman who is, in essence, a man. Her bodily functions are curtailed by her soul. Whether we can extend this to a man who is only attracted to other men is speculative since Luria says nothing about the soul in relation to sexual desire. However, given Luria's comments in other places about barrenness (and the curse of barrenness from the Bible through classical Judaism), I will argue that this interpretation is at least suggestive. The plasticity here is further supported by the notion of impregnation that enables a woman with a male soul to, in essence, become a woman, albeit temporarily, in order to have a child. I say temporarily because after the birth, that female soul departs (either to the daughter or, in rare cases, back to where it came from) leaving the woman barren, and male, once again. The ability for that woman to have another child, as Vital explains below, can produce quite gruesome results:

> In this case [when a woman has a male soul], it is impossible for this woman to have another child without that same soul reentering her body once again. Hence, if the [first] child was a girl, this daughter would have to die, creating the possibility of her soul reentering the body of her mother to aid in her [new] pregnancy, after which the soul of the new daughter will be that same soul. . . . It is also possible that sometimes the first daughter will not have to die and another [female] soul can enter the mother [via ʿ*ibbur*] and she will become pregnant and give birth to a [second] daughter. That soul will then achieve the full status of *gilgul*.[139]

The reason that Vital uses the caveat "sometimes" regarding another ʿ*ibbur* is that there are limits to the number of soul impregnations (generally three) that are possible in any one body. More to the point, however, is the notion that to have a second child the woman who has a male soul must import a female soul in order to function as a woman, requiring, at times, the birth and death of a child to do so. Scholars have suggested that the prominence of *gilgul* in Safed in the sixteenth century was a way of justifying the unusually high child mortality rate at that time due to plagues and illness.[140] Luria himself died of such a plague. For our purposes, this discussion strengthens the notion suggested above that gender in the Lurianic corpus is a fluid and liminal category[141] and that *mishkav zakhur*, as an act of de- and regendering not only has an impact on the cosmic realm but also on the functions, and identity, of the physical body.

At the end of *Shaʿar ha-Gilgulim*, Vital relates a conversation with Luria that personalizes the impact of *mishkav zakhur* on the bodies and souls of the participants and their spiritual descendants. The discussion focuses around Vital's wife, Hannah, and the death of Vital's daughter, Angela:

He [Luria] said to me [Vital] that of all the sparks at the root of
my soul, none are closer to me than those of R. Akiva. Everything that happened to him will happen to me. He told me my
wife Hannah is the *gilgul* of Kalba Shavua, the father-in-law of R.
Akiva.[142] Since he [Kalba Shavua] was the penetrated partner
like a woman, he came back as a woman,[143] [first as] the wife of
Abaya because he was also from the root of R. Akiva. . . . Afterward, he was reincarnated in my wife Hannah. Because she is
the *gilgul* of a male, she can only give me daughters and not sons
because she is a man (*lifi s'he zakhar*). . . . He told me she became
pregnant with the soul of the wife of Tyranus Rufus the evil one
who later married R. Akiva, as is known.[144]

The text goes on to talk about the death of Vital's daughter, Angela
and later his wife, Hannah. Luria tells him that he will marry a more elevated woman later who will better represent the union of R. Akiva and
the wife of Tyranus Rufus.[145] In any event, this text illustrates the earlier
discussion in the realia of Vital's life. While we do not know anything
about the homosexual liaison between Kalba Shavua and a male partner, we do know that this act, now personalized, resulted in the construction of a woman with a male soul, who is here described as a male
(*lifi s'he zakhar*), supporting our basic claim from the more metaphysical
discussions in *Sha'ar ha-Yihudim* and *Sha'ar Ruah ha-Kodesh* of the transmorphing of gender resulting from *mishkav zakhur*. This transmorphing
is only possible because each human being already contains the inherent possibility of both genders. In some cases, as in *Sha'ar ha-Gilgulim*,
the dominant soul gender is other than the physical gender.[146] In different cases, the female nature of *ima*'s effluence (even as it acts as male
inside *zeir anpin*) holds the potential to change the receptive male into
a woman through desire, thus creating the condition of male–male
intercourse.

Conclusion

As I read and reread these passages on *mishkav zakhur* through the lens
of pre-Lurianic literature and feminist theory, a few things come into
relief. First, it seems quite plausible that Luria understood homosexual
desire as natural in the sense that the feminine is an integral part of
the male body and could easily become an object of desire for another
male. On the naturalness of homosexual desire, he was very much
aligned with his Muslim environment. The extent to which this meta-

physical reification of the inherent, albeit not active, bisexuality of the male and female (re: *Sha'ar ha-Gilgulim*) reflects Muslim thinking in that period is a topic for further research. It is true that Luria held that acting on that desire causes all kinds of de- and regendering that are destructive and thus forbidden. The question of constructivist versus essentialist notions of gender looms large in Luria's depiction of sex differentiation. I think that Luria's position is neither constructivist nor essentialist, in that gender for him is so fluid and is determined by so many factors (*gilgul*, desire, etc.) other than biology that the body is but one instantiation of an otherwise changing dynamic.

In exploring the gender–sexual orientation debate through Luria, I have found that the most cogent depiction is suggested by William D. Hart in an essay on homosexuality in Black churches in America: "Sexual Orientation and the Language of Higher Law." In this essay, Hart rehearses the arguments about the formation of nature verses nurture (to simplify an otherwise complex argument) and comes out with the following conclusion:

> From my perspective, sexual orientation *isn't* a social construct, if by construct one means unnatural and easy to change. On the contrary sexual orientation is one aspect of our nature that is least malleable and most difficult to change. What follows from this? That sexual orientation is fundamental to our identity, its soul, secret truth, and destiny? Not at all. All that need follow is that in constructing our identity, some aspects of our nature are less malleable than others. That doesn't make them truer, more natural, prototypically natural; it simply makes them more difficult to deal with.[147]

What Hart suggests is that the nature/nurture dichotomy is false because social identity is part of nature and nature is a piece of one's social identity. Taking this back to Luria, gender identity is not purely natural if by that we mean biological and unalterable. Desire for the opposite sex may be natural but that opposite sex can be easily instantiated in the same sex. Or, the nature of biology can be a veil for a soul inheritance that undermines biology. Desire is powerful enough to make a man a woman, or a woman a man, both of which already exist in each body. Nature is itself a construction, and human desire, even when it manifests as transgression, can be reconstructed.

To return once more to Butler, constructivist positions always reiterate norms outside themselves. However, to simply be satisfied with the bottom line that Luria maintains the prohibition of male homosexuality (which he surely does) is, in my view, to do an injustice to the creative and atypical nature of Lurianic physics, metaphysics, and psychology. Luria's contribution to the discussion of sexuality and sexual orientation in Judaism is found in the way in which he utilizes the performativity of desire and a quasi-constructivist approach to gender in order to destabilize the essentialist model to which he remains anchored.

4

NUMBERS
Balaam, Moses, and the Prophecy of the "Other":
A Lurianic Vision for the Erasure of Difference

inclusion is exclusion
—Daniel Boyarin, *Border Lines*

The adversity of exclusion can be made to go
hand in hand with the gifts of inclusion.
—Amartya Sen, *Identity and Violence*

Inversion, in other words, must simultaneously
be a perversion that is subversive.
—Mark C. Taylor, *Erring: A Postmodern A/Theology*

Ring the bells that still can ring
Forget your perfect offering
There is a crack in everything
That's how the light gets in.
—Leonard Cohen, "Anthem"

Especially since the rise of Christianity and Islam, Jews have concerned themselves with defining the nature and fabric of the Jewish claim of particularism[1] in relation to, and as distinct from, the non-Jewish other.[2] But not only the non-Jewish other. The other is not only the non-Israelite/Jew but also the other that lives in the midst of the community, inside the Jewishness of the Jew.[3] The fear is not only of the non-Jewish other but of the Jewish "other," the Jew who stands in opposition to the operative definition of *Judaism*. Esther Benbassa and Jean-Christoffe Attias argue that otherness is not merely a part of Jewish identity; it stands at the very center of how Judaism views itself: "Biblical thought and rabbinical Judaism have obviously never ceased to secrete this imagined other. The reason is that Judaism has defined itself, to a large extent, as a 'counter-religion'. It constructs itself and conceives of itself in confrontation with an external enemy, that is, however, simultaneously a standing internal temptation: idolatry."[4] Sacha Stern puts it more starkly: "The rabbinic image of the non-Jew is xenophobic in the extreme."[5] The other who is Christian, of course, begins as an internal other that becomes external, and Islam views itself to some extent in the trajectory of Judaism or at least Abrahamic and Mosaic prophecy. In Kabbala the other, who is often demonic, is sometimes depicted as internal to the self whose power is generated through interaction with the sacredness of the human soul. Being empowered by the sacred, the demonic is, in some way, always a part of the sacred it opposes.[6]

In the Bible, the external other, for example, Balaam, is portrayed in the Lurianic imagination as sharing a soul with Moses. And he is viewed as connected to the ʿerev rav (mixed multitude, Exod. 12:39) who also constitute a kind of "internal other" to Israel. Like the ʿerev rav, Balaam is both outside and inside, an external threat and internal temptation. So while the other is, as Boyarin suggests, "different," she is also the same, a difference that is rooted in sameness, the other that is also always the self. As Jonathan Z. Smith notes, comparison is always the manipulation of difference "to achieve some stated cognitive end."[7] So the question regarding Balaam and Israel is not only about difference per se but about how that difference reflects sameness (Balaam/Moses) and how that sameness reflects an internal difference (Israelite/convert).

W. D. Davis claims that the relationship of Israel to the gentile world may have been the most pressing theological problem of the first century.[8] The claim of exclusivity that lies at the center of the Israelite covenant is often in tension with the messianic and eschatological claim endemic to Judaism, especially in the Hebrew Prophets, predicting a utopian future where exclusivist claims (at least conventionally understood) are effaced or at least transformed.[9] The extent to which Paul's ostensible move to universalize the covenant founded on his reading of the eschatology of the Hebrew Prophets (with all its caveats) should not be underestimated as exhibiting an internal tension among Ancient Israelites.[10] While modernity—which brought emancipation and later the promise of religious pluralism to Jews—certainly presents unique challenges to traditional Jewish claims of covenantal exclusivity, modernity does not create the tension.[11] Rather, negotiating exclusivity and universality, being inside and outside, self and other, underlies much of the Ancient Israelite and later Jewish tradition, beginning in the Bible, and becomes especially prominent among post-rabbinic mystical Judaisms that stress utopian redemption. This is especially true when Jews find themselves in close proximity, geographically or theologically, to the (monotheistic) "other" (Christianity and Islam). I argue that sixteenth-century Safed is such an environment, one where the Islamic other (the tolerant Ottoman Empire) and the "(ex)-Christian" other (returning conversos) create a unique nexus that informs Lurianic exegesis on this question of identity, not only on the more obvious question of "who is a Jew?" but also on the more subtle question, "what is the difference between the Jew and the gentile?"[12]

In its early period (until the middle of the second century CE), Rabbinic Judaism seemed to largely follow the biblical model of exclusiveness. That is, the identity *Israelite* was determined by tribal and blood lineage and, while one could enter the tribe through marriage, there was little recourse to become an Israelite in any formal sense although many Hellenes integrated into Jewish communities informally.[13] Nor was there much desire on the part of Israelites to make an "outsider" an Israelite, although outsiders readily entered into Jewish communities sometimes without any formal conversion.[14] The lack of a legislated conversion procedure in this early period has been interpreted to mean that identity in the Bible was largely, if not exclusively, tribal and familial and not about belief or behavior.[15] Alternatively, in this period no one who was an Israelite could erase that affiliation even through sin or nonbelief.[16] William Scott Green writes, "Whatever their differences, these two claims[17] represent the position that most ancient Jews shared a common national or religio-ethnic self-definition . . . and that in such a context otherness meant being outside the 'Jewish community,' or bereft of 'Jewish identity,' or excluded from 'the Jewish people.' According to this model, one was either in or out; there appears no middle range."[18] This observation does not account for the existence of gentiles who lived among Jews, participated in Jewish rituals, and had the status of partial Jews in the Jewish community. Josephus Flavius notes in numerous places gentiles who revered Jewish customs and participated in Jewish life-cycle events (and not only as observers).[19] While Ancient Israelite religion may not have been as missionizing as early Christianity (both Jewish and Pauline), conversion, institutional and cultural, was not uncommon.[20] While the permeability of Jewish identity defining both Jew and non-Jew in the pre-rabbinic and rabbinic period did not efface the centrality of ethnicity as the backbone of Jewish identity, it did push the "ethnicity doctrine" into a more mythic realm.[21] Particularism remained and the myth of Jews as descendants of the "sons/tribes of Jacob" still survived, but Jewish particularity ("in" and "out") now stretched beyond the confines of a purely tribal identity.

The Hebrew prophets expressed a more universalistic model of inclusiveness.[22] However, in almost all cases, this utopian universalism was a vision of the future.[23] And prophetic utopianism in any event does not erase ethnicity as much as erase the absolute hierarchy inherent in biblical ethnic reasoning. As Denise Buell has argued, universalism in Christianity (and, I would add, Judaism), does not erase ethnicity as much as refashion it in a way that is conducive to a utopian vision.[24] This does not necessarily mean that universalism, however limited, was an invention of Christianity.[25] H. W. F. Saggs argues that pre-Mosaic patriarchal religion may have contained "a tint of universalism" that was erased with the introduction of the Mosaic God.[26] Jon Levenson further suggests that the categories of universalism and particularism and ethnicity more generally do not apply to the Hebrew Bible. While the Hebrew Bible begins with a universal and not particular notion of God and humanity (Gen. 1:1–2:3 and 2:4–24) and moves to posit a "chosen" people (e.g., Exod. 6:7; 19:19; Deut. 7:8), that move is not necessarily exclusivist in that Israel's covenant mandates responsibility to the non-Israelite other (Exod. 23:9; Lev. 19:33, 34; Deut. 23:8). Levenson argues that while divine election in the Hebrew Bible makes "universalism" impossible, election does not make Israelite religion hopelessly particularistic.[27] In any case (that is, whether a pre-Mosaic universalism preceded Mosaic religion or whether universalism grew as a tributary from it), classical post-biblical Judaism made clear distinctions between self and other even as those distinctions may not have always been applied to the masses.

Shaye Cohen sums up the biblical worldview on this question as follows: "Does the Hebrew Bible contain the idea that a non-Israelite can somehow become an Israelite by believing in the one true God? The answer is no. The Tanakh has adumbrations, intimations, harbingers of the idea, but not the idea itself."[28] Cohen argues that the Jewish notion of including the "outsider" into the Jewish fold (i.e., conversion) begins in the second century and is largely the result of Israel moving away from constituting cultural affiliation and citizenship outside of ethnicity, a shift common in Hellenism. Another factor was the fledging Christian movement that, while not fully severed from Judaism until much later, had already drawn certain definitive boundaries, via Pauline theology, separating Jewish non-Christians and Jewish Christians.[29]

The details of these arguments are not at issue here. Suffice it to say that for various reasons theories about exclusivity and separation from the surrounding culture, including Christianity, were a vital issue for the rabbis, not only as a way of distinguishing Jew from gentile but as way of distinguishing between what would become Judaism and Jewish/Christianity. Thus Daniel Boyarin writes, "In a precise mirror of the contemporary Christian move in which ethnic difference is made religious, for the latter rabbis religious difference has been ethnicized; Christians are no longer seen as a threatening other *within* [my italics] but as an entity fully other, as separate as the gentiles had been for the Jews of temple times."[30]

Especially toward the end of late Antiquity when Christianity took hold as a distinct and dominant religion and attracted the attention of the rabbis, the "other" became more complicated because it included an "internal other" who, after the fourth century, became a dominating power.[31] While it is true that after the conversion of Constantine (and even sometime before) the Christian was no longer considered a Jew,[32] the very claim of Christianity as the New Israel produced a new set of issues about Israel's exclusive covenantal experience.[33] The other was now (also) internalized, and was an "other" that grew up in the same theological universe yet interpreted that universe in ways that undermined the rabbinic construction of covenant. It was here that orthodoxy, and Judaism, really begins.[34] Hence, the rabbis, among other things, were very invested in making distinctions—who was in and who was out (e.g., Mishna Sanhedrin 10:3), and who was an Israelite/Jew and who was not.[35]

In the sixteenth century, especially in Safed, the exercise of distinguishing self and other undergoes another development. Many conversos, now free (or forced) to travel beyond the borders of the Iberian Peninsula (Spain and Portugal), sought to reenter the Jewish fold. Many were born and raised Christian and, even as they practiced Christianity, maintained a clandestine Jewish identity. In returning, many demanded full rights as Jews.[36] In such cases, "otherness" takes on another layer—a community whose claim to Jewishness includes the past practice of another (competing) religion and the identification with that religion. Yet for many legal authorities, past religious affiliations did not efface their identity as Jews because their conversion to Christianity was deemed involuntary. It is true that most returning conversos abandoned their old allegiances (Christianity) to embrace Judaism. But even with the abandonment, sincere or not, we still have a case in which the self and other (in this case Christianity) are embodied simultaneously in an individual who now seeks reentry into the community of Israel. The question as to whether or how much the ex-Christian can erase decades and sometimes generations of Christian education was an issue debated in the sixteenth century by rabbinic leaders. While the exclusivity doctrine is surely maintained in sixteenth-century Judaism, the converso phenomenon (from Christian back to Jew) challenged earlier notions of Jewishness and the question "Who is a Jew?" was renewed.[37] One result among many was the emergence of new messianic possibilities, in part because the boundaries of self and other were being effaced.[38]

As I argued in the previous chapters, the converso phenomenon is an important social and intellectual context of Lurianic Kabbala that influences both its metaphysics and its construction of social reality. In this chapter I argue that Lurianic depictions of Balaam as the prophetic other suggest ways in which the rabbinic desire for exclusiveness, extending from the Deuteronomist School in the Bible, is problematized. I suggest that the converso phenomenon, in theory and in practice, may be generating this reading, at least in part. Luria's erasure, or at least effacement, of rabbinic notions of other does not mean that Luria is presenting a competing claim of universality in any conventional sense.[39] Rather, the particularity he is claiming is nuanced by the idea, based on his theory of the human soul, that the other is, in fact, always also the self. The biblical narrative viewed through the lenses of Lurianic metaphysics, here the Balaam narrative in particular, exhibits the thinning of the opacity separating the self and the other (Moses/Israel, Balaam/nations), enabling the otherness of the other to disappear or at least become transparent. Underlying all this, of course, is Luria's eschatology, his belief in the absorption or eradication of the demonic (the unredeemable other) through the encounter with the holy.

If I am correct that Luria, following the Zohar, depicts the soul descendants of Adam as only including Israel (also meaning that it is only Israel who is "created in the image of God"),[40] then the notion of the "other" of any human is only that dimension that is not rooted in Israel. Yet this dimension, deemed the demonic (*kelipot*), has no lasting existence. In fact it has no true existence at all.[41] The eradication of the demonic through *tikkun* is the eradication of the other, or, the disappearance of the particular in favor of a universal that is defined as simply "human." The conventional distinction between Jew and gentile would fall away because each one is dependent on the existence of the other; the gentile other is thus a temporary category. This does not mean that all gentiles will become Jews in the future, because Jewishness is also a temporary category, an exilic instantiation of the human in a world not-yet-redeemed. Rather, all will become fully human in the future, humanity defined here as a full disclosure of the image of God.[42] The locution "will become" does not mean that this does not already exist. In Lurianic metaphysics, the future is already embedded in the present. The future is the disclosure of an already existing reality that is concealed. Thus the categories of self and other, Jew and gentile, are false in the sense that they are a result of a world not fully disclosed. Yet they are true in that it is only through this dichotomy that the fully human self is revealed.

As I illustrated in previous chapters, the Lurianic doctrine of the soul knows no particularistic boundaries. In this chapter I argue that the particularistic and irreconcilable differences between the self and the other, a distinction that classical Judaism was very invested in defending, is deconstructed in Luria's understanding of the full disclosure of the covenant. The divinity of the human soul, rooted in Adam, is reconstructed and liberated from its profane elements. While in the preredemptive world this divine soul is most fully manifest in a people called Israel, Israel (which in the future will simply be "the human") is incomplete until the lost remnants of the Adamic soul, buried in the "other" of the non-Israelite, returns to its source. In the end, then, we will have to determine why Luria would not agree with Paul that, in the messianic moment, "there is no Jew, no Greek" (Gal. 3:28).

Before exploring how this unfolds in Luria's rendering of the Balaam narrative, I will briefly examine the rabbinic use of the Balaam story and then the Zohar's ontology of evil to present the particularity and exclusivity that Luria deconstructs.

The Gentile Prophet as a Tool for Concrete Exclusivity: The Rabbinic Use of Balaam

The episode of Balaam (Num. 22:2–25:9) has always been viewed as problematic in the history of Jewish literature. Balaam is not an overtly negative personality in Numbers.[43] While he agrees to curse Israel for money, he consistently acknowledges that he can only fulfill the will of God (e.g., Num. 22:18). In the deuteronomic tradition (Deut. 23:5–6) Balaam's intentions are made explicit: *But the Lord your God refused to heed Balaam; instead the Lord your God turned the blessing into a curse for you for the Lord your God loves you.* Whereas there is no mention of Balaam's inner feelings in Numbers, in Deuteronomy Balaam *desires* to curse Israel and it is God who turns (*ve-yahafokh*) Balaam's curse into a blessing. Balaam's evil intentions are extended in the prophetic tradition as well and also filter into the Septuagint translation of the Bible.[44] In Deuteronomy and beyond, Balaam is envisioned as an arch enemy of Israel.[45] Alexander Rofe argues that this deuteronomic shift is aligned with Deuteronomy's general worldview of Israel's uniqueness. "This view [of discrediting Balaam in Deuteronomy] works well with Israel being chosen as a holy nation unto God (Deut. 7:6). It can no longer acknowledge that the nations (*bnei nekhar*) have any positive contribution to make to the history of Israel. This history [only] reveals the uniqueness of Israel and God's grace [upon them]. Therefore, we also see the erasure of the purpose of Jethro in Deuteronomy regarding the organization of a court system in Israel (Deut. 1:9–18)."[46] It is thus the doctrine of exclusivity in Deuteronomy that makes Balaam's apparent virtuous character impossible. He becomes, at best, a prophet against his will, and his blessings are God's and not his own.

This is even more evident regarding prophecy (Deut. 18:13–20). After Moses, true prophecy is exclusively an Israelite phenomenon. On this reading of Deuteronomy, Balaam, as a post-Mosaic non-Israelite prophet, must be an enemy, one who combines prophecy and magic in an attempt to destroy Israel. If his prophetic powers were true, which the Bible takes for granted, and his intentions were noble, his prophecy would threaten the exclusivist doctrine being espoused in Deuteronomy.

In short, the demonization of Balaam coincides with the claim of exclusivity of Israel after Sinai. He becomes a prototypic "other," not the more benign other of earlier biblical strata but the other who attempts to undermine God's covenant with Israel, even outside Israel's purview.[47] It is only divine intervention that saves Israel from the curses that Balaam was hired, and desired, to speak.

This trajectory of Balaam as a signpost for contentious otherness dominates the rabbinic imagination concerning Balaam. Balaam as an individual becomes the embodiment of all the other nations in the rabbinic imagination. His personality is envisioned as the collective mind of the gentile toward Israel. And his imagined spiritual life becomes a leitmotif for non-Jewish religions, particularly Christianity.

Rabbinic literature is replete with aggadic material about Balaam.[48] For our limited purposes, Rabbinic Judaism asks two fundamental questions about this narrative, the latter of which serves as a foundation for post-rabbinic Jewish philosophy and Kabbala. The first question, which is really two related questions, is literary. If we begin with the notion that Moses wrote the entire Torah during the forty-year period in the desert (excluding the last verses relating to his death), the question arises how Moses knew about what was going on between Balak and Balaam? The story is an odd interlude separating the on-going narrative of Israel's life in the desert and shows no apparent connection to the lives of the Israelites.[49]

A second and more discomfiting dimension of the Balaam story is the apparent recognition of the prophecy of a non-Israelite after the revelation at Sinai. Here the question is theological. The rabbis had no difficulty recognizing prophecy of non-Israelites before the covenant. However, after Sinai, after Israel was chosen by God, the continuation of legitimate prophecy for those not present at the event was viewed as problematic and threatening. Rather than solving this through talmudic dialectics, the rabbis seem to make it more difficult by equating the prophecy of Balaam and Moses (we will explore those equations below). In short, the rabbis must come up with a strategy that legitimates non-Israelite, post-Sinai prophecy and answer why this non-Israelite prophecy is important enough to occupy three chapters in the Book of Numbers. In fact, they do more than that—they creatively turn this narrative, which has the potential to weaken the exclusive nature of the

God–Israelite communication, into a post-Sinai episode that strengthens the covenant, finally excluding the non-Israelite from any claim to it. The elevated status of Balaam's prophecy becomes a tool against any gentile claim to covenant. Even after Sinai, the nations are given a prophetic equal in stature to Moses and still they fail. Balaam becomes a leitmotif that erases any protest against Israelite uniqueness. For the rabbis, the Balaam story coupled with the Moses–Balaam equation drives a wedge between the truth claims (via prophecy and revelation) of Judaism versus the truth claims (via prophecy) of any other religion.

The equation of Balaam and Moses, the villain and the hero, is viewed by some scholars of rabbinics as having a polemical tone. With the emergence of Christianity, the rabbis of late Antiquity were confronted with Christian claims of legitimacy, one of them being the prophecy of Jesus.[50] In an illuminating essay on this subject, "Homilies of the Sages on Gentile Prophecy and on the Episode of Balaam," Efrayim Urbach discusses the nature of rabbinic responses to Christianity through the lens of Balaam's prophecy.[51] He contests earlier scholarly opinions of men such as Abraham Geiger, among others, in the late nineteenth and early twentieth centuries who argued that Balaam serves as a foil for Jesus in rabbinic literature.[52] However, he does not discount the possibility that rabbinic texts, including those dealing with Balaam, are polemical against the fledgling Christian religion.[53] In particular, Urbach chooses Mishna Avot de-Rebbe Natan (second version) chapter 45,[54] "Everyone who has these three traits is from the disciples of Abraham and everyone who has these three traits is from the disciple of Balaam." On this early rabbinic passage Urbach states:

> Particularly noteworthy is the phrase "disciples of Abraham" that does not appear in all of rabbinic literature aside from this text [and Mishna Avot]. The phrase "disciples of Abraham" does not refer to those from the seed of Abraham (*zera*) or his progeny (*banav*), phrases that are more common when referring to [the nation of] Israel. The word "disciples" (*talmidim*) refers to those who accept the teachings of Abraham and walk in his ways. This does not negate the possibility that those students may not be from his seed or progeny. It is therefore possible that the disciples of Abraham, like the disciples of Balaam, are not the children of Abraham but those that walk in his [Abraham's] ways and distance themselves from the ways of Balaam.[55]

Urbach goes on to cite New Testament sources that make similar distinctions, albeit with different intentions. The phrase "the doctrine (lit., law) of Balaam" (*torat Balaam*) appears in Revelations 2:14 (known to be a Jewish-Christian text) and 2 Peter 2:15, *Which have forsaken the right way, and are gone astray, following the way of Balaam son of Beor, who loved the wages of unrighteousness.*[56] As is known, Paul often uses Abraham (and being a descendant of Abraham) as a motif describing faith and not law, that is, as an argument against the Jews and Jewish-Christians who believed the law remained in effect after Christ (e.g., Rom. 4:2, 13–16). This is especially true in Paul's diatribe against the Jewish-Christians in Galatians 3 and Romans 9:7.[57] The faith of Abraham is embodied *in Christ* and no longer is the property of Abraham's biological seed.[58] *And if you are in Christ, then you are Abraham's seed, and heirs according to the promise* (Galatians 3:29).[59] Paul also refers to Christian gentiles as "children of Abraham" (Gal. 3:7), using "children" euphemistically.

The Mishna in Avot and Avot de-Rebbe Natan juxtapose Abraham (here his disciples or those who live according to his teachings) and Balaam. Unlike Mishna Sanhedrin 10:2 or Paul's Romans 9–11, there is no intent to define "Israelite." The juxtaposition of Abraham and Balaam is noteworthy for two reasons: first, the use of the term *talmidim* (disciples) instead of *zera* (seed) or *banim* (children). This is uncharacteristic of rabbinic teaching when discussing Abraham and his progeny. Second, because the juxtaposition of Abraham and Balaam is unprecedented in rabbinic literature even as this comparison does have a linguistic foundation.[60] Urbach argues that the Abraham–Balaam equation may have originally been a motif used for an internal dispute between Jewish-Christians who believed in the continued efficacy of mitzvot, and the disciples of Paul who wanted to erase or at least thin the distinction between Israel and the gentiles.[61] Given the odd turn-of-phrase *talmidei Avraham* in Avot and Avot de-Rebbe Natan, Urbach suggests that perhaps the rabbis adopted this motif to distinguish between Jews and those who adhered to "another prophet," meaning Jesus. Moreover, the failure of Balaam's prophecy developed in rabbinic literature (the Bible tells us nothing of Balaam's failure as a prophet) deepens the argument for the exclusivity of Jews against gentiles who are disciples of a prophet whose prophecy is true but who is a "false" prophet.[62] By this I mean his prophecy originates from a place that is rooted in holiness (sharing a dimension of Moses' soul) but that he does not hold the status of a true prophet.

Urbach's argument here is useful for numerous reasons. While he rejects the overt use of Balaam to portray Jesus, he does not deny that the rabbis may have been reacting, via biblical exegesis, to Christianity as they knew it.[63] At least early on, Balaam's prophecy is fully acknowledged as true prophecy, but it is deemed an utter failure. Perhaps Balaam is prefigured as one, as opposed to Abraham, who prophecies the end of mitzvot and the universality of the divine message.[64] If a non-Israelite can be a true prophet, then why is it that God's will can only be lived through mitzvot (Paul, of course, argues in favor of this point)? The result of this admittedly speculative theological–polemical move in Mishna Avot de-Rebbe Natan (viewing Balaam as challenging Jewish claims of exclusive divine authority) potentially undermines the uniqueness of the Sinai covenant. The Mishna's depiction of the traits of Balaam responds to this implied challenge by claiming that such a stance results in the collapse of morality (the three traits of Balaam—an evil eye, haughtiness, and arrogance are all moral categories).[65] If we follow Urbach and suggest that it is at least feasible that the rabbis in these passages may have been responding to the theological challenge of Christianity by using the tools of an inner-Christian polemic—Jewish-Christian arguments against Paul—certain possibilities arise. By reclaiming Abraham, not his "seed" but the morality of his teaching, and juxtaposing him to Balaam, not as Jesus or false prophet but as a prophet who failed to instill upon his disciples basic moral qualities, the rabbis reconfigure Judaism's value in a world where there is now competition as to who owns the covenant.[66] The rabbis, of course, never make the theological critique overt, and I acknowledge that this idea is somewhat speculative. But it is significant, in my view, that the mishna is not simply saying that the abrogation of mitzvot makes one a "disciple of Balaam." The disciples of Balaam are those who follow a leader (or prophet) who fails to instill upon his community basic moral values.

From another angle, this battle may also be against Paul's own metaphorical use of "the children of Abraham" as an example of those who choose faith over law. Following Urbach's analysis, I would suggest the rabbis actually dislodge the "disciples of Abraham" from the "children of Abraham" in order to make a statement about exclusivity—not the exclusivity of genealogy but the unique message of Torah though Moses that cannot be supplanted after Balaam (i.e., the gentiles) was given the opportunity and failed. On this reading of Avot de-Rebbe Natan and Mishna Avot, the rabbis are arguing for particularity not based on genealogy but the moral certitude of the Abrahamic message as interpreted solely by Moses. This makes sense precisely because they may have been faced with a competing narrative (Christianity) that was being espoused by biological Jews.

Much of rabbinic and post-rabbinic discussions about Balaam are founded on a short passage at the end of Sifre Devarim, an early halakhic Midrash on Deuteronomy. Commenting on the verse, *And there has not risen a prophet since in Israel like Moses* (Deut. 34:10), the midrash states, "None has arisen in Israel, but one has arisen among the nations. And who is he? Balaam son of Beor."[67] The midrash then proceeds to compare the differences between Moses and Balaam (not the substance of their respective prophecies but how they each absorbed prophecy). The midrash is surprisingly value-free, and Moses and Balaam both seem to have certain advantages and disadvantages. Yet this correlation, giving Balaam a stature equal to Moses, becomes a leitmotif in subsequent midrashim and later in Kabbala. The fact that Sifre concludes its discussion on Deuteronomy, the final book of the Pentateuch, with something that seems to attenuate the stature of Moses (by discussing another gentile prophet equaling his stature) is fascinating and deserves a separate study. While subsequent midrashim embellish this comment to strengthen the Israelite covenant, the silence of Sifre stands out.

In the trajectory of the rabbinic tradition, Balaam's prophecy raises the question of non-Israelite prophecy more generally. We read in the Tannaitic midrash Seder ʿOlam,

> There was not a city in Erez Israel that did not have prophets. However, all prophecy that was necessary for posterity was written and all prophecy that was merely useful for the moment was not written . . . these were prophets that existed before Abraham. After Abraham the prophets were Balaam and his father (Beor), Job from Erez Utz, Elifaz the Yemenite, Beldad ha-Sukhi, Zofer ha-Neʿemati, and Elijah son of Birkha'el the Buzite. These were prophets who prophesied to the nations before the giving of the Torah. When the Torah was given to Israel, *ruah ha-kodesh* ceased among the nations.[68]

This midrash begs the obvious question: But Balaam prophesied after Sinai?! An answer is given in Leviticus Raba 1:12.

> Said R. Isaac. "There was prophecy among the nations until the erection of the Tent of Meeting. Once the Tent of Meeting was erected prophecy ceased from among them, as it says, I held him fast I would not let him go (Song of Songs 3:4)." They said to him, behold Balaam prophesied [after the Tent of Meeting]. He said to them, he prophesied for the good of Israel. . . .[69]

In other words, there is dispensation for the otherwise unassailable position that God speaks only to Israel after the Sinai covenant and its more permanent instantiation in the Tent of Meeting. What is accomplished here is simply another dimension of exclusion. After Sinai, God's will can be manifest *only* as it relates to Israel, even if spoken from the mouth of a non-Israelite. In fact, this midrash espouses an even deeper claim of exclusion because now the nations of the world have direct access to God *only* when it serves to benefit Israel.[70] Balaam is the example of one who was given the power of prophecy for the sake of expressing divine will about Israel through a non-Israelite conduit.

The more interesting rabbinic turn here is the extension of Balaam as a prophet of the gentiles. This midrashic strain exhibited in Tanna de be-Eliyahu and later in Midrash Tanhuma in fact undermines the midrashic trajectory here. If Balaam is a prophet for gentiles, then his prophetic gift is not for the Israelites but in order to provide a correlate to Moses to enable the gentile to have the same access to divine will as Israel. In this case, the Balaam narrative serves a more extended purpose—to diffuse any future protest by the nations of any covenantal claim.[71]

> After Noah came into the world, the Holy One said to Shem. Shem, you had my Torah—if it had been kept at all among the first ten generations, do you suppose that I would consider destroying My world on account of them and their transgressions? Now prophesy to them in the hope that they will take My Torah upon themselves. So for four hundred years Shem prophesied to all the nations of the world, but they were not willing to heed him. After him came Eliphaz son of Barachel, Zophar the Naamathite. . . . and the last of all of them, Balaam son of Beor. There was not a thing in the world that the Holy One did not reveal to Balaam. Why? Because otherwise all the nations of the earth would have spoken up to Him and said: Master of the Universe, had you given us [as well as Israel] a prophet like Moses, we would have accepted [Your] Torah. Therefore the Holy One gave them Balaam son of Beor who in his native intelligence surpassed Moses.[72]

Balaam is positioned here as the final gentile prophet, the "last chance" for the nations to recognize God's Torah (in the more general sense of the term). There are two advantages that he has over the other pre-Mosaic prophets of the gentiles. First, coming after Sinai, divine will is already manifest and, it would appear, is more readily accessible. Second, coming concomitant with Moses, Balaam's prophetic gift must at least match that of Moses in order to make possible the gentile acceptance of Torah. The midrash here is even willing to grant Balaam superior status to balance the weight of Sinai on the other side. Here we view the position, reiterated in Midrash Tanhuma, that Balaam is essentially a prophet to and for the gentiles. More than that, he is a biblical character who embodies the gentile spirit ("do not be like the disciples of

Balaam"). As Urbach argued, the mishna in Avot de-Rebbe Natan does not conflate disciple with seed.

Midrash Tanhuma begins its discourse on Balaam by stressing his presence in the Torah as a message to the nations:

> And Balak saw (Num. 22:2). This is like it is written, *The Rock!—His deeds are perfect, His ways are just* (Deut. 32:4). God did not give the nations an opening (*pithon peh*) in the future to say "You God have abandoned us and did not give us what you gave to Israel." What did God do [to prevent this accusation]? Just as he raised kings, wise men, and prophets in Israel, he did the same for the nations. He chose kings, prophets and wise men of Israel correlate to those of the nations. He appointed King Solomon as ruler of the world (*melekh ʿal kol ha-aretz*), and so too Nebuchadnezzar, as it is written [about him], *All the nations shall serve him, his son and his grandson . . .* (Jer. 27:7). . . . He appointed Moses to Israel, who spoke with God whenever he wanted. And he appointed Balaam with him, who spoke to God whenever he wanted.[73]

This midrash mirrors the earlier Tanna de be-Eliyahu passage except that it extends the parity beyond Balaam's prophecy to include governance and legislation. That is, the nations had as much opportunity as Israel to recognize God's sovereignty and create a moral and just society; their failure to do so cannot be blamed on divine preference. Attempting to justify the irreconcilable exclusivity of Israel, Tanhuma brackets Sinai as a final stage of othering the other and suggests that even after Sinai divine appointment of gentile kings, legislators, and prophets continued, if only to strengthen the Israelite covenantal claim that their election is earned and not solely delivered by divine fiat.

> See the difference between the prophets of Israel and the prophets of the [idolatrous] nations. The prophets of Israel warn the nations of their sins, as it is written, *I gave you a prophet for the nations* (Jer. 1:5). Prophets of the nations are destructive and attempt to destroy humanity's claim to immortality (*ʿolam ha-bah*). Moreover, all the prophets of Israel act with mercy on Israel and the nations. So Isaiah said, *Therefore, like a lyre my heart moans for Moab, and my very soul for Kir-heres* (Isa.16:11). And Ezekiel says, *Now you, O mortal (ben adam) intone a dirge for Tyre* (Ezek. 27:2). The prophets of the nations [on the other hand] act with anger; this one [Balaam] tried to destroy an entire people for no reason.[74]

The caricature of Israelite and non-Israelite prophets is beside the point here. The direction of this midrashic approach is twofold. First, it serves to answer the obvious question as to what the Balaam narrative is doing in the Torah. Second, based on Urbach's comments on Avot de-Rebbe Natan, this may be a polemical tool to undermine the Christian claim of the prophecy of Jesus or to deflect any other claim of access to the divine in a post-biblical world. The midrashic trajectory here is to humanize the success of Israel and the failure of the nations—interestingly, to minimize divine fiat in order to maximize the claim of exclusivity. Both Israel and the nations had prophets, and each one's prophets heard God's word. One heeded his message and one distorted it. Covenantal exclusivity is the consequence of human behavior rather than divine design. The conclusion to this midrash answers the question of why this narrative is here altogether. "Hence, the Balaam story was written [in the Torah] to reveal why God withdrew the Holy Spirit [*ruah ha-kodesh*] from the nations. They had it, and look what they did with it."

What remains ambiguous is that the Balaam story happens *after* Sinai. In order to make this chronology fit the midrashic use of Balaam, the rabbis reinvent the story as a lesson about Sinaitic exclusivity in retrospect.[75] Israel merited Sinai because the nations were already discredited. The illustration of their failure appears *after* Sinai in the failed prophetic episode of Balaam.[76]

This limited foray into rabbinic readings on Balaam suggests a number of points that will become relevant when we turn to the Lurianic material. First is the unequivocal position that Balaam's prophecy was true.[77] In fact, it is precisely the truth of his prophetic vocation that is crucial—without Balaam being a true prophet the rabbinic use of Balaam to buttress the artifice of covenantal exclusivity would fail.

Second, Balaam's failure is moral—as a prophet he could not translate God's word into a message that resulted in the creation of a moral world. By using the phrase *disciples of Balaam,* Avot determines that his failure as a prophet was a moral failure.[78] In this case, the rabbis curiously mirror earlier New Testament usages of Balaam's error.

Third, there appear to be two distinct and in many ways incompatible midrashic trajectories at play. The first is less common and less convincing. Bothered by the question of how a prophet can rise from among the nations after Sinai and why this is deemed important enough to include in the Torah, the rabbis posit that Balaam's prophecy exists to serve Israel alone. That is, exclusivity is solidified at Sinai and Balaam is the non-Israelite (prophetic) affirmation of that exclusivity. After all, Balaam's blessings (Num. 23: 9, 10, 21, 24) are such strong confirmations of the covenant that some were included in the traditional Jewish liturgy!

The second and more interesting midrashic reading views Balaam as a prophet to the nations. The nations had prophets (Balaam being the last and most prominent)[79] who could convey the true divine message, and yet the nations consistently fail to heed the call. For the rabbis, this removes non-Israelite claims against the unjustness of Israel's election. While this implies that election is bracketed until the nations and their prophets fail, the ultimate end is the same. However, two things extend from this: (1) prophecy is taken away from the nations; and (2) the absence of non-Israelite prophecy can no longer be an argument against Israel's exclusive covenant with God. Finally, the extension of Balaam as an embodiment of "the nations" procured in midrash more generally becomes a dominant trope in the kabbalistic tradition and in Luria in particular. However, as we will see, Balaam is not merely an archetype of the nations but rather of a particular non-Israelite community: the *'erev rav,* who in fact were quite close, and even inside, Israel.[80]

In Lurianic teaching, the literary questions and the more overt questions concerning theological challenges to Israel are not prominent. The latter question as to Balaam's relationship to Israel does play an important role but one that concerns an inner-Israelite struggle concerning the question of its own exclusivity. That is, it deals with who is included and who is excluded among the Israelites. The Sifri's correlation of Moses and Balaam becomes paramount, not as a tool to finalize exclusivity but as a way of viewing Balaam as part of the redemptive process—a figure whose prophecy and death contribute to purging the world of the final barrier separating exile and redemption. In midrash, Balaam is a leitmotif for exclusivity, while in Luria he is a central tenet of its erasure. Before examining Luria's writings on Balaam we must briefly map the Zohar's metaphysical demonization of Balaam, extending the rabbinic idea into an ontology of evil. It is this depiction of Balaam that Luria inherits—it is the lens through which he and his disciples read the rabbis. And it is this ontological rendering that serves as the foundation of his deconstruction.

From Prophet to Demon and toward Reconciliation: Balaam as the Dark Other in the Zohar

Rabbinic tradition certainly set the stage for the demonization of Balaam in the Zohar. The apparently innocuous depiction of Balaam in Numbers is effaced in midrashic and aggadic literature, based on the rabbinic reading of Deuteronomy 23:5–6.[81] What remains is the portrait of Balaam as a villain and enemy of Israel. As is almost always the case in zoharic hermeneutics, the Zohar adapts the basic framework of rabbinic teaching and reconstitutes it for its own metaphysical ends.[82] In doing so, I claim that it sets the stage for the Lurianic reconciliation between Balaam and Moses, admittedly through Balaam's death, whereby Balaam, via *gilgul*, becomes an Israelite and completes an important prerequisite for redemption. A detailed study of Balaam in the Zohar is surely a desideratum and beyond the narrow focus of this study. Here I will simply sketch some of the salient points in the Zohar's construction of Balaam as an example of its dialectical understanding of evil in preparation for a more in-depth examination of how Luria and his circle move beyond the Zohar in their analysis.

As stated in the introduction to this chapter, I am arguing that in the Lurianic tradition Balaam is an interesting case of an "other" (Jesus? Christian? converso?) who threatens the Israelite/Jewish covenant by, among other things, challenging its particularistic and exclusivist covenantal claims. While the claim that rabbinic texts, especially early ones, may be influenced by, or are responding to, Jesus or Christianity is contestable.[83] By the Middle Ages this is well known.[84] Paradoxically, even though each community defines itself in opposition to the other, in many cases they deploy the shared language and similar mythic constructs in order to do so. Israel Yuval notes, "[In the Middle Ages] to be a Christian meant to be anti-Jewish, to reject any alternative interpretation other than Christianity. The opposite was also true: to be Jew in the Middle Ages meant to be anti-Christian, because Christianity offered an alternative interpretation to Judaism. Negation of the 'other' was an indispensable stage in the process of defining one's identity."[85] Yet, as Yuval continues, both sides used biblical characters and similar ancient myths to make opposite claims: either Christianity was true or Judaism was true. As we will presently see, whereas the Zohar never overtly compares Balaam to Christianity, its demonization of Balaam fits nicely into its more general demonization of the "other," with the Christian "other" being a primary target.[86]

Whereas Balaam is an instantiation of the *Sitra Ahra* (the demonic "other side") in both the Zohar and later in Luria, Lurianic texts focus on Balaam's soul as rooted in holiness (he is the "other side" of Moses), a soul that must be reintegrated into the Israelite community. The result is that Balaam, the advocate of the universal, becomes subsumed in the particular and, in that way, deconstructs the particularistic nature of the particular without destroying the particular as such. The Zohar introduces the notion of the ontological status of evil (*Sitra Ahra*) and its roots in the divine.[87] Luria suggests that conversion (either actual conversion or soul-conversion through *gilgul* and *'ibbur*) is one way that the demonic is neutralized or rather, having its roots revealed, yielding

a reconciliation that moves the world closer to redemption. It is a movement from zoharic containment to absorption. The relevance of conversion as a metaphysical motif should not be viewed in isolation but as
a reification of a concrete reality in sixteenth-century Safed. What I am
suggesting here is that the depiction of Balaam in rabbinic literature as
a foil for Christianity interestingly leads us to Luria's depiction of
Balaam as the villain whose actions enable him to realize his true (holy)
nature and initiate his yearning to return to his roots embodied in his
desire to "die an upright death" (Num. 23:10).[88]

The Zohar's reification of biblical figures into metaphysical and cosmic tropes, thereby (one could argue) mythologizing the "fictive narrative" of the Bible is well known. What we find in the Zohar when examining depictions of the Balaam narrative is a case where the Zohar
takes the rabbinic initiative of viewing the Numbers episode through
the lens of Deuteronomy 23:5–6 and, taking significant license, reconstructs Balaam as a demonic character, part of a larger cast (the serpent, Esau, Amalek et al.), all of whom represent evil forces attempting
to undermine Israel's covenant with God.[89] From the context of this
chapter, these figures challenge the exclusivist doctrine of Israel (i.e.,
the covenant) protesting the unworthiness of Israel as a partner in
God's covenant. In some cases, including that of the serpent in the garden and Balaam, the demonic serves to show Israel unfit for the covenantal task (and in almost all cases they are correct even as Israel is subsequently saved and forgiven by God). Specifically with Balaam, the
Zohar develops the rabbinic notion that the two angels who protest
against Adam's creation in midrashic tradition, Azzah and Azael, are
teachers of Balaam, thus connecting Balaam's attempt to curse Israel
with the angelic desire to undermine the very creation of humanity.[90]
As stated above, the demonic does not represent the dark forces that
wish to destroy Israel as much as a force to undermine Israel's covenant
with God. Hence, a religion such as Christianity that seeks to undermine Israel's particularistic claim in favor of a notion of a more inclusive covenant would constitute an expression of the demonic.

For example, the Zohar suggests a correlation between Balaam and
Amalek demonizing Balaam as unredeemable.[91] The Zohar even goes
further in equating Balaam with the serpent who tempted Eve (and
then Adam) in the garden.[92] The Zohar in general downplays the prophetic mission of Balaam, making him almost exclusively a magician
and charlatan.[93] While the Zohar does offer numerous interpretations
of Sifri Devarim's equation of Moshe and Balaam (see below), it does
not primarily view this equation in terms of prophecy but rather in
terms of leadership (Moses—Israel, Balaam—gentiles).

Perhaps the biggest break between the rabbis and the Zohar, one that turns the Balaam trajectory around, is the equation of Balaam with the *Sitra Ahra*. *Prima fascia*, one would assume that the Zohar's cosmology of good and evil would solidify, even more than rabbinic literature, Balaam as a villain without redemption. However, as Elliot Wolfson has shown, the apparently dualistic world of the Zohar contains an essential dialectical twist.

The examples Wolfson offers in his essay describing the Zohar's ontology of evil center around Egypt and Pharaoh. Using the Exodus story, he illustrates how the Zohar constructs a battle between good and evil that is both external and internal to God. "The intrinsic relationship of Egypt to magic was developed at length by the author of the Zohar. The old aggadic theme, however, is transformed by the theosophic system of the Kabbalah. That is Egypt's special relation to magic underscores Egypt as the seat of demonic power, for according to the Zohar, magic is the force of the demonic, the *Sitra Ahra*, which corresponds to the divine."[94]

Since the Zohar views Balaam as an extension of the generic demonic category, it is thus predictable that it erases any semblance of prophecy with regard to Balaam and views him exclusively as a magician.[95] We will see that Luria reverses the Zohar's erasure of Balaam as prophet and focuses precisely on the metaphysical roots of his prophecy.[96] For Luria, Balaam's prophecy constitutes a yet unexplored category—prophecy that is neither true nor false. It is rooted in a demonic part of the Godhead but one that can be and must be redeemed to complete the process of reconciliation. This offers a new reason for the inclusion of the story in the Pentateuch. Similar to the story of Moses killing the Egyptian task-master (Exod. 2:11–14) and the mention of the ʿerev rav (Luria, following a passing remark in the Zohar, links Balaam to the ʿerev rav),[97] the Balaam narrative juxtaposes Moses with a character who is "outside" (yet rooted "inside") and must be integrated back inside to procure the final *tikkun*. And, both the ʿerev rav and Balaam share dimensions of their soul with Moses. Balaam does not represent a corrupt element of the holy (i.e., the prophetic) in the Zohar but the demonic that is embodied in magic. His potential for rehabilitation, like Pharaoh's, is far less clear. More strongly, Balaam is likened to Amalek in the Zohar.[98] Regarding Amalek, the Zohar teaches that he must be wiped out and not transformed.[99]

Yet the story in the Zohar is more complex than it appears, and Luria may not be deviating as far from the Zohar as it seems. In one Zohar passage, we find a disagreement as to whether Balaam, as the *Sitra Ahra*, has any access to the sacred (*kedusha*). Underlying this disagreement is whether or not God gives non-Israelites access to the holy. This hearkens back to the rabbinic discussion concerning the question of prophecy, but here it is about the esoteric knowledge of practical Kabbala (via *torat ha-sephirot*) as the vehicle of magic. In both the rabbis and the Zohar, Balaam becomes an example of exclusivity. However, in the Zohar as opposed to the rabbis there is no final answer about the potential for Balaam's rehabilitation. This, I argue, serves as the precedent Luria and his disciples use to make a case for Balaam as the "outsider" who, rooted in the "inside," works his way back into the embodied Israel:

> Balaam said to Balak: Come and see what can be done to them [Israel]. All of the magic and sorcery in our power (lit., from our crowns) is rooted in their higher *malkhut* (*me-kizpah de-malkhuta de-leayla*). And it [that is, this higher *malkut* or *zeir anpin*][100] is bound to them (i.e., Israel), as it is written, *The Lord their God is with them, and their King's claim in their midst* (Num. 23:21). Said Rabbi Yehuda, "Heaven forbid that Balaam knew anything about the lofty holiness (*be-kedusha de-leayla*). God did not allow any other nation to have conscious access in His glory except his holy children, as it is written, *And he sanctified them (lit. made them holy), and they were holy*" (Lev. 11:44). Only those called holy (*kadosh*) can have access to holiness (*kedusha*). And [only] Israel is holy, as it is written, *for you are a holy nation* (Deut. 14:2).[101]

The initial comment in this passage suggests that Balaam knew that his magical powers were rooted in the divine. Rabbi Yehuda does not contest that ontological claim; nor does he contest that Balaam in fact used these powers in an attempt to destroy Israel. He only contests that Balaam knew about it.[102] That is, he contests that any non-Israelite (after Sinai) can have the consciousness to know the roots of supernatural power. Without this distinction, that is, between what was actually true and what Balaam knew to be true, Rabbi Yehuda would be guilty of Gnostic or Manichean heresy. With the distinction, he acknowledges that all power is from God, but Balaam, as demonic or more generally as a non-Israelite, could not apprehend the source of his own power. In some way, Rabbi Yehuda's position regarding sorcery is a reflection of Balaam's own admission in Numbers about his ability to prophesize. The first position in the Zohar, reflecting the comment about Balaam in Deuteronomy, runs counter to the biblical narrative of the episode by arguing that Balaam intended to curse Israel using his *knowledge* of *torat ha-sephirot*.

In a sense this passage is mired in the same dilemma as the rabbinic discussion about prophecy. However, now it is transferred to the practice of sorcery. If only Israel is holy and prophecy is a consequence of holiness, then only Israel can be prophets. If only Israel is holy and the apprehension of divine power (*kosmin ve-harashin* or its correlate *torat ha-sephirot*) is holiness, then only Israel can apprehend how (even gentile) magic is rooted in the divine. Even though the Zohar remains agnostic on this point, the die has been cast and this discussion will take a decidedly anti-Rabbi Yehuda turn in the Lurianic corpus precisely because Luria is unwilling to acknowledge that what is "outside" is not also "inside." As we will presently see, much of this is based on his creative reading of Sifri Devarim's equation of Moses and Balaam. Therefore, before moving to Luria, I will briefly review how the Zohar understand the Sifri Devarim passage to highlight the contrast between it and Luria's counter-rabbinic reading.

There are two passages about Moses and Balaam in the Zohar that are instructive in understanding the Zohar's multivalent reading of this episode and its implications. These passages employ, one explicitly and the other by implication, the rabbinic equation of Moses and Balaam to achieve disparate ends—the first to illustrate the irreconcilable difference between Moses/Israel and Balaam/the nations; the second to suggest that it is Moses and Balaam, and only them, who see how the outsiders (Balaam/the nations) are already included within the insiders (Moses/Israel) and that the future will reveal to all how Israel's exclusivity doctrine must be deconstructed. In fact, it is this very perception that marks the distinctiveness of their prophecies which, in terms of perspective, are antithetical and in terms of substance are identical. I suggest it is the second approach in the Zohar that opens the way for Luria's sympathetic reading of Balaam as the outsider who desires to be included.

The context of the first passage is Moses' vision at the burning bush (Exod. 3:2). In the midst of this discussion, concentrating on the uniqueness of Moses' prophecy, the Zohar cites the well-known Sifri passage about Moses and Balaam:

> Said Rav Dimi, "But it is written, *No other prophet arose in Israel like Moses*" (Deut. 34:10). Says Rabbi Joshua ben Levi "*No other prophet arose in Israel*, but among the nations another rose. And who is this? This is Balaam." He (Rabbi Yohanan) replied, "What you said is very good. Be silent!" When Rabbi Shimon bar Yohai arrived they asked him about this. He opened and said, "Heaven forbid that the dirty tar from the cutting of ʿ*arazim* should be mixed with a ripe persimmon. Rather, this is what it means when it says, 'among the nations another rose. And who is this? This is Balaam.' Moses' actions are rooted above and Balaam's below.

Moses utilizes the holy crown of the supernal king and Balaam utilizes the lower crowns that are not from holiness. On this it is written, The *Israelites put Balaam ben Beor, the auger, to the sword* (Josh. 13:22). And if you think there is more about this, go ask his she-ass." Rabbi Yossi rose and kissed his hand, saying, "the stone that was in my heart just departed." We learn from this that there is above and below, right and left, mercy and severity, Israel and the nations. Israel utilizes the higher holy crowns and the nations the lower crowns that are not holy. These from the right and these from the left. The higher prophets are separated from the lower prophets, the prophets [who draw] from holiness and the prophets who do not draw from holiness.

Said Rabbi Yehuda, "Just as Moses is distinct from all prophets who prophesy from the holy, so Balaam is different from all prophets and sorcerers whose prophecy is not from the holy. In every case, Moses is above and Balaam is below and there are innumerable levels between them."[103]

Based loosely on the Sifri's equation between Moses and Balaam, this passage suggests that the equation is not between Moses and Balaam per se but rather stresses their similarity with respect to other prophets of their genre (Jewish and gentile). Each one has unparalleled access to the roots of their respective prophecies. Employing the rabbinic trope that Moses = Israel and Balaam = the nations, this disparity is extended to both sets of people—the covenanted and the uncovenanted. Each draws sustenance from its prophetic source, one from the right and one from the left. Finally, Rabbi Yehuda, whom we read in the passage above, enters to teach that this distinction is irreconcilable. The levels that separate Moses and Balaam are vast and insurmountable and the nature of their prophecies forever disparate. What we essentially have here is an ontologized version of the rabbis—what is inside (Israel) can never include the outside (the nations) because the very roots of their respective prophecies are incompatible. While both sources may stem ultimately from the one God, there is nothing they have in common. Exclusivity is maintained and hardened with the cement of a seemingly dualistic metaphysic.

If one stopped here, the Zohar would not have contributed much to the discussion about Balaam regarding exclusivity and universalism. But there is another approach in the Zohar that more fully develops what Wolfson argues is the dialectical tenor of zoharic metaphysics more generally. The context of this second passage is the Zohar's suggestion that Pharaoh had three advisers (or wise men): Jethro, Job, and

Balaam. At different times, and for different reasons, Jethro and Job repent, yet Balaam does not:

Balaam did not repent (*lo shav ve lo he-adar*) because the murkiness (*tenufa*) of the *Sitra Ahra* was attached to him. Even so, he was able to gaze [at *kedusha*][104] from afar, that is, from the murky and unclean place of the *Sitra Ahra*. This is because the *Sitra Ahra* has a narrow emanation of light that shines [in/from above it] as it is written, *surrounded by a radiance* (Ezek. 1:4). This small gaze was a gaze from a distance and did not include all things. When he was gazing at this small place from this light it was as if he was behind a wall. He spoke [from/about the gaze] but he did not know about what he spoke. Gazing at this light is done with a closed eye. A man rolls his eyes [back in his head] and sees this concealed emanation (*nehora satima*)—and he does not see. This is hinted at in the words *satum eyin* (Numbers 24:3). It is established that *satum* in the verse means closed (*satum*, םותס spelled with a *samakh* ס and not a *shin* ש).[105] It is all one. There is no *Sitra Ahra* that does not contain a narrow small [emanation] from holiness, as is the case with most dreams—amidst all the straw there is one good seed of wheat beside all these small forms that are all defiled, about which Balaam knew.[106]

The Zohar sets up a situation in which Balaam, here an embodiment of the *Sitra Ahra,* has access to a small dimension of holiness via this narrow emanation of light that penetrates the realm of the demonic. His inability to repent was due to the infusion of the *Sitra Ahra* even as he was cognizant of the dimension of the holy that existed therein. In fact, this narrow emanation informs his prophecy (as Rabbi Yehuda argued above) even though he was not aware of the nature or roots of his prophetic voice. In opposition to the more malicious portrait of Balaam in the Zohar, Balaam appears here as a pathetic figure, cognizant of his sullied state and even somewhat aware of something "behind the wall" but unable to utilize it, react, or understand it.

The second part of this passage explains Moses' relationship to holiness (*kedusha*) in a way that strikingly mirrors Balaam. The juxtaposition is informed by the rabbinic analogy in Sifri Devarim but frames that analogy in a manner that views Moses and Balaam as sharing a similar space of being "outside looking in":

Happy is the portion of Moses who is above all realms of holiness and sees what no other human was able to see. Just as Balaam saw a narrow emanation of light, as behind a wall from the *Sitra*

Ahra, so too Moses, from his lofty place as from behind a wall, saw a narrow dark emanation. And this [disclosure] is not at all times, just as for Balaam it was not at all times.

Happy is the portion of Moses, the faithful prophet, upon whom it is written, *An angel of God appeared to him in a blazing fire out of a bush* (Exod. 3:2). The bush: this is surely because the *kedusha* was attached to him, which means that everything was attached to him, pure and impure. There is no purity except through/by means of (*migo/metokh*) impurity. This is the secret of the verse, *Who can produce a clean thing out of an unclean thing?* (Job 14:4).[107]

While Moses and Balaam stand outside *kedusha,* both were privy to a narrow ray that gave each access to *kedusha.* Balaam saw it as light, Moses saw it as darkness. Both had only intermittent visions of this realm. Both are connected in that, as outsiders (pure and impure) they have limited access to the realm of holiness. The second section draws this out, and puts them in even closer proximity to each other—Moses, as the embodiment of holiness (yet one who was so "holy" he was above holiness) contains Balaam (the impure) within himself. And, offering a reading of a partial verse from Job (excising the crucial climax, *No one!*) the Zohar suggests that Moses (as pure) is also dependent on Balaam ("there is no purity except through impurity").

The contemporary anthology of Zohar commentaries compiled by Abraham ha-Levi Bar Lev, entitled *Yedid Nefesh,* offers an instructive comment on this passage worth reproducing. It is based on Hayyim Vital's reading of this Zohar passage in question.

"This is because the *Sitra Ahra* has a narrow emanation of light that shines [in] from above it . . ." This hints at the great wisdom of Balaam, who was ensconced in the *Sitra Ahra.* Others who act from the *Sitra Ahra* are not able to apprehend anything from the pure realm. The reason is known: the end of the limits of the holy is the place where the impure begins. Balaam's knowledge of the impure was so comprehensive that he reached the highest realm of the impure. At that instant he realized something small from the realm of the pure. We also find this in Zohar 2.269 that the seventh palace of impurity has a small passageway (*petah katan darko*) in which a small element of the light of holiness enters. Balaam had reached a full understanding of impurity and was thus able to gaze from that passageway that opened up to the holy. Others, however, who had not reached that high place (of the *Sitra Ahra*) were not able to apprehend purity at all![108]

The dialectical rendering of pure and impure in this comment deserves a more lengthy analysis than I can offer here. Suffice it to say that Vital, according to Bar Lev, views Balaam as one who is privy to a vision of the pure/holy as a consequence of having absorbed the full extent of the impure realm. It is only the deepest realm of impurity, which is "the seventh palace" or highest realm, where the narrow alley passing to the holy exists. While the Zohar does not describe the contents of the vision of either Moses or Balaam, from Vital's reading we can conjecture that the narrow vision of Moses and Balaam, that which others could not see (because they were either not pure enough or not impure enough) was precisely the understanding that both pure and impure are contained in each other and are mutually dependent. The experience of this realization is the apex of human comprehension (prophecy?) and it is something only Moses and Balaam achieved. Thus the Sifri's equation now means that Moses and Balaam shared something no other human beings shared, a realization, through vision, that purity and impurity were dialectally intertwined and mutually dependent. The comment that Moses' vision of the holy was "dark" and Balaam's was "light" supports this suggestion. For Moses, holiness was dark because he stood above it (in true light), while for Balaam it was light because he stood below it (in darkness). Yet what they saw was identical: they saw how light and dark, the self and other, were included in the opposite.

I suggest that this text's observation about Balaam, one that is uncharacteristic in the body of the Zohar, may serve as the beginning of Luria's analysis (even as he does not cite it). Moses and Balaam are mirror images of each other—they both know what they could not articulate, that to be outside is always also to be inside and only via exclusion can one understand that the self, to be fully itself, must contain that which lies outside it, which, in truth, is always contained within it.

Luria's Balaam and Moses: Separated at Birth?

In the previous sections on rabbinic and zoharic literature I argued that the postbiblical depiction of Balaam is essentially founded on two points. The first point concerns the villainous intentions of Balaam implied in Deuteronomy 23:5–6, *But the Lord your God refused to heed Balaam; instead the Lord your God turned the blessing into a curse for you for the Lord your God loves you.* This is the lens through which Balaam is understood in postbiblical literature. The second point involves the equation in Sifri Devarim of Balaam and Moses as equal in prophecy and stature. The Zohar's reification of these biblical personalities presents us with a number of narratives describing this relationship, both the similarities and differences, between Balaam and Moses, one occupying the realm of the demonic and the other the realm of the sacred. While the Zohar's depiction of the Balaam–Moses equation is largely dualistic, in the last Zohar passages analyzed there is a hint of a more substantive correlation between them.

Lurianic exegesis begins with this basic premise and reframes the Balaam episode within its own specific exegetical scheme. This functions on two levels simultaneously—first on the metaphysical or cosmological plane of *sephirot* and *parzufim* (mostly founded on the sins of Adam and Eve and Cain and Abel); and second on the theory of soul construction and metempsychosis that is used to describe the roots of Balaam and Moses' souls and those who inherit Balaam's soul after his death. I suggest here that delineating the soul construction of Balaam is the Lurianic way of understanding Balaam's ontological similarities to Moses based on Sifri's equation of the two biblical figures. Different from the rabbis or the Zohar, in Lurianic exegesis this relationship is internalized—that is, it is not simply about Balaam as the prophet of the gentiles and Moses as the prophet of the Israelites/Jews (this first appears in rabbinic midrash and is then reiterated in the Zohar). Nor is it simply about the demonic versus the sacred. Rather, what is stressed is the fundamental similarity between Balaam and Moses through an understanding of their cosmological genealogy. The roots of their souls are identical and each one contains a part of the soul of the other in need of reconciliation. In this sense, the Lurianic reading of Balaam corresponds quite closely to what we read earlier regarding Moses and the ʿerev rav (in fact, in Lurianic exegesis, Balaam is considered to be the "Moses" of the ʿerev rav).[109] This theory of *gilgul* is then deployed as the primary tool of exegesis, tracking the postmortem history of Balaam through a variety of biblical and rabbinic figures.

Another distinguishing factor in the Lurianic analysis of Balaam is that it seems to be linked strongly to conversion, an idea that resonates with the converso phenomenon in sixteenth-century Safed. As I discussed in earlier chapters, conversion plays a crucial role in Lurianic Kabbala and may very well have been influenced by conversos returning to Judaism in the mid-sixteenth century.[110] The trope of conversion also plays an important role in the Zohar, but the Lurianic fraternity seems to stress the central role of conversion in the redemptive process, a process that requires the final ingathering of lost sparks embedded in the demonic "other."[111] The Lurianic discussion of conversion is inextricably tied to *gilgul*—in fact, in Lurianic Kabbala, conversion is not a viable category without *gilgul*. Therefore, when speaking about *gilgul*, especially as it crosses boundaries from gentile (Balaam) to Israelite, we are also speaking about a kind of conversion, one that is achieved via separating holy sparks from their demonic context enough to enable those sparks to attach themselves to a holy (Jewish) soul that can then be embedded in a Jewish body. I suggest that this is precisely what happens in the Balaam episode, according to Luria.

Therefore, in Lurianic Kabbala conversion is not only achieved via normal legalistic means. Or perhaps, the impetus to convert and the legal procedure that facilitates conversion are the result of either a Jewish soul occupying a non-Jewish body or a gentile soul already containing dimensions of a Jewish soul. The legalistic framework of conversion is simply the manifestation or completion of a process initiated at birth. The context that makes conversion possible—that is, the existence of a Jewish soul in a gentile body—is achieved in various ways, often tied to soul migration. Death and *gilgul* are two prefatory stages that create the context for eventual conversion.[112] Both are phenomena that purge sin, separating good from evil, enabling a dimension of a soul previously trapped in the demonic to be liberated enough to inspire conversion in a new body. Regarding Balaam and Moses we read, "In this way, when the good of Moses is cleansed from the evil of Balaam, it is inevitable that some good sparks from Moses will remain with Balaam that will require redemption by means of many deaths and *gilgulim*, as it is known. This is true for all souls."[113] The convert is considered one who contains a "Jewish" soul as a result of various factors, in most cases as a result of *gilgul* or ʿ*ibbur*.[114] Luria interprets Balaam's sincere desire to convert in Numbers 23:10: *Who can count the dust of Jacob, Number the dust-cloud of Israel? May I die the death of the upright/righteous, may my fate be like theirs.*[115] These words are viewed as a sign that the pure dimension of his soul has become dominant.

What emerges from this analysis is a theory of otherness that deconstructs the dualism of previous interpretations. Balaam's evil dissipates as a result of his indirect encounter with Israel and, more importantly, Moses. This encounter (unbeknownst to either Israel or Moses) and Balaam's subsequent death (an "upright/righteous death"; Num. 23:10)[116] serves as a *tikkun* allowing him to be reincarnated as an Israelite. The part of his soul that is bound to Moses is severed from its demonic shell and is able to return to its roots in Israel. Thus the demonic (rooted in the divine) has come full circle and through Balaam (perhaps only through Balaam) Moses completes his mission of fixing the blemished remnant of the soul of Abel, a process that began with Moses' birth.

We will begin with a concise description of Balaam and Moses that is also tied to the ʿ*erev rav*, all viewed from the context of the sin of the golden calf:

[To understand] the sin of the golden calf one must know the intentions of the ʿerev rav in this episode. You already know from [our explanation of] the verse *A new king arose in Egypt* (Exod. 1:8)[117] how this implicated Balaam and the ʿerev rav. That is, how they are both from the extraneous matter and poison of Moses, whose soul is rooted in *daʿat* of *zeir anpin* in the realm of *yesod* of *abba*. However, there were still some remnants of holiness [in the souls of the ʿerev rav and Balaam]. Therefore, Moses was diligent and struggled with all his might to bring the ʿerev rav under the canopy of the *shekhina*. This is also why we read regarding Balaam: *No other prophet arose in Israel like Moses* (Deut. 34:10). Says Rabbi Joshua ben Levi, "*No other prophet arose in Israel,* but among the nations another rose. And who is this? This is Balaam." You also know from the verse *And Rachel stole her father's household idols* (Gen. 31:19) that Laban the Aramean was reincarnated in Balaam son of Beor.[118] Beor was the son of Laban and the father of Balaam. That entire family is from one [soul] root, all of whom are extraneous remnants of Moses. . . .[119]

This text schematically draws the genealogy of Laban (both physical and spiritual) through the ʿerev rav and Balaam, all of whom are attached to Moses. It specifically views the progeny of Laban as the perpetrators of the golden calf. This connection is later made more explicit, in the following short excerpt: "Balaam was the evil side of Moses. . . . Moses is from the higher *daʿat* (*daʿat elyon*) of *zeir anpin* from the *yesod* of *abba*. Therefore it [i.e., Moses' *daʿat*] is called *elyon*. This is connected to what we already said that Balaam is from the *kelipah* opposite this very *daʿat*. Hence the verse, *And he [Balaam] knew this higher knowledge (daʿat elyon)* (Num. 24:16).[120] The sons of Balaam, Yonus and Yombaros, are also from *daʿat* and they were the evil instigators of the ʿerev rav. Hence the ʿerev rav are also from *daʿat*."[121]

The interconnectedness of Balaam and Moses is made more explicit further in this same homily:

It is known that Balaam is the evil side of Abel and Moses is the good side of Abel. It is known that when silver is cleansed with dirt the dirt is put to the fire [after the cleansing process] in order to remove the remaining elements of silver. This is the way [it was with Moses and Balaam]. When the good of Moses is cleansed from the evil of Balaam it is inevitable that some good sparks from Moses will remain with Balaam. These sparks needed to be redeemed by means of many deaths and reincarnations, as is known. . . .[122]

In *Likkutei Torah* (88a) there is an addition to this statement that says "and this is the reason that Balaam was able to perceive what he perceived [that is, he was able to achieve true prophecy]" referring to Sifri Devarim's affirmation of Balaam's prophecy. That is, Balaam's prophecy is rooted in the remnants of Moses' soul embedded in Balaam's soul. This is developed a bit further at the beginning of the discussion on Balaam in *Likkutei Torah:*

> The secret of Balak is that he is from the soul of Cain because he is a descendant of Jethro. The secret of Balaam is that he is from Abel as it states, *And another prophet did not rise like Moses.* . . . Balaam is the evil side of Abel. On this is written, *And they saw him [Moses], and he was good (tov)* (Ex. 2:2).[123] This means that with his birth Moses fixed [the blemish in] Abel and the goodness of Abel (*tov*) was thus embodied in Moses and the evil in Balaam. This is why they both have equal standing, this one for Israel and this one for the nations. This is hinted in the verse, *Some time later, Abraham was told, "Milcah has borne children to your brother Nahor"* (Gen. 22:20). The acronym of *he banim le-Nahor* (the children of Nahor) is HeVeL (Abel). The evil side of Abel is reincarnated in Laban son of Nahor. It is already known that Balaam is a reincarnation of Laban (that is, the evil side of Abel that Laban inherits from Nahor).[124]

The underlying assumption here is that good and evil were intermingled in all of creation due to the sins of Adam and Eve and Cain and Abel until the birth of Moses. In Lurianic Kabbala, the consequence of all sin is the admixture of good and evil. *Tikkun* is always that which separates good from evil, although in a preredemptive world separation often results in remnants of the good trapped in the (separated) evil, thus requiring more draconian measures to facilitate the final separation. In fact, this was the purpose (and need) of Jacob and his sons' descent into Egypt.[125] Moses' birth ("it was good"—*ki tov*) began the rectification of Abel by separating the good from the evil, beginning the final rectification of the sin. This rectification of Abel was further developed in Moses' encounter with the burning bush.[126] However, even when the separation was complete (as it was at the burning bush), the good did not achieve full disclosure until the remnants of the good embedded in the evil were finally redeemed. The separation (*tikkun*) invariably left the evil side of Abel homeless, severed from its good roots (yet also containing remnants of the good). Balaam became the new home for this yet unredeemed dimension of Abel. Thus Balaam (as embodying the evil side of Abel without the good) was, in a sense, created by Moses through his birth and encounter with the burning bush. Balaam also contains remnants of the good of Abel that Moses has yet to redeem. Hence, Moses (via Israel) must redeem those sparks in order to complete the redemptive process. The sign of this redemption is apparent when Balaam is able to reenter Israel, as he does in the Lurianic schema through *gilgul.*

On this reading, Balaam's encounter with Israel in Numbers provides the necessary context for the final rectification of Balaam (and thus Israel) completed through his reentry into Israel. It is likely that this is Luria's implicit answer to the talmudic question as to why the Balaam episode is in the Torah. The episode allows for the holy sparks embedded in Balaam (sharing the soul of Abel with Moses) to be redeemed before Israel enters Erez Israel. This story also harkens back to Luria's interpretation of Moses killing the Egyptian taskmaster (Exod. 2:11–13).

In the following text from *Sha'ar ha-Gilgulim,* we are introduced to the same basic position from a slightly different angle, here focusing more specifically on transmigration as the link connecting Balaam and Moses:

We already explained that the *ruah* [of any soul] does not transmigrate (*mitgalgel*) until the *nefesh* transmigrates first and is rectified (*ve-tushlam le-hitaken*). After that the *ruah* can transmigrate and become rectified and afterward the *neshama.* Behold [as a result of the sin of Cain and Abel], Abel's *nefesh* and *ruah* were blemished (*mekulkalim*) [meaning that] good and evil were intermingled in them. But his *neshama* was completely good. This is the process of the transmigration of his soul. First his *nefesh* transmigrated in the following manner and was given to Seth the son of Adam.[127] At that point the evil [in Abel's *nefesh*] departed and was given to Balaam, the evil one. The admixture of good and evil in the *nefesh* of Abel is hinted at in the letters of his name. The good is hinted at in the letter ה of הבל. This was given to Seth. This is the secret of the verse *laying the world at his feet* תחת רגליו שתה (Psalms 8:7). שתה is ה "שת. And we already know that this psalm is about Moses, as it says, *That you have made him little less than divine* (Psalm 8:6). The evil in the soul of Abel is hinted at in the letters בל. This is the secret of the verse, *He did not do so for any other nation; of such rules they know nothing* משפטים בל ידעום

(Psalms 147:20). These two letters (בל) refer to the *kelipot,* as it is written, *Bel (בל) is bowed* (Isaiah 46:1).[128] These two letters were given to Balaam, the evil one, בל of בלעם. You already know that when evil is purged from good some sparks of holiness will inevitably remain embedded in the evil. This is the meaning of the rabbinic dictum that Balaam was equated with Moses. That is, they both come from one realm. Moses was also from Seth (from the good within him), as we explained. Hence, the small amount of good in Balaam was given to Nabal the Carmelite[129] where it began to be rectified.[130]

This small amount of goodness constitutes a very small dimension of Abel's soul, as it is only treating the *nefesh* or lowest level of the five-part soul. However, it nicely ties Moses to Balaam, through Abel and Seth using, among other things, the tradition that Psalm 8 is dedicated to Moses. The relevant point here is that even though Balaam inherits the evil of Abel, part of the good of Abel is also given to Balaam and needs to be redeemed in order for the *nefesh* of Abel to complete its *tikkun*. Moses inherits the soul of Seth, Abel, and a new soul that has not yet come into this world. Part of Abel's good soul goes to Seth (Adam and Eve's son born outside the Garden of Eden who is considered unblemished by Adam's sin or by the sins of Cain and Abel). Moses also acquires the remaining good from Abel that was not given to Seth. Once the good is separated from the evil, the evil is free to transmigrate alone and, in this case, ends up as Balaam. While one would think from this text that Balaam's evil is not directly connected to Moses but rather to the birth of Seth, Luria (or Vital) bases this whole case on Psalm 8, which he argues is all about Moses. If we return to the verse in Psalm 8 that serves as the foundation of this short text, we see that *laying the world at his feet,* the linguistic basis for Seth's acquisition of the good of Abel, is really about Moses. Moses is the complete manifestation of Seth as "wholly good" and thus it is only with or through Moses that Balaam's soul is constituted. That is, the evil part of Abel could not act independently until the good was separated from it through Moses. Moses' *tikkun* created the evil nature of Balaam. And, more importantly, the evil soul of Balaam (the remaining parts of Abel's yet unredeemed soul) cannot be rectified as long as it remains disconnected from its source (now found in Moses). This entire trajectory has no sound foundation in the Bible. Rather, it is based on the implied intention of Balaam in Deuteronomy, on *Sifri*'s reading of Balaam and Moses, and on the Zohar's subsequent ontological demonization of Balaam. But what results is not a call to eradicate Balaam but to foster another separation, this time between the demonic nature of Balaam's soul and the remnants of holiness that lie within it. The final moment of that *tikkun*, facilitated though Balaam's death, is also his conversion.

The Metaphysical Nature of Balaam's Soul
and Its Transmigration History

In the previous section we viewed Luria's rendition of the midrashic correlation between Balaam and Moses, a correlation that underlies almost all classical readings of Baalam. In order to better understand Luria's particular rendering of the Balaam narrative we need to clarify two additional points: first, the metaphysical roots of Balaam's soul—that is, its origins in the cosmological map of Lurianic *parzufim;* second, the trajectory of the transmigration of Balaam's soul, where it came from before its instantiation in Balaam and where it went after Balaam's death. After that we can better understand Luria's reading of Numbers 23:10 as an act of redemptive conversion.

By way of introduction, I will briefly review the basic contours of the Lurianic myth of *parzufim* before moving to an analysis of the relevant texts at hand. Lurianic cosmology is largely a reification of the Genesis narrative focusing on Adam and Eve and the triune relationship between Jacob, Leah, and Rachel. For our limited purposes, the map of Lurianic cosmology includes Jacob/Israel (as *zeir anpin*) and Rachel and Leah and his female consorts. *Zeir Anpin* is the male body and his two wives, Rachel (the beloved wife, Gen. 30:18) and Leah (the subsidiary wife, Gen. 30:30) constitute the primary female potencies. Both female potencies are in a competitive role in that only one can couple (*meyahed*) with *zeir anpin* at a time. While Rachel is the preferred partner, she is also the one who is often exiled from her proximate relationship to Jacob in order to make way for the more frequent *yihud* between Jacob and Leah to take place.[131]

The physical proximity of Leah and Rachel to *zeir anpin* and to each other is paramount. Both are attached to the back of *zeir anpin,* Leah from the base of the brain of *zeir anpin* (the place of the *sephirah daʿat*) to mid-torso, and Rachel from the mid-torso (or lower chest cavity) of *zeir anpin* (the place of the bottom third of the *sephirah tiferet*) to the bottom of *zeir.* They are only "face-to-face" with Jacob/*zeir anpin* when they are in a state of union that occurs during the daily times of prayer (including the midnight vigil of *tikkun hazot*), Shabbat, and festivals while Leah occupies the top half and Rachel the bottom half of *zeir anpin.* There is some overlap between them. It is in this overlap that Luria locates the origin of Balaam's soul. When *zeir anpin* and *nukva* are not in a state of face-to-face union, the heels of Leah are embedded in the head (*keter*) of Rachel. And, the lights of the top half of *zeir anpin* emanate to Leah first and are then only transferred to Rachel through her (this overlap becomes crucial in locating the origin of Balaam's soul). However, Rachel receives the emanation of the bottom half of *zeir* without any intermediary and Leah does not receive any of that light. Moreover, as we will see, the light Rachel receives from *zeir anpin* is more direct because it does not have to pass through any intermediary shells inside the body of *zeir anpin*. Rachel thus has the distinct advantage of a more gentle light emanating from the lower body of *zeir anpin* and the disadvantage of only receiving the light from the upper body of *zeir anpin* through the heels of her sister and co-wife.

The place of the higher *parzufim abba* and *ima* are also important here. *Abba* and *ima* (whose roots are above *zeir anpin*) both descend into the body of *zeir anpin* and occupy different places in his cosmic body. Generally, the female potency (*yesod*) of *ima* reaches to the chest cavity inside *zeir anpin*. The male potency of *abba* (which is embedded inside *yesod* of *ima*) extends further to the very male potency (*yesod*) of *zeir anpin*. However, because *abba* and *ima* are in a state of perpetual union, the *yesod* of *abba* is enveloped inside *yesod* of *ima* inside the male body of *zeir anpin*. The male potency is thus diminished in the upper half of the body of *zeir anpin* since it is surrounded by its own vessel and the light and vessel of *yesod* of *ima*. However even as the *yesod* of *abba* begins where *ima*'s ends (*tiferet* or midtorso of *zeir anpin*), it extends in a revealed state (that is, no longer enveloped inside *ima*) until *yesod* of *zeir anpin*. Hence the light of *abba* in the lower half of *zeir* is much stronger and more potent. Even though *yesod* of *ima* ends in *tiferet* of *zeir,* there are remnants of lights of her *yesod* (in a much diminished state) that extend to his lower body. However, those lights are in a vulnerable state because they are no longer protected by the vessel of her *yesod* and therefore are easily accessible to the demonic forces that are perpetually waiting to suckle from any unprotected light. This will all become relevant in the texts we will now examine.

One last introductory remark. In the Lurianic system, Rachel and Leah are "created," or at least empowered, by the effluence of *zeir anpin* that flows into their cosmic bodies. This is Luria's rendition of Genesis 2:21–23. The lights of *zeir anpin* that construct Rachel and Leah are largely composed of the lights of *abba* and *ima* that emanate out of *zeir anpin* to their female progeny. The constitution of both Rachel and Leah are thus determined by the substance and directness of that light as it emanates out of *zeir anpin* into their respective bodies. The danger is as follows: if emanated light does not find a vessel to contain it (the vessel being a dimension of the cosmic bodies of Rachel or Leah), it will become vulnerable to the demonic realm (*hizonim* or *kelipot*). In such a case, divine light is used as fuel to empower evil that traps it until the light is redeemed in some manner.[132] As I mentioned in the first chapter, it is the admixture of good and evil that is consequent of original sin. When the demonic is fueled by the good, it produces evil in the world. If the demonic is in a state of potential redemption (*kelipot nogah*), the good can become dominant and can transform the demonic to holiness. This is part of Luria's general understanding of conversion. If the demonic is unredeemable, it must be eradicated in order to rescue the good that lies within.

With this brief introduction to one small dimension of the Lurianic myth, we can now move to one of the most comprehensive texts delineating Balaam's metaphysical origins. The underlying assumption of this section of a much longer homily is that Balaam is a reincarnation of Laban, the father of Rachel. Hence the starting point of this exercise begins with an elaborate interpretation of the verse, *Meanwhile Jacob had gone to shear sheep and Rachel stole her father's household idols (terapim)* (Gen. 31:19). This verse is used to explore the status of Rachel, both in relationship to Leah and to Jacob.[133] More specifically, it speaks about idolatrous (demonic) dimensions of (cosmic) Rachel's constitution. We will begin in the middle of this homily from *Sha'ar ha-Pesukim*. While relevant, the detailed interpretation of the word *terapim* (household idols) that underlies this reading to describe Rachel is not essential.[134]

> It is important to know what Balak and Balaam share. We already explained *and Rachel stole her father's household idols (terapim)* (Gen. 31:19). The middle third of *tiferet* of *zeir* is where the lights of *yesod* of *ima* are in a revealed state from the back of *zeir*. This is the place where *keter* of Rachel begins, engulfed within her [*keter*] the two heels of Leah. These heels are *the household idols (terapim;* Gen. 31:19). . . . Leah is [or becomes] the *malkhut* of *ima* that is within *zeir*. As a result Leah contains lights from both *abba* and *ima*. The head of Leah is situated opposite the back of *da'at* of *zeir* [the base of his skull] that contains *yesod* of *abba* . . . the *yesod* of *abba* is enveloped in the *yesod* of *ima*. The *yesod* of *ima* is embedded in the empty middle space of the skull of *zeir* that is called *da'at*. Hence, when the lights of *yesod* of *ima* are emanated to [the head] of Leah they have to pass through two barriers; the vessel of *yesod* of *ima* and the head of *zeir* after which they can enter the head of Leah and permeate her entire body until her heels, which are enveloped in *keter* of Rachel.[135]

Here we are introduced to the emanation process whereby Leah is constructed out of the lights of *yesod* of *ima*, albeit with a diminished dimension of that light because it is weakened each time it passes through a barrier. The fact that the light of *yesod* of *ima* is enclosed in the vessel of *ima* has a positive and a negative consequence. Positively, it is protected from any demonic forces. Negatively, when it emanates out of the body of *zeir anpin* it is weakened as a result of having to have passed through various barriers. This results in the vulnerable and weakened constitution of Leah, who bears many children but is unloved by her spouse (*God saw that Leah was unloved and opened her womb;* Gen. 30:31). The other salient point here is that Rachel receives some of this diminished light mediated through the "heels" of Leah (also representing the *household idols* she stole from Laban). That is, she "steals" or borrows that which belongs to Leah (the *terapim* are the heels of Leah) but are also embedded in her body.[136] Thus the demonic is part of Rachel, albeit in a temporary and liminal way. This is will become relevant later on. The homily continues:

This is what we mean by the *terapim*. The place of the heels of Leah constitute radical severity (*din gamur*) since they are composed of only small amounts of diminished lights (*'orot muatim*) emanated from a place of concealed light [light enveloped inside the vessel of *yesod* of *ima* and inside the shell of *zeir*]. . . . This is particularly the case since these diminished lights are located in the heels [of Leah] that house the most sever dimension of *din*. In such a case (and place) the *kelipot* attach themselves to [this light]. These lights of *ima* that descend to the heels of Leah rupture and desolate (*bol-kim*)[137] *keter* of Rachel. Entering into her body in that way sends out a remnant of light that is taken by the demonic (*hizonim*). . . . These remnants of light are represented in Balak for two reasons. First, linguistically the lights that enter Rachel by means of *balika* (BLKa) and rupture are hinted at in the letters of the name BaLaK.[138]

Balak is constituted of light that is (1) diminished in stature; and (2) enters into Rachel in a violent and destructive manner. The light that he receives is already the property of the demonic realm, originating in *ima* yet stripped of her nurturing inclination. As we will presently see with Balaam, his origins are similar but somewhat less destructive and less demonic, and hold more potential for redemption:

Regarding Balaam, he is constituted mostly from the lights of *da'at* [should be *yesod*] of *abba*. The lights of *abba* that emanate to Leah must pass through three barriers; *yesod* of *abba, yesod* of *ima*, and the head of *zeir*. Only then are the revealed and able to enter the head of Leah. These lights also permeate Leah until her heels. These lights also break through [the heels of Leah] and are given to *keter* of Rachel. *Keter* of Rachel is known as a permeable place because it envelops the two hells of Leah and absorbs them.

We must note that Rachel is composed of revealed light because of her place in the lower half of *zeir anpin*. Therefore she embodies more mercy (*rahamim*) than Leah. However, in this place [that is, *keter* of Rachel that intersects with the heels of Leah] her light [*rahamim*] is darkened because it has to traverse so many vessels. Take, for example, the light that emanates from *yesod* of *ima* that ends in the chest cavity of *zeir anpin* and breaks through the vessel of the back of *tiferet* [of *zeir anpin*] exiting [*zeir anpin*] and entering Rachel. This light must first break through the vessel of the back of the head of Rachel that is connected to the body of *zeir anpin*, after which it must break though two more barriers, the two heels of Leah [in the head of Rachel], each of which has two barriers, front and back. Afterward it must break through the front side of the head of Rachel and only then can it become absorbed in her *keter* (which is on her front side). Invariably, this light is weakened and diminished and is thus susceptible to the demonic. . . . Therefore, the light that reaches *keter* of Rachel (which has absorbed the heels of Leah) has already been infected with the demonic. This is the place of Balaam. That is, Balaam originates in *keter* of Rachel that has absorbed the heels of Leah. Balaam is constituted by the lights of [*yesod*] of *abba* that entered Leah and descended through her to *keter* of Rachel. Balak is from the light of *ima* in the heels of Leah and Balaam is from the light of *abba* that travels through the heels of Leah and becomes embedded in *keter* of Rachel.[139]

Here the essential difference between Balak and Balaam is that Balak is located *in* the heels of Leah, the place of the demonic, while Balaam, also being infected with this demonic dimension, is actually from *keter* of Rachel. One consequence is that Rachel's body exhibits a stronger dimension of mercy and potential. Regarding Azzah and Azael (two angelic figures originating in midrash whom we will discuss below), we read in *Sha'ar ha-Pesukim* that "the place of Balak is the very roots of *din* (*takhlit hadinim*). The light that emanates out and Azzah is formed from the right heel and Azael from the left heel. Balaam is not from the emanation of the light of the heels themselves but from the emanation of *keter* of Rachel that absorbs the emanation of the two heels [of Leah]. Therefore, he also learned all his wisdom from Azzah and Azael, absorbed from them through *keter* of Rachel."[140] While both figures (Balak and Balaam) are deemed evil and enemies of Israel, in the Lurianic imagination Balak appears unredeemable whereas Balaam, rooted in *keter* of Rachel, has more potential to be become "upright" (Num. 23:10) or at least part of the Israelite nation.

Azzah and Azael: The Two Angelic Teachers of Balaam

One of the more enigmatic episodes in Genesis is the short description of the Nephilim in Genesis 6:1–4. In verse 4 we read, *It was then, and later too, that the Nephilim appeared on earth—when the divine beings cohabited with the daughters of men, who bore them offspring. They were the heroes of old, the men of renown.* Much has been written about the Nephilim ("fallen angels") and the role these verses play in the Primeval Cycle of Genesis. Our limited interest will focus on the reception of these verses in classical Israelite and Jewish religion as a motif that points to the emergence of evil, in particular the evil of idolatry and magic as it relates to Balaam. There are numerous intertestamental traditions that identify these Nephilim as angelic figures who play a role in the (mis)education of humanity. In the Zohar and later in Luria, these angelic figures (two of whom are Azzah and Azael) are connected to Balaam. In one textual strain in the Zohar they are depicted as the heavenly teachers of Balaam who instruct him in sorcery; in another strain (in Lurianic teaching) they are viewed as sharing the same demonic soul-root with Balaam in the heels of the cosmic Leah. I have not located any overt connection between Azzah and Azael (or the Nephilim) and Balaam in any Jewish literature before the Zohar, even though this connection is not far-fetched. Until such pre-zoharic text is found, we can assume that this connection is the product of the Zohar's creative interpretive impulse. As is often the case, Luria integrates the Zohar into his metaphysical worldview by situating Azzah and Azael in a particularly vulnerable part of the cosmos. Unlike the main thrust of the Zohar, Luria departs from the more unequivocal demonic depiction of Balaam as an unredeemable sorcerer and enemy of Israel.[141]

The origin of the Nephilim/Azaah, Azael connection is the pseudopigraphic text 3 Enoch, chapter 5.[142] This text is likely influenced by earlier stories of the angels and Nephilim in 1 Enoch and Jubilees (second century BCE), where these Nephilim (or their descendants the "giants" or "watchers") were the source of the constructive knowledge of working with metals and other materials (this is the angel Asael in 1 Enoch 8:1) and the destructive knowledge of nature manipulation, magic, and sorcery.[143] In line with the verse in Genesis, these Nephilim are not unequivocally evil. However, as Annette Yoshiko Reed writes, "In contrast [to 1 Enoch], 3 Enoch 5 (7–8) describes the angels Uzzah, Azzah and Azael in a wholly negative manner, by associating them with the idolatry of the Generation of Enosh (5:9)."[144] This seems to refer to the reception of these angels in rabbinic and post-rabbinic Judaism, although one cannot be certain that these later texts draw directly from 3 Enoch 5.

Many Bible scholars assume that these Nephilim are destroyed in the flood and thus only play a role in predeluvian human civilization.[145] However, the survival of these angels (or the Nephilim of Genesis 6:1–4) is a matter of dispute. There is mention of Nephilim in Numbers 13:33 (as the giants who lived in Canaan) and perhaps Ezekiel 32:27, which may suggest that these Nephilim or their offspring actually survived the flood.[146] Another possibility, one more in concert with the kabbalistic traditions of the Zohar and Luria, is that these Nephilim survive as angelic spirits and continue to influence human society by directing certain individuals toward evil behavior, particularly through the use of sorcery.[147] The Zohar uses a late midrashic tradition where Azzah and Azael are depicted as angels who argue with God about creating Adam, claiming that they could also succeed if given a chance on earth. God then sends them to earth as a test and they immediately succumb to their evil inclinations and cohabit with earthly women.[148] Thus they become the perennial enemies of humanity in the heavens and the teachers of those who seek to destroy Israel.

The likely sources of Azzah and Azael in post-rabbinic literature are the few places where they surface in rabbinic literature.[149] The original text in 3 Enoch 5 and its precursors in 1 Enoch and Jubilees are not likely the places where the Zohar and Luria become aware of these destructive angels. In its discussion of the creation of Adam, the Zohar adopts the rabbinic position that these angels argued with God against creating Adam and were sent to earth to test their resolve (Gen. 6:1–4).[150] The more creative adaptation in the Zohar comes in its narrative of Balaam. In at least two texts, the Zohar tries to determine the origin of Balaam's "super wisdom" (דעת עליון Num. 24:16) and what the Torah means when it says *And beholds the visions from the Almighty* (Num. 24:5 and 16).[151] These words occur as Balaam begins his prophecy about Israel; for the Zohar, they represent the source of that prophecy (which the Zohar views mostly as sorcery). The Zohar renders Numbers 24:16 as Balaam's acknowledgment of the source of his wisdom. That is, *he obtains knowledge from the Most High [from those who] behold visions from the Almighty, Prostrate but with eyes unveiled.* The Zohar suggests the figures are Azaah and Azael, presumably the angelic Nephilim (the Zohar never employs the term Nephilim in this context) who "fall [to earth] but with their eyes open." As we will see, this enables Luria to extend this idea to write,

As we discussed in the homily of Balak and Balaam and Azzah and Azael, their roots are the four lights from the heels of Leah that is where the demonic receives its sustenance. Therefore Balaam went *from the hills of the east* (Num. 23:7). That is, he went

to Azzah and Azael, as the Zohar writes.[152] Before Balaam went
to Balak he closed himself off in these mountains with Azza and
Azael, as it is written, *From Aram has Balak brought me, Moab's king
from the hills of the east* (Num. 23:7).[153]

The continuation of this homily will become relevant later on. For
now, it exhibits the way in which Luria absorbs the Zohar's correlation of
Azzah and Azael, the Nephilim who remain proactive spirits, and frames
Balaam's knowledge and power as rooted in these anti-Adamic angels
who taught humanity the art of sorcery. The portrayal of the Nephilim in
earlier Jewish texts such as Jubilees and 1 Enoch that focus on the sexual
perversity of the divine–human erotic encounter has been transformed
in midrashic and post-rabbinic literature to spirits that continue to teach
the ways of sorcery in order to prove humanity's unworthiness of the covenant. The Zohar connects these spirits to Balaam thereby making the
Balaam episode a replay of the midrashic rendering of Genesis 6:1–4 in
which the angels attempt to convince God not to create (or later, to destroy) Adam. In "the book of Balaam" Balaam plays the role of the
Nephilim (the disciples of Azzah and Azael) and Moses the new Adam.
This dramatic replay is made more explicit in the context of an internal
battle over Abel's soul in *Sefer ha-Likutim:*

> You already know that Moses and Abel are from the same root.
> From this you can understand why Moses wrote "his book, the
> book of Job, and the book of Balaam." You can also understand
> the rabbinic dictum (Midrash Deuteronomy Raba 1:4) that the
> blessings Balaam offered to Israel should have been recited by
> Moses. They were recited by Balaam so that the evil angel would
> answer "amen." You will also understand the rabbinic dictum on
> "another prophet will not rise in Israel like Moses. Not in Israel
> but among the nations one will rise. Who is this? This is Balaam."
> The meaning of all this is that both [Moses and Balaam] were
> from the same root, the root of Abel, Moses from the good and
> Balaam from the evil. This is how Moses [could have] written the
> book of Balaam. This was in order to subjugate the evil inclination
> of Balaam. . . . He thus says *[I] gaze upon Shadai* (Num. 24:16). This
> means he understood *Shadai* through a veil (*masakh*) and did have
> a direct vision of *Shadai*. Further, when Balaam says, *My message
> was to bless* לקחתי ברך הנה (Num. 23:20), the first letter of each word
> constitutes HeVeL (Abel). Balaam's intention was to take the ה
> from HeVel (the good of Abel) and subjugate it to the evil side of
> Abel in order to facilitate the domination of good over evil.[154]

Here Balaam's encounter with Israel was intended to undermine Israel's viability as a covenantal partner with God. Inside this mythic depiction, Balaam intends to usurp the good side of Abel (Moses) that empowers this divine–human relationship. Moses could have easily written this "book" because, sharing a soul-root with Balaam, he could have predicted this was coming. In fact, according to this he likely knew this confrontation was inevitable and, perhaps, anticipated its arrival as it presented the possibility for Moses to complete the *tikkun* of his own soul. Whatever the intentions of Balaam (spelled out only in Deuteronomy), they backfired. Instead of cursing Israel, he blessed them and, in doing so, subjugated his own evil to the remnants of the good within him. It appears the battle between Adam and Azzah and Azael (mentioned explicitly later on in this short homily) returns in the Balaam story. However, in the case of Genesis, Azzah and Azael fail in their goal to undermine Adam. As a result, they become disembodied spirits that continue their struggle, now focusing on what the kabbalistic worldview holds are the true inheritors of Adam: Israel. In Numbers, Moses successfully completed the task in order to finalize this particular struggle, redeeming his lost sparks embedded in Balaam and bringing them back to Israel.

I will move now more directly into the Lurianic rendering of the myth of Azzah and Azael and Balaam in order to illustrate Luria's subtle equivocation regarding how Balaam's evil nature distinguishes him from the more demonic character of Balak. Unlike the Zohar, the Lurianic use of Azzah and Azael takes place almost exclusively in the context of Balaam. The discussion occurs in three places, in two texts from *Sha'ar ha-Pesukim* and *Likkutei Torah* and in a few short references in *'Etz Hayyim:*

We must now explain what the Midrash[155] and Zohar (3.208b) teach regarding the verse *He who obtains knowledge from the Most High, And beholds visions from Shadai, They descend*[156] *but with eyes unveiled* (Num. 23:16). This refers to Azzah and Azael. Know that Azzah and Azael are the two angels that are rooted and created from the two lights that emanate from the two heels of Leah that are embedded in *keter* of Rachel. From there they are attached to Balak as we already explained. They are the very telos of *dinim* (severity) and extensions of their light (*ha'aratam*) emanate outward. . . . Balaam does not originate from the extension of these heels themselves but from the extension of *keter* of Rachel where these lights are embedded. Therefore, he studied with Azzah and Azael and learned their wisdom and was also nurtured by them by means of *keter* of Rachel. . . . Since Azzah and

Azael are revealed in this place [the two heels of Leah] they are called "beholders of the vision of *Shadai.*"

From this you will understand what the rabbis and the Zohar (1.35a) mean when they say that Azzah and Azael protested the creation of Adam. God brought them down from their lofty place (*me-makom kedushatam*), upon which it is written *the Nephilim were in the land* (Gen. 6:4). They did not protest more than other angels for no reason. The reason [behind their protest of creating Adam] was that in the beginning [before Adam was created] *zeir anpin* and *nukva* were "back to back," at which time Leah and Rachel were one above the other, as we explained. The two heels of Leah were hidden inside *keter* of Rachel, at which time Azzah and Azael were able to sustain themselves from that place [the nexus of Leah and Rachel]. God's will to create Adam and Eve was that through their actions, *nukva* would be fixed enough to sustain a "face-to-face" union [with *zeir anpin*]. This is the secret of the verse *And there was no man to till the soil* (Gen. 2:5). If *zeir anpin* and *nukva* united "face to face" [requiring the turn of Rachel to the front of *zeir anpin*] the heels of Leah would no longer be embedded in *keter* of Rachel. Therefore, all the light that emanated from the heels of Leah to *keter* of Rachel, the place where Azzah and Azael dwelled, would now be nullified. Those lights would now emanate from the front of [the head of] Rachel and there is no place for the demonic in the front, as is known. The only place of the demonic is from the back. Hence, Azzah and Azael would disintegrate with the creation [and success] of Adam. They protested the creation of Adam because of the damage it would cause to them.[157]

For our limited purposes, this text reiterates a crucial distinction between Balak and Balaam.[158] The root of Balak's soul is in the heels of Leah, the very source of diminished light (descending through the body of Leah) and thus the source of the demonic. On the other hand, Balaam is rooted in *keter* of Rachel, the place where the demonic Azzah and Azael thrive, though it is not essentially demonic. Rather, it houses the demonic as long as *zeir anpin* and *nukva* are "back to back." The evil dimension of Balaam's place is not the heels of Leah but rather *keter* of Rachel. On this reading he draws power from Azzah and Azael only as long as *zeir anpin* and *nukva* are "back to back." When Rachel turns, however, Balaam remains in *keter* of Rachel while Balak remains in the heels of Leah; Azzah and Azael (and their sorcery) evaporate.

If I am correct that the Balaam narrative featuring Azzah and Azael in the Zohar and Luria replays the Genesis narrative of Adam and Azzah and Azael (Balaam playing Azzah and Azael, Moses playing Adam) we can see how Balaam is redeemed from his encounter with Moses/Israel. That is, through mitzvot Moses and Israel create the context for the "face-to-face" unity of *zeir anpin* and *nukva*, albeit temporarily. Balaam witnesses this as he gazes at Israel (Num. 23:9–10, and 24:5–6) and understands that the "face-to-face" union of *zeir anpin* and Rachel liberates him from the demonic forces from which he originates (*keter* of Rachel). His "intended" curse (if we read this all through Deut. 23:6) thus becomes a blessing and he continues to curse the evil nations (Num. 23:20–23). Even if we accept Deuteronomy 23:6 as the appropriate lens, from Luria's reading one could posit that Balaam's "intention" to curse was *before* he encountered the beauty of Israel, here understood as the potential for a "face-to-face" union of *zeir anpin* and Rachel. His realization from that encounter turned his curse into a blessing. Separated from the place of the demonic through the turning of Rachel (or at least its potential via mitzvot), Balaam not only blesses Israel but also desires to become one with her: *May I die a death of the upright / May my fate be like theirs!* (*yesharim/yeshurun* or Israel; Deut. 32:15; Num. 23:10). What remains in Balaam are the sparks of holiness that are the severed part of Moses' soul (the soul of Abel) that were enveloped in the demonic power fed to Balaam through the heels of Leah embedded in *keter* of Rachel. Moses cannot redeem these souls, as he never meets Balaam. However, through Balaam's death and reincarnation, conversion takes place, thereby bringing these sparks back into the Israelite community where they can function in a constructive way.

From Laban to Nabal the Carmelite and Dying an "Upright Death": From Gentile Prophet to Repentant Israelite

Lurianic Kabbala is primarily interested in the soul history of Balaam as a way of understanding his place in the biblical narrative and the mythic–cosmic history of Israel. Lurianic exegetical texts frequently use the hermeneutical method of dramatic replay as a way of presenting a seamless historical and cosmological narrative. For Luria, the historical and the cosmological are, if not identical, then inextricable.

By dramatic replay, I mean that biblical episodes are almost always read through the lens of earlier episodes.[159] Luria's notion of this is founded on the principle of metempsychosis—later biblical and rabbinic figures are reincarnations of earlier figures returning to complete something that remained incomplete in the original narrative. In Lurianic teaching, the esoteric understanding of the Bible requires one to know the soul construction of each character in order to understand their previous incarnations.

Balaam presents us with a particularly interesting example. While he is presented in post-biblical Judaism as an archenemy of Israel, Numbers is far more ambiguous about his intentions (as opposed to Amalek or even Balak). Lurianic Kabbala takes this ambiguity as license to proffer a Balaam who, in the end, not only desires to become an Israelite/Jew but succeeds in doing so. Moreover, it is precisely this transference/conversion (from gentile prophet to Israelite) that completes Moses' mission. I thus propose that conversion lies at the center of the Balaam narrative in the Lurianic imagination.[160]

As discussed earlier, the focus on conversion in sixteenth-century Safed is not without a historical anchor. The influx of conversos to Ottoman Palestine in those decades (and after) was significant; a number of important Lurianic kabbalists were either conversos themselves or came from converso lineage. Thus, while we have no direct evidence that the interpretations of the ʿerev rav or Balaam (intertwined in Lurianic exegesis) are a conscious response to the historical challenges of sixteenth- and seventeenth-century Ottoman Palestine, this study uses these exegetical instances to argue that history and myth are indeed categories that inform and, more importantly, construct each other.

Balaam is actually situated in the middle of a particular soul trajectory that extends from Nahor, to Laban, and finally to Nabal the Carmelite (the husband of Abigail, wife of King David; I Sam. 25). This soul trajectory contains remnants of Moses' soul that are only recovered when Balaam dies and, via *gilgul*, is "converted to an Israelite (Nabal)." Before moving to Nabal it is worth citing a startling text regarding the transformation and conversion of Balaam.

This secret is explained at length regarding the *gilgul* of Balaam son of Beor.[161] The first *gilgul* was from Laban the Aramean.[162] Balaam was partially rectified (*nitkan*) by means of his being killed [by Pinhas]. From that point onward [his soul] became part of the holy (*kedusha*). First, it was reincarnated in Nabal (NBL) the Carmelite, who shares the letters of [the name] Laban (LBN). From this point [the soul] continued on a path of *tikkun*. One should not be surprised at this after knowing the rabbinic dictum that Balaam was a prophet of the gentiles and merited *ruah ha-kodesh*. It states in Midrash Tanhuma,[163] *"From Aram (ARM) has Balak brought me* (Num. 23:6); that is, I come from the lofty ones (HRM"M) from the place where the Patriarchs are distinguished." And the sages say . . . "but from the gentiles a prophet did arise like Moses. He was Balaam." You also know that from the time of Israel's exodus from Egypt all their souls were mixed with good and evil. From this point, they began to be clarified. This trajectory will continue until the coming of the messiah. I have said enough! What is meant by "from here onward"[164] is that after Balaam was killed he received some dimension of atonement. God did what He did in entering him into the realm of the holy.[165]

This text is essentially a spin on a passage from the Zohar (3.194a) where R. Shimon warns his son Eliezer of the strange and concealed ways of God. Luria uses his reading of Balaam as one example of this phenomenon. One would think that the verse, *the name of the wicked will rot* (Prov. 10:7) could easily refer to the eradication of evil. In fact, Luria suggests that this is not at all the case. Evil (here Balaam) not only is *not* destroyed, but in this case is transformed (converted?) into Israel undergoing a progressive series of rectifications (*tikkunim*) that continue until the time of the messiah. We read further on in *Sha'ar Mamrei Rashbi* that

> With evil ones, [*gilgul*] works the opposite [to that of righteous ones]. Every *gilgul* lessens the evil and thus equalizes the holy sparks that are initially in the minority. Hence an evil person must die many times and his body must rot many times. By means of this process his soul is diminished and the evil "rust" that is attached to [the holy sparks] separate from the evil. By this means the soul is purified until which time only the good remains. This is the secret of the verse *the name of the evil will rot* (Prov. 10:7).[166]

Luria then directs the reader to a series of rabbinic passages that allude to this trajectory, demonstration that Balaam's soul originated in Laban and ended up in Nabal the Carmelite. Luria claims that Balaam merits authentic *ruah ha-kodesh* and thus his claim (according to Midrash Tanhuma) that he comes from the place of the Patriarchs (AR"M [Aram] = HRM"M [the lofty ones]) is true! Finally, R. Shimon's statement to Eliezer in the Zohar "from here on . . ." referring to God's strange ways, Luria reads as a sign of Balaam's atonement, entrance into Israel, and subsequent *tikkun*.

Luria situates Balaam between Laban and Nabal the Carmelite. Laban lives before Israel and Israel emerges partially through him (as the father of Rachel and Leah). Nabal the Carmelite is an Israelite, albeit an unsavory one, and his death results in King David's marriage to

Abigail. In this next text Luria traces the lineage from Laban to Nabal as a trajectory of *tikkun*. While Balaam is not mentioned (he is surely conspicuous in his absence), it is Balaam's encounter with Israel that creates the context for Laban's entrance into the Israelite people.

Laban (LBN—לבן) is a hint to wisdom (*hokhma*) that is called LeVaNon לבנן (white). Jacob is *zeir anpin* and Rachel is *nukva*. Therefore Laban is the father-in-law of Jacob.[167] It is known that gold is more valuable than silver,[168] and therefore *gevurot* are more valuable than *hasadim*, as the sages say, "The righteous sit with crowns on their heads."[169] These crowns are the female (*nukva*) *gevurot*, who sit on the crown of her spouse, who is *hesed*. This is at the time when the *gevurot* have been sweetened. However, before that time, surely *hasadim* are more valuable than *gevurot*. Hence, before Laban is rectified he is called *hokhma*, which is hinted at in the L'B (ל"ב) of Laban representing the "32 (לב) paths of wisdom" only after which you have the נ of Laban representing the 50 (נ) gates of understanding (*bina*) which is feminine. However, after the *tikkun* is proffered through Nabal the Carmelite the feminine (crown) of her spouse, which is *bina*, returns to its original place is the word Nabal (נבל). *Hokhma*, which constitutes the (לב) paths of wisdom, is also fixed. That is, now the נ comes before the ל as it does in the aleph-bet. After Laban is fixed through Nabal the Carmelite, who is *bina*, this is called "the world to come." Therefore, he (Laban and Nabal) has a portion in the world to come.[170]

Through a wordplay of the names Laban (לבן) and Nabal (נבל), Luria illustrates the extent to which Laban's pre-*tikkun* status is exhibited in the ordering of the letters of his name. That is, he contains all the right components but they are not in the proper order. Nabal represents the onset of the state of *tikkun* where the letters representing wisdom and understand (*hokhma* and *bina*) are situated so that *bina* sits atop *hokhma* (לב), as is the case in the redemptive image of the righteous sitting with their crowns (spouses) on their heads. What this text does not tell us is that this whole process moving from pre-*tikkun* to *tikkun*, is facilitated by Balaam who is the *gilgul* of Laban and is reincarnated in Nabal, entering Israel by means of his encounter with Israel and his *(upright) death*. It is likely that the reordering of letters here (a common sign of *tikkun* in Lurianic teaching) is one that can only occur when the soul in question becomes part of the Israelite people—that is, when the soul undergoes conversion. Balaam is the vehicle for this conversion.

Balaam's part as the facilitator of this *tikkun* (Laban-Nabal) is developed in *Sha'ar ha-Gilgulim*. In this next text, Laban is only mentioned parenthetically, the text focusing on the movement from Balaam to Nabal:

Laban was reincarnated in Balaam and afterward in Nabal the Carmelite. Balaam the evil one was involved in sorcery but his only real power was in orality, that is, in his ability to curse [through speech]. When he is killed, Balaam is reincarnated as a stone, that is, inorganic matter [lit., silent matter] in order to atone for the sins he committed with his mouth.[171] When he is later reincarnated as Nabal the Carmelite he comes back into this world in order to actively fix [his sin of speech]. Then he disrespects David by saying, *Who is David, who is the son of Jesse* (I Sam. 25:10)? David wanted to kill him (I Sam. 25:13) because Nabal came to fix the sin of the evil speech of Balaam and only continued the same sin by cursing David, the King of Israel. [When Nabal hears of this] he remembers that he was first reincarnated as a stone to fix the evil speech of Balaam and now he cursed [David] and revisited that sin. Therefore, [we read] *his wife told him everything that happened [regarding David]; and his courage died within him, and he was a stone* (I Sam. 25:37).[172] That is, he remembered that he was first reincarnated as a stone [to fix a sin that he again committed]. Therefore, it is not written "he became a stone" but "he was a stone" והוא היה לאבן. Behold Nabal was a great man. We should not be surprised that he knew this. It is also possible a prophet or sage told him this. It is also possible he saw this in the stars.[173]

It appears that the history of this soul lineage, a lineage tied to Moses, is one of fixing speech. Laban is the one who has *terapim*, sometimes interpreted as "speaking idols." Rachel steals them and they occupy the space of the demonic Azzah and Azael, who argue with God against creating Adam and also teach humanity sorcery and magic. This is the place of Balaam, who comes with the power of speech. He ostensibly intends to curse Israel but blesses Israel instead. His blessing begins the transformation of speech but he is still outside Israel and thus his soul cannot be fully rectified. This final soul rectification occurs through conversion via *gilgul* into Nabal. Nabal is also tested and fails. Like Balaam, once he fails he realizes his mistake and, traumatized, dies (I Sam. 25:38). His death appears to be the beginning of the *tikkun* of his soul, including the souls of Balaam and Laban. Although to my knowledge Luria does not make this connection, this plays well into the fact that Moses' deficiency was one of speech (Exod. 6:13 and 30). That is, these individuals who inherit a part of Moses' soul have the power of speech that Moses lacks. However, it is used by them for evil purposes and thus must be rectified before they can be reunited with Moses. Balaam begins this process and Nabal completes it with David. In both cases (Balaam and Nabal) it is ultimately death that finalizes the *tikkun*.

At the outset of this section I mentioned the method of dramatic replay as a tool of Lurianic exegesis. This method comes into play in the Lurianic reading of Nabal by tying the narrative first back to Moses and then back to Adam. It is Adam, after all, who is first confronted by the demonic forces of Azzah and Azael that need to be nullified in order to complete the *tikkun*. As is often the case in Lurianic exegesis, all roads lead back to Genesis 2–4 and the Adam narrative. Uncharacteristic of post-rabbinic Jewish exegesis (but quite common in Christianity), it is this biblical episode (often refracted through the lens of the Jacob story) that holds the entire history of biblical religion:

It is written in the Zohar that every male places one dimension of his *ruah* in his wife during their first intercourse when she is made a vessel [for him].[174] This *ruah* is a spark of his soul. Jacob placed one *ruah* in Rachel and one in Leah. The *ruah* he placed in Rachel became Benjamin. . . . The *ruah* that he gave to Leah was reincarnated in Abigail the prophetess, the wife of Nabal the Carmelite. This (seminal drop) should have yielded a male but it was given to a female because of Laban's sin of forcing Jacob to work [seven more years] for his [preferred] wife [Rachel]. Therefore, the *ruah* that was given to Leah that was from Jacob [during their first intercourse] was implanted in a woman, who was Abigail. That is why it is written *Here is the present which your maidservant has brought to my lord* (I Sam. 25:27) using the masculine form of the verb "to bring." This is a hint that her root is masculine and not feminine. . . . All this means the following: Laban was reincarnated in Nabal the Carmelite. Since Jacob worked for Laban he gave a part of his *ruah* to Abigail [through Leah] who married Nabal to work for him as a wife works for her husband. The secret reason why all these *gilgulim* were necessary is as follows: The face of Jacob was like the face of Adam.[175] Adam brought forth two seminal drops of holiness in his encounter with the serpent. Hence he [Jacob] had to work all those years guarding the flock of Laban the Aramean, who is from the serpent, until he was able to gather those two drops who became Rachel and Leah, as we read in Zohar. Afterward, when Laban was reincarnated in Nabal the power of the serpent still existed.

Hence he [David] had to work more years guarding the flock of Nabal until he was able to get the other drop of Leah, who is Abigail, who eventually becomes his wife. David was a *gilgul* of Adam. Therefore he had to extract from Nabal the other drop that was still in the possession of the serpent. Hence David had to do what Jacob did with Laban, that is, he had to guard the flocks of Nabal.[176]

Here Nabal plays the role of Laban and David plays Jacob. It seems that the narrative is replayed because the first instance did not yield the desired results. This may mean that Laban's soul could not be fully rectified because he remained outside Israel and was thus reincarnated in Balaam as a path back inside. Nabal then becomes the "Jewish" Laban through the death/repentance of Balaam. Once Laban's tarnished soul is integrated into Israel, the Jacob/Laban narrative has to be replayed in order for the *tikkun* of Laban's soul (the evil of Abel that was later separated from the good in Abel's soul through Moses). This projects itself back to Adam ("David is the *gilgul* of Adam"). Abigail becomes the child from the yet unredeemed seminal drop of Adam that Jacob tried but failed to retrieve through Leah. The reason for Jacob's failure is not clear from this text.[177] Perhaps it is because Jacob did not love Leah and thus he could not facilitate this *tikkun,* whereas he could do so with his beloved Rachel. If this is correct, then David and Abigail replay the relationship of Jacob and Leah without the distraction of Rachel. On this reading, it is Balaam who makes all this possible. As we read above, Balaam separates from the demonic (the heels of Leah) when he witnesses Israel who, through the mitzvot, produce the face-to-face union of Rachel and Jacob, liberating *keter* of Rachel (Balaam) from the heels of Leah (Balak and Azzah and Azael).

The final example of this trajectory exhibits a messianic tenor not overt in the other texts we have seen. Here Luria speaks specifically about the role of *gilgul* in the messianic drama. Given the connection made in numerous places between *gilgul* and conversion, is it plausible to assume that *gilgul* may be, in fact, a veiled term for conversion or at least a possible method of conversion?

Raise your eyes and look about [they are all gathered and come to you] (Isa. 60:4).[178] Behold the acronym of נקבצו באו לך (*they are all gathered and come to you*) is Nabal (נבל). This, as we explained, in *Sha'ar ha-Gilgulim.* All the souls in a body must be rectified before redemption. No holy spark, however small, will be abandoned. Even Balaam, who had some holy sparks, was reincarnated in Nabal the Carmelite. This is the beginning of his rectification in the realm of holiness (*kedusha*). From there, all the [holy] sparks that were within him were rectified. In this way, the roots of all souls will be rectified before redemption, after which we will be redeemed. Therefore it is written, *Raise your eyes and look about [they are all gathered and come to you].* That is, the [lost] sparks of all the souls of your children that were scattered about in the realm of the demonic will be *gathered and come to you* and be rectified in holiness. Even the [holy] sparks of Balaam that were reincarnated in Nabal, "those despised mortal men," (Isa. 33:7) *will come to you.*[179]

The basic premise of gathering the sparks is a common theme in the Lurianic vision of redemption. In this sense this text is not noteworthy. However, the fact that Luria chooses to interpret Isaiah's redemptive vision of the gathering of God's children using Balaam and Nabal as the primary example seems original. Perhaps the notion of scattered sparks in Lurianic Kabbala does not apply only, or even predominantly, to those Jews who have abandoned religious practice (this is the more contemporary reading). It more likely applies to those Jews/conversos who became New Christians and who were now making their way back to their ancestral religion, or to those gentiles who were converting to Judaism for a variety of other reasons. The final phase of redemption is thus not only maximizing Jewish observance among Jews but the conversion of ex-Jews or non-Jews (back) into the fold. Hence, the example used here is Balaam, the gentile prophet who becomes an Israelite (through death and *gilgul*) as a result of his witnessing the glory of Israel in the desert. The subtle insertion of Isaiah 33:7 at the end of this passage is instructive. It may be that those who are deemed "despised moral men" may hold the key to Israel's redemption. The converso phenomenon occupying so much attention among Jewish jurists and the general population seems to loom here just below the surface. The outsider, who is also the alienated insider, may be the focus of Luria's exegetical agenda in his reading of the "Book of Balaam."

The final piece to this exegetical puzzle is how Luria interprets the verse constituting the end of Balaam's prophecy, *May my soul* (נפשי) *die the death of the upright, may my fate be like theirs* (Numbers 23:10).[180] The rabbinic tradition understands this verse as Balaam's desire for final acceptance or simply the recognition of the greatness of Israel.[181] Others, such as Nahmanides and those that follow him suggest that Balaam desired that his death and fate be likened to the covenantal fate of Israel and not "be among those in Gehenna who are destroyed."[182] In any case, almost all readers of this verse view it as Balaam's desire to share

the special relationship that Israel has with God. None (to my knowledge) read it as Balaam's desire to convert and no one reads it as a prophetic proclamation about conversion that comes true! Yet this is precisely how the Lurianic tradition understands this verse and, in my
view, the entire Balaam narrative.

> Balaam prophesied about himself and said *may my fate be like theirs.*
> If this was false prophecy it would not have been included in the
> Torah, God forbid. Because it is true we must understand his
> words. He could have said "May I die an upright death, may my fate
> be like theirs." However, this is a hint that he knew that he would
> not die an upright bodily death but rather the death of evildoers,
> killed by the sword. But he also knew that his soul alone would be
> reincarnated in Nabal the Carmelite who was an Israelite. Hence
> "I will die an upright death." The letters of upright (ישרים) are also
> the letter of straight/righteous (יושר). *My fate [will] be like theirs,* this
> means that I [Balaam] will become an Israelite. Just like they are
> Israelites in body and soul, I too will be like them in body and soul
> since I will be reincarnated as Nabal the Carmelite.[183]

As we discussed above, Nabal was hardly a righteous figure but he was an
Israelite. This seems to be the main point. Thus our text continues: "It
was not possible to fully rectify Nabal himself without many *gilgulim* as is
hinted at in the verse, *the name of the wicked will rot*" (Prov. 10:7). This text,
and the others that will follow, offer a strong reading of how *gilgul* can
function as a tool of conversion. Conversion does not complete the *tikkun*
of a soul but enables it to enter into Israel and thus continue the trajectory of rectification through subsequent incarnations. The very possibility of the rectification of these sparks is dependent on Balaam's desire to
become an Israelite. Conversion through *gilgul,* even when it requires
death (as it usually does), becomes a central tenet in redemption.

The next example uses a similar motif but ties the Balaam death/
conversion back to Cain killing Abel and Moses killing the Egyptian
taskmaster. It thus views the Balaam–Nabal trajectory as part of a larger
phenomenon:

> *If Cain is avenged sevenfold then Lemeh seventy-sevenfold* (Gen. 4:24).
> Moses had seven names and killed the Egyptian taskmaster who
> was a *gilgul* of Cain. Jethro also had seven names. When [Moses]
> killed the Egyptian he killed him with the divine name [the forty-
> two letter name of God] in order to elevate the Egyptian's soul
> which then attached itself to Jethro. [The soul] then converted

and was atoned for the sin of idolatry. But there was no desire to
kill Balaam the evil one with the name of God but only with a defiled sword. Hence regarding Balaam it does not say "May I die an
upright death" but, *May my soul die an upright death.* His soul died
an upright death in being reincarnated in Nabal the Carmelite
but his body died a defiled death [of the sword].[184]

Here our episode is juxtaposed to the story of Moses and the Egyptian
taskmaster. For our limited purposes the difference between Moses'
killing the Egyptian (Ex. 2:12) and Pinhas's killing of Balaam (Num.
31:8) is that the latter understood that the dimension of Balaam that
was defiled must be totally destroyed; that is, there could be no bodily
redemption for Balaam. The Egyptian is reincarnated as a righteous
gentile (Jethro) who then "converts" while Balaam is reincarnated as an
Israelite. The latter loses all biological connections to his previous life
(he is converted through *gilgul*) while the former retains his biological
status as a gentile while inheriting a soul that is now prepared for conversion. In a sense, this juxtaposition only highlights this innovative
reading of Balaam and Nabal. "Death by the defiled sword" liberates
the holiness within Balaam, severing all connections to his body and
thus enabling the sparks to traverse the biological and, in Luria's imagination, ontological barrier separating the Jew from gentile.[185] Apparently, Balaam's bodily evil was such that a more spiritual death (by
means of the divine name) would have sufficiently separated the body
from the soul enough to accomplish the necessary task of liberating the
holy sparks trapped in his *kelipah.*

This final excerpt ties together themes introduced in the previous
two texts. This time, however, it uses the Zohar's understanding of the
death of Balaam as a foundation for its interpretation. This presents
new challenges as the Zohar adopts the standard translation of *nafshi* in
Numbers 23:10 as an idiomatic expression for Balaam more generally.
This undermines Luria's distinction between body and soul illustrated
earlier. In what follows, Luria takes the verse in a slightly different direction, asking whether this "prophecy" (dying an upright death) is
true or not. Underlying this is the assumption mentioned above that
Balaam's prophecy is true and that this proclamation must also be fulfilled. Yet the Talmud teaches that Balaam did not, in fact, die a righteous death but the defiled "death of the sword" at the hands of Pinhas.
Hence, for Luria the fulfillment of Balaam's words (referring only to
himself) does not occur through the death of Balaam proper but only
in Balaam after he becomes an Israelite, arguably identifying Balaam
even more strongly with future Israelite characters:

May my soul die the death of the upright, may my fate be like theirs (Num. 23:10). This is difficult after we see that this was not achieved with Balaam. That is, he did not *die an upright death*. The Zohar states that Pinhas did not want to kill him with the divine name but only with a defiled sword that had the figure of the serpent [referring to the serpent in the Garden of Eden] engraved on it.[186] This was precisely in order that he should *not die an upright death*. If so, why does the Torah contain superfluous things (*devarim betalim*) God forbid? One must know the secret of the matter. Balaam was reincarnated as Nabal נבל which is hinted at in the acronym **N**abal, **B**alaam, **L**aban (NBL). When David wanted Nabal to give him [from his shearing] Nabal refused (I Sam. 24:5–11). Afterward, *the Lord struck Nabal and he died* (I Sam. 25:38). He died on his bed, an upright death.[187] This is how the rabbis read the verse, *Those murderous and treacherous men, they shall not live out half their days* (Ps. 56:24). That is, they will only live 33 לג years.[188] This is the secret of [the verse] *[This mound shall be witness and this pillar shall be witness] that I am not to cross to you past this mound* לגה *...* (Gen. 31:52). Laban says this [to Jacob] and Laban is Nabal.[189] This is the secret of, *Like a partridge* (דג) *hatching what she did not lay. So is one who amasses wealth by unjust means. In the middle of his life it will leave him and in the end he will be proved a fool* (באחריתו יהיה נבל) (Jer. 17:11).[190] Afterward Nabal was reincarnated in Barzalai the Giladi (this must be through *ʿibbur*—soul impregnation—because Barzalai was very old in the days of David).[191] How could he be a *gilgul* of Nabal who lived in the days of David? Perhaps you will say old age unnaturally came upon him. If I err may God forgive me. Therefore Barzalai gave David and his men bread to eat in order to atone for what he did not give in his first *gilgul* [that is, in Nabal] (II Sam. 19:34). Barzalai also died "on his bed" and this is *an upright death* (II Sam. 19:40). Hence there were two upright deaths, one with Nabal and one with Barzalai. However, the completion of the *gilgul* [of Balaam] was only with Chimham (כמהם) son of Barzalai (II Samuel 19:39). This is the meaning of, *may my fate be like theirs* אחריתי כמהו [literally, may my fate be like Chimham].[192]

In one sense this text exhibits that even if one were to accept the standard idiomatic translation of *nafshi* in Numbers 23:10 one would need to show how Balaam's prophecy of dying an upright death (referring to conversion) could be fulfilled. Balaam enters Israel through *gilgul* and begins a process of *tikkun* that moves from the more nefarious Nabal to the righteous Barzalai who cannot join David (perhaps symbolic of not being able to fully integrate in to the messianic trajectory) because of his age. His son Chimham, also carrying the soul rooted in Balaam, finally unites with the Davidic army: *The king passed on to Gilgal, with Chimham accompanying him; and all the Judite soldiers and part of the Israelite army escorted him across* (II Sam. 19:41).[193] In Chimham, Balaam becomes a fully participating member of the Israelite people and Balaam's prophecy in Numbers 23:10 is fulfilled.

This entire trajectory stresses the notion that being "outside" is also already being "inside." The process of *gilgul* is in this regard not only a path toward *tikkun* but also a method of conversion or reentry into Israel. The extent to which this relates to, responds to, or is influenced by the existence of an attentive converso audience remains unknown. However, one can see how these teachings can be words of solace for returning Jews and perhaps more importantly as consolation for their relatives who died as New Christians or chose to remain "outside" the theater of Judaism. The trajectory of Balaam's soul from the evil side of Cain under the demonic influence of Azzah and Azael to the fully integrated Chimham points to a notion of exclusion that is also inclusion. Moreover, linking this to David in II Samuel suggests that conversion as reentry is not only desirable but an essential, perhaps the central, motif of Lurianic messianism.

5

DEUTERONOMY

The Human and/as God:
Divine Incarnation and the "Image of God"

Deuteronomy is Israel's book of *Imitatio Dei*
—Solomon Schechter

Man is an end to himself only by virtue of the divine in him
—G. W. F. Hegel, *Reason in History*

Anyone who repudiates idolatry is called a Jew
—b.T. Megillah 13a

Deuteronomy and the Deuteronomic circle constitute perhaps the most influential component of the Hebrew Bible. Deuteronomy is a book scholars have determined represents a reformist trend in Ancient Israel taking shape roughly around the reigns of Hezekiah and Josiah (640–609 BCE) (2 Kings 18:1–8; 23:4–25), revising earlier biblical traditions.[1] There are parts of Deuteronomic literature that are likely of much later origin, perhaps the product of the postexilic period. Framed ostensibly as a repetition of the previous four books of the Pentateuch, Deuteronomic innovations altered the structure and form of earlier biblical traditions and were a fairly systematic revision the Covenant Code (Exod. 20:23–23:19). There are numerous themes that Deuteronomy introduces to the biblical corpus. The four most well known are (1) the centralization of ritual worship around the Tent of Meeting/Temple in Jerusalem (Deut. 12:10–16), revising earlier traditions that apparently allowed worship at other venues (Exod. 20:19–23); (2) the humanistic turn of the statutory law of the Covenant Code; (3) the replacement of the anthropomorphic notion of God with the more abstract concept of the divine name who has no form (Deut. 4:12; 12:5; 26:2); and (4) the emergence of a written text, composed by Moses, that replaces Moses and becomes the central witness of the covenant (Deut. 31:9, 26).[2] In Deuteronomy, God does not dwell in the tabernacle as other priestly strata suggest (Exod.25:8; 29:45; and Num. 16:3).[3] Rather, it is the *name* of God, His name serving as a represented manifestation on earth that dwells in the tabernacle and later the Temple.[4] Moses, as prophet, is replaced by the "text" (Moses as author of the text, or Moses as the text?) creating a suggestive correlation between the body and the word. This last "innovation"—moving from divine body to divine name—will inform my use of Deuteronomy as a frame for the Lurianic discussion of *theosis* and incarnation.[5]

Structurally, Deuteronomy is the last will and testament of Moses. From beginning to end it is a Mosaic rendition of the Torah that Jewish tradition termed *mishneh torah* (a repetition of the law).[6] We know, however, that Deuteronomy is far from a repetition. Bernard Levinson puts it succinctly: "[T]heir [the Deuteronomic] concern was to implement their own agenda; to effect a major transformation of all spheres of Judean life—culturally, politically, theologically, judicially, ethically and economically. . . . The authors of Deuteronomy sought to implement a comprehensive program of religious, social, and political transformation that left no area of life untouched."[7] The revolutionary nature of Deuteronomy may be the first in a long list of revolutionary trends in Judaism that have become canonical, including the work of Yohanan ben Zakkai and Yavneh resulting in the Mishna and subsequently the talmudic tradition,[8] Moses Maimonides and the medieval rationalist tradition, and the Zohar and the subsequent canonical tradition of medieval and modern Kabbala. All these trends act under the guise of "tradition" but each has its own reformist agenda. And each renewal claims its own particular authoritative anchor. In the case of the Lurianic tradition, this revision (founded on the basic principles of the zoharic corpus) revolutionized the metaphysical, ritual, and liturgical structure of early modern Judaism in most of Europe, the Levant, Maghreb, and Yemen.

Moving back to Deuteronomy, we find another implied dimension of this reformist tradition that will be the focus of this chapter. Deuteronomy offers its reader a complex and often confusing rendition of the erasure of the person, Moses, who is replaced by the book, or law (Deut. 31:1–5). Even though Moses appoints Joshua as a successor (Deut. 3:28; 31:7–8, repeating and perhaps revising Num. 27:19), it is clear that Joshua does not replace Moses. Moses' replacement, if there is one, is the "book of the law" (Deut. 31:9).[9] More than the other books of the Pentateuch, Deuteronomy has the semblance of a book, a coherent formation of Israel's rights and responsibilities that some call a covenantal constitution. Moses is the main speaker in Deuteronomy and arguably its only significant character. The point of the book is to prepare for Moses' death and the survival of the book without him.[10] While Deuteronomy concludes with his death (Deut. 34), the entire book anticipates this event. At various places in Deuteronomy, Moses situates the book as his replacement, trying to convince Israel that they should now turn their attention to the book and away from him (Deut. 31:13, 26).[11] Jean-Pierre Sonnet expresses this succinctly: "Now that Moses' mediating mission has come to an end, the elders are reunited with God's word, receiving it 'in proper hands'—'and he gave it to them.' The lethal encounter face to face, oral communication, gives way, thanks to the written medium, to a life-giving transmission and repetition."[12] That is, the book now becomes an embodiment of the theophany at Sinai from which the people can read and understand God's covenantal requirements. Moses as teacher replaces Moses as prophet. The law, in time, will even replace Moses as teacher (Deut. 30:11–14).

In Deuteronomy, especially in its retelling of the Sinai theophany, the voice of Moses (as prophecy) is always viewed as mediating between God and the people (Deut. 5:23–24). After Sinai, the book of the law emerges and it is also mediated through Moses as teacher.[13] There was an unspoken mutuality between Moses and the law as he slowly revealed it, through teaching, to Israel (Deut. 4:5; 5:31; 6:1). The basis of his authority is that he possessed the law; therefore, the law was only accessible to Israel through him. Yet in Deuteronomy Moses slowly yet consistently extricates himself from the book, first by telling his audience (most of whom did not witness Sinai) that, in fact, revelation is in their possession in the form of the law and since they now have it, they no longer need him. One of his last acts as leader is to forcefully inaugurate his replacement as the Torah itself.[14]

This move from person to text, from human being to language, dominates Deuteronomy. But the transition is not clean and becomes a topic for further reflection in the history of Judaism in general and Kabbala in particular.[15] In Deuteronomy it is almost impossible to differentiate between the mediator (Moses) and the mediated (Torah). In fact, it is arguably the case that one of Moses' primary goals is precisely to introduce that distinction, as he knows that is the only way the covenant will survive.[16] Israel makes it quite clear that they have no access to the word of God except through Moses; that is, no access to divine language is available except through (a quasi-divine) person.[17] They are thus fully justified in fearing his absence (Exod. 32; Deut. 5:5, 25–28). Moses knows this and responds by suggesting that the words of God can be "taken to heart" and through recitation can guide them in the right path (Deut. 6:7–9; 30:11–14). A hyperliteral rendering of internalizing Torah ("taken to heart"), making it a part of each Israelite as a replacement for Moses, is quite suggestive and may inform our kabbalists in their understanding of how *zelem elohim* (the image of God)—as the letters of Torah—is, in a sense, the internalized Torah, the divine name that constitutes the Jewish body.[18] And, through devotion and meditation those letters can rise and become the fully realized (divine) human.

The person is thus not completely effaced in light of the law, but the law is internalized in the person (Deut. 30:14). The transition from person to text initiated by the Deuteronomists was never fully implemented in the kabbalistic tradition. In rabbinic Judaism—arguably the place where this transition finally matures—the person took the role of interpreter of the law and thus fulfilled another kind of mediation that is central to the covenant. In the Zohar, Shimon bar Yohai moves back toward a role that may be more reminiscent of pre-rabbinic Israelite religion. His messianic status in the Zohar portrays him as a holder of secrets. He is not simply an interpreter of the law in the rabbinic mode, but one who reveals that which has never been disclosed.[19] The portrait of Shimon bar Yohai in the Zohar is a link in the chain of kabbalistic and prekabbalistic Jewish literature that portrays the mystic as more than an interpreter of the text but one who, in some sense, *is* the text. That is, his very person, or body, embodies the divine message. This elevated status of the person as divine text spills over into Lurianic teaching. In the hagiographical literature that describes his life, Luria more closely resembles a prophetic or even Mosaic figure than a rabbinic sage. Yet as rabbinic Jews (loosely defined), kabbalists view the text as the template for inspiration and even for experience. Nevertheless, the inspired reader—for example, the mystic—may be more than an "interpreter" in the rabbinic sense. Some kabbalists also extend the deconstructed text (the Torah as divine letters) beyond the words on the page to the fabric of the human body, in particular to the body of the mystic. The reader who reads Torah is made up of the same stuff of the text he or she is reading. For many kabbalists, inspired mediation through interpretation required the inner resources of the divine nature of the human, the letters of Torah internalized.

The rabbinics scholar and theologian Solomon Schechter called Deuteronomy "Israel's book of *Imitatio Dei*." The reason behind this assertion is not clear, although one could surmise he may have been pointing to Deuteronomy's humanistic turn away from the earlier Covenant Code.[20]

But even if this is not the case, Schechter's observation may be true in another sense. In Kabbala, beginning perhaps with *Sefer Yezeriah* 4:4 and continuing with Abraham Abulafia and the Zohar, the transition from person to text is also interpreted to mean the internalization of text in the person.[21] The oblique biblical image of God (*zelem elohim*), referring to the human, is taken in Kabbala to mean that the human is composed of the letters of the Torah—the human, as image of God, is comprised of the same matter as the text of God.[22] The zoharic identity of God, Torah, and Israel is mediated through the letters of Torah. Thus the human is divine and the divine, human, creating an ostensible symmetry that makes incarnation at the very least reasonable, perhaps even inevitable.[23] The actualization of those letters in the human both fixes and externalizes the image of God as *zelem elohim*, an image many kabbalists, along with Paul, Augustine and other Christians, deem broken—or at least compromised—through the sin of Adam and Eve.[24] For these kabbalists, the text does not replace the person but defines him. The occasion for this actualization is mediated in the form of the Hebrew letters, through the recitation of liturgy or study.[25] It is the human engagement with the text in some form that enables the devotee to actualize his own *zelem*, or perhaps more accurately, to reconstruct his fractured *zelem*.

My exploration of the theme of *zelem elohim* in Lurianic Kabbala through a Deuteronomic lens is thus predicated on Schechter's comment, albeit understood quite differently than he might have intended.[26] This exercise is, in a very real sense, a return to the beginning of this book, back to Genesis 1:26 and the construction of the human through the notion of original sin. If the sin damaged the status of *zelem elohim* and if that act prevents the final unfolding of the covenant (i.e., redemption), one needs to inquire as to the rectification of *zelem elohim* (or *tikkun ha-zelem*). In one sense, the notion of *tikkun ha-zelem* can function as a response to Paul's notion that original sin can never be rectified without the appearance of one whose *zelem* was never broken—Jesus as the product of virgin birth.[27] An answer to the question regarding *tikkun ha-zelem* requires an understanding of the nature, or metaphysics, of the term *zelem elohim;* that is, in what ways is the human the image of the divine?[28] As mentioned earlier, the kabbalists are far too hyper-literal and visually oriented to accept any metaphorical rendering of *zelem elohim* common among medieval rationalist interpreters.[29] The term *zelem elohim*, of course, does not appear in the book of Deuteronomy, nor is it a part of larger Deuteronomic nomenclature. However, Deuteronomy does develop the transition from person to text (initiated earlier) that is quite suggestive in this regard. The verse, *the thing is very close to you*, in your mouth and in your heart, *to observe it* (Deut. 30:14) speaks directly to the issue of an internalized Torah. This trajectory becomes even more pronounced in Jeremiah's prophecy of redemption. *See, a time is coming—declared the Lord—when I will make a new covenant with the House of Israel and the House of Judah. It will not be like the covenant I made with their fathers. . . . But such a covenant I will put My teaching into their innermost being and inscribe it upon their hearts. . . . No longer will they need to teach one another and say to one another "Heed the Lord": for all of them, from the least to the greatest, shall heed me—declares the Lord* (Jer. 31:31–34). Moreover, diminishing the emphasis of the divine form in favor of the divine voice and divine name (Deut. 4:12; 12:5; and 26:2) lends itself to an internalized vision of God, one that dwells in the deep recesses of the human being. The kabbalistic notion of the letters of the sacred text as constitutive of the human and the fact that classical Kabbala entertains or, at least, seems compelled by, an incarnationalist theology (that is, the mystic as having access to divine power by embodying the letters of Torah via contemplation) will serve as an entry point of my analysis.[30] Given the Deuteronomic interplay between human and text, I will use Deuteronomy as a frame for the Lurianic notion of the human–divine encounter *in* the human as an understanding of *zelem elohim*.[31]

Is Judaism Incarnational?

It is conventional wisdom among students of Judaism that incarnation is exclusively a Christian concept—that is, it is "un-Jewish." While it became an anchor of Christianity, incarnation's roots lie deep inside the latter phases of late antique (proto) Judaism and find expression in various apocryphal and pseudepigraphic texts, many of which where written by Israelites/Jews in the pre-Christian era.[32] The nexus between the human and the divine was vexing for a burgeoning Israelite monotheism founded on a scripture that presented God anthropomorphically and described the human as created "in the image of God" (Genesis 1:26).[33] Mystics were even more apt to complicate any claim of opacity between the human and the divine in their quest for an intimate experience of the supernal realm. Hence, the wider definition of incarnation as the indwelling of the divine in the human—of the divine having a body—of the human being transformed into a divine being—is not as foreign to biblical Israel or pre-rabbinic "Judaism" and even rabbinic tradition, as we might think.[34] Once Judaism is confronted with a more doctrinally cohesive Christianity in the Middle Ages, most semblances of incarnation in Judaism are diffused, concealed, or reinterpreted.[35]

In medieval Kabbala, incarnation was not erased but reframed. Elliot Wolfson observes this when he writes:

Pitched in the heartland of Christian faith, one encounters the logocentric belief in the incarnation of the word in the flesh of the person Jesus, whereas in the textual panorama of medieval kabbalah, the site of the incarnational insight in the ortho-graphic inscription of flesh into word and the consequent con-version of the carnal body into the ethereal, luminous body, fi-nally transposed into the literal body, the body that is the letter, hyperliterally, the name that is the Torah. . . . For Christians, the literal body is embodied in the book of the body; for Jews, the literal body is embodied in the body of the book.[36]

Here Wolfson suggests an inversion of the incarnational trajectory, in Kabbala from body to text and not word into flesh (as we read in John 1: 1–14). The inversion does not dismantle incarnation but, in fact, places it squarely in the arena of Deuteronomy, a book in which Moses, as person, transfers his authority and his mediating role to a text. In Wolfson's language, "the literal body [the body of Moses] is embodied in the body of the book [the Torah]." To oversimplify for a moment, in Christianity the divinity of the book—the word (which is itself a re-placement for Moses) becomes the flesh of Jesus. In Judaism, at least ac-cording to some kabbalists, the book (more specifically the letters therein) is envisioned as the "body" of God and then becomes, more obliquely, part of the literal body of the Jew. To complicate this assess-ment, in Lurianic literature (following the trajectory of earlier Kabbala from Abulafia and Gikatillia) we find that the book (Torah) is also im-planted in the literal body, the body of those who study it. By engaging with that "literal body," or the book (the literal body in the actual body), the letters that constitute the flesh of the reader—is divinized. This divinization, or incarnation, of one who encounters the "literal body" of the book is not a one-time historical event, as in much (but not all) of Christianity.[37] It is, rather, a full disclosure of *zelem elohim*, the divine that is "imaged" in the human until it can become manifest through devotion. To become divine, then, is nothing more than to be-come fully human, an idea I will suggest has a correlate in the concept of *theosis* in Eastern Orthodox Christianity. By incarnationalism, then, I do not mean the exclusive Christian notion of God being incarnate in one human being at one time, as is the case with Jesus Christ. Rather, I refer to the broader notion that the human being is, in essence, poten-tially divine (in Christianity *because* of the incarnation),[38] and that such divinity can become manifest and experienced as the "actual" body.

This expansive and democratized notion of incarnation, or *theosis*, draws heavily from Eastern Orthodox doctrine, specifically from the way it conceives of ethics as love and love as fulfilled through the event of the divine becoming human in Jesus of Nazareth.[39] For Eastern Orthodoxy, the event of incarnation makes possible the incarnation of divine love in the human, any human, such that divine love or *agape* is a vehicle for human–divine love of another, who is loved as human–divine.[40] And it is this expression of love that is the essence of the ethical.[41] The notion of *theosis* or human–divine similitude is viewed as possible for all because it occurred at one time. "Incarnation also presents the theanthropic vocation as a new moral imperative. . . . Clement of Alexandria undoubtedly had this in mind when he wrote in the *Protreptikos*, 'The Word of God became man that you also may learn from a man how man becomes God.'"[42] The instantiation of divine/human similitude now becomes possible, and should be the goal, for all human endeavors. This is summarized nicely in the following way: "After the incarnation, God is united to humankind through the sacrament of the Eucharist and is manifested as light within one's inner being. . . . This interpretation of the theory of the uncreated light can be found not only among the hesychast monks, but more generally, in the teaching of the Orthodox Church regarding the renewal and *theosis* (deification) of humanity. By participating in the uncreated grace or energy of God, humankind itself becomes a god by grace."[43] This notion of human deification does not mean that there ceases to be any distinction whatsoever between humans and the divine through *theosis*. It means, however, that in the Incarnation, Jesus contains within Himself "the fullness of divinity," while we only receive "from that fullness" because His fullness has become manifest in the world.[44] Stripped of its particular Christian language and imagery, I argue that the Lurianic texts we will examine come close to this assessment.

Thus, while it is often argued that Judaism and incarnationalism are incompatible,[45] the story is more complex. Divine embodiment, even in a human being, is neither historically nor philosophically at odds with the way Jews have fashioned the Jewish religion.[46]

In rabbinic literature, divine indwelling (a term not identical to but also not absolutely distinct from incarnation) is manifest most prominently in the realms of physical space (the Temple), history, the collective body of Israel (Knesset Israel), the holiness of Jerusalem (or the entirety of the Land of Israel), and perennial providence (*hashgakha peratit*). This also includes cosmic and metaphorical representations of God in human form, such as God performing mitzvot in Heaven and experiencing the plethora of human emotions.[47] The divinity of Torah, or Torah as the embodiment of God, and the indwelling of God among those who study Torah is yet another example in which Judaism quite easily acknowledges divine presence within its ostensibly aniconic worldview.[48] In certain medieval mystical formulations, specifically those regarding prayer, it has been shown that rabbinic "indwelling" passes over the incarnational thinking.[49] In the texts Elliot Wolfson reads, God is envisioned as human and, by extension, the human is fashioned as divine. This constitutes a kind of inversion of Christian incarnation but it is incarnation nonetheless—in this case the human form becomes a cosmic divine body in the human imagination.

I argue here that incarnational thinking as an idea, when detached but not wholly severed from its historical and theological roots in Christianity—the one-time mysterious embodiment of God in Jesus of Nazareth (John 1:45–46)—is not antithetical to kabbalistic Judaism and, in fact, provides certain kabbalists with a framework for thinking through the relationship between text and person that Deuteronomy introduces. Incarnational thinking in Judaism tests the elasticity of the normative rabbinic idea that there is an absolute distinction separating the human and the divine (an idea that is fundamental to halakha). That is, while there may be a distinction between *being* God and being *with* God or a residence *for* God, the latter two are aspects of incarnational thinking, broadly defined.[50]

If classical Judaism does not affirm the definition of incarnation the way it is described in Christianity (which it does not), it is justified to ask why I would choose the weighty term *incarnation* to describe these Jewish texts.[51] The reason is that this idea, admittedly employed as a theoretical construct (divine embodiment fulfilled) plays a role in the Jewish mystical tradition. That is, certain strains of Kabbala move beyond the more conventional notion of divine indwelling to the radical notion of divine embodiment.[52] More to the point, the (re)turn of Lurianic and earlier kabbalistic texts to incarnational thinking may also inform the extent to which the Christian notion is born out of ancient Jewish (mystical) sources, thus closing a circle of the Jewish–Christian mystical imagination.[53] The question of direct historical influence is relevant here but not determinative. My thesis does not stand or fall on whether any direct influences can be documented. This is because I argue that incarnational thinking already exists in pre-rabbinic (and thus pre-"Jewish") Israelite thinking. This is not to say that sixteenth-century Kabbala draws from these pre-rabbinic sources (although it may). It only suggests that the theological structure of what became Judaism already contains elements that can be interpreted through an incarnational lens.

As I argued throughout this book, sixteenth-century Safed and the later Lurianic teaching in seventeenth-century Italy provides an interesting nexus between Judaism and Christianity wherein Kabbala became a vehicle for conversos to reenter Judaism. Conversos also contributed to the teaching of Kabbala to Christians, resulting in the more fully developed Christian Kabbala of early modernity, compared to its earlier precedent in the fourteenth century.[54] From another vantage point, Wolfson has shown the extent to which this incarnational thinking is already deeply embedded in the Zohar, a textual tradition read closely by Lurianic kabbalists. Hence, while the larger historical context of returning conversos may inform Lurianic reading, it surely does not do so exclusively. The Zohar was constructed in a deeply pious Christian environment that both influenced it as well as elicited from it a polemical response.[55] Lurianic Kabbala was not born in an overtly Christian environment; its host culture was Muslim—yet Christian resonances may have seeped in subversively through the converso community.

In both Judaism and Christianity, divine embodiment or incarnation in human beings is based on the biblical notion of humans created in the divine image or *zelem elohim* (Gen. 1:27).[56] The kabbalistic texts under consideration suggest a hyperliteral interpretation of *zelem elohim* (the human as "the image of God"), distinguishing themselves from the metaphorical way this notion has been interpreted.[57] In classical Judaism, indwelling is an idea holding that God takes up temporary residence in the world, but this presence does not transform the physical space it occupies into something divine.[58] From Deuteronomy we learn that this "presence" is in fact God's name, with letters that also appear in/as God's text. There is a disagreement as to whether divine residence is temporary or permanent; that is, whether divine residence in Erez Israel, Zion,[59] the Temple,[60] or the people Israel is contingent upon Israel's behavior or a permanent part of Israel's "body."[61] The practical consequence of this debate concerns levels of sacredness regarding objects or space, denoting specific ways in which these "embodied" physical objects should be treated. Regarding the human as *zelem elohim,* the sages understood this largely as the way the Bible distinguishes between the human and other creatures.[62] *Zelem elohim* is not generally interpreted to suggest the divinity of the human.[63] While the physical body remains (as it does in Jesus), the individual's perspective of selfhood is transformed (with Jesus it is also his disciple's perspective of him). This move, I argue, points beyond the conventional Jewish notion of "indwelling."[64] Martin Buber alludes to this when he writes, "In the measure in which the fire of God shining above men in infinite distance and majesty is enkindled in the innermost chambers of the self, thus, in the measure in which the 'divine image' *becomes concrete reality* [my italics] the difference between autonomy and heteronomy is dissolved in a higher unity within the community living in the living certitude of the tradition."[65] The *concrete reality of the divine image* points to the incarnational thinking I am suggesting. The separation between the human and divine is sustained through the imperfection of the human, that is, his or her inability to disclose the divine letters that are embedded within. It thus represents the human inability to become fully human by disclosing the divine image. If and when those "letters" are disclosed, the "imaging" of the divine is replaced by a divination, however temporary, of the human. Eastern Orthodoxy calls this process *theosis* and founds this possibility on the one-time (permanent) incarnation of Jesus. Our kabbalistic texts do not need that historical event to make a similar claim. For them, it appears that a hyperliteral reading of Genesis 1:26 suffices when aided by the transition from divine anthropomorphic presence in the Covenantal Code or early priestly writings to God's presence as the divine name in the Deuteronomic school.[66]

Deuteronomy and the Divine Text in/as the Human:
The Case of Hoshana Raba

In the following section I will illustrate the way in which a series of Lurianic texts construct the notion of *zelem elohim* as textual (that is, that the human being is comprised of letters of Torah),[67] based on a reading of the nocturnal ritual of Torah study during the night of Hoshana Raba, the final night of the festival of Sukkot. Deuteronomy plays a central role in this kabbalistic ritual, as Luria directed his disciples to recite the entire Book of Deuteronomy during the first part of the night of Hoshana Raba, after which they were to recite penitential prayers or study Kabbala until morning prayers (approximately forty-five minutes before sunrise).[68] In the next section I will illustrate how the divine image in the human is activated and fully disclosed through the engagement with the divine text of Torah in the mystical practice of study and prayer more generally. The human as *divine text-concealed* engaging with Torah as *divine text-revealed* results in a *theosis* whereby the human, becoming fully human, also becomes divine. And as "divine," he no longer requires the protective garb that *zelem* provides.

Hoshana Raba is a minor festival on the last, or seventh, day of the festival of Sukkot. Its origins lie in the Ancient Israelite religion at the time of the Temple when pilgrims would circle the altar seven times holding ʿaravot (willow branches), reciting verses of praise to inaugurate the beginning of the rainy season. It is also the culmination of the water libations common on Sukkot that also mark the autumnal transition from the dry summer to a rainy winter.[69]

Kabbala, especially the Zohar and later Lurianic Kabbala, adds significance to this day, suggesting it serves as the conclusion to the Day of Atonement. For the Lurianic kabbalists, following the Zohar, Hoshana

Raba was the "day of the final sealing": the day of the second seal of judgment following the first seal in the final service (*neilah*) of Yom ha-Kippurim (YK).[70] Hence, there are certain customs on Hoshana Raba (some of
which were initiated by Luria) that resemble those of YK, among them
the donning of the white garment (*kittel*) by the prayer leader (*sheliah
zibur*), the solemn intonation of the liturgy similar to that of both Rosh
Ha-Shana and YK, the lighting of candles in the synagogue as on the eve
of YK, and immersion in a ritual bath (*mikveh*) on the morning of
Hoshana Raba (the custom of mikveh on YK is the afternoon preceding
the festival).[71] For our kabbalists, the notion of Hoshana Raba as the final
closing of the period of judgment and thus the final opportunity to alter
any negative divine decree, takes on a life of its own. For our purposes,
there is a significant connection between Hoshana Raba and Deuteronomy in that Luria directs his students to recite the entire Book of Deuteronomy during the first part of the night of Hoshana Raba. This is because
Deuteronomy and Hoshana Raba represent the final stages of their respective projects, the seal of Torah and the period of judgment respectively. As we will see, both are called "seal" (חותם) and are also depicted as
a manifestation of *malkhut* or the feminine. In *Sha'ar ha-Kavannot* Vital
writes as follows:

> On the evening of Hoshana Raba the second external seal is
> made, the "seal within the seal" that is given to the *sephirah mal-
> khut*, the crown/corona of *yesod*. This seal is weaker than the first
> seal (on YK) because it only has the three "fillings" of the name
> *ehyeh* [אהיה] . . . but the actual letters themselves (of *ehyeh*) are not
> present [in this seal].[72] It is thus weaker than the first seal (which
> is constituted by the actual letters). . . . *Malkhut* does not take
> from the three forms of *eyeh* but only from their impression/rem-
> nant [העורתם]. However since this seal is drawn initially from *ima* it
> still has the power to avert the demonic and thus it is called *seal*.

With this one can understand the Zohar and the Tikkunei Zohar when
they teach that Deuteronomy is called "Mishneh Torah" which is *malkhut*.[73]
It is known that the term *mikra* [lit., to read or recite but also used as a
noun to refer to Torah] is a feminine description of Torah. When *zeir anpin*
emanates its effluence to the *yesod* (vaginal cavity) of its feminine, this *yesod*
is called Torah. And when this "impression" is emanated to its *malkhut* and
creates a seal, it is called Mishneh Torah. Torah is the first four books of
the Pentateuch and Mishneh Torah is the secret name of Deuteronomy
which teaches and repeats what was said in Torah.[74] The creation of the
first seal of the *yesod* of the feminine occurs when the world is judged dur-

ing the *neilah* service of YK and the judgment is either for life or death.
Now (on Hoshana Raba) the second seal of *malkhut* is made in which the
world is judged a second time. The first inner seal was the time of the judgment and thus the primary seal. Now we are dealing with the outer seal
that is about the transference of the writ of judgment sealed during *neilah*
of YK and given to the emissaries of doom, as is written in the Zohar.[75]

This text suggests a feminization of Deuteronomy whereby the Mishneh Torah (Deuteronomy) and Hoshana Raba, as the outer and weaker
seals of judgment, represent the final instantiation of divine effluence
in *malkhut*.[76] These two dimensions of finality—the final destinations of
the divine word (Torah) and judgment (YK)—are connected to *zelem*,
as divine image, through the double entendre of *zelem* as "image" and
"shadow." This triadic equation (Deuteronomy, Hoshana Raba, and
zelem) is ritualized in the following manner:[77]

> The dominant time of judgment on Hoshana Raba is the first
> part of the night, after which time the seal of *malkhut* is com-
> plete. Therefore immediately after midnight one who is judged
> for death will see his *zelem* [divine image] above his head, heaven
> forbid.[78] This is also the time people would go out and look at
> their *zelem* (shadow) in the light of the moon that only rises after
> midnight. It is thus a custom to engage in Torah study the first
> part of the night (until the rising of the moon) by reciting the
> Book of Deuteronomy that is called Mishneh Torah. One should
> intend with this reading to create the seal of *malkhut* which is the
> numerical value of Mishneh (395).[79]

The moon, classically defined as feminine, serves to illuminate the nature of the final judgment as to whether the seal of *malkhut* was sufficient
to ward off any negative judgments pending from YK.[80] But there are two
seals and thus two *zelems* of *malkhut* here; the first is Hoshana Raba itself
and the second is Deuteronomy. The recitation of Deuteronomy on
Hoshana Raba night serves as the (temporary) protective seal of divinity
while the *zelem* of the individual departs to witness the final moment of
divine decree.[81] As Deuteronomy is the divine text that is itself a seal it is
deployed to construct the second seal of *malkhut* in the soul in order to
protect the feminine lights of the soul from external danger. This is
needed when the part of the *zelem* that normally serves this purpose is absent. The connection of *zelem* to judgment (*din*), and thus to Hoshana
Raba, is made explicit at the end of this homily referring to an apparent
contradiction in the Zohar regarding the temporary separation of the
zelem from the human on the night of Hoshana Raba:

Now I will explain an apparent contradiction in the Zohar. In one place the Zohar teaches that the *zelem* departs from the head [of a person] on the night of Hoshana Raba (Zohar 2.142a). In another it teaches that the *zelem* only departs from a person thirty days before his death (Zohar 1. 2.17b).[82] This is how these texts can be reconciled. On Hoshana Raba night the *zelem* departs in order to be instructed [about] what has been decreed upon it. During this time, permission is also given to the demonic to have temporary dominion over the individual and kill him. Since the *zelem* departs from the person that evening, it is as if the person already gave himself over to the demonic at the time of the decree and thus has nothing more to fear. On this, see Zohar 2. 231a. [After midnight] the *zelem* returns to its place because without it a person could not continue to live, as it is written, *Man walks about as a mere shadow (zelem)* [אך בצלם יתהלך איש] (Ps. 39:7) [read now as, *Man can only exist with his* zelem/*image of God*]. The *zelem* returns to him until thirty days before his death, after which it departs and does not return during the last thirty days of life. . . .[83]

The precariousness of Hoshana Raba seems to trump even YK, as tradition teaches that on YK the day itself (*'azumo shel-yom*) atones.[84] But apparently this atonement isn't complete until Hoshana Raba. For Luria, Hoshana Raba is the day when the final decree containing anything remaining after repentance and atonement on YK is passed on to angelic messengers. Proper observance of this day (that is, the recitation of Deuteronomy in accord with Lurianic custom) can create the final outer seal for *malkhut* necessary in order to ward off evil energy. The danger of the day is imagined here as temporary death via the departure of the *zelem* during the first part of the night, leaving the individual susceptible to demonic forces. This temporary state of divine absence within the human must then be accommodated by the recitation of Deuteronomy which serves as a temporary divine seal until midnight when the *zelem* returns. In this case, engagement with Torah is an example of embodiment in that the words of Torah become a temporary (divine) dimension of the human body, loosely construed, when its permanent divinity temporarily departs.

A more explicit connection between *zelem* and the divine nature of the human body is suggested by Luria in the juxtaposition of two verses in Scripture (*Let us make man in our image* [zelem]—*From my flesh I will see God* [eloha]—Gen. 1:26 and Job 19:26). The notion that the Job verse relates to the male circumcised phallus has been thoroughly examined by Wolfson in numerous studies. In Luria, the verse may have a wider lens and apply to the entire human body:

Regarding immature consciousness (*mohin de-katnut*) we should
know that the human was formed (*nozar*) in the *image of God*
(Gen. 1:26) and *From my flesh I will see God* (*eloha*) (Job 19:26). The
structure (*dugmat*) of a person comes from one drop that originates in the brain[85] of the father and enters into the womb of the
mother where it begins its existence and takes on form
(*zurah*) . . . The mature consciousness (*mohin de-gadlut*) comes
from the inside of *abba* and *ima*. Hence, their existence is the secret of the verse *zelem elohim* (אלוהים) and *zelem adonai* (יהוה).[86]

It is noteworthy that the text chooses the word *form* (*nozar*) instead of the
biblical term *created* (*bara*). The obvious reason is that the text refers to the
formation of the human embryo and not the "creation" of Adam by God.
However, the term *nozar* is also suggestive in that it describes the formation of the Hebrew alphabet in Kabbala (*zurat 'otiot*). The relationship between the word *image* (*zelem*) and God (*eloha*) may be the key to understanding this odd juxtaposition of verses. In the Zohar, especially in Sabba
de-Mishpatim, the term *eloha* is often used to represent the garment (*lev-
ush*) of the soul, a name of God that protects the soul when it descends
into the world. In the following text the flesh clearly refers to the phallus,
but for our purposes it sets up the important use of the term *eloha:*

The other began speaking and said, *From my flesh I see God* (Job
19:26). What does it mean *From my flesh;* it should say "from myself"? But, it means really from my flesh! What is this? As it is
written, *the sacred flesh will pass away from you, for you exalt while performing your evil deeds* (Jer. 11:15) as it is written, *And my covenant
will be on their flesh as an everlasting covenant* (Gen. 17:14).[87]

In Sabba de-Mishpatim, the Zohar's analysis of a section of Exodus, the
term *eloha* is made more explicit.[88]

Do not go out like slaves (Exod. 21:7). That is, when it [the soul]
leaves the scale on the side of joy, God will imprint it and seal it
with one [signet] ring and spread over it His precious garment.
And what is this [garment]? It is the divine name *eloha*. And this
is its clothing. God will spread over it the precious garment of
majesty (*le-vusha yakira de-malka*). . . . as it is written, *in the days
when eloha watched over me* (Job 29:2).[89]

These passages from the Zohar may help clarify Luria's juxtaposition of
Genesis 1:26 and Job 19:26. The "God" that one sees when gazing at his

"flesh" is the divine name *eloha,* which is the garment of the soul that God bequeaths to the soul when it descends to the world. This divine name is the *zelem,* as in the words "*in the image of God He created them.*" It could then be that the term *nozar* is a double entendre, meaning both the physical formation of the embryo in the womb and the fact that this *zelem* is constructed with letters of a divine name that already maintain a specific divine form (*zura*). The implicit identification of *zelem* in *zelem elohim* with the name *eloha* points toward a rendering of the human as a name or names of the divine. More is needed, however, to solidify this claim.

One obvious question is the following: if, according to *Sefer Yezeriah,* all of creation is formed from the Hebrew letters, in what way is the human different?[90] In the Hebrew Bible, the description of the human created "in the image of God" appears to distinguish the human from all other creatures. Yet Luria's rendering of *zelem* as the divine name *eloha* does not clarify the ways in which the human is categorically "other" and closer to the divine than the rest of creation. Moreover, strong statements of human distinctiveness are explicit throughout the Lurianic corpus.[91]

One response to this question comes in the context of a discussion about the ritual to remain awake and study through the entire night on Hoshana Raba (discussed above). This also points to a more explicit statement of *theosis* in Luria's discussion of Torah study in *Pri ʿEtz Hayyim* below. Luria mentions that on the night of Hoshana Raba the individual is quite vulnerable because his *zelem* departs from him only to return the next morning.[92] Implied is that his protective garment departs, leaving his soul vulnerable. Thus Torah study (engagement with the divine letters of the text) serves as the temporary protective layer of the human soul when its *zelem* (a divine name) is elsewhere. That is, the divine names that constitute Torah, when recited and studied, provide the same protection for the soul as the divine name *eloha* that departed. This notion is born out of an apparent contradiction between two verses (Ps. 39:7 and Song of Songs 2:17 [also 4:6]). The text below is a section of a much longer homily on the festival of Sukkot in *Shaʿar ha-Kavvanot,* illustrating the relationship between the soul and the divine name.

We will now explain clearly the notion of the *zelem* departing from the person on the night of Hoshana Raba. . . . It is written in one verse, *Man walks about as a mere shadow (zelem)* [אך בצלם יתהלך איש] (Ps. 39:7). We can infer from this that there is one *zelem.* In that verse it is also called *zelem* and not [the more common term for shadow] *zel* [צל]. We read in another verse, *When the day descends and the shadows (ha-zelalim)* [הצללים] *flee* (Song of Songs 2:17). We can infer from this that there are two "images" (*zelalim*). And, they are not called *zelamim* [צלמים] but *zelalim* [צללים]. There are obvious oddities in these verses. . . . Know that the soul (*nefesh*) is called by five [divine] names that correspond to the five times *borkhei nafsi* (blessed in my soul) is mentioned in Psalms 103 and 104. . . .

We will now explain the specifics of the five parts of the world of ʿ*azilut* and from there you will understand [the four lower worlds]. The human body is derived from the feminine side of *malkhut*. We see that the physical body completes its development during the nine months of pregnancy. There are three levels below the five levels of the soul. These are the three *zelalim* צללים (shadows, images). The highest of these three is called *zelem* צלם. The two lower parts are each called *zel* צל. Each one of the lower two is missing the letter *mem* (מ). This is the secret of the verse *Man walks about as a mere shadow (zelem)* [אך בצלם יתהלך איש] [now read as, *but man only walks with (his) zelem*] (Ps. 39:7).[93] The secret of the verse *When the day descends and the shadows (ha-zelalim)* [הצללים] *flee* (Song of Songs 2:17) is that there is a *zelem* above the one mentioned in Psalms derived from those two [*zelalim* that flee in Song of Songs].

Regarding these three *zelamim:* the five parts of the soul are implanted in the vaginal cavity (*yesod*) and the womb (*rehem*) of the woman and the body develops during the nine months of pregnancy. At that point [at the time of birth] a force emerges emanating from her cervix כלי החותם אשר ביסוד הנקבה[94] (as was explained in our explanation of the *neilah* service on YK) that is comprised of the three names of *ehyeh* [אהיה] spelled with *yods, hays,* and *alefs* which numerically add up to "seal"/cervix [חותם].[95] The power of this force coming from this "seal" is engraved on the soul of the individual and not on the body. When the higher soul (*neshama*) descends into this world to enter the body it comes [to the body] enveloped in this "seal." By means of this "seal"/cervix it is protected from the demonic forces. These (three) *zelamim* are from the remnants of that force that emerges from the seal of the female.

The impression of the force of the cervix that becomes engraved in the *neshama* of the person is comprised of three names of *ehyeh* [אהיה], as we explained. It is divided into the same three parts (*yods, hays,* and *alefs*). This is how to understand, *And God Elohim created Adam in his image, in the image (zelem) of Elohim He created him* (Gen. 1:27) and *But man only walks with (his) zelem]* (Ps. 39:7).[96]

Therefore, a person who has his *zelem* and the two [lower] *zelalim* which are the three names of *ehyeh* numerically equaling "seal" חותם, is protected from those *shadim* (demonic ghosts) who do not have the lower *zel* and whose seal is incomplete.[97]

In this homily we see a more developed notion of how dimensions of the soul are constituted by divine names. It appears here as if these names in the human serve to shield it from the negative external forces that would invariably destroy it. When the divinity (as *zelem*) departs, the human appears hopelessly vulnerable. Therefore, on Hoshana Raba when the *zelem* departs, one must engage with another form of divinity, the letters of Torah, specifically those letters that constitute the "seal" of Torah (Deut.) to provide protection from the ever-present forces of negativity.

The question that will occupy the final section of this chapter is: can Torah during other parts of the year serve to embellish or further disclose these divine letters in the human soul such that they dominate the human condition? That is, can the divine letters of Torah activate, as it were, the dormant divinity in the human, enabling the individual to achieve divine status?

Imagio Dei and Incarnation through Reading

As mentioned earlier, any incarnational theology in Lurianic Kabbala and Kabbala more generally must include the Torah as divine text and the human as created "in the image of God." This is because the text of Torah is what Jews—rabbinites and kabbalists alike—determine is divine in nature. The reversal of John's creed "the word becomes flesh" to "the flesh becomes word" as a basis for Jewish incarnational thinking has already been mentioned.[98] Given recent scholarship on this question, I think it is safe to say that the nexus between divine text and (divine) human in Judaism is far more complex, especially in Kabbala, than normative Judaism would have us believe.[99] Thus far I have been exploring this complexity through the prism of *zelem elohim*, the biblical description of humanity's "divine" nature, framing that discussion in terms taken from Deuteronomy, a book that explores the nexus between text (Torah) and person (Moses). The larger question about Christian influence, cultural and theological, looms large. Christianity has formulated its position on the relationship between the human and the divine, a problem that is biblical in origin, placing it at the very center of its Christology. While living with the blurred distinction between the human and the divine may have been less vexing for Israelites before Christianity, as intertestamental literature indicates, after Christianity classical Judaism carefully rejected any hint of crossover between the human and God. Yet Kabbala, for many reasons, may have been less invested in this defensive posture.

In the case of sixteenth-century Safed, the forces pushing against the ostensibly opaque lines of Jewish defense were stronger. More importantly, some pressure may have been exerted from internal sources. As I have noted throughout this book, conversos were plentiful in Safed and, in more than a few instances, became members of mystical fraternities. This phenomenon grew even more prominent in Sabbateanism in the seventeenth century.[100] Therefore, without making any concrete claims about overt influences, as none can be adequately traced, I offer here a reading of a Lurianic text edited by an early seventeenth-century student of a known converso as an example of incarnational thinking in early modern Judaism.

I argue that the engagement between divine text and (divine) person through the act of reading illuminates the dormant divine nature of the human, disclosing the full potential of human beings as carriers of the divine name. The exposure of the divine "nature" of the reader (which I have called a Jewish *theosis*) collapses any significant distinction between person and text.[101]

The text that will serve as the foundation for this section is found in *Pri 'Etz Hayyim*. There are essentially two theories as to the origin of the text we have now as *Pri 'Etz Hayyim*, the first by Joseph Avivi, and the second by Menahem Kallus.[102] Avivi largely bases his theory on Poppers's introduction to "Derekh 'Etz Hayyim," a large text that is only extant in manuscript. He suggests that what we now have as *Pri 'Etz Hayyim*, first published in Kraków in 1785, constitutes just the first part of Poppers's larger *Pri 'Etz Hayyim*, which Poppers completed in 1650. This earlier text includes material from Vital, Jacob Zemah, and others. Kallus offers a slightly different genealogy, arguing that Poppers's work is more simply a redaction of material that originated in earlier Vitalean versions of his own corpus and not the original work of Zemah. In any case, there is agreement that our *Pri 'Etz Hayyim* is from Meir Poppers, who was a student of the ex-converso Jacob Zemah, redacted in Jerusalem and later in Kraków in the middle of the seventeenth century.

The section in *Pri 'Etz Hayyim* dealing with Torah study or Talmud Torah, which will be the focus of this section, also appears in truncated form in Vital's *Sha'ar ha-Yihudim*, although in the latter text the discussion is not in the context of any performance of a particular mitzvah.[103] In most other discussions of Talmud Torah, in Luria and elsewhere, the frame of the discussion centers around the mitzvah itself. Curiously, in the printed edition of *Pri 'Etz Hayyim*, the title of the section is *Hanhagat ha-Limud*, which I would translate as "The Performance of Study." The latter part of the section deals with what texts one should study and how one should study them, a topic that has been amply treated in various articles by Lawrence Fine and in his recent book *Physician of the Soul*.[104] The first

section, however, situates the act of study, or reading (how does one translate *le-asok*?), in a dramatic, almost theatrical, context that amounts to an
imaginal depiction of the human being threatened by demonic forces
that seek to undermine the act. The notion of the divine name (as letters)
in the human protecting the individual against the demonic is a common
trope in Lurianic Kabbala, as we witnessed above in the discussion of the
recitation of Deuteronomy on Hoshana Raba:

> In the performative act of Torah (בעת שעוסק בתורה) one should en-
> vision oneself as one who is being overpowered by the forces of
> Samael and the serpent (סמאל ונחש ומצולת ים) because of the letters
> צל being masculine and מות being feminine. One should con-
> stantly contemplate the divine name אהיה, never allowing it to be
> removed from one's eyes in order that these forces not over-
> power you and that you are not overcome by the יצר הרע (evil
> inclination).[105]

The divine name *ehyeh* אהיה and the term *zel* צל are familiar to us from the
previous section. This name (*ehyeh*) constitutes one dimension of "the divine image" embedded in the body that protects the individual from danger. The text never explains why the act of study or reading should put
one in such a precarious position. That is, why begin a discussion on the
commandment of Torah study, arguably the quintessential divine command as described in Mishna Peah 1:1, as an act that is dangerous and
ominous? I suggest that the act—or performance—of reading Torah
here activates a divine dimension of the human being that attracts the sa-
tanic forces hoping to deflect the concentration of the actor, thus diminishing the impact of the "incarnational act." It is not that the divine name
protects the individual, but that engaging with the divine names of Torah
through study activates the divine name in the person; such activation *attracts* the demonic. To read is thus to become (more) Godlike (to live as
the fully disclosed "image of God"), and becoming Godlike both activates and subsequently diffuses the potency of demonic energy. It is noteworthy that the *Sha'ar ha-Yihudim* parallel does not include the dark theatrical setting that frames the *Pri 'Etz Hayyim* text, beginning only with the
notion of the human as created in the image of God, something that only
comes later in *Pri 'Etz Hayyim*. I suggest that in *Sha'ar ha-Yihudim* (see extract immediately below), the mention of the image of God at the outset
creates an incarnational image but that the image is still placed within
the more conventional framework of supernal *tikkun* (the first definition
mentioned above; that is, *tikkun* as cosmic repair).[106] The relevant passage
from *Sha'ar ha-Yihudim* begins as follows:

It is fitting for a man to imagine (ולעריך לכוין) as if he is the house
and seat of ʿazilut ha-kadosh because *in the image of God, he made
man.* During the times of study and prayer this is even more important. In this manner one can unite to worlds until the supernal holiness rests on him.[107]

The depiction of the act of reading in *Pri ʿEtz Hayyim* uses this model but
adds something absent in *Shaʾar ha-Yihudim*. The first part of the following
texts appears in both versions, and the second part only appears in *Pri ʿEtz
Hayyim.*

Part I (in both *Shaʾar ha-Yihudim* and *Pri ʿEtz Hayyim*). This is how
one should imagine (יכוין) being the house of ʿazilut: A person
should view his head as the seat of יהוה with the vowel *kamatz*. Its
two *mohin*, that is, *hokhma* and *bina*, are also יהוה with a *patah* and
zire, and his two arms יהוה with a *segol*. When he comes to his
body, the יהוה takes a *holem*, his hands [alt. version his legs] with
kibutz and *hirek*, *yesod* with a *shuruk*, and the *atara* of *yesod* does not
take a vowel as it stated in Tikkunei Zohar.
     Part II (only in *Pri ʿEtz Hayyim*). One should also imagine that a
person (*adam*) is the 63-letter name of יהוה. He should imagine that
his ears are the 63-letter name without the final ה and perhaps with
this (final ה?) he will be able to hear some supernal holiness during
prayer or study. His nose is also the 63-letter name as חוטם is the numerical equivalent of 53. Perhaps with this (imagining) he will
smell from holy odor (רוח קדושה). His mouth is also the 63-letter
name. With the 22 letters and five oral openings of the mouth, he
can apprehend the spirit of God that speaks within him (רוח ה״ ידבר
בו) and his work will be on his tongue during study and prayer. All
this depends on the strength of his imagining and his cleaving.

Both texts suggest that the human body consists of various permutations
of the divine name. The second text suggests that it is the name that corresponds to the world of *beriah*, the world where separation and form begins. This is also the angelic world that may point back to the text cited
above, on the demonic interest in preventing this act, which results in the
divination of the human body.
     In the beginning of this text we read: "You should constantly con-
template the divine name אהיה never allowing it to be removed from
your eyes in order that these forces not overpower you so that you are
not overcome by the *yezer hara.*" The term *yezer hara* here is quite curious. It is a term, of course, that serves as the template for sin, the qual-

ity that separates the human from the divine. Could it be that the result of reading by imagining oneself as a divine name actualized through absorbing the letters of the divine word (in Torah or in liturgy) could bring one to a realm beyond human sin (the angelic world of *beriah*)— that is, to become a divine being?[108] If this is so, then the act of reading Torah is, in fact, a full recovery of *zelem*, reconciliation, the divination of the body, and an instance of incarnation. In fact, following the text just cited Luria adds the following:

> There is no doubt if a person performs this way for a period of time he will apprehend all that he desires. He will be like one of the angels who abide in the heavens. This is the secret of the verse, *Know Him in all your ways* (Prov. 3:6). This is especially the case if you think this way constantly and do not allow this to pass from your thought. Remember this in your heart![109]

I would suggest that the verse *Know Him in all your ways* should be translated here as "experience Him, the divine name, in/as your entire being." To achieve this is to achieve a kind of divinity where sin, depicted here as the *yezer hara*, no longer holds sway, where *imitatio dei* is fulfilled through *imago dei* which is the recovery of *zelem* through a kind of incarnation.[110] This incarnation is different from the formal notion in Christianity in that it may be fleeting and is not limited to one person at one moment in history. It may be closer to the notion of *theosis* described by Eastern Orthodoxy.

Finally, there is also a hint of Maimonidean language in the above passage worth noting. Discussing individual providence (*hashgakha peratit*), Maimonides notes that one is protected by providence as long as one is engaged in contemplating the divine.[111] Luria offers an internalized rendition of this idea: when one is in such a state that the divine letters within him are activated and fill his body, he will "be like one of the angels who abide in the heavens"; that is, he will no longer be human or, perhaps, only then will he be fully human. Luria departs from Maimonides by suggesting that by achieving such as state on a consistent basis (through the practical application of *kavvanot* or contemplative practices), one may reach a permanent state of divine embodiment. This recalls later theories of *devekut* (divine cleaving) in early Hasidism that suggest the *zaddik* or righteous one may reach a state where he no longer needs the mitzvot to remain bound with God.[112] Whether this last claim in Lurianic teaching is true would require much more textual analysis than I have provided in this chapter. What I have shown is that the Lurianic texts examined argue for a strong—one might say, hyperliteral—reading of *zelem elohim* such that the boundaries separating the human from the divine are translucent, if not, in certain circumstances, transparent.

Conclusion

This chapter argues that the Deuteronomic reforms elucidated by biblical scholarship may have resonated quite deeply in the mystical imaginations of sixteenth-century kabbalists. That is, the Deuteronomic transition from person to text, from human (prophetic) witness to the "book of the law" as the core "proof" of the covenant, and from the divine form to the divine voice seem to have captured the attention of many of our kabbalists. In this, Luria is not unique. The Deuteronomic transition from person to text (Moses—Torah) was noticed by many in the Jewish interpretive tradition long before Luria and surely before biblical scholarship. The kabbalists, however, complicate this transition and use it to thin the barrier separating the human from the text and, by extension, the human from the divine. Whereas for John, the text (as Word) becomes human/flesh in Jesus (John 1:1–14), for our kabbalists the text as divine has a correlate in the human as *zelem elohim*. The divine text (as divine names) and the *zelem elohim* in the human (also comprised of divine names according to these kabbalists) become activated through the engagement of text and person in the performance of study. What Luria and his disciples provide is a series of texts that elucidate this way of thinking, including the ways in which we can activate and fully disclose that *zelem elohim*, creating a kind of Jewish *theosis*.

I will conclude this chapter with two basic avenues for further inquiry. First, a parenthetical yet potentially significant aside needs to be expressed about the reception and dissemination of Lurianic Kabbala. Kabbala, at least from the time of the Zohar, viewed its own teachings as a superior dimension of Torah. More than that, it was viewed as necessary to foster redemption.[113] In some cases, Kabbala was Torah that could be available to non-Jews.[114] Why were some conversos so compelled by Lurianic Kabbala? Why were Christians so drawn to it? And why did Lurianic kabbalists, and perhaps even some kabbalists before Luria, teach Kabbala, which they surely believed was Torah, to gentiles?[115] We know from b.T. Sanhedrin 59a and Hagigah 13a that Torah study, in the rabbinic mind, was restricted to Jews or to those aspiring to convert to Judaism.[116] Torah was not something gentiles needed to know (outside the Noahide laws the rabbis claimed non-Jews had to follow). The Talmud states quite explicitly that Torah was forbidden to gentiles.[117] Following that line of thinking, the Zohar limits the study of

Torah to one who is circumcised (i.e., the male Jew).[118] Yet we know of at least some Lurianic kabbalists who may have taught Kabbala to Christians, and not only to conversos who were returning to Judaism.[119] This feature becomes even more prominent in Sabbateanism, which emerged only a decade after the redaction of *Pri 'Etz Hayyim* by Poppers (it should be noted that Shabbetai Zvi's primary disciple and the architect of one branch of Sabbateanism, Nathan of Gaza, allegedly studied as an adolescent with the Lurianic kabbalist Jacob Zemah, Poppers's teacher in Jerusalem).[120] I am suggesting that the overt program among some Sabbateans to teach Kabbala to gentiles as part of its redemptive program may not have been a deviation but rather a specific mutation of earlier Lurianic doctrine. This thesis is complicated by two facts: first, Moses Cordovero spoke stridently against teaching Kabbala to gentiles and against the authenticity of Christian Kabbala more generally (the two are not, by definition, identical).[121] He clearly knew about Christians studying Kabbala and, from his comments, also knew about Jews teaching them and was unequivocally opposed to both.

Second, Luria, perhaps in partial response to his limited knowledge of Christian Kabbala and Jews teaching gentiles in Italy, desperately tried to limit the dissemination of his own teachings to his small fraternity (in fact, Vital was allegedly buried with some of his manuscripts of Lurianic teaching). And yet we know that in subsequent generations some Lurianic kabbalists (most likely conversos who had relations with the gentile world in Europe) did, in fact, teach Kabbala to gentiles. Was this simply an aberration, or is there something in Lurianic teaching that justified this behavior? In some way, this Lurianic theory of secrecy also may point to its opposite: that is, perhaps secrecy is so important before the end-time precisely because the final *tikkun* will require the dissemination of "true" Kabbala to Christians in order to diffuse the distorted Kabbala that had developed in Christianity until then.

This can be illustrated by an entry in Vital's dream diary *Sefer Hizyonot*.[122] Vital recounts a dream in which he is captured by "Caesar of Rome" (likely referring to the Pope). The Pope demands that he reveal to him some of the secrets of the Kabbala. Vital begins to reveal to him "a little bit of the wisdom of the Kabbala" and then suddenly awakens. As we have seen, Vital certainly considered himself a messianic figure. Could the disclosure of "true" Kabbala as a corrective to its distortion among Christians be a necessary part of the final stage of disclosure? Could the dissemination of Kabbala outside the Jewish sphere, in its proper time and measure, itself be considered a redemptive act?

This last possibility should be coupled with some curious similarities between Lurianic doctrine and Christian teaching that I attempted to illustrate in this book and should at least raise questions for scholars of early modern Judaism in general and early modern Kabbala in particular. The second question is related to the first. Was it only reading Kabbala that held the potential for the divination of the human body? Why not Bible, Talmud, Legal Codes?[123] In the first part of this chapter I investigated the Lurianic custom of reciting the entire Book of Deuteronomy on Hoshana Raba. After one's completion of that ritual, it was advised to continue studying Kabbala for the remainder of the night. Is there any connection between the exclusivity of the study of Kabbala during these sacred times and the teaching of Kabbala to gentiles? Was Kabbala, as the Torah of ʿazilut (the cosmic dimension where there are no distinctions), the Torah of the *Etz ha-Hayyim* (the Tree of Life in the Garden of Eden) and perhaps (also) the Torah *for* the gentile in order to facilitate the final reconciliation of the Jew and the other?[124] Was the Torah of ʿazilut, from this perspective, a Torah drawn from a realm in which the distinction between Jew and gentile did not exist, a realm where there was only the human in a divinized body? In his book *Paul and the Torah*, Lloyd Gaston argues that for Paul the gospel was not meant to supplant Torah or undermine God's covenant with Israel. Rather, it was meant to spread Torah and God's covenant with Israel to the gentile world.[125]

In *Sefer ha-Gilgulim*, Hayyim Vital unabashedly states that only Jews are created *be-zelem elohim*, a notion that is rooted in zoharic teaching and likely even earlier, and appears throughout the Lurianic corpus.[126] Is this statement ontological or historical? If redemptive Torah, i.e., Kabbala, facilitates the recovery of *zelem* and only Jews are created *be-zelem elohim*, why teach Torah to the gentile at all? Could it be that for some of Luria's disciples (some of whom were conversos) the limitation of *zelem* as applying only to the (born?) "Jew" is a temporary state that will be overcome in the future?[127] Or, that while in a preredeemed world only "biological" (or converted) Jews are *be-zelem elohim*, in a world redeemed all humans will exhibit their "hidden" sparks of divinity because the unredeemable dross will be eliminated? That is, in the redeemed world, is the Jew simply a euphemism for the fully realized human? While we can never know the answer to this question, a parallel discussion about Erez Israel and the Diaspora may be illustrative. In his *Megillat ha Megalleh*, Abraham bar Hiyya (d. ca. 1136) addresses a question of the fate of those who are buried in the Diaspora during the time of resurrection. The Talmud argues that those bodies will roll underground until they reach Erez Israel and then be resurrected (he coins the term *gilgul ha-mehilot*). Bar Hiyya disagrees and writes,

> For this reason God has dispersed Israel among the nations in every settlement. When they arise from their graves in the future

they will remain in their places and continue to dwell there. And all of the places in the world will be called Erez Israel. Or [the geographic] Erez Israel will expand so much that it will contain the entire world.[128]

This startling excerpt is part of Bar Hiyya's text that ostensibly "reveals" the secrets of the messianic era (thus the work is called "The Scroll of the Revealer"). While there is no direct parallel between expanding Erez Israel such that it encompasses the entire world or indicating that the world will simply become Erez Israel in the future, to the dissolution of Jew as defining a specific faith community or ethnic group, I think Bar Hiyya's comment at least suggests a similar line of thought.[129]

I argued throughout this book, most pointedly in the chapter on Balaam and gentile prophecy, that the erasure or at least reconfiguration of the difference between Jew and gentile produces a tension that underlies much of Lurianic metaphysics, psychology, and physiology founded on *gilgul neshamot*. It also relates to Vital's infatuation with conversion as a redemptive trope, as I illustrated in chapter 2.[130] There I argued that the larger historical context of returning conversos and the permeability of boundaries implicit in that phenomenon should be considered when examining Lurianic exegesis and metaphysics. In chapter 4 on Balaam, I suggested that *gilgul* also serves to traverse the ostensibly opaque boundaries separating Jew and gentile. In short, can we say that Luria and his disciples may have envisioned their kabbalistic teaching in a manner similar to Lloyd Gaston's claim about Paul or Abraham Bar Hiyya's depiction of Erez Israel in the future? That is, that the recovery of *zelem* is also the expansion of *zelem*, from the Jew to the human—from the human to the divine?[131]

If my readings of these and other Lurianic texts about *zelem elohim* are plausible and there is indeed something lurking underneath Lurianic kabbalists' willingness to disseminate Kabbala (perhaps even to the gentile world) after Luria's death (and against his explicit wishes!), we may have a curious case whereby one of the most Judeo-centric and parochial strains of early modern Jewish thinking is subverting its own parochialism. In this case, Sabbateanism and later Hasidism (which limited Sabbateanism's universalizing of Kabbala to Jews) indeed adhere to Luria's redemptive project. As many others have noticed regarding Lurianic Kabbala, and as exhibited in Sabbateanism, Lurianic mystics did not view messianism as a product solely of divine fiat. As messianic activists they walked the delicate line between bringing the end and "forcing the end." The extent to which this "end" requires thinning the barriers separating Jew and gentile through a combination of metaphysical and exegetical rereadings of the biblical narrative is one of the central questions of this book.

CONCLUSION

The real power of hermeneutical consciousness is our ability
to see what is questionable.
—Hans Georg-Gadamer, "The Universality of
the Hermeneutical Problem"

The initial phases of the scholarly study of Kabbala placed great emphasis
on kabbalistic myth and metaphysics and its relationship to normative
(i.e., rabbinic) Judaism. To a lesser extent, Kabbala was examined in comparative perspective, viewed as a Jewish engagement with cosmology and
connected to the development of contemplative practices to cultivate
mystical gnosis. Early scholars were also fascinated by the mystical here-
sies of Shabbetai Zvi and Jacob Frank, for polemical, political, as well as
historical reasons. Some Jewish historians (e.g., Heinrich Graetz) used
these heretics to illustrate the ways in which mysticism was not compatible
with normative Judaism. Others (e.g., Gershom Scholem) used them to illustrate the perennial tension that exists between legalistic religion and
its (necessary) subversive antinomian underside.

In recent years scholars have paid closer attention to the ways kabbalistic cosmology emerges from and subsequently influences Jewish ritual and law and the various hermeneutical practices used by kabbalists to construct their metaphysic systems. In this study I hoped to add another dimension to this scholarly discussion. Focusing primarily on the Lurianic fraternity in sixteenth-century Safed, I examined the kabbalistic relationship to, and construction of, history (local and global; covenantal and universal) and the absorption, integration, and transformation of Christian and Muslim ideas and ethos resulting from the proximity of these traditions to Safadean mystics through conversos and the tolerant Ottoman host culture in Erez Israel.[1] I examined Lurianic kabbalists as readers of Scripture who used Scripture as a template for interpreting and constructing historical reality. I argued that Lurianic engagement with Scripture has at least two goals. The first goal is to reconstruct the scriptural narrative by building a cosmic–mythic edifice from Scripture that can then be used to (re)interpret it. The second is that Lurianic Kabbala uses its newfangled scriptural reality, now reified as a metaphysical template, to construct a historical narrative focusing on local events that it views as paradigmatic to Israel's redemptive history.

The core of my argument contends that Scripture stands at the center of Lurianic literature, much more so than initially imagined. Those familiar with this literature are aware that for the most part Lurianic Kabbala is not focused on scriptural exegesis in any conventional sense. Yet while Luria does not often engage in midrashic or kabbalistic interpretation in the manner of the Zohar, his entire cosmology is founded on a creative interpretation of Genesis. For those familiar with Lurianic metaphysics, this is obvious. However, I argue that Luria's use of Genesis as the foundation of his cosmological myth is also an exegetical act, one that rewrites the Genesis narrative and then uses that rewritten "myth" (as *nimshal*) as a template to understand Scripture as metaphor. Using metempsychosis (*gilgul*) as a hermeneutical trope, the remainder of the Torah, and by extension Jewish history, is refracted through the seminal events and characters in Genesis. What we have, then, is a literary genre that is not exegetical in the conventional sense but is deeply engaged and intertwined with the scriptural narrative as a grand metaphor that it claims to disclose through its cosmological interpretation.

Metempsychosis or *gilgul neshamot* underlies Luria's entire exegetical enterprise. While *gilgul* is surely not new in Luria, his use of it as an exegetical template for systematically interpreting Scripture and Jewish history is innovative.[2] In my view, *gilgul* as a systematic mode of interpreting Scripture and, by extension, human civilization, undermines the now traditional concept of "the decline of the generations" (*yeridat ha-dorot*).[3] A rabbinic idea first concretized by Shrera Gaon (eighth century CE), *yeridat ha-dorot* has largely become orthodox doctrine with few dissenters in the traditional world. It asserts that the further we move away from the originary moment of revelation, the more diffuse and less accessible truth becomes. Thus earlier authorities, in both legislative and nonlegislative matters, are given more weight than present authorities.[4] This idea becomes a centerpiece in the normative Jewish construction of authority and tradition in matters of both law and doctrine.

Luria undermines this idea in two ways. First, he makes the startling assertion, as recorded by his disciple Hayyim Vital, that all kabbalistic teaching after Moses Nahmanides (who died at the end of beginning of the fourteenth century) is unreliable and should be avoided.[5] He posits that kabbalistic tradition after Nahmanides was invalidated through corrupt transmission and misunderstanding until he came on the scene and, through inspiration (Elijaic revelation) and his own unique (messianic) soul, was able to reconstruct the authentic Kabbala that had been lost after the close of the thirteenth century. This proclamation discounts more than two hundred years of kabbalistic activity, including the kabbalistic work of his elder colleague and teacher Moshe Cordovero. This comment further suggests that even before redemption and the reemergence of prophecy as a new form of authority, individuals could essentially undermine, or transcend, tradition through forms of inspiration. It could be argued that this was a political ploy to gain the absolute authority he thought he deserved, or needed, to justify his creative kabbalistic innovations (or, perhaps, a ploy by his disciples against his detractors after his death). Taken alone, this proclamation would not be enough to argue that Luria undermines the traditional doctrine of *yeridat ha-dorot*. At most it was a singular attestation of one charismatic personality. However, this personal challenge to the structure of Jewish authority was supported in a more systematic way through the use of *gilgul* as a hermeneutical trope.

Gilgul neshamot as a tool of exegesis implies that everyone *in the present* (individuals and entire generations) is a composite of everyone *in the past.* Individuals from the past return through soul fragments in numerous individuals to complete acts not completed in previous lives (individual or collective) or to repent from sins or blemishes that remained intact after their previous deaths. Each human soul is thus a composite of many previous soul fragments in need of completion and liberation from the corporeal world. The weight of that liberation, and the particular personality and psychological make-up of any individual is thus an extension of the previous lives he or she carries. Human existence becomes a vessel for past sins. Not only does this concept arguably flatten the descending trajectory of human history (*yeridat ha-dorot*); it also potentially argues that later generations are, in fact, superior in that they have the power, and responsibility, to complete what previous generations could not. As each generation progresses, it liberates soul fragments from returning to the world, ultimately exhausting human agency as part of the redemptive process and leaving the final erasure of exile to divine fiat. As a hermeneutical trope, *gilgul* is thus more than a creative way to interpret Scripture or a novel way to deploy Kabbala as the basis for New Age psychology—it is a subversive method that challenges the very notion of authority, and thus power, in a traditional world.

Moving back to the issues about the centrality of Scripture more generally, Luria's focus on Scripture manifests itself ritually in numerous ways. The study of Torah (study usually implies the study of Torah through the prism of Lurianic doctrine) and more specifically recitation (recitation either of Tanakh, Mishna, or the Zohar) is ritualized throughout the Lurianic corpus. For example, Luria institutes a ritual of reciting the weekly portion each Friday by reciting each passage twice and the Aramaic translation (Targum) once. While this practice has roots in rabbinic tradition and was likely practiced by individuals before Luria, Luria's ritualizing this practice speaks to the way he envisions the Pentateuch as the glue that hold his metaphysics together. Through this weekly practice the adept not only develops an intimate relationship to the Pentateuch but, given that the Torah is envisioned as the grand cosmic metaphor in the Lurianic imagination, the adept comes to understand Lurianic cosmology in a deeper way. The metaphor or *mashal* (Torah) is recited in order to inform its reader more deeply of the esoteric Torah that is its meaning or *nimshal* (Lurianic Kabbala). The weekly recitation of the Torah portion thus has a utilitarian as well as a theurgic–cultic function. It integrates the metaphor into the consciousness of the adept who spends much of his time studying the kabbalistic–mythic "meaning" of the metaphor.[6]

The centrality of Scripture as metaphor plays another role in Lurianic Kabbala. Like many of their kabbalistic predecessors, Luria's circle maintained a hyperliteral reading of the rabbinic midrash that states, "God gazed into the Torah and created the world." That is to say, the Torah is not simply God's covenantal gift to Israel but is the template and metaphor for all reality. History is thus constructed through, and interpreted out of, Torah. Gershom Scholem focused on the Lurianic myth of creation (*zimzum* and divine rupture or *shevirat ha-kelim*) as the ideational foundation for exile in the Lurianic imagination (*zimzum* and divine rupture have no scriptural anchor and, in fact, arguably precede Genesis 1 in time).[7] In this study I focus more specifically on the biblical narrative as the lens through which the Lurianic circle constructed their historical reality. Underlying this "reality" was the aftermath of the Spanish expulsion

that consisted, in part, of conversos returning to Judaism, a phenomenon
that implied a kind of unconversion. That is, the returning converso was
undoing the act of conversion that made him or her (or their parents)
Christians, a trajectory that held overt redemptive possibilities in the eyes
of some kabbalists. The converso phenomenon is a fascinating epoch in
Jewish history with broad implications and has been amply studied by historians of the Jewish and Christian Middle Ages and early modernity.
The identity of the converso—living simultaneously as a Jew and non-
Jew—has been viewed as reflecting Jewish modernity.[8]

There has been a lacuna, however, between the historians who work
with historical documents and archival material on this question and
those who read and interpret the mystical literature that was produced
in this period. The ostensible reason for this is that the mystical literature in question does not overtly address its own historical context, leaving little for the historian to work with. However, as New Historians
have argued, history is not only born from historical documents but is
also embedded in literature, art, and other cultural phenomena that
never explicitly relate to persons or events. I used that approach as a hypothesis to examine Lurianic ideas, taught between 1570 and 1572 and
later redacted through the middle of the seventeenth century, with an
eye toward understanding if indeed this literature (and I do treat it as
literature) substantiates New Historicists' claims.

I discovered, among other things, that these kabbalists may not have
been as divorced from realia as we conventionally think—that their
mystical teaching, conscious or otherwise, may reflect, respond to, and
reconstruct the challenges of the day, and sometimes in surprising
ways.[9] More generally, I argued that the ostensibly parochial and insular posture of these mystical circles exhibits an acute consciousness of
difference (Jew–gentile; heterosexual–homosexual; esoteric Torah–ex-
oteric Torah; God–human) and the mystics in question entertained
various ways in which these differences can be, will be, perhaps even
should be, erased or transformed. I am not arguing that this school in
any way represents a proto-modern perspective. It does not. As far as we
know, these adepts were uncompromising in their piety and halakhic
behavior and rarely ventured too far outside their Judeocentric world,
intellectually or culturally. And yet, perhaps even against their will, the
outside world of Christianity and Islam may have penetrated, sometimes deeply, into their own Judeocentered universe.

The literature is surely opaque enough to be interpreted in various
ways. Contemporary ultra-Orthodox Jewish groups that use Lurianic
Kabbala (and its subsequent influence) as "proof" of their absolutist ideologies and uncompromising attitudes toward the gentile "other" have a

strong case.[10] I do not intend to offer an apologetic reading of Lurianic Kabbala nor redeem it from the clutches of extremist ideologies. I do attempt, rather, to reread this material outside the rigid traditional lens that has become the norm in some of these communities, a lens that Lurianic Kabbala admittedly helped create. My reading points more to the ways in which insular mystical literary and ideational constructs, in this case Lurianic Kabbala, sometimes undermine their own agenda.

Scholem argued that the engine that drives the mystical mind has a subversive, one might now add, deconstructive edge.[11] The mystical quest, in its continued and always unsuccessful attempt to "experience the non-experientiable reality" through the depth of tradition,[12] is arguably by nature undermining—and then recovering, only to undermine again—its commitment to normativity as the "norm" in mystical literature is often pushed to the limit and in many cases points beyond it. This mystical "subversion" does not come about by lifting the arduous burden of practice. But it does sometimes come about by the hypernomian creation of new rituals and rigidity in practice. As others have argued, we must seriously consider the extent to which hypernomianism is itself an act of subversion. More pointedly, for our kabbalists, is the extent to which the cosmic lenses through which these practices are performed sometimes undermine basic doctrines of normative rabbinic and post-rabbinic Judaism. This book argues that viewed through a New Historicist lens, this kabbalistic school is not an insular and removed mystical fraternity divorced from its cultural surroundings, both Jewish and non-Jewish. Deeply traditional, it can also be quite subversive (subversion itself coming from and through the "tradition"), thus raising the question, first suggested by Scholem, about the relationship between pietism and heresy in the mystical imagination.

I have reserved the final word on this matter for Charles Mopsik (d. 2004), eminent scholar of Kabbala who died in the prime of his life yet still managed to produce an impressive body of work from which I have greatly benefited. I never met him (I arrived in Paris on sabbatical to work on this book in early November 2004 in time to attend a memorial service marking the thirtieth day of his passing). I read his work with great interest and admiration, both for its clarity and its courage. On the matter at hand Mopsik writes:

> Whereas normative religious institutions which dominated doctrinal truths applied social pressure and exercised their symbolic violence to impose a pre-established and universal model on individual singularities, certain mystical movements were able to bridge the gap between the traditional religious framework and the

broad range of effects, drives, self concepts, alterity and modes of rational being. . . . The social censure of these movements in their original environments, the more or less deliberate sidelining of their concepts in highly orthodox 'catechisms' deserves study in its own right. Nevertheless kabbalists were and are perceived as sufficiently subversive to be subject to silent evincing. Even though most of the kabbalists considered themselves to be perfectly Orthodox, the key factor here is that the society of the time viewed them with distrust. Their ideas and religious considerations have been received differently throughout history, which also merits further investigation.[13]

Finally, this book, both in spirit and substance, is a gesture toward the creativity, ingenuity, and dark complexity of my teacher Dovid Din who, like Mopsik, left this world in the prime of his life yet unlike Mopsik left almost nothing in writing. His life embodied the paradox of being both inside and outside simultaneously, an "excluded insider" and "included outsider," which amounts to the same thing. He was my first initiation into the imaginative world of Lurianic metaphysics which, like him, is dark yet light, parochial yet enlightened, pious yet subversive, authentic yet innovative, traditional yet heretical. This is my gift to his memory.

6th of Av 5766
July 31, 2006

NOTES

Introduction

1. The influence of Lurianic Kabbala is a debated issue among scholars. Following Gershom Scholem, Yosef Haim Yerushalmi argues that Lurianic Kabbala changed the very way Jews thought about history and memory. Its myth, even for theose not adept in mysticism, became a dominant trope of Jewish thinking in modernity. See Yerushalmi, *Zakhor: Jewish History and Jewish Memory*, pp. 72–74. Moshe Idel argues that Scholem's argument about the widespread influence of Lurianic Kabbala is exaggerated. See Idel, *Hasidism: Between Ecstasy and Magic*, pp. 33–43. Idel focuses primarily on the impact of Lurianic literature and doctrine on Hasidism while Yerushalmi (pace Scholem) argues that Lurianic myth infected the larger arena of Jewish thinking more generally.

2. Edward Said defines a concerned reader as one who has "convergent political concerns in the contemporary world and a genuine historical curiosity about what produced this situation . . . [and tries] to carry out his or her concerns in a conscious and rational way, with lines of force emerging out of the past for transformation in the present." Edward Said, "Overlapping Territories: The World, the Text, and the Critic," in *Power, Politics, and Culture: Interviews with Edward Said* (Cambridge: Harvard University Press, 2006), pp. 58, 59. Responding to a question about history and the study of texts, Said continues, "I think there's no doubt that one does organize one's study out of concerns in the present; to deny that is simply bad faith. You're interested in things for all kinds of contemporary reasons . . ." A fourth case [about why people work on what they do] is the uncovering of affiliations that are usually hidden from history. Not only relationships but texts that are normally affiliated with each other. That's not as interesting as what I'm asking, which is what were these texts connected to that enables them? For another assessment of the invested nature of scholarship, see Bruce Lincoln, "Scholarship as Myth," in his *Theorizing Myth: Narrative, Ideology, and Scholarship* (Chicago: University of Chicago Press, 2000), pp. 207–216; and Robert Orsi, *Between Heaven and Earth*, pp. 177–204.

3. In general, see Ezra Zion Melammed, *Bible Commentaries*, 2 volumes [Hebrew]; Moshe Greenberg, *Jewish Biblical Exegesis: An Introduction; Early Biblical Interpretation*, James Kugel and Rowan Greer, eds. (Philadelphia: Westminster, 1988); Simon Rawidowicz, "On Interpretation," in Rawidowicz, *Studies in Jewish Thought* (Philadelphia: JPS, 1974), pp. 45–80; Beryl Smalley, *The Study of the Bible in the Middle Ages* (South Bend, Ind.: University of Notre Dame Press, 1964); Frank Talmage, "Apples of Gold: The Inner Meaning of Sacred Texts in Medieval Judaism," in *Jewish Spirituality*, ed. Arthur Green (London: Routledge & Kegal Paul, 1986), pp. 313–355. On Kabbala, see Gershom Scholem, "The Meaning of Torah in Jewish Mysticism," in *On Kabbala and Its Symbolism* (New York: Schocken Books, 1965), pp. 32–86; Elliot Wolfson, "Beautiful Maiden without Eyes: *Peshat* and *Sod* in Zoharic Hermeneutics," in *The Midrashic Imagination* (Albany, N.Y.: SUNY Press, 1993), pp. 155–204; idem. "The Hermeneu-

tics of Visionary Experience: Revelation and Interpretation in the Zohar," *Religion* 18 (1988): 311–345; Eric Segal, "The Exegetical Craft of the Zohar," *AJS Review* (1992): 31–48; Moshe Idel, *Kabbala: New Perspectives* (New Haven: Yale University Press, 1988), pp. 200–249; idem. *Absorbing Perfections*, esp. pp. 80–110, 250–271, 429–437; idem. "PaRDes: Some Reflections on Kabbalistic Hermeneutics," in *Death, Ecstasy and Other Wordly Journeys*, pp. 249–268; Michael Fishbane, "The Book of *Zohar* and Exegetical Spirituality," in Fishbane, *The Exegetical Imagination* (Cambridge: Harvard University Press, 1998), pp. 105–122; and my "From Theosophy to Midrash: Lurianic Exegesis and the Garden of Eden," *AJS Review* 22, no. 1 (1997): 37–75.

4. Idel's *Absolute Perfections* (cited above) devotes a number of chapters to the question of scriptural exegesis. See esp. pp. 26–79 and 429–437. In this study I concentrate on one kabbalistic school, viewing its relationship to Scripture as a lens through which to construct reality and then to use that construction to interpret its world.

5. On the function of reading as a spiritual exercise in midrash and earlier Kabbala (Zohar), see Michael Fishbane, *The Exegetical Imagination*, esp. pp. 105–122.

6. This is done throughout the history of the Bible. In fact, the Hebrew Bible as a text is arguably a "rabbinic text," that is, a text formed, chosen, and canonized in the early rabbinic period. What was included and excluded from the biblical canon was at least somewhat dependent on the ways in which the biblical text in question expressed "orthodox" rabbinic views. The Old Testament of the Christian Bible is not simply the Hebrew Bible but includes texts the rabbis excluded and, more pointedly, reordered later books. The Hebrew Bible ends with Ezra and Nehemiah, which dovetails with the rabbinic centrality of Torah and then 2 Chronicles 36:22–23, which speaks of the reconstruction of the Temple as a look toward the future redemption. The Christian Bible (King James) ends with the prophet Malachi that concludes with a more eschatological and utopian vision of redemption with no mention of a reconstructed Temple. But see Sid Leimen who argues that the canon was decided as early as the 2nd century BCE and rabbinic discussions of canonicity mentioned in the Mishna (2nd century) are largely concerning "inspired texts" rather than authoritative ones. Leimen, *The Canonization of Hebrew Scripture: The Talmudic and Midrashic Evidence* (Camden, Conn.: Archon Books, 1976).

7. This observation has been informed by Stephen Greenblatt and the New Historians but also by Robert Alter's important notion of the Bible as "prose fiction" and Daniel Boyarin's extension of the argument to include midrash as "literary theory." Alter's comment that the Bible should be read as "prose fiction" does not deny the historical nature of the Bible's project but suggests that fiction, as a literary device, was one way the Bible told its story, moving away from the purely mythic and epic depictions of earlier literature. See Robert Alter, *The Art of Biblical Narrative* (New York: Basic Books, 1981), esp. pp. 23–62; and Herbert Schneidau, *Sacred Discontent* (Berkeley: University of California Press, 1977). Boyarin, juxtaposing Alter with Meir Sternberg's theory of the defictionalized historiography of the Bible, suggests that midrash, through its use of parable and exemplification (*dugma*), functions as literary theory to the fictionalized history of the biblical narrative. Boyarin suggests that in midrash we can overcome the inexorable debate between Alter and Sternberg. He states that "[t]he rabbinic interpretation of biblical narrative suggests, then, a way out of the dilemma posed by Alter and Sternberg. Historiography and fiction for the Rabbis are not alternative genres to

one or the other of which biblical narrative must be assigned, but different semiotic functions within the text. That is why it is possible for them to speak of the clearly historiographical narratives of the Torah as having a *mashal,* a term which always signifies fiction for them." See Boyarin, "Take the Bible for Example: Midrash as Literary Theory," in Boyarin, *Sparks of the Logos* (Leiden: Brill, 2003), pp. 89–113 (quotation from p. 112). Here I suggest that Lurianic exegesis is not merely reinserting myth into the "fictionized" biblical narrative but rather creating drama using the Bible as its basic script (accompanied by midrashic and zoharic fictionized spins on the Bible) but deconstructs and revalues the narrative and its characters so that they come to represent a story that resembles but does not mirror the Hebrew Bible. The implicit assumption among Lurianic kabbalists is that Luria's metaphysics is the inner Torah and the Bible merely a garment concealing the esoteric truths.

8. That is, the Torah is the *mashal* of its kabbalistic interpretation. See my essay "From Theology to Midrash: Lurianic Exegesis and the Garden of Eden," *AJS Review* 22, no. 1 (1996): 37–75. For one classic example of this, see Ephraim Urbach, "Rabbinic Homilies on Gentile Prophets and the Episode of Balaam," [Hebrew] in Urbach, *Me-Olamom shel Hakhamim,* pp. 537–554. I will discuss Urbach's work more carefully in the chapter on Balaam's prophecy. For now, suffice it to say that while Urbach rejects earlier attempts to view the rabbinic depiction of Balaam as Jesus, he accepts that rabbinic literature of this nature is indeed responding to Christianity.

9. The idea that symbols, ritual, doctrinal, or metaphysical are signs of social and cultural commentary is the thesis of Mary Douglas' *Natural Symbols,* 2nd ed. (New York: Routledge, 2003). More relevant for us is the use of body symbols as reflections of social reality. See John G. Gager, "Body-Symbols and Social Reality: Resurrection, Incarnation, and Asceticism in Early Christianity," *Religion* 12 (1982): 345–363.

10. There are a few important exceptions. One is Yehuda Liebes's "Christian Influences on the Zohar," in his *Studies in the Zohar,* pp. 139–161. Another is Elliot Wolfson's *Language, Eros, Being* (New York: Fordham University Press, 2005), pp. 190–260 and Wolfson's other studies on Christian Kabbala cited there. Cf. Moshe Idel, *Kabbalah and Eros* (New Haven: Yale University Press, 2005), pp. 47, 48.

11. The centrality of election as the foundation of the biblical and later Jewish covenant is explored by David Novak in his *Election of Israel* (Cambridge: Cambridge University Press, 1995).

12. Michael Fishbane, "Martin Buber's *Moses,*" in his *Garments of Torah* (Bloomington: Indiana University Press, 1989), p. 96. Fishbane's full citation makes his intention clearer. "But the relationship between 'historical understanding' and 'personal transformation' is surely a delicate one; and with great men of spirit, like Martin Buber, the boundaries may be completely obscured." I think this assessment is also true of Luria.

13. A similar observation is expressed by Seth Schwartz in his depiction of Jacob Neusner's historical reconstruction of Rabbinic Judaism. "In his [Neusner's] view the documents [i.e., rabbinic texts] did not simply reflect reality but constituted attempts to construct it, that is, they are statements of ideology." See Seth Schwartz, *Imperialism and Jewish Society from 200 BCE to 640 CE* (Princeton: Princeton University Press, 2001), p. 8. Cf. Shaye Cohen, "The Significance of Yavne: Pharisees, Rabbis, and the End of Sectarianism," *HUCA* 55 (1984): 27–53, and most recently Daniel Boyarin, *Border Lines: The Partition of Judeo-Christianity* (Philadelphia: University of Pennsylvania Press), pp. 151–201.

14. See Mary Douglas, *Natural Symbols*, 2nd ed. (New York: Routledge, 1996), p. 158. "Anyone who finds himself living in a new social condition must, by the logic of all we have seen, find that the cosmology he used in his old habitat no longer works. We should try to think of cosmology as a set of categories that are in use. It is like lenses which bring into focus and make bearable the manifold experience of change."

15. The notion of Kabbala and textuality more generally as a double mirror is first suggested by Elliot Wolfson in *Through a Speculum That Shines*, pp. 393–397. This image is explained by Wolfson more recently as follows, "There is no gap between praxis and interpretation, and hence the scholarly exegete is not outside the process he/she is describing—the speculum [*Through a Speculum That Shines*] ends with an image of the double mirror, which for me is the most appropriate symbol to convey the art of reading—the text as mirror of the reader and the reader as mirror of the text—what do we see in this double mirror. Each other." Cited in Barbara Galli, "Postface," in Wolfson, *Pathwings* (Barrytown, N.Y.: Barrytown Station Hill, 2004), p. 223.

16. This is not a claim unique to Lurianic Kabbala although I do think the Lurianic context provided a distinctive nexus among these three traditions. On the importance of the Christian and Islamic context of the Zohar, see Isaiah Tishby, *Wisdom of the Zohar*, vol. 1, pp. 68–71.

17. This claim of influence and response to Christianity in Kabbala is not new. See Yehuda Liebes, "Christian Influences on the Zohar," in his *Studies in the Zohar*, pp. 139–161; Arthur Green, "Shekhina, The Virgin Mary, and the Song of Songs," *AJS Review* 26, no. 1 (2002): 21; Peter Shaefer, "Daughter, Sister, Bride, and Mother Images: Images of Femininity of God in Early Kabbala," *Journal of the American Academy of Religion* 68 (2000): 222–242; and *Mirror of His Beauty: Feminine Images of God from the Bible to Early Kabbala* (Princeton, N.J.: Princeton University Press, 2002), pp. 209–216. Wolfson understands the nature of influence in a more nuanced way. See his *Language, Eros, Being*, pp. 190–260.

18. Ronald C. Keiner, "The Image of Islam in the Zohar," *Mekharei Yerushalayim* 8 (1989): 49.

19. Most of our knowledge about this fraternity and about their relationship to the world comes through hagiographic material such as *Shivhei Ha-Ari* and the later *Toldot ha-Ari* that is not very reliable. Another text perhaps more accurate, albeit viewed from one very invested perspective, is Hayyim Vital's diary *Sefer Hizyonot*. This diary was written throughout Vital's life. An abbreviated version was published in 1826. The first complete version from manuscript was edited by A. Z. Aescoli and published by N. Ben-Menachem. The latest edition, the one used in this book, was published by the Shuvi Nafsi Institute in Jerusalem in 2002. An English translation of the Aescoli edition appears in *Mystical Autobiography*, translated and introduced by Morris Faierstein (New York: Paulist Press, 1999).

20. In fact, the remainder of Keiner's essay is precisely about making those very inferences in order to argue that we can indeed find an image of Islam in the Zohar.

21. Stephen Greenblatt, *Shakespearean Negotiations: The Circulation of Social Energy in Renaissance England* (Berkeley: University of California Press, 1989), p. 147.

22. Stephen Greenblatt, *Renaissance Self-Fashioning: From More to Shakespeare* (Chicago: University of Chicago Press), p. 5. See the discussion of this notion in Sonja Laden, "Greenblattian Self-Fashioning and the Construction of 'Literary History,'" in *Critical Self-Fashioning: Stephen Greenblatt and the New Historicism*, ed. Jurgen Pieters (Frankfurt am Main: Peter Lang, 1999), pp. 68 and 69.

23. See, for example, the collection of essays in Ismar Schorsch, *From Text to Context: The Turn to History in Modern Judaism* (Hanover, N.H.: University Press of New England, 2003) and, most recently, Nils Roemer, *Jewish Scholarship and Culture in Nineteenth-Century Germany: Between History and Faith* (Madison: University of Wisconsin Press, 2005).

24. See Stephen Greenblatt, "Toward a Poetics of Culture," in *The New Historicism*, H. Aram Veeser, ed. (New York: Routledge, 1989), pp. 1–14.

25. Louis Montrose, "The Poetics and Politics of Culture," in *The New Historicism*, p. 23.

26. On the ways texts as "documents" not only describe but also reflect on their subjects, see Dominick LaCapra, *History and Criticism*, pp. 19–51.

27. One could argue similarly when examining mystical texts. See, for example, Moshe Idel, *Messianic Mystics* (New Haven: Yale University Press, 1998), p. 4. "Scholarship in the humanities in general, and in the realm of mysticism in particular, should not be seen as a matter of arguments in a court. It is not judicial truth that is at stake here but an effort to penetrate zones of human consciousness that have been neglected. No regular forensic procedures are available. The attempts to unravel the processes taking place here involves a great amount of speculation in order to extrapolate from the scant literary evidence what happened in the consciousness of an aspirant to messianic status."

28. See Ann Rigney, "Literature and the Longing for History," in *Critical Self-Fashioning: Stephen Greenblatt and the New Historicism*, p. 33.

29. Another way of saying this is that the texts in question seek to give the reader an experience of the past, be it the mythic past of the Sinai desert or the contemporary moment in the author's life. On this, see F. R. Ankersmit, "Historicism: An Attempt at Synthesis," in *History and Theory* 34 (1995): 143–161. In some sense, then, I am sympathetic to Moshe Idel's criticism of Scholem's theory about Jewish messianism. See Idel, *Messianic Mystics*, pp. 1–37.

30. Ann Rigney, "Literature and the Longing for History," pp. 21–43; and Stephen Greenblatt, "Toward a Poetics of Culture," both in *The New Historicism*, pp. 1–14. Stephen Greenblatt captures this when he says "[the] significance [of these texts] for us is not that we may see through them to underlying and prior historical principles but rather that we may interpret the interplay of their symbolic structures with those perceivable in the careers of their authors and in the larger social world as constituting a single, complex process of self-fashioning and, through the interpretation, come closer to understanding how literary and social identities were formed in this culture." See Stephen Greenblatt, *Renaissance Self-Fashioning*, p. 6.

31. Louis Montrose, "Professing the Renaissance: The Poetics and Politics of Culture," in *The New Historicism*, p. 20. Cf. Robert Carroll, "Poststructuralist approaches: New Historicism and Postmodernism," in *The Cambridge Companion to Biblical Interpretation*, John Barton, ed. (Cambridge: Cambridge University Press, 1998), pp. 50–66.

32. Safed was surely not the only community where returning conversos were an issue at this time. Nor is there scholarly consensus that it was a "burning" issue. Abraham David, in his *To Come to the Land* (Tuscaloosa: Alabama University Press, 1999), argues that it dominated Safadean discourse during these decades, although he does not produce much hard evidence to support his claim. Others see it as less intense an issue. In any event, there is little doubt that conversos did play a role in Safadean Jewry during this time and, given the messianic tenor of the mystical community, it is plausible that someone like

Vital could have viewed this immigration as meaningful in that regard. See David, "Safed, foyer de retour au judaïsme de 'conversos' au XVIe siècle," in *Revue études juives* 146, nos. 1–2 (1986): 63–83.

33. The converso population, both in northern and southern Europe, comprised a very diverse community. For a schematic typology, see Jose Faur, *In the Shadow of History: Jews and Conversos at the Dawn of Modernity* (Albany, N.Y.: SUNY, 1992), pp. 41–52. Cf. Yosef Kaplan, "Wayward New Christians and Stubborn New Jews: The Shaping of Jewish Identity," *Jewish History* 8, no. 1–2 (1994): 27–41; and "From Apostasy to Judaism: The Portuguese Jews in Amsterdam," in *Binah: Studies in Jewish History*, vol. 1, pp. 99–117.

34. The notion of the apostate not being fully a Jew is a hotly debated topic in halakhic discussions stemming from the Gaonic period, which responded to conversions of Jews to Islam. See Salo Baron, *Social and Religious History of the Jews*, vol. 3, pp. 11–113. For an in-depth overview and discussion, see Gerald Blidstein, "Who Is Not a Jew?—the Medieval Discussion," *Israel Law Review* 11 (1976): 269–290. Blidstein states (p. 285), "He is a Jew, but as the geonim had argued in the case of the apostate *levir*, he is not 'your brother' (referring to Deuteronomy 23:20–21 and Leviticus 25:35–37 regarding taking interest from an Israelite or foreigner), he does not share your values and commitment. The biblical 'brother' is not a biological relation but an axiological, ideological one." This notion of adjudicating Jewish identity by anything other than biology is a radical notion that is debated in halakhic literature. For a review and analysis, one that addresses Rashi's position that Jewishness must remain solely a matter of biology, see Jacob Katz, "Although He Has Sinned He Remains a Jew" [in Hebrew], *Tarbiz* 27 (1958): 203–217. More generally, see Aaron Lichtenstein, "Brother Daniel and the Jewish Fraternity," *Judaism* 12, no. 3 (Summer 1963): 260–280. Regarding Christians not considering conversos fully Christian, see Ben Zion Netanyahu, *The Origins of the Inquisition* (New York: New York Review of Books, 1995), pp. 848–854.

35. For one example, see *Likkutei Torah*, p. 56a. "This generation is a *gilgul* of the generation of the desert and the *ʿerev rav* and Moses is in the midst of all of them." Other examples will be examined in subsequent chapters.

36. The notion of the *ʿerev rav* as converts is an important element in Vital's reading. This idea is first articulated in Mekhilta d'Rebbe Shimon bar Yohai and cited in Rashi on Exodus 12:38. See the discussion below. The notion that the *ʿerev rav* desired to convert in Egypt, perhaps before the beginning of the exodus, makes their case stronger. In fact, this would render them the opposite of "the apostate with regard to the whole Torah" (*meshumad l'kol ha-Torah kula*). Maimonides explains the logic of such an apostate as follows: "What good is it for me to adhere to Israel who are lowly and oppressed? It is better for me to adhere to those who are strong." Maimonides, *Mishneh Torah*, "Laws of Teshuva" 3:9. If it is the case that the *ʿerev rav* expressed sincere interest in converting while Israel was still in Egypt ("lowly and oppressed"), their merit should be great.

37. As we will see, Vital apparently follows an isolated Zohar passage that suggests that the *ʿerev rav* contained fallen Israelites as well. If I am correct that Vital follows this zoharic trajectory, the correlation to the converso community is even stronger.

38. The Egyptian background of Moses plays a prominent, albeit silent, role in Vital's depiction of the *ʿerev rav* as "Moses' people." As it is impossible that Vital could have even entertained what Freud made famous—Moses' Egyptian lineage—it becomes plausible that at least some of the *ʿerev rav*, like Moses,

were assimilated Israelites. As we will see, such an assertion is entertained in the Zohar and becomes, I argue, more prominent in Vital's reading. This notion of the *ʿerev rav* as "fallen Jews" makes the connection of the *ʿerev rav* to the conversos more believable. On Moses as an Egyptian, see Sigmund Freud, *Moses and Monotheism* (New York: Vintage Books, 1939); Jan Assmann, *Moses the Egyptian: The Memory of Egypt in Western Monotheism* (Cambridge: Harvard University Press, 1997); and Martin Buber's response to Freud in his *Moses* (Oxford: East and West Library, 1961).

39. See Yosef Hayyim Yerushalmi, *From Spanish Court to Italian Ghetto* (New York: Columbia University Press, 1971), p. 12. "But, when thousands of Jews had been baptized within the space of a few decades, it seems as though the Jews had been transported bodily, though under another guise, into the very midst of the Christian social fabric. Here was a new and ambiguous breed that fitted into no familiar category, somehow neither Jew nor Christian." Yerushalmi argues this phenomenon was the case far more among the Portuguese Jews than the Spanish, the former of which underwent swift communal conversion leaving no "Jewishness" behind to serve as a point of reference.

40. The question of volitional versus forced conversion is paramount here. The former are called "conversos" and the latter "*ʿanusim.*" For example, Yizhak Baer argues that Don Isaac Abrabanel's lenient attitude toward the conversos made little distinction between forced or volitional conversion. Ben Zion Netanyahu argues that Abrabanel's attitude only applies to the *ʿanusim* and not to those who chose to convert. See Yizhak Baer, "The Messianic Movement in Spain" [Hebrew], *Zion* 3 (1934): 71; Ben Zion Netanyahu, *The Marranos of Spain from the Late 16th Century to the 17th Century According to Hebrew Sources*, pp. 177–203; A. A. Sicroff, "The Marranos—Forced Converts or Apostates," *Midstream* 12 (1966); and Ran Ben-Shalom, "The Converso as Subversive: Jewish Traditions or Christian Libel?" *Journal of Jewish Studies* 50, no. 2 (1999): 259–260. On the use of these terms and their distinctions, see Yosef Kaplan, "The Problem of Conversos and New Christians" [Hebrew], in M. Zimmerman, M. Stern, and Y. Salmon, eds., *Studies in Historiography*, pp. 117–144, 530; and Shaul Regev, "The Attitude towards *Conversos* in 15th and 16th Century Jewish Thought," *Revue des études Juives* 149 (1990): 118 and 119. Another position is articulated by Gerson Cohen, in his review of Netanyahu's *The Marranos of Spain* in *Journal of Jewish Social Studies* 29, no. 3 (1967): 181. Cohen is reluctant to put too much weight on the "halakhic" debate about the Jewishness of many conversos and places more emphasis on their own-self-identification: "It follows that no matter how Christianized the Marrano way of life may have become, and was given evidence of becoming further, they need not—and, apparently did not—cease to be a Jewish group historically, sociologically, or even religiously."

41. The status of a Jew who "converts" to another religion is not unique to this period. There are already responsum in the Gaonic period (8th century CE) that address this issue. In this period Yom Tov Sahalon argued that *ʿanusim* (forced converts and their descendants) did not require any conversion ritual. This lenient position, however, was not universally accepted. See, for example, the Gaonic work *Shaʿarey Zedek* (Salonica, 1792) 3.6.11 and others cited in Norman Roth, *Conversos, Inquisition, and the Expulsion of the Jews from Spain* (Madison: University of Wisconsin Press, 2002), pp. 7, 8 and notes 18 and 19, p. 381.

42. This is, of course, not exclusive to the Holy Land or even southern Europe. See Elisheva Carlebach, *Divided Souls, Converts from Judaism in Germany* (New Haven: Yale University Press, 2001), 1500–1750, esp. pp. 47–66.

43. The status of a Jew who openly practices another religion has a long history in Jewish literature. Maimonides takes quite a radical stance by saying that a voluntary convert (specifically to an idolatrous religion) is no longer a Jew, suggesting that Jewishness is not inextricably tied to biology. See, for example, Maimonides, *Mishneh Torah* "Laws of Idolatry," 2:5. This is more complex in Maimonides because he does hold that in the case of an apostate who marries a Jew, the marriage is still valid. See *Mishneh Torah*, "Laws of Illicit Relations," 13:17. R. Menahem ha-Meiri makes a similar, but not identical, claim in his *Beit ha-Behira* to *Avodah Zara*, p. 61, although Meiri does say that one remains Jewish only for marriage and divorce. In both cases, however, the reference is specifically to "idolaters." See, for example, *Beit ha-Behira* to Gittin, pp. 257, 258; *Beit ha-Behira* to Horayot, p. 279, and the recent discussion on these and other texts in Moshe Halbertal, *Between Torah and Wisdom: Rabbi Menahem ha-Meiri and the Maimonidean Halakhists in Provence* [in Hebrew] (Jerusalem: Magnus, 2001), pp. 91–96 and 101–103. See the extensive discussion in Jacob Katz, "Tolerance in the Thought of Rabbi Menahem ha-Meiri in Law and Philosophy" [in Hebrew], *Zion* 18 (1953): 15–30; *Halakha and Kabbala*, pp. 271–291 and 243–246. In English, see Jacob Katz, *Exclusiveness and Tolerance: Studies in Jewish–Gentile Relations in Medieval and Modern Times*. The difference between Maimonides and Meiri on this point may be that both hold one can erase one's Jewishness. For Maimonides this occurs by taking on another idolatrous religion. For Meiri it is only by abandoning religion altogether. While Maimonides' position articulated above may include Christianity, it specifically, albeit by implication, excludes conversion to Islam, a religion Maimonides holds is monotheistic. In both cases, however, this refers to one who converts willingly and may exclude conversos, especially those from Portugal, who were converted en mass against their will. On the important distinction between the forced convert (ʿanus) and one who converts under pressure, see Cohen, *Conversos*, pp. 5–9.

44. See Yerushalmi, *From Spanish Court*, p. 380. For this and other examples, see Miriam Bodian, *Hebrews of the Portuguese Nation: Conversos and Community in Early Modern Amsterdam* (Bloomington: Indiana University Press, 1997), pp. 100–103. Interestingly, while it is surely true that, in rabbinic literature, circumcision is not related to original sin, in Kabbala it surely is. See Elliot R. Wolfson, "Circumcision and the Divine Name: A Study in the Transmission of Esoteric Doctrine," *Jewish Quarterly Review* 78 (1987): 77–112.

45. A similar locution is used by Maimonides to distinguish between what the Israelites experienced versus what Moses experienced. See *The Guide of the Perplexed*, II:33, p. 364 in the Strauss/Pines edition: "This is the proof that it was he [Moses] who was spoken to and that they heard the great voice, it says: *When ye heard the voice* (Deut. 5:20). And it also says: *Ye heard the voice of words but saw no figure; only a voice* (Deut. 4:12). It does not say: *Ye heard the words.* Thus every time when their hearing words is mentioned, it is their hearing the *voice* that is meant, *Moses* being the one who heard the words and reported them to them." Maimonides reads this narrative to strengthen Israel's dependency on Moses in the same way Vital uses it to strengthen the ʿerev ravʾs dependency on Moses. By arguing that Israel, in fact, did hear the *words*, and not just the voice, Vital subverts the Maimonidean reading by liberating Israel from Moses in that they no longer needed him as an intermediary. It is impossible to tell whether Vital is basing himself on Maimonides' reading of these verses, but it is striking how he offers a similar reading while subverting Maimonides' intent by substituting the ʿerev rav for the Israelites. For an interesting reading of this Maimonidean text, see James A. Diamond, *Mai-

monides and the Hermeneutics of Concealment (Albany, N.Y.: SUNY Press, 2002), pp. 8 and 9.

46. For a discussion of this in rabbinic literature, see Ephraim Urbach, *Hazel, Pirkei Emunot v Deᶜot*, pp. 29–51. On the relationship between divine indwelling and the human being, see pp. 190–195; and Yair Lorberbaum, *Zelem Elohim: Halakha v Aggadah* [Hebrew] (Jerusalem: Schocken, 2004).

47. I use mutation in the positive sense here, drawing from the biological sciences that view mutation simply as "a description of a sudden and significant development in the species." See Larry Hurdato, *One Lord: Early Christian Devotion and Ancient Jewish Monotheism* (Philadelphia: Fortress, 1998), pp. 99–124 and esp. p. 162 n. 20. Hurdato suggests that the Christian notion of incarnation is a "mutation" of a Jewish idea. Hurdato's use of mutation is helpful because as it maintains a link between the ancient Jewish early Christian idea it also suggests that postbiblical Judaism still has the core notion of divine embodiment that Christianity "mutates." Given that fact, it is not far-fetched to posit that later Judaisms could make similar kinds of "mutations."

1. Genesis

"And Adam's Sin Was (Very) Great" is from SeG, p. 103.

1. See Rashi's comment to Genesis 1:1. When he asks, "Why not begin the Torah with 'this month will be to you . . .'"—that is, the first collective commandment—he is asking about the utility of the entire book since Genesis only contains a few mitzvot that could have been included elsewhere. Cf. Nahmanides on Genesis 1:1, who argues that creation is a necessary prelude to Sinai, in that belief in creation makes revelation, and thus the covenant, possible.

2. See Wolfson, *Venturing Beyond*, pp. 17–128.

3. See Segal, *Paul the Convert*, pp. 65–67.

4. See, for example, Romans 5:12–21, 6:3–11; 7:7–25; 8:9, and I Corinthians 15:21–22. For a general discussion of these passages, see F. R. Tenant, *The Sources of the Doctrine of the Fall and Original Sin* (New York: Schocken, 1903), pp. 248–272; and N. P. Williams, *The Ideas of the Fall and of Original Sin* (London: Longmans Green, 1927). More recently, see Tatha Wiley, *Original Sin* (New York: Paulist Press, 2002), esp. pp. 13–36. The pre-Christian Jewish antecedents to what would later be known as original sin appear in various apocryphal and pseudepigraphic literatures. For example, see Sirah 8:5; I Enoch 2:23–24; IV Ezra 3:4, 20–22, 4:30–31; 7:92; Book of Adam and Eve, 9; and Ben Sira 25:24. On these and other passages, see Tenant, *Sources*, pp. 145–234; and Samuel Cohen, "Original Sin," reprinted in Cohen, *Essays in Jewish Theology* (Cincinnati, Ohio: HUC Press, 1987), pp. 219–272. I will not deal with these sources in detail as much scholarly work has already been done on them and, in fact, these early sources really predate the doctrine of original sin that is more relevant to this chapter. However, it is important to note the extent to which the doctrine, and its early formulation in Paul, is not made out of whole cloth but was an integral part of the pre-Christian Jewish conversation. The most one can say is that rabbinic Judaism (and by this I mean late rabbinic Judaism; i.e., after the 4th century), which itself contains remnants of this early debate, may have rejected the notion of inherited sin.

5. See Wiley, *Original Sin*, pp. 37–55.

6. In fact, the sin is repeated, sometimes by implication, numerous times in the Hebrew Bible, although it never takes on a doctrinal tone. See, for example, Genesis 6:5–8; 11:1–9; Isaiah 2:7–12; 10:12, 33:14; 22:11. In other passages, e.g.,

Genesis 8:21 and 6:5–8, God recognizes the sin of Adam but implies that his actions will not be inherited by his progeny. That is, God can and will forgive human sin. These verses make a biblical notion of original sin highly unlikely. Samuel Cohen concludes, "the theodicy of the Bible completely ignores the fall. The suffering of the righteous is nowhere justified on the ground of the sinfulness transmitted by Adam to his posterity." Cohen, *Original Sin*, p. 227. While I think this might be somewhat overstated, and surely seen through Jewish lenses, I generally agree that the notion of inherited sin is not an overt biblical motif.

7. Two examples of this phenomenon in Judaism are the doctrines of the messiah and resurrection, each of which has antecedents in the Bible (the Messiah in particular) but grows exponentially in the Second Temple period. See Jacob Neusner, *Messiah in Context: Israel's History and Destiny in Formative Judaism; Judaisms and their Messiahs at the Turn of the Christian Era* (Philadelphia: Fortress, 1984); and, most recently, Lawrence Shiffman, "Messianism and Apocalypticism in Rabbinic Texts" (forthcoming).

8. There are many early, and even later, rabbinic sources that point to a notion of inherited sin. For example, see Pirkei de-Rebbe Eliezer, 13 and 21; Genesis Raba 12:5; Leviticus Raba 21:4; Deuteronomy Raba 11:9. Cohen suggests three basic categories of early rabbinic treatment of the issue: (1) corruption of the race as hereditary; (2) Adam's sin as punished through his progeny; (3) all sin is the result of Adam's own actions. He suggests that in the end the rabbis opt for (3) while Paul opts for (1). Most recently, see Alan Cooper, "A Medieval Jewish Version of Original Sin: Ephraim of Luntshits on Leviticus 12," *Harvard Theological Review* 97, no. 4 (2004): 445–459.

9. See Joel Rembaum, "Medieval Jewish Criticism of the Christian Doctrine of Original Sin," *AJS Review* (1982/83): 353–382. Cf. the case of Nahmanides, who argues against any notion of Adam's fall as that of original sin, in Bezalel Safran, "Rabbi Azriel and Nahmanides: Two Views of the Fall of Man," in *Rabbi Moses ben Nahman: Explorations in His Religious and Literary Virtuosity*, I Twersky, ed. (Cambridge: Harvard University Press, 1983), esp. pp. 86–99. Nahmanides argues that Adam, since he had no will, could not be guilty of the sin, and therefore Judaism does not recognize the doctrine of original sin. "As a result of this second creation, the 'fall,' Adam and Eve were converted into physical beings from their state of spiritualized bodies. . . . But their incipient humanity was not a curse; it was an opportunity. Within their human context, people were summoned to recognize the Creator, a summons which Nahmanides repeatedly formulates as the goal of human beings in the world" (p. 97). Cf. Nahmanides' comments to Exodus 13:16; Leviticus 17:11; and Deuteronomy 32:26. At the conclusion of his essay, Safran entertains the possibility that Nahmanides' position on these verses may have been part of his overarching anti-Christian polemic (p. 106).

10. For example, see Deborah Schechterman, "The Doctrine of Original Sin and Maimonidean Interpretation in Jewish Philosophy of the 13th and 14th Centuries" [Hebrew], *Da'at* 20 (Winter 1988): 65–90; Daniel Lasker, "Original Sin and Its Atonement According to Hasdai Crescas," *Da'at* 20 (Winter 1988): 127–135; Alan Cooper, "An Extraordinary Sixteenth-Century Biblical Commentary: Eliezer Ashkenazi on the Song of Moses," in *The Frank Talmage Memorial Volume* 1:129–150; and idem. "A Jewish Version of Original Sin: Ephraim of Luntshits on Leviticus 12," unpublished paper presented at *AJS Conference*, December 2002. I want to thank Professor Cooper for his assistance and for making this paper available before its publication, as well as for his subsequent insight on these mat-

ters. I am very much indebted to the work of Daniel Boyarin who has shown the extent to which Judaism and Christianity, at least in their classical phases, have fluid boarders and are, in a deep sense, twins. In particular, see Boyarin, *Dying for God: Martyrdom and the Making of Christianity and Judaism*; *Border Lines: The Partition of Judeo-Christianity;* and a contemporary and confessional addition in "Interrogate My Love," in *Wrestling with Zion: Progressive Jewish American Responses to the Israeli–Palestinian Conflict*, Tony Kushner and Alisa Solomon (New York: Grove, 2003), pp. 198–204. Cf. Zohar 2:237a/b.

11. Cohen, *Original Sin*, pp. 271, 272. Cohen even acknowledges that Luria seems to have adopted a marginal view (he calls it "most fantastic forms"), drawn from the Zohar. But Cohen is simply citing from Samuel Abba Horodetzky's *Torat Haari* and did not investigate the sources himself. See Cohen, "Original Sin," p. 255. Had he done so, his intuitions would have been confirmed tenfold. It is interesting to note here that Cohen's essay was first published in 1948 before a real understanding in the scholarly community of the ways in which Lurianic Kabbala deeply influenced "conventional" Judaism. Thus his attempts to marginalize Lurianic teaching, while understandable in context, cannot bear the weight of subsequent scholarship.

12. In fact, original sin was a hotly debated topic in medieval Jewish and Christian polemics. See, for example, in Nahmanides *"Sefer ha-Vikuah"* in *Kitvei Ramban*, pp. 309, 310. On the issue of biblical exegesis as a tool of these polemical issues, see Elazar Touitou, "Peshat and Apologetics in the Commentary of Rashbam in the Story of Moshe in the Torah" [Hebrew], *Tarbiz* 51 (1982): 227–238.

13. Others claim that original sin was, in fact, far more normative in the rabbinic imagination than conventionally thought. See, for example, Joel Kaminsly, "Paradise Regained: Rabbinic Reflections on Original Sin," in *Jews, Christians, and the Theology of the Hebrew Scriptures*, Alice Bellis and Joel Kaminsky, eds. (Atlanta, Ga.: Society of Biblical Literature, 2000), pp. 15–43.

14. This conjecture is the premise of Alexander Altmann's thesis regarding the debate between Isaac Aboab and Saul Morteira on the Jewish doctrine of eternal punishment in 17th-century Amsterdam. Altmann argues that Aboab, basing himself on Lurianic Kabbala (he was a student of Abraham Herrera who studied with Israel Sarug), argues against the doctrine of eternal damnation in part to address the returning conversos who wondered whether they could, in fact, return to Judaism. Altmann writes, "The point pressed home by Aboab and his faction was the assurance of ultimate salvation for all Jewish souls. It was prompted, we suggest, by a sense of concern for Marranos who had, as yet, not returned to the fold or, having returned, either had been remiss in their duties or had relapsed into their old ways. In other words, the issue at stake was the recognition of all Marranos as inseparably belonging to the people of Israel and sharing in its election and privileges" (p. 17). See Altmann, "Eternality of Punishment: A Theological Controversy within the Amsterdam Rabbinate in the Thirties of the Seventeenth Century," in *Academy of Jewish Research: Proceedings*, vol. XL (1972), pp. 1–40. In his *Nishmat Hayyim*, Aboab, using the resources of Kabbala, rejects the Christian doctrine of eternal damnation, whereas the talmudist Saul Morteira essentially defends the notion of eternal damnation as a "Jewish" doctrine. The question of Christian influence on Kabbala was not explored in detail by Gershom Scholem, some say intentionally so. Scholem was reticent to acknowledge these cultural influences in his attempt to present Kabbala in a more insular light. See Idel, *Messi-*

anic Mystics, p. 30; and more in-depth in Amnon Raz-Krakotzkin, "'Without Regard for External Considerations'—The Question of Christianity in Scholem and Baer's Writings" [Hebrew], *Mada'ey ha-Yahadut* 38 (1998): 73–96.

15. In general, see Abraham David, *To Come to the Land: Immigration and Settlement in 16th Century Erez-Israel*, pp. 95–172, and chapter 2 of this study.

16. The influences went both ways. Jose Faur notes, "Many of the conversos had joined the clergy and occupied positions of power and prestige within the Church, in the academic world and the world of letters. Knowingly or unknowingly, these 'new Christians' were now introducing concepts and perspectives that were shaped by Jewish tradition, thus undermining the world of 'old Christians'." Faur, *In the Shadow of History* (Albany, N.Y.: SUNY Press, 1992), p. 30. Faur does not discuss the opposite scenario, that is, new Christians again becoming Jews and bringing with them Christian ideas that became part of Judaism. For this and other examples, see Miriam Bodian, *Hebrews of the Portuguese Nation: Conversos and Community in Early Modern Amsterdam*, pp. 100–103. Interestingly, while it is true that in rabbinic literature circumcision is not related to original sin, in Kabbala it surely is. See Elliot R. Wolfson, "Circumcision and the Divine Name: A Study in the Transmission of Esoteric Doctrine," *Jewish Quarterly Review* 78 (1987): 77–112.

17. The extent to which Lurianic Kabbala becomes intermingled with Christian sources is more easily determined in the 17th century, when Renaissance humanism served as another intellectual nexus between Judaism and Christianity. See, for example, in David Ruderman, *The World of a Renaissance Jew: The Life and Thought of Abraham ben Mordecai Farissol* (Cincinnati, Ohio: HUC Press, 1981); Moshe Idel, "Differing Conceptions of Kabbalah in the Early Seventeenth Century," in I. Twesky, B. Septimus, eds., *Jewish Thought in the Seventeenth Century* (Cambridge: Harvard University Press, 1987), pp. 152, 153; and Modena's *Ari Nohem*, p. 96, cited in Idel idem., p. 168. In Sabbateanism this becomes a crucial issue. For example, Scholem discusses the extent to which Christians used Kabbala as a way of interpreting the sin of Adam. See Scholem, *Sabbatei Sevi* (Princeton, N.J.: Princeton University Press, 1973), p. 77.

18. Bezalel Safran puts it this way: "To identify for a given writer the state from which Adam fell is to reconstruct that writer's conception of the ideal human being and the ideal human condition. This idea will be found to be all-pervasive in that writer's thought system. . . . At a minimum, such a scheme provides a helpful perspective on the matter. At best, it may provide the key to his thought." Safran, "Rabbi Azriel and Nahmanides: Two Views of the Fall of Man," p. 75. On mitzvot as the antidote for Adam's sin, see b.T. Kiddushin 30b: "The Holy One said to Israel, My child, I created the evil inclination, and I created Torah as its antidote. If you busy yourselves with Torah, you will not be given over to its power." The implied correlation between "the evil inclination" and Adam's sin is replete in rabbinic literature. Moreover, Christians were known to make the correlation between *originale paccatum*, or original sin, and the evil inclination. For example, see the 13th-century Dominican, Raymond Martini, as cited and discussed in Jeremy Cohen, "Original Sin and the Evil Inclination—A Polemicists' Appreciation of Human Nature," *Harvard Theological Review* 73, nos. 3–4 (1980): 495–520. Martini is discussed on pp. 496–499.

19. While the sexual nature of the sin is common, almost canonical, in rabbinic sources and later in the Zohar, Luria adds another dimension widening the transgressive nature of the act. See LiT, p. 18a, "Adam ha-Rishon slept with his wife while she was a menstruate and during the week (instead of waiting

until Shabbat)." On talmudic sources, see b.т. Shabbat 146a; b.т. Yebamot 103b; and b.т. Avodah Zara 22b; and see also Zohar 3.231a.

20. Scholem, *Major Trends*, pp. 245–286; and idem. "The Exile from Spain" [Hebrew] in *Devarim b-Go*, vol. 1, pp. 262–269. Idel has challenged Scholem's historiosophic assumption in *Messianic Mystics*, pp. 154–182, but does not deny a strong messianic impulse in 16th-century Kabbala. Neither places much emphasis on the converso phenomenon and the messianism/millenarianism that existed in that community. On this, see Matt Goldish, "Patterns in Converso Messianism," in *Millenarianism and Messianism in Early Modern European Culture*, in M. Goldish and R. Popkin, eds. (Dordrecht, The Netherlands: Kluwer Academic Publishers, 2001), vol. 1, pp. 41–64.

21. See Moshe Idel, "On the History of the Term *Zimsum* in Kabbala and Scholarship" [Hebrew], *Mekharei Yerushalayim* 10 (1992): 59–112.

22. On the correlation between the *zimzum* myth and original sin, see Scholem, *Major Trends*, p. 279. This is made explicit in SeLi, 3b, "The vessels descended twice. The first time they descended by themselves as they were not able to hold the great light. The second time they were forced to descend because of Adam's sin." Cf. my "Origin and the Overcoming of the Beginning: *Zimzum* as a Trope of Reading in Post-Lurianic Kabbala," in *Beginning/Again: Toward a Hermeneutic of Jewish Texts* (New York: Seven Bridges, 2002), pp. 163–214; and E. R. Wolfson, "Divine Suffering and the Hermeneutics of Reading: Philosophical Reflections on Lurianic Mythology," in R. Gibbs and E. R. Wilson, eds., *Suffering Religion* (London: Routledge, 2002), pp. 101–162.

23. For a preliminary discussion, see Isaiah Tishby, *Torat ha-Ra ve-ha-Kelippah* (Jerusalem: Magnus, 1982), p. 91.

24. An exploration as to the possible correlation between the Lurianic second *zimzum* and the Christian second coming is a desideratum.

25. This will be discussed at length in the next chapter. On conversion and messianism more generally, see Alan Segal, "Messianism and Conversion: Outline for a New Approach," in J. Charlesworth, ed., *The Messiah* (Minneapolis: Fortress, 1987), pp. 296–340.

26. See EH Gate 8, chapter 3. Cf. the discussion of this text in E. R. Wolfson, "Divine Suffering and the Hermeneutics of Reading," p. 131. Wolfson notes that the death of the Kings of Edom is inextricably tied to Adam's seminal emission, "an offense that is not fully rectified except by the coming of the Messiah." Cf. idem. p. 159 n. 169.

27. There are important exceptions. Alan Cooper analyzes a similar exegetical move by the 16th-century Jewish exegete Ephraim of Luntshits. See Cooper, "A Medieval Jewish Version of Original Sin," esp. p. 452.

28. On Paul and original sin, see Henri Blocher, *Original Sin: Illuminating the Riddle* (Grand Rapids, Mich.: Erdmanns, 1987), pp. 63–82.

29. Gary Anderson, *The Genesis of Perfection* (Louisville, Ky.: Westminster John Knox), pp. 209–210.

30. The universalist nature of Paul's and subsequent versions of early Christianity is now under revision. See Denise Buell, "Rethinking the Relevance of Race for Early Christian Self-Definition," *Harvard Theological Review* 94, no. 4 (2001): 449–476; and idem. "Race and Universalism in Early Christianity," *Journal of Early Christian Studies* 10, no. 4 (2002): 429–468. Cf. George W. E. Nickelsburg, "The Incarnation: Paul's Solution to the Universal Human Predicament," in Burger A. Pearson, ed., *The Future of Early Christianity: Essays in Honor of Helmut Koester* (Minneapolis: Fortress, 1991), pp. 348–357.

31. See variants in b.T. Yebamot 103b and b.T. Avodah Zara 22b. This observation about the Zohar's rewriting of the talmudic text is discussed in Alan Cooper, "A Medieval Jewish Version of Original Sin": 445–450.

32. For a Lurianic interpretation, see his comment to Zohar Idra Raba cited in ZHR, p. 73d and a more lengthy interpretation in ZHR, pp. 75b–d.

33. Zohar 1.52b. I borrowed freely from Cooper's lucid translation in "A Medieval Jewish Version of Original Sin": 448. Cf. SeG, p. 3. Vital reads the mitzvah of procreation and the antidote to the sin, both of Adam and the calf in that, "by means of it [procreation] one brings holy souls out from *kelipot.*" There are other kabbalistic positions in this period of kabbalistic activity that offer alternative erasures of Adam's sin. See, for example, Joseph ibn Gikitillia, *Sha'arei Orah* 1, pp. 66–68 and Jonathan Garb, *Manifestations of Power* [Hebrew] (Jerusalem: Magnus), pp. 101, 102.

34. This rabbinic dictum becomes the dominant position in the Zohar. See Zohar 1.36b; 84b–85a; and 202b–203a. For more sources, see Tishby, *Wisdom of the Zohar,* pp. 382–385, and the discussion in E. R. Wolfson, "Divine Suffering and the Hermeneutics of Reading," pp. 116 and 117. See especially Zohar 1.126a where the Zohar makes a correlation between magic and sorcery, which is only found in women, and the insemination of Eve.

35. The correlation between Sinai and Adam's sin is explicit in ShP, p. 22b (bottom): "The secret of this passage [b.T. Sanhedrin 146a] is that the Israelites in Egypt had not yet rectified the sin of Adam and the sins they committed in the generation of the flood and the Tower of Babel and Sodom. . . ." The text continues that Moses had to complete the rectification of Abel and Jethro and the rectification of Cain before the serpent's poison would disappear and they could stand at Sinai. Here it appears that Sinai does not erase the poison but is its culmination. Cf. Isaiah Horowitz, *Shenei Luhot ha-Brit,* 1:92.

36. The Shabbat version does inquire about converts who, it suggests, did not stand at Sinai.

37. See b.T. Yevamot 103b. Cf. b.T. Avodah Zara 22b; and b.T. Shabbat 145b–146a. Underlying this is the rabbinic idea that gentiles do not contain a human soul like Jews. See Genesis Raba 34:13. This is sometimes relegated only to idolaters (see Ezek. 34:31), but the distinction between idolaters and gentiles more generally in rabbinic literature is complicated.

38. See SeL p. 7b "*vayehi Adam.*" Luria suggests, following Tikkunei Zohar 110b, that the word *bereshit* is divided to read *bara* (BaR) *sheit* (ShYT). The second word alone means six. The two first letters of the second half of the word (*shin, yud*) represent the six (*shin, sheit*) hand breaths of Moses' tablets, and the *yud* (10) the Ten Commandments. Thus creation was completed at Sinai. *Shin tav* (ת ש) without the *yud* (י) spells the name of Adam's third son, Seth, who had the potential to fix the sin of his father but needed the *yud* that came, through Moses, at Sinai. However, when Moses broke the tablets, seeing the sin of the calf, the *yud* departed and what was left was *shin tav* or *Sheit*, Adam's son's incomplete name. As a *gilgul* of Seth and Abel, Moses momentarily rectified their souls and this prepared the world for the final rectification of Adam's sin. However, the sin of the calf destroyed that moment in Moses' and Israel's history.

39. One modern argument for the position of Pelagius can be found in Elaine Pagel's *Adam, Eve, and the Serpent* (New York: Random House, 1988). Cf. Anderson, *The Genesis of Perfection,* pp. 64–67, and Peter Brown, *Augustine of Hippo: A Biography* (Berkeley: University of California Press, 2000), pp. 390–399.

40. On the calf narrative and its connection to Genesis 3, see Gary Ander-

son, *The Genesis of Perfection*, pp. 205–207. Cf. Cooper, "A Medieval Version of Original Sin," pp. 448–450. See Zohar Hadash on Ruth, p. 83a. Zohar Hadash argues that the sin of the serpent disappeared "when Song of Songs was revealed to the world" (83a bottom).

41. I think one can see this in the way the Zohar envisions itself as the corrective to the Torah. By corrective I simply mean that the Zohar offers dimensions of revelation that are inaccessible in other Torah texts. See, for example, Zohar 2.99a ff. Cf. the discussion in R. Kalonymous Kalman Shapira, *Hakhsharat ʿAvreikhim* (Jerusalem, 1962), pp. 31, 32.

42. Midrash Raba to Numbers, 4:20 and Yalkut Shemoni to Exodus 17:261.

43. ShG, intro. 33, pp. 255, 256.

44. This can be seen in many places in the Zohar, particularly regarding the virtuosi's ability to augment the feminine in prayer. See the rereading of Psalm 103:20 in Zohar 3.191a; Idel's discussion in *Kabbalah and Eros*, p. 215; Liebes, *Studies in the Zohar*, pp. 46–47; and Wolfson, *Venturing Beyond* (New York: Oxford University Press, 2006), pp. 214, 215, and n. 101. This became particularly popular in the 16th century. See Yehuda Hayat's *Minhat Yehuda* (Mantua, 1558; written in 1498), introduction, and more generally in Elior, "Messianic Expectations," *Revue de Etudes Juives* 145 (1986): 35–38.

45. Luria's picture is quite a bit darker than that of the Zohar. In SeG, "Sod Hibuk ha-Kever," p. 105, we read, "No person is even saved from the poison of the serpent until the messianic days. Even those that die with the 'kick of the snake' [that is, without sin] still retain the 'poison of the serpent'."

46. The relationship of conversos to Protestantism as subverting their Catholic oppressors may be relevant here. On this, see H. H. Ben Sasson, "The Reformation in Contemporary Jewish Eyes," *Israel Academy of Science and Humanities* (1970): 4–12.

47. But see Elliot Wolfson, "Ontology, Alterity, and Kabbalistic Anthropology," *Exemplaria* 12 (2000), p. 138. "I do not think it would be far off the mark in saying the aggadic myth (b.T. Yevamot 103b) comes remarkably close to the conception of original sin enunciated in Christian tradition, for the claim it makes is that the ontological status of humanity was changed with the insemination of Eve by the serpent. The antidote to this seminal pollution is Torah, the efficacy of which will be fully realized only in the time of the messiah when the evil force in the world will be completely eradicated and non-Jews will be purified in the manner that Jews were purified at Sinai." While it is true that the full disclosure of Torah must wait for the messianic era, it seems to me the Zohar's position that the sin of the golden calf is a replay of the sin in the garden makes an even stronger case for original sin (still by implication) that emerges explicitly later in Luria.

48. Paul's conversion stands at the center of his whole approach to Christ. See 1 Corinthians 15:9. More generally, see Alan Segal, *Paul the Convert: The Apostolate and Apostasy of Saul the Pharisee* (New Haven, Conn.: Yale University Press, 1992), esp. pp. 117–149. On the necessity of incarnation as the solution to original sin in Paul, see George Nickelsburg, "The Incarnation: Paul's Solution to the Universal Predicament," pp. 348–357.

49. See Lawrence Fine, *Physician of the Soul* (Stanford, Calif.: Stanford University Press, 2003), pp. 178–186. Another manifestation of the popularity of these ideas in a conversion community can be found in the converso participation in Sabbateansim, in the mid to late 1600s. Conversos seemed to be disproportionately attracted to Sabbateanism, contributing to the strength of the movement. See, for example, Richard Popkin, "R. Nathan Shapiro's Visit to

Amsterdam in 1650," *Dutch History* I (1984): 185–205; Jacob Barnai, "The Development of Community Organizational Structures: The Case of Izmir," in *Jews, Turks, Ottomans* (Syracuse, N.Y.: Syracuse University Press, 2002), pp. 40–42; and most recently Matt Goldish, *The Sabbatean Prophets* (Cambridge: Harvard University Press, 2004), esp. pp. 138–140.

50. The case of Jacob Zemah (17th-century Jerusalem) is instructive. Zemah was an important editor of Lurianic texts who was born and raised a Christian and reentered Judaism in his late teens. On Zemah, see Gershom Scholem, "The Life of R. Jacob Zemah, His Works and Writings" [Hebrew], *Keriat Sefer* 26, no. 2 (1950): 185–194.

51. Most prominently, see Gershom Scholem, *Major Trends in Jewish Mysticism*, pp. 244–286. Four recent and important exceptions to this rule are (1) Elliot Wolfson, "Weeping, Death, and Spiritual Descent," in J. Collins and M. Fishbane, eds., *Death, Ecstasy, and Other Worldly Journeys* (Albany, N.Y.: SUNY Press, 1995), pp. 207–247; (2) Lawrence Fine's *Physician of the Soul: Healer of the Cosmos*, esp. pp. 7–14; (3) Yehuda Liebes, "Two Young Roes of a Doe" [Hebrew], *Mekharei Yerushalayim* 10 (1992): 113–170; and, most recently, (4) Menahem Kallus, "The Theurgy of Prayer in the Lurianic Kabbala," especially his comments on the Scholem/ Tishby school on pp. 30–70. All these attempt, in different ways, to revise Scholem's basic approach to the Lurianic school. Cf. Pinhas Giller, *Reading the Zohar* and my "From Theosophy to Midrash: Lurianic Exegesis and the Garden of Eden," pp. 37–75. Scholem does discuss Adam's sin briefly in *Major Trends*, pp. 279–281, and later in *Kabbala*, pp. 162–165, but it is not a major theme in his writings on Luria. Isaiah Tishby's *Torat ha-Ra ve-ha-Kelippah be-Kabbalat ha-Ari*, is to date the only full length scholarly work in Hebrew on Lurianic Kabbala (excluding Meroz and Kallus's unpublished dissertations) that deals extensively with Adam's sin but does not engage in a systematic analysis. Rather, it provides a schematic overview based largely on *'Etz Hayyim*. See idem., pp. 91–104. He does not address the issue of original sin at all and does not enter into a discussion about the comparative implications of Lurianic doctrine. Fine's *Physician of the Soul* deals with Adam's sin in a circumspect way, discussing it only as it relates to the larger metaphysical system. On pp. 142–144, he does discuss the fall and even mentions original sin in passing but does not explore the extent to which this doctrine is, in fact, a deep rendering of original sin. See especially his comment on p. 152.

52. See my "From Theosophy to Midrash," pp. 37–75.

53. The two-volume *Torat ha-Gilgul* includes older editions of both of these works plus some of the classic commentaries.

54. Menahem Kallus's recent dissertation argues that, in fact, the human (and earthly) correlation to the divine is far more complex in the Lurianic system than either Scholem and Tishby claimed. The latter argued that Luria's metaphysics was highly theistic, breaking from the more pantheistic system of Cordovero and earlier emanationists. Kallus exhibits how a close and wide-lens reading of Luria's corpus shows Luria to be far less theistic and more pantheistic than previously thought. See Kallus, "The Theurgy of Prayer in the Lurianic Kabbala," pp. 26–72.

55. For example, see Gershom Scholem, "The Concept of the Astral Body," in J. Neugroschel, trans., *On the Mystical Shape of the Godhead* (New York: Schocken, 1991), pp. 251–273.

56. Lurianic causality is surely a fundamental part of the system, and a careful study of this phenomenon is a desideratum in Luria scholarship. That is,

the notion of *mayyim nukvin* (feminine waters) through *yihud* (union) rising to initiate the descent of *mayyim dekhurin* (masculine waters) is a backbone of its metaphysical system.

57. See Rachel Elior, "The Metaphorical Relation between Man and God and the Significance of Visionary Reality in Lurianic Kabbala" [Hebrew], in *Mekhkarei Yerushalayim* 10 (1992): 47–57.

58. For a general discussion of this in kabbalistic literature, see Scholem "The Concept of the Astral Body," in *The Mystical Shape of the Godhead*. I deal with this issue in depth in the final chapter of this study. Cf. Charles Mopsik, "Genesis 1:26–27: L'Image de Dieu, le couple humain et le statut de la femme chez les premiers cabalists," in *Le sexe des âmes* (Paris: Editions de L'Eclat, 2003), pp. 149–217. In English, see Mopsik, *Sex of the Soul* (Los Angeles: Cherub, 2005), pp. 75–114.

59. See, for example, in Luther's *Lectures on Romans*, pp. 302 and 304. On earlier patristic doctrines, see Henri Rondert, *Original Sin: The Patristic and Theological Background* (Shannon, Ireland: Ecclesia, 1972). More cursory discussions can be found in Tatha Wiley, *Original Sin*, esp. pp. 37–55.

60. ShMR, p. 33d. It is interesting that this text refers to both Adam and Eve as distinct, as if they were separate. This is quite uncharacteristic. Cf. ShMR, p. 9a/b; LiT, p. 13; ShG, intro. 31, p. 221; and SeG, chapter 31, p. 61. But see ShG, intro. 32, p. 244, where Vital states that there are various "new souls" that Adam did not merit and thus were not included in Adamic sin and not in need of any *tikkun*. Cf LiT, p. 51a. Cf. ShMR, p. 54d which states: "the earthly Adam hints to (or includes) the ten sephirot of ʿazilut including all of ʿazilut together from the highest ʿarikh ʿanpin until the end of *nukva* of *zeir ʿanpin*." Cf. EH, Gate 16, chapter 5 and Kallus, "The Theurgy of Prayer," pp. 141 and 142.

61. Thus, as Elliot Wolfson has noted, when the Zohar refers generically to *bar nash* (the human) the intention is usually the circumcised (that is, male) Jew. See Elliot Wolfson, "Ontology, Alterity, and Kabbalistic Anthropology," *Exemplaria* 12 (2000): 141, 142, 145; and *Venturing Beyond*, pp. 4, 5 and esp. n. 15 where Wolfson takes on many of the apologetic universalist readings of Kabbala on the question of the human and the Jew. On the Zohar's notion of the sin transforming the nature of Adam, see Zohar 3.83a (bottom) and 83b. The notion that only man, and not woman, is created in the image of God is made quite explicit in I Corinthians 11:7: *For a man should not have his head covered, for he is the image and reflection of God; but woman is the reflection of man.*

62. ShG, intro. 31, pp. 233, 234.

63. ShP, p. 4a. Cf. LiT, p. 16. *Likkutei Torah* also states that animals can rectify their sin by being sacrifices. However, they sinned again in the flood, as it states: *for all flesh has corrupted its ways on earth* (Gen. 6:12). This is interpreted by b.T. Sanhedrin 108a as referring to the animals who were mating with other species.

64. Rashi's comment to Genesis 6:12 is built on the linguistic use of *all flesh had corrupted its ways on earth* (Gen. 6:12) in addition to what we read in 6:5: *The Lord saw how great was man's wickedness on earth.* But see Nahmanides' critique of Rashi's use of Sanhedrin 83a as plain-sense reading.

65. This is made explicit in LiT, p. 13. See PEH, "The Gate of Rosh Ha-Shana 1," where Luria suggests that the days between Rosh Ha-Shana and the culmination of Sukkot (*Shemini ʿAzeret*) contain the power to begin the process of rectification for the coming year. However, this is all equivocal and the sin cannot, ultimately, be rectified without messianic salvation. A similar trope is

repeated regarding the Kiddush on Shabbat Eve. See EH, Gate 6, chapter 8; and Kallus, "The Theurgy of Prayer," p. 152.

66. See Zohar 3.83a/b. For a Lurianic reading of this passage, see LiT, p. 16a.

67. ShP, p. 3b (bottom). This is likely an extension of the rabbinic notion of Adam "seeing from one end of the world to the other." See Genesis Raba 12:6.

68. But see SeG, chapter 35, p. 70; and ZHR, pp. 82d, 83a where Vital states that "there are some [souls] that were not included in Adam. These are the secret of new souls." This source appears to suggest that there were/are souls who were not present during Adam's sin. In other texts they were initially present in Adam (as Adam includes all souls) but they departed immediately before the sin and thus do not inherit the blemish of original sin.

69. SeG, chapter 2, p. 3. Vital here is explicit that mitzvot cannot complete the separation of good and evil that was mixed by the sin. "This is the meaning of the notion that the 'evil inclination' was created with Adam. All one's days, one must strive to separate the evil that is mixed in with it [the good] through Torah and mitzvot. In any event, he will never succeed in separating them completely. Only death separates the evil completely." See also ShMR, p. 37a, "Come now and see what damage Adam's sin did in deeply drawing down the worlds such that it is impossible [for the human] to raise them up [to where they were before] even on *minha* (the afternoon service) of Shabbat."

70. SeG, "Sod Hibuk ha-Kever," p. 105.

71. In ShP p. 20c we read, "When Adam sinned all those souls from him descended to the *kelipot* and were divided into the 70 nations. . . ." We know from ShG that the souls in Adam were divided into three basic parts, only the latter of which descended into the *kelipot*. This text apparently refers to those souls who would become the gentile nations. Thus, at least here, all human souls were encompassed in Adam before the sin *in potentia* and, as a result of the sin, the seventy nations were born, that is, born in sin.

72. SeG, chapter 31, pp. 71, 72 and chapter 35, p. 80. Cf Tikkunei Zohar, tikun 69, p. 112.

73. ShG, intro. 28, p. 205. Aaron Agasi adds an important caveat to this statement in his gloss Bnei Aaron #3: "This refers to all the worlds . . . but those places that directly relate to one's son it is the opposite. One is obligated to fix the portion related to his soul that is connected to Adam. That is the very reason he came to the world. . . ." Cf. SeG, chapter 22, that full rectification will not occur in the messianic era but only with resurrection. This notion of original sin also appears in Sabbatean literature a century later. See, for example, R. Elijah ha-Kohen ha-Ittamari of Izmir, *Midrash Eliyahu* (Warsaw, 1878), p. 11a, cited in Bezalel Naor, *Post-Sabbatean Sabbateanism* (Spring Valley, N.Y.: Orot, 1999), p. 36. R. Moshe Hayyim Luzatto writes that Moses destroyed Amalek but not the "remnant" (*roshem*) of Amalek, which is internal to Israel (Joshua) and continues to weaken them. The commandment to blot out "the rememberance of Amalek" (*zekher Amalek*) is to destroy the remnant of Amalek that exists even after Moses destroyed Amalek. See Ramhal, "Kinat ha-Shem Zivaot" in *Ginzei Ramhal* (Bnei Brak, 1984), p. 108.

74. This was the result of the cosmic rupture, *shvirah*. See Tishby, *Torat ha-Ra*, p. 91.

75. But see SeG, "Sha‘ar ha-Nevuah," p. 100. "Know that all souls, whether new souls or old, were created, at the time of creation, with a back-to-back union. After Adam sinned the *shekhina* was exiled and enveloped in the *kelipot*. All the souls were exiled with her and descended below into the *kelipot*. When a righteous

person [I think this refers to a kabbalist or one initiated into the esoteric teaching] performs a mitzvah or makes a contemplative unification (*yihud be-kavannah gemura*) he can raise a new soul from the *kelipot* and elevate it through the secret of the feminine waters (*mayim nukvin*) which will result in a face-to-face union." This seems to imply that the sin was not solely responsible for humanity's depraved state but that all souls, at the moment of creation, were already deficient. This text requires further analysis and clarification. Cf. Tishby, *Torat ha-Ra*, p. 91.

76. See EH, Gate 39, Drush 1 where face-to-face unions are possible, albeit temporal.

77. On this, see also LiT, p. 88b where this is used to discuss the soul of Balaam as rooted in the *kelipot* that attached themselves to the face-to-face union below.

78. SeLi, p. 5b.

79. SeLi, p. 3a (bottom), b (top).

80. SeLi, p. 3a.

81. See, for example, Tikkunei Zohar, tikun 69, p. 116a.

82. SeLi, p. 3a/b. Cf. SeD, p. 173a. On the apparent superfluous repetition of the word *Adam* that serves as the basis of Luria's reading, see Reuven Kimelman, "The Seduction of Eve and the Exegetical Politics of Gender," *Biblical Interpretations* 4, no. 1 (1996): 1–39.

83. See, for example, R. Moses Nahmanides, *Sefer ha-Vikuah*, in *Kitvei Ramban*, vol. 1, p. 310. Cf. Bezalel Safran, "Rabbi Azriel and Nahmanides: Two Views of the Fall of Man," in *Rabbi Moses Nahmanides [Ramban]: Explorations of His Literary of Religious Virtuosity*, pp. 75–106.

84. See EH, Gate 39, chapter 1. Cf. Tishby, *Torat ha-Ra*, p. 94.

85. ShMR, p. 35d. Cf. SeG, chapter 16, p. 33. In SeG Vital notes that if Adam had not sinned he would have remained immortal and, in order for him to become mortal, he had to attain a portion of the lowest realm, *ʿasiah*. This was done by a comprehensive descent of his entire body.

86. The Zohar claims *Etz ha-Daʿat* was from the world of *yezeriah*. See Zohar 1.27a. The continuation of this text suggests that *yezeriah* of the Zohar is before the sin. The tree subsequently descends to *ʿasiah*.

87. This is true even on the afternoon of Shabbat considered to be the time when Adam reaches the highest place in the cosmos. See ShMR, pp. 38a and 80: "Since the sin caused a deep descent of the worlds, it is impossible for us now to elevate the worlds, even on *minha* of Shabbat." *Minha* on Shabbat is understood to be the highest realm humans can occupy. Cf. LiT, p. 13a/b and ShK. "Gate of Keriat Shma," chapter 1, p. 19b/c. On Shabbat as restitution, see Kallus, "The Theurgy of Prayer," pp. 152ff.

88. See as described in Genesis Raba 14:1 and Midrash Tanhuma 1.

89. This notion has its source in Genesis Raba and more explicitly in Zohar 1.36b (top) and 2.229b; these state that before the sin, Adam's "skin" was made of light (*ʾohr*) and after the sin it transformed to flesh (*ʿor*), a wordplay replacing the *alef*, in the first case, with an *ayin* in the second. Cf. SeLi, p. 7c "vayehi Hanokh."

90. ShP, p. 3d and EH 49:4.

91. See ShP, 2b–d; LiT, p. 15b; ZHR, p. 76a and more extensively ShG, intro. 32, p. 244, Intro. 33, pp. 252ff and SeG, chapter 6, p. 17. Here it understood that those "new souls" did not take part in the sin as implied in the biblical words, *evil cannot abide with you* (Ps. 5:5). Note that the phrase in Psalms is referring to God, and Vital turns it so that it refers to the soul that was not part of Adam's sin. This may be significant in that such a soul is, in effect, divine be-

cause it has sinned and thus is not mortal. Cf. SeG, chapter 35, p. 70 for another rendering of new souls.

92. See ShG, intro. 29, p. 218; intro. 31, p. 237; ShP p. 4a.; and ShG, intro 33, p. 252. "Enoch, who is Metatron, took the *neshama* of *zihara 'ilah* and Cain took the *nefesh* of *zihara 'ilah.*" Cf. SeG, chapter 15, p. 31 and idem. "Sha'ar ha-Nevuah," p. 95.

93. SeL, p.6b. Cf. ShG, intro. 29, p. 216, intro. 31, pp. 239, 242; SeG, chapter 22, p. 40.

94. SeLi, p. 8a.

95. LiT, p. 15b.

96. See ibid., p. 19a on Moses' failed messianic mission. "Enoch achieved the level of *hayye* and Moses only the level of *neshama*. But Messiah will reach the level of *yehida* [the highest level]. Moses would have achieved the status of angel [as did Enoch] if he had not sinned in trying to save and fix the *'erev rav*, which he failed to do. . . ." Thus the messiah is a figure who does transcend original sin and fixes humanity in that light.

97. The Christological resonances of these passages are worth exploring. That is, it seems the possibility does exist that a human can inherit this pre-sin Adamic soul and, if so, transcend death.

98. On the detailed damages done to the cosmos and the material world as a result of the sin, see EH, Gate 48, chapter 3 and Tishby, *Torat ha-Ra*, p. 99. In the Lurianic system it is more difficult to divide the physical from the spiritual than it is in more neoplatonic systems. Therefore, in discussing the fall, earlier kabbalists more influenced by neoplatonic doctrine could easily separate the soul from original sin, relegating the consequence of the sin to the degraded material body. Regarding Azriel of Gerona, Bezalel Safran notes: "A clear pattern emerges from R. Azriel's notions concerning the beginning and the end of time. The body is a hindrance to spirituality; it is a consequence of original sin and must be overcome if the ideal state is to be retrieved. Since the soul failed to achieve union with the divine in the ideal disembodied state, governed by the strict justice in Binah, it should now do better in a physical state, governed by justice and compassion." Bezalel Safran, "Rabbi Azriel and Nahmanides: Two Views of the Fall of Man," p. 81. In Luria, the soul, and not just the body, is implicated in the sin and, thus, no part of the human being escapes unscathed. On R. Azriel and neoplatonism more generally, see Alexander Altmann, "The Motif of the Shells in Azriel of Gerona," *Journal of Jewish Studies* 9 (1958): 73–80.

99. See ShG, intro. 31, p. 239. See Zohar 1.36b; and SeLi, p. 7d.

100. SeG, chapter 31, p. 63.

101. See SeG, chapter 16, pp. 31, 32.

102. See SeD, pp. 160–163; and ZHR, pp. 65d, 66a.

103. See SeG, chapter 22, p. 40. "After the sin, *nefesh, ruah,* and *neshama* of *'azilut*, called *zihara 'ilah*, departed from Adam as did every *keter* of all ten *sephirot* of all four worlds."

104. ShP, 4a.

105. As we will see, this second level of *halato shel 'olam* is divided into two distinct dimensions, the higher of which is inherited by Cain and Abel. See ShG, intro. 29, p. 218.

106. This undermines the basic claim of those who deny Judaism has a doctrine of original sin. See, for example, in S. S. Cohen, "Original Sin."

107. But see ZHR, p. 80c, d where Luria takes up the issue of repentance and its impact on original sin. There he argues that original sin is located in the

upper realms of the soul (*ruah* and above) and repentance generally has an impact on sins done in the lower realm of the *nefesh*. However, ascetic acts, the Day of Atonement, and death can purify sins of this upper realm but still not purify the soul from the poison of the serpent that was implanted in Eve.

108. SeG, "Sod Hibuk ha-Kever" p. 103. See SeG, chapter 1, pp. 1 and 2 (top). "At the time of Sinai the poison was erased and death was overcome. This is the meaning of *herut ʿal ha luhot*, they were liberated from death and subjugation to all nations. Death and the other nations only have dominion over Israel because of the evil portion that is in them [that is, in Israel]. However, at the time of the golden calf, good and evil were once again mixed in Israel, the poison returned, and death retuned like before. But see Zohar 1.168a and Nahmanides' comment to Numbers 19:2, where he states that one who dies with the "kick of the serpent" does not attain the status of defilement of the dead (*tumaʿat meit*). Cf. Tosefot to b.T. Baba Meziah 114b s.v. "mahu."

109. On the doctrine of *gilgul* in 16th-century Safed more generally, see Scholem, "Le-Heker Torat ha-Gilgul be-Kabbala be-Meah ha-Shelosh 'Esre," *Tarbiz* 16 (1955–45): 135ff; "*Gilgul:* The Transmigration of Souls," in *On the Mystical Shape of the Godhead*, pp. 197–250; Rachel Elior, "The Doctrine of Transmigration in *Galya Raza*," reprinted in *Essential Papers in Kabbala*, pp. 243–269; Yehuda Liebes, "Gilgula," in *Perakim be-Milon Shere ha-Zohar*, pp. 291–327; Dina Ripsman Elyon, *Reincarnation in Jewish Mysticism and Gnosticism* (Lewiston, Maine: Edwin Mellen, 2003); Yigal Arikha, *Reincarnation: Reality that Exceeds All Imagination* [Hebrew] (Kefar Saba, Israel: Aryeh Nir, 2001); Rami Shekalim, *Torat ha-Nefesh ve-ha-Gilgul b'Reshit ha-Kabbala* (Tel Aviv: Rubin Moss, 1998); Avraham Amos, *Be-gilgul Hozer: Gilgul in Kabbala and Other Sources* [Hebrew] (Israel, 1997); Dov Ber Pinson, *Reincarnation and Judaism: The Journey of the Soul* (Northvale, N.J.: Jason Aronson, 1999); Pinhas Giller, *Reading the Zohar* (Oxford: Oxford University Press, 2002), pp. 37–42; and Lawrence Fine, *Physician of the Soul*, pp. 304–358. *Gilgul* also played a prominent role in the antikabbalistic writings of Judah Aryeh Modena and Elijah del Medigo in the 17th century. On the controversy about *gilgul* in Kandia, for example, see Efrayim Gottlieb, *Studies in Kabbalistic Literature* [Hebrew], J. Hacker, ed. (Tel Aviv, 1976), pp. 370–396. On Modena's argument against the authenticity of *gilgul*, see Idel, "Different Conception of Kabbala in the Early 17th Century," pp. 160–162 and n. 119. Modena and others make use of Saadia Gaon's famous repudiation of *gilgul* in his *Emunot ve-Deʿot* 6:7. Cf. Hayyim Yerushalmi's discussion in *From Spanish Court to Italian Ghetto: Isaac Cardoso*, pp. 256–258 and Menahem Azaria D'Fano's *Gilgulei Neshamot* (Lemberg, 1865), reissued with the commentary "Me'ir 'Eyin" of Yeruham Leiner of Izbica (Jerusalem: Yarid Books, 1998). It should also be noted that *gilgul* played a prominent role in the writings of David ibn Zamra (RaDBaZ), Luria's teacher in Egypt who also immigrated to Safed. See, for example, the important distinction between *ʿibbur* and *gilgul* in his *Metsudat David*, p. 27d. Cf. Melila Helner, "*Gilgul* in the Kabbalistic Works of Rabbi David ben Zamra" [Hebrew], *Peʿamim* 43 (1990): 16–50. Most recently on this question from a wider historical lens, see Mark Verman, "Reincarnation and Theodicy: Traversing Philosophy, Psychology, and Mysticism," in *Beʿerot Yizhak: Studies in Memory of Isadore Twersky*, pp. 399–426.

110. On new souls, see ShG, intro. 12, pp. 111–117: 32; intro. 32, p. 244; and SeG, chapter 6, p. 15. Cf. Luria's commentary to "*Sabba de-Mishpatim*" in ZHR, pp. 63c, 83a–c. Note that the term *new soul* is used in various contexts. For example, souls whose roots are in Cain and Abel are called "new souls" juxta-

posed to those souls ("old souls") not rooted in Cain and Abel who cannot rise up to the level of *nefesh* of ʿ*azilut* (the root of Cain and Abel's soul). See ShG, intro. 35, p. 261 and ZHR, pp. 82d, 83a. In SeG, p. 17, we read that "new souls" are those few not included in Adam and the "old souls" are all souls included in Adam. In yet another version, we read, "Souls are divided into two general categories: first, new souls that were not a part of Adam, and second, old souls that were a part of Adam. New souls are also divided into two categories: first, those from the world of ʿ*azilut*. Second, those from [the three lower worlds] *yezeriah, beriah,* and ʿ*asiah*. The souls from this latter category were also embedded in the *kelipot* as a result of Adam's sin even though they were not enveloped in Adam." SeG, chapter 14, p. 28, chapter 35, p. 70 and chapter 35, p. 79.

111. This is most prominent in Paul, Romans 5. Cf. Romans 8:3 where Jesus is presented as a new Adam, one who did not sin. See Otfried Hofius, "The Adam-Christ Antithesis and the Law: Reflections on Romans 5:12–21," in James Dunn, ed., *Paul and the Mosaic Law* (Grand Rapids, Mich.: Eerdmanns, 2001), pp. 165–296; and Henri Blocher, *Original Sin,* pp. 68–81. Cf. C. E. B. Cranfield, *A Critical and Exegetical Commentary on the Epistle of the Romans* (Edinburgh: T&T Clark, 1975), vol. 1, p. 290: "We may assume that by the former statement Paul means that all other men (Jesus alone excepted) were constituted through sinners through Adam's misdeed in the sense that, sin having once obtained entry into human life through it, they all in their turns live sinful lives." For a discussion of the nature of the soul of the messiah in Lurianic Kabbala, see Yehuda Liebes, "Two Young Roes of a Doe: The Secret Sermon of Isaac Luria before His Death," pp. 122–126.

112. See, for example, in SeG, chapter 19, p. 38. "It is impossible to achieve the level of Adam before the sin. He achieved *neshama* of the *neshama* of *hokhma* of ʿ*azilut*. The Messiah will also achieve this. But Moses only achieved the *ruah* and the *neshama* of *zihara* ʿ*ilah*." Cf. LiT, p. 50.

113. For example, Alexander Altmann posits that *gilgul,* as a tool in the larger doctrine of tikun in Lurianic Kabbala, was important for Isaac Aboab's rejection of eternal punishment in his *Nishmat Hayyim,* a doctrine Altmann argues is influenced by the converso phenomenon. See Altmann, "The Eternality of Punishment," *Academy of Jewish Research: Proceedings* XL (1972), esp. 22 and 23. The use of *gilgul* was multifaceted, especially in the 16th century. See Rachel Elior, "The Doctrine of Transmigration in the Book *Galya Raza,*" in L. Fine, ed., *The Essential Papers in Kabbala* (New York: New York University Press, 1992).

114. It would appear that the entire Lurianic corpus is only concerned with the Jewish soul. See, for example, ZHR, p. 79d, "It is known that God only created the world for the sake of the souls of Israel. . . ." However, defining precisely what constitutes "the soul of Israel" is a more complex matter that will be taken up later in the chapter on Balaam and gentile prophecy.

115. SeG, chapter 3, p. 5. Cf. ShK, p. 1a.

116. B.T. Yevamot, 62a. It also serves as a foundation for the inverted conversion of Shabbetai Tzvi. That is, the notion of permeable boundaries and liminal space and identity (national/gender) is prominent in Lurianic teaching. See SeG, chapter 3, ShG, intro. 36.

117. In the case of ʿ*ibbur* it is different in that some instances of ʿ*ibbur* are solely to aid other souls already in the world.

118. SeG, chapter 35, p. 69.

119. Luria's two treaties on *gilgul,* redacted and edited by Hayyim Vital and others, are *Shaʿar ha-Gilgulim* and *Sefer ha-Gilgulim.* I used the 1990 Jerusalem

reprint of *Sha'ar ha-Gilgulim* with R. Shimon Agassi's Bnei Aaron. For *Sefer ha-Gilgulim* I used the 1986 Bnei Brak reprint. These two texts are collected in a two-volume collection, *Torat ha-Gilgul* (Jerusalem: Ahavat Shalom, 1982). This set contains both texts, Agassi's commentary, "Bnei Aaron," "Ha-Alot Aaron," R. Yehuda Padaya's "Megillat Setarim" on repentance, R Elijah Mani's gloss to *Sha'ar ha-Gilgulim*, "Mazkir Shalom," and R. Shimon Aggasi's "Khizyonot 'u Gilui Eliahyu."

120. Fine deals with Cain and Abel's sin in a circumspect way in a larger discussion about *gilgul* and Hayiim Vital. See Fine, *Physician of the Soul*, pp. 333–339.

121. An important exception to this is Rabbenu Bahya ibn Asher's "Commentary to the Torah," which revisits the Cain and Abel story numerous times, especially in the Moses narratives in Exodus. Given that Bahya was strongly influenced by Spanish Kabbala immediately preceding the Zohar, this may be the exception that proves the rule. We find numerous references to Cain in particular in Rashi and Nahmanides outside Genesis 4 but these references are still quite scant.

122. This is particularly true in one lengthy discussion in Tikkunei Zohar, tikun 69, pp. 100a–119b.

123. Given Rashi's commitment to a lack of chronology in the Torah (*"eyn mukdam u mukhar be-Torah"*) this bears no problem for his plain-sense meaning. For some examples, see Rashi on Genesis 6:3; 35:28; Exodus 19:11; 31:18; Leviticus 8:2; and Numbers 9:1.

124. Cf. Zohar 1.60b, 61a; Zohar Hadash on Ruth, p. 83b; and ShG, chapter 28, p. 202. See Zohar Hadash on Ruth, p. 79d, where it states explicitly that Cain and Abel were born outside the Garden of Eden.

125. This reading is implied in Targum Pseudo-Jonathan to Genesis. See *Targum Pseudo-Jonathan to the Pentateuch: Text and Concordance*, p. 5 cited in Wolfson, "Ontology," p. 137.

126. See, for example, EH, Gate 36, chapter 2.

127. There are many examples in late medieval and early modern Jewish literature that argue that Eve is more culpable than Adam. This approach largely centers on the biblical distinction (Lev. 12) between the birth of a son versus the birth of a daughter. On this, see Alan Cooper, "A Medieval Jewish Version of Original Sin," pp. 450–459.

128. ShK, "Drush 1 for Rosh Ha-Shana," p. 90c. The notion of the serpent impregnating Eve with Cain is articulated quite early in Targum Psuedo-Jonathan to Genesis 4:1.

129. Ibid. Cf. Zohar 1.14.

130. In SeG, chapter 30, p. 61 Vital offers another version of this statement: "while there are midrashim that disagree with this [that Cain and Abel were born after the sin] Zohar 3.77a agrees with our position. [According to the Zohar] the day Adam was created, he ate from the tree, copulated with Eve, and Cain and Abel were born."

131. See Zohar Hadash on Song of Songs, p. 63c where the Zohar suggests that Cain is from the serpent but his body is from Adam.

132. ShP, p. 2d, "blemish" #7 and #8.

133. ShP, p. 4c. For another similar version, see SeG, chapter 25, pp. 48 and 49.

134. See ShG, intro. 36, p. 279; and SeD, p. 150a.

135. Tikkunei Zohar circumvents this problem when it implies that Abel was born from a different ejaculation. See Tikkunei Zohar, tikun 69, p. 119a.

136. The separation of Adam from his wife after the death of Abel is a rabbinic

concept in origin. See Genesis Raba 20:11 and b.T. Eruvin 18b. It is developed in the Zohar as a leitmotif of Adam's sin. See Meir Benayahu, "Spirits of Harm and their Reparation" [Hebrew], in *Sefer Zikharon le-ha-Rav Yizhak Nissim* (Jerusalem: Yad ha-Rav Nissim, 1985), pp. 81–104; and Fine, *Physician of the Soul*, pp. 178–179.

137. LiT on Ezekiel, p. 123. Cf. Avraham David Azulai, *Hesed le-Avraham*, 4:52. See also Zohar Hadash on Ruth, p. 78c. "Rebbe opened and said: Adam had a soul to his soul; Eve just had a soul. Cain and Abel? Abel is from one seed from Adam with Eve that is called a holy spirit. Abel had an evil spirit from the left that is called 'mixed' (*kelayim*). It was confused and was not essential, the demonic that was not from Adam and Eve." The Zohar does not tell us the root of Abel's soul but one can surmise his soul-root is from the serpent. Luria puts Cain and Abel closer together, both being from Adam and Eve and the serpent. Luria rejects the utter demonization of Abel that the Zohar presents. The root of these 130 years can be found in b.T. Yevamot 28b. There, however, it is viewed as an act of heroism. "R. Meir said, Adam ha-Rishon was a righteous person (*hasid gadol*). When he saw he was responsible for [the] death [of Abel] he fasted for 130 years and separated from his wife 130, and boils grew on his skin for 130 years. . . ."

138. See SeD, p. 150b which states explicitly that Abel was born from a different union than Cain: "When Adam and Eve coupled to give birth to Abel, the *mayyin nukvin* of Rachel had already been completed with the birth of Cain."

139. On the description of the generation of the desert as *dor de'ah* (the generation of knowing), see Zohar 2.62b; Zohar Hadash, end of parshat Hukkat; "Sha'ar ha-Klalim" (printed in EH), chapter 11, pp. 9 a/b.

140. SeG, chapter 30, p. 71.

141. Lurianic Kabbala suggests that male masturbation is the most egregious sin. It is even more egregious than sexual union with a forbidden woman (*'arayot*) that results in *mamzerim* (that is, even sex with a married woman or blood relative!). Hence, it would make sense that original sin is, or at least includes, masturbation. See, for example, in ShK, "Drushei Layla" #7, pp. 56b–d. "In all of the prohibitions of the Torah, even the strictest, none really (*mamash*) produce demons (*mazikin*) like masturbation (*zera le-vatala*). Hence, it is even worse than one who has sex with a forbidden woman (*'arayot*) when she gives birth to physical *mamzerim* in this world. The truth is one who transgresses this prohibition is enveloped in demons who testify against him, but the emission of prohibitive seed is more grave." This notion filters into later Hasidic literature and is the occasion for one of the Baal Shem Tov's most provocative teachings on the recitation of Psalm 108 immediately before the commencement of Shabbat. See printed in Rivka Shatz-Uffenheimer's, *Hasidut ke-Mystica* (Jerusalem: Magnes, 1968), pp. 194–223. In English, see *Hasidism as Mysticism: Quietistic Elements in Hasidic Thought* (Princeton, N.J.: Princeton University Press, 1993), pp. 342–382.

142. A similar assertion is made about the seed that is the product of male–female union. See EH, "Sha'ar ha-Klalim," p. 9c and the chapter on Leviticus in this study.

143. Ezekiel is referred to as "son of Adam" throughout his prophetic book. See Ezekiel 2:1, 3, 6, 9:3:1, 3, 4, 10, 25. See LiT, p. 124; ShP, p. 46c,d; and SeD, p. 153b. The notion of spilled seed as creating lofty souls is also discussed in the soul origin of the ten martyrs of rabbinic literature as rooted in the seed emitted from the fingertips of Joseph during Potifar's seduction. See EH, Gate 31, chapter 2; ShG, intro. 26, 181f.; intro. 38. Cf. SeD, p. 150a (top).

144. LiT, ibid. "Therefore, Ezekiel is always called '*ben Adam*.' All other souls

are from Adam and Eve, from *zeir anpin* and *nukva*, but Ezekiel was from Adam alone, from the drop of a male seed without the feminine." Cain is also likened to this, as he contains the seed that preceded Adam's insemination of Eve. Cf. ShD, p. 149b: "When the *gevurot* go out first they do not establish their proper place and take the place of the *hasadim*. Hence they cannot yet pass over to the feminine (*nekava*). Therefore, they are pure masculinity (*zekharim gemurim*)."

145. ShG, intro. 38, pp. 202, 203.

146. See LiT, 18a; and my discussion of these and other sources in Lurianic Kabbala and Hasidism in *Hasidism on the Margin* (Madison: University of Wisconsin Press, 2004), pp. 124–137.

147. Op. cit.

148. Op. cit.

149. Tikkunei Zohar, p. 99b and Zohar Hadash on Ruth, p. 78d. The Zohar, in fact, likens Cain to the demonic and the serpent. Cf. Tikkunei Zohar, pp. 117a–119b.

150. According to SeL, p. 6c (bottom) Na'amah is Cain's twin–mate whom he wants to subjugate to the status of mistress by stealing Rachel from Abel. Cain says to Abel, "Take Leah [Abel's first twin] alone and I will take Rachel [Abel's second twin] and Na'amah [Cain's twin] will be a mistress [*pilegesh*]." On Na'amah as demonic, see Zohar 1.9b, 19b, 55b, 2.114b, 3.76b; Zohar Hadash, p. 19d; and Tikkunei Zohar, tikun 69, 119a.

151. SeG, chapter 26, p. 52. Cf. ShG, intro. 35, p. 273. SeLi, pp. 6c/d offers another reading. Cain is the embodiment of *parzuf* Jacob (the bottom half of *zeir anpin*) and Abel is Israel (the top half of *zeir anpin*). As the bottom half, Cain descends first and is also concealed. When Abel/Israel descends he does so with two mates, Rachel and Leah, Cain only having one twin called Na'amah. Cain claims that Rachel (*shekhina*—whose place is opposite the bottom half of *zeir anpin*) is rightfully his (as he occupies that space). Abel counters that God's will was that both should be his because "Rachel is rooted with me (Cain) in the higher sphere of *abba* and *ima*, that is from the power of *malkhut* of *abba*. From this rift we read, *and Cain rose up [to kill] Abel*."

152. See Genesis Raba 32:5; and Exodus Raba 31:17.

153. This is a paraphrase of Genesis 6:12, *for all flesh had corrupted its ways on earth*. Rashi, employing b.T. Sanhedrin, understands this in a sexual way, describing animals mating with animals of other species. Luria's turn of phrase gives it a meaning closer to masturbation, "*darkam*" (inferring "seed"), linking it to the sin of Er and Onan in Genesis 38:9. For a later use of this phrase, see Avraham Azulai, *Hesed le-Avraham* 4:52.

154. LiT, p. 124. Cf. SeLi, 6d; and SeD, p. 153b.

155. On Cain's sin being a sin of "*ervah*" or sexual misconduct, see Tikkunei Zohar, tikun 69, p. 119b.

156. On this, see my "From Theosophy to Midrash: Lurianic Exegesis and the Garden of Eden," and David Stern, *Parables in Midrash: Narrative and Exegesis in Rabbinic Literature* (Cambridge: Harvard University Press, 1991), pp. 4–45, and 227–232. Stern does not deal with Lurianic material but offers important observations about Sefer Bahir and the Zohar.

157. See Genesis Raba 22:7. The midrash constructs this as a quasi-halakhic argument, Cain invoking his right as a first-born, due a double portion. This is reminiscent of the rabbis' rendering of Korah's claim for the priesthood in Numbers.

158. On the importance of the eighteen wives in Lurianic Kabbala, see SeD, pp. 93–95; and ShM, "Parshat Shoftim," pp. 48b–51b.

159. SeG, chapter 27, p. 57.

160. These *malkhuyot* are the last female components of *parzufim* or *sephirot*. Hence, if a *parzuf* has ten *sephirot* it will have ten *malkhuyot*, one corresponding to each *sephirah*. "The influence of the *malkhuyot* of *abba* and *ima* emanate outside, as we see with Jacob (i.e., Rachel and Leah). They are two which are four: (1) the *malkhuyot* of *abba* which stays in its place (and serves as the last *sephirah* in *parzuf abba*); (2) the *malkhuyot* of *ima* in its place; (3) the *malkhuyot* of *abba* that is enveloped in *nezah, hod,* and *yesod* of *ima;* and (4) the *malkhuyot* of *ima* that emanates outward in the place of the knot of the head phylactery (the base of the skull) of *zeir anpin* and is called Leah, the wife of Jacob." SeG, chapter 27, p. 57.

161. "Abel, who is *yesod* of *abba*, has two twin sisters who are the two *malkhuyot* of *abba*. The *yesod* of *ima*, who is Cain, only has one twin [that remains with him], the *malkhuyot* of *ima*. The fourth *malkhuyot* [Cain's second twin] emanated outside . . . and thus he cannot unify with her. Hence he was jealous of Abel on account of that extra twin, which is really extra (*yetera mamash!*) because the inner mate is really essential. . . . Therefore Cain wanted to take her. He also wanted her because even though her origin is from *yesod* of *abba*, she is really on the margin of the open feminine root in *yesod* of *ima*." SeD, p. 156c.

162. ShP, pp. 5c/d (top).

163. LiT p. 124 cited and discussed above.

164. We do have a few scant allusions to Abel's sin in Zohar 3.11b and Tikkunei Zohar, tikun 69.

165. On this, see Daniel Boyarin, *Intertextuality and Midrash*, esp. pp. 1–21.

166. See SeG, chapter 3, p. 5.

167. For another rendition, see Tikkunei Zohar, tikun 69, p. 110b. There the **Sh** (ש) represents the three animals of Ezekiel's chariot, and the **M** (מ) and **H** (ה) represent the face of Adam on the chariot. Cf. Tikkunei Zohar, tikun 69, 119a. See Zohar Hadash on Ruth, p. 83b where the Zohar creates a triune equation between Moses, Seth, and Sinai, arguing that Moses comes into his fullness as Seth at Sinai, thus removing the poison of the serpent that was implanted in Eve.

168. See b.T. Hagigah 14b. See also Alon Goshen-Gotstein, *The Sinner and the Amnesiac: The Rabbinic Invention of Elisha ben Avuya and Eliezer ben Arach* (Stanford, Calif.: Stanford University Press, 2000), pp. 89–124; Jeffrey Rubenstein, *Talmudic Stories: Narrative, Art, Composition and Culture*, pp. 64–104; and Yehuda Liebes, *Heto shel Elisha* (Jerusalem: Akadamon, 1990). For another approach to Abel's sin, see ShM, "parshat Kedoshim," pp. 24b–25a. In this text Abel's sin, tied to a discussion of the prohibition of *shatnez* (wearing wool and linen together) was intended to rectify Cain's sin yet failed to do so. This is likely based on the discussion of Cain and Abel and *shatnez* in Zohar Hadash on Ruth, p. 79d. Cf. Gershom Scholem, *Heker Kabbalat R. Yizhak ha-Cohen* (Jerusalem: Akademon, 1934), pp. 136–138; and Tishby, *Torat ha-Ra*, p. 136.

169. Cf. ShP on Psalm 146, p. 51a. There Luria states that Abel's sin, like Cain's was "unredeemable" (*she-lo haya lo teshuah*).

170. LiT, p. 33a.

171. Genesis 4:3, *Yayehi me-ketz ha-yomin. JPS Tanakh* translates this idiomatically as "in the course of time." However, Luria's hyperliteralism reads it "from the *ketz yomim.*" On the notion of *ketz* as damaging to creation, see ShG, intro. 36, p. 283. Vital delineates three errors of "the end" (*ketz*) in Jacob, Samuel, and R. Akiba. *Ketz* seems to mean here the calculation of the end which, Vital

suggests always darkens the creation. See Tikkunei Zohar, tikun 69, p. 113b; and Targum Yonatan to Genesis 4:3.

172. On the distinction between the *yamim* and *yamin* regarding Cain, see Zohar Hadash, on Song of Songs, ma'amar #5; Zohar Hadash on Ruth, p. 83b; and Zohar 2.181b. The reason the ט is used instead of the נ regarding Cain is that Cain is from the demonic, left side, and not the side of the right (*yomin*). Abel is thus *kez ha-yamin* or "darkness from the side of the right," i.e., *yamin*.

173. SeL, p. 7b.

174. For the most extensive discussion of this, see EH, Gate 13, chapters, 12, 13, 14. A shorter and more opaque version is found in LiT. p. 37a. The details of the 370 lights are a complex calculation in Lurianic metaphysics that is not directly relevant to our specific concerns.

175. Cf. PEH, "Gate of Prayer," chapter 2, pp. 5 a/b and EH ibid., p. 69b.

176. ShP, p. 9b. Both ShP and LiT, 33a argue the rectification of Abel's sin was at the *akedah* while SeLi 7b maintains it was at the burning bush. In both cases, the sin and its tikun were in the realm of vision.

177. ShP, p. 7b. Our text continues to interpret the last clause of the *mishna*: "He said [to the skull]: Because you drowned others, you were drowned, and eventually those who drowned you will be drowned." The floating skull also refers to Moses, whose mother set his basket floating on the river. The drowning refers to the Egyptians, who were drowned at the sea (Exod. 15:4). Cf. b.T. Sukkah 53a and Rashi there. I want to thank my friend and colleague Aryeh Cohen for helping to clarify this mishna in its talmudic context.

178. EH, "Shaʿar ha-Kelalim," chapter 10, p. 9a.

179. See Menahem Recanati, *Taʿamei ha-Mitzvot*, p. 17b who states that Abel sinned with "gazing" and Moses rectified that sin by concealing his eyes from the *shekhina* at the burning bush.

180. For example, see my "From Theosophy to Midrash," pp. 58–75. Cf. Tikkunei Zohar, tikun 69, p. 117b; and my discussion in *Hasidism on the Margin*, pp. 92–96.

181. SeG, chapter 27, p. 57.

182. In general, these texts speak about the tikun of Cain and not Abel's sin. The rectification of Abel's sin will result in redemption. See LiT, p. 117a, "This is the meaning of **Bela Ha-mavet Le-nezah** (HVL) (*He will destroy death forever;* Isaiah 25:8). That is, Messiah cannot come until Abel's sin is rectified. Moses is the *gilgul* of Abel. In every generation [the Moses of that generation] must redeem the soul sparks from the demonic realm. At that time, Messiah will come." Cf. LiT, p. 103b.

183. The question is implied in Zohar 2.14b.

184. Actually it is three parts, but the fourth part here (Egypt) is already rectified and prepared. On the four-part process of tikun more generally, see ShG, intro. 22; ShHM, p. 42b; and ShP, pp. 31a.157, 158. On the four possible times of *gilgul*, see Tikkunei Zohar, tikun 69, p. 117 b (top).

185. See ShP, p. 19c and ShK, p. 79a/b. On three *gilgulim* as the limit after which the soul does not return, see Tikkunei Zohar, tikun 69, p. 115a.

186. Genesis Raba, 38; and Zohar 1:71.

187. The connection of the biblical term *ra* or wicked to spilling seed was made earlier in a section of this text not cited here. The connection is built on the use of the term *ra* (evil) describing the sin of Er: *Er, the first-born of Yehuda, acted wickedly (ra) in the eyes of God* (Gen. 31:7). Cf. Psalms 5:5: *For you are not a God who desires wickedness (lo yagurkha ra).*

188. ShP, p. 21a. See an augmented version in ShK, "Drush le-Pesah," 1, pp. 79a/b.

189. See SeL, p. 41b where the "mixed multitude"—*ʿerev rav* is viewed as rooted in Cain.

190. LiT, p. 69.

191. See ShHM, p. 47b; and ShP, p. 20c. This is based on b.T. Pesahim 87b, "Why was Israel exiled among the nations? It was so that they could make converts."

192. ShP. p. 20c. 130 years as a time of tikun is also viewed through the 130 years Jacob suffered from losing Joseph. See EDT, p. 55a. On the correlation of Adam and Jacob, see ShMR, p. 13c (bottom), "Jacob, who is Adam, fixed his blemish and thus merited two wives, marrying both like *zeir anpin.*" This correlation predates Luria and his circle and can be found in Meir Ibn Gabbai's *Avodat ha-Kodesh* 4:5; and Joseph Gikitillia's *Shaʿarei ʿOrah* 5:6.

193. This is not original in Luria. In b.T. Sota 12a (cited in Rashi on Exodus 2:1) we read that Yoheved was 130 years old when Moses was born. We also read that Amram, Moses' father, separated from his wife (in some readings divorced her) after Pharaoh's edict to kill all Israelite sons. The word "he took" (*ve-yikakh*) in Exodus 2:1 thus refers to his remarriage to her. In this talmudic passage we have the two components that serve Luria's correlation between Moses and Adam, first, the 130 years and second, the separation. Although the 130 years does not mark the time of separation, the connection is implied in the Talmud. Yoheved, who is 130 when Moses is born, was herself born at the time of Israel's descent into Egypt. Thus she becomes a marker for the generation in Egypt who dwelled there 130 years in order to fix the souls of Adam's 130 years of masturbation. See ShP, p. 19c. Cf. LiT, p. 69.

194. See Midrash Tanhuma, 9 and Rashi on Exodus 2:11. Cf. Exodus Raba 1:29. For the mention of the son of Shelomit bat Divri and his evil deed, see Leviticus 24:10–12. The midrash assumes that this son was born from the rape in Exodus 2:11 that Moses avenged. Moses is commanded in Leviticus to take this son out of the camp and have him stoned. According to Luria it is because this son inherits the evil side of Cain that was not fixed. Hence, for him there is no redemption.

195. Note that *JPS Tanakh* translates *brother* idiomatically as *kinsmen.* However, the hyperliteralism of kabbalistic exegesis reads *brother* (*me-akhiv*) literally; that is, the Egyptian was from his brother, that is, Cain. This necessarily shifts the noun *brother* from a description of *ish ivri* to *ish mizri.*

196. But see Ibn Ezra on Exodus 2:11 where he writes "from his brother," referring to the familial relation of the Hebrew to Moses. This is difficult for the reason Luria mentions, i.e., the Hebrew is from Dan and Moses is from Levi. Perhaps ibn Ezra means that there is a marital relation, but this is never explained. Cf. the explanation in Midrash Yalkut Shemoni 2:166.

197. SeG, chapter 33, p. 65. The connection between Cain and Abel and Moses and the Egyptian can be found in Tikkunei Zohar, tikun 69, p. 113a. The use of the term *ruah ha-kodesh* in Luria is complex. Fine suggests that it is used almost interchangeably with prophecy. See Fine, *Physician of the Soul,* pp. 281–285. The justification of a seemingly transgressive act through the use of *gilgul* preceded Luria. In *Sefer ha-Peliah,* an anonymous medieval kabbalistic work, David is justified in killing Uriah because Bathsheba was a *gilgul* of Eve and, maintaining that he was a *gilgul* of Adam, he had to marry her in order to facilitate the tikun. See *Sefer ha-Peliah,* p. 60c/d.

198. See ibid. Luria notes that Moses' act was not committed with malice or re-venge but "with great love" in his attempt to rectify the good side of Cain.

199. See SeD, p. 155a. "The secret of the three *gilgulim* of Cain, the Egyptian taskmaster, and Jethro constitute the *roshei tevot* (KMY) *if anyone kills Cain, sevenfold vengeance (sevataim yakum)*."

200. SeG, p. 66. On the good in Cain going to Jethro, see Tikkunei Zohar, tikun 69, pp. 115b, 119a; and Zohar 3. 117b. On Jethro more generally in Lurianic Kabbala, see SeD, pp. 157a/b.

201. This is discussed at length in chapter 2 of this study.

202. Mekhilta de-Rebbe Yishmael, "parshat Yitro."

203. See b.T. Sota, 12a; Megilah, 13a.

204. ShP, p. 6a. Cf ShP, 5d; and Tikkunei Zohar p. 99b. This text contains a short preface by Shmuel Vital, stating that he found this fragment that explains the verses in question differently than the previous texts and includes it simply because he does not want to exclude any text in his possession. If we look at the previous text (5c/d) the general thrust of the interpretation, at least regarding our interests, is the same.

205. Moreover, the evil part of Cain that is "killed" by Moses is not destroyed but reemerges as Amalek. The tikun is thus not complete. See ShP, pp. 35d/36a.

206. On the terms *katnut* and *gadlut* in late Kabbala, see Mordecai Pachter, "Clarifying the Terms *Katnut* and *Gadlut* in the Kabbala of the Ari and a History of its Understanding in Hasidism" [Hebrew], *Mekharei Yerushalayim* 10 (1992): 171–210; and Zvi Mark, "The Status of *Katnut* and *Gadlut* in R. Nahman and their Source in Lurianic Kabbala" [Hebrew], *Da'at* 46 (2001): 45–80.

207. *But the LORD was wrathful with me on your account* (Deut. 3:26).

208. The *yovel* or Jubilee year is the fiftieth year, completing a cycle where all land goes back to its original owner and all contracts are completed. See Leviticus 25:10–12.

209. LiT, p. 92.

210. LiT, pp. 86a, 86b (top). But see LiT on Jeremiah, p. 122b (bottom), where it clarifies this generalization and says that during the generation of the desert (and during the period of the patriarchs) there was a face-to-face union opposite the chest (*tiferet*) of *zeir anpin*.

211. LiT, p. 86b. The staff of Moses contains the lights that emanate from *yesod* of *abba* and constitutes a *parzuf* in its own right. See EH, Gate 32, chapters 1 and 2; ShP, p. 35c.

212. Ibid.

213. We also know that Hayyim Vital, the main collector and redactor of Lurianic texts, was a student of Moses Cordovero when he was the head of a seminary of Portuguese Jews (almost all of whom were conversos) in Safed. On this, see the next chapter.

214. Even Fine's study on the life of Luria, *Physician of the Soul*, acknowledges that we know little about the day-to-day activities of this fraternity, especially as it relates to their engagement with the world around them. So simple and fundamental a question as to what language they spoke to one another has never been decisively determined. Abraham David's many studies using official archival documents about Safed during this period also does not give us much to work with in terms of the fraternity's relationship to the larger Safed community, much less an account of their attitude toward the many conversos in their midst.

215. Joel Rembaum, "Medieval Criticism of the Christian Doctrine of Original Sin," *AJS Review* 7–8 (1982/83): 380.

216. On the more specific question regarding the way Kabbala serves as a bridge between Judaism and Christianity, see Elliot Wolfson, "Language, Secrecy and the Mysteries of Law: Theurgy and the Christian Kabbala of Johannes Reuchlin," *Kabbala* 13 (2005); and, most recently, *Language, Eros, Being*, pp. 190–260.

2. Exodus

1. Walter Cohen, "Political Criticism of Shakespeare," in J. E. Howard and M. F. O'Conner, eds., *Shakespeare Reproduced: The Text in History and Ideology* (N.Y.: Routledge, 1987), p. 34. Cohen's comment is meant to undermine Greenblatt's thesis that one can construct "history" from "literature." For a defense of Greenblatt on this point, see Sonja Laden, "Greenblattian Self-Fashioning and the Construction of 'Literary History,'" *Critical Self-Fashioning*, pp. 72, 73.

2. See Vital, *Sefer Hezyonot*, p. 222 discussed in Yehuda Liebes, "Two Young Roes of a Doe" [Hebrew], *Mekharei Yerushalayim* 10 (1992): 120.

3. "One should consequently not be surprised to find among them [i.e., medieval and Renaissance historians] the inclination to rely heavily on the Bible and the present history in what modern authors would call an intertextual way. This meant, for instance, the use of biblical style, continuous implicitly or explicit comparisons of the protagonists of the historian's tale with biblical personalities, discovering in contemporary history the typological significance of Biblical events . . . and so on." See Robert Bonfil, "Jewish Attitudes toward History and Historical Writing in Pre-Modern Times," *Jewish History* 11, no. 1 (Spring 1997): 29. Cf. Joseph Hacker, "On the Intellectual Character and Self-Perception of Spanish Jewry in the Late Fifteenth Century" [Hebrew], *Sefunot*, n.s. 17 (1983): 21–95.

4. This is similar to Michael Fishbane's "hermeneutical transference" discussed in his *Garments of Torah* (Bloomington: Indiana University Press, 1989), p. 96. Ben-Zion Netanyahu uses a similar approach in his *The Marranos of Spain: From the Late XIVth to Early XVIth Century According to Contemporary Hebrew Sources* (New York: American Academy for Jewish Research, 1966). See Gerson Cohen's review essay on Netanyahu in *Journal of Jewish Social Studies* 29, no. 3 (1967): 178. A good survey of the different positions on this issue also can be found in Yirmiyahu Yovel, "The New Otherness: Marrano Dualities in the First Generation," *The 1999 Swig Lecture*, pp. 1 and 2 (also at http://www.usfca.edu/judaicstudies/yovel .html, accessed February 21, 2005). Moshe Idel suggests a category of reading called "systematic arcanization" whereby a response to a new cultural phenomenon is read back into classical literature. While not New Historicism as such, it has a similar resonance. See Moshe Idel, *Absorbing Perfections*, p. 6.

5. The notion of the apostate not being fully a Jew is a hotly debated topic in halakhic discussions stemming from the Gaonic period, which was responding to conversions of Jews to Islam. See Salo Baron, *Social and Religious History of the Jews* (New York: Columbia University Press, 1983), vol. 3, pp. 11–113. For an in depth overview and discussion, see Gerald Blidstein, "Who Is Not a Jew?—the Medieval Discussion," *Israel Law Review* 11 (1976): 369–90. For a review and analysis that addresses Rashi's position that Jewishness must remain solely a matter of biology, see Jacob Katz, "Although He Has Sinned He Remains a Jew" [Hebrew], *Tarbiz* 27 (1958): 203–217. Regarding Christians not considering conversos fully Christian, see Ben-Zion Netanyahu, *The Origins of the Inquisition*, pp. 848–854.

6. See Schechter, "Safed in the Sixteenth Century," *Studies in Judaism*, Second Series (Philadelphia: JPS, 1938), pp. 202–306; Abraham David, *To Come to*

the Land: Immigration and Settlement in Sixteenth-Century Erez-Israel; Lawrence Fine, *Safed Spirituality,* pp. 1–24; Mordecai Pachter, *Mi-tsefunot Tsefat* (Jerusalem: Zalman Shazar Institute, 1994); Meir Benayahu, *Toldot ha-Ari;* and David Tamar, *Mekhkarim be-toldot ha-Yehudim be-Eretz Yisra'el u-be-Italia,* pp. 69–80.

7. On this, see Abraham David, *To Come to the Land.* All page references are from the English ed. Cf. David Tamar, *Mekhkarim be-toldot ha-Yehudim be-Erez Yisra'el u ve-artsot ha-mizrakh;* and David Tamar, *Mekhkarim be-toldot ha-Yehudim be-Erez Yisrael u-be-Italia,* pp. 69–80, 124–130, 141–159.

8. See Shmuel Avitsur, "Safed—Center for the Manufacture of Woven Woolens in the Fifteenth Century" [Hebrew], *Sefunot* 6 (1962): 43–69.

9. See Don Isaac Abrabanel's commentary to Isaiah 43:6. Cf. Abraham David, "The Spanish Exiles in the Holy Land," in H. Belmont, ed., *The Sephardi Legacy* (Jerusalem: Magnus), 2 volumes, 2:79–81; and Yizhak Baer, "The Messianic Movement in Spain" [Hebrew], *Measaf Zion* 5 (1933): 76, n. 1.

10. For example, see Jacob Katz, *Halakha and Kabbala* [Hebrew] (Jerusalem: Magnus, 1984); and Zvi Werblowsky, *Joseph Karo: Lawyer and Mystic* (New York: Oxford University Press, 1962).

11. The notion that exegesis often functions as a tool to respond to contemporary events is well documented. For example, see Alan Segal's discussion of the binding of Isaac in early Christian and Jewish interpretation, "The Sacrifice of Isaac in Early Judaism and Christianity," in Alan Segal, *The Other Judaisms of Late Antiquity* (Atlanta: Scholars, 1987), pp. 109–130.

12. In his *History of the Jews in Christian Spain,* 1:243 Yizhak Baer suggests that mystics in medieval Spain "participated actively in the efforts to raise the level of religious and moral life." This comment is a critique of Gershom Scholem's position that mystical fraternities are insular groups who are not seriously engaged in the contemporary conflicts of the larger community. On the religion of Safed in these decades more generally, see Pinhas Giller, "The Common Religion of Safed," *Conservative Judaism* 55, no. 2 (2003): 24–37. Cf. Lawrence Fine, *Physician of the Soul,* pp. 19–40.

13. On this point, my approach is much more aligned with Moshe Idel who posits that new centers of kabbalistic activity among Jews in the 16th century, resulting from the expulsion, widened the scope of intellectual concerns and included direct responses to new sociological phenomena. While Idel does not discuss the converso immigration to Safed, this could be included in his sociological perspective. See Moshe Idel, "On Mobility, Individuals and Groups: Prolegomenon for a Sociological Approach to Sixteenth-Century Kabbala," *Kabbalah: Journal of the Study of Jewish Mystical Texts* 3 (1998): 145–173.

14. This sharply changes after he met Luria. His subsequent writing exhibits a density and attention to cosmological detail almost unmatched in the history of kabbalistic literature. Interestingly, it appears Vital continued to edit this work even after his discipleship with Luria, yet the text shows almost no Lurianic influence.

15. Cordovero's two popular works, *Tomar Devorah* and *Or Ne'erav* had tremendous impact in nonkabbalistic circles in both Sephardic and Ashkenazic communities. See Ira Robinson, *Moses Cordovero's Introduction to Kabbalah: An Annotated Translation of His Or Ne'erav* (Hoboken, N.J.: Yeshiva University Press, 1994); Ira Robinson, "Moses Cordovero and Kabbalistic Education in the Sixteenth Century," *Judaism* 93 (1990): 155–162; and Brakha Sack, *Sha'are ha-kabbala shel R. Moshe Cordovero* (Beer Sheva: Beer Sheva University Press, 1995), pp. 11–32.

16. For a precedent in the Zohar, see Zohar 1.25a.

17. Jews, now conversos, were permitted to leave Portugal by royal decree in 1507, one year after the massacre of conversos in Lisbon in 1506. On this, see Ben Zion Netanyahu, *The Marranos of Spain: From the Late Fourteenth to the Early Sixteenth Century*, updated and expanded, pp. 211–215; Abraham David, "Safed, foyer de retour au judaïsme de 'conversos' au XVIe siècle," in *Revue études juives* 146, nos. 1–2 (1986): 63–82. Cf. idem. "Safed as a Center for the Resettlement of *Anusim*" [Hebrew], *Proceedings for the Second International Congress for Research of the Sephardic and Oriental Heritage* 1984, pp. 183–204; and "The Spanish Exiles in the Holy Land," in *The Sephardi Legacy*. After the forced conversion of Portuguese Jews in 1497, all Jews from that land were New Christians. On a detailed discussion of this phenomenon, see Cecil Roth, *A History of the Marranos* (Philadelphia: JPS, 1959); and Yosef Hayyim Yerushalmi, *From Spanish Court to Italian Ghetto*, pp. 1–50.

18. More generally, see Norman Roth, *Conversion, Inquisition, and the Expulsion of the Jews from Spain* (Madison: University of Wisconsin Press, 1995), esp. pp. 48–116. On the Portuguese Conversos in particular, see Miriam Bodian, *Hebrews of the Portuguese Nation: Conversos and Community in Early Modern Amsterdam*, esp. pp. 96–131.

19. Many of the immigrants temporarily settled in other Mediterranean cities such as Solonika before arriving in Safed around 1525. For a brief overview of the conversos of Solonika and their history, see David F. Altabe, "Portuguese Jews of Solonika," in *Studies of the History of Portuguese Jews from Their Expulsion in 1497 through Their Dispersion* (New York: Sehev-Hermon, 2000), pp. 119–125. A more detailed account can be found in Joseph Hacker, "On the Intellectual Character and Self-Perception of Spanish Jewry in late Fifteenth Century" [Hebrew], *Sefunot: New Series* 17 (1983): 37–59; and idem. "The Jewish Community in Solonika in the Fifteenth and Sixteenth Centuries" [Ph.D. diss., Hebrew University, 1978]. More generally, see A. Danon, "La Communaute Juive de Solonique au de 16e Siecle," *Revue des études Juives* 8 (1999): 110–124; and Netanyahu, *The Marranos of Spain*, pp. 211–215.

20. The rise of messianic hope among conversos did not begin with their arrival in Erez Israel. See Haim Beinart, "A Prophesying Movement in Cordova in 1499–1502" [Hebrew], *Zion* 44 (1980): 190–200; Rene Levene-Melammed, *Heretics of Daughters of Israel? The Crypto-Jewish Women of Castille* (Oxford: Oxford University Press, 1999), pp. 45–72; Stephen Sharot, *Messianism, Mysticism, and Magic* (Chapel Hill: University of North Carolina Press, 1982), pp. 76–86; and Anita Novinsky, "Marranos and Marranism—A New Approach," *Jewish Studies* 40 (2000): 19. However, the common belief in the messiah rising in the Galilee made many believe they had the best chance of being reabsorbed in that vicinity. More generally, see Aaron Zeev Aescoly, *Jewish Messianic Movements* [Hebrew] (Jerusalem: Bialik Institute, 1987), pp. 253–439; Rachel Elior, "Messianic Expectations and Spiritualization of Religious Life in the Sixteenth Century," *Revue des études Juives* 145 (1986): 35–49; David Ruderman, "Hope Against Hope: Jewish and Christian Messianic Expectations in the Late Middle Ages," in A. Mirsky, A. Grossman, and Y. Kaplan, eds., *Exile and Diaspora* (Jerusalem: Yad ben Zvi, 1991), pp. 185–202; and most recently Matt Goldish, "Patterns in Converso Messianism," in *Millenarianism and Messianism in Early Modern Culture*, pp. 41–63. In the 17th century, Sabbateanism also had a certain cache with conversos. On this, see Gershom Scholem, "Redemption through Sin," in *The Messianic Idea in Judaism* (New York: Schocken, 1995), pp. 114ff; Yerushalmi, *Spanish Court*, 303–313; Yosef Kaplan, "The Attitude of the Leadership of the 'Portuguese' Community in Amsterdam

to the Sabbatean Movement" [Hebrew], *Zion* 39 (1974): 198–216; Richard Popkin, "Jewish Christians and Christian Jews in the Seventeenth Century," in R. Popkin and G. Weiner, eds., *Jewish Christians and Christian Jews: From the Renaissance to the Enlightenment* (Dordrecht, The Netherlands: Kluwer Academic Publishers, 1994), pp. 57–72; Jacob Barnai, "Christian Messianism and Portuguese Marranos: The Emergence of Sabbateanism in Smyrna," *Jewish History* 7 (1993): 119–126; David Halperin, Abraham Miguel Cardozo, pp. 37–59; and, of course, Gershom Scholem, *Sabbatai Sevi: Mystical Messiah*, pp. 518–545, 749–764.

21. Based on Zohar 1:119a.

22. Reversion back to Judaism was not unique to this period or to the Holy Land. Throughout the sordid history of the conversos there are many instances of reversion back to Judaism, most, but surely not all, happening after the expulsion and outside the Iberian Peninsula. See David M. Gitlitz, *Secrecy and Deceit: The Religion of the Crypto-Jews* (Albuquerque: University of New Mexico Press, 2002), pp. 578–580. On the converso immigration to Erez Israel more generally, see Joseph Hacker, "The Relationship and Immigration of Spanish Jews to the Land of Israel" [Hebrew], *Katedra* 36 (1985): 3–34.

23. Cited in R. Elijah Mizrachi *Responsa* (Constantinople, 1560), #47; and R. Joseph ibn Habib *Nimukei Yosef* on Rif to b.T. Yevamot 16b. On this, see Gerald Blidstein, "Who Is Not a Jew?—The Medieval Discussion," *Israel Law Review* 11 (1976): 378 and n. 29. Cf. David Novak, *The Election of Israel*, pp. 177–200. See, for example, R. Shlomo ibn Adret, *Teshuvot ha-Rashba* 5:66, cited in Novak p. 197 and other sources in n. 125.

24. It is true that in some respects this makes it easier, as they could simply undergo conversion and the problem would be solved. But, for those who maintained a Jewish identity (however ambiguous), even as they practiced Christianity, this may not have been so easily accepted. In some way this goes back to Ben-Zion Netanyahu and Gerson Cohen's disagreement about defining Jewishness cited earlier. The use of the talmudic dictum "even though he sinned he is still Israel" (b.T. Sanhedrin 43b–44a) underwent a transformation in the early Middle Ages when Jews were confronted with the choice of conversion to Christianity or death. On this, see Jacob Katz, *"Af al pi She-Hata Yisrael Hu"* Tarbiz (1958): 203ff. R. Yakov Emden is one who stated explicitly that one who is an apostate forfeits his or her right to being considered a Jew. See Emden, *She'alt Yavetz* 1:28; Novak, *The Election of Israel*, p. 192; and idem. *Jewish Social Ethics*, pp. 223, 224.

25. See Isaiah Tishby, *Messianism on the Generation of the Expulsion in Spain and Portugal* [Hebrew] (Jerusalem: Zalman Shazar, 1985), pp. 66–81. "The development of messianic expectation . . . became stronger after the expulsion from Spain and peaked around the year 1500, almost a full decade after the Spanish expulsion and in the wake of the expulsion from Portugal. Messianic expectation in the year 1500 was intertwined with the messianic fervor among the conversos in Spain and other groups in the Diaspora . . . Among the conversos there were prophetic declarations regarding the coming of the Messiah in 1499 and this phenomenon expanded in 1500 . . ." (Tishby, p. 73). Cf. David M. Gitlitz, *Secrecy and Deceit*, pp. 103–110. Cf. Richard Popkin, "The Marrano Theology of Isaac La Peyrere," *Studi Internazionali di Filosophia* 5 (1973): 97–126; idem, *Isaac La Peyrere: His Life, Work, and Influence* (Leiden: Brill, 1987), pp. 69–79; and Matt Goldish, *Sabbatean Prophets*, pp. 45–49. Gerson Cohen notes in passing that part of the rationalization of conversion to Christianity of Marranos was that, "[t]hey knew that the Messiah must come and soon, and they were sure that those who could justify their inner-most intentions would also be re-

deemed." Gerson Cohen, "Messianic Postures of Ashkenazim and Sephardim," reprinted in Marc Saperstein, ed., *Essential Papers on Messianic Movements and Personalities in Jewish History* (New York: New York University Press), p. 228.

26. See, for example, Abraham David, "Demographic Changes in the Safed Community of the Sixteenth Century," in R. Dan, ed., *Occident and Orient: A Tribute to the Memory of A. Schreiber* (Budapest: Akademiai Kiado, 1988), pp. 83–93; "The Spanish Exiles in the Holy Land," in *The Sephardi Legacy*, vol. 2: 77–108; "The Jewish Settlement in Palestine at the Beginning of the Ottoman Empire (1517–1599)," *The Jewish Settlement in Palestine 634–1881*, pp. 81–141.

27. On Zemah, see Gershom Scholem, "The Life of R. Jacob Zemah, His Works and Writings" [Hebrew], *Keriat Sefer* 26, no. 2 (1950): 185–194. It is noteworthy that Zemah was a teacher of Nathan of Gaza, later Shabbatei Zevi's main disciple. It is worth exploring the possible connections between Sabbatean doctrine and converso religiosity, especially given that Abraham Miguel Cardozo, a disciple of Nathan of Gaza, was himself a converso. For a preliminary discussion about Sabbateanism and Christianity, see Moshe Idel, *Messianic Mystics*, pp. 205 and 206. See Sharot, *Messianism, Mysticism, and Magic*, pp. 76–86; and Yerushalmi, *From Spanish Court to Italian Ghetto*, p. 4. Yerushalmi notes the extent to which some offspring of conversos were attracted to mysticism within the Catholic Church. Moshe Idel notes that Zemah links some Lurianic ideas to Christianity. While Idel correctly notes that Zemah is utilizing the works of Giordano Bruno, it is also worth considering Zemah's own Christian past and its impact on his willingness to adopt Christian ideas to his otherwise conservative Lurianism. See Idel, "Differing Conceptions of Kabbalah in the Early 17th Century," in *Jewish Thought in the Seventeenth Century*, p. 196.

28. The relationship of conversos to Jewish mysticism is complex and liminal. While we do have some indication of conversos being attracted to Kabbala, many were also strong advocates of rationalism in Renaissance Italy and, in fact, virulently anti-Kabbala. This was especially true in the 17th century. See Moshe Idel, "Differing Conceptions," pp. 137–140. Cf. his discussion of David Farrar and the controversy surrounding him on pp. 152, 153.

29. It is also the case that the Portuguese conversos were quite homesick and many traveled back and forth to their homeland, maintaining dual identities and at times dual families! One example of this is the testimony of Father Pantaleao de Aveiro, who traveled to Safed to visit the Portuguese conversos in the 16th century and was impressed by the desire of many of them to return to Portugal. On this, see Anita Novinsky, "Marranos and Marranism—A New Approach," *Jewish Studies* 40 (2000): 8. This seems common is earlier periods as well. See, for example, Shlomo ibn Adret, *Teshovot ha-Rashba*, vol. 6, p. 179, and Haym Soloveitchik, "Religious Law and Change," *AJS Review* 12, no. 2 (Fall 1987): 214 and n. 15.

30. See David, *To Come to the Land*, p. 105 and n. 32. See also Yerushalmi, *From Spanish Court to Italian Ghetto*, p. 39 n. 57. The ex-Marrano Isaac ben Nahmias always signed his name followed by *baʿal teshuva*. The notion of conversos engaging in severe acts of penance is common both among Sephardic and Ashkenzic Jews. See, for example, in Yosef Hayyim Yerushalmi, "The Inquisition and the Jews of France in the Time of Bernard Gui," *Harvard Theological Review* 63 (1970): 363, 364.

31. See Isaiah Tishby, "Rabbi Moses Cordovero as He Appears in the Treatise of Rabbi Mordecai Dato" [Hebrew], *Sefunot* 7 (1963): 24 as cited in David, *To Come to the Land*, pp. 105 and 213 n. 31.

32. See, for example, in R. Moshe Alsekh, *Romemot 'El* (Zolkiew, 1764), on Psalms 44:24. There is an interesting passing reference in Vital's ShG, a text compiled, if not written, long after the converso controversy. Discussing why Vital went against his master's expressed request not to reveal to others the nature of his (Vital's) soul, Vital states, "I thought I was doing a great mitzvah in order to bring merit to all those who were 'returning' (*hozrei be-teshuva*) . . ." It would be interesting to explore who he was referring to. That is, who in Safed was "returning" in that way? The text continues to tell the story that after Vital conveyed to others how Luria told him the roots of his soul, Luria was flooded with visitors (these *ba'alei tehsuva*) who wanted to know the roots of their soul. Luria angrily lamented to Vital, "this is the reason that I no longer have any time to study with you . . . you are the cause of all these people wanting to see me—and I am a humble man. . . ." See ShG, intro. 38, p. 351.

33. David, *To Come to the Land*, p. 104. Cf. R. J. Z. Werblowsky, "Tikkunei Tefilot le-Rav Shlomo ha-Levi Alkabetz," *Sefunot* 6 (1962): 152. Moreover, in numerous places Moshe Cordovero writes about the merging of Islam and Christianity into Judaism as a final phase of exile. On this, see Reuven Kimelman, *Lekha Dodi ve-Kabbalat Shabbat: Their Mystical Meaning* [Hebrew] (Jerusalem: Magnes, 2003), pp. 82–134. We know that Vital considered himself a student of Alkabetz from the statement in ShG, intro. 39, p. 380, where he refers to Alkabetz as "my teacher," an attribution he usually restricts to Cordovero and Luria.

34. See Hayyim Z. Dimitrovsky, "Beit Midraso shel R. Ya'akov Berab be-Safed," *Sefunot* 7 (1963): 41–102. On the *semikha* (ordination) controversy in general, see Jacob Katz, "The Controversy on the *Semikha* between Rabbi Jacob Berab and Ralbah" [Hebrew], *Zion* 16 (1951): 28–45; *Halakha ve Kabbala*, pp. 213–236; and "The Dispute Between Jacob Berab and Levi ben Habib over Renewing Ordination," in *Binah: Studies in Jewish History*, vol. 1, pp. 119–141. Cf. Hayyim Z. Dimitrovsky, "New Documents Regarding the *Semikha* Controversy" [Hebrew], *Sefunot* 10 (1966): 113–192; and Meir Benayahu, "The Renewal of *Semikha* in Safed" [Hebrew], *Sefer Yovel for Yizhak Baer* (Jerusalem, 1971), pp. 248–269. For an interesting legal discussion on the *semikha* controversy, see Robert Cover, "Folktales of Justice," in M. Minow, M. Ryan, A. Saret, eds., *Narrative, Violence, and the Law: The Essays of Robert Cover* (Ann Arbor: University of Michigan Press, 1995), pp. 187–195.

35. Abraham David, "Demographic Changes," p. 87.

36. ShG, intro. 39, p. 381. The notion of Vital being from the root of Cain is an underlying trope in the entire treatise. Much of the latter part of ShG is an extended discussion of the roots of Vital's own soul as told to Vital by Luria. For a preliminary analysis of Vital's soul, see Menahem Kallus, "Pneumatic Mystical Possession and the Eschatology of the Soul in Lurianic Kabbala," in *Spirit Possession in Judaism* (Detroit: Wayne State University Press, 2003), pp. 163–168.

37. One clear exception to this rule is the work of Isaac Abrabanel, especially his *Mashmi'ah Yeshu'ah* (Tel Aviv, 1960), among other thinkers of that period, who overtly addressed political and cultural issues in their commentary to Scripture. See Eric Lawee, "The Messianism of Isaac Abrabanel, Father of the [Jewish] Messianic Movements of the Sixteenth and Seventeenth Centuries," in *Millenarianism and Messianism*, pp. 1–39. Another example might be the early 15th-century philosopher Joseph Albo. Scholars have argued that his three fundamental principles of Judaism, as a critique of Maimonides' thirteen principles, may have been an attempt to support the "Jewishness" of conversos who, according to Maimonides' standards, would no longer be considered Jews. On this, see Shaul

Regev, "The Attitude Toward the Conversos in Fifteenth and Sixteenth Century Jewish Thought," *Review des études Juives* 146 (1987): 120 and 121. I am also not addressing Scholem's thesis about kabbalistic tradition in this period as a response to the expulsion. Scholem's position deals more with the existential or psychological impact of a historical event on metaphysical doctrine. Here I am speaking about the reconstruction of a whole biblical–rabbinic category in order to take a stand on a contemporary issue in the community of the mystic. While there are similarities, the two cases are quite different.

38. Also see Moses Nahmanides' comment to Numbers 9:14. For an incisive analysis of Rashi's use of the ʿerev rav in the golden calf episode, see Kalman Bland, *The Artless Jew* (Princeton, N.J.: Princeton University Press, 2000), pp. 117–129. Bland argues that Rashi uses the calf as a critique of contemporary Christianity. "Rashi's historiography of the golden calf was therefore double hinged: He made the past coincide with the present and the present reenact the past. His hostility toward the idolatrous 'mixed multitude' of ancient Egyptians carried over and ran parallel to his hostility toward the seductive and increasingly oppressive Christianity of his own day" (p. 120). Cf. Rashi on Song of Songs 2:7 and 3:5 and Bland's analysis on p. 120. I would argue that Vital is also using this narrative to comment on his situation. However, instead of using it to criticize Christianity he uses it to argue that conversos who are practicing Christians should be allowed to return to their Jewishness by simply abandoning these practices. To do this he essentially offers a fairly sympathetic, although in no way accepting, view of Christian worship. However, Vital does adopt Rashi's basic premise that the golden calf episode is an example of Christianity, thereby turning the tables on Christian exegetes who use Israel's sin with the calf as proof of Israel as idolaters. See Bland, p. 120; and Sarah Kamin, "Rashi's Commentary on Song of Songs" [Hebrew], *Tarbiz* 22, no. 1 (1983): 41–58; and Pier Cesare, *The Golden Calf and the Origins of Anti-Jewish Controversy*, trans. David Ward (Atlanta, Ga.: Scholars, 1990).

39. It is interesting that most medieval commentators (e.g., ibn Ezra, Rashbam, Ramban) do not use the term "convert" to describe the ʿerev rav. Rabbi Samuel ben Meir or Rashbam (1085–1174), Rashi's grandson does not think the ʿerev rav were involved at all in the golden calf, thus protesting against the midrashic myth of God's conversation with Moses in Egypt. Moreover, the more popular Mekhilta de-Rebbe Yishmael does not refer to them as "converts." See Mekhilta de-Rebbe Yishmael, "Parshat Bo," 14. The Zohar 3.263a tempers this assertion by saying that "their conversion . . . was not for the sake of heaven." The midrash never makes such an assertion discrediting the ʿerev rav's conversion.

40. Exodus Raba 18:10.

41. Ibid., 20:2.

42. Note that Targumn Onkelos reads "riffraff" as ʿaravravin (mixed)—etymologically and phonetically very close to ʿerev rav. I used "riffraff" as suggested by the *New JPS Tanakh* translation.

43. Midrash Tanhuma, Parshat B'helakotkha, chapter 17.

44. It is noteworthy that Nahmanides, while not openly disagreeing with Rashi or ibn Ezra does not identify the riffraff with the ʿerev rav. He claims that the riffraff were dissatisfied with the manna. As we will see, in many readings the ʿerev rav did not eat the manna, or at least did not merit that the manna tasted however they wanted it to taste. That being the case, perhaps Nahmanides did not agree that the riffraff were the ʿerev rav, especially since such identification is part of a rabbinic disagreement and is never made unequivocally in rabbinic literature.

45. In fact, the ambiguity of the sages' relationship to converts in general, expressed in the oft-cited rabbinic quip, "converts are like a sore for Israel," lies shallow beneath the surface of the entire rendition of the *ʿerev rav.* See b.T. Yebamot 47b, 109b; b.T. Kiddushim 70b. See also Zohar 2.182a. The Zohar adds the words "on live flesh" (*be-basar hayye*) to the talmudic phrase. The Zohar's locution is adopted by some exegetes. See, for example, R. Bahya ibn Asher of Saragossa, *Rabbenu Bahya ʿal ha-Torah*, vol. 2, p. 322. For a study that traces this ambivalence about conversion, see Yosef Kaplan, "Political Concepts in the World of the Portuguese Jews of Amsterdam during the Seventeenth Century: The Problem of Exclusion and the Boundaries of Self-Identity," in Y. Kaplan, H. Mechowlan, R. Popkin, eds. *Menasseh ben Israel and His World* (Leiden: Brill, 1989), pp. 45–62.

46. Midrash Tanhuma, Parshat Ki Tisa, chapter 21. Cf. Zohar 3.376b.

47. See, for example, EDT p. 173a (top).

48. The notion of messiah is not limited to Moses here. The fact that Vital and Luria had messianic pretensions is well known. See, David Tamar, "The Ari and Vital as Messiah ben Joseph" [Hebrew], in his *Mekharim be-Toldot ha-Yehudim be-Erez Yisrael u be-Italia*, pp. 211–229. Cf. Harris Lenowitz, *The Jewish Messiahs* (New York: Oxford University Press, 1998), pp. 125–147. Hence Vital's role in arguing for the absorption of the conversos can be likened, perhaps, to Moses' arguing for the inclusion of the *ʿerev rav.* It is the messianic figure who must complete the process of absorption. Moreover, the fact that Luria died in a plague in August 1572, a mere three years before the expected messianic date of 1575, may underscore, for Vital, that the delayed process of absorbing the conversos may have been a cause of Luria's untimely death and thus his failed messianic mission. The notion of the dual messiah appears in rabbinic literature but may have originated in Qumran literature that predates rabbinic doctrine and served, of course, as a template for Christianity. For example, see S. Talmon, "Typen der Messiaserwartung un die Zeitensende," in H. W. Wolf, ed., *Probleme biblischer Theologie* (Munich: Kaiser, 1971), pp. 571–588; and John J. Collins, "Patterns of Eschatology and Qumran," in J. D. Bittalperl, J. D. Levenson, eds., *Traditions in Transformation* (Winona Lake, Ind.: Eisenbrauns, 1981), pp. 351–375.

49. There are many places in the Zohar where the *ʿerev rav* are depicted as evil. For a correlation of the *ʿerev rav* to Amalek, see Tikkunei Zohar, tikun 69, p. 119b (top). For Vital's view on this, see EDT, p. 187b. This becomes truer in light of modern ultra-Orthodox critiques of modern Judaism in general and Zionism in particular. For a good example of this phenomenon, see R. Hayyim Elazar Shapiro, *Darkei Hayyim ve-Shalom* (Jerusalem, 1970), p. 8. More generally, see Alan Nadler, "The War on Modernity of R. Hayyim Elazar Shapira of Munkacz," *Modern Judaism* 14 (1994): 233–264, esp. pp. 241, 242; and Aviezer Ravitzky, *Messianism, Zionism and Religious Radicalism* (Chicago: University of Chicago Press, 1996), pp. 67ff.

50. The golden calf is a flash point between Judaism and nascent Christianity. For example, the broken tablets (precipitated by the golden calf, Exod. 32) is viewed by Christianity as God's rejection of Israel as elected, see Epistle of Barnabas 4:8, 18. For example, see Michael Chernick, "Some Talmudic Responses to Christianity, Third and Fourth Centuries," *Journal of Ecumenical Studies* 17 (1980): 393–406; Eugene Mihaly, "A Rabbinic Defense of the Election of Israel: An Analysis of Sifre Deuteronomy 32:9," *Hebrew Union College Annual* 35 (1964): 103–143; and Anthony Saldarini, *Matthew's Christian-Jewish Community* (Chicago: University of Chicago Press, 1994), pp. 19, 20.

51. See Zohar 3.237a.

52. See Zohar 2.45b.
53. Ibid. Cf. Zohar 3.279a. Unless otherwise indicated all translations from the Zohar are mine.
54. b.T. Sanhedrin 97a.
55. b.T. Shabbat 146a.
56. See b.T. Hulin fol. 139a and Tikkunei Zohar, tikun 69.
57. Zohar 1. 28b. Cf. Zohar Hadash, "Yithro," fourth essay. Cf. Tikkunei Zohar, tikun 69, p. 113a (bottom). The ʿ*erev rav* are also given the spiritual lineage of Esau and Ishmael. See Zohar 3.246b; and Tikkunei Zohar, #21.
58. See Vital, ShG, intro. 33, p. 36a/b; and intro. 34.
59. See, for example, the Vilna Gaon's comment to Song of Songs 2:11. "*For now the winter is past, the rains are over and gone. The winter is past*, this the exile among the nations. *The rains are over and gone*, this is the domination of the ʿ*erev rav* who are more difficult for Israel than the nations because they are "rain" (*geshem*) that constantly deter Israel. They are like a difficult wife who is constantly causing strife between Israel and their father in heaven." This is cited and discussed in R. Isaac Hutner, *Pahad Yizhak* (Brooklyn, N.Y.: Gur Aryeh Institute, 1995) on Shavout #39, p. 202. Bahya ibn Asher reads Moses' killing of the taskmaster as fixing the sin of Cain, who is embodied in the Egyptian. See his *Rabbenu Bahya ʿal ha-Torah* to Exodus 2:12.
60. Zohar 2.181a/b.
61. On the ʿ*erev rav* not partaking of the manna, see Zohar 2.191b. Cf. Joseph of Hamadam who suggests that the consumption of the manna resulted in a collective "knowledge of God." As the ʿ*erev rav* did not consume the manna, they would not have this experience and thus their connection to divine will in the desert would be attenuated. On this, see Jeremy Zwelling, "Joseph of Hamadan's '*Sefer Tashak:* Critical edition with Introduction'" (Brandeis University, Ph.D. diss., 1975), p. 309; and Joel Hecker, *Mystical Bodies, Mystical Meals*, pp. 99–100.
62. Ibid., 2.181b.
63. Elliot Wolfson argues that the Zohar does not generally advocate the eradication of evil but rather its "containment." In this case, containment can be viewed as a kind of integration of redeemable evil, leaving the remainder as subjugated but still viable. See Wolfson, "The Left Contained in the Right: A Study in Zoharic Hermeneutics," *AJS Review* 11 (1986): 19. Cf. Wolfson's position on Lurianic theodicy and redemption in "The Engenderment of Messianic Politics," in Peter Schaefer and Mark Cohen, eds., *Toward the Millennium* (Leiden: Brill, 1998), p. 210. Gershom Scholem makes a similar case for the dialectical rather than dualistic nature of good and evil in the Zohar in *On the Mystical Shape of the Godhead*, pp. 72–78. Scholem does mention that the Zohar takes on both the dualistic and the dialectical position. Isaiah Tishby argues that Lurianic doctrine can only support the complete and utter eradication of evil, which includes the annihilation of the nations once all sparks are rectified via tikun or conversion. See Tishby, *Torat ha-Ra*, pp. 134–143. I think Tishby's reading is much too strong and not nearly as nuanced as the material demands.
64. b.T. Yebamot 24b. For a kabbalistic rendition of the talmudic passage in the spirit of Vital, see Abraham Azulai, *Hesed le-Avraham*, "maʿayan shishi," nahar 7, p. 243.
65. On the problem of conversion in Kabbala more generally, see Elliot R. Wolfson, "Othering the Other: Conversion and the Eschatological Overcoming of Difference," in *Venturing Beyond—Limits of Law and Laws of Limit: Engendering a Kabbalistic Ethos* (Oxford: Oxford University Press, 2006), pp. 129–185.

I'd like to thank Professor Wolfson for making this manuscript available to me before its publication. See also Vital, ShG, intro. 12, p. 114: "The fifth level of souls, which is the worst of all, are souls that come from the body of converts who convert." This seems incongruous with Vital's earlier assessment of converts in his EDT.

66. See also Zohar 3.238b; and 3. 246b. This is also cited in Vital's ShP, p. 36a.

67. The Zohar's use of Genesis passages describing humankind to refer only to Israel is noteworthy. The Zohar's position in general is that only Israel is the descendant of Adam and Eve. Here God's promise of humanity's ruling over all of creation is read as the redemptive promise of Israel ruling over all of humanity, thus distinguishing between Israel and the rest of humankind. See, for example, Zohar 3. 28a.

68. See Mishna Halah 1:1.

69. See also Zohar 3.232b.

70. Zohar 2.120b. Cf. Zohar 3.125b. On the Zohar and conversion more generally, see Wolfson, *Venturing Beyond*, pp. 165ff.

71. But see Zohar Hadash, Yithro, "*sartutin de-mitzkha*," where the ʿ*erev rav* are identified as identical to the gentile nations.

72. In his defense of the conversos, Isaac Abrabanel likens the future redemption to the Exodus from Egypt, claiming that the sinners who have been forced to abandon their faith will return to God. Abrabanel, here quite close to Vital's suggestive reading, never to my knowledge uses the ʿ*erev rav* as a biblical example of this act of return. See Isaac Abrabanel, *Mashmia Yeshuah*, p. 511. Cf. the lengthy discussion of Abrabanel's defense of the conversos in Shaul Regev, "The Attitude Toward the Conversos," pp. 123–128; and Ram Ben-Shalom, "The Conversos as Subversive: Jewish Traditions as Christian Libel?" *Journal of Jewish Studies* 50, no. 2 (1999): 260–264.

73. The notion of the retrieving of the lost Ten Tribes as a prerequisite to the messianic era is quite common. See Rabbi Akiba's position in Mishna Sanhedrin 10:3; Tosefta Sanhedrin 8:12; *Halakhot Gedolot* (Tel-Aviv, 1962), 84a. Also see the references to Isaac Karo in his *Toldot Yizhak*, written in 1518 (Warsaw, 1877), 156a, 163b and the discussion in Abba Hillel Silver, *A History of Messianic Speculation in Israel* (New York: Macmillan, 1927), pp. 115 and 116. Cf. R. Menahem ha-Meiri, *Beit ha-Behira* to b.T. Yebamot, p. 69; and Blidstein, "Who Is Not a Jew?" p. 372 and n. 12. I have not found any source that explicitly posits the ʿ*erev rav* as the Ten Tribes, but such a position would not be far-fetched given their desire to covert upon hearing God's message to Moses. The Ten Tribes did become a part of converso messianic speculation. See, for example, in David M. Gitlitz, *Secrecy and Deceit*, p. 106. The immanent return of the Ten Tribes also appears in the literature of Safed in the early decades of the 16th century and in R. Hayyim Vital's own diary. See David Tamar, "An Epistle from Safed Regarding the Ten Tribes—Dated Either 1526 or 1625" [Hebrew], *Sefunot* 6 (1962): 305–310; and Vital, *Sefer Hizyonot*, p. 71.

74. But see Zohar 3.230a where the ʿ*erev rav* are aligned with Lilith, the demonic first wife of Adam. It seems that the Zohar is somewhat ambiguous about the ʿ*erev rav*. On the one hand, it extends the general rabbinic depiction to metaphysical proportions. On the other hand, it seems to view them dialectically, simultaneously demonic yet a necessary part of the redemptive process.

75. As I indicated above, the general tenor of the Zohar does not reflect this more temperate dialectical view. My point in focusing on this passage is to highlight what may be the foundation of Vital's use of the ʿ*erev rav* to vindicate

the conversos, suggesting that the notion of a fallen Jew and his or her reabsorption into Israel may play an important part in the drama of redemption.

76. In terms of the *ʿerev rav* at Sinai, the midrash equates them with the "riffraff" (*asafsuf*) who complained to Moses in the desert. One would assume that their appearance after Sinai would assume they were also at Sinai. See Numbers Raba 16.24 and Midrash Tanhuma "*be-ha-alotkha*" 17. In the Middle Ages, they became the scapegoats for the sin of the golden calf. See ibn Ezra on Numbers 31.18; Rabbenu Bahya, *Perush Rabbenu Bahya on the Torah* to Exodus 22:8; Exodus 24:5; Leviticus 17:1; and Deuteronomy 21:14. On the *ʿerev rav* in Kabbala more generally, see Yehuda Liebes, "The Haredi Community in Jerusalem and the Judean Desert Sect" [Hebrew], *Mekhkarei Yerushalayim* 2, no. 3 (1982): 142–145.

77. To my knowledge, Vital never cites Nahmanides in his discussions of the *ʿerev rav* in EDT.

78. Nahmanides' *Commentary to the Torah*, Exodus 19:1. Translation mine.

79. See Yovel, "The New Otherness: Marrano Dualities in the First Generation," 3: "What marked the Conversos' existential situation was a new way of being Other . . . The otherness—this being Other within—was expressed first in religious terms, either as dissent from Christianity or as dissent within Christianity, and also as religious laxity or, on the contrary, as exaggerated zeal. . . . At the same time, the Conversos became estranged from the Jews. Though Jews and Marranos have sometimes socialized and associated on a practical level, their more fundamental relation was severance and alienation. Therefore, the Conversos, as a traditional Other's Other, were doubly estranged."

80. This is clearly the case among many descendants of forced conversions in Portugal. See Y. H. Yerushalmi, *From Spanish Court to Italian Ghetto*, pp. 34–42; and Roth, *Conversos*, 8–9. Cf. Cecil Roth, "The Religion of the Marranos," *Jewish Quarterly Review* n.s. 12 (1931): 1–35.

81. See Yerushalmi, *From Spanish Court to Italian Ghetto*, pp. 42–43. "A much more volatile potential was represented by the Marranos during the sixteenth and seventeenth centuries, bringing with them ideas and attitudes which derived, not merely from a different Jewish environment, but from a life lived in a totally gentile world."

82. Vital is altering the verse here. The verse simply reads, "You saw that I spoke to you from the heavens." Vital adds "alone" and "to you and not to them."

83. EDT, 75d.

84. EDT, 77b.

85. They are defined as "converts" from the time they left Egypt and not as a result of experiencing Sinai. See Exodus 12:30 and Rashi ad loc. Cf. Rabbenu Bahya ben Asher, *Rabbenu Bahya ʿal ha-Torah* to Leviticus 22:27. On the notion of the "proximate other" and its implications, see Jonathan Z. Smith, "What a Difference a Difference Makes," in *To See Ourselves as Others See Us*, pp. 3–48.

86. See Zohar 2.105a.

87. Zohar 2.45b.

88. It is not clear whether this "other kind of faith" (*emunah akheret*) refers to a faith different from what they had before or a faith different from that of Israel, who experienced divine speech at Sinai.

89. EDT, 77c/d.

90. See Nahmanides to Exodus 19:1. Nahmanides suggests that the separation between the *ʿerev rav* and the Israelites only occurs when they camp at Mount Sinai. Before that, they traveled together.

91. Vital argues that this consistent rejection by God changes toward the

end of the desert narrative, where He accepts their repentance and places them under the protection of the *Shekhina*. See EDT, pp. 187d–188a.

92. See Zohar 2.7a.

93. EDT, 77c.

94. See, for example, Yerushalmi, *From Spanish Court to Italian Ghetto*, p. 47 and n. 69. Conversion to Christianity as a response to the disappointment of unfulfilled messianism was also not uncommon among conversos. See, for example, Shem Tov ibn Shem Tov, *Derashot* (Jerusalem, 1973), fol. 21a; and Roth, *Conversos*, p. 11 and n. 18. Cf. Elisheva Carlebach, *Divided Souls*, pp. 67–87.

95. See Zohar 2.181b.

96. The "re-Judaization" process for Portuguese Jews in particular was quite difficult. Much can be gained from Isaac Pinto, a Portuguese ex-converso, who describes the plight of these totally uneducated Jews in their attempt to reenter the Jewish community. See Miriam Bodian, *The Hebrews of the Portuguese Nation*, pp. 97–106.

97. See Zohar 2.120b and 3.125b. Another possibility, suggested by Abrabanel, is that the conversos constitute two distinct communities: the first are those who were forced to convert (*ʿanusim*) and are therefore not responsible for their Christian practices. These people will be "returned to God" in the messianic future. The second group consists of Jews who willingly converted for financial or political gain. This second group will be cut off from Israel. See Abrabanel, *Mashmiʿa Yeshuʿah*, pp. 513–514; and Shaul Regev, "The Attitude Toward the Conversos," p. 128. Along these lines one could posit that the entire *ʿerev rav* were fallen Israelites and that their test in the desert was to determine the roots of their fallen-ness. Those who repented for the sin of the golden calf are accepted and returned to Israel. Those who do not are destroyed. In all fairness this requires grafting Abrabanel onto Vital, which is problematic. First of all, Vital never mentions Abrabanel's discussion (we do not know if he had access to his text), and second, Abrabanel never uses the *ʿerev rav* as a biblical mirror in describing the conversos. However, as mentioned above, he does align the future redemption to the Exodus event without giving us too many details.

98. See, for example, Exodus Raba 42.6.

99. See Zohar 1.25a and EDT, 64b.

100. For Vital, what is at stake here is nothing less than the redemption of Israel, an idea that would have resonated well with the already messianic-minded converso community. See Shaul Regev, "The Attitude Toward the Conversos," esp. pp. 122 and 133: "According to the commentators and preachers of the era of the Spanish-Portuguese exiles, the *Conversos* are considered so integral a part of the Jewish people that the ultimate redemption of the Jews will not be possible without the presence of the *Conversos*" (p. 122). Cf. Ram Ben-Shalom, "Conversos as Subversive," p. 262. What Vital adds is that the same was true of the *ʿerev rav*, even as God tried to prevent Moses from taking them out with the Israelites. Moses' insistence can thus be seen as part of his messianic mission.

101. On messianism in Vital and his belief in his own messianic vocation, see David Tamar, "The [Messianic] Expectations in Italy for the Year of Redemption in 1575" [Hebrew] and "The Ari and R. Hayyim Vital and the Messiah son of Joseph" [Hebrew], both in Tamar, *Mekhkarim be-toldot ha-Yehudim be-ʿEretz Yisrael u veʾItalia*.

102. See, for example, Zohar 2.45b and 2.181a.

103. It is interesting that throughout EDT Vital often speaks about the *ʿerev rav* in the first person.

104. EDT, 104c.

105. See Rashi on b.T. Ked 62b. Cf. Maimonides' "Letter to a Proselyte," cited in Lichtenstein, "Brother Daniel and the Jewish Fraternity," *Judaism* 12, no. 3 (1963): 270. See Maimonides, *Teshuvot ha-Rambam*, p. 293.

106. See Genesis Raba 51.2; Rashi on Genesis 19:24; and Exodus 12:29: "Whenever we have the word *And YHVH* (*ve-YHVH*) it refers to God and his Bet Din. The *'vav'* is the language of addition."

107. On the ʿ*erev rav* not being under the Cloud of Glory, see EDT, p. 64b.

108. EDT, p. 104d. The reading of this episode as "not idolatry" is not uncommon in medieval exegesis. While Rashi and others argue unequivocally that it was idolatry, others challenge that position. Nahmanides, for example, in his comment to Exodus 32.1, argues that the act was not idolatrous. Joseph Bekhor Shor of Orleans, a French Tosafist, also claims that the Israelites were only asking for a substitute for Moses and at no time intended the golden calf for idolatrous purposes. On an analysis of Bekhor Shor, see Kalman Bland, *The Artless Jew*, pp. 124–125. It is interesting that commentators like Rashi who view the sin as idolatry are committed to the ʿ*erev rav* as the culprits, while Nahmanides, who does not place the ʿ*erev rav* at the center of this episode, also does not see the sin as idolatry. Hence, Israelite participation, and even instigation, is not as problematic.

109. The notion of doing something "for the sake of God" and having it turn into idolatry appears in many places in scriptural exegesis. See, for example, in Hayyim ben Attar *Or ha-Hayyim* on Exodus 32:4; and Rabbi David Kimhi's (Radak) comments on 1 Kings 12:30. Cf. the discussion of how acting for God can easily become acting against God in Joel Teitelbaum's ʿ*Al ha-geʾula ve-ʿal ha-temura*, pp. 4–10. Teitelbaum uses the episode of the golden calf as a biblical mirror of the Zionist agenda, deeming Zionism as a form of good intentions that, in the end, became idolatrous and disastrous for the Jewish people.

110. On this more generally in classical Judaism, see Alan Segal, *Two Powers in Heaven*, pp. 3–32 and 84–97.

111. I did not reproduce all the verses cited in the text to make this argument. The verses are Exodus 20:19, Deuteronomy 4:36, Exodus 19:20, and 2 Samuel 22:10.

112. EDT, 78b.

113. EDT, 106c.

114. EDT, 106d.

115. The idea that the doctrine of the *sephirot* can be likened to the mediation of Jesus should not be so surprising. In a famous response against Kabbala, Rabbi Isaac ben Sheshet (Ribash) severely criticizes the doctrine of the *sephirot*, drawing a parallel to the Christian doctrine of the Trinity. A similar comment is made by Abraham Abulafia about the *sephirot* in *Ve-Zot le-Yehuda*, p. 19. Cf. Idel, *Messianic Mystics*, p. 60. Moreover, the rise and popularity of Christian Kabbala is, in many respects, based on this premise. For some examples, see Gershom Scholem, "The Beginnings of Christian Kabbala," *The Christian Kabbala*, pp. 17–51; Chaim Wirszubski, *Pico della Mirandola's Encounter with Jewish Mysticism* (Cambridge: Harvard University Press, 1989); *Three Studies in Christian Kabbala* [Hebrew] (Jerusalem, 1975) and *A Christian Kabbalist Reads the Torah* [Hebrew] (Jerusalem, 1977); and Elliot R. Wolfson, "Messianism in the Christian Kabbala of Johann Kemper," *Millenarianism and Messianism in Early Modern European Culture*, vol. 1, pp. 139–187.

116. See Amos Funkenstein, "History, Counter History, and Narrative," in his *Perceptions of Jewish History* (Berkeley: University of California Press, 1993), pp. 39–49.

117. On this, see Leivy Smolar and Moshe Aberbach, "The Golden Calf Episode in Postbiblical Literature," *HUCA* 39 (1968): 91–116.

118. Acts 7 is basically a sustained praise of Moses, retelling his righteous life, and an attempt to see Jesus as the inheritor of the Mosaic covenant. Israel's rejection of Moses in the calf episode is used as proof of the Israelites' inability to accept Moses and subsequently the truth of Jesus as savior.

119. Smolar and Aberbach, "The Golden Calf," pp. 100–101.

120. Ibid. 100. Cf. Augustine, *Exposition on Psalms* 62:5; 74:13; and his *Second Discourse on Psalms* 34:25 and 26.

121. See the rabbinic sources cited in Smolar and Aberbach, "The Gold Calf Episode," pp. 102–105, 107–109, 112. For a stronger reading, see b.T. Avodah Zara 4b: "Said Rebbe Yeshouah ben Levi, 'Israel only sinned with the golden calf to provide an opening to penitents,' as it says, *May it be in their hearts that they should revere me always* (Deut. 5:26)." The talmudic discussion continues, juxtaposing the sin of David and the sin of the calf, arguing that both were necessary to provide proof of individual and collective repentance as part of the covenantal relationship.

122. See Smolar and Aberbach, "The Golden Calf," p. 116: "The early Church made polemical use of the sin of the golden calf for which it blamed the Jews of its time, claiming that God had forever rejected them on account of this sin and that the covenant between God and the Jews was consequently void. The result was that in rabbinic literature, despite frank admissions designed for internal use, Aaron, the Israelites, and the eternity of the covenant between God and the Jewish people were vigorously defended." While this is surely true, Vital offers a different approach by making the ʿerev rav "Christians" and likening their worship of Jesus as God to the ʿerev rav's failure in maintaining the absolute distinction between the calf (*elohim*) and God (YHVH). However, Vital uses this not to polemicize against Christians but against those Jews who were unwilling to accept conversos back into the Jewish community.

123. On the notion of the converso as subversive and thus counter-historical, see Ram Ben-Shalom, "The Converso as Subversive: Jewish Traditions or Christian Libel?"

124. On this, see Moshe Halbertal and Avishai Margalit, *Idolatry*, pp. 180–213.

125. See Judah ha-Levi, *Sefer Kuzari* 1:97. This section in the *Kuzari* has attracted a lot of attention in terms of ha-Levi's attitude toward other religions and his definition of idolatry. While surely placing mediated worship below Judaism, ha-Levi readily acknowledges that Jews also utilize forms of mediated worship, albeit not as pronounced as other religions. Cf. b.T. Ket 112a/b. Like ibn Ezra, ha-Levi argues that the sin of the calf was improper monotheistic worship and not idolatry. In the words of Halbertal and Margalit, "Halevi, who defends the Israelites in the commission of this sin and claims that they did not worship an alien god but rather worshiped God in a way that they were not commanded to, interprets the prohibition on making pictures as a prohibition relating to methods of worship," *Idolatry* (Cambridge: Harvard University Press, 1992), p. 187. Given Halbertal and Margalit's definition, it could be argued that, according to Vital, the calf would have been a legitimate form of worship for the ʿerev rav, since they were not commanded against such worship not having heard God's words at Sinai. The sin may then simply have been inciting Israel into participating with them even as Israel may not have complied. Again, what emerges here is Vital's tolerant view of the basis of mediated worship as a tool to enable the conversos to return.

126. The notion of idolatry as fallen monotheism is not uncommon in medi-

eval Jewish sources. See, for example, Abraham ibn Ezra's "Long Commentary" on Exodus 20:1–17 and Bland, *The Artless Jew*, pp. 132–133. Cf. Maimonides' *Mishneh Torah*, "Laws of Idolatry" 1:1–3.

127. In this regard I think Vital only utilizes part of ibn Ezra's position that idolatry is mistaken monotheism. For Vital, the sin of the calf was mistaken monotheism but not idolatry.

128. Here Vital is following the medieval quasi-rationalist tradition of ibn Ezra, ha-Levi etc. and not the more strident position of the Zohar.

129. In this he follows Abraham ibn Ezra, Judah ha-Levi, Nahmanides, R. Joseph Bekhor Shor, Samuel ben Meir (Rashbam), and others. However, whereas they viewed the sin as occurring in Israel, Vital understands it totally in the camp of the *ʿerev rav*. At most, Israel is silent when challenged by the *ʿerev rav* in Exodus 32:4.

130. EDT, 105a.

131. EDT, 105d.

132. I was unable to locate any direct midrashic or zoharic source for this statement.

133. EDT, 105d.

134. Ibid.

135. The motif of the golden calf and the sufferings of the New Christians at the hands of the inquisitors is not uncommon. See, for example, the inquisitional testimony of Isabel Alveras in 1570, who states that the New Christians are suffering for all of Israel (because of the sin of the golden calf), and the atonement for that sin would bring about the messianic age. Cited and discussed in Goldish, "Patterns in Converso Messianism," p. 46.

136. The notion and status of mediated worship for non-Jews has a long history. For some relevant studies, see Daniel Lasker, *Jewish Philosophical Polemics against Christianity* (New York: Ktav, 1977), pp. 45–134; David Berger, *The Jewish-Christian Debate in the High Middle Ages: A Critical Edition of the Nizzahon vetus with an Introduction, Translation and Commentary* (Northvale, N.J.: Aronson, 1996); Jacob Katz, *Exclusiveness and Tolerance* (New York: Oxford University Press, 1961); and Moshe Halbertal, *Between Torah and Wisdom: Rabbi Menahem Hameʾiri and the Maimonist Masters of Halakha in Provence* [Hebrew] (Jerusalem: Magnes, 2000), esp. pp. 90–108.

137. The Inquisition in 1478 was instituted specifically to deal with the problem of judaizing conversos. There is a long history of Jews persecuting returning apostates. In general, see Jacob Katz, *Exclusiveness and Tolerance*, pp. 67–81, 148–150; Yosef Hayyim Yerushalmi, "Assimilation and Racial Anti-Semitism: The Iberian and the German Models," *Leo Baeck Memorial Lecture* 26 (1982); Elisheva Carlebach, *Divided Souls*, pp. 24–32 and notes there; Gerald Blidstein, "Who Is Not a Jew?—The Medieval Discussion," pp. 369–391; Edward Fram, "Perception and Reception of Repentant Apostates in Medieval Ashkenaz and Premodern Poland," *AJS Review* 21, no. 2 (1996): 299–339. Cf. Yerushalmi, "Assimilation": 17–18.

138. Yosef Hayyim Yerushalmi, "Assimilation," p. 10. In general, see Roth, *Conversos*, pp. 11–14 and notes.

139. This is certainly also true of formal converts. See b.T. Yebamot 46b. The attitude toward converts in not monolithic in rabbinic culture, and, for similar reasons, the same may have been true for conversos. On Vital and converts, interpreting b.T. Yebamot 46b, see SeG, chapter 8, pp. 19–21. The notion that the conversos were the living exemplars of the sin of the golden calf plays a prominent role in Sabbatean literature, especially in the works of Abraham Miguel

Cardozo. See, for example, Bruce Rosenstock, "Abraham Miguel Cardoso's Messianism: A Reappriasal," *AJS Review* 23, no. 1 (1998): 63–104, esp. 90 n. 32.

140. The phenomenon of conversos' syncretistic forms of worship was not uncommon, yielding a Judaism that had Christian values and ideas as its rationalization. Vital may very well have been responding to this well-known phenomenon by using the ʿ*erev rav*'s mistake as a guide to reassimilation into the Jewish fold. On the Christian foundations of converso Judaism, see David M. Gitlitz, *Secrecy and Deceit*, esp. pp. 99–182 and 569–571; Matt Goldish, "Patterns in Converso Messianism," *Millenarianism and Messianism*, vol. 1, p. 42; and Richard Popkin, "Marranos, New Christians, and the Beginning of Anti-Trinitarianism," *Jews and Conversos at the Time of the Expulsion*, pp. 143–161. Some ex-Jews, such as Johann Kemper, had a more conscious and calculated notion of Judaism founded on Christianity. See the penetrating analysis by Elliot R. Wolfson in "Messianism in the Christian Kabbalah of Johann Kemper," *Millenarianism and Messianism*, vol. 1:141–143. Cf. Yovel, "The New Otherness: Marrano Dualities in the First Generation," p. 10.

141. The notion of the disappearance of both Christianity and Islam, or perhaps more accurately, the total nullification, via absorption, of both into Judaism was a prominent idea among Kabbalists, especially in 16th-century Safed. Reuven Kimmelman recently argued that this motif is one theme of the hymn "Lekha Dodi," written by R. Shlomo Alkabetz in 16th-century Safed. See Kimmelman, *The Mystical Meaning of Lekha Dodi and Kabbalat Shabbat* [Hebrew], pp. 82–133.

142. On *gilgul* in general, see Gershom Scholem, *On the Mystical Shape of the Godhead*, pp. 197–250; Most recently, see Lawrence Fine, *Physician of the Soul*, pp. 300–360; Menahem Kallus, "Pneumatic Mystical Possession and the Eschatology of the Soul in Lurianic Kabbala," *Spirit Possession In Judaism*, pp. 163–168; and Mark Verman, "Reincarnation and Theodicy," pp. 399–427. None of these studies address the issue of *gilgul* as an exegetical tool which is distinctive in the Zohar-Luria trajectory.

143. The correlation between returning conversos and the messiah is not uncommon. Abraham Michael Cardozo argued in this vein. Joseph Kaplan notes, "[According to Cardoso] their [the conversos'] return to Judaism was interpreted as an omen and sign of the beginning of the redemption process. The words of the prophet that state 'but do not profane my holy name and more with your idolatrous gifts' (Ezekiel 20:39) came to pass in the form of crypto-Jews who left Spain and joined the Jewish community." See Kaplan, "From Apostasy to Return to Judaism: The Portuguese Jews in Amsterdam," in J. Dan, ed., *Bina: Studies in Jewish History* (New York: Praeger, 1989), vol. 1, p. 110. As far as I know, Vital is the only one who reifies this idea through the lens of the ʿ*erev rav*, arguing that the ʿ*erev rav* share Moses' (messianic) soul. When the ʿ*erev rav* "return," Moses' soul is/will be complete and Israel (as embodied in Moses' soul) will be redeemed.

144. See Zohar 3.282a.

145. See EDT, 173c/d.

146. Vital is certainly taking the verse out of context and, in my view, offering a radical interpretation. It is not, as Deuteronomy states, that the "portion" of God is Israel's election. Rather, it is that the name YHVH is the root and origin of Israel, like the soul of Moses is the origin of the ʿ*erev rav*. Or, as he states later on, the ʿ*erev rav* are under the provenance of *Elohim*, who is, in effect, incarnate in Moses, while Israel is under the provenance of YHVH. In either case, I would suggest that *helko*, or portion, is taken literally and not metaphori-

cally, as it is in Deuteronomy. The idea of Israel being God's portion is similarly employed by a contemporary of Vital, R. Abraham Azulai in his *Hesed le-Avraham* "ma ʿayan sheni," nahar 45, p. 74.

147. EDT, pp. 186d, 187a. See also ShG, intro. 20, p. 143. This text suggests that the in last generation (*be-dara batra*) the entire generation of the desert including the ʿ*erev rav* will be reincarnated, "and Moses will also rise with them." Cf. *Sefer Baʿal Shem Tov ʿal ha-Torah*, vol. 2, p. 464.

148. The depiction of Moses' sinning by supporting the ʿ*erev rav*, which is prominent in the Zohar (e.g., Zohar 1.28b), is also used to identify Luria himself to Moses' failed messianic mission. On this, see Yehuda Liebes, "Two Young Roes of a Doe," p. 118 and n. 33.

149. See EDT, 173a. Cf.SeL, 52a; ShP, p. 22a; and Liebes, "Two Young Roes and a Doe," 120.

150. ʿ*Inyane Shabbatai Zevi*, A. Friedman, ed. (Berlin, 1912), p. 88 cited and discussed by Elliot Wolfson in, "Messianism in the Christian Kabbalah of Johann Kemper," 1:165. Cf. Jacon Sasportas, *Zizat Novel Zvi*, p. 291; Yerushalmi, *From Spanish Court*, pp. 303–306; and David J. Halperin, *Abraham Miguel Cardozo: Selected Writings* (New York: Paulist Press, 2001), p. 55. It was actually not uncommon among converso messianists that a converso would actually be the messiah. See Gitlitz, *Secrecy and Deceit*, pp. 103–109. This is especially true of Sabbatean messianism where Cardozo, a converso, conflates the conversion and messianism of Sabbatai Zvi in light of a Converso. See Matt Goldish, "Patterns in Converso Messianism," pp. 42–43. Vital's Moses is a kind of converso who becomes both the messiah and the redeemer of the ʿ*erev rav;* or, the messiah because he redeems the ʿ*erev rav*, even as his mission ultimately fails.

151. See ShG, intro. 38, p. 369.

152. The reference here is to the *parzuf,* Jacob, situated within the larger *parzuf* of *zeir anpin.*

153. See also R. Meir Poppers ed., LiT, p. 49b.

154. EH 2, vol. 2, gate 32, chapter 2, pp. 35d–36b.

155. Note that the JPS Tanakh translates ʿ*am rav mi-Yisrael* simply as "Israelites," which can only be maintained outside the Zohar's hermeneutics of substitution. Hence, I altered the translation to "people," which sets up Vital's reading.

156. EDT, 187c.

157. See b.T. Shabbat 146a. This ties the sin of Adam and Eve to Sinai where the Talmud relates that the poison of the serpent, first implanted in Genesis 3, now ceases to have any power of Israel. Apparently, at least according to Vital, the ʿ*erev rav* were at Sinai but, not hearing God's words, did not merit liberation from the serpent's poison. This reading fits very well with the ʿ*erev rav* as guilty of making the golden calf and not the Israelites. If the Israelites were no longer burdened by the poison of the serpent, how could they have made the calf? There is a disagreement as to whether the sin of the calf revived the serpent's poison in the Israelites.

158. EDT, 187d.

159. Ibid.

160. On the relationship between the messiah (Moses?) and the convert, see Vital, SeG, chapter 35, p. 99.

161. On the Exodus as the correction of the sin of Adam and the re-membering of his fallen body, see ShP, pp. 20a–23b.

162. See David Tamar, "The AR'I and R. Hayyim Vital and Messiah the Son of Joseph," in *Mekhkarim be-toldot ha-Yehudim be-Erez Yisrael uve-'Italia*, pp. 115–

123. Moshe Idel is much more skeptical of translating Luria's messianic metaphysics to his person. See Moshe Idel, *Messianic Mystics*, pp. 154–182.

163. See Vital's introduction to *Shaʿar ha-Hakdamot* printed as the introduction to EH 4d (top). Vital's language is quite interesting. He describes Kabbalah more generally and Luria's teachings in particular as "revealing one hands breath and concealing two." This is a play on the statement attributed to R. Eliezer in b.T. Ned 20b: "[it] reveals one hand breath and conceals two." This description of esotericism is, of course, not limited to Kabbalah. Moses Maimonides, in the introduction to his *Guide of the Perplexed*, makes a similar argument regarding his own philosophical esotericism. Cf. Maimonides, *The Guide of the Perplexed*, 1.18.

164. See Yizhak Baer, *The History of the Jews of Spain*, vol. 2, pp. 143–145.

165. On this phenomenon more generally, focusing on Western Europe and Amsterdam, see Yosef Kaplan, *From New Christians to New Jews* [Hebrew] (Jerusalem: Zalman Shazar, 2003).

166. Christianity's suspicion of the conversos is well known and documented and was the source of inquisitions and expulsions in both Spain and Portugal. Cf. Isaac Abrabanel's comment to Exodus 20:33. It is also worth noting that some scholars blamed the Reformation and the fracturing of the Catholic Church on the descendants of conversos who, as Judaizers, attempted to destroy the Church from within. See, for example, L. I. Newman, *Jewish Influence on Christian Reform Movements;* H. H. Ben Sasson, "The Reformation in Contemporary Jewish Eyes," *Israel Academy of Science and Humanities* 4, no. 12 (1970); "Jews and Christian Sectarians," *Viator* 4 (1973): 369–385; and Ram Ben-Shalom, "The Converso as Subversive," pp. 279–284. On the attitude of the reformers toward converting the Jews more generally, see Christopher M. Clark, *The Politics of Conversion: Missionizing Protestants and the Jews in Russia* (Oxford: Oxford University Press, 1995).

167. We have earlier kabbalistic cases (e.g., R. Joseph Hamadan) where conversion is viewed as a necessary part of the redemptive process. See the discussion in Idel, *Kabbalah and Eros*, pp. 114–117.

168. In this last sense I think there is an ideational link between Vital and Luria and Abraham Miguel Cardozo's "Marrano Messiah." Cardozo, as noted, believed the messiah was one who must embody this notion of "crossing-over," either, as in his case, born a Christian (converso) and then becoming a Jew or, as in Sabbatai Zvi's case, being born a Jew and crossing over (ostensibly) into Islam. This apparently deviant understanding of the personhood of the messiah has, I believe, deep roots in the Lurianic tradition, as I have exhibited in this chapter.

3. Leviticus

1. For a preliminary study, see Moshe Idel, "Sexual Metaphors and Praxis in the Kabbala," in *The Jewish Family: Metaphor and Meaning*, David Kraemer, ed. (New York: Oxford University Press, 1989), pp. 197–224. Cf. Elliot Wolfson, "Gender and Heresy in the Study of Kabbala" [Hebrew], *Kabbala: Journal for the Study of Jewish Mystical Texts* 6 (2001): 231–262.

2. On Eros and Kabbala, see Yehuda Liebes, "Eros and the Zohar" [Hebrew], *'Alpayim* 9 (1994): 67–119; Wolfson *Through a Speculum that Shines* (Princeton, N.J.: Princeton University Press, 1995), esp. pp. 326–392; "Crossing Gender Boundaries in Kabbalistic Ritual and Myth," in *Circle in the Square* (Albany, N.Y.: SUNY Press), pp. 79–121. Also you have "alternative" codes of law written by kabbalists and their disciples, SA ha-Ari, SH ha-Rav, etc. While not deviant

in substance, although sometimes they are, the whole notion of an alternative code is a subversive act, even if its result is an increase of pious demands.

3. See Elliot Wolfson, "Beyond Good and Evil: Hypernomianism, Transmorality, and Kabbalistic Ethics," in *Crossing Boundaries: Essays on the Ethical Status of Mysticism*, G. W. Barnard and J. J. Kriplal, eds. (New York: Seven Bridges, 2001), pp. 103–156. Cf. Talya Fishman, "A Kabbalistic Perspective on Gender-Specific Commandments," *AJS Review* 17 (1992): 199–245.

4. See Gershom Scholem, *Major Trends in Jewish Mysticism*, p. 292.

5. On the centrality of halakha as the success of Lurianic Kabbala, see Moshe Idel, "Differing Conceptions of Kabbalah in the Early 17th Century," in *Jewish Thought in the Seventeenth Century*, I. Twersky and B. Septimus, eds. (Cambridge: Harvard University Press, 1987), p. 138. Idel notes that the centrality of *ta'amei ha-mitzvot*, and the halakhic underpinnings of 16th-century Lurianic Kabbala more generally, disappears in the Renaissance Kabbala of the early 17th century, which may provide an important link between orthodox Lurianism and Sabbateanism. Cf. Scholem, *Sabbatai Sevi*, pp. 86 and 87.

6. See David Halperin, *The Construction of Homosexuality* (Chicago: University of Chicago Press, 1988), esp. pp. 1–25; and John Boswell, *Christianity, Social Tolerance and Homosexuality* (Chicago: University of Chicago Press, 1980). There are two recent book-length studies of homosexuality in Judaism: Steven Greenberg, *Wrestling Between God and Men: Homosexuality in the Jewish Tradition* (Madison: University of Wisconsin Press, 2003) and Rabbi Chaim Rapoport, *Judaism and Homosexuality: An Authentic Orthodox View* (London: Vallentine Mitchell, 2003). Greenberg's book gives a creative reading of the sources in an attempt to wedge an opening for the acceptance of homosexuality in Jewish Orthodoxy. Rapoport's is an analysis of the prohibition, using a plethora of classical sources but offering no new insights. He does argue for tolerance and compassion but remains steadfast in the unalterable prohibitive nature of the act. While Greenberg does use some recent theoretical studies of gender and homosexuality, his weakness, in my view, is in his overt attempt to convince a community that will not be convinced. Rapoport seems quite unaware of recent studies on gender and bases his argument exclusively on classical sources. It is more erudite than Greenberg's but far less creative and synthetic.

7. The texts that will serve as the foundation of this chapter include *Sha'ar ha-Yehudim*, *Sha'ar Mamrei Rashbi*, and *Sefer ha-Kelalim*. All three texts overlap yet each one contains certain elements absent in the others. I do not engage in the complex bibliographical debates about reaction here. I am concerned, rather, with the text as text, with what it offers a reader interested in the construction of gender through a kabbalistic lens.

8. See Yaron Ben-Na'eh, "Mishkav Zakhur be-Hevra ha-Yehudit be-Ottomonit," *Zion* 65 (2001): 171–200; and Ruth Lamdan, "Deviations from Normative Ethical Rules in the Jewish Communities in Erez Israel and Egypt in the Sixteenth Century" [Hebrew], in *Eros, Erusin, and Issurim*, I. Bartal and I. Gafni, eds. (Jerusalem, 1998), pp. 119–130.

9. Commenting on a colleague, Israel Najara, Vital notes that, among other things, he was guilty of homosexual acts committed in a drunken state. Then, more generally, he comments about Damascus: "There is much homosexuality and much perversion and delay of justice in this land." R. Hayyim Vital, *Sefer Hizyonot* (Jerusalem, 2002), p. 89. An English translation can be found in Morris Faierstein, *Spiritual Autobiography* (New York: Paulist Press, 1999), p. 71. On Najara, see Meir Benayahu, "R. Israel Najara," [Hebrew] *Asufot*

4 (1990): 203–284. For a latter source explicitly mentioning the prevalence of homosexual acts among Jewish males, see R. Isaac Molkho, *'Orhot Yashar* (Salonica, 1769), 145a cited in Ben-Na'eh, "Mishkav Zakhur," p. 183.

10. *Shulkhan Arukh*, Eben ha-Ezer, 24:1. "Israel should not be suspect in the transgression of (male) homosexual acts and bestiality. Therefore, there is no prohibition of being alone [with another male or an animal]. . . . However, in our generation there are many guilty of these prohibitions and it is recommended to avoid being alone with another male." The commentaries on this precept interestingly substitute time for place in Karo's statement. For example, R. Yoel Sirkus's commentary (known as the Bayit Hadash) states, "The Rav (Karo) writes this because in his place of residence (*medinato;* i.e., Safed) this transgression was commonplace." This comment is cited by most commentators to this chapter. From this, one could posit that the commentators, many of whom lived in Christian, and not Muslim, lands, some of whom lived in the same century as Karo, recognized that the Ottoman Empire, including Erez Israel, was a place where homosexual acts were not unusual. In his commentary Beit Schmuel, R. Schmuel Feorda adds that in his land, what Karo demands is supererogatory and not obligatory. However, he continues, regarding two males who lie together [presumably for the purposes of warmth], this is prohibited, all the more so if it is two single men.

11. On the prohibition of single males residing in Jerusalem, see Azriel Shohar, "The Jews in Jerusalem in the 18th Century" [Hebrew], *Zion* 1 (1936): 396. Cf. the discussion in Ruth Lamdan, *A Separate People: Jewish Women in Palestine, Syria, and Egypt in the Sixteenth Century* (Leiden: Brill, 2000), pp. 127–138. Lamdan argues that the root of the prohibition is an attempt to prevent licentious behavior between single Jewish males and Jewish and gentile women. Ben-Ne'ah extends this to include the fear of homosexual male liaisons. Ben-Ne'ah's position is supported by sources Lamdan herself cites. For example, citing Toledano's regulation #8, p. 50 (cited in Lamdan on p. 28), we read, "While some fathers marry off their children around the age of 13 or 14, others wait until they are 25 years of age or more in the hope of contracting a more advantageous match. These end up *committing a number of transgressions which carry the death penalty* [italics hers]." It would seem to me the only two transgressions relevant here that would carry the death penalty would be sex with a married woman or homosexuality. While the former is surely possible, and probably did indeed occur, given Ben Ne'ah's evidence the latter is at least as, or perhaps more, possible, since it did not carry the added danger of confronting the wrath of the woman's husband and family or the danger of producing a *mamzer.*

12. There is a disagreement in the sources as to whether female homosexuality is biblical or rabbinic. See b.T. Yebamat 76a; Maimonides, *Sefer ha-Mitzvot*, negative commandment #353; *Tur Shulkhan Arukh* "Even ha-Ezer," 20; and *Shulkhan Arukh* "Even ha-Ezer" 20:2. For more sources, see Rapoport, *Judaism and Homosexuality*, pp. 2–5 and notes, pp. 142–144. One of the few studies that deals with female homoeroticism in classical Kabbala is Elliot Wolfson's "Fore/giveness On the Way: Nesting in the Womb of Response," in *Luminal Darkness* (Madison: University of Wisconsin Press, 2007). I want to thank Professor Wolfson for making this chapter available to me before publication. In general, see Bernatte Brooton, *Love Between Women: Early Christian Responses to Female Homoeroticism* (Chicago: University of Chicago, 1996), esp. pp. 61–71. The curious absence of female homoeroticism in Lurianic Kabbala should not be surprising. The kabbalistic system is a male-centered and male-dominated metaphysics. The female plays, at best, a marginal role in

the metaphysical construct of the Kabbala even given the prominence of the *shekhina*. While the *sephirah malkhut* and the more obsequious *shekhina* play major roles in the kabbalistic imagination, they do so largely in relation to, and not distinct from, their male counterpart, which is not the case for the male. For some illustrative studies, see Gershom Scholem, "The Feminine Element in the Divinity," in his *The Mystical Shape of the Godhead*, pp. 140–196; Yehuda Liebes, "Eros and the Zohar" [Hebrew], *'Alpayim* 9 (1994): 67–119; Elliot R. Wolfson, "Erasing the Erasure/Gender and the Writing of God's Body in Kabbalistic Symbolism," in *Circle in the Square* (Albany, N.Y.: SUNY Press, 1995), pp. 49–78; Yoram Jacobson, "The Feminine Aspect in Lurianic Kabbala," in *Major Trends: Fifty Years After;* Peter Schafer, Joseph Dan, eds. (Tubingen: Mohr, 1993), pp. 239–255. On female homoeroticism in classical Judaism more generally, see Michael Satlow, "They Abused Him Like a Woman: Homoeroticism, Gender Blurring, and the Rabbis of Late Antiquity," *Journal of the History of Sexuality* 5 (1994): 16ff; Daniel Boyarin, "Are There Any Jews in 'The History of Sexuality'?" *Journal of the History of Sexuality* 5, no. 3 (1995): 339, 340; and Bernadette Brooton, *Love Between Women*, pp. 61–71.

13. See John Boswell, *Christianity, Social Tolerance, and Homosexuality*, pp. 92–100; Robin Scroggs, *The New Testament and Homosexuality: Contextual Background for a Contemporary Debate* (Philadelphia, 1983); David F. Greenberg, The *Construction of Homosexuality*, pp. 274–279; David F. Greenberg and Marcia H. Bystryn, "Christian Intolerance of Homosexuality," *American Journal of Sociology* 28, no. 3 (1982): 515–548; Michael Satlow, "And They Abused Him Like a Woman," p. 24; Boyarin, "Are There Any Jews," p. 350; and Martti Nissinen, *Homoeroticism in the Biblical World: A Historical Perspective* (Minneapolis: Fortress, 1998), p. 106. It is not insignificant that Paul's most sustained discussion about the prohibition of male–male sex (Rom. 1:26–32) never mentions Leviticus 18 or 20, although, as Nissinen notes, "It can be assumed that Paul has Leviticus in mind." Boswell posits that the Leviticus passages as the basis for Christian notions of the prohibition are problematic. "The irrelevance of the verses (Leviticus 18:22 and 20:13) was further emphasized by the teaching of both Paul and Jesus that under new dispensation it was not the physical violation of Levitical precepts which constituted 'abomination' but the internal infidelity of the soul. . . . Within a few generations of the first disciples, the majority of converts to Christianity were not Jews, and their attitude toward Jewish law was to say the least ambivalent" (Boswell, p. 102). According to Boswell, Christianity is wed to the story of Sodom as the source of the biblical prohibition. As he shows, the biblical story is far from explicit and most early pre-Christian Jewish commentators are not at all convinced that the sin of Sodom was one of male homosexuality. As we will see, Lurianic texts do not employ the Sodom story in their discussions. Moreover, they equate the sin of Sodom with the sin of "spilling seed" more generally, like the sin of Adam, and not with male–male intercourse. Cf. D. S. Bailey, *Homosexuality and the Western Christian Tradition* (London: Longmans, Green, and Co., 1955).

14. For example, Genesis Raba 26:5, 50:5,7; Leviticus Raba 23:9. In other instances, the sin of Sodom is interpreted as a sin of arrogance and injustice. See b.T. Sanhedrin 109a; b.T. Baba Batra 12b; 59a, 168a/b. There is a possible connection to be made between the sin of arrogance and male–male intercourse. See, for example, Mekhilta Beshalakh (Horowitz, ed., p. 140) cited and discussed in Satlow, p. 19. While this text does not speak about Sodom, it draws a correlation between the sin of arrogance and the insertive homosexual partner. While this may be a forced reading of the sources that state the sin as one of inhospitality, it is worth noting.

15. In terms of the interpretive tradition of the Leviticus verses, Steven Greenberg, in *Wrestling Between God and Men* (see pp. 74–85), offers some very creative and insightful possibilities as to new approaches to these verses. The two major early Jewish sources that interpret the Sodom sin as one of homosexuality are Philo Judeaus of Alexandria and Flavius Josephus. These Jewish authors were strongly influenced by Hellenistic culture more generally, and their understanding of male–male sex as "unnatural" (with Paul) seems to be a product of that influence. On Sodom in Josephus, see *Antiquities* 1.194–204. Cf. *Against Apion* 2.199. In Philo, see *On Abraham* 135–136. More generally, see Satlow, "And They Abused Him Like a Woman," pp. 7–9, Nissinen, *Homoeroticism in the Biblical World*, pp. 93–97; Boswell, pp. 128–130; and Scroggs, "The New Testament and Homosexuality," pp. 88–91. On the adaptation of Hellenistic values into Judaism through Philo more generally, see Samuel Sandmel, *Philo of Alexandria: An Introduction* (New York: Oxford University Press, 1979), p. 122.

16. See, for example, Boswell, Halperin, Nissenen, Olyan, Boyarin, and Satlow. There is a disagreement among Jewish jurists on how to read Maimonides on the biblical nature of female homosexuality. Some, like Moshe d' Trani (Keryat Sefer on Maimonides *Sefer ha-Mitzvot* #15) and Hayyim Rosen (*Zofnat Paʿaneah*, Dvinsk, vol. 1, nos. 90 and 113), hold it is a biblical prohibition while most others, including the 20th-century jurist Moshe Feinstein, hold that it is rabbinic. See Norman Lamm, "Judaism and the Modern Attitude to Homosexuality," *L'Eylah* 1, no. 3 (1977).

17. I will ignore Olyan's discussion in his essay on those biblical passages as it relates to more formal and technical Bible scholarship, as that is not relevant to our subject.

18. See Olyan, p. 184.

19. Ibid., pp. 201 and 202, against Howard Elberg-Schwartz, *The Savage in Judaism* (Bloomington: Indiana University Press, 1990).

20. Olyan, pp. 186, 187, 189, 199, 204.

21. Ibid., p. 195.

22. See, for example, in Boyarin, pp. 351, 353 and n. 43; Halperin, pp. 48–50; Nissinen, pp. 93f and the appendix, "Creation, Nature, and Gender Identity," pp. 135–140; and more generally, on the topic of natural law and Judaism, David Novak, *Natural Law and Judaism* (Cambridge: Cambridge University Press, 1998), esp. pp. 62–91; and, more specifically, "Religious Communities, Secular Society, and Sexuality: One Jewish Opinion," in *Sexual Orientation and Human Rights in American Religious Discourse*, S. Olyan and M. Nussbaum, eds. (New York: Oxford University Press, 1998), pp. 17–23. On the question of the unnaturalness of homosexuality, Novak is more circumspect. He offers three definitions of nature: (1) nature as what is necessary; (2) nature as what is real; and (3) nature as a desire to procreate. It is only in this third definition that heterosexuality is privileged, according to Novak. This notion of homosexuality as unnatural because is makes procreation impossible is based in Philo, who is one of the earliest proponents of this argument. See Boswell, p. 155; Nissinen, pp. 93–97. For another rendering of the various meanings of "nature," see Nissinen, pp. 135–139. On sex and procreation in classical Judaism, see David Biale, *Eros and the Jews* (Berkeley: University of California Press, 1997), pp. 33–59, and Daniel Boyarin, *Carnal Israel: Reading Sex in Talmudic Culture* (Berkeley: University of California Press, 1993), pp. 53–57.

23. On the notion of purity as a basis of the Levitical laws more generally, see Mary Douglas, *Purity and Danger* (London: Routledge, 1984), pp. 42–58; Olyan, p. 205, Jerome Walsh, p. 205.

24. On this, see b.T. Sanhedrin 54 a/b and Mishna Sanhedrin 7:4.

25. Walsh, p. 204.

26. Olyan, p. 205.

27. Satlow, pp. 2 and 3.

28. Boyarin, p. 348.

29. Walsh, p. 208.

30. Olyan, p. 205.

31. Walsh, p. 207.

32. Satlow, p. 9.

33. Ibid., pp. 2 and 10, where Satlow states unequivocally that only the active partner is culpable in the Bible. This is in concert with Olyan. Jerome Walsh challenges Olyan's conclusions on this matter. I am not sure if that dispute would impact Satlow's analysis since by the time this prohibition reaches the rabbis in late Antiquity, dual culpability was already normative.

34. Ibid., p. 23.

35. Boswell's main thesis, that Christianity's negative attitude toward homosexuality is drawn from host cultures, is challenged by the "constructivist" school, most prominently by David Halperin in *One Hundred Years of Homosexuality*, esp. pp. 41–53. For a defense of the "moral" case against homosexuality as endemic to Christianity, see Richard Hays, *The Moral Vision of the New Testament* (San Francisco: Harper San Francisco, 1996).

36. Boyarin's work on this question has developed considerably since then. See, for example, his *Unheroic Conduct* (Berkeley: University of California Press, 1997), esp. pp. 221–270.

37. See Michel Foucault, *The History of Sexuality*, Robert Hurley, trans. (New York: Vintage Books, 1990), esp. "Scientia Sexualis," pp. 53–73; and David Halperin, *One Hundred Years*, pp. 15–39.

38. See Satlow, p. 19. This idea is developed by Moses Maimonides in his discussion about circumcision. See Maimonides, *Guide of the Perplexed*, two volumes, Shlomo Pines, trans. (Chicago: University of Chicago, 1963), vol. 2, Part III: 49, p. 609. On this, see Josef Stern, "Maimonides on the Circumcision and the Unity of God," in *The Midrashic Imagination*, Michael Fishbane, ed. (Albany, N.Y.: SUNY Press, 1993), pp. 131–154. Cf. Nisinen on Josephus and Philo, p. 94. This is also true of Christian views of gentiles. See William L. Countryman, *Dirt, Greed, and Sex: Sexual Ethics in the New Testament and Their Implications for Today* (Philadelphia: Ausburg Fortress, 1988), p. 117.

39. Satlow, p. 19.

40. See Thomas Thurston, "Leviticus 18:22 and the Prohibition of Homosexual Acts," in *Homophobia and the Judeo-Christian Tradition*," M. L. Stemmeler and J. M. Clark, eds. (Dallas, Tex.: Monument, 1990), pp. 7–23.

41. Boyarin, "Are There Any Jews in 'The History of Sexuality'?" p. 341.

42. The notion of cross-dressing, or transvestism, is not foreign to medieval culture. See Vern L. Bullough, "Transvestism in the Middle Ages," in *Sexual Practices in the Medieval Church*, V. L. Bullough and J. Brundage, eds. (Buffalo, N.Y.: Prometheus Books, 1982), pp. 43–54.

43. Ibid. Cf. Halperin, *One Hundred Years*, pp. 88–112.

44. Ibid., pp. 339–343.

45. The issue of homoeroticism in Kabbala, specifically in the theosophic tradition, has been explored by Elliot Wolfson in "Eunuchs Who Keep the Sabbath: Becoming Male and the Ascetic Ideal in Thirteenth Century Jewish Mysticism," in *Becoming Male in the Middle Ages*, J. J. Cohen and B. Wheeler, eds.

(New York: Garland, 1997), pp. 151–185, esp. pp. 165–174; and *Language, Eros, Being* (New York: Fordham, 2005), pp. 296–332. Cf. the yet unpublished essay by Joel Hecker, "Kissing Kabbalists: A Mystical Gesturer between Men and with God," delivered at the conference of the American Academy of Religion, 2002. I want to thank Dr. Hecker for providing me with a copy of his paper.

46. The notion that any gender also contains its opposite is common in many religious traditions, especially in Hinduism. See, for example, in Vern L. Bullough and Bonnie Bullough, *Cross Dressing, Sex, and Gender* (Philadelphia: University of Pennsylvania Press, 1993), pp. 6–10.

47. For Philo, unnatural sex constituted not only same-sex relations but any sexual act not done for the sake of procreation. Intimacy is not a criteria of sexuality for Philo, be it homosexual or heterosexual. More strongly, engaging is such sexual activity is deemed "unnatural." Philo openly criticized men who married barren women and rejected sexual pleasure as having any benefit whatsoever. See Philo, *On Special Laws*, F. H. Colson, ed. and trans. (London: William Heinemen, 1958), III:113; and Vern L. Bullough, "The Sin Against Nature and Homosexuality," in *Sexual Practices and the Medieval Church*, V. L. Bullough and J. Brundage, eds. (Buffalo: Prometheus Books, 1982), pp. 57, 58. Cf. Michael Goodich, *The Unmentionable Vice: Homosexuality in the Later Medieval Period* (New York: Dorset Books, 1979). More generally, see James T. Noonan, *Contraception: A History of its Treatment by the Catholic Theologians and Canonists* (Cambridge: Belknap Press of Harvard University, 1966). The prominence of natural law as the foundation for the Christian prohibition of homosexuality comes from Thomas Aquinas. See Aquinas, *Basic Writings of St. Thomas Aquinas*, vols. 1 and 2, Anton C. Pegis, ed. (New York: Random House, 1945), pp. 750, 775, 776. Cf. the use of natural law theory in John Finnis, *Natural Law and Natural Rights* (Oxford: Clarendon, 1980) and a critique of Finnis in Martha Nussbaum, *Sex and Social Justice*, pp. 299–331. Following Philo (and more directly Paul) and the Hellenistic influence on Jewish, or late Israelite, notions of sexuality, the Church canonized "unnatural" sexual practices as any practice (with any partner) that does not potentially lead to procreation. Homosexuality is included in this category not because it is a sexual act with the same gender but because it is an act that cannot result in procreation. Judaism could not adopt this stance because the sages explicitly acknowledge sexual pleasure (especially for the woman) and intimacy as part of legitimate sexuality. See, for example, in David Novak, "Religious Communities, Secular Society, and Sexuality: One Jewish Opinion," in *Sexual Orientation*, pp. 15–17. Hence, some Jewish (and Christian) interpreters sever homosexuality from nonprocreative heterosexuality more generally and call it, and only it, "unnatural." This move has little basis in classical sources, both Jewish and Christian. Novak uses the natural law argument as only one piece of his justification for the prohibition of homosexuality. He designates homosexuality as part of the category of *gilluy ῾arayot* (illicit sexuality including incest), making it one of the Noahide laws. Hence, from a Jewish perspective, he argues homosexuality is a universal prohibition extending to all of humanity. This case is also supported by Rapoport in *Judaism and Homosexuality*, p. 4.

48. Sigmund Freud, "Three Lectures on Sexuality," in Sigmund Freud, *Sexuality: Three Essays on the Theory of Sex* (London: Penguin Books, 1953), pp. 46–170. Carl Jung treats this issue as well. See *Man and His Symbols*, Carl Jung, ed. (New York: Doubleday, 1964).

49. There are many studies on the messianism in Lurianic Kabbala. On the latest statement of messianism in Luria, see Moshe Idel, *Messianic Mystics*, pp. 154–182 and notes.

50. The messianism of Luria's fraternity is a complex issue. For some relevant discussions, see Scholem, *Major Trends in Jewish Mysticism*, pp. 244–286; Lawrence Fine, *Physician of the Soul, Healer of the Cosmos*, pp. 300–360; and Moshe Idel, *Messianic Mystics*, pp. 154–182.

51. The historical work on this period does analyze the general Islamic context in which the Safed kabbalists worked, but none of them delve into the intellectual, theological, and cultural influence that may underlie Lurianic Kabbala. The most recent and comprehensive analysis of the Lurianic circle in its historical context is Lawrence Fine's *Physical of the Soul*. While Fine's thorough work provides the reader with important doctrinal and historical data, he does not relate Lurianic doctrine to its Islamic or Ottoman context. See esp. pp. 20–27. See Abraham David, *To Come to the Land*; Mordecai Pachter *Me-Zefunot Safed* (Israel: Zalman Shazar Institute, 1994); Meir Benayahu, *Toldot ha-Ari* (Jerusalem, 1967); David Tamar, *Mekharim be-oldot ha-Yehudim be-rez Yisrael u be-Italia*; and *Aliyah v Hityashvut be-Erez Yisrael be-Meah ha-Shishit* (Jerusalem: Reuven Moss, 1993); and Schmuel Avitsur, "Safed—Center for the Manufacture of Woven Woolens in the Fifteenth Century" [Hebrew], *Sefunot* 6 (1962): 43–69.

52. See Fine, *Physician of the Soul*, pp. 27–39.

53. Vital was born in 1542, apparently in Safed. An intellectual biography of Vital is still a desideratum. See Scholem, *Kabbala* (New York: Dorset Books, 1974), pp. 442–448.

54. The tolerant and sometimes embracing relationship between the Ottoman Empire and its Jews has been well documented. For some examples, see Salo Baron, *Social and Religious History of the Jews*, vol. 18: 120ff; Stanford Shaw, *The Jews of the Ottoman Empire and the Turkish Republic* (New York: New York University Press, 1991); and Halil Inalcik, "Foundations of Ottoman-Jewish Cooperation," in *Jews, Turks, Ottomans*, Avigdow Levy, ed. (Syracuse, N.Y.: Syracuse University Press, 2003), pp. 3–14.

55. See Jeremy A. Bellamy, *Sex and Society in Islamic Popular Literature*, in *Society and the Sexes in Medieval Spain* (Malibu, Calif: Udena, 1979), pp. 23–42; and Jim Wafer, "Muhammad and Male Homosexuality," in *Islamic Homosexualities: Culture, History, and Literature*, S. O. Murray and W. Roscoe, eds. (New York: New York University Press, 1997), pp. 87–97.

56. Quran 7:80–84; 11:77–83; 21:74; 22:43; 26:165–185; 27:56–59; 29:27–33. In colloquial Arabic, homosexuals are called *qaum Lut* (Lot's people) and the homosexual is called a *Luti* (Lotist). As noted by Khalid Duran, this is quite odd given that Lot, in fact, distanced himself from his community because of their behavior. See Khalid Duran, "Homosexuality in Islam," in *Homosexuality and World Religions*, Arlene Swidler, ed. (Valley Forge, Pa.: Trinity Press International, 1993), pp. 181, 182.

57. See Bellamy, *Sex and Society*, p. 89; and Jehodeda Sofer, "Sodomy in the Law of Muslim States," in *Sexuality and Eroticism among Males in Moslem Societies*, A. Schmitt and J. Sofer, eds. (New York: Harworth, 1992), pp. 1–24. In actuality, homosexuality does not even warrant the more formal punishment (*hadd*) but the more flexible notion of *taʾzir*.

58. For example, see A. Abu-Khalil, "A Note on the Study of Homosexuality in the Arab/Islamic Civilization," *Arab Studies Journal* 1–2 (1993): 32–34; M. Daniel, "Arab Civilization and Male Love," in *Reclaiming Sodom*, J. Goldberg, ed. (New York: Taylor & Francis, 1994), pp. 59–65; Khalid Duran, "Homosexuality and Islam," pp. 195–197; and Yaron Ben-Na'eh, "*Mishkav Zakhor* Among Jews in the Ottoman Empire" [Hebrew], *Zion* 65 (2001): 174.

59. On this, also see Boswell, *Christianity*, pp. 195ff.

60. Steven O. Murray, "The Will Not to Know: Accommodations of Male Homosexuality," in *Islamic Homosexualities*, pp. 14–54. Cf. Everett K. Rowson, "Two Homoerotic Narratives from Mamluk Literature," in *Homoeroticism in Classical Arabic Literature*, J. W. Wright Jr. and E. K. Rowson, eds. (New York: Columbia University Press, 1997), p. 166. Rowson discusses the Hanbalite response to the Sufi practice of gazing at young boys. Even the strict and rigid Hanbalite legalists acknowledge the naturalness of homoerotic desire, while strictly prohibiting it. On the use of young boys as objects of contemplation, see William C. Chittick, *The Sufi Path of Love: The Spiritual Teachings of Rumi* (Albany, N.Y.: SUNY Press, 1983), p. 288. "Certain Sufis, such as Awhad al-Din Kirmani and Fakhr al-Din Iraqi, seem to have made systematic use of outward objects in the world as supports for the contemplation of the inward Witness. These two figures in particular are known for meditating upon the Witness as reflected in the person of young boys, a practice for which they were often blamed by other Sufis, including Shams-I Tabrizi himself." Paul Fenton connects this practice to the Sufi practice of gazing at the face and form of one's master. See Fenton, "The Influence of Sufism on Safed Kabbala" [Hebrew], *Mahanayim* 6 (1994): 177. As Fenton notes, this practice had deep influence among kabbalists, particularly Moses Cordovero and the circle of Isaac Luria. For Fenton's more expanded discussion, see his "Influences Soufies sur le development de la Qabbale a Safed: le cas de la visitation des tombes," in *Experience et écriture mystiques dans les religions du livre*, P. Fenton and R. Goetschel, eds. (Leiden: Brill, 2000), pp. 163–190.

61. Khlaid Duran, "Homsexuality and Islam," pp. 190–192 and Sofer, "Sodomy in the Law of Muslim States." Islamic tradition, going back at least to the 9th century has dealt with the desire for cross-dressing and becoming the other sex. For example, the 9th-century Quran exegete Al-Bukhari wrote an entire treatise on the subject of individuals who desire to become the opposite sex. See Abu ad Allah ibn al-Bukhari, *Sahih*, Muhammad Assad trans. (Lahore, Pakistan: Awafat, 1938). More generally, see Unni Wikan, "Man becomes Woman: Transsexualism in Oman as a Key to Gender Roles," *Man* (new series) 12 (1977): 304–319. Cf. Bullough/Bullough, *Cross Dressing*, pp. 12–14.

62. See Jim Wafer, *Islamic Homosexualities*, p. 91. John Boswell, *Christianity*, pp. 278–283, notes that the commonality of homosexuality in Muslim societies was used against them by Christians. This is true among Jews as well. The rabbis often view the "gentile" Other as, among other things, guilty of homosexuality, thereby making it a deplorable act for Jews. See, for example, in Josephus Antiquities 15:2; b.T. Shabbat 17b, 149b; Tosefta Avodah Zara 3:2; and Mishna 2:1. Cf. Lewis John Eron, "Homosexuality and Judaism," in *Homosexuality and World Religions*, Arlene Swidler, ed. (Valley Forge, Pa.: Trinity Press International, 1993), p. 116. Boswell argues that this natural law argument against homosexuality is rare in early Christianity (which shares much of the cultural context of rabbinic Judaism), and appears most prominently in medieval Christianity influenced by Hellenism.

63. Rowson, "Two Homoerotic Narratives from Mamluk Literature." See also Wright Jr., "Masculine Allusion and the Structure of Satire," in *Homoeroticism in Classical Arab Literature*, p. 7: "it is important to consider further the tension that exists in Islamic texts between homoerotic beauty and homosexual activities. Clearly, there is a recognition that men can be inspired by masculine beauty and homoerotic intimacy."

64. See Jim Wafer, pp. 90 and 91. More generally, see Lois Griffith, *Theory of Profane Love among the Arabs: The Development of the Genre* (New York: New York

University Press, 1971). Cf. Vern L. Bullough, "The Sin Against Nature and Homosexuality," in *Sexual Practices and the Medieval Church,* pp. 55–71. Khalid Duran, however, claims that Islam does view homosexuality as a sin against nature. See Duran, "Homosexuality and Islam," p. 183.

65. Rowson, "Two Homoerotic Narratives from Mamluk Literature," p. 159. See also Ben-Na'eh, *"Mishkav Zakhur,"* p. 177, who notes that the legal prohibition against public displays of homosexuality in the Ottoman Empire were largely for reasons of "protecting social order."

66. Norman Roth, "Jewish ʿArabiyya and the Renaissance of Hebrew in Spain," *Journal of Semitic Studies* 28, no. 1 (Spring 1983): 63–84.

67. See Joseph Hacker, "The Exiles from Spain in the Ottoman Empire in the 17th Century: Community and Culture" [Hebrew], in *Moreshet Sefard,* Hayyim Beinart, ed. (Jerusalem, 1992), and Ben-Ne'ah, *"Mishkav Zakhur,"* p. 173.

68. See Hayyim Shirmann, "The Ephebe in Medieval Hebrew Poetry," *Sefarad* 15 (1955): 55–68; and Norman Roth, "'Deal Gently with the Young Man': Love of Boys in Medieval Hebrew Poetry of Spain," *Speculum* 57, no. 1 (1982): 22 and 23.

69. For a more contemporary example, see Neal Kozodoy, "Reading Medieval Hebrew Love Poetry," in *AJS Review* 2 (1977): 111–129. A more scholarly position can be found in the work of Raymond P. Scheindlin in "A Miniature Anthology of Medieval Hebrew Love Poems," *Prooftexts* 5 (1985): 269–300 and later in *Wine, Women, and Death* (Philadelphia: JPS, 1986). In response to these positions, see Normon Roth, "'Fawn of My Delights': Boy-Love in Hebrew and Arabic Verse," in *Sex in the Middle Ages,* Joyce E. Salisbury, ed. (New York: Garland, 1991), pp. 158–162. For a list of some earlier studies that outright reject the homoerotic nature of these poems, see pp. 164–166.

70. Roth, "Deal Gently," p. 24.

71. Yom Tov Assis, "Sexual Behavior in Mediaeval Hispano-Jewish Society," in *Jewish History: Essays in Honor of Chimen Abramsky,* A. Rapoport-Albert and S. Zipperstein, eds. (London: Peter Haban, 1988), p. 51.

72. See Assis, ibid., pp. 50–51, who refers to numerous cases and the Muslim influence. A good example of how these kinds of transgressions are "covered up" can be found in Lewis John Eron, "Homosexuality and Judaism," in *Homosexuality and World Religious,* pp. 103–134. Eron's analysis of classical sources is quite useful. However, he concludes, from the paucity of legal responsa on this issue, that it simply was not widely practiced. He states: "very few Jews were perceived to have sexual relationships with members of their own sex, so such relationships were not understood as a major social problem" (104). Ben-Na'eh illustrates, at least in Ottoman Erez Israel, that there were quite a number of rabbinic edicts that dealt with this issue, and it was, if not a major social problem, surely one that merited the attention of the rabbinic leadership.

73. Norman Roth shows how this is false even in the Middle Ages, citing responsa from R. Shlomo ibn Adret from Spain, Elijah Mizrahi from Turkey, and others on this topic. See Roth, "Fawn of My Delights," pp. 163 and 164.

74. See *Shaʿar ha-Kavannot,* 71d, 72a; Yehuda Liebes, "Sabbath Meal Songs Established by the Holy ARI" [Hebrew], *Molad* 4 (1972): 540–555; and Fine, *Physician of the Soul,* 253, 254.

75. Roth, p. 161.

76. See Fishbane, *The Exegetical Imagination* (Albany, N.Y.: SUNY Press, 1998), pp. 105–122; *Biblical Myth and Rabbinic Mythmaking* (Oxford: Oxford Uni-

versity Press, 2004), pp. 253ff; and most recently Elliot Wolfson, *Language, Eros, Being,* esp. pp. 1–45, 261–295.

77. See, for example, in Wolfson, *Language, Eros, Being,* pp. 296–332.

78. Roth, "Deal Gently with the Young Man," p. 51; and Fine, *Physician of the Soul,* pp. 78–123.

79. Ruth Lamdan, "Deviations," p. 119.

80. See Abraham David, *To Come to the Land,* pp. 6–8, 95–114.

81. Landam, "Deviations," p. 125; and Meir Benayahu, *Toldot ha-Ari,* pp. 159, 160.

82. R. Joseph Karo, *Shulkhan Arukh,* "Even ha-Ezer" 24:1. Cf. Maimonides, *Mishneh Torah* "Issurei Biah" 22:2. Interestingly, many Ashkenazi rabbis disagreed with Karo's position and ruled in accordance with Maimonides, who permitted two males to be alone together. See the Polish-born Joel Sirkus, *Bayit Hadash* on Tur Shulkhan Arukh, "Even ha-Ezer" 24. Cf. Efon, "Judaism and Homosexuality," pp. 118, 119.

83. See Fine, *Safed Spirituality* (New York: Paulist Press, 1984), pp. 61–83; and *Physician of the Soul,* 179–186. More generally in Judaism, see Efrayim Urbach, "Askesis and Suffering in Talmudic and Midrashic Sources" [Hebrew], in *Yizhak F. Baer Jubilee Volume,* Salo Baron, ed. (Jerusalem, 1960), pp. 48–68; and Steven Fraade, "Ascetical Impulses of Ancient Judaism," in *Jewish Spirituality I: From the Bible to the Middle Ages,* A. Green, ed. (New York: Crossroad, 1986), pp. 253–288; A. Lazeroff, "Bahya's Asceticism Against Its Rabbinic and Islamic Background," *Journal of Jewish Studies* 21 (1973): 11–38; Elliot Wolfson, "Eunuchs Who Keep the Sabbath: Becoming Male and the Ascetic Ideal in Thirteenth-Century Jewish Mysticism," in *Becoming Male in the Middle Ages,* J. J. Cohen and B. Wheeler, eds. (New York: Garland, 1997), pp. 151–185; "Martyrdom, Eroticism, and Asceticism in Twelfth-Century Ashkenazi Piety," M. A. Signer, J. H. Van Enger, eds., *Jews and Christians in Twelfth-Century Europe* (South Bend, Ind.: Notre Dame University Press, 2001), pp. 171–220. On the relationship between asceticism and mysticism more generally, see Bernard McGinn, "Asceticism and Mysticism in Late Antiquity and the Early Middle Ages," in *Asceticism,* V. Wimbush and R. Valantasis, eds. (New York: Oxford University Press, 1995), pp. 58–74.

84. Lamdan, "Deviations," pp. 126, 127, 130; and Ben-Na'eh, "*Mishkav Zakhur,*" p. 188.

85. The proliferation of kabbalistic ethical literature in Safed during this period is an illustration of the extent to which the mystics understood the need for reeducating the community. See, for example, R. Elijah Da Vidas's *Reshit Hokhma,* R. Moses Cordovero, *Tomer Devorah,* R. Eliezer Azkiri, *Sefer Haredim,* esp. 41 a/b; R. Natan Shapira, *Mazat Shemorim,* 9a; and R. Judah Hayyat's *Sefer Zafnat Pa'aneah.* Cf. Ben-Ne'ah, p. 191; Joseph Dan, *Jewish Ethics and Jewish Mysticism* (Seattle: University of Washington Press, 1986), pp. 76–103. On Hayyat, see Idel, "R. Yehuda Hallewah and his *Zafnat Pa'aneah*" [Hebrew], *Shalem* 4 (1984): 119–138.

86. See Ben-Ne'ah, "*Mishkav Zakhur,*" p. 174.

87. See Joseph Hecker, "The Spanish Exiles in the Empire in the Sixteenth Century—Community and Culture," *Moreshet Sefard* 8, Hayyim Beinhart, ed. (Jerusalem: Magnes, 1992), pp. 477, 478. Cf. Ben-Na'eh, "*Mishkav Zakhur,*" p. 173 and n. 7.

88. See Ben-Ne'ah, "*Mishkav Zakhur,*" pp. 196, 197.

89. Judith Butler, *Bodies that Matter* (New York: Routledge, 1993), esp. pp. 233–236.

90. On this, see *Playing with Gender: A Renaissance Pursuit,* Jean Brink, Mary-anne Horowitz, and Alison Coudert, eds. (Urbana: University of Illinois Press, 1991); and Bullough/Bullough, *Cross Dressing,* pp. 74–90.

91. *Sha⁽ar ha-Yihudim* (SHY) (Yeshivat ha-Hayyim ve ha-Shalom, n.d.), pp. 36d–37a. Another manuscript version, Bodleian Library, 1782, fol. 177b, is cited in Elliot R. Wolfson, *Circle in the Square* (Albany, N.Y.: SUNY Press, 1995) p. 223 n. 145. Another version, slightly amended, appears in *Sha⁽ar Ruah ha-Kodesh* 16a. Yet another version that I will discuss later appears in *Sha⁽ar ha-Kelalim,* printed at the beginning of *⁽Etz Hayyim,* standard eds. In *Sha⁽ar ha-Kelalim,* this introduction is absent.

92. SHY 36d.

93. It may be worthwhile to compare Luria's approach to the Quran 4:16: "If two (men) among them are guilty of such acts then punish them both. But if they repent and reform, let them be, for God accepts repentance and is merciful." The leniency of the Quran on this is quite striking and is reflected in other ap-proaches, just as tolerant, in Hadith and Sha'ria literature mentioned above. More generally, see Jim Wafer, "Muhammad and Male Homosexuality," pp. 87–96.

94. See Ben-Ne'ah, *"Mishkav Zakhur,"* p. 190 (writing about the 17th cen-tury): "The author (of this edict) does not see *mishkav zakhur* as an independent (prohibitive) category and expresses this with the same breath as other trans-gressions—e.g., immodesty, Sabbath desecration, general licentiousness etc. . . . The lack of any unique relation to male–male intercourse supports the theory of (Michel) Foucault that, until modernity, sodomy was not considered any more transgressive than other prohibited (heterosexual) offense. Its status was like that of other offenses and no more" [my translation].

95. The delineation of *zeir anpin* is a central tent of the Lurianic system. For some examples, see Vital, *EH,* vol. 2, Palace 5, Gate 31, pp. 32c–34d; OzH, pp. 25d–27d; AdY, pp. 122–136; and R. Efrayim Penzari, SeD, 96–106. Cf. Pinhas Giller, *Reading the Zohar* (Oxford: Oxford University Press, 2001), pp. 113–119.

96. See, for example, in ShG, intro. 39, p. 376 in Bnei Aaron ed.

97. Zohar 1.246a/b. Cf. Wolfson, *Language, Eros, Being,* pp. 82 and 83. The no-tion of *bina,* usually viewed as female, being male is not as surprising as it may sound. Jesus is also viewed as a female. See, for example, Caroline Walker Bynum, *Jesus as Mother: Studies in Spirituality in the High Middle Ages* (Berkeley: University of California Press, 1982), pp. 110–169. There is a similar kind of androgyny or gen-der playing regarding Moses. See Aaron Wildavsky, *The Nursing Father: Moses as Political Leader* (Birmingham: University of Alabama Press, 1984).

98. See Zohar, Idra Raba 190b. But see Penzari, SeD, pp. 144, 145, where it is only the *levushim* (garments) and not the *'orot* of *ima* that descend.

99. Jaques Lacan, "The Phallic Phase and the Subjective Import of the Cas-tration Complex," in Lacan, *Feminine Sexuality,* J. Mitchell and J. Rose, eds., trans. J. Rose (New York: Pantheon Books, 1982), pp. 99–122.

100. *Sha⁽ar ha-Kelalim,* printed at the beginning of EH, standard eds., p. 19c. For an English rendition of this text, see Elijah Klein, *The Kabbala of Creation: The Mysticism of Isaac Luria, Founder of Modern Kabbala* (Berkeley, Calif.: North Atlantic Books, 2005).

101. R. Moshe Zakuto, cited in R. Menahem Halperin's gloss to *Sha⁽ar ha-Kelalim,* p. 19c.

102. The narrative in Genesis 36 about the deaths of the Kings of Edom is the mythic foundation of the Lurianic notion of divine rupture (*shevirat ha-kelim*). See, for example, EH, Palace 2, Gate 2, chapters 2 and 3, pp. 40c–44b.

103. SeG, chapter 24, p. 46.

104. SeD, p. 149a.

105. Jacques Lacan, "The Meaning of the Phallus," in his *Feminine Sexuality*, pp. 74–85.

106. Ibid., pp. 79 and 82; and Butler, *Bodies that Matter*, p. 96. Cf. EH, Gate 21, chapter 3, p. 105a, where the Hebrew word for masculine, *zakhar*, signifies memory [*zakhur*], arguing that the loss of masculinity is the loss of the ability to remember Torah, based perhaps as an interpretation of *nashim daʿatan kalot*. Cf. ShRK, 16d and *Shaʿar ha-Kelalim*, p. 19c. On *daʿatan kalot* (b.T. Kiddushin 80b), see *Taʿamei ha-Mitzvot*, printed in R. Meir Poppers, LiT, "parshat terumah," p. 65b.

107. ShY, p. 35d.

108. On the impossibility of homosexual desire, see Butler, *Bodies that Matter*, p. 127.

109. Butler, *Bodies that Matter*, pp. 102 and 103.

110. ShRK, p. 16d.

111. The notion of one gender becoming the other through erotic arousal already exists in the Zohar. See, for example, Zohar 1. 66b and 53b discussed in Wolfson, "Eunuchs Who Keep the Sabbath," pp. 166 and 167. Wolfson notes, "To arouse the supernal male, the female must assume a role that is characteristically masculine; what facilitates the assumption of this role is the insemination of the female by the male mystic. . . . The erotic union of the male mystic and the feminine Shekhinah results in the mutual transformation of the two; the masculine below is feminized and the feminine above is masculinized." Hence, the whole notion of the plasticity of gender is already deeply embedded in the zoharic imagination that Luria had so thoroughly absorbed. What Luria does is translate the metaphysical and vertical transmorphing of gender in the Zohar to the horizontal plane of two male bodies. Wolfson makes a claim in "Eunuchs" that, far from being transgressive, homoeroticism as the unity of the mystic with the "male" God is that which arouses heterosexual Eros: "from the human perspective heterosexual Eros is fulfilled in the homoerotic union of the male mystic and God" (171). Moreover, he alludes to the communal nature of this homoeroticism in the kabbalistic fraternity in the zoharic corpus that only feeds the close-knit nature of the Lurianic circle.

112. Butler, *Bodies that Matter*, p. 98.

113. Ibid., p. 139.

114. Zohar 1.50a.

115. ShY, p. 36d. Cf. *Zohar ha-Rakiya*, p. 73c.

116. Butler, *Bodies that Matter*, p. 111.

117. Ibid., p. 234.

118. More strongly, the whole dichotomy of essentialist/constructivist is problematic. While Butler aptly problematizes this structure, she is still, to some degree, wed to its premises. For a penetrating critique of this dichotomy, and Butler's use of it, see William D. Hart, "Sexual Orientation and the Language of Higher Law," in *Sexual Orientation and Human Rights in American Religious Discourse*, pp. 208, 209.

119. See Wolfson, "Crossing Gender Boundaries in Kabbalistic Myth and Ritual," in *Circle in the Square* (Albany, N.Y.: SUNY Press, 1995), pp. 79–121; "Gender and Heresy in Kabbala" [Hebrew], *Kabbala: Journal for the Study of Jewish Mystical Texts* 6 (2001): 231–262; and most recently, *Language, Eros, Being*, pp. 46–110. In these last two studies Wolfson extends his thesis to show how gender dimorphism is a theme that filters through the entire theosophic kabbalistic tradition. Basing

himself on the distinction between sex and gender, gender being a symbolic and not a biological construction, Wolfson argues that the movement from male to female (and back again) is common, gender being a station in the mythic life of the *sephirot* or *parzufim*. In the Lurianic material we have been exploring we see an example where the biological human (i.e., flesh and blood man or woman) is also viewed in this symbolic way, each human containing within him/her both male and female. The actualization of these potentialities is at least somewhat dependent on human behavior. Another example of this that supports Wolfson's approach can be found in R. Shneur Zalman of Liady's *Siddur Tefillot me-kol Ha-Shana* (Brooklyn, N.Y.: Kehot, 1981), p. 125 a/b.

120. Butler, *Bodies that Matter*, p. 95.

121. The notion of the human body containing both genders, and thus being able to transmorph from one to the other is not unique to the theosophic tradition. It also exists in the ecstatic writings of Abraham Abulafia. See Abulafia, *Imre Shefer* (Jerusalem, 2001), pp. 101–103.

122. See Charles Mopsik, *Le sexe des âmes: Aleas de la difference sexualle dans la Cabale* (Paris: Editions de L'Eclat, 2003), esp. pp. 79–105. In English, see Mopsik, *Sex of the Soul: The Vicissitudes of Sexual Difference in Kabbala* (Los Angeles: Cherub, 2005), pp. 38–50.

123. Saʿadia Gaon, *Emunot ve Deot*, 4:7.

124. See Gershom Scholem, "The Transmigration of Souls," in *The Mystical Shape of the Godhead*, pp. 197–250; Rachel Elior, "The Doctrine of Transmigration in *Galya Raza*," in *Essential Papers in Kabbala*, Lawrence Fine, ed. (New York: New York University Press, 1995), pp. 243–269; Ronit Meroz, "Selections from Ephraim Penzari: Luria's Sermon in Jerusalem and the Kavvanah in Taking Food" [Hebrew], *Jerusalem Studies in Jewish Thought* 10 (1992): 211–258; and Lawrence Fine, *Physician of the Soul*, pp. 304–358. This idea first appears in Kabbala in *Sefer ha-Bahir* (late 12th century). See Scholem, "Transmigration," in *The Mystical Shape of the Godhead*, pp. 199–201. For some medieval kabbalistic sources, see Meroz, pp. 226–230. Most recently, see Menahem Kallus, "Pneumatic Mystical Possession and the Eschatology of the Soul in Lurianic Kabbala," in *Spirit Possession in Judaism: Cases and Contexts from the Middle Ages to the Present*, Matt Goldish, ed. (Detroit: Wayne State University Press), pp. 159–185. Cf. Raza Lea Hovav-Machboob, "The Ari's Doctrine of Reincarnation" (DHL thesis, The Jewish Theological Seminary of America, 1983). This idea begins to gain prominence in zoharic literature (late 13th century), yet it is limited primarily to the question of levirate marriage in *Sabba de-Mishpatim*. See Pinhas Giller, *Reading the Zohar* (New York: Oxford University Press, 2001), pp. 37 and 38.

125. b.T. Sanhedrin 106b. Cf. Zohar 16a; 2.91a; 102a; 3.164b. The Zohar does not mention *gilgul* in relation to this *migdal*. This is apparently Luria's (or Vital's) invention. In the talmudic discussion. this *migdal* is likely the Temple (*Beit ha-Mikdash*), as Doag was viewed as an expert in the laws of the Temple. The connection, if there is any, between the Temple and *gilgul* is unknown to me.

126. See ShG, intro. 8, pp. 76 and 77. There Vital addresses the issue of women and *gilgul* by saying that women can sometimes be reincarnated with their husbands for certain reasons, "even though they do not need to be reincarnated."

127. See ShG, intro. 4, p. 47. "A righteous person (*zaddik*) who engages in Torah, especially if he is from the ancient ones, is not judged in Gehenna. But, he still must become purified from his sins in order to enter the Garden of Eden. Therefore, he has no choice but to be reincarnated."

128. ShG, intro. 9, pp. 78, 79. Cf. SeG, chapter 13, p. 26f.

129. See, for example, in SeG, chapter 11, p. 25.

130. See SeG, intro. 4, pp. 47, 48; intro. 20, p. 141; and intro. 22, pp. 152, 153.

131. See ShG, intros., 6, 7, and 12; SeG, chapters 7 and 35, p. 79. Luria allegedly told Vital that a portion of Vital's soul was "new"—a compliment of the highest order. See Vital, *Sefer ha-Hezyonot*, 154, 192, and 292; and Kallus, "Pneumatic Mystical Possession," pp. 160–163.

132. On ʿibur (impregnation of souls), see ShG, intro. 3; SeG, chapter 5; and Hovav-Machoob, "The Ari's Doctrine," pp. 55–65.

133. SeG, chapter 5.

134. See SeG, chapter 13, p. 27. "There are numerous kinds of sins that cause the change of a man to a woman, on the blessing, [Blessed be you, of God] who did not make me a woman. One of them is *mishkav zakhur*, which is just punishment (*mida ke-neged mida*)."

135. See SeG, chapter 13, p. 27. The "feminine waters" represent the potency of the female (even if she may be male, as in Israel in relation to God) to activate male desire above that results in the descent of the (male) light/seminal fluid resulting in impregnation or *tikkun*.

136. This is because at the time of conception the female body, in this case, is inhabited by a male soul, hence rendering a circumstance much like *mishkav zakhur*.

137. SeG, pp. 81, 82.

138. See Anne Bolin, "Transsexualism and the Limits of Traditional Analysis," *American Behavioral Scientist* 31 (1987): 41–65; and Gilbert Herdt, "Representations of Homosexuality: An Essay on Cultural Ontology and Historical Comparison, Part 1," *Journal of the History of Sexuality* 1, no. 3 (1991): 481–504.

139. SeG, p. 82.

140. See Ronit Meroz, "Selections from Ephraim Penzari," pp. 226ff.

141. See, for example, in ShP, p. 5a. "When a higher light descends downward, as long as it retains its strength, it is called masculine (*zakhar*). When it reaches its place and loses its strength, it is called feminine (*nekava*)." Thus, labels of gender are relative and not static.

142. B.T. Ketubot 62b and b.T. Nedarim 50a.

143. The term *nirva*, from the root RVA, refers to sodomy or pederasty. See b.T. Sanhedrin 9b and b.T. Avodah Zara 24a.

144. ShG, introduction 39, p. 340. On R. Akiva marrying the wife of Tyranus Rufus (Governor of Judea, 1st century), see b.T. Avodah Zara 20a. Cf. b.T. Nedarim 50b; Baba Batra 10a; Sanhedrin 65b.

145. Vital's anguish about only having daughters was not uncommon. In fact, during this period we have a collection of letters from Jerusalem that addresses the "burden of having daughters" (*zarat ha-bat*). See as cited and discussed in Ruth Lamdan, *A Separate People: Jewish Women in Palestine, Syria, and Egypt in the Sixteenth Century* (Leiden: Brill, 2000), pp. 25, 26. Luria's explanation and solution to this social dilemma must have been quite welcome to men since it put the burden of infertility on the woman's soul.

146. Another case is Avigail, the wife of Nabel the Carlemite and then the wife of King David. Vital states in ShG, intro. 36, p. 300, that Avigail had a male soul.

147. Ibid., p. 209.

4. Numbers

1. Or, as Daniel Boyarin suggests, "difference." "Rather than the negatively loaded term 'particularism' we can easily rename this Jewish resistance with the

positive marked 'difference' and, as such, it has functioned as a model for politics of difference of repressed people of color, women, and gays." Daniel Boyarin, "The Subversion of the Jews: Moses' Veil and the Hermeneutics of Supersession," in Boyarin, *Sparks of the Logos* (Leiden: Brill, 2003), p. 184. Boyarin is talking about Israel's insistence on living a corporeal existence despite Paul's critique and how that stubbornness has, in effect, enabled Israel to survive. While I agree that *particularism* is a term that has been used unfairly against Judaism, I think *difference*, while more nuanced, can be viewed as softening the often hard-edged claims made by the rabbis and their spiritual and intellectual progeny (especially the mystics) about their place in humanity. Yehezkel Kaufmann's history of the birth of Jewish particularism in *Galut ve Nekhar* suggests that Israel experienced alienation from its host environment only with the rise of Christendom and Islam, two competing "monotheisms." He is making a similar point to Boyarin from the opposite direction. That is, because nonmonotheistic religions are generally more tolerant of other religions, even monotheisms, they are also less threatening to Jews. When Jews lived under competing monotheisms they were more alienated by their host culture and also needed to be more strident in defining their unique particularistic nature because of their theological proximity to their surroundings.

2. Much of this rests on the biblical and rabbinic notions of divine election. See, for example, Deuteronomy 7:6–8; Samuel 2: 23; Amos 3:2; b.T. Berakhot 6a; Hagigah 3a; More generally, see David Frank, ed., *A People Apart: Chosenness and Ritual in Jewish Philosophical Thought* (Albany, N.Y.: SUNY Press, 1993), and David Novak, *The Election of Israel*. Shaye Cohen argues that this preoccupation with the other begins in earnest in the 2nd century CE and underlies the rabbinic construction of conversion to a nascent Judaism. "This, in this period, even though Jews were becoming more nationalistic and particularistic they were becoming more universalistic by extending citizenship to other peoples and allowing individuals to convert to Judaism." Shaye J. D. Cohen, *The Beginnings of Jewishness: Boundaries, Varieties, Uncertainties* (Berkeley: University of California Press, 1999), p. 138. Navigating the boundaries of difference between Jew–Christian and Christian–Jew is also evident in early Christianity, based largely on Paul's self-definition as being (and remaining?) a "Hebrew born of Hebrews." See Phillippians 3:4–7. Cf. Romans 11:1; Paula Fredrikson, "What 'Parting of the Ways'? Jews, Christians, and the Ancient Mediterranean City," in A. Becker, A. Y. Reed, eds., *The Ways That Never Parted* (Tubingen: Mohr-Srebed, 2003), pp. 35–63; and Andrew S. Jacobs, "A Jew's Jew: Paul and the Early Christian Problem of Jewish Origins," *Journal of Religion* 86, no. 2 (April 2006): 258–286.

3. Jonathan Z. Smith's term *proximate other* is quite useful here. Smith argues that all "otherness" as much as it used in comparison between "near neighbors" still implied difference. That is, the construct of otherness implies by definition a dimension of sameness such that distinctions become relevant. "Remoteness," Smith argues, guarantees our "indifference." See Smith, "What a Difference a Difference Makes," in J. Neusner, E. Freirich, eds., *To See Ourselves as Others See Us* (Chico, Calif.: Scholars, 1985), pp. 3–48. Cf. idem. "Scriptures and Histories," in *Method and Theory on the Study of Religion* 4 (1992): 104, 105.

4. Esther Benbassa and Jean-Christoff Attias, *The Jew and the Other*, G. M. Gushgarian (Ithaca, N.Y.: Cornell University Press, 2004), p. 64.

5. Sacha Stern, *Jewish Identity in Early Rabbinic Writings* (Leiden: Brill, 1994), p. 4.

6. On the question of the other in Kabbala, see Wolfson, *Venturing Beyond*, pp. 26–41 and 129–165.

7. Jonathan Z. Smith, *To Take Place: Toward Theory in Ritual*, pp. 13, 14.

8. W. D. Davis, "From Schweitzer to Scholem: Reflections on Sabbatai Zvi," *Journal of Biblical Literature* 96 (1976): 529–558. Jon Levenson puts it this way: "There is probably nothing that has attracted so much attention and generated so much controversy as the biblical idea that the Jews are the chosen people." Levenson, "The Universal Horizon of Biblical Particularism," in *Ethnicity in the Bible*, p. 143.

9. This division is suggested by Yezhezkel Kaufman when, writing about the prohibition of idolatry, he states, "While the same viewpoint [i.e., that only Israel is prohibited in idolatry] underlies the doctrine of the prophets, they regard the past and present dichotomy of mankind as a passing phase. At the end of days all men shall worship YHWH. In contrast, the faith of the Torah sees no end to this division. It has no dream for the end of idolatry. The eschatological visions of the Torah lack the motif of a universal religious conversion." Kaufman, *The Religion of Israel*, p. 164. David Novak contests this view and argues that the difference between the Torah's view of the distinction between Israelites and gentiles is one of degree and not of kind. That is, Novak claims that the universal prophetic vision still contains the particular and perhaps even exclusivist notion of the Torah. See Novak, *The Image of the Non-Jew in Judaism* (New York: Edmin Mellen, 1983), p. 113.

10. In fact, it has been noted that Paul's universalizing impulse draws not from Hellenism but from Jewish sources with which he was intimately familiar. See Wayne Meeks, "A Nazi New Testament Reads His Bible," in *The Idea of Biblical Interpretation; Essays in Honor of James Kugel* (Leiden: Brill, 2004), pp. 513–545. Cf. Denise Buell and Caroline Johnson Hodge, "The Politics of Interpretation: The Rhetoric of Race and Ethnicity in Paul," *Journal of Biblical Literature* 123, no. 2 (2004): 240. Others have argued that conversion in Christianity is intended to fulfill a universalism latent in Judaism. See Arthur Darby Nock, *Conversion: The Old and the New in Religion from Alexander the Great to Augustine of Hippo* (Baltimore, Md.: Johns Hopkins Press, 1988), pp. 187–190, cited in Buell and Johnson Hodge, *The Politics*, p. 240, n. 22; and Lloyd Gaston, *Paul and the Torah* (Vancouver: University of British Columbia Press, 1987), pp. 116–134.

11. See David Novak, *The Election of Israel*. It is quite telling that Spinoza, whose *Theological/Political Treatise* is arguably the first deep experiment of Judaism and modernity is also the first to jettison the category of election. More generally, see Arnold Eisen, *The Chosen People in America* (Bloomington: Indiana University Press, 1984).

12. On the first question, see Gerald Blidstein, "Who Is Not a Jew?—the Medieval Discussion," *Israel Law Review* 11 (1976): 369–390 and my discussion in the previous chapter on Exodus. On the kabbalistic response to Christianity and Islam, see Wolfson, *Venturing Beyond*, pp. 129–185.

13. Following Daniel Boyarin I include Jewish-Christians as Israel. See Boyarin, *Border Lines: The Partition of Judeo-Christianity*. The notion that Jewish exclusivity was based on Judaism viewing itself as the exclusive monotheism is inaccurate. For example, the rabbis put these words in the mouth of a "pagan" in conversation with Rabbi Akiva: "We both know that in our heart there is no reality in idolatry." See b.T. Avodah Zara 55a.

14. This observation is challenged in Vital's interpretation of the ʿerev rav in his ʿEtz ha-Daʿat Tov (EDT). Vital argues, via the lens of biblical interpretation, that conversion was always a pressing issue in Ancient Israel. For another view, see Stern, *Jewish Identity in Early Rabbinic Writing*, pp. 88–95 and Alan Segal, "Conversion and Messianism: Outline of a New Approach," in *The Messiah*, James

292   Notes to page 145

Charlesworth, ed. (Minneapolis: Fortress, 1987), pp. 296–323. As I argued earlier, this reflects Vital's social setting far more than the biblical narrative. But see S. McKnight, *A Light among the Gentiles: Jewish Missionary Activity in the Second Temple Period* (Minneapolis: Fortress, 1991), who argues that the boundaries between Jew and Greek were quote permeable in an earlier period.

15. See Cohen, *The Beginning of Jewishness*, pp. 119–125. Cf. Idel, "Messianic Ideas and Zionist Ideas," pp. 73–81, who argues that even the messianic idea in Pentateuchal Israelite religion was not universalistic but about the normalization of Israel in its land. But Jon Levenson argues that this lack of a conversion procedure may have been an expression of universalism since Ancient Israelite religion did not require one to be an Israelite to be living divine will. Levenson, "The Universal Horizon," in *Ethnicity in the Bible*, pp. 160–163. Cf. Jacob Milgrom, "Religious Conversion and the Revolt Model for the Formation of Israel," *Journal of Biblical Literature* 101 (1982): 169–176.

16. See Ephrayim Urbach, "Self-Isolation or Self-Affirmation in Judaism in the First Three Centuries: Theory and Practice," in E. P. Saunders, ed., *Jewish and Christian Self-Definition, Volume Two: Aspects of Judaism in the Greco-Roman Period* (Philadelphia: JPS, 1981), pp. 269–298; and Lawrence Shiffman, "At the Crossroads: Tannaitic Perspectives on the Jewish Christian Schism," in ibid., pp. 115–156.

17. The two claims he is addressing are (1) that one's Jewishness was founded on accepting the notion of election (Urbach); and (2) that one's Jewishness could not be erased even with disbelief (Shiffman).

18. William Scott Green, "Otherness Within: Towards a Theory of Difference in Rabbinic Judaism," pp. 51, 52 in J. Neusner and E. S. Frerichs, *To See Ourselves as Others See Us: Christians, Jews, "Others" in Late Antiquity* (Atlanta: Scholars, 1985).

19. For example, see Josephus, *Against Apion* 2.11, 40; *Jewish War* 2.20.2; 7.3.3; and *Antiquities* 3.8.9; 20.8.11. See Louis Feldman, *Jew and Gentile in the Ancient World* (Princeton, N.J.: Princeton University Press, 1993), pp. 177–287; and David C. Sinn, "Christianity and Ethnicity in the Gospel of Matthew," in *Ethnicity in the Bible*, pp. 172–177.

20. See Alan F. Segal, "The Costs of Proselytism and Conversion," in *Society of Biblical Literature 1988 Seminar Papers*, pp. 350–353; Feldman, *Jew and Gentile*, pp. 342–382; and Joseph Rosenbloom, *Conversion in Judaism: From the Biblical Period to the Present* (Cincinnati, Ohio: HUC Press, 1978), pp. 35–66.

21. See Sasha Stern, *Jewish Identity*, pp. 135–138; and Christine Hayes, *Gentile Impurities and Jewish Identity* (Oxford: Oxford University Press, 2002).

22. It should be noted that many scholars argue that Rabbinic Judaism also contains certain universalistic tendencies. See, for example, Lloyd Gaston, "Alongside the fundamental postulate 'All Israel have a share in the world to come' (Mishna Sanhedrin 10:1) stands the corollary concerning the righteous concerning the 'righteous among the nations of the world who have a share in the world to come' (Tosephta Sanhedrin 13:2). It is precisely Israel's universalistic perspective, which allows non-Jews to relate to God in their own way that enables Israel to have her own particularity in relating to God through the Sinai covenant." Gaston, *Paul and the Torah*, p. 23. What Gaston fails to note here, although he implies it elsewhere, is that Israel gets to determine what constitutes righteousness. This is embodied in the seven Noahide laws. Thus, it is not that Israel is open to salvation of the non-Jew through their religion. This is only so if their religion conforms to Judaism's understanding of righteousness.

23. For some examples, see Isaiah 56, Zechariah 14; Terence Donaldson, "Proselytes or 'Righteous Gentiles'? The Status of Gentiles in Eschatological Pilgrimage Patterns of Thought," *Journal for the Study of the Pseudepigrapha* 7 (1990): 3–27; and Cohen, *The Beginnings of Jewishness*, pp. 122. Cf. Jon Levenson, "The Universal Horizon of Biblical Particularism," pp. 143–169, esp. p. 145.

24. See Denise Buell, "Rethinking the Relevance of Race for Early Christian Self-Definition," *Harvard Theological Review* 94, no. 4 (2001): 449–476; and "Race and Universalism in Early Christianity," *Journal of Early Christian Studies* 10, no. 4 (2002): 429–468. Especially useful is her interpretation of aggregative notions of ethnicity—that is, ethnicity determined by a common ancestor. Buell notes, "Nonetheless, aggregative strategies can serve universalizing ends. *We can view universalizing arguments as instances of aggregative ethic reasoning.* This is especially the case when the totalizing categories most commonly found in oppositional ethnic reasoning are used in the context of aggregative arguments" (445). I will argue in the second part of this chapter that Luria views ethnicity is a similar way when it comes to Balaam. That is, Balaam becomes a Jew, via *gilgul*, because he already has a share in the ancestry of Ancient Israel, either through his soul inheritance (through Moses) or through his connection to the *ʿerev rav*.

25. The notion of Christian universalism is largely a product of Pauline theology. Therefore, the legitimacy of such a claim rests on how one reads Paul. One of the classic modern formulations distinguishing the universal nature of Christianity and the particularism of Judaism can be found in F. C. Baur's *The Church History of the First Three Centuries*, vol. 1, edited by A. Menzies (London: Williams and Norgate, 1878) and his *Paul, the Apostle of Jesus Christ* (London: Williams and Norgate, 1876), esp. pp. 309ff. Krister Stendhal debunked the claim of Paul's exclusion of the Jews and began a new era of Pauline scholarship. See his *Paul Among Jews and Gentiles*. Other important studies in this regard are E. P. Sanders, *Paul and Palestinian Judaism* (London: SCM, 1977), and James D. G. Dunn, *Jesus, Paul, and the Law* (Louisville, Ky.: Westminster, 1990); Daniel Boyarin's *A Radical Jew: Paul and the Politics of Identity* (Berkeley: University of California Press, 1997) contributed to the discourse on Paul by arguing that Paul's universalism was (1) not really universalist and (2) dangerous to the extent that it was considered universalist. Boyarin argues (p. 96) that Paul uses Jewish particularism and expands that beyond biological ethnicity. In doing so he creates a "coersive sameness" (p. 236) that is not universalist in any positive sense. For a recent engagement with Boyarin's work on Paul and Paul scholarship on this issue more generally, see John M. G. Barclay, "'Neither Jew Nor Greek': Multiculturalism and the New Perspective on Paul," in *Ethnicity in the Bible*, pp. 197–214 (his response to Boyarin is from 206–214).

26. See H. W. F. Saggs, *The Encounter with the Divine in Mesopotamia and Israel* (London: Athlone, 1978), p. 38, cited in Levenson, "The Conversion of Abraham to Judaism, Christianity, and Islam," in *The Idea of Biblical Interpretation*, p. 11.

27. Levenson, "The Universal Horizon," pp. 143–169. In fact, Levenson acknowledges that postbiblical Judaism may have distorted the universal resonance of the biblical period, both in traditional and progressive forms. He writes, "Ironically, secularization can also result in the opposite extreme, an exaggerated particularism purchased at the cost of the universal dimension of Judaism. I am thinking, for example, of the currently common habit of stressing Jewish survival as a goal in its own right" (169).

28. Cohen, *The Beginnings of Jewishness*, p. 130.

29. See Daniel Boyarin, *Border Lines*, esp. pp. 1–36, 74–89. Interestingly,

Boyarin argues that the concept of heresy (*hairesis*) in Judaism (and Christianity) emerges at almost the same time Cohen argues conversion emerges, that is, in the middle of the 2nd century. See Boyarin, *Border Lines*, p. 41. The question as to who Paul's opponents really were, i.e., Jewish Christians or nonbelieving Jews, is a matter of scholarly debate. See the discussion in Lloyd Gaston, *Paul and the Torah*, pp. 18–21.

30. Boyarin, *Border Lines*, p. 220.

31. This starts as early as the fourth Gospel. Pre-Christian Israel certainly had other sectarian examples of "internal others," e.g., the Zadokim, Sadducees, Baitousin, etc. See Jean le Moyne, *Les Sadduceens* (Paris: Librarie Le Coffre, 1972), pp. 63–118; Moses Gaster, *The Samaritans: Their History, Doctrines, and Literature* (London: British Academy, 1925); and Lester L. Grabbe, *Judaic Religion in the Second Temple Period* (London: Routledge, 2000), pp. 183–209. However, Christianity posed a particular threat because of its popularity and dominance, especially after Constantine. The question is Jewishness more generally, whether a Christian could be a Jew and vice versa. See Daniel Boyarin, *Dying for God: Martyrdom and the Making of Christianity and Judaism* (Stanford, Calif.: Stanford University Press), pp. 1–41; Shaya Cohen, "Those Who Say They Are Jews and Are Not: How Do You Know a Jew in Antiquity When You See One?" in Shaye Cohen and Ernst Frerichs, eds., *Diasporas in Antiquity* (Atlanta, Ga.: Scholars, 1993), pp. 1–45; and *The Beginnings of Jewishness*, pp. 25–68. While there are other sectarians before Christians, e.g., the Zaddokites, the Baitousins, etc., they did not pose the same threat as Christianity, especially after Constantine.

32. See Boyarin, *Border Lines*, esp. pp. 74–86.

33. The concept of the New Israel as instituted by Paul does not necessarily refer to the end of the Old Israel. Krister Stendahl has argued that Paul's New Israel includes gentiles in the covenant of Israel, thus expanding the notion of election and not superseding Israel's election. See Stendahl, "The Apostle Paul and the Introspective Conscience of the West," *Harvard Theological Review* (1963): 199–215.

34. See Boyarin, *Border Lines*, pp. 22–36 and 37–73.

35. See Gerald Blidstein, "Who Is Not a Jew?—the Medieval Discussion," *Israel Law Review* 11 (1976): 369–290; and Jacob Katz, "Although He Has Sinned He Remains a Jew" [in Hebrew] *Tarbiz* 27 (1958): 203–217. This question also stands at the center of Pauline theology. Understanding Romans 9–11 is crucial for understanding how Paul breaks down the Jewish claim of exclusivity through his own exegesis on the Torah. See Gaster, *Paul and the Torah*, pp. 15–34.

36. See Yosef Hayyim Yerushalmi, *From Spanish Court to Italian Ghetto*, pp. 21–50; and Matt Goldish, "Patterns in Converso Messianism," in *Millenarianism and Messianism in Early Modern Culture*, pp. 41–63.

37. See Gerald Blidstein, "Who Is Not a Jew?—the Medieval Discussion," 269–290; and Aaron Lichtenstein, "Brother Daniel and the Jewish Fraternity," *Judaism* 12, no. 3 (Summer 1963): 260–280.

38. On this, see Isaiah Tishby, *Messianism in the Time of the Expulsion from Spain and Portugal* [Hebrew] (Jerusalem: Zalman Shazar, 1985), pp. 73–81. There are even converso traditions that the messiah will be a Marrano. See Gitlitz, *Secrecy and Deceit*, pp. 103–110. Moreover, the phenomenon of conversion as redemptive plays a central role in Sabbateanism, making it logical that Sabbateanism would be an attraction for some conversos. See Matt Goldish, *The Sabbatean Prophets*, pp. 99–101. Citing Abraham Miquel Cardoso, Jacob Sasportas writes, "It was also two years ago that it was told to me that the king mes-

siah was destined to wear the clothes of the converso [*ʿanus*], because of which the Jews would not recognize him; and in fine, that he was destined to be a *converso* like me." Cited in Sassportas, *Zizat Novel Zvi*, p. 293.

39. Scholem claimed that Luria's vision has real universalist intent. "The vision of Lurianic kabbala went even further; it embraced all creation. In it the sum total of the world process, starting with *tzimzum* (contraction), was represented as a Gnostic drama, a drama of failure and reconstruction, but one needed to achieve what had been seminal in it and had never existed before. Here Redemption was not only the goal of history, which thus gave it meaning, but the goal of the whole universe as such." Scholem, "Reflections of Jewish Theology," in *Jews and Judaism in Crisis: Selected Essays* (New York: Schocken, 1976), p. 285.

40. This is actually made explicit by Vital in the beginning of SeG, p. 1. The question about Vital's apparent unabashed admission that only "Jews" are from Adam needs to address the Lurianic understanding of Israel. Perhaps it is a category that transcends conventional ethnic boundaries to include the entirely of humanity in some eschatological future. That is, does conversion become for Luria and his disciples the sine qua non of Judaism? See also Wolfson, "Ontology, Alterity, and Ethics in Kabbalistic Anthropology," in *Exemplaria* 12 (2000): 129–155.

41. In a short summary of kabbalistic views on this point, David Novak states the following: "Everything real is in truth a manifestation of the Godhead. In fact, Israel is the only human manifestation of the Godhead; she is the microcosm, and the full ten *sefirot* are the macrocosm of the panentheistic being. Accordingly, Israel and humanity are synonymous. There is no humanity outside Israel. In this divine scheme, the nations of the world have no human reality for all intents and purposes." *The Election of Israel*, p. 17. Novak's insight, drawn from the Zohar, is essentially correct. However, his use of that insight to deny the usability of kabbalistic doctrine to contemporary theories of election is problematic. In the later Kabbala (Zohar and onward) all material existence (Jewish and non-Jewish bodies) constitute a form of the demonic (*kelipah* or *kelipah nogah*). The non-Jewish soul is a composite of divine and extraneous elements. The Jewish soul is fully divine. Accordingly, the nonhumanity of the non-Jew in kabbalistic parlance is only that dimension of his or her soul that is not divine. The process of redemption is the eradication or transformation of that non-humanity thus revealing the humanity rooted in all souls. The dialectic of divine and mundane or, as the Zohar states "the left contained in the right," is discussed in Elliot Wolfson, "The Left Contained in the Right: A Study in Zoharic Hermeneutics," *AJS Review* 11 (1986): 27–52. Novak's overly dualistic representation of this kabbalistic schema does not capture the more nuanced dimensions of its presentation. Whether or not kabbala is a usable resource for cotemporary theories of election is another matter. I am not that optimistic that it can be without significant revisions. And, it is true that if we determine Jew and non-Jew simply as bodies in the world, the Kabbala would deny humanity to the non-Jew. However, the Kabbala's determination of person is more complicated, requiring the inclusion of the soul construction which, even in the case of the non-Jew contains divine elements.

42. The erasure of the categories *Jew* and *gentile* has a correlate in some medieval authors who suggested the erasure of the categories Land of Israel and Diaspora in the messianic future. For example, in *Megillat ha-Megalleh* (Berlin, 1924), p. 110, Abraham bar Hiyya makes the following comment about the messianic future: "For this reason God has dispersed Israel among the nations in every settlement on earth, to enable them in the future, when they rise form their graves, to dwell in their places and inhabit all the dwelling places on

earth, and all the lands of the earth will be called 'Erez Yisrael.' The Land of Israel will be greatly expanded, so as to fill the entire world." See Moshe Idel, "Some Conceptions of the Land of Israel in Medieval Jewish Thought," in Ruth Link-Salinger, ed., *A Straight Path: Essays in Honor of Arthur Hyman* (Washington, D.C.: Catholic University of America Press, 1988), p. 125.

43. See Alexander Rofe, *"The Book of Balaam" (Numbers 22:2–24:25): A Study in Methods of Criticism and the History of Biblical Literature and Religion* [Hebrew] (Jerusalem: Simon, 1979), esp. pp. 45–49. The benign assessment of Balaam is also the basis of Josephus' retelling of the episode. See Geza Vermes, *Scripture and Tradition: Haggadic Studies* (Leiden: Brill, 1973), p. 174. The positive assessment of Balaam goes further in pre-rabbinic and early Christian. See Judith Baskin, *Pharaoh's Counselors: Job, Jethro, and Balaam in Rabbinic and Patristic Literature* (Chico, Calif.: Scholars, 1983), esp. p. 99; and Jay Braverman, "Balaam in Rabbinic and Early Christian Traditions," in S. B. Hoenig and L. D. Sritskin, eds., *Joshua Finkel Festscrift* (New York: Yeshiva University Press, 1974), pp. 41–50. This benign or even positive assessment of Balaam is not uniform in this period. See Louis Feldman, "Philo's Version of Balaam," in *Henoch* 25 (2003): 301–319. Feldman shows that Philo, independent of rabbinic influence, gives a "completely negative portrait" of Balaam (304).

44. Rofe, *"The Book of Balaam,"* p. 46.

45. This interpretation dominates rabbinic tradition. See, for example, b.T. Sanhedrin 105b where every word of Balaam's blessing is understand by the rabbis as intending to be a curse. Cf. Lamentations Raba 28:142; and Targum Yerushalmi to Numbers 22:22. Yet there is also a tradition that when he saw Israel's tents he really did desire to bless them. b.T. Baba Batra 60a; and Numbers Raba 2.4.

46. Alexander Rofe, *"The Book of Balaam,"* p. 48 [my translation].

47. The rabbinic demonization of Balaam stands out in a lengthy discussion of his intentions in Tanna de be-Eliahyu, Seder Eliyahu Raba, chapter 28, pp. 142–143.

48. For an extensive collection of this material, see Louis Ginzberg, *Legends of the Jews*, vol. 2, pp. 758–784.

49. b.T. Baba Batra 14b. Cf. P.T. Sota 5:6.

50. The conventional wisdom that Jews were not seriously concerned with Christianity until the Middle Ages has been refuted by Israel Yuval. See his *"Two Nations in Your Womb": Perception of Jews and Christians in the Middle Ages* (Berkeley: University of California Press, 2003), p. 41. Marc Hirschman, in *A Rivalry of Genius: Jewish and Christian Biblical Interpretation in Late Antiquity*, Batya Stein, trans. (Albany, N.Y.: SUNY Press, 1996), argues that rabbinic texts, some as early as the 2nd century but surely by the 4th century, are explicitly responding to Christianity.

51. Efrayim Urbach, "Homilies of the Sages on Gentile Prophecy and on the Episode of Balaam," *Me-Olamot shel Hakhamim* [Hebrew] (Jerusalem: Magnus, 1988), pp. 537–554. Cf. idem. "When Did Prophecy Cease?" [Hebrew], *Tarbiz* 17 (1946): 1–11.

52. A stronger case is made by Levi Ginsburg, "Some Observations on the Attitude of the Synagogue Towards the Apocalyptic-Eschatological Writings," *Journal of Biblical Literature* (1922): 115–136. Cf. Abraham Geiger, "Bileam und Jesus," *Judische Zeitschrift* 6 (1868): 31–37. On Geiger's theory, see Susannah Heschel, *Abraham Geiger and the Jewish Jesus* (Chicago: University of Chicago Press, 1998), esp. pp. 127–161. The question of Balaam as a foil for Jesus was also entertained by

Travers Herford, *Christianity in Talmud and Midrash* (London: Williams and Nor-gate, 1908), p. 65 and refuted by Ginzberg, *Legends*, vol. 2, p. 761, n. 722. Ginz-berg notes in *Legends*, vol. 2, p. 796, n. 855 that "[t]he different legends concern-ing the death of Balaam show many points of resemblance to those of the death of Jesus. But this does not furnish any basis for the hypothesis that Balaam is used as a cryptic name for Jesus." The talmudic reference is to b.T. Sanhedrin 106b. Cf. Samuel Sandmel, *We Jews and Jesus*, p. 28, n. 1; Jacob Lauterbach "Jesus in the Talmud," in *Rabbinical Essays;* and David Berger, "Three Typological Themes in Early Jewish Messianism: Messiah Son of Joseph, Rabbinic Calculations, and the Figure of Armilua," *AJS Review* 10, no. 2 (1985): 159–162.

53. On this, see the material collected in Travers Herford, *Christianity in Mi-drash and Talmud;* and David Aaron, "Imagery of the Divine and the Human: On the Mythology of Genesis Rabba 8/1," *Journal of Jewish Thought and Philoso-phy* 5 (1995): 1–62.

54. Cf. Mishna Avot 3:14 and Magan Avot on that mishna.

55. Urbach, "Homilies," p. 276 [my translation]. Interestingly, in his *Commen-tary to the Mishna*, Maimonides conflates disciples of Abraham (*talmidei Avraham*) and children of Abraham (*zera Avraham*), employing Isaiah 41:8. Ovadia Bartenura makes the same correlation. See Maimonides, *Commentary to Avot* 5:19, p. 466. The purpose of this conflation is unclear. Did Maimonides read "disciple" as "seed," or was it an attempt to universalize "seed" to mean "disciple"? That is, is this an attempt to erase the universal (*disciple*) in the particular (*seed*) or erase the particular in the universal? If it is the latter, than Maimonides' comment, in its attempt to universalize the Abrahamic teaching, is actually quite Pauline.

56. Another similar reference can be found in Jude 1:11: *Woe unto them! For they have gone in the way of Cain, and ran greedily after the error of Balaam for reward and perished in the gainsaying of Korah*. In general, see Jay Braverman, "Balaam in Rabbinic and Early Christian Traditions."

57. *Neither, because they are the seed of Abraham, ate they all children; but, in Isaac they shall be called seed* (Rom. 9:7). In Galatians, see 3:7,8, 14, 29. See Andrew Ja-cobs, "A Jew's Jew: Paul and the Early Christian Problem of Jewish Origins," *Journal of Religion* 86, no. 2 (2006): 266.

58. In John 8:33–40 the usage is a more ambiguous. The crowd says "we are Abraham's seed" (8:33), and Jesus replies, "I know you are Abraham's seed but you seek to kill me, because my word has no place in you" (8:37). Jesus then rebukes them, saying, "If you were Abraham's children you would do the works of Abra-ham" (8:39). Here the seed motif is maintained but the correlation between seed and behavior is introduced as if to say, "how can you be the seed of Abraham if you act against his will." See Caroline Johnson Hodge, "If Sons, then Heirs: A Study of Kinship and Ethnicity in Paul's Letters" [Ph.D. diss., Brown University, 2002].

59. There is also an interesting discussion as to whether Rabbinic Judaism de-fined *seed* and *Israelite* purely biologically. See Mishna Sanhedrin 10:2 and 3 and the discussion in Bruce Chilton and Jacob Neusner, *Judaism in the New Testament: Practices and Beliefs* (London: Routledge, 1995), pp. 71–76. Regarding *Rabbinic Ju-daism*, they conclude, "The main point is inescapable: 'Israel' are those who have a portion in the world to come, and excluded from 'Israel' are those whose actions, including acts of bad faith, deny them their portion. If Israel is to be divided, it is not between ethnic and religious components, but among religious components" (76). They want to distinguish between Paul's criteria for "Israel" which is being "in Christ," and their religious criteria which is correct belief in the future (world to come), but more interestingly they deny the ethnic criteria as determinant.

60. See Genesis 19:27; 21:14; 22:3; and Numbers 22:13; and 22:21.

61. The extent to which Paul wanted to erase the distinction between Israel and the gentiles is not uncontested. Recent scholarship on Paul and early Christianity suggests that (1) Paul's message may have been intended primarily for the gentile leaving the Jew to continue mitzvot and believe in Jesus; and (2) early Christianity may have been more particular and less universal than conventionally thought. Paul's notion of race is discussed in Denise Buell and Caroline Hodge, "The Politics of Interpretation: The Rhetoric of Race and Ethnicity in Paul," *Journal of Biblical Literature* 123, no. 2 (2004): 235–252. Cf. Denise Buell, "Race and Universalism in Early Christianity," *Journal of Early Christian Studies* 10, no. 4 (2002): 429–468. Cf. John M. G. Barclay, "'Neither Greek nor Jew': Multiculturalism and the New Perspective on Paul," in *Ethnicity in the Bible*, pp. 197–214.

62. Perhaps the contemporary distinction between a false prophet and a failed prophet made by Yitz Greenberg is useful here although that would still equate Christianity with the disciples of Balaam. See Irving Yitz Greenberg, "The Relationship of Judaism and Christianity: Toward a New Organic Model," in E. Fisher, A. J. Rudin, and M. H. Tanenbaum, *Twenty Years of Jewish–Catholic Relations* (New York: Paulist Press, 1980), pp. 197–203; and more recently Byron L. Sherwin, "'Who Do You Say That I Am?'" in B. Bruteau, ed., *Jesus through Jewish Eyes* (New York: Orbis Books, 2001), pp. 31–44. Cf. Abraham David Azulai, *Hesed le-Avraham*, 3:9.

63. Urbach's denial of the Balaam–Jesus motif follows Louis Ginzberg and Joseph Klausner. See Ginzberg, *The Legends of the Jews* (New York: Macmillan, 1925), vol. 2, p. 761, n. 722; and Klausner, *Jesus of Nazareth*, pp. 32–35.

64. Interestingly, Paul uses Abraham to make the opposite claim. See Galatians 3:8,9, *And Scripture foreseeing that God would justify the heathen through faith, preached before the message of Abraham saying, 'In you shall all the nations be blessed'* (Gen. 12:3). *So then those who are of faith are blessed with faithful Abraham.* On Balaam and the universalization of faith, see Midrash Tanhuma Balak 11 and Urbach, "Homilies," p. 288.

65. For a detailed account of how these traits are moral in nature, see Maimonides, *Commentary to Avot*, p. 465. This reflects the attitude of the New Testament references, almost all of which fault Balaam for his agreeing to take reward from Balak—to profit from his prophetic powers.

66. In a telling extension of the immoral valuation of Balaam, the rabbis take considerable license in their reading of Numbers 22:30, *I am the she-ass upon whom you have ridden.* b.T. Sanhedrin 105a–b reads this to means that Balaam had sex with his she-ass and thus is guilty of bestiality. The notion of Balaam's sins as sexual in nature (and thus acts of immorality) are common in rabbinic literature. See, for example, Leviticus Raba 1:13. Much of this stems from the rabbis juxtaposition of Numbers 25:1 and 31:16, where Balaam is blamed for instigating the seduction of Israel with the Midianite woman. Cf. Sifri to Numbers 131 and 157; Tanhuma Buber 4:147; Numbers Raba 20:23 and 22:4. Balaam's enticing Israel to sexual immorality also appears in Philo's *Moses* 1.54, 55 and 1.295–299 and Josephus in *Antiquities* 4.129–130. On the Zohar's use of this motif, see Zohar 3.206b.

67. Sifri Devarim, #357, p. 430. In English, see *Sifrei on Deuteronomy*, Reuven Hammer trans., p. 383.

68. Midrash Sefer 'Olam, chapter 21, pp. 162 and 163.

69. Leviticus Raba 1:12, p. 27 in Margolit ed. See b.T. Baba Batra 15b which claims that gentile prophecy continued until Moses' death.

70. The notion that the nations only have access to God through the covenant

with Israel is common in rabbinic discussions about election. For example, see David Novak, *The Election of Israel*, pp. 241–255. Novak's attempt to posit Israel's election as including the nations (against the more exclusivist position of Michael Wyschogrod in *The Body of Faith*) still must view the nations "walking in God's ways" as including a recognition of Israel's election as unique and unalterable.

71. There is another midrashic trajectory that places the concrete exclusion of the nations in the Sinai event itself. See Sifri Devarim #343, pp. 396–397 in the Finkelstein ed. This tradition holds that God initially offered the Torah to the nations who rejected it. Similarly, the nation's reasons for rejecting the Torah there are largely moral demands that the nations could not accept.

72. Tanna de be-Eliyahu, Margolit ed., p. 141. For this excerpt, I used the English translation, *Tanna Debe Eliyyahu*, William Braude and Israel Kapstein, trans., p. 349.

73. Midrash Tanhuma, Parshat Balak, 1.

74. Ibid.

75. Rabbinic tradition suggests that Balaam's demand that Balak build seven altars (Num. 23:29) is his challenge to the exclusivity of the Israelite covenant, the altars representing the seventy nations. See Numbers Raba 20:18; Tanhuma Buber 3:16; Tanhuma "Parshat Zav" 4.

76. This raises the question as to whether Balaam had free will. One response to this was already proffered by Maimonides in his analysis as to how Pharaoh could have been liable for acts done without free will. See his *Eight Chapters*, chapter 8. Maimonides' analysis of Balaam surely does not resolve the issue but at least acknowledges that one must confront the apparent illogicality of the episode.

77. Even the rabbinic position that held he was a magician acknowledges that he was also a prophet. See b.T. Sanhedrin 106a that asks, "Can he be a (true) prophet and a magician? First he became a prophet and then he became a magician." Cf. Midrash Tanhuma, S. Buber, ed. "Parshat Balak" 5.

78. This picture cannot come solely from Numbers but, in fact, emerges from Deuteronomy 23:5, where it is implied that Balaam wanted to curse Israel and was not merely hired to do so. One could argue that Balaam's passivity in Numbers also contributes to this. Instead of saying, "I can speak only what God puts in my mouth," he could have criticized Balak for wanting to curse Israel in the first place. This, I would argue, is not strong enough to serve as the foundation for the rabbinic depiction of Balaam. See other examples in Joshua 13:2; Micha 6:5; and Nehemiah 13:2. Even though the use of the term *disciples of Balaam* only appears in Mishna Avot 5;19 and Avot de-Rebbe Natan 2:45, the notion of Balaam's evil nature as a moral failure appears often in rabbinic interpretation.

79. Lamentations Raba 28:142.

80. In fact, see ShP, p. 36c where Vital says there are two dimensions in Israel, one Israel themselves and the second the ʿerev rav.

81. See Lamentations Raba 28:142; and Targum Yerushalmi to Numbers 22:22. On the status of the non-Jew in the Zohar's ontology more generally, see Elliot Wolfson, "Ontology, Alterity, and Ethics in Kabbalistic Anthropology," 129–155. Wolfson notes (p. 135), "In some measure, the attitude expressed in zoharic literature, and confirmed in other kabbalistic sources, elaborates a position articulated in earlier rabbinic texts, which in turn echo ethnocentric tendencies evident in parts of the Hebrew Bible."

82. More generally, see Elliot Wolfson, "Beautiful Maiden without Eyes: *Peshat* and *Drash* in Zohar Hermeneutics," pp. 155–203. The demonization of

Balaam can also be found in Moshe de Leon's Hebrew writings. See Moshe de Leon's *Sefer Shekel ha-Kodesh*, Charles Mopsik ed., pp. 14, 15; Dorit Cohen-Alloro, "The Secret of the Garment in the Zohar" [Hebrew] [Ph.D. diss., Hebrew University, Jerusalem, 1987], pp. 75–81. In terms of rabbinic demonization of Balaam, see Targum Pseudo-Jonathan to Numbers 24:3; and 31:8; Midrash Tanhuma, "Parshat Balak" 4 and 5 and Numbers Raba 20:18. Most recently, see Joel Hecker, *Mystical Bodies, Mystical Meals* (Detroit: Wayne State University Press, 2005), pp. 157–162. Hecker notes (p. 244, n. 66) that it is plausible that the demonization of Balaam, at least in the medieval period, may be a polemic against Christianity. Cf. Wolfson, *Venturing Beyond*, p. 140 and n. 46.

83. Both Daniel Boyarin and Marc Hirschman most recently claim that by the 4th century there is no doubt that rabbinic texts are responding to Christian theological claims. Both suggest that this likely existed much earlier, even to the 2nd-century rabbinic literature. See Boyarin, *Border Lines*, pp. 98–111; and Marc Hirschman, *A Rivalry of Genius*, esp. pp. 13–23.

84. On the Zohar in particular, see Isaiah Tishby, *Wisdom of the Zohar*, pp. 68–71. Cf. Yehuda Liebes, *Studies in the Zohar*, p. 244 n. 92, cited in Wolfson, "Ontology," p. 150.

85. Israel Jacob Yuval, "Jews and Christians in the Middle Ages: Shared Myths, Common Language," in R. S. Wistrich, ed., *Demonizing the Other: Anti-Semitism, Racism and Xenophobia* (Amsterdam: Harwood Academic Publishers, 1999), p. 104. Cf. Yehuda Liebes, "Christian Influences on the Zohar," in *Studies in the Zohar* (Albany, N.Y.: SUNY Press, 1993), pp. 139–161.

86. Zohar Hadash on Ruth, p. 78d makes an interesting comment about this dichotomy: "I will give you a great opening. All of Israel prostrates before their God. The god of Esau (Christianity) bows down to them. How do we know this? There is a hint in the verse, *And Elohim Came to Balaam* (Numbers 23:2) [in a dream] his god came and prostrated before him. *And [Elohim] came* to his home and spoke to him from his window [some say, dream]." The intentional misreading here of "Elohim" as Balaam's god and not God undermines the entire narrative of Balaam as a true prophet, something the Zohar implies.

87. Elliot Wolfson's reading of these relevant zoharic texts has shown that the demonic within the Godhead is only one dimension of evil that needs to be contained. See Wolfson, "Left Contained in the Right: A Study in Zoharic Hermeneutics," pp. 27–52. It is also the case that the Zohar generally has a negative assessment of conversion more generally. See Zohar 1.25a; 2:12b; 120b; 3:125b; Tikkunei Zohar 18, pp. 30b; 36b.

88. The positive assessment of conversion is not unequivocal in Lurianic teaching. See, for example, SeL, p. 88c; and the discussion in Wolfson, *Venturing Beyond*, pp. 165ff.

89. On Balaam and Esau, see Zohar 1.170a. On Balaam and the serpent, see 1.171b. On Balaam and Amalek, see 2.195a; 3.281b and Tikkunei Zohar, p. 124b.

90. Zohar 1.25b; 37a; and 126a.

91. See Zohar 3.281b. There is no overt correlation between Balaam and Amalek in the rabbinic corpus. However, in b.T. Sota 11a we read of Laban (who is genealogically connected to Balaam in the rabbinic imagination) enticing Amalek to war against Israel. For sources in determine Balaam's genealogical connection to Laban, see b.T. Sanhedrin 105a; and Genesis Raba 57:3. But see b.T. Sanhedrin 106b that claims that Balaam could not have been a close relative of Laban, There is also a linguistic connection made in the Zohar between Balaam (who does not bless willingly) and Esau (who does not kiss Jacob with good will). See Zohar

Notes to pages 160–168

1.117b. In the Middle Ages, Esau becomes the biblical motif of Edom, or Christianity. See Gerson D. Cohen, "Esau as Symbol in Early Medieval Thought," in A. Altman, ed., *Jewish Medieval and Renaissance Studies* (Cambridge: Harvard University Press, 1967), pp. 19–48.

92. Zohar 1.170a. Cf. LiT, p. 88b.

93. Zohar 2.69 a/b; 2.264a.

94. Wolfson, "Left Contained in the Right," 33, 34. For Zohar sources on magic as the source of the demonic, see ibid., p. 33, n. 30 and p. 34, n. 31. The connection between Balaam and Laban, already in rabbinic literature, is expanded here when Laban is also considered a magician. See Zohar 1.161b; 167a.

95. The Zohar even views Balaam's knowledge of the *sephirot* through magic. See Zohar 3.207b; 3.208a; 3.212a/b.

96. In Luria, it is Balak who takes on the dominant role of magician. The Zohar does not sharply distinguish between Balak and Balaam. The hatred of Israel of both is viewed as gratuitous. See, for example, Zohar 3.189b.

97. Zohar 1.25a remarks in passing that Balaam is included in one of the five kinds of the ʿerev rav; nefalim, giburim, ʿanakim, rafaʿim, and ʿamalakim, but it never develops this notion. Cf b.T. Sota 11a where Amalek is mentioned in regard to Balaam. The strong connection, introduced in rabbinic literature is between Laban and Balaam. This will also play a prominent role in Luria. See b.T. Sanhedrin 105a, Targum Yerushalmi to Numbers 22:25, and Zohar 1.111b.

98. Zohar 3.281b. We will see that Luria adopts this correlation but uses it in a different way.

99. Zohar 2.66a; 65b.

100. Yehuda Ashlag suggests the "*hu*" here refers to *zeir anpin* and not *malkhut*. See *Sefer ha-Zohar im Perush ha-Sulam*, 3, "vayishlakh," p. 11 n. to #37.

101. Zohar 1.167a/b. Cf. 3.207b, where the Zohar states that Balaam knew magic through the *sephirot*, a position that appears to counter R. Yehuda's position above.

102. Rabbi Yehuda's claim that Balaam did not know what he was saying has precedent in Philo. See Philo, Life of Moses 1.272 as cited in Feldman, "Philo's Version of Balaam," p. 308.

103. Zohar 2. 21b, 22a.

104. There is no mention of what Balaam was gazing at. However, in the parallel passage about Moses, using the same locution, the object of the gaze (i.e., *kedusha*) is made explicit.

105. The JPS Tanakh translates it as "whose eye is true" but notes (note g) "Other 'whose eyes is (or, eyes are) open.' Meaning of Hebrew uncertain."

106. Zohar 2.69a/b. Cf. ShMR, p. 18a.

107. Zohar 2.69b. Cf. Zohar 2:237a/b and the discussion in Wolfson "Ontology," pp. 153–155.

108. *Sefer ha-Zohar Im Perush Yedid Nefesh*, vol. 6 (Petah Tikva, Israel, 1994), p. 14. This comment is drawn from Vital's reading of this Zohar passage. Cf. "Iyunim," p. 12, s.v. "*odkha be-goyim.*"

109. Interestingly, in Vital's early EDT the ʿerev rav are considered at times closer to Moses than Israel. See EDT, p. 173a (top). Cf. EH Gate 32, chapter 2.

110. Conversion served as a strong motif in late Antique Jewish Messianism as well. See Alan Segal, "Conversion and Messianism: Outline for a New Approach," in *The Messiah: Developments in Earliest Judaism and Christianity*, James Charlesworth, ed. (Minneapolis: Fortress, 1987), pp. 296–340.

111. One of the more sustained and startling Lurianic texts on conversion

can be found in ZHR, pp. 91a–94c. In relation to Balaam, see LiT, p. 89a. Much of this is a play on the rabbinic dictum "the messiah will not come (lit., ben David) until all the souls will be embodied." See b.T. Yevamot 63b; and Niddah 13b.

112. See, for example, ShMR, p. 46c.

113. ShP, p. 37c and LiT, p. 18a where Luria notes that Balaam inherits holy sparks from Abel. The notion of "many *gilgulim*" (exceeding the conventional notion of three as a maximum) is an early idea that may be rooted in Sefer Bahir #3, 3–12.

114. See ZHR, p. 93a where three categories of converts are delineated. The first category is created when the father of the convert achieves merit by saving a Jew. "He merits that his son will have a soul that is rooted in holiness, which is from the highest dimension of *kelippah* close to *kedusha*. He [the son] will then convert and attach himself to *kedusha*.

115. The notion that a sign of true blessing is to be included in the blessing of Israel appears in numerous places. See Genesis 12:3; 22:18; and 28:14. However, only here is it stated by a non-Israelite.

116. Literally "a death of the upright (*yesharim*)" a play on *yeshurun*, a euphemism for Israel. See Deuteronomy 32:15 and Nahmanides to Numbers 23:10. This apparent request by Balaam to be connected to Israel in his death is taken literally in Lurianic exegesis and becomes the basis of his notion of Balaam being reincarnated as an Israelite.

117. ShP, pp. 20c–22b.

118. On this, see EH, Gate 38, chapter 3, pp. 61a/b.

119. ShP, p. 31a. Cf. p. 20c–21d; 37b/c and Zohar 2. 181a. On the ʿ*erev rav* and Balaam, see EH, Gate 32, chapter 2. This correlation does not come from the Zohar. It seems to emerge from Luria's correlation of Moses and the ʿ*erev rav* with his interpretation of Sifri equation of Moses and Balaam.

120. It is noteworthy that JPS Tanakh translates the term "*daʿat elyon*" as "knowledge from the Most High," understanding "*elyon*" as a reference to God. In typical fashion Luria views *daʿat elyon* as a noun referring to a place in the cosmic anthropos. Cf. EH Gate 8, chapter 4.

121. ShP, p. 37b. Cf. ShP, p. 31a. On the sons of Balaam as the instigators in the episode of the calf, see Zohar 2. 191a and 194a. Cf. ShG, intro. 22, p. 162. Cf. ZHR, p. 66b.

122. Ibid. Cf. LiT, p. 88a, "Just as Moses was from *daʿat elyon* from the *yesod* of *abba* that is in *zeir anpin*, so too Balaam *mamash!*"

123. Cf. ZHR, pp. 92b (bottom).

124. LiT, p. 87b. Cf. EH Gate 38, chapter 3.

125. See ShP, pp. 20c–22d; EH, Gate 48, chapter 3, pp. 110a–d; ZHR, p. 94a; and ShMR, p. 46c.

126. LiT, p. 88a. "In the beginning [Moses' birth] the tikun was not complete. Only the first letter of Moses of his name and the first letter of the name of Abel (Hevel - ה). What remained was the ש referring to Seth - שת and the "לב of Hevel. These letters correspond to לבת. This was fixed with the burning bush. Thus it is written And the angel appeared to him in a blazing fire out of the burning bush (בלבת אש) (Exodus 2:2)."

127. This is stated explicitly in Tikkunei Zohar. See Tikkunei Zohar, tikun 70, p. 111b, "Seth is the first *gilgul* of Abel."

128. "BeL" is an epithet for *Lord* and became an alternate name for the Babylonian God Marduk.

129. He will be important later on as he is the Jew who carries the soul of Balaam. He is the first husband of Abigail, the wife of David. See 2 Samuel 2:2.

130. ShG, intro. 29, p. 210.

131. This is an obvious play on the biblical narrative of Rachel's plight as the beloved who is childless. Rachel's exile, her separation from Jacob, is the foundation of the Lurianic nocturnal ritual of Tikun Hazot. On this, see my "Conjugal Union, Mourning, and Talmud Torah" *Daat* 36 (1996): xvii–xlv; and Moshe Idel, *Messianic Mystics*, pp. 308–320.

132. This dimension of the Lurianic system, that is, the notion of power and how it is used and abused, is developed comprehensively in Jewish mysticism more generally in Jonathan Garb's *Manifestations of Power in Jewish Mysticism: From Rabbinic Literature to Safadean Kabbalah* [Hebrew] (Jerusalem: Magnus, 2005), esp. pp. 47–72; 185–248.

133. An extended meditation on this verse can be found in EH, Gate 38, chapter 3; and ShP, pp. 15d–16d.

134. For an explanation of the *terapim* and their relationship to Laban and Balaam through the angelic enemies of Azzah and Azael, see EH Gate 38, chapter 3, p. 62b/c and Gate 49, chapter 3, pp. 110b–d.

135. ShP, p. 36a.

136. See EH, Gate 38, chapter 3, p. 62a (toward the bottom). "Sometimes Rachel steals from Leah the middle third (of *tiferet*) which are called *terapim*. She takes it/them for herself because it is the property of her father."

137. See Isaiah 24:1. *Behold, The LORD will strip the earth bare, and lay it waste.*

138. ShP, p. 36b.

139. Ibid.

140. ShP, p. 37a. On Balaam learned from Azzah and Azael, see EH, Gate 38, chapter 3, p. 62b (bottom). This appears to be based on Zohar 1.126a; and 3.208a.

141. Joel Hecker notes, correctly I believe, that in the Zohar Balaam "is one of the Zohar's favorite targets for vilification, rivaled in human ignominy only by Pharaoh and Esau." Hecker, *Mystical Bodies, Mystical Meals*, p. 156.

142. See Annette Yoshiko Reed, "From Asael and Semihazah to Uzza, Azzah, and Azael: 3 Enoch 5 (#7–8) and Jewish Reception-History of 1 Enoch," *Jewish Studies Quarterly* 8, no. 2 (2001): 105–136.

143. See, for example, 1 Enoch 7:1; 8:3; 9:6–8a; 13:2b and 16:3. In Jubilees, see 8:3; 10:1–11; 11:8. More generally, see Loren T. Stuckenbrick, "The 'Angels' and 'Giants' of Genesis 6:1–4 in Second and Third Century BCE Jewish Interpretation: Reflections on the Posture of Early Apocalyptic Traditions," in *Dead Sea Discoveries* 7, no. 3 (2000): 354–377. On Azael and magic, see Gershom Scholem, *Jewish Gnosticism, Merkabah Mysticism, and Talmudic Tradition* (New York: JTS, 1960), pp. 84–93.

144. Reed, "From Asael," p. 116. For example, whereas 1 Enoch has these angels teaching humans about the use of metal, in 3 Enoch 5 humans are taught by them to build idols from "silver, gold, precious stones, and pearls." But see Ronald Hendel, "Of Demigods and the Deluge: Toward an Interpretation of Genesis 4:1–6," in *Journal of Biblical Literature* 106, no. 1 (1987): 16 where he argues that the wholly negative depiction appears in 1 Enoch as Jubilees 4–5 as well.

145. See, for example, Ronald Hendel, "Of Demigods and the Deluge," *Journal of Biblical Literature* 106, no. 1 (March 1987): 21.

146. See Reed, "From Asael," p. 357. "Within the literary context of the Pentateuch, these ominous dwellers of Canaan could have been readily interpreted

as descendants of the Nephilim of Genesis 6:1–4. Such a connection would again presuppose that somehow they escaped the great flood unless, again, Noah was to be considered one of their number." See also Abraham ibn Ezra to Genesis 6:4, where he suggests that the giants who dwell in the land of Canaan are the descendants of the Nephilim.

147. This appears to be the position taken by Luria. See EH, Gate 49, chapter 3. In terms of sexuality impropriety, later texts, including the rabbis and the Zohar (who view Balaam as sexually perverse) do not connect the sexual activity of the Nephilim (Azzah and Azael) as extending to Balaam. On the rabbinic and zoharic view of Balaam's sexual perversity, see b.T. Avodah Zara 4b; Sanhedrin 105a/b; Targum Pseudo Jonathan to Numbers 22:30; and Zohar 1.125b.

148. See Yalkut Shimoni on Genesis 6:44.

149. See, for example, b.T. Yoma 67b where the scapegoat on Yom Kippur (Azazel) is viewed as the tikun of the "episode of Azzah and Azael." Cf. Tanna d' be-Eliyahu 25; Pesikta Rabati 34; Yalkut to Genesis 6:44, to Leviticus 16:572; and to Deuteronomy 31:1044.

150. See, for example, Zohar 1.23a; 137a (tosafot) and 1.55a.

151. Zohar 3. 194a/b; and 208 a/b.

152. See Zohar 3. 208a.

153. EH, Gate 38, chapter 3, pp. 63b/c.

154. SeL, p. 54c.

155. I have not located a midrashic source that connects Numbers 23:16 to Azzah and Azael.

156. The JPS TANAKH translates נופל as "prostrate," but the use of the verb in the Zohar and Luria refers to "descending" like the Nephilim who descended to earth in Genesis 6:4.

157. ShP, p. 37a. Cf SeLi, p. 54a; and LiT, pp. 88b, 89a.

158. Cf. SeLi, p. 54c.

159. This is distinct from the rabbinic notion of "the events of the fathers are signs for the children" (*maʿaseh avot siman le-banim*). See Midrash Tanhuma 9; and Nahmanides on Genesis 12:6.

160. The notion of a soul going from gentile to Israelite or from Israelite to gentile and then back again is not unusual in the Lurianic tradition. See, for example, the case of King Jeroboam (I Kings 12–15). Moshe Hayyim Luzzato claims part of his soul departed when he sinned and was reincarnated in a gentile. This soul then became part of the soul of the father of R. Akiva and later of R. Akiva himself. Luzzatto, "Kinat ha-Shem Zivaʿot," reprinted in *Ginzei Ramhal* (Bnei Brak, 1984), p. 104.

161. The secret being referred to here is from Zohar 3.194b (toward the bottom). The context of the Zohar passage is about seminal emission but more specifically about the verse . . . *but the name of the wicked rots* (Proverbs 10:7). R. Shimon tells his son Eliezer that God does what He does and these things are all very hidden and concealed. However, he continues, since this fraternity already knows some of these secrets I will reveal some of the others.

162. Cf. ShP, p. 37b.

163. Midrash Tanhuma, Parahat Balak, 12, pp. 416, 417.

164. This is taken from Zohar 3.194a. R. Shimon says to his son something like, "and so it goes my son; God does what He does, . . ." referring to divine action that seems to contradict our understanding of how God works.

165. ShMR, p. 46c.

166. Ibid.

167. That is, as *hokhma* (*abba*) is the cosmic father of *zeir anpin*, Laban, as *hokhma*, is the father (in-law) of Jacob/*zeir anpin*.

168. See Zechariah 13:9.

169. Avot de-Rebbe Natan 1:1,8.

170. EH, Gate 38, chapter 3, p. 62a/b. It is interesting that Luria reads Nabal's name as the fixing of Laban and ignores Scripture's own wordplay, *For he [Nabal] is just what his name says: His name means 'boor' and he is a boor* (I Sam. 25:25).

171. The notion of humans being reincarnated into subhuman forms is quite common in Lurianic Kabbala. See Gershom Scholem, "Gilgul: The Transmigration of Souls," in *The Mystcial Shape of the Godhead.*

172. JPS Tanakh translates this verse as "he became like a stone," which makes more sense in context. However, the hyperliteral translation would be "he was like a stone" or even "he was a stone." This is how Luria reads the verse as pointing to his remembering his past as a stone.

173. ShG, intro. 22, p. 163a.

174. I have not found the exact Zohar passage quoted here. For related passages regarding this one dimension of *ruah*, see Zohar 2. 99b; 101b–102b. I would like to thank Menahem Kallus for pointing me to these passages.

175. See b.T. Baba Mezia 84a; Baba Batra 58a; Zohar 1. 35b; 142b; 2.11a. This also appears in many places in the Lurianic corpus. Cf. Elliot Wolfson, "The Image of Jacob Engraved upon the Throne: Further Reflections on the Esoteric Doctrine of the German Pietists," in *Along the Path* (Albany, N.Y.: SUNY Press, 1995), pp. 1–62.

176. ShG, intro. 36, p. 300.

177. See Zohar 2.126b that argues that Jacob's attempt to correct the jealousy of Rachel and Leah (sisters and co-wives) was not completely successful.

178. It is unclear whether the verse in question is Isaiah 60:4 or 49:18, *Look up around you and see, they are all assembled, are come to you.* The context of both verses is the prophet's messianic vision.

179. ShP, p. 45a.

180. Note that most English translations have *May I die the death* (JPS TANAKH), or *Let me but die* (*The Five Books of Moses*, Robert Alter, trans.) or *Let me die . . .* (*The Harper Collins Study Bible, New Revised Standard Edition*). These translations all render *nafshi* (lit., soul) as idiomatic, which works from a biblical perspective. Luria builds his reading precisely on the existence of the word *nafshi* denoting something different than the "I."

181. For example, see Midrash Tanhuma, Parsaht Balak, 7; and Tana de be-Eliahyu Raba 21.

182. See Nahmanides to Numbers 23:10. Cf. Ibn Ezra on this verse, who takes a slightly different approach. Jacob Milgrom suggests that this desire "to share the fate of Israel" is a blessing that every nation will desire to receive from God. Cf. Genesis 12:3; 22:18; and 28:14. See *The JPS Torah Commentary, Numbers*, p. 197. This only reaffirms the notion that this verse has nothing to do with becoming an Israelite, that is, conversion.

183. ShMR, p. 46c.

184. LiT, p. 19a.

185. See ShP, p. 37c. There Luria states more explicitly (referring to Zohar 3.194b), "His body died with a defiled sword *but* his soul was reincarnated afterward as an Israelite, who are called *yesharim* from the name *Yisrael*. Then [his soul] was rectified. That is what is meant by *May my soul die a righteous death.*" What interests me here is the use of the term *but* ('*aval*) in this sentence. Does

it function to connect the following clause (and therefore is closer to *thus*)? If so, it is precisely his defiled death that enables his holy soul to become liberated from his body and enter Israel.

186. Zohar 3.194b.

187. To my knowledge, this interpolation is based on b.T. Rosh Ha-Shana 18a that states that Nabal died during the ten days of repentance between Rosh ha-Shana and Yom ha-Kippurim, a time the rabbis state is a time of an "upright death." Cf. b.T. Ketubot 103, "It is a good sign for one who dies the evening following Yom Ha-Kippurim." Cf. ShP, p. 37c (bottom) and n. #11, "Our teacher (Luria) includes the night following Yom ha-Kippurim as part of the ten days of repentance." This may be because Luria held that the final seal of the season of repentance is not until Hoshana Raba, the final day of the festival of Sukkot.

188. b.T. Sanhedrin 106b; and Midrash Numbers Raba 14:1. In both cases this is speaking about the death of Balaam at the hands of Pinhas.

189. Laban/Nabal is thus saying to Jacob/Israel, "I will not cross beyond this mound, that is, I will not survive beyond thirty-two years (half my life)."

190. On this, see b.T. Hulin 140b. Thus, Nabal, who amassed wealth and would not share it with David, will expire in the middle of his life. The linguistic connection at the end of the verse (באחריתו יהיה נבל) connects this both to Numbers 23:10 and to Nabal.

191. See ShG, intro. 36, p. 296. II Samuel 19:33. *Barzalai was very old, eighty years old; and he had provided the king [David] with food during his stay at Mahanaim, for he was a very wealthy man.*

192. LiT, p. 89a. Cf. ShP, p. 37d, "The words כמוהו and כמוהם are equal in the numbers of letters and the letters are very close to one another."

193. It may be significant, although to my knowledge not mentioned, the etymological similarity of *Gilgal* and *gilgul*.

5. Deuteronomy

I have not been able to locate where Schechter makes this comment. It is recorded by Martin Buber in his essay "Imitatio Dei," reprinted in Buber, *Israel and the World*, p. 75.

1. See Moshe Weinfeld, *Deuteronomy and the Deuteronomic School* (Oxford: Clarendon, 1972) and more recently "Deuteronomy and the Present State of Inquiry," in D. L. Christensen, ed., *A Song of Power and the Power of Song: Essays on the Book of Deuteronomy* (Winona Lake, Ind.: Eisenbrauns, 1993), pp. 21–35. On Josiah and the Deuteronomist school more generally, see Marvin Sweeney, *Josiah: The Lost Messiah of Israel* (Oxford: Oxford University Press, 2001), pp. 33–39 and 137–169. The Deuteronomist history, originally documented by Martin Noth, consists of most of Deuteronomy, Joshua, Judges, I and II Samuel, and I and II Kings.

2. See Jan-Pierre Sonnet, *The Book within the Book: Writing in Deuteronomy* (Leiden: Brill, 1997), pp. 134–147 and Michael Fishbane, "Varia Deuteronimica," *Zeitschrift für die alttestamentliche Wissenschaft* 84 (1972): 350–351.

3. Aside from earlier traditions, see I Samuel 4:4; II Samuel 6:2; Psalms 80:2; II Kings 19:15.

4. Weinfeld, *Deuteronomy*, pp. 191–209.

5. On this, see Elliot Wolfson, "The Body in the Text: A Kabbalistic Theory of Embodiment," *The Jewish Quarterly Review* 95, no. 3 (2005): 488. "The goal for the kabbalist—indeed what justifies his being called a kabbalist—is to receive the secret of the name, that is, to cleave to YHWH, the archaic Deuteronomistic injunc-

tion interpreted in a manner very close to the twelfth-century neoplantonically influenced philosophers, primarily of the Andulusian cultural background. . . ."

6. The term *Deuteronomy* literally means "second law" and was likely an instruction to future kings to make a "copy of the law." See Herb Marks, "Introduction to Deuteronomy," in Marks, *Norton Companion to the Hebrew Bible* (forthcoming). I want to thank Professor Marks for all his advice and wisdom on the entire manuscript and on this chapter in particular. I also thank him for making his text available to me before its publication.

7. Bernard Levinson, *Deuteronomy and the Hermeneutics of Legal Innovation* (New York: Oxford University Press, 1997), pp. 16 and 20.

8. For a possible deathbed confession of ben Zakkai's recognizing his radical program, see b.T. Berakhot 28b.

9. See Sonnet, *The Book within the Book*, pp. 128–143.

10. See Dennis T. Olson, *Deuteronomy and the Death of Moses: A Theological Reading* (Minneapolis: Fortress, 1994), pp. 6–22.

11. On this, see Steven Weitzman, "Sensory Reform in Deuteronomy," in *Religion and the Self in Late Antiquity* (Bloomington: Indiana University Press, 2006), p. 131.

12. Sonnet, *The Book within the Book*, p. 139.

13. On this, see Patrick D. Miller, "'Moses My Servant': The Deuteronomic Portrait of Moses," in D. L. Christenson, ed., *A Song of Power and the Power of Song* (Winona Lake, Ind.: Eisenbrauns, 1993), pp. 301–312.

14. See Miller, "Moses my Servant," p. 311. "The Book of Deuteronomy says that all that is needful for your life as a community under God, guided and blessed by the Lord, is found in these words Moses spoke and taught as charged by the Lord. Nothing more is needful. . . . The people now have the word of the Lord which Moses taught, and that will be their guide in the land that the Lord has promised. Israel is to now live by the Torah that Moses has taught and in a very real sense does not need Moses."

15. Most recently, see Elliot R. Wolfson, "Flesh Becomes Word: Textual Embodiment and Poetic Imagination," in his *Language, Eros, Being*, pp. 190–260, and "The Body in the Text: A Kabbalistic Theory of Embodiment," *The Jewish Quarterly Review* 95, no. 3 (2005): 479–500.

16. See Deuteronomy 18:15–19, where Moses promises Israel that God will raise up a new prophet "like me" to serve as mediator. The tradition subsequently rejects this and distinguishes Moses' prophetic stature as categorically superior to that of any other prophet. See Maimonides, "Laws of the Foundation of the Torah," *Mishneh Torah*, chapters 6 and 7.

17. See, for example, Deuteronomy 5:23, 24. *For what **mortal** ever heard the voice of the living God speak out of the fire, as we did, and lived? You go closer and hear all the Lord our God says, and then you tell us everything that the Lord our God tells you, and we will willingly do it.* Moses here seems to be contrasted with any *mortal*, implying his unique prophetic status.

18. The tradition that only the Jew (male Jew) is considered *zelem elohim* is rooted in the Zohar and adopted by Lurianic kabbalists. See, for example, Zohar Hadash on Ruth, p. 78c/d. The Zohar states that only the Jewish body is constructed from YHWH and thus a Jew should not mate with a gentile, because their soul does not come from that divine name. On the Torah as the names of God, see Nahmanides, "Introduction" to his commentary on Genesis. On this more generally, see Gershom Scholem, "The Name of God and Linguistic Theory in Kabbala," *Diogenes* 79 (1982): 59–80. This tradition is devel-

oped in Abulafia. See Moshe Idel, *Language, Torah, and Hermeneutics in Abraham Abulafia* (Albany, N.Y.: SUNY Press, 1989), pp. 29–81; idem. "The Concept of Torah in the Hekhalot and its Evolution in Kabbala [Hebrew]," *Mekharei Yerushalayim* 1 (1981): 23–49; Joseph Dan, *Esoteric Theology of the Ashkenazi Hasidim* [Hebrew], pp. 124ff; and Elliot Wolfson, "The Mystical Experience of Torah Study in German Pietism," in *The Jewish Quarterly Review* (July 1993): 47–51.

19. See Yehuda Liebes, "The Messiah of the Zohar: On R. Shimon bar Yohai as a Messianic Figure" in his *Studies in the Zohar* (Albany, N.Y.: SUNY Press, 1995), pp. 1–84, and the more extensive Hebrew version, "Messiah of the Zohar," in *The Messianic Idea in Jewish Thought: In Honor of the Eightieth Birthday of Gershom Scholem* (Jerusalem: Israeli Academy of Sciences and Humanities, 1982), pp. 87–236. On Luria as a messianic figure, see Liebes, "Two Young Roes of a Doe: The Secret Sermon of Isaac Luria before His Death" [Hebrew], *Mekharei Yerushalayim* 10 (1992): 67–119; and, most recently, Lawrence Fine, *Physician of the Soul*, pp. 322–358.

20. See Weinfeld, *Deuteronomy*, pp. 179–189. Cf. Wolfson, *Language*, pp. 204 and 520, n. 124, and *Abraham Abulafia* (Los Angeles: Cherub, 2000), pp. 141, 142. It is more likely that Schechter also had in mind the rabbinic interpretation of *imitatio dei* as an act emulating the divine attributes of compassion and mercy. See, for example, p.T Peah 15b; b.T. Sota 14a; Genesis Raba to Genesis 23:19 and 49:29; Sifre Devarim 11:22; and Pesikta Rabati, 14b.

21. We see this quite early in the kabbalistic tradition. There is a tradition taught in the name of Isaac the Blind: "Adam himself is constructed by the letters, and when that edifice was constructed the supernal spirit that guides him guides everything. . . ." See Scholem, *Kabbala in Provence* (Jerusalem: Akademon, 1970), appendix p. 13, and Wolfson, *Language*, p. 208, and more explicitly, "Abulafia affirms that the human body, that is, the corporeality stripped of its course materiality, is constituted by these very letters" (241). Cf. idem, "Anthropomorphic Imagery and Letter Symbolism in the Zohar," pp. 155–158.

22. In fact, Lurianic Kabbala follows *Sefer Yezeriah* that the entire creation is composed of combinations of letters, the human constituting a microcosm of existence. See LiT, p. 6. Cf. Elliot Ginsburg, "Zelem Elohim: Some Thoughts on God and Person in Zoharic Kabbalah," in *In Search of the Divine: Some Unexpected Consequences of Interfaith Dialogue*, Larry Shinn, ed. (St. Paul, Minn.: Paragon House, 1987), pp. 61–94.

23. Wolfson puts it this way: "When examined from a kabbalistic perspective, anthropomorphism in the canonical texts of Scripture indicates that human and divine corporeality are intertwined in a mesh of double imaging through the mirror of the text that renders the divine body human and the human body divine." *Language*, p. 246.

24. On the rabbinic understanding of *zelem elohim* as metaphor, see Yair Lorberbaum, *Zelem Elohim: Halakha and Aggada* [Hebrew], pp. 27–82. In Kabbala, see Charles Mopsik, "Genesis 1:26–27: L'Image de Dieu, le couple humain et le statut de la femme chez les premiers cabalists," in *Le sexe des âmes*, pp. 149–217. On Augustine's notion of the condition of the human as sinful, see chapter 1 of this study.

25. See the discussion in Scholem, "The Concept of Kavvanah in the Early Kabbalah," in A. Jospe, ed., *Studies in Jewish Thought: An Anthology of German-Jewish Scholarship* (Detroit: Wayne State University Press, 1981), pp. 165–180; Moshe Idel, *Kabbalah: New Perspectives*, pp. 42–49; and Wolfson, *Language*, pp. 209 and 521, n. 129.

26. Although *zelem elohim* is not part of Deuteronomic nomenclature, from the perspective of the kabbalists (for whom these distinctions are meaningless) the Deuteronomic shift from God as body to divine name is deployed to offer a rendering of *zelem elohim* as the divine name within the human.

27. See Paul Galatians 4:4–7; Romans 7, 8:3; and more generally, George Nickelsburg, "The Incarnation: Paul's Solution to the Universal Human Predicament," pp. 348–357.

28. The notion of the divine–human similitude as the form of the body dominates the biblical depiction, both in Genesis and in Ezekiel 1:26–28. This depiction also extends to the rabbinic tradition. See Alon Goshen-Gottstein, "The Body of God in Rabbinic Literature," *Harvard Theological Review* 87 (1994): 171–195 and more specifically "Judaisms and Incarnational Theologies," esp. pp. 229–242. In Ezekiel, the human in the divine image is used as a polemic against idolatry. Idols are misrepresentations of God's presence and only the human is the true representation of divine presence. See John F. Kutsko, *Between Heaven and Earth: Divine Presence and Absence in the Book of Ezekiel* (Winona Lake, Ind.: Eisenbrauns, 2000), pp. 63–76. Lurianic tradition also makes a correlation between idolatry and murder, the latter viewed as the severance of "the image of God" in the human leaving a lifeless body. Just as idolatry is an act that causes the departure of the *shekhina* from Israel, so is murder the destruction (or departure) of the *elohim* in the *zelem elohim* leaving an empty shell. This reading appears sensitive to Kutsko's analysis of Ezekiel, who uses *zelem elohim*, as a case against idolatry. See also LiT, p. 5b.

29. For example, see Maimonides *Guide* 1:1. In terms of rabbinic understandings of *zelem*, Goshen Gottstein writes, "according to my anthropomorphic readings of the rabbis I suggest that the bodily meaning is the only meaning of *zelem* in rabbinic literature. . . . Instead of asking 'Does God have a body?' we should inquire 'what kind of body does God have?'" Goshen-Gottstein, "The Body as Image of God in Rabbinic Literature," p. 174. I would agree and simply suggest a reversal of the equation. If God has a body in rabbinic literature through the phrase *zelem elohim* referring to the human, what can we say of the human body as divine? On this, see the discussion of "theomorphism" in Lorberbaum, *Zelem Elohim*, pp. 101–104, citing Franz Rosenzweig, *Naharayim*, Y. Amir, trans. (Jerusalem: Mosad Bialik, 1978), p. 35.

30. On this, see Garb, *Manifestations of Power*.

31. On the incarnational dimensions of Kabbala as structural, see Wolfson, *Language*, esp. p. 256; idem, "Anthropomorphic Imagery and Letter Symbolism in the Zohar" [Hebrew], *Jerusalem Studies in Jewish Thought* 8 (1989): 147–181; "Judaism and Incarnation: The Imaginal Body of God," in T. Frymer-Kensky, D. Novak, P. Ochs, D. Sandmel, and M. Signer, *Christianity in Jewish Terms* (Boulder, Colo.: Westview, 2000), pp. 239–254; and my "Ethics Disentangled from the Law: Incarnation, the Universal, and Hasidic Ethics," *Kabbala* 15 (Fall 2006).

32. The idea that serving a human being in Christianity is rooted in Ancient Judaism and is not a product of Christianity's adapting Hellenistic pagan ideas is argued in Larry Hurtado's *One God One Lord: Early Christian Devotion and Ancient Jewish Monotheism*, esp. pp. 17–40. Cf. Lars Thunberg, "The Human Person as Image of God," in B. McGinn and J. Meyendorff, eds., *Christian Spirituality* (New York: Crossroads, 1995), pp. 293–295; and Jacob Neusner, *Torah: From Scroll to Symbol in Formative Judaism* (Philadelphia: Fortress, 1985), pp. 4ff; idem, *Incarnation of God: The Character of Divinity in Formative Judaism* (Philadelphia: Fortress, 1988), pp. 188–192; and Wolfson, "Judaism and Incarnation," pp. 246–251.

33. See, for example, Margaret Barker, "The High Priest and the Worship of

Jesus," in C. Newman, J. Davila, and G. Lewis, eds., *The Jewish Roots of Christological Monotheism* (Leiden: Brill, 1999), pp. 93–111; and Crispin H. T. Fletcher, "The Worship of Divine Humanity as God's Image and the Worship of Jesus," in *The Jewish Roots of Christological Monotheism*, pp. 112–128.

34. The notion of incarnation as the divine *in* the human is part of early Christianity's understanding as well. See, for example, John 13:31–14:29 and Philippians 2. More generally, see Goshen-Gottstein, "Judaisms and Incarnational Theologies," *Journal of Ecumenical Studies* 39, nos. 3–4 (2002), esp. 229–234.

35. There are numerous rabbinic examples where the messiah is called by a divine name (YHVH, Adonai, or 'El). See b.T. Baba Batra 75b and Rashi ad loc; Lamentations Raba 1:51; and Idel, *Messianic Mystics*, pp. 23 and 41. On the question regarding how Jews responded to Christian doctrine that reinterpreted notions rooted in its own tradition, see Idel, p. 24: "Or to mention another main question that haunted Jewish messianism, the emergence of Christianity, a messianic religion drawing upon Jewish sources and attempting to reinterpret some of the messianic claims cherished by the Jews, problematized some of the earlier Jewish concepts, which were marginalized in order to make a clearer distinction between Judaism and Christianity."

36. Wolfson, *Language*, p. 191. It is also interesting to note that the staunch antikabbalist Aryeh Leone of Modena criticized Kabbala partially because he believed it led to kabbalists converting to Christianity! See Idel, "Differing Conceptions of Kabbala in the Early Seventeenth Century," pp. 137–200, esp. pp. 166–168; and *Enchanted Chains* (Los Angeles: Cherub, 2005), pp. 194 and 195.

37. See Wolfson, *Language*, p. 257, where he notes that the incarnational thinking in the Zohar may indeed be a "polemical ploy," albeit one that accepts the wider framework of incarnational thinking.

38. See Georgios Mantzaridis, *The Deification of Man* (Crestwood, N.Y.: St. Vladimir, 1984), pp. 15, 29, and 31. On the extent to which this notion of the deification of man has become the backbone of Orthodox doctrine, see J. Gross, *La divinisation du crétien les peres grecs, contribution historique à la doctrine de la grâce* (Paris, 1938). Cf. Jaques Maritain, *Integral Humanism: Temporal and Spiritual Problems of a New Christendom*, Joseph W. Evans, trans. (New York: Scribner, 1968).

39. See Vigen Guroian, *Incarnate Love: Essays in Orthodox Ethics* (South Bend, Ind.: University of Notre Dame Press, 1987). This notion extends at least back to Plotinus and Pseudo-Dionysius.

40. The notion of the Incarnation as constant in all of humanity and (re)lived through the sacraments is the basis of the work of the 14th-century Greek theologian and saint Nicholas Cabasilas (ca. 1322–1395). See especially his *Life in Christ*, Carmino J. de Catanzaro, trans. (New York: SVS, 1974). In Cabasilas, and his better-known predecessor St. Gregory Palamas (1296–1359), the notion of *theosis*, or the divination of the human, plays a central role. Relevant to our concerns, both suggest that the Incarnation of Christ "makes of us a temple of his divinity and enlightens our soul from within" (p. 26). A thorough treatment of this in the work of St. Gregory Palamas can be found in Georgios Mantzaridis, *The Deification of Man*.

41. Mantzaridis, *The Deification of Man*, p. 71. "Love of God is the root of all virtue. . . . Love of God bears fruit in the form of love of one's neighbor, which is the 'sign' of the believer's love for Jesus Christ and the starting point of all social virtue." For the use of *theosis* as a model for Hasidic ethics, see my "Ethics Disentangled from the Law: Incarnation, the Universal and Hasidic Ethics," *Kabbala* 15 (Fall 2006): 31–75.

42. Mantzaridis, p. 15. Maximus the Confessor defines *theosis* this way: "A firm and trustworthy basis of hope for the deification of human nature is God's incarnation, which makes of man a god in the same measure as God Himself became man" (p. 14). Cf. David S. Yaego, "Jesus of Nazareth and Cosmic Redemption: The Relevance of St. Maximus the Confessor," *Modern Theology* 12 (1996).

43. *The Encyclopedia of Religion*, 2nd ed., 2005, vol. 6, p. 3699.

44. St. Gregory of Palamas, *Defense of the Hesychasts* 3, 1, 34, cited in *The Deification of Man*, p. 31.

45. See, for example, Geza Vermes, *The Changing Faces of Jesus*, p. 37. "No biblical or post-biblical Jewish writer ever depicted a human being literally as divine, nor did Jewish religious culture agree to accommodate the Hellenistic notions of 'son of God' and 'divine man.' The designations, common in the terminology of ruler worship in imperial Rome and in the description of charismatic personalities in Hellenism, remained taboo in Judaism." David Blumenthal is a bit more uncertain of this absolute negation. See his "*Tselem:* Toward an Anthropomorphic Theology of Image," in *Christianity in Jewish Terms*, pp. 345 and 346. On the one hand he argues that "the doctrine of the incarnation is not beyond the Jewish theological imagination" and then equivocates by saying "Judaism cannot accept the doctrine of incarnation." Perhaps Blumenthal is making a distinction, one that sits at the very center of my argument, that the notion of incarnation must be distinguished from its particular Christian instantiation. If this is correct, it undermines Vermes's position that the idea itself is a product of Hellenistic and not Jewish thinking. This thesis, common among many Jewish theologians, has been duly challenged by Larry Hurtado, *One Lord One God.*

46. Michael Wyschogrod writes that "it must be emphasized that the Jewish objection to an incarnational theology cannot be based on a priori grounds, as if something in the nature of the Jewish concept of God made his appearance in the form of humanity a rational impossibility." Michael Wyschogrod, "A Jewish Perspective on Incarnation," *Modern Theology* 12, no. 2 (1996): 204. On incarnationalism and Judaism more generally, see Jacob Neusner, *The Incarnation of God: The Character of Divinity in Formative Judaism;* David Stern, "*Imitatio Hominus:* Anthropomorphism and the Character(s) of God in Rabbinic Literature," *Prooftexts* 12 (1992): 151–174; Alon Goshen-Gottstein, "The Body of God in Rabbinic Literature," pp. 171–195; Elliot Wolfson, "Iconic Visualization and the Imaginal Body of God: The Role of Intention in the Rabbinic Concept of Prayer," *Modern Theology* 12 (1996): 137–162; "Judaism and Incarnation: The Imaginal Body of God," in *Christianity in Jewish Terms;* and Michael Fishbane, "Some Forms of Divine Appearance in Ancient Jewish Thought," in J. Neusner, E. Frerichs, and W. Sarna, eds., *From Ancient Israel to Modern Judaism: Essays in Honor of Marvin Fox* (Atlanta, Ga.: Scholars, 1989), vol. 2, pp. 261–270. In a slightly different way, Daniel Boyarin's *Border Lines: The Partition of Judeo-Christianity* makes a similar point. Boyarin argues, however, that while logos theology (the divine embodiment in the Word) is endemic to Judaism, transference from Word to human (Jesus) is not.

47. See B.Talmud Avodah Zara, 3b; Menahot, 29b and 53b. Cf. Alon Goshen-Gottstein, "The Body as Image of God in Rabbinic Literature," and Elliot R. Wolfson, "Images of God's Feet: Some Observations on the Divine Body in Judaism," in H. Eilberg-Schwartz, ed., *People of the Body: Jews and Judaism from an Embodied Perspective* (Albany, N.Y.: SUNY Press, 1992), pp. 143–181.

48. Jacob Neusner, *Torah: From Scroll to Symbol in Formative Judaism*, p. 4; Wolfson, "Judaism and Incarnation," pp. 246–251; and Ephraim Urbach, *Hazal* (Jeru-

salem: Magnus, 1976), pp. 28–52. On aniconism and Judaism more generally, see Kalman Bland, *The Artless Jew.*

49. Wolfson, "Iconic Visualization," p. 139 and "Judaism and Incarnation," pp. 251–253.

50. See Geza Vermes, *The Changing Faces of Jesus,* pp. 45–53.

51. Jacob Neusner offers a Jewish definition of incarnation as follows: "The description of God, whether in allusion or narrative, as corporeal; exhibiting traits of emotion like those of human beings; doing deeds that women and men do in the way in which they do them." Neusner, *The Incarnation of God,* p. 17. While this definition may suffice for classical rabbinic Judaism, I find it inexact when applied to our texts. This is because Neusner's definition and the texts he cites in his book are focused on how humans describe God as human. Our texts are more interested in describing how humans are divine. The latter, I suggest, is much closer to the Christian idea.

52. Neusner acknowledges that Judaism rejects the "particular framing" of Christian incarnation, but, in concert with Wyschogrod, this rejection is not in principle, only in fact. See Neusner, *The Incarnation of God,* p. 6, and Wolfson, "Judaism and Incarnation," p. 240. Larry Hurtado suggests another model in his *One God One Lord,* pp. 99–124, saying that the Christian notion of incarnation is a "mutation" of a Jewish idea. He does not imply "mutation" in the negative sense but rather the way it is used in the biological sciences, as "a description of a sudden and significant development in the species" (p. 162, n. 20). Hurtado's notion of mutation is helpful because as it maintains a link between the ancient Jewish–early Christian ideas it also suggests that postbiblical Judaism still has the core notion of divine embodiment that Christianity "mutates." Given that fact, it is not far-fetched to posit that later Judaisms could make similar kinds of "mutations."

53. Michael Wyschogrod writes, "My claim is that the Christian teaching of the incarnation of God in Jesus is an intensification of the teaching of the indwelling of God in Israel by concentrating that indwelling in one Jew rather than leaving it diffused in the people of Jesus as a whole. From my perspective such a severing of any Jew from his people is a mistake because, biblically, God's covenantal partner is always the people Israel and not an individual Jew." Wyschogrod, "Incarnation of God's Indwelling in Israel," in his *Abraham's Promise: Jewish and Jewish-Christian Relations* (Grand Rapids, Mich.: Eerdmans, 2004), p. 178. Wyschogrod here admits that the Incarnation as doctrine is a distinction in degree and not in kind from the Jewish notion of indwelling. In this spirit, I suggest that our texts extend divine indwelling beyond its conventional borders until it reaches the limits of incarnational thinking. This would satisfy Wyschogrod because the kabbalistic texts in question do not limit incarnation to one person but present it as a possibility to all.

54. On the history of Christian Kabbala more generally, see Joseph Dan, *The Christian Kabbalah: Jewish Mystical Books and Their Christian Interpreters,* and Chaim Wirszubski, *Pico della Mirandola's Encounter with Jewish Mysticism.* On Lurianic Kabbala and its influence on subsequent Christian Kabbala, see Idel, "Jewish Thinkers versus Christian Kabbala," pp. 60–63; and more generally p. 50, n. 2.

55. Tishby noticed this in his "God, Torah, Israel are One" [Hebrew], *Keriat Sefer* 50 (1975): 668–674. More generally, see Yehuda Liebes, "Christian Influences on the Zohar," in Liebes, *Studies in the Zohar,* pp. 139–161. Most recently, see Wolfson's comment in *Language,* p. 260.

56. In Christianity, see Lars Thunberg, "The Human Person as Image of God,"

in *Christian Spirituality*, pp. 293–295. In Judaism, see Urbach, *Hazal*, pp. 190–194; and Yair Lorberbaum, *Zelem Elohim: Halakha and Aggadah*, esp. pp. 84–105.

57. The notion of divine indwelling in Judaism applies to the land of Israel and the Temple, e.g., to Exodus 40:35, 36; and I Kings 8:13. For some examples, see Exodus 25:8, *And let them make me a sanctuary that I may dwell among them;* and Deuterony 33:15, *Since the LORD moves about in your camp to protect you . . . ;* Jeremiah 49:38; Mekhilta de-Rebbe Yishmael, Sidra de-Piskha, chapter 14; and Sifri Bamidbar, Parshat Zav, p. 94.

58. The idea of indwelling is also a part of early Christianity, especially regarding the tabernacle. See, for example, Craig R. Koester, *The Indwelling of God: The Tabernacle in the Old Testament, Intertestamental Jewish Literature, and the New Testament.*

59. See, for example, Psalms 84:2; 132:12–14; Ezekiel 19:3, 4; 34:1–4.

60. Ezekiel 10:3, 4; 43:1–4.

61. For a discussion of this disagreement between the school of R. Akiva and the sages, see Urbach, *Hazal*, pp. 40–43.

62. See, for example, Pirkei Avot 3:4; Sifra, "Kedoshim" 4:12; Urbach, *Hazal*, pp. 191–193; Lorberbaum, *Zelem Elohim*, pp. 84, 89–101.

63. There is, however, a correlation drawn between the human and the Temple, for example, that does make such a connection. See Lorberbaum, *Zelem Elohim*, pp. 436–453.

64. For the classical depiction of indwelling and also the rabbinic construction of "the image of God" in man, see Ephraim Urbach, *Hazal*, pp. 29–52 and 189–226.

65. See Martin Buber, "Love of God and Love of Neighbor," in *Hasidism and Modern Man* (Atlantic Highlands, N.J.: Humanities Press International, 1988), p. 223.

66. The kabbalists, of course, do not accept the documentary hypothesis and thus they would not agree with this assessment. However, they are surely sensitive to the overt change from the anthropomorphic imagery to the exclusive presentation of presence as name in Deuteronomy.

67. Cf. *Sefer Temunah*, p. 25a, and Wolfson's comment in *Speculum*, p. 329. Cf. "The Mystical Experience of Torah Study in German Pietism," in *The Jewish Quarterly Review*, pp. 43–77.

68. See ShK, "Drush on Sukkot" #6, pp. 106b–d. This homily will be analyzed in detail below.

69. See Mishna Sukkah 4:2; and b.T. Sukkah 45a. For the notion of Sukkot being the time "the waters are judged," see b.T. Rosh ha-Shana 16a and Ta'anit 2b. The idea of Hoshana Raba being the day the waters are judged appears to be kabbalistic and not of rabbinic origin. Since Hoshana Raba is the final day of Sukkot, this does not constitute much of an innovation. The custom of circling the *bimah* in the synagogue comes as a remembrance of a Temple custom of circling the altar. The genealogy of the custom is unclear. Rabbi Yohanan argues it is a "secret" of the latter prophets and thus deserves a blessing. Rabbi Joshua argues it is merely a custom of the prophets and thus does not require a blessing. See b.T. Sukkah 44b and *Tur Shulkhan Arukh* 2, no. 644, p. 359b. There is no special sanctity of the night of Hoshana Raba given in rabbinic literature. However, we do see in the Middle Ages, even by texts not necessarily influence by the Zohar, that the night of Hoshana Raba has particular power. For example, see *Sefer Hasidism* #453 and Bahya ben Asher, *Rabbenu Bahya ʿal ha-Torah* on Numbers 14:9. Cf. to Deut. 33:21, where Bahya states that the day is called Hoshana Raba

because it marks the twenty-six days from creation (on the 25th of Elul), the number twenty-six equaling the numerical value of יהוה .

70. See Zohar 1.220a and 2.242a. The use of the plural *"kippurim"* as opposed to *"kippur"* already suggests, to these kabbalists, a second atonement apart from Yom Kippur. Kabbalistic renderings of Hoshana Raba precede the Zohar. See, for example, Eliezer of Worms (12th-century Rhineland), *Hokhmat ha-Nefesh*, E. Weiss, ed. (Bnei Brak, 1987), p. 63 and his *Sodei Razzaya*, "Hilhot Nevuah," I. Kamhelar, ed. (Jerusalem, 1936), p. 49 and the discussion in Idel, *Enchanted Chains*, pp. 109–114.

71. This similarity is noted in *halakhic* literature as well. See Joseph Karo, *Shulkhan Arukh*, "Laws of Lulav," #663:1.

72. The notion of the "filling of the divine names" is a Lurianic practice whereby any divine name can be spelled simply, i.e., היהא or "filled out" with *alefs* as follows: אלף ה"א יו"ד ה"א or with *yods:* אלף ה"י יו"ד ה"י or with *hays:* אלף ה"ה יוד ה"ה. This can be done with any of the various divine names; thus one reaches different numerical values for each permutation, maximizing the different valences of divine presence.

73. See Zohar 3.261a and Tikkunei Zohar 46a.

74. For an expanded explanation, see SeK, p. 285b.

75. ShK, p. 106c. The notion of Mishneh Torah (Deuteronomy) as *malkhut* is already in the Zohar. See Tikkunei Zohar, tikun 21, p. 46a.

76. For a gender analysis of YK in Kabbala more generally, see Elliot Wolfson, "Fore/giveness On the Way: Nesting in the Womb of Response," in Wolfson, *Pathwings*, pp. 11–136. Wolfson shows how YK is engendered as feminine, the union of *malkhut* with *binah*, as a state of female homoeroticism brought about by the withholding of sexual energy (founded on the prohibition of sexual contact on YK). But he notes that this ostensible feminine engendering also is related to the masculinization of *binah*. For Luria, even though YK may be masculine juxtaposed to Hoshana Raba, Neilah on YK already takes on this feminine quality. See SeK, p. 283b, "On Neilah of YK the *yesod* of Rachel is created. This *yesod* is the vessel and receptacle to receive its seed."

77. The relationship between ritual and metaphysics is a debated issue among ritual theorists. Some, following Clifford Geertz, argue that ritual is not indicative nor informative about metaphysics but represents a culture's style and ethos. On this, see Kevin Schilbrack, "Ritual Metaphysics," *Journal of Ritual Studies* 18, no. 1 (2004): 77–88. In Lurianic Kabbala, it seems clear that ritual is, in fact, the very embodiment of metaphysics. Schilbrack argues (p. 79), "But the goal [of ritual] in any case is to provide visible, tactile instantiation to teachings that might otherwise seem merely conceptual. The goal is to have the ritual participants perceive metaphysical truths 'in the flesh.'" I would argue this is an accurate description of our case.

78. The *zelem* of each individual departs during the first part of the night. It should return, however, after midnight. If one still sees his/her *zelem* "above them" after midnight, it is sign of impending death.

79. ShK, p. 106c. For another similar version with slight alterations, see PEH, "Sha'ar Lulav" chapter 4, p. 150b. The numerology is as follows: the second seal is made up of three names of *ehyeh* אהי"ה the first spelled with *yods* (140), the second with *alefs* (122), and the third with *hays* (130). This comes to 392. If you add one for each name you have 385, the value of *"mishneh."* See Mordecai Moshe Karfman, "Minhat Cohen," commentary to *Shulkhan Arukh ha-Ari Z'L* (Jerusalem: Hatam Sofer Institute, 1984), p. 170.

80. There is a correlation in the Zohar between the moon and YK. Rosh ha-Shana is the only festival when the moon is new (and thus hidden). The Zohar notes that the judgment of Rosh Ha-Shana is not sealed until YK, when the moon reaches the first stage of fullness. See Zohar 3.100b.

81. The notion of the "seal" as a protection against the demonic forces is explicit in SeK, p. 284c: "This seal is also a protection of the feminine light against the demonic forces because their attachment is primarily to the feminine."

82. See also Zohar 1.157b and 3.104b.

83. ShK, p. 106c.

84. See b.T. Yoma 85b–87a and b.T. Keritut 7a.

85. The term *moah* literally means "brains" and often, as in this case, refers to the physical object of the human brain. In other cases, e.g., above, especially when referring to the two states of human development (immature and mature), it more accurately translates as consciousness. The concept of spermogenesis (the notion that male sperm originates in the brain) was a common trope in medieval medicine adopted by the Zohar and its later interpreters. On this, see D. Jacquart and C. Thomasset, *Sexuality and Medicine in the Middle Ages*, pp. 53ff.

86. EH vol. 1, Gate 6, chapter 1, p. 103:3. Cf. ShMR, p. 53b (bottom) and SeK, p. 287a. The notion of *zelem adonai* is unclear. On this, see MeSh, Gate 5, part 1, chapter 13, p. 43a (bottom), where this is stated more explicitly, though no explanation is given as to its source. See Jacob Zemah's gloss on that passage: "I could not find a reference to *zelem havaya* הו'ה in any verse. Perhaps it is hinted at in the verse שמחו השמים ותגל הארץ where the last letter of each word spells מלצו and the first letter of each word spells הו'ה."

87. Zohar 1.94a. More generally, see Wolfson, *Speculum*, pp. 342 and 343, and "Circumcision, Visionary Experience, and Textual Interpretation," reprinted in *Essential Papers in Kabbala*, pp. 206ff.

88. On the Sabba de-Mishpatim, see Pinhas Giller, *Reading the Zohar*, pp. 35–68.

89. Zohar 2.96b. Cf. 2.97b. I want to thank Menahem Kallus for bringing this text to my attention. On the use of the image of the signet ring in this context, see SeK, p. 287a.

90. The notion that the creation is formed through Hebrew letters in not solely a kabbalistic idea based on *Sefer Yezeriah*. For example, see Midrash Raba on Ruth, chapter 5, on grace after meals. Cf. Zohar 3.218a and Nahman of Bratslav, *Likkutei MoHaRan* 1:19, 7.

91. See, for example, ShMR, p. 60d. "Regarding what is said about 'Perek Shira,' i.e., that all who recite it every day merit many great [spiritual] levels, this is the reason: It is known that God made Adam in His image. Therefore, just as all the [supernal] worlds are dependent and take hold of the divine stature of God (*shiur kumato Yitbarakh*) called Supernal Adam (*Adam ha-Elyon*) who sits on the throne, so too the lower worlds are dependent and take hold of the stature of lower Adam, and they are all blessed through him."

92. The ritual of Torah study on Hoshana Raba is a Lurianic invention, as is the same custom on the night of Shavout. On ritual innovation in Luria in general, see Scholem, "Tradition and New Creation in the Ritual of the Kabbalists," in his *On the Kabbalah and Its Symbolism* (New York: Schocken, 1965), pp. 118–157.

93. This means that to be a full person one needs all three *zelamim*.

94. See PEH, "Sha ʿar le-Yom ha-Kippurim," #5, p. 145c, and idem. "Sha ʿar ha-Lulav," #4, pp. 149c–150b. Cf. SeK, p. 183a, where we read, "the seal is the point of Zion in the female," denoting the entry point to the womb.

95. For an explanation of the various spelling permutations of the divine name to constitute different dimensions of divine presence, see Fine, *Physician of the Soul*, pp. 276–281.

96. The understanding of these two verses appears to be as follows: there are three references to *zelem* in these verses, each reference referring to one manifestation of the full spelling of *ehyeh*.

97. ShK, pp. 106d–107a. This is based loosely on b.T. Yebamot 122a and Zohar 1.120a. For more on *shadim* in this context, see SeK, p. 287b.

98. Most recently, see Wolfson, *Language*, pp. 190–260. For a formulation of text that is different, yet shares some interesting parallels, see Steven Kepnes's study of Martin Buber's hermeneutics, *The Text as Thou* (Bloomington: Indiana University Press, 1992).

99. Recently, see Daniel Abrams, *Ha-Guf ha-Elohi* (Jerusalem: Magnus, 2004), pp. 21–28. The notion that the human body is comprised of divine letters is not an original kabbalistic idea but is rooted in rabbinic Midrash. See Midrash Tanhuma to Genesis 11. Cf. the discussion in Tikva Frymer-Kensky, *Motherprayer: The Pregnant Women's Spiritual Companion* (New York: G.P. Putnam and Sons, 1995), pp. 52–58 and notes, and her "The Image, The Glory, and the Holy," in W. Schweiker, M. Johnson, and K. Jung, eds., *Humanity Before God: Contemporary Faces of Jewish, Christian, and Islamic Ethics* (Minneapolis: Fortress, 2006), pp. 137 and 138.

100. See Matt Goldish, *Sabbatean Prophets*, and "Patterns in Converso Messianism," in *Jewish Messianism in the Early Modern World*, pp. 41–64.

101. See Kallus, *Theurgic Prayer in Lurianic Kabbala*, pp. 198–205. I am not claiming this is unique to Lurianic Kabbala, as similar themes are present in earlier kabbalistic literature, particularly *Sefer ha-Meshiv*, a set of texts likely written in the late 15th century. *Sefer ha-Meshiv* was available to Vital and likely had a strong impact on the Lurianic tradition. See Moshe Idel, *Enchanted Chains*, pp. 114–121 and n. 162, for numerous studies on this work. Idel sums up his theory on *Sefer ha-Meshiv* as follows: "Thus God as name, as prayer, and as Torah characterize attempts to envision the divinity in terms of certain ritualistic concepts that also function as techniques, and create forms of continua between man and God. All these are cataphatic modes of religion, conceptualizing the existence of a deep-seated affinity between man, the technique, and God" (p. 121).

102. See Joseph Avivi, *Binyan Ariel*, pp. 68–71; Kallus, *Theurgy*, p. 159 n. 83; and Moshe Ya'akov Hillel's introduction to *Sefer ha-Kavannot ha-Yashan* (Jerusalem: Ahavat Shalom Institute, 2004), pp. 14–17.

103. See ShY, "*Sha'ar ha-Yehudim u Nevuah ve-Ruah ha-Kodesh*," p. 15c.

104. See Fine, *Physician of the Soul*, pp. 207–219. Cf. Fine, "Recitation of the Mishnah as a Vehicle for Mystical Inspiration: A Contemplative Technique Taught by Hayyim Vital," *Revue des études juives* 141, no. 1–2 (1982): 183–199; and "The Study of Torah as a Theurgic Rite in Lurianic Kabbala," in D. Blumenthal, ed., *Approaches to Judaism in Medieval Times* (Atlanta, Ga.: Scholars, 1988), vol. 3, pp. 29–40.

105. PEH, p. 84d.

106. Cf. ShRK, p. 57b.

107. ShY, p. 15c.

108. This idea is debated in early Hasidism regarding the status of the *zaddik*. On one reading in Shneur Zalman of Liady's *Sefer ha-Tanya*, the *zaddik gamur* (complete righteous person) is one who simply does not have a *yezer hara* or, in our terms, one who cannot sin and thus has achieved *theosis*. See *Sefer ha-Tanya*,

chapters 1 and 10. Cf. my "The Divine/Human Messiah and Religious Deviance: Some Reflections on the Origins of Chabad's 'Rebbesim,'" in *Reaching for the Infinite* (forthcoming).

109. PEH, p. 83d (bottom).

110. See Kallus, *Theurgy*, p. 199. "We find here that the practitioner is transforming himself into a 'dwelling place' for the emanation of the Divine manifestation, in order to pray effectively with the *Kavvanot.*" I suggest a stronger reading here. It is not simply that the "reader" makes himself a "dwelling place" but that the letters that are activated within him make him divine. Thus, the *yezer hara* disappears and he loses the very distinction between the human and the divine, the susceptibility to sin. Whether this is a permanent or transitory state is another important issue, one that distinguishes between incarnation in a more formal sense, and *theosis*. In any event, the transformative nature of this encounter with the divine letters of Torah through study seems quite clear.

111. Maimonides, *Guide of the Perplexed* III: 51, pp. 621, 622 (in Pines ed.). Cf. a similar locution in Isaac of Acre, *Meʿirat ʿEinayim*, Amos Goldreich, ed. (Jerusalem, 1984), p. 127, and Ephrayim Gottlieb, *Studies in Kabbalistic Literature* [Hebrew], Joseph Hacker, ed. (Jerusalem, 1976), p. 235.

112. See Miles Krassen, *Uniter of Heaven and Earth* (Albany, N.Y.: SUNY Press, 1998), pp. 43–80, and 107–122; and my *Hasidism on the Margin* (Madison: University of Wisconsin Press, 2004), pp. 201–248.

113. On this, see Jacob Katz, *Halakha and Kabbalah;* Rachel Elior, "The Dispute of Position of the Kabbala in the Sixteenth Century," pp. 177–190; and idem, "Messianic Expectations."

114. Yet rabbinic society in the Middle Ages put its own onerous restrictions on the study of Kabbala for Jews. On this, see Moshe Idel, "Le Toldot ha-Issure Lilmod Kabbala lifnei Gil Arba'im," *AJS Review* 5 (1980): 1–20 [Hebrew section]. Idel notes (pp. 11–13) that this restriction of studying Kabbala until the age of forty was adapted by many Christian Kabbalists as well.

115. On the accessibility of Lurianic Kabbala to Christians, see Allison P. Coudert, *The Impact of Kabbala in the Seventeenth Century* (Leiden: Brill, 1999).

116. In the talmudic discussion, R. Meir argues that "even a gentile who studies Torah is like a High Priest." The Talmud concludes this only applies to a gentile who studies the seven Noahide commandments of which he is obligated. The Zohar Hadash on Ruth, p. 82a, argues that R. Meir's position is referring to a high priest who is an ignoramus. The equation is as follows: just like a high priest who is an ignoramus, his divine service is not considered valid and he receives no reward, so too a gentile who studies Torah will receive no reward since he was not commanded to do so. Maimonides has an odd position on this matter. He held that it is permissible to teach commandments (he does not stipulate only Noahide commandments) to Christians (who he believed were idolaters) because they recognize the divinity of Scripture, while it is forbidden to teach Torah to Muslims (whom he held were monotheists), because they did not believe in the divinity of Scripture. See *Teshuvot ha-Rambam* 1: 284, 285.

117. See b.T. Sanhedrin 59a. "An idolater (ʿoved kokhavim) who studies Torah (ʿosek be-Torah) is liable to the death penalty (hayyav mita), as it is written, *Moses commanded the law to us (lanu) as an inheritance*—to us and not to them." Rashi ad loc suggests the reason the idolater is forbidden from studying Torah is that it would constitute stealing as Torah is the inheritance of Israel. This would suggest that the prohibition has nothing to do with idolatry but applies to all gentiles at all times. This seems to be the accepted interpretation. See, for ex-

ample, Jacob Joseph of Polnoy's *Toldot Ya'akov Yosef*, vol. 2, p. 59a, where he changes the language of the talmudic passage to read: "A gentile (*goy*) who studies Torah is liable to the death penalty." The Talmud is ultimately not satisfied with this reading because the punishment for theft is not death. Hence it reads "inheritance" (*morasha*) as "fiancée" (*me-ursa*). Hence the gentile who studies ('*osek*) Torah is committing an act of adultery (*gilluy arayot*).

118. See Elliot Wolfson, "Circumcision, Vision of God, and Textual Interpretation: From Midrashic Trope to Mystical Symbol," reprinted in *Papers in Essential Kabbala*, p. 496. And yet, the Venetian rabbi Elijah Menahem Halfan in the early 16th century argued that teaching Kabbala to non-Jews was under the talmudic ban of teaching secrets to the gentiles. See David Kaufmann, "Elijah Menachem Helfan on Jews teaching Hebrew to Non-Jews," *Jewish Quarterly Review* (OS) vol. IX (1896/7): 500–508; and Idel, "Jewish Thinkers versus Christliche Kabbalah" (Ostfildern: Thornbeche Verlag, 2003), pp. 53 and 54.

119. One example would be the converso Abraham Cohen Herrera. See Nissim Yosha, *Myth and Metaphor* [Hebrew] (Jerusalem: Magnus, 1994), pp. 21–50. In general, Christian kabbalists learned Kabbala either from Jewish apostates or conversos. See Scholem, *Kabbala*, pp. 196–220; Idel, "Jewish Thinkers versus Christian Kabbala," p. 50; and *Absorbing Perfections*, pp. 461–481. Even though Pico della Mirandola's main teacher was the apostate Flavius Mithredates, it is likely that he also had Jewish teachers, one being Yehuda Allemano. In the 17th century, given the return of many conversos, the story gets more complicated. See Klaus Reichert, "Christian Kabbalah in the Seventeenth Century," in *The Christian Kabbala*, pp. 127–147. We do not have any explicit evidence that kabbalists state it is permissible to teach gentiles Kabbala. The closest case may be that of Yehuda Ashlag, who implies this in numerous places, and his disciples Krokovsky (who published some of the early English translations of Kabbala in the United States) and later Phillip Berg of The Kabbala Center. I want to thank Professor Boaz Huss for his help with this question. On Ashlag, see D. Hansel, "The Origin and Thought of Rabbi Yehuda Halevi Ashlag: Simsum of God or Simsum of the World," *Kabbalah* 7 (2002): 37–46, and Garb, *The Chosen Will Become Herds* (Jerusalem: Carmel Books, 2005), pp. 57–64, 99–110.

120. On Nathan and his kabbalistic training, see Scholem's preface to Nathan's *derashot* in *Be-Ikvot Moshiah* (Jerusalem: Tarshish, 1944), pp. 9–13; and Avraham Elkayam, "On the 'Knowledge of the Messiah'—The Dialectic of the Erotic Peak in the Messianic Thought of Nathan of Gaza" [Hebrew], *Tarbiz* 65 (1996): 637–670.

121. See Cordovero's comment on Tikkunei Zohar, cited in Brakha Sack, *Be-Sha'arei ha-Kabbala shel Moses Cordovero*, p. 37, n. 22, and Idel, "Jewish Thinkers," p. 55.

122. *Sefer Hizyonot*, p. 68, and *Spiritual Autobiographies*, Morris Faierstein trans. (New York: Paulist Press, 1999), pp. 98, 99.

123. The superiority of Kabbala over Talmud is made quite explicit in Vital's introduction to *Sha'ar Hakdamot*, printed as the introduction to EH, p. 5 (English pagination), left column, and ShK, second part, eighth gate. More generally in the 16th century, see Twersky, "Talmudists, Philosophers, Kabbalists," pp. 446–449.

124. See, for example, "Introduction" to EH, p. 6 (English pagination), right column. This also resonates in the Zohar when it depicts itself as the Torah where the demonic has been eradicated. See Zohar 3:124b, Zohar Hadash 94a; and Wolfson, *Venturing Beyond*, pp. 269, 270.

125. Lloyd Gaston, *Paul and the Torah*, pp. 116–134.

126. SeG, p. 1. And see b.T. Sanhedrin 59a where it states, "Jews are called Adam, gentiles are not called Adam." This idea is pervasive in the Zohar and subsequent Kabbala influenced by the Zohar. See Wolfson, *Venturing Beyond*, pp. 42–58. On the other hand, see b.T. Megillah 13a, "Anyone who repudiates idolatry is called a Jew."

127. On this question, see Kimelman, *The Mystical Meaning of Lekhah Dodi and Kabbalat Shabbat* [Hebrew], pp. 82–133.

128. *Megillah ha-Megalleh* (Berlin, 1924), p. 110. See this text discussed in Idel, "Some Conceptions of the Land of Israel in Medieval Jewish Thought," pp. 125 and 126.

129. It is, of course, worth considering the talmudic dictum "Anyone who repudiates idolatry is called a Jew" (b.T. Megillah 13a) in this context. While it is not wholly clear what the sages meant by this, one could see that from a messianic perspective, if one understands the messianic era as the complete eradication of idolatry, all humanity will, by definition, be called Jews.

130. It is very likely that this infatuation with conversion comes both from the converso context and the centrality of conversion in parts of the Zohar, particularly the Tikkunei Zohar. See Wolfson, *Venturing Beyond*, pp. 165–185.

131. In *Venturing Beyond*, p. 113, Elliot Wolfson argues that for Vital, "non-Jewish nations come into being as a consequence of Adam's transgression. In the ideal state of purity and innocence, the human form is homologized as a Jew; the existence of all other human beings is due to sin and imperfection." See Vital ShP, 55b,c. For an interesting contemporary comment that may be based on this kabbalistic tradition, see Zalman Schachter-Shalomi (with Daniel Seigel), *Credo of a Modern Kabbalist* (Canada: Trafford, 2005), p. 382. "When it comes time to *avodah*/prayer we are limited now to making a *minyan* only with Jews. . . . However, just as we said that, in the future, anyone who shares a vision of God is served in many different ways can be included in *Yisra'el*, so I can imagine that there will be a time when we will go to any mall and other gathering place and ask who would like to tune in for a moment to God's oneness. Any ten such people will then gather and do the equivalent of '*Kadosh, kadosh, kadosh*/Holy, holy holy' and then go back to their work."

Conclusion

1. The relationship between Kabbala and Christianity and Islam has been examined in depth by numerous scholars. For example, see Ron Kiener, "The Image of Islam in the Zohar," Yehuda Liebes, "Christian Influences in the Zohar," and most recently Elliot Wolfson in *Venturing Beyond*, pp. 129–185. Cf. Reuven Kimmlemen, *Lekha Dodi*. My analysis builds on these studies and examines the more unconscious dimensions of how Lurianic Kabbala could have been responding to its host environment's ideology, absorbing certain ideas and responding polemically (albeit covertly) to others. I am also more interested in the way these kabbalists use the biblical narrative as a template to engage these ideas.

2. See Gershom Scholem, "*Gilgul*" in *On the Mystical Shape*, pp. 197–250; Pinhas Giller, *Reading the Zohar*, pp. 36–68; and most recently, Mark Verman, "Reincarnation and Theodicy" in *Be'erot Yizhak*, pp. 399–426. For other noteworthy studies, see Verman, p. 401 n. 7.

3. See Kellner, *Maimonides on the 'The Decline of the Generations' and the Nature of Rabbinic Authority*.

4. This idea has its caveats, For example, the rabbis construct a legal category of "the law is like the later authorities" (*hilkhata ke-batrei*), but this usually applies to those already within a particular historical epoch. That is, in the rabbinic period, later rabbinic authorities may have their way but post-talmudic medieval authorities cannot undermine the decisions of those in the earlier rabbinic period.

5. See "Hakdama le-Shaʿar Hakdamaot," printed as the "Hakdama le-ʿEtz Hayyim."

6. The ritualization of recitation has been examined by Lawrence Fine, "The Study of Torah as a Theurgic Rite in Lurianic Kabbalah" and *Physician of the Soul*, pp. 207–212. In addition, this focus of recitation realized an important publication entitled *Hok le-Yisrael*, which is a multivolume guide to the recitation of Tanakh, Mishna, Talmud, and Zohar according to Lurianic custom. Cf. the new *Shaʿagat ha-Ari* (Jerusalem, 2005) devoted to the customs of study according to Luria.

7. On this, see my "Origin and Overcoming the Beginning," in A. Cohen and S. Magid, eds., *Beginning/Again* (New York: Seven Bridges, 2002), pp. 163–214; and Wolfson, "Divine Suffering and the Hermeneutics of Reading," in *Suffering Religion*, pp. 101–162.

8. See, for example, Elaine Marks, *Marrano as Metaphor: The Jewish Presence in French Writing*.

9. This is not unusual. See Yerushalmi, *Zakhor*, p. 31.

10. For another statement in the vein, see Wolfson, *Venturing Beyond*, pp. 25, 26; and Garb, *The Chosen Will Become Herds*, pp. 71–98.

11. For example, see Scholem, *On the Kabbalah and its Symbolism*, pp. 8–11; and Wolfson, *Venturing Beyond*, pp. 232, 233. The tension between law and spirituality was also the central focus of the work of Isadore Twersky. This is most apparent in two essays, "Religion and Law," pp. 69–73; and "Talmudists, Philosophers, Kabbalists: The Quest for Spirituality in the Sixteenth Century," pp. 431–457. Twersky argued that law in Judaism was always challenged by the underlying desire for "spirituality" and that tension is, in fact, the articulation of the law in its healthiest state. Yet he held that although there was tension, there was never really any chasm between rational, mysticism, and tradition. Twersky's work consistently maintains that law stood at the center of all normative Judaism, even of the more radical rationalist and mystical kinds. For him, then, Sabbateansim was an aberration from even the mystical traditions of Judaism, whereas for Scholem it was one particular manifestation that, while deviant, was hardly derivative. See Bernard Septimus, "Isadore Twersky as a Scholar of Medieval Jewish History," pp. 15–24.

12. Wolfson, *Venturing Beyond*, p. 3.

13. Mopsik, *Sex of the Soul*, p. 51.

BIBLIOGRAPHY

Non-Lurianic Primary Sources

Abravanel, Isaac. *Mashmi'a Yeshu'ah*. Königsberg, 1860.

Abu ad Allah ibn al-Bukhari. *Sahih*. Trans. Muhammad Assad. Lahore, Pakistan: Awafat Publications, 1938.

Abulafia, Abraham. *'Imre Shefer.* Jerusalem, 2001.

Adret, Shlomo Ibn. *Teshuvot Ha-Rashba*. Standard edition.

Agasi, Aaron. *Bnei Aaron (on Sha'ar ha-Gilgulim)*. Jerusalem, 1990.

Alsekh, Moshe. *Romemot 'El*. Zolkiew, 1764.

Aquinas. *Basic Writings of St. Thomas Aquinas*, vol. 1 and 2. Ed. Anton C. Pegis. New York: Random House, 1945.

Augustine. *Exposition on Psalms*, standard edition.

———. *Second Discourse on Psalms*.

Azkiri, Eliezer. *Sefer Haredim*. Jerusalem: Yeruham, 1990.

Azriel of Gerona. *Perush 'Al 'Eser Sephirot*. In Meir ibn Gabbai, *Derekh Emunah*. Berlin, 1850.

Azulai, Avraham David. *Hesed le-Avraham*. Amsterdam, 1685.

Bahya ibn Asher of Saragossa. *Rabbenu Bahya 'al Ha-Torah*, vol. 2. Jerusalem: Mossad ha-Rav Kook, 1994.

Bar Hiyya, Abraham. *Megillat Ha-Megillah*. Berlin, 1924.

Cordovero, Moses. *Tomer Devorah*. London, 2003.

Da Fano, Menahem Azaria. *Gilgulei Neshamot*. Lemberg, 1965. Reissued with the commentary "Me'ir Eyin" of Yeruham Leiner of Izbica. Jerusalem: Yarid Books, 1998.

Da Vidas, Elijah. *Reshit Hokhma*. Jerusalem, 1972.

De Leon, Moses. *Sefer Shekel ha Kodesh*. Ed. Charles Mopsik. Los Angeles: Cherub, 1996.

Eliezer of Worms, *Hokhmat ha-Nefesh*. Ed. E. Weiss, Bnei Brak, 1987.

———. *Sodei Razzaya*, "Hilkhot Nevuah." Ed. I. Kamhelar, Jerusalem, 1936.

Gabbai, Meir ibn. *Avodat Ha-Kodesh*. Two volumes. Jerusalem, 1992.

Gaon, Sa'adia. *Emunot ve Deot*. Israel: Sura Institute, n.d.

Gikitillia, Joseph ibn. *Sha'arei 'Orah*. Two volumes. Ed. Yosef ben Shlomo. Jerusalem: Bialik Institute, 1996.

Gregory of Palamas. *Defense of the Hesychasts*. Cited in *The Deification of Man*. Georgios Mantzaridis. Crestwood, N.Y.: St. Vladimir, 1984.

Habib, Joseph Ibn. *Nimukei Yosef.* Standard editions of Babylonian Talmud.

Ha-Ittamari of Izmir, R. Elijah Ha-Kohen. *Midrash Eliyahu*. Warsaw, 1878.

Ha-Levi, Judah. *Sefer Kuzari.* Jerusalem, 1959.

Horowitz, R. Isaiah. *Shenei Luhot Ha-Brit*. Five volumes. Jerusalem, 1993.

Hutner, Isaac. *Pahad Yizhak*. Eight volumes. Brooklyn, N.Y.: Gur Aryeh Institute, 1995.

Isaac of Acre. *Me'irat 'Einayim*. Ed. Amos Goldreich. Jerusalem, 1984.

Josephus, Flavius. *Antiquities*. In *The New Complete Works of Josephus*. Trans. William Whiston, commentary by Paul L. Maier. Grand Rapids, Mich.: Kregel, 1999.

———. *Against Apion*. In *The New Complete Works of Josephus*. Trans. William Whiston, commentary by Paul L. Maier. Grand Rapids, Mich.: Kregel, 1999.

———. *Jewish Wars*. In *The New Complete Works of Josephus*. Trans. William Whiston, commentary by Paul L. Maier. Grand Rapids, Mich.: Kregel, 1999.

Karfman, Mordecai Moshe. "Minhat Cohen." Commentary to *Shulkhan Arukh Ha-Ari Z'L*. Jerusalem: Hatam Sofer Institute, 1984.

Karo, Isaac. *Toldot Yizhak*. Warsaw, 1877.

Luzzatto, Moses Hayyim, "Kinat ha-Shem Ziva'ot." In *Ginzei Ramhal*. Ed. Hayyim Friedlander, Bnei Brak, 1984.

Maimonides. *Commentary to Avot*. Standard edition.

———. *Eight Chapters*. Standard edition.

———. *Guide of the Perplexed*. Trans. Shlomo Pines. Chicago: University of Chicago Press, 1963.

———. *Moreh Nevukhim*. Jerusalem, 1960.

———. *Mishneh Torah*. Six volumes. Standard edition.

———. *Teshuvot ha-Rambam*. Ed. J. Blau. Jerusalem, 1960.

Menashe ben Israel. *Nishmat Hayyim*. Jerusalem, 1967.

Mizrachi, Elijah. *Responsa*. Constantinople, 1560.

Molkho, Isaac. *'Orhot Yashar*. Salonica, 1769.

Nahman of Bratslav. *Likkutei Moharan*. Jerusalem: Breslov Institute, 1976.

Nahmanides, *Commentary on the Torah*. Two volumes. Jerusalem: Mossad ha-Rav Kook, 1959.

———. *Kitvei Ramban*. Two volumes. Jerusalem: Mossad ha-Rav Kook, 1963.

Nathan of Gaza. *'Inyane Shabbatai Zevi*. Ed. A. Friedman. Berlin: Mekize Nirdamim, 1912.

Philo. *The Works of Philo: Complete and Unabridged*. Trans. C. D. Yonge. New York: Hendrikson, 1993.

Recanati, Menahem. *Ta'amei Ha-Mitzvot*. London: Ozar Hokhma, 1962.

Rosen, Joseph. *Zofnat Pa'aneah*. Jerusalem, 1989.

Sefer Hasidism Jerusalem: Mossad ha-Rav Kook, 1989.

Sefer Ha-Zohar 'Im Perush Yedid Nefesh. Six volumes. Petah Tikva, Israel, 1994.

Shapira, Kalonymous Kalman. *Hakhsharat 'Avreikhim*. Jerusalem, 1962.

Shapira, Natan. *Mazot Shemorim*. 1776.

Shem Tov Ibn Shem Tov. *Derashot*. Jerusalem, 1973.

Shneur Zalman of Liady. *Sefer Ha-Tanya*. Brooklyn, N.Y.: Kehot, 1979.

———. *Siddur Tefillot me-Kol ha-Shana*. Brooklyn, N.Y.: Kehot, 1981.

Sifrei on Deuteronomy. Trans. Reuven Hammer. New Haven: Yale University Press, 1986.

Sirkus, Joel. *Bayit Hadash*. In *Tur Shulkha Arukh*. Standard edition.

Tanna Debe Eliyyahu. Jerusalem: Lewin-Epstein, 1978.

Tanna Debe Eliyyahu. Trans. William Bruade and Israel Kapstein. Philadelphia: JPS, 1981.

Targum Pseudo-Jonathan to the Pentateauch: Text and Concordance. E. G. Clark and W. E. Aufrecht, J. C. Hurd, and F. Spitzer. Hoboken, N.J.: Ktav, 1984.

Teitelbaum, Joel. *'Al ha-ge'ula ve-'al ha-temura*. New York, 1967.

Torat Ha-Gilgul. Two volumes. Jerusalem: Ahavat Shalom, 1982.

Secondary Sources

Aaron, David. "Imagery of the Divine and the Human: On the Mythology of Genesis Rabba 8/1." *Journal of Jewish Thought and Philosophy* 5 (1995): 1–62.

———. "Shedding Light on God's Body in Rabbinic Midrashim: Reflections on the Theory of the Luminous Adam." *Harvard Theological Review* 90, no. 3 (1997): 299–314.

Abrams, Daniel. *Ha-Guf ha-Elohi ha-nashi be-Kabalah: Iyun ba-tsurot shel ahavah gufanit u-miniut nashit shel ha-Elohot* [Hebrew]. Jerusalem: Magnes, 2004.

Abu-Khalil, A. "A Note on the Study of Homosexuality in the Arab/Islamic Civilization." *Arab Studies Journal* 1, no. 2 (1993): 32–34.

Aescoly, Aaron Zeev. *Jewish Messianic Movements* [Hebrew]. Jerusalem: Bialik Institute, 1987.

Altabe, David F. "Portuguese Jews of Solonika." In *Studies of the History of Portuguese Jews from Their Expulsion in 1497 through Their Dispersion*. New York: Seher-Hermon Press, 2000.

Alter, Robert. *The Art of Biblical Narrative*. New York: Basic Books, 1981.

Altmann, Alexander. "Eternality of Punishment: A Theological Controversy within the Amsterdam Rabbinate in the Thirties of the Seventeenth Century." In *Academy of Jewish Research: Proceedings*, vol. XL (1972): 1–40.

———. "*Homo Imago Dei* in Jewish and Christian Theology." *Journal of Religion* 48 (1968): 235–259.

———. "Lurianic Kabbala in a Platonic Key: Abraham Cohen Herrera's *Puerta del Cielo*." In *Jewish Thought in the Seventeenth Century*, ed. B. Septimus and I. Twersky. Cambridge: Harvard University Press, 1987.

———. "The Motif of the Shells (*Quelipot*) in Azriel of Gerona." *Journal of Jewish Studies* IX (1958): 73–80.

Amos, Avraham. *Be-gilgul Hozer: Gilgul in Kabbala and Other Sources* [Hebrew]. Israel, 1997.

Anderson, Gary. *The Genesis of Perfection*. Louisville, Ky.: Westminster John Knox, 2001.

Ankersmit, F. R. "Historicism: An Attempt at Synthesis." *History and Theory* 34 (1995): 143–161.

Apfelbaum, Abba. *Moses Zakuto: His Life, Works, and Approach to Kabbala* [Hebrew]. Lvov, 1926.

Arikha, Yigal. *Reincarnation: Reality that Exceeds All Imagination* [Hebrew]. Kefar Saba, Israel: Aryeh Nir, 2001.

Assis, Yom Tov. "Sexual Behavior in Mediaeval-Hispano-Jewish Society." In *Jewish History: Essays in Honor of Chimen Abramsky*, ed. A. Rapoport-Albert and S. Zipperstein. London: Peter Haban, 1988.

Assmann, Jan. *Moses the Egyptian: The Memory of Egypt in Western Monotheism*. Cambridge, Mass.: Harvard University Press, 1997.

Avitsur, Schmuel. "Safed—Center for the Manufacture of Woven Woolens in the Fifteenth Century" [Hebrew]. *Sefunot* 6 (1962): 43–69.

Badiou, Alain. *Saint Paul: The Foundation of Universalism*. Stanford, Calif.: Stanford University Press, 2003.

———. "Eight Theses on the Universal." In *Theoretical Writings*, ed. and trans. Ray Brassier and Alberto Toscano. New York: Continuum, 2004.

Baer, Yizhak. *History of the Jews in Christian Spain*. Philadelphia: JPS, 1961.

———. "The Messianic Movement in Spain" [Hebrew]. *Measaf Zion* 5 (1933): 61–77.

Bailey, D. S. *Homosexuality and the Western Christian Tradition.* London: Longmans, Green, and Co., 1955.

Barclay, John M. G. "'Neither Jew nor Greek': Multiculturalism and the New Perspective on Paul." In *Ethnicity in the Bible,* ed. Mark Brett. Leiden: Brill, 2002.

Barker, Margaret. "The High Priest and the Worship of Jesus." In *The Jewish Roots of Christological Monotheism,* ed. C. Newman, J. Davila, and G. Lewis. Leiden: Brill, 1999.

Barnai, Jacob. "Christian Messianism and Portuguese Marranos: The Emergence of Sabbateanism in Smyrna." *Jewish History* 7 (1993): 119–126.

———. "The Development of Community Organizational Structures: The Case of Izmir." In *Jews, Turks, Ottomans,* ed. Avigdor Levy. Syracuse, N.Y.: Syracuse University Press, 2002.

Baron, Salo. *Social and Religious History of the Jews.* New York: Columbia University Press, 1983.

Barr, James. "The Image of God in the Book of Genesis—A Study of Terminology." BJRL 51, no. 1 (Autumn 1968): 11–26.

Baskin, Judith. *Pharaoh's Counselors: Job, Jethro, and Balaam in Rabbinic and Patristic Literature.* Chico, Calif.: Scholars, 1983.

Baur, F. C. *The Church History of the First Three Centuries,* vol. 1, ed. A. Menzies. London: Williams and Norgate, 1878.

———. *Paul, the Apostle of Jesus Christ.* London: Williams and Norgate, 1876.

Beinart, Haim. "A Prophesying Movement in Cordova in 1499–1502" [Hebrew]. *Zion* 44 (1980): 190–200.

Bellamy, Jeremy A. "Sex and Society in Islamic Popular Literature." In *Society and the Sexes in Medieval Spain,* ed. Afaf Lutfi al-Sayyid-Marsot. Malibu, Calif.: Undena, 1979.

Ben Sasson, H. H. "The Reformation in Contemporary Jewish Eyes." *Israel Academy of Science and Humanities* 4, no. 12 (1970).

Benayahu, Meir. "R. Israel Najara" [Hebrew]. *Asufot* 4 (1990): 203–284.

———. "The Renewal of *Semikha* in Safed" [Hebrew]. In *Sefer Yovel for Yizhak Baer,* ed. S. Baron and S. Ettinger [Hebrew]. Jerusalem: Ha-Hevrah ha-Historit ha-Yisraelit, 1960.

———. "Spirits of Harm and Their Reparation" [Hebrew]. In *Sefer Zikharon le-Ha-Rav Yizhak Nissim.* Jerusalem: Yad ha-Rav Nissim, 1985.

———. *Toldot Ha-Ari.* Jerusalem: Ben Tzvi Institute, 1967.

Benbassa, Esther, and Jean-Christoff Attias. *The Jew and the Other,* trans. G. M. Goshgarian. Ithaca, N.Y.: Cornell University Press, 2004.

Ben-Na'eh, Yaron. "*Mishkav Zakhur b'Hevra Ha-Yehudit b'Ottomonit.*" *Zion* 65 (2001): 171–200.

Ben-Shalom, Ram. "The Conversos as Subversive: Jewish Traditions as Christian Libel?" *Journal of Jewish Studies* 50, no. 2 (1999): 260–264.

Benz, Ernst. *The Eastern Orthodox Church,* trans. Richard and Clara Winston. Garden City, N.Y.: Doubleday, 1963.

Berger, David. "Three Typological Themes in Early Jewish Messianism, Messiah son of Joseph, Rabbinical Calculations, and the Figure of Armilus." *AJS Review* 10, no. 2 (1985): 141–164.

Berger, David, ed. and trans. *The Jewish-Christian Debate in the High Middle Ages: A Critical Edition of the Nizzahon Vetu with an Introduction, Translation, and Commentary.* Northvale, N.J.: J. Aronson, 1996.

Biale, David. *Eros and the Jews.* Berkeley: University of California Press, 1997.

Bland, Kalman. *The Artless Jew: Medieval and Modern Affirmations and Denials of the Visual.* Princeton, N.J.: Princeton University Press, 2000.

Blidstein, Gerald. "Who Is Not a Jew?—the Medieval Discussion." *Israel Law Review* 11 (1976): 369–390.

Blocher, Henri. *Original Sin: Illuminating the Riddle.* Grand Rapids, Mich.: Eerdmans, 1997.

Blumenthal, David. "*Tselem:* Toward an Anthropomorphic Theology of Image." In *Christianity in Jewish Terms,* ed. Tikva Frymer-Kensky, David Novak, Peter Ochs, David Fox Sandmel, and Michael A. Signer. Boulder, Colo.: Westview, 2000.

Bodian, Miriam. *Hebrews of the Portuguese Nation: Conversos and Community in Early Modern Amsterdam.* Bloomington: Indiana University Press, 1997.

Bolin, Anne. "Transsexualism and the Limits of Traditional Analysis." *American Behavioral Scientist* 31 (1987): 41–65.

Bonfil, Robert. "Change and Cultural Patterns of a Jewish Society in Crisis: Italian Jewry at the Close of the Sixteenth Century." *Jewish History* 3, no. 2 (1988): 11–30.

————. "Jewish Attitudes toward History and Historical Writing in Pre-Modern Times." *Jewish History* 11, no. 1 (Spring 1997): 7–40.

Boswell, John. *Christianity, Social Tolerance and Homosexuality.* Chicago: University of Chicago Press, 1980.

Boyarin, Daniel. *A Radical Jew: Paul and the Politics of Identity.* Berkeley: University of California Press, 1994.

————. "Are There Any Jews in 'The History of Sexuality'?" *Journal of the History of Sexuality* 5, no. 3 (1995): 339–340.

————. *Border Lines: The Partition of Judeo-Christianity.* Philadelphia: University of Pennsylvania Press, 2004.

————. *Carnal Israel: Reading Sex in Talmudic Culture.* Berkeley: University of California Press, 1993.

————. *Dying for God: Martyrdom and the Making of Christianity and Judaism.* Stanford, Calif.: Stanford University Press, 1999.

————. "Interrogate My Love." In *Wrestling with Zion: Progressive Jewish American Responses to the Israeli-Palestinian Conflict,* ed. Tony Kushner and Alisa Solomon. New York: Grove, 2003.

————. *Intertextuality and Midrash.* Bloomington: Indiana University Press, 1990.

————. "The Subversion of the Jews: Moses' Veil and the Hermeneutics of Supersession." In Boyarin, *Sparks of the Logos.* Leiden: Brill, 2003.

————. "Take the Bible for Example: Midrash as Literary Theory." In Boyarin, *Sparks of the Logos.* Leiden: Brill, 2003.

————. *Unheroic Conduct.* Berkeley: University of California Press, 1997.

Braverman, Jay. "Balaam in Rabbinic and Early Christian Traditions." In *Joshua Finkel Festscrift,* ed. S. B. Hoenig and L. D. Sritskin. New York: Yeshiva University Press, 1974.

Brink, Jean, Maryanne Horowitz, and Alison Coudert, eds. *Playing with Gender: A Renaissance Pursuit.* Urbana: University of Illinois Press, 1991.

Brooton, Bernatte. *Love Between Women: Early Christian Responses to Female Homoeroticism.* Chicago: University of Chicago, 1996.

Buber, Martin. "Love of God and Love of Neighbor." In *Hasidism and Modern Man.* Atlantic Highlands, N.J.: Humanities Press International, 1988.

————. *Moses.* Atlantic Highlands, N.J.: Humanities, 1988.

Buell, Denise. "Race and Universalism in Early Christianity." *Journal of Early Christian Studies* 10, no. 4 (2002): 429–468.

———. "Rethinking the Relevance of Race for Early Christian Self-Definition." *Harvard Theological Review* 94, no. 4 (2001): 235–251.

Buell, Denise, and Caroline Johnson Hodge. "The Politics of Interpretation: The Rhetoric of Race and Ethnicity in Paul." *Journal of Biblical Literature* 123, no. 2 (2004): 235–251.

———. "Rethinking the Relevance of Race for Early Christian Self-Definition." *Harvard Theological Review* 94, no. 4 (2001): 449–476.

———. "The Sin against Nature and Homosexuality." In *Sexual Practices and the Medieval Church*, ed. V. L. Bullough and J. Brundage. Buffalo, N.Y.: Prometheus Books, 1982.

———. "Transvestism in the Middle Ages." In *Sexual Practices in the Medieval Church*, ed. V. L. Bullough and J. Brundage. Buffalo, N.Y.: Prometheus Books, 1982.

Bullough, Vern L., and Bonnie Bullough. *Cross Dressing, Sex, and Gender.* Philadelphia: University of Pennsylvania Press, 1993.

Butler, Judith. *Bodies that Matter.* New York: Routledge, 1993.

Bynum, Caroline Walker. *Jesus as Mother: Studies in Spirituality in the High Middle Ages.* Berkeley: University of California Press, 1982.

Cabasilas, Nicholas. *The Life in Christ,* trans. Carmino J. de Catanzaro. New York: SVS, 1974.

Carlebach, Elisheva. *Divided Souls: Converts from Judaism in Germany, 1500–1750.* New Haven, Conn.: Yale University Press. 2001.

Casey, Maurice. *From Jewish Prophet to Gentile God: The Origins and Development of New Testament Christology.* Louisville, Ky.: Westminster John Knox, 1991.

Cesare, Pier. *The Golden Calf and the Origins of Anti-Jewish Controversy,* trans. David Ward. Atlanta, Ga.: Scholars, 1990.

Chajes, Jeffrey. *Between Worlds.* Philadelphia: University of Pennsylvania Press, 2003.

Chernick, Michael. "Some Talmudic Responses to Christianity, Third and Fourth Centuries." *Journal of Ecumenical Studies* 17 (1980): 393–406.

Chilton, Bruce, and Jacob Neusner. *Judaism in the New Testament: Practices and Beliefs.* New York: Routledge, 1995.

Chipman, J., trans. *Hasidism as Mysticism: Quietistic Elements in Hasidic Thought.* Princeton, N.J., and Jerusalem: Princeton and Magnus, 1993.

Chittick, William C. *The Sufi Path of Love: The Spiritual Teachings of Rumi.* Albany, N.Y.: SUNY Press, 1983.

Clark, Christopher M. *The Politics of Conversion: Missionizing Protestants and the Jews in Russia.* Oxford: Oxford University Press, 1995.

Cohen, Gerson D. "Esau as Symbol in Early Medieval Thought." In *Jewish Medieval and Renaissance Studies,* ed. Alexander Altmann. Cambridge: Harvard University Press, 1967.

———. "Messianic Postures of Ashkenazim and Sephardim." Reprinted in *Essential Papers on Messianic Movements and Personalities in Jewish History,* ed. Marc Saperstein. New York: New York University Press, 1992.

———. "Review of *The Marranos of Spain* by B. Netanyahu." In *Jewish Social Studies* 29, no. 3 (1967): 178–184.

Cohen, Jeremy. "Original Sin and the Evil Inclination—A Polemicists' Appreciation of Human Nature." *Harvard Theological Review* 73, no. 3–4 (1980): 496–520.

Cohen, Samuel. "Original Sin." Reprinted in Cohen, *Essays in Jewish Theology.* Cincinnati, Ohio: HUC Press, 1987.

Cohen, Shaye J. D. *The Beginnings of Jewishness: Boundaries, Varieties, Uncertainties.* Berkeley: University of California Press, 1999.

———. "The Significance of Yavne: Pharisees, Rabbis, and the End of Sectarianism." *Hebrew Union College Annual* 55 (1984): 27–53.

———. "Those Who Say They Are Jews and Are Not: How Do You Know a Jew in Antiquity When You See One?" In *Diasporas in Antiquity,* ed. Shaye Cohen and Ernest Frerichs. Atlanta, Ga.: Scholars, 1993.

Cohen, Walter. "Political Criticism of Shakespeare." In *Shakespeare Reproduced: The Text in History and Ideology,* ed. J. E. Howard and M. F. O'Conner. New York: Routledge, 1987.

Cohen-Alloro, Dorit. "The Secret of the Garment in the Zohar" [Hebrew]. Ph.D. diss., Hebrew University, Jerusalem, 1987.

Collins, John J. "Patterns of Eschatology and Qumran." In *Traditions in Transfromation,* ed. B. Halpern and J. D. Levenson. Winona Lake, Ind.: Eisenbrauns, 1981.

Cooper, Alan. "An Extraordinary Sixteenth-Century Biblical Commentary: Eliezer Ashkenazi on the Song of Moses." In *The Frank Talmage Memorial Volume,* 2 volumes, ed. Barry Walfish. Haifa: Haifa University, 1993.

———. "A Medieval Jewish Version of Original Sin: Ephraim of Luntshits on Leviticus 12." *Harvard Theological Review* 97, no. 4 (2004): 445–459.

Coudert, Allison P. *The Impact of Kabbala in the Seventeenth Century: The Life and Thought of Francis Mercury von Helmont (1614–1698).* Leiden: Brill, 1999.

Countryman, William L. *Dirt, Greed, and Sex: Sexual Ethics in the New Testament and Their Implications for Today.* Philadelphia: Ausburg Fortress, 1988.

Cover, Robert. "Folktales of Justice." In *Narrative, Violence, and the Law: The Essays of Robert Cover,* ed. M. Minow, M. Ryan, and A. Sarat. Ann Arbor: University of Michigan Press, 1995.

Cranfield, C. E. B. *A Critical and Exegetical Commentary on the Epistle of the Romans.* Edinburgh: T&T Clark, 1975.

Dan, Joseph, ed. *The Christian Kabbalah: Jewish Mystical Books and Their Christian Interpreters.* Cambridge: Harvard College Library, 1997.

———. *Esoteric Theology of the Ashkenazi Hasidim* [Hebrew]. Jerusalem: Bialik Institute, 1968.

———. *Jewish Ethics and Jewish Mysticism.* Seattle: University of Washington Press, 1986.

———. *Kabbala: A Very Short Introduction.* New York: Oxford University Press, 2006.

Daniel, M. "Arab Civilization and Male Love." In *Reclaiming Sodom,* ed. J. Goldberg. New York: Taylor & Francis, 1994.

Danon, A. "La communaute juive de Solonique au de 16ᵉ Siècle." *Revue des études juives* 8 (1999): 110–124.

David, Abraham. "Demographic Changes in the Safed Community of the Sixteenth Century." In *Occident and Orient: A Tribute to the Memory of A. Schreiber,* ed. R. Dan. Budapest: Akademiai Kiado, 1988.

———. "The Jewish Settlement in Palestine at the Beginning of the Ottoman Empire (1517–1599)." In *The Jewish Settlement in Palestine 634–1881,* ed. Alex Carmel, Peter Schafer, and Yossi Ben-Artzi. Wiesbaden, 1990.

———. "Safed as a Center for the Re-Settlement of *Anusim*" [Hebrew]. In *Proceedings for the Second International Congress for Research of the Sephardic and Oriental Heritage 1984,* ed. A. Haim. Jerusalem: Misgav Yerushalayim, 1991.

———. "Safed, Foyer, De retour au judaïsme de conversos au XVI Siècle." *Revue des études juives* 146 (1978): 63–82.

———. "The Spanish Exiles in the Holy Land." In *Moreshet Sepharad: The Sephardi Legacy*, ed. H. Beinart. Jerusalem: Magnes, 1992.

———. *To Come to the Land: Immigration and Settlement in 16ᵗʰ-Century Eretz-Israel*, trans. Dena Ordan. Tuscaloosa: University of Alabama Press, 1999.

Davis, W. D. "From Schweitzer to Scholem: Reflections on Sabbatai Zvi." *Journal of Biblical Literature* 96 (1976): 529–558.

———. "New Documents Regarding the *Semikha* Controversy" [Hebrew]. *Sefunot* 10 (1966): 113–192.

Diamond, James A. *Maimonides and the Hermeneutics of Concealment*. Albany, N.Y.: SUNY Press, 2002.

Dimitrovsky, Haym Z. "Beit Midraso shel R. Yaʿakov Berab be-Safed." *Sefunot* 7 (1963): 41–102.

———. "New Documents Regarding the *Semikha* Controversy" [Hebrew]. *Sefunot* 10 (1966): 113–192.

Donaldson, Terence. "Proselytes or 'Righteous Gentiles'? The Status of Gentiles in Eschatological Pilgrimage Patterns of Thought." *Journal for the Study of the Pseudepigrapha* 7 (1990): 3–27.

Douglas, Mary. *Natural Symbols*. London: Routledge, 1970.

———. *Purity and Danger*. London: Routledge, 1984.

Dunn, James D. G. *Christology in the Making: A New Testament Inquiry into the Origins of the Doctrine of the Incarnation*. Philadelphia: Westminster, 1980.

———. *Jesus, Paul, and the Law*. Louisville, Ky.: Westminster, 1990.

Duran, Khalid. "Homosexuality in Islam." In *Homosexuality and World Religions*, ed. Arlene Swidler. Valley Forge, Pa.: Trinity Press International, 1993.

Elberg-Schwartz, Howard. *The Savage in Judaism*. Bloomington: Indiana University Press, 1990.

Elior, Rachel. "The Dispute on the Position of the Kabbalah in the Sixteenth Century." *Mekharei Yerushalayim* 1 (1981): 177–190.

———. "The Doctrine of Transmigration in *Galya Raza*." Reprinted in *Essential Papers in Kabbala*, ed. Lawrence Fine. New York: New York University Press, 1992.

———. "Messianic Expectations and Spiritualization of Religious Life in the Sixteenth Century." *Revue des études juives* 145 (1986): 35–49.

The Encyclopedia of Religion. 2nd edition. New York: Thomson/Gale, 2005.

Eron, Lewis John. "Homosexuality and Judaism." In *Homosexuality and World Religions*, ed. Arlene Swidler. Valley Forge, Pa.: Trinity Press International, 1993.

Faierstein, Morris. *Jewish Mystical Autobiographies*. New York: Paulist, 1999.

Faur, Jose. *In the Shadow of History: Jews and Conversos at the Dawn of Modernity*. Albany, N.Y.: SUNY Press, 1992.

Feldman, Louis. *Jew and Gentile in the Ancient World*. Princeton, N.J.: Princeton University Press, 1993.

———. "Philo's Version of Balaam." *Henoch* 25 (2003): 301–319.

Fenton, Paul. "Influences Soufies sur le Development de la Qabbale a Safed: Le Cas de la Visitation des Tombes." In *Experience et ecriture mystiques dans les religions du livre*, ed. Paul Fenton and Roland Goetschel. Leiden: Brill, 2000.

———. "The Influence of Sufism in Safed Kabbala" [Hebrew]. *Mahanayaim* (1994): 170–179.

Fine, Lawrence. *Physician of the Soul, Healer of the Cosmos: Isaac Luria and His Kabbalistic Fellowship*. Stanford, Calif.: Stanford University Press, 2003.

———. "Recitation of the Mishnah as a Vehicle for Mystical Inspiration: A Contemplative Technique Taught by Hayyim Vital." *Revue des études juives* 141, no. 1–2 (1982): 183–199.

——. *Safed Spirituality*. New York: Paulist, 1984.
——. "The Study of Torah as a Theurgic Rite in Lurianic Kabbala." In *Approaches to Judaism in Medieval Times*, vol. 3, ed. David Blumenthal. Atlanta, Ga.: Scholars, 1988.
Finnis, John. *Natural Law and Natural Rights*. Oxford: Clarendon, 1980.
Fishbane, Michael. *Biblical Myth and Rabbinic Mythmaking*. Oxford: Oxford University Press, 2004.
——. *The Exegetical Imagination: On Jewish Thought and Theology*. Cambridge: Harvard University Press, 1998.
——. "Martin Buber's *Moses*." In Fishbane, *Garments of Torah*. Bloomington: Indiana University Press, 1989
——. "Some Forms of Divine Appearance in Ancient Jewish Thought." In *From Ancient Israel to Modern Judaism: Essays in Honor of Marvin Fox*, vol. 2, ed. J. Neusner, E. Frerichs, and N. Sarna. Atlanta, Ga.: Scholars, 1989.
——. "*Varia Deuteronimica*." *Zeitschrift fur die alttestamentliche Wisenschaft* 84 (1972).
Fishman, Talya. "A Kabbalistic Perspective on Gender-Specific Commandments." *AJS Review* 17 (1992): 199–245.
Fletcher-Louis, Crispin H. T. "Alexander the Great's Worship of the High Priest." *Early Jewish and Christian Monotheism* (2004): 71–102.
——. "The High Priest as Divine Mediator in the Hebrew Bible: Daniel 7:13 as a Test Case." In *Society for Biblical Literature SP* 36. Atlanta, Ga.: Scholars, 1997.
——. "The Worship of Divine Humanity as God's Image and the Worship of Jesus." In *The Jewish Roots of Christological Monotheism*, ed. C. Newman, J. Davila, and G. Lewis. Leiden: Brill, 1999.
Foucault, Michel. *The History of Sexuality*, two vols., trans. Robert Hurley. New York: Vintage Books, 1990.
Fraade, Steven. "Ascetical Impulses of Ancient Judaism." *Jewish Spirituality I: From the Bible through the Middle Ages*, ed. Arthur Green. World Spirituality Series 13. New York: Crossroad, 1986.
Fram, Edward. "Perception and Reception of Repentant Apostates in Medieval Ashkenaz and Premodern Poland." *AJS Review* 21, no. 2 (1996): 299–339.
Frank, David H., ed. *A People Apart: Chosenness and Ritual in Jewish Philosophical Thought*. Albany, N.Y.: SUNY Press, 1993.
Fredrikson, Paula. "What 'Parting of the Ways' Jews, Christians and the Ancient Mediterranean City." In *The Ways that Never Parted*, ed. Adam Becker and A. Y. Reed. Tubingen: Mohr-Siebeck, 2003, pp. 35–63.
Freud, Sigmund. *Moses and Monotheism*. New York: Vintage Books, 1939.
——. "Three Lectures on Sexuality." In Freud, *Sexuality: Three Essays on the Theory of Sex*. London: Penguin Books, 1953.
Frymer-Kensky, Tikva. "The Image, The Glory, and the Holy." In *Humanity before God: Contemporary Faces of Jewish, Christian, and Islamic Ethics*, ed. W. Schweiker, M. Johnson, and K. Jung. Minneapolis: Fortress, 2006.
——. *Motherprayer: The Pregnant Women's Spiritual Companion*. New York: G.P. Putnam Sons, 1995.
Funkenstein, Amos. "History, Counter History, and Narrative." In A. Funkenstein, *Perceptions of Jewish History*. Berkeley: University of California Press, 1993.
Gager, John G. "Body-Symbols and Social Reality: Resurrection, Incarnation, and Asceticism in Early Christianity." *Religion* 12 (1982): 345–363.
Gamlieli, Devorah bat-David. *Psychoanalysis and Kabbala: The Masculine and Feminine in Lurianic Kabbala*. Los Angeles: Cherub, 2006.

Garb, Jonathan. *The Chosen Will Become Herds* [Hebrew]. Jerusalem: Carmel Books, 2005.

———. *Manifestations of Power in Jewish Mysticism: From Rabbinic Literature to Safadean Kabbalah* [Hebrew]. Jerusalem: Magnes, 2005.

Gaster, Moses. *The Samaritans: Their History, Doctrines, and Literature.* London: British Academy, 1925.

Gaston, Lloyd. *Paul and the Torah.* Vancouver: University of British Columbia Press, 1987.

Geiger, Abraham. "Bileam und Jesus." *Judische Zeitschrift* 6 (1868): 31–37.

Giller, Pinhas. "The Common Religion of Safed." *Conservative Judaism* 55, no. 2 (2003): 24–37.

———. *Reading the Zohar.* New York: Oxford University Press, 2002.

Ginsburg, Elliot. "*Zelem Elohim:* Some Thoughts on God and Person in Zoharic Kabbalah." In *In Search of the Divine: Some Unexpected Consequences of Interfaith Dialogue,* ed. Larry Shinn. St. Paul, Minn.: Paragon House, 1987.

Ginsburg, Levi. "Some Observations on the Attitude of the Synagogue Towards the Apocalyptic-Eschatological Writings." *Journal of Biblical Literature* 41, no. 1–2, A Symposium on Eschatology (1922): 115–136.

Ginzberg, Louis. *Legends of the Jews.* Two volumes. Philadelphia: JPS, 2003.

Gitlitz, David M., and Ilan Stavans. *Secrecy and Deceit: The Religion of the Crypto-Jews (Jewish Latin America).* Albuquerque: University of New Mexico Press, 2002.

Goldish, Matt. "Patterns in Converso Messianism." In *Millenarianism and Messianism in Early Modern European Culture,* vol. 1, ed. M. Goldish and R. Popkin. Dordrecht, The Netherlands: Kluwer Academic, 2001.

———. *The Sabbatean Prophets.* Cambridge: Harvard University Press, 2004.

Goodich, Michael. *The Unmentionable Vice: Homosexuality in the Later Medieval Period.* New York: Dorset Books, 1979.

Goshen-Gottstein, Alon. "The Body of God in Rabbinic Literature." *Harvard Theological Review* 87 (1994): 171–195.

———. "Judaism and Incarnational Theologies: Mapping out the Parameters of Dialogue." *Journal of Ecumenical Studies* 39, nos. 3–4 (2002): 219–247.

———. *The Sinner and the Amnesiac: The Rabbinic Invention of Elisha ben Avuya and Eliezer ben Arach.* Stanford, Calif.: Stanford University Press, 2000.

Gottleib, Efrayim. *Studies in Kabbalistic Literature* [Hebrew], ed. J. Hackler. Tel Aviv, 1976.

Grabbe, Lester L. *Judaic Religion in the Second Temple Period.* London: Routledge, 2000.

Green, Arthur. "Shekhina, The Virgin Mary, and the Song of Songs." *AJS Review* 26, no. 1 (2002): 1–52.

Green, William Scott. "Otherness Within: Towards a Theory of Difference in Rabbinic Judaism." In *"To See Ourselves as Others See Us": Christians, Jews, "Others" in Late Antiquity,* ed. J. Neusner and E. S. Frerichs. Atlanta, Ga.: Scholars, 1985.

Greenberg, David F. *The Construction of Homosexuality.* Chicago: University of Chicago Press, 1990.

Greenberg, David F., and Marcia H. Bystryn. "Christian Intolerance of Homosexuality." *American Journal of Sociology* 28, no. 3 (1982): 515–548.

Greenberg, Irving Yitz. "The Relationship of Judaism and Christianity: Toward a New Organic Model." In *Twenty Years of Jewish–Catholic Relations,* ed. Eugene J. Fisher, A. James Rudin, and Marc H. Tanenbaum. New York: Paulist, 1986.

Greenberg, Steven. *Wrestling Between God and Men: Homosexuality in the Jewish Tradition.* Madison: University of Wisconsin Press, 2003.

Greenblatt, Stephen. *Renaissance Self-Fashioning: From More to Shakespeare.* Chicago: University of Chicago Press, new edition, 2005.
———. *Shakespearean Negotiations: The Circulation of Social Energy in Renaissance England.* Berkeley: University of California Press, 1989.
———. "Toward a Poetics of Culture." In *The New Historicism,* ed. H. Aram Vesser. New York: Routledge, 1989.
Greene, John T. *Balaam and His Interpreters: A Hermeneutical History of the Balaam Traditions.* Atlanta, Ga.: Scholars, 1992.
Griffith, Lois. *Theory of Profane Love among the Arabs: The Development of the Genre.* New York: New York University Press, 1971.
Gross, J. *La divinization du crétien les peres grecs, contribution historique à la doctrine de la grâce.* Paris, 1938.
Guroian, Vigen. *Incarnate Love: Essays in Orthodox Ethics.* South Bend, Ind.: University of Notre Dame Press, 1987.
Hacker, Joseph. "The Exiles from Spain in the Ottoman Empire in the Seventeenth Century: Community and Culture" [Hebrew]. In *Moreshet Sefard,* ed. Hayyim Beinart. Jerusalem, 1992.
———. "The Jewish Community in Solonika in the Fifteenth and Sixteenth Centuries" [Hebrew]. Ph.D. diss., Hebrew University, 1978.
———. "On the Intellectual Character and Self-Perception of Spanish Jewry in the Late Fifteenth Century" [Hebrew]. *Sefunot,* n.s. 17 (1983): 21–95.
———. "The Relationship and Immigration of Spanish Jews to the Land of Israel" [Hebrew]. *Katedra* 36 (1985): 3–34.
Halbertal, Moshe. *Between Torah and Wisdom: R Menachem ha-Meiri and The Maimonidean Halakhists in Provence* [Hebrew]. Jerusalem: Magnes, 2000.
Halbertal, Moshe, and Avishai Margalit. *Idolatry.* Cambridge: Harvard University Press, 1992.
Halperin, David. *The Construction of Homosexuality.* Chicago: University of Chicago Press, 1988.
———. *One Hundred Years of Homosexuality.* New York: Routledge, 1990.
Hansel, David. "The Origin and Thought of Tabbi Yehuda Halevi Ashlag: Simsum of God or Simsum of the World." *Kabbalah* 7 (2002): 37–46.
Hart, William D. "Sexual Orientation and the Language of Higher Law." In *Sexual Orientation and Human Rights in American Religious Discourse,* ed. Saul M. Olyan and Martha C. Nussbaum. New York: Oxford University Press, 1998.
Hayes, Chrsitine. *Gentile Impurities and Jewish Identity.* Oxford: Oxford University Press, 2002.
Hays, Richard. *The Moral Vision of the New Testament.* San Francisco: Harper San Francisco, 1996.
Hecker, Joel. "Kissing Kabbalists: A Mystical Gesturer between Men and with God." Lecture delivered at the conference of the American Academy of Religion, 2002.
———. *Mystical Bodies, Mystical Meals.* Detroit: Wayne State University Press, 2005.
Hendel, Ronald S. "Of Demigods and the Deluge: Toward an Interpretation of Genesis 6:1–4." *Journal of Biblical Literature* 106, no. 1 (March 1987): 13–26.
Herdt, Gilbert. "Representations of Homosexuality: An Essay on Cultural Ontology and Historical Comparison, Part 1." In *Journal of the History of Sexuality* 1, no. 3 (1991): 481–504.
Herford, Travers. *Christianity in Midrash and Talmud.* London: Williams & Norgate, 1903.

Heschel, Susannah. *Abraham Geiger and the Jewish Jesus.* Chicago: University of Chicago Press, 1998.

Hirschman, Marc. *A Rivalry of Genius: Jewish and Christian Biblical Interpretation in Late Antiquity,* trans. Batya Stein. Albany, N.Y.: SUNY Press, 1996.

Hodge, Caroline Johnson. "If Sons, then Heirs: A Study of Kinship and Ethnicity in Paul's Letters." Ph.D. diss., Brown University, 2002.

Hofius, Otfried. "The Adam–Christ Antithesis and the Law: Reflections on Romans 5:12–21." In *Paul and the Mosaic Law,* ed. James Dunn. Grand Rapids, Mich.: Eerdmans, 2001.

Hovav-Machboob, Raza Lea. "The Ari's Doctrine of Reincarnation." DHL thesis, The Jewish Theological Seminary of America, 1983.

Hurdato, Larry. *One Lord One God: Early Christian Devotion and Ancient Jewish Monotheism.* Philadelphia: Fortress, 1988.

Idel, Moshe. *Absorbing Perfections: Kabbalah and Interpretation.* New Haven, Conn.: Yale University Press, 2002.

——. "The Concept of Torah in the *Hekhalot* and Its Evolution in Kabbala" [Hebrew]. *Mekharei Yerushalayim* 1 (1981): 23–49.

——. "Differing Conceptions of Kabbalah in the Early Seventeenth Century." In *Jewish Thought in the Seventeenth Century,* ed. Isadore Twersky and Bernard Septimus. Cambridge: Harvard University Press, 1987.

——. *Enchanted Chains: Techniques and Rituals in Jewish Mysticism.* Los Angeles: Cherub, 2005.

——. "Jewish Thinkers versus Christian Kabbala." In *Christliche Kabbala.* Ostfildern: Jan Thornbecke Verlag, 2003.

——. *Kabbalah: New Perspectives.* New Haven, Conn.: Yale University Press, 1988.

——. *Kabbala and Eros.* New Haven, Conn.: Yale University Press, 2005.

——. *Language, Torah, and Hermeneutics in Abraham Abulafia,* trans. Menahem Kallus. Albany, N.Y.: SUNY Press, 1989.

——. "Le-Toldot ha-Issure Lilimod Kabbala lifnei Gil Arbaʿim." *AJS Review* 5 (1980): 1–20 [Hebrew section].

——. "Messianic Ideas and Zionist Ideas" [Hebrew]. In *Ha-Zionut v'Hazara l'Historia,* ed. S. Eisenstadt and M. Lisk. Jerusalem: Ben Zvi Institute, 1999.

——. *Messianic Mystics.* New Haven, Conn.: Yale University Press, 1998.

——. "On Mobility, Individuals and Groups: Prolegomenon for a Sociological Approach to Sixteenth-Century Kabbalah." *Kabbalah: Journal for the Study of Jewish Mystical Texts* 3 (1998): 145–173.

——. "On the History of the Term *Zimsum* in Kabbala and Scholarship" [Hebrew]. *Mekharei Yerushalayim* 10 (1992): 59–112.

——. "R. Yehuda Hallewah and His *Zafnat Paʿaneah*" [Hebrew]. *Shalem* 4 (1984): 119–138.

——. "Sexual Metaphors and Praxis in the Kabbala." In *The Jewish Family: Metaphor and Meaning,* ed. David Kraemer. New York: Oxford University Press, 1989.

——. "Some Conceptions of the Land of Israel in Medieval Jewish Thought." In *A Straight Path: Essays in Honor of Arthur* Hyman, ed. Ruth Link-Salinger. Washington, D.C.: Catholic University of America Press, 1988.

Inalcik, Halil. "Foundations of Ottoman-Jewish Cooperation." In *Jews, Turks, Ottomans,* ed. Avigdow Levy. Syracuse, N.Y.: Syracuse University Press, 2003.

Jacobs, Andrew S. "A Jew's Jew: Paul and the Early Christian Problem of Jewish Origins." *Journal of Religion* 86, no. 2 (April 2006): 258–286.

Jacobson, Yoram. "The Feminine Aspect in Lurianic Kabbala." In *Major Trends: Fifty Years After,* ed. Peter Schafer and Joseph Dan. Tubingen: Mohr, 1993.

Jung, Carl, ed. *Man and His Symbols.* New York: Doubleday, 1964.

Kallus, Menahem. "Pneumatic Mystical Possession and the Eschatology of the Soul in Lurianic Kabbala." In *Spirit Possession in Judaism: Cases and Contexts from the Middle Ages to the Present,* ed. Matt Goldish. Detroit: Wayne State University Press, 2003.

———. "The Theurgy of Prayer in the Lurianic Kabbala." Ph.D. diss., Hebrew University, 2003.

Kamin, Sarah. "Rashi's Commentary on Song of Songs" [Hebrew]. *Tarbiz* 22, no. 1 (1983): 41–58.

Kaminsky, Joel. "Paradise Regained: Rabbinic Reflections on Original Sin." In *Jews, Christians, and the Theology of the Hebrew Scriptures,* ed. Alice Bellis and Joel Kaminsky. Atlanta, Ga.: Society of Biblical Literature, 2000.

Kaplan, Yosef. "The Attitude of the Leadership of the 'Portuguese' Community in Amsterdam to the Sabbatean Movement" [in Hebrew]. *Zion* 39 (1974): 198–216.

———. "From Apostasy to Return to Judaism: The Portuguese Jews in Amsterdam." In *Bina: Studies in Jewish History,* vol. 1, ed. J. Dan. New York: Praeger, 1989.

———. "Political Concepts in the World of the Portuguese Jews of Amsterdam during the Seventeenth Century: The Problem of Exclusion and the Boundaries of Self-Identity." In *Menasseh ben Israel and His World,* ed. Y. Kaplan, H. Mechoulan, and R. Popkin. Leiden: Brill, 1989.

———. "The Problem of the Conversos and the 'New Christians' in Recent Historical Studies." In *Studies in Historiography,* pp. 117–144.

Kaplan, Yosef, H. Mechoulan, and R. Popkin, eds. *Menasseh ben Israel and His World.* Leiden: Brill, 1989.

Katz, Jacob. "Although He Has Sinned He Remains a Jew" [Hebrew]. *Tarbiz* 27 (1958): 203–217.

———. "The Controversy on the *Semikha* between Rabbi Jacob Berab and Ralbah" [Hebrew]. *Zion* 16 (1951): 28–45.

———. "The Dispute Between Jacob Berab and Levi ben Habib over Renewing Ordination." In *Binah: Studies in Jewish History,* vol. 1, ed. Jospeh Dan. New York: Praeger, 1989.

———. *Exclusiveness and Tolerance: Studies in Jewish–Gentile Relations in Medieval and Modern Times.* New York: Oxford University Press, 1961.

———. *Halakhah and Kabbalah: Studies in the History of Jewish Religion—Its Various Faces and Social Relevance* [Hebrew]. Jerusalem: Magnes, 1984.

Kaufman, Yehezkel. *Golah ve Nekhar,* two volumes [Hebrew]. Tel Aviv, 1929–1930.

———. *History of Israelite Religion.* Eight volumes. Jerusalem: Mossad Bialik, 1966.

———. *The Religion of Israel.* Ed. Moshe Greenberg. Chicago: University of Chicago Press, 1960.

Kaufmann, David. "Elijah Menachem Helfan on Jews Teaching Hebrew to Non-Jews." *Jewish Quarterly Review* (old series) IX (1896/7): 500–518.

Keiner, Ronald C. "The Image of Islam in the Zohar." *Mekharei Yerushalayim* 8 (1989): 43–65.

Kepnes, Steven. *The Text as Thou.* Bloomington: Indiana University Press, 1992.

Kimelman, Reuven. *Lekha Dodi ve-Kabbalat Shabbat: Their Mystical Meaning* [Hebrew]. Jerusalem: Magnus, 2003.

———. "The Seduction of Eve and the Exegetical Politics of Gender." *Biblical Interpretations* 4-1 (1996): 1–39.

Klausner, Jacob. *Jesus of Nazareth.* New York: Macmillan, 1925.
———. *The Messianic Idea in Israel,* ed. W. F. Stinespring. New York: Macmillan, 1955.
Klein, Eliahu. *The Kabbalah of Creation: The Mysticism of Isaac Luria, Founder of Modern Kabbalah.* Berkeley, Calif.: North Atlantic Books, 2005.
Koester, Craig R. *The Indwelling of God: The Tabernacle in the Old Testament, Intertestamental Jewish Literature, and the New Testament.* Washington, D.C.: Catholic Biblical Association of America, 1989.
Kozodoy, Neal. "Reading Medieval Hebrew Love Poetry." *AJS Review* 2 (1977): 111–129.
Krassen, Miles. *Uniter of Heaven and Earth.* Albany, N.Y.: SUNY Press, 1998.
Kutsko, John F. *Between Heaven and Earth: Divine Presence and Absence in the Book of Ezekiel.* Winona Lake, Ind.: Eisenbrauns, 2000.
Lacan, Jacques. "The Meaning of the Phallus." In *Feminine Sexuality,* ed. J. Mitchell and J. Rose, trans. J. Rose. New York: Pantheon Books, 1982.
———. "The Phallic Phase and the Subjective Import of the Castration Complex." In *Feminine Sexuality,* ed. J. Mitchell and J. Rose, trans. J. Rose. New York: Pantheon Books, 1982.
LaCapra, Dominick. *History and Criticism.* Ithaca, N.Y.: Cornell University Press, 1987.
Laden, Sonja. "Greenblattian Self-Fashioning and the Construction of 'Literary History'." In *Critical Self-Fashioning: Stephen Greenblatt and the New Historicism,* ed. Jurgen Pieters. Frankfurt am Main: Peter Lang, 1999.
Lamdan, Ruth. "Deviations from Normative Ethical Rules in the Jewish Communities in Erez Israel and Egypt in the Sixteenth Century" [Hebrew]. In *Eros, Erusin, and Issurim,* ed. I. Bartal and I. Gafni. Jerusalem: Merkaz Shazar, 1998.
———. *A Separate People: Jewish Women in Palestine, Syria, and Egypt in the Sixteenth Century.* Leiden: Brill, 2000.
Lamm, Norman. "Judaism and the Modern Attitude to Homosexuality." *Encyclopedia Judaica Year Book* (1974): 194–205.
Lasker, Daniel. *Jewish Philosophical Polemics Against Christianity.* New York: Ktav, 1977.
———. "Original Sin and Its Atonement According to Hasdai Crescas." *Da'at* 20 (Winter 1988): 127–135.
Lazeroff, A. "Bahya's Asceticism Against Its Rabbinic and Islamic Background." *Journal of Jewish Studies* 21 (1973): 11–38.
Le Moyne, Jean. *Les Sadduceens.* Paris: Librairie LeCoffre, 1972.
Leiman, Sid Z. *The Canonization of Hebrew Scripture: The Talmudic and Midrashic Evidence.* New Haven: Connecticut Academy of Arts and Sciences, 1991.
Levenson, Jon. "The Conversion of Abraham to Judaism, Christianity, and Islam." In *The Idea of Biblical Interpretation: Essays in Honor of James L. Kugel,* ed. Hindy Najman and Judith H. Newman. Leiden: Brill, 2003.
———. "The Universal Horizon of Biblical Particularism." In *Ethnicity in the Bible,* ed. Mark Brett. Leiden: Brill, 2002.
Levine Melammed, Renee. *Heretics of Daughters of Israel? The Crypto-Jewish Women of Castille.* Oxford: Oxford University Press, 1999.
Levinson, Bernard. *Deuteronomy and the Hermeneutics of Legal Innovation.* New York: Oxford University Press, 1997.
Lichtenstein, Aaron. "Brother Daniel and the Jewish Fraternity." *Judaism* 12, no. 3 (Summer 1963): 260–280.
Lieberman, Saul. *Hellenism in Jewish Palestine.* New York: JTS, 1950.

Liebes, Yehuda. "Christian Influences on the Zohar." In *Studies in the Zohar*, trans. A. Schwartz, S. Nakache, and P. Peli. Albany, N.Y.: SUNY Press, 1993.

————. "Eros and the Zohar" [Hebrew]. *'Alpayim* 9 (1994): 67–119.

————. "The *Haredi* Community in Jerusalem and the Judean Desert Sect" [Hebrew]. *Mehkare Yerushalayim* 1, no. 3: 142–145.

————. *Heto shel Elisha.* Jerusalem: Akademon, The Hebrew University Students Printing and Publishing House, 1990.

————. "Messiah of the Zohar." In *The Messianic Idea in Jewish Thought: In Honor of the Eightieth Birthday of Gershom Scholem.* Jerusalem: Israeli Academy of Sciences and Humanities, 1982.

————. "The Messiah of the Zohar: On R. Shimon bar Yohai as a Messianic Figure." In *Studies in the Zohar.* Albany, N.Y.: SUNY Press, 1993.

————. "Sabbath Meal Songs Established by the Holy ARI" [Hebrew]. *Molad* 4 (1972): 540–555.

————. *Studies in the Zohar*, trans. A. Schwartz, S. Nakache, and P. Peli. Albany, N.Y.: SUNY Press, 1993.

————. "Two Young Roes of a Doe: The Secret Sermon of Isaac Luria before His Death" [Hebrew]. *Mekharei Yerushalayim* 10 (1992): 113–170.

Lincoln, Bruce. *Theorizing Myth: Narrative, Ideology, and Scholarship.* Chicago: University of Chicago Press, 2000.

Lorberbaum, Yair. *Zelem Elohim: Halakha and Aggada* [Hebrew]. Jerusalem: Schocken, 2004.

Magid, Shaul. "Conjugal Union, Mourning, and Talmud Torah in R. Isaac Luria's Tikkun Hazot." *Da'at* 36 (1996): 27–45.

————. "The Divine/Human Messiah and Religious Deviance: Some Reflections of the Origins of Chabad's 'Rebbeism'." In *Reaching for the Infinite*, ed. Lawrence Schiffman and Elliot Wolfson (forthcoming).

————. "Ethics Disentangled from the Law: Incarnation, the Universal, and Hasidic Ethics." *Kabbala* 15 (2005): 31–76.

————. "From Theosophy to Midrash: Lurianic Exegesis and the Garden of Eden." *AJS Review* 22, no. 1 (1997): 37–75.

————. *Hasidism on the Margin.* Madison: University of Wisconsin Press, 2004.

————. "Origin and the Overcoming of the Beginning: *Zimzum* as a Trope of Reading in Post-Lurianic Kabbala." In *Beginning/Again: Toward a Hermeneutic of Jewish Texts*, ed. S. Magid and A. Cohen. New York: Seven Bridges, 2002.

Mantzaridis, Georgios. *The Deification of Man.* Crestwood, N.Y.: St. Vladimir, 1984.

Maritain, Jaques. *Integral Humanism: Temporal and Spiritual Problems of a New Christendom.* Trans. Joseph W. Evans. New York: Scribner, 1968.

Mark, Zvi. "The Status of *Katnut* and *Gadlut* in R. Nahman and Their Source in Lurianic Kabbala" [Hebrew]. *Da'at* 46 (2001): 45–80.

Marks, Herbert. "Introduction to Deuteronomy." In H. Marks, *Norton Companion to the Hebrew Bible.* Forthcoming.

McGinn, Bernard. "Asceticism and Mysticism in Late Antiquity and the Early Middle Ages." In *Asceticism*, ed. V. Wimbush and R. Valantasis. New York: Oxford University Press, 1995.

McKnight, S. *A Light Among the Gentiles: Jewish Missionary Activity in the Second Temple Period.* Minneapolis: Fortress, 1991.

Meeks, Wayne. "A Nazi New Testament Reads His Bible." In *The Idea of Biblical Interpretation: Essays in Honor of James Kugel.* Leiden: Brill, 2004.

Melammed, Ezra Zion. *Bible Commentaries* [Hebrew]. Tel Aviv: Ha-Mekhira ha-Reshit, Yavne, 1975.

Meroz, Ronit. "Selections from Ephraim Penzari: Luria's Sermon in Jerusalem and the Kavvanah in Taking Food" [Hebrew]. *Jerusalem Studies in Jewish Thought* 10 (1992): 211–258.

Mihaly, Eugene. "A Rabbinic Defense of the Election of Israel: An Analysis of *Sifre* Deuteronomy 32:9." *Hebrew Union College Annual* 35 (1964): 103–143.

Miles, Margaret. *Word Made Flesh: A History of Christian Thought.* Oxford: Blackwell, 2004.

Milgrom, Jacob. *The JPS Torah Commentary: Numbers.* Philadelphia: Jewish Publication Society, 1990.

———. "Religious Conversion and the Revolt Model for the Formation of Israel." *Journal of Biblical Literature* 101 (1982): 169–176.

Miller, Patrick D. "'Moses My Servant': The Deuteronomic Portrait of Moses." In *A Song of Power and the Power of Song: Essays on the Book of Deuteronomy,* ed. Duane L. Christensen. Winona Lake, Ind.: Eisenbrauns, 1993.

Montrose, Louis. "Professing the Renaissance: The Poetics and Politics of Culture." In *The New Historicism,* ed. Harold Veeser. New York: Routledge, 1989.

Moore, Michael S. *The Balaam Traditions: Their Character and Development.* Atlanta, Ga.: Scholars, 1990.

Mopsik, Charles. "Genesis 1:26–27: L'Image de Dieu, le couple humain et le statut de la femme chez les premiers cabalists." In *Le sexe des âmes—Aléas de la différence sexuelle dans la Cabale.* Edition de l'eclat, 2004.

———. *Sex of the Soul: The Vicissitudes of Sexual Difference in Kabbala.* Los Angeles: Cherub, 2005.

———. *Le sexe des âmes: Aleas de la difference sexualle dans la Cabale.* Paris: Editions de L'Eclat, 2003.

Murray, Steven O. "The Will Not to Know: Accommodations of Male Homosexuality." In *Islamic Homosexualities: Culture, History, and Literature,* ed. S. O. Murray and W. Roscoe. New York: New York University Press, 1997.

Nabarro, Assaf. "'Tikkun': From Lurianic Kabbalah to Popular Culture." Ph.D. diss., Ben Gurion University of the Negev, 2006.

Nadler, Alan. "The War on Modernity of R. Hayyim Elazar Shapira of Munkacz." *Modern Judaism* 14 (1994): 233–264.

Naor, Bezalel. *Post-Sabbatean Sabbateanism.* Spring Valley, N.Y.: Orot, 1999.

Netanyahu, Ben-Zion. *The Marranos of Spain: From the Late Fourteenth to the Early Sixteenth Century, according to Contemporary Hebrew Sources.* New York: American Academy for Jewish Research, 1966.

———. *The Origins of the Inquisition in Fifteenth-Century Spain.* New York: New York Review Books, 1995.

Neusner, Jacob. *The Incarnation of God: The Character of Divinity in Formative Judaism.* Philadelphia: Fortress, 1988.

———. *Messiah in Context: Israel's History and Destiny in Formative Judaism.* Philadelphia: Fortress, 1984.

———. *Torah: From Scroll to Symbol in Formative Judaism.* Philadelphia: Fortress, 1985.

Neusner, Jacob, W. S. Green, and E. Frerichs, eds. *Judaisms and Their Messiahs at the Turn of the Christian Era.* Cambridge: Cambridge University Press, 1987.

Newman, L. I. *Jewish Influence on Christian Reform Movements.* New York: Columbia University Press, 1925.

Nickelsburg, George. "The Incarnation: Paul's Solution to the Universal Human Predicament." In *The Future of Early Christianity: Essays in Honor of Helmut Koester,* ed. Birger A. Pearson. Minneapolis: Fortress, 1991.

Nissinen, Martti. *Homoeroticism in the Biblical World: A Historical Perspective.* Minneapolis: Fortress, 1998.

Nock, Arthur Darby. *Conversion: The Old and the New in Religion from Alexander the Great to Augustine of Hippo.* Baltimore, Md.: Johns Hopkins Press, 1988.

Noonan, James T. *Contraception: A History of Its Treatment by the Catholic Theologians and Canonists.* Cambridge: Belknap Press of Harvard University, 1966.

Novak, David. *The Election of Israel.* Cambridge: Cambridge University Press, 1995.

———. *The Image of the Non-Jew in Judaism.* New York: Edwin Mellen, 1983.

———. *Jewish Social Ethics.* New York: Oxford University Press, 1992.

———. *Natural Law and Judaism.* Cambridge: Cambridge University Press, 1998.

———. "Religious Communities, Secular Society, and Sexuality: One Jewish Opinion." In *Sexual Orientation and Human Rights in American Religious Discourse,* ed. S. Olyan and M. Nussbaum. New York: Oxford University Press, 1998.

Novinsky, Anita. "Marranos and Marranism—a New Approach." *Jewish Studies* 40 (2000): 5–20.

Nussbaum, Martha. *Sex and Social Justice.* New York: Oxford University Press, 1999.

O'Collins, Gerald. *Incarnation.* New York: Continuum, 2003.

Olson, Dennis T. *Deuteronomy and the Death of Moses: A Theological Reading.* Minneapolis: Fortress, 1994.

Orsi, Robert. *Between Heaven and Earth.* Princeton, N.J.: Princeton University Press, 2004.

Pachter, Mordecai. "Clarifying the Terms *Katnut* and *Gadlut* in the Kabbala of the Ari and a History of Its Understanding in Hasidism" [Hebrew]. *Mekharei Yerushalayim* 10 (1992): 171–210.

———. *Me-Zefunot Safed.* Jerusalem: Zalman Shazar Institute, 1994.

Pagel, Elaine. *Adam, Eve, and the Serpent.* New York: Random House, 1988.

Pinson, Dov Ber. *Reincarnation and Judaism: The Journey of the Soul.* Northvale, N.J.: Jason Aronson, 1999.

Popkin, Richard. *Isaac La Peyrere: His Life, Work, and Influence.* Leiden: Brill, 1987.

———. "Jewish Christians and Christian Jews in the Seventeenth Century." In *Jewish Christians and Christian Jews: From the Renaissance to the Enlightenment,* ed. R. Popkin and G. Weiner. Dordrecht, The Netherlands: Kluwer Academic, 1994.

———. "The Marrano Theology of Isaac La Peyrere." *Studi Internazionali di Filosophia* 5 (1973): 97–126.

———. "Marranos, New Christians, and the Beginning of Anti-Trinitarianism" [Hebrew]. In *Jews and Conversos at the Time of the Expulsion,* ed. Y. T. Assis. Jerusalem: Zalman Shazar Center, 1999.

———. "R. Nathan Shapiro's Visit to Amsterdam in 1650." In *Dutch History* I (1984): 185–205.

Ra'ayon ha-Meshikhi be-Yisrael. Jerusalem: National Israel Academy of Sciences, 1982.

Rapoport, Chaim. *Judaism and Homosexuality: An Authentic Orthodox View.* London: Vallentine Mitchell, 2003.

Ravitzky, Aviezer. *Messianism, Zionism, and Religious Radicalism,* trans. Michael Swirsky and Jonathan Chipman. Chicago: University of Chicago Press, 1996.

Rawidowicz, Simon. "On Interpretation." In Rawidowicz, *Studies in Jewish Thought.* Philadelphia: JPS, 1974, pp. 45–80.

Raz-Krakotzkin, Amnon. "'Without Regard for External Considerations': The

Questions of Christianity in Scholem and Baer's Writings" [Hebrew]. *Ma-daʿey ha-Yahadut* 38 (1998): 73–96.

Redman, Barbara. "One God: Toward a Rapprochement of Orthodox Judaism and Christianity." *Journal of Ecumenical Studies* 31, nos. 3–4 (Summer/Fall 1994): 307–331.

Reed, Annette Yoshiko. "From Asael and Semihazah to Uzza, Azzah, and Azael: 3 Enoch 5 (#7–8) and Jewish Reception–History of 1 Enoch." *Jewish Studies Quarterly* 8, no. 2 (2001): 105–136.

Regev, Shaul. "The Attitude Toward the Conversos in Fifteenth- and Sixteenth-Century Jewish Thought." *Revue des études juives* 146 (1997): 117–134.

Reichert, Klaus. "Christian Kabbalah in the Seventeenth Century." In *The Christian Kabbalah*, ed. Joseph Dan. Cambridge: Harvard College Library, 1997.

Reinhard, Kenneth. "Universalism and the Jewish Exception: Lacan, Badiou, Rosenzweig." In *Umbr(a): A Journal of the Unconscious* (2005): 43–72.

Rembaum, Joel. "Medieval Jewish Criticism of the Christian Doctrine of Original Sin." *AJS Review* 7, no. 8 (1982/83): 353–382.

Rigney, Ann. "Literature and the Longing for History." In *Critical Self-Fashioning: Stephen Greenblatt and the New Historicism*, ed. Jurgen Pieters. Frankfurt am Main: Peter Lang, 1999.

Ripsman Eylon, Dina. *Reincarnation in Jewish Mysticism and Gnosticism*. Lewiston, N.Y.: Edwin Mellen, 2003.

Robinson, Ira. "Moses Cordovero and Kabbalistic Education in the Sixteenth Century." In *Judaism* 93 (1990): 155–162.

———. *Moses Cordovero's Introduction to Kabbalah: An Annotated Translation of His Or Neʿerav*. Hoboken, N.J.: Michael Scharf Publication Trust of Yeshiva University, 1994.

Roemer, Nils. *Jewish Scholarship and Culture in Nineteenth-Century Germany: Between History and Faith*. Madison: University of Wisconsin Press, 2005.

Rofe, Alexander. *"The Book of Balaam" (Numbers 22:2–24:25): A Study in Methods of Criticism and the History of Biblical Literature and Religion*. Jerusalem: Simor, 1979.

Rondert, Henri. *Original Sin: The Patristic and Theological Background*. Shannon, Ireland: Ecclesia, 1972.

Rosenblum, Joseph. *Conversion in Judaism: From the Biblical Period to the Present*. Cincinnati, Ohio: Hebrew Union College Press, 1978.

Rosenzweig, Franz. *Naharayim*, trans. Y. Amir. Jerusalem: Mosad Bialik, 1978.

Roth, Cecil. *A History of the Marranos*. Philadelphia: Jewish Publication Society, 1959.

———. "The Religion of the Marranos." *Jewish Quarterly Review* n.s. 12 (1931): 1–35.

Roth, Norman. *Conversion, Inquisition, and the Expulsion of the Jews from Spain*. Madison: University of Wisconsin Press, 1995.

———. "'Deal Gently with the Young Man': Love of Boys in Medieval Hebrew Poetry of Spain." *Speculum* 57, no. 1 (1982): 20–51.

———. "'Fawn of My Delights': Boy-Love in Hebrew and Arabic Verse." In *Sex in the Middle Ages*, ed. Joyce E. Salisbury. New York: Garland, 1991.

———. "Jewish ʿArabiyya and the Renaissance of Hebrew in Spain." *Journal of Semitic Studies* 28, no. 1 (Spring 1983): 63–84.

Rowson, Everett K. "Two Homoerotic Narratives from Mamluk Literature." In *Homoeroticism in Classical Arabic Literature*, ed. J. W. Wright Jr. and E. K. Rowson. New York: Columbia University Press, 1997.

Rubenstein, Jeffrey. *Talmudic Stories: Narrative, Art, Composition, and Culture*. Baltimore, Md.: Johns Hopkins University Press, 2003.

Ruderman, David. "Hope Against Hope: Jewish and Christian Messianic Expectations in the Late Middle Ages." In *Exile and Diaspora*, ed. A. Mirsky, A. Grossman, and Y. Kaplan. Jerusalem: Yad ben Tzvi, 1991.

———. *The World of a Renaissance Jew: The Life and Thought of Abraham ben Mordecai Farissol*. Cincinnati, Ohio: Hebrew Union College Press, 1981.

Sack, Brakha. *Sha'are ha-kabbala shel R. Moshe Cordovero*. Beer Sheva: Beer Sheva University Press, 1995.

Safran, Bezalel. "Rabbi Azriel and Nahmanides: Two Views of the Fall of Man." In *Rabbi Moses ben Nahman: Explorations in His Religious and Literary Virtuosity*, ed. I. Twersky. Cambridge: Harvard University Press, 1983.

Saggs, H. W. F. *The Encounter with the Divine in Mesopotamia and Israel*. Jordon Lectures in Comparative Religion. London: Athlone, 1978.

Said, Edward. *Orientalism*. New York: Vintage Books, 1979.

———. "Overlapping Territories: The World, the Text, and the Critic." In *Power, Politics, and Culture: Interviews with Edward Said*. Cambridge: Harvard University Press, 2006.

Saldarini, Anthony. *Matthew's Christian: Jewish Community*. Chicago: University of Chicago Press, 1994.

Sanders, E. P. *Paul and Palestinian Judaism*. London: SCM, 1977.

Sandmel, Samuel. *Philo of Alexandria: An Introduction*. New York: Oxford University Press, 1979.

Sarachek, Joseph. *The Doctrine of the Messiah in Medieval Jewish Literature*. New York: Hermon, 1968.

Sasportas, Jacob. *Zizat Novel Zvi*, ed. by Isaiah Tishby. Jerusalem: Mosad Bialik, 1954.

Satlow, Michael. "They Abused Him Like a Woman: Homoeroticism, Gender Blurring, and the Rabbis of Late Antiquity." *Journal of the History of Sexuality* 5 (1994): 1–25.

Schaefer, Peter. "Daughter, Sister, Bride, and Mother Images: Images of Femininity of God in Early Kabbala." *Journal of the American Academy of Religion* 68 (2000): 221–242.

———. *Mirror of His Beauty: Feminine Images of God from the Bible to Early Kabbala*. Princeton, N.J.: Princeton University Press, 2002.

Schechter, Solomon. "Safed in the Sixteenth Century: A City of Legists and Mystics." In *Studies in Judaism, Second Series*. Philadelphia: JPS, 1938.

Schechterman, Deborah. "The Doctrine of Original Sin and Maimonidean Interpretation in Jewish Philosophy of the Thirteenth and Fourteenth Centuries" [Hebrew]. *Da'at* 20 (Winter 1988): 65–90.

Scheindlin, Raymond P. "A Miniature Anthology of Medieval Hebrew Love Poems." *Prooftexts* 4 (1984): 269–300.

———. *Wine, Women, and Death*. Philadelphia: JPS, 1986.

Schneidau, Herbert. *Sacred Discontent*. Berkeley: University of California Press, 1977.

Scholem, Gershom. "The Beginnings of Christian Kabbala." In *The Christian Kabbala*, ed. Joseph Dan. Cambridge: Harvard College Library, 1997.

———. "The Concept of Kavvanah in the Early Kabbalah." *Studies in Jewish Thought: An Anthology of German-Jewish Scholarship*, ed. A. Jospe. Detroit: Wayne State University Press, 1981.

———. "The Concept of the Astral Body." In *On the Mystical Shape of the Godhead:*

Basic Concepts in Kabbala, trans. Joachim Neugroschel. New York: Schocken, 1991.

———. *The Establishment of Kabbala in Provence* [Hebrew], ed. Rivka Schatz. Akadamon, 1970.

———. "The Exile from Spain." [Hebrew]. In *Devarim be-Go*. Tel Aviv: Am Oved, 1976.

———. "The Feminine Element in the Divinity." In *On the Mystical Shape of the Godhead: Basic Concepts in Kabbala*, trans. Joachim Neugroschel. New York: Schocken, 1991.

———. "*Gilgul:* The Transmigration of Souls." In *On the Mystical Shape of the Godhead: Basic Concepts in Kabbala*, trans. Joachim Neugroschel. New York: Schocken, 1991.

———. "Good and Evil in the Kabbalah." In *On the Mystical Shape of the Godhead: Basic Concepts in Kabbala*, trans. Joachim Neugroschel. New York: Schocken, 1991.

———. *Heker Kabbalat R. Yizhak Ha-Cohen*. Jerusalem: Akadamon, 1934.

———. *Jewish Gnosticism, Merkabah Mysticism, and Talmudic Tradition*. New York: JTS, 1960.

———. *Kabbala*. New York: Dorsett, 1974.

———. "Le-Heker Torat Ha-Gilgul be-Kabbala be-Meah ha-Shelosh Esre." *Tarbiz* 16, no. 45 (1955): 135–150.

———. "The Life of R. Jacob Zemah, His Works and Writings" [Hebrew]. *Keriat Sefer* 26, no. 2 (1950): 185–194.

———. *Major Trends in Jewish Mysticism*. New York: Schocken, 1941.

———. "The Name of God and Linguistic Theory in Kabbala." *Diogenes* 79 (1982): 59–80.

———. *Perkei Yesod be-Havant ha-Kabbalah u' Semaleha* [Hebrew]. Jerusalem: Magnus, 1976.

———. "Reflections of Jewish Theology." In *Jews and Judaism in Crisis: Selected Essays*. New York: Schocken, 1976.

———. *Sabbatai Sevi: Mystical Messiah*, trans. R. J. Zwi Werblowsky. Princeton, N.J.: Princeton University Press, 1973.

———. "*Sitra Ahra:* Good and Evil in the Kabbalah." In *On the Mystical Shape of the Godhead*. Gershom Scholem. New York: Schocken Books, 1991.

———. "Toward an Understanding of the Messianic Idea in Judaism." In *The Messianic Idea in Judaism*. New York: Schocken, 1971.

———. "Tradition and New Creation in the Ritual of the Kabbalists." In *On the Kabbalah and Its Symbolism*. New York: Schocken, 1965.

———. "The Transmigration of Souls." In *The Mystical Shape of the Godhead*, ed. Joachim Neugroschel. New York: Schocken, 1991.

Schorsch, Ismar. *From Text to Context: The Turn to History in Modern Judaism*. Hanover, N.H.: Brandeis University Press, 1994.

Schwartz, Dov. *Ha-Raᶜayon ha-Meshikhi be-Hagot a-Yehudot b'Yemei ha-Benayim*. Ramat Gan: Bar Ilan, 1997.

Schweid, Eliezer. "The Rejection of the Diaspora in Zionist Thought: Two Approaches." In *The Essential Papers on Zionism*, ed. Yehuda Reinharz and Anita Shapira. New York: New York University Press, 1996.

Scroggs, Robin. *The New Testament and Homosexuality: Contextual Background for a Contemporary Debate*. Philadelphia: Fortress, 1983.

Segal, Alan. "The Costs of Proselytism and Conversion." In *Society of Biblical Literature 1988 Seminar Papers*. Atlanta, Ga.: Scholars, 1988.

———. "Messianic and Conversion: Outline for a New Approach." In *The Messiah*, ed. James Charlesworth. Minneapolis: Fortress, 1987.

———. *Paul the Convert: The Apostolate and Apostasy of Saul the Pharisee*. New Haven, Conn.: Yale University Press, 1992.

———. "The Sacrifice of Isaac in Early Judaism and Christianity." In *The Other Judaisms of Late Antiquity*. Atlanta, Ga.: Scholars, 1987.

———. *Two Powers in Heaven*. Leiden: Brill, 1977.

Shapiro, Hayyim Elazar. *Darkei Hayyim v Shalom*. Jerusalem, 1970.

Sharot, Stephen. *Messianism, Mysticism, and Magic*. Chapel Hill: University of North Carolina Press, 1982.

Shatz-Uffenheimer, Rivka. *Hasidut Ke-Mystica*. Jerusalem: Magnus, 1968.

Shaw, Stanford. *The Jews of the Ottoman Empire and the Turkish Republic*. New York: New York University Press, 1991.

Shekalim, Rami. *Torat Ha-Nefesh v Ha-Gilgul be-Reshit ha-Kabbala*. Tel Aviv: Rubin Moss, 1998.

Sherwin, Byron L. "Who Do You Say That I Am?" In *Jesus through Jewish Eyes*, ed. Beatrice Bruteau. New York: Orbis Books, 2001.

Shiffman, Lawrence. "At the Crossroads: Tannaitic Perspectives on the Jewish Christian Schism." In *Jewish and Christian Self-Definition, Volume Two: Aspects of Judaism in the Greco-Roman Period*, ed. E. P. Saunders. Philadelphia: JPS, 1981.

———. "Messianism and Apocalypticism in Rabbinic Texts." Forthcoming.

Shinn, Larry, ed. *In Search of the Divine*. New York: Paragon House, 1987.

Shirmann, Hayyim. "The Ephebe in Medieval Hebrew Poetry." *Sefarad* 15 (1955): 55–68.

Shohar, Azriel. "The Jews in Jerusalem in the Eighteenth Century" [Hebrew]. *Zion* 1 (1936): 377–410.

Sicroff, Albert.A. "The Marranos—Forced Converts or Apostates." *Midstream* 12, no. 8 (1966): 71–75.

Silver, Abba Hillel. *A History of Messianic Speculation in Israel*. New York: Macmillan, 1927.

Sinn, David C. "Christianity and Ethnicity in the Gospel of Matthew." In *Ethnicity in the Bible*, ed. Mark Brett. Leiden: Brill, 2002.

Smalley, Beryl. *The Study of the Bible in the Middle Ages*. South Bend, Ind.: University of Notre Dame Press, 1964.

Smith, Jonathan Z. "Scriptures and Histories." In *Method and Theory on the Study of Religion* 4 (1992): 104, 105.

———. *To Take Place: Toward Theory in Ritual*. Chicago: University of Chicago Press, 1987.

———. "What a Difference a Difference Makes." In *To See Ourselves as Others See Us*, ed. by J. Neusner and E. Frerichs. Chico, Calif.: Scholars, 1985.

Smolar, Leivy, and Moshe Aberbach. "The Golden Calf Episode in Postbiblical Literature." *Hebrew Union College Annual* 39 (1968): 91–116.

Sofer, Jehodeda. "Sodomy in the Law of Muslim States." In *Sexuality and Eroticism among Males in Moslem Societies*, ed. A. Schmitt and J. Sofer. New York: Harworth, 1992.

Soloveitchik, Haym. "Religious Law and Change: The Medieval Ashkenazic Example." *AJS Review* 12, no. 2 (Fall 1987): 205–221.

Sonnet, Jan-Pierre. *The Book within the Book: Writing in Deuteronomy*. Leiden: Brill, 1997.

Stanislawski, Michael. "The Yiddish *Shevet Yehuda*: A Study in the Ashkenization of a Spanish-Jewish Classic." In *Jewish History and Jewish Memory*. Boston: University Press of New England, 1998.

Stendhal, Krister. "The Apostle Paul and the Introspective Conscience of the West." *Harvard Theological Review* (1963): 199–215.

———. *Paul among Jews and Gentiles*. London: SCM, 1977.

Stern, David. "*Imitatio Hominus:* Anthropomorphism and the Character(s) of God in Rabbinic Literature." *Prooftexts* 12 (1992): 151–174.

———. *Parables in Midrash: Narrative and Exegesis in Rabbinic Literature*. Cambridge: Harvard University Press, 1991.

Stern, Joseph. "Maimonides on the Circumcision and the Unity of God." In *The Midrashic Imagination: Jewish Exegesis, Thought, and History*, ed. Michael Fishbane. Albany, N.Y.: SUNY Press, 1993.

Stern, Sacha. *Jewish Identity in Early Rabbinic Writings*. Leiden: Brill, 1994.

Stuckenbrick, Loren T. "The 'Angels' and 'Giants' of Genesis 6:1–4 in Second and Third Century BCE Jewish Interpretation: Reflections on the Posture of Early Apocalyptic Traditions." *Dead Sea Discoveries* 7, no. 3 (2000): 354–377.

Sweeney, Marvin. *Josiah: The Lost Messiah of Israel*. New York: Oxford University Press, 2001.

Swidler, Arlene, ed. *Homosexuality and World Religions*. Valley Forge, Pa.: Trinity Press International, 1993.

Talmon, S. "Typen der Messiaserwartung un die Zeitensende." In *Probleme biblischer Theologie*, ed. H. W. Wolf. Munich: Kaiser, 1971.

Tamar, David. *Aliyah ve Hityashvut b'Erez Yisrael b'Meah Ha-Shishit*. Jerusalem: Reuven Moss, 1993.

———. "The Ari and Vital as Messiah ben Joseph" [Hebrew]. In *Mekharim b'Toldot ha-Yehudim b'Erez Yisrael u b'Italia*. Jerusalem: Reuven Mass, 1973.

———. "An Epistle from Safed Regarding the Ten Tribes—Dated Either 1526 or 1625" [Hebrew]. *Sefunot* 6 (1962): 305–310.

———. *Mekharim be-Toldot ha-Yehudim be-Erez Yisrael u be-Italia*. Jerusalem: Rubin Mass, 1973.

———. "The [Messianic] Expectations in Italy for the Year of Redemption in 1575" [Hebrew]. In *Mekharim be-Toldot ha-Yehudim be-Erez Yisrael u be-Italia*. Jerusalem: Rubin Mass, 1973.

Taubes, Jacob. *The Political Theology of Paul*. Stanford, Calif.: Stanford University Press, 2004.

Tennant, F. R. *The Sources of the Doctrine of the Fall and Original Sin*. New York: Schocken Books, 1903.

Thomasset C., and Jacquart, D. *Sexuality and Medicine in the Middle Ages*. Princeton, N.J.: Princeton University Press, 1988.

Thunberg, Lars. "The Human Person as Image of God." In *Christian Spirituality*, ed. B. McGinn and J. Meyendorff. New York: Crossroads, 1995.

Thurston, Thomas. "Leviticus 18:22 and the Prohibition of Homosexual Acts." In *Homophobia and the Judeo-Christian Tradition*, ed. M. L. Stemmeler and J. M. Clark. Dallas, Tex.: Monument, 1990.

Tishby, Isaiah. "God, Torah, Israel Are One" [Hebrew]. *Keriat Sefer* 50 (1975): 668–674.

———. *Messianism in the Time of the Expulsion from Spain and Portugal* [Hebrew]. Jerusalem: Zalman Shazar Center, 1985.

———. *Mishnat ha-Zohar*. 2 vols. Jerusalem: Mossad Bialik, 1957.

———. "Rabbi Moses Cordovero as He Appears in the Treatise of Rabbi Mordecai Dato" [Hebrew]. *Sefunot* 7 (1963).

———. *Torat Ha-Ra v Ha-Kelippah be Kabbalat ha-Ari.* Jerusalem: Magnes, 1942, rpt. 1991.

———. *Wisdom of the Zohar: An Anthology of Texts,* trans. David Goldstein. New York: Oxford University Press, 1989.

Touitou, Elazar. "Peshat and Apologetics in the Commentary of Rashbam in the Story of Moshe in the Torah" [Hebrew]. *Tarbiz* 51 (1982): 227–238.

Twersky, Isadore. "Talmudists, Philosophers, Kabbalists: The Quest for Spirituality in the Sixteenth Century." In *Jewish Thought in the Sixteenth Century,* ed. Bernard Cooperman. Cambridge: Harvard University Press, 1983.

Urbach, Efrayim. "Askesis and Suffering in Talmudic and Midrashic Sources" [Hebrew]. In *Yizhak F. Baer Jubilee Volume.* S. Baron and S. Ettinger, eds. Jerusalem: He-Hevral Ha-historit ha-Yisraelit, 1960.

———. *Hazal.* Jerusalem: Magnes, 1976.

———. "Homilies of the Sages on Gentile Prophecy and on the Episode of Balaam." In *Me-Olamot shel Hokhamim* [Hebrew]. Jerusalem: Magnes, 1988.

———. "Self-Isolation or Self-Affirmation in Judaism in the First Three Centuries: Theory and Practice." In *Jewish and Christian Self-Definition, Volume Two: Aspects of Judaism in the Greco-Roman Period,* ed. E. P. Saunders. Philadelphia: JPS, 1981.

———. "When Did Prophecy Cease?" [Hebrew]. *Tarbiz* 17 (1946): 1–11.

Usque, Samuel. *Consolation for the Tribulations of Israel,* trans. Martin A. Cohen. Philadelphia: JPS, 1965.

Vermes, Geza. *The Changing Faces of Jesus.* New York: Viking Books, 2001.

———. *Scripture and Tradition: Haggadic Studies.* Leiden: Brill, 1973.

Wafer, Jim. "Muhammad and Male Homosexuality." In *Islamic Homosexualities: Culture, History, and Literature,* ed. S. O. Murray and W. Roscoe. New York: New York University Press, 1997.

Walsh, Jerome. "Leviticus 18:22 and 20:13: Who Is Doing What to Whom?" *Journal of Biblical Literature* 120, no. 2 (2001): 201–209.

Weinfeld, Moshe. *Deuteronomy and the Deuteronomic School.* Oxford: Clarendon, 1972.

———. "Deuteronomy and the Present State of Inquiry." In *A Song of Power and the Power of Song: Essays on the Book of Deuteronomy,* ed. Duane L. Chrsitensen. Winona Lake, Ind.: Eisenbrauns, 1993.

Weitzman, Steven. "Sensory Reform in Deuteronomy." In *Religion and the Self in Late Antiquity,* ed. D. Brakke, M. Satlow, and S. Weitzman. Bloomington: Indiana University Press, 2005.

Werblowsky, R. J. Z. *Joseph Karo: Lawyer and Mystic.* New York: Oxford University Press, 1962.

———. "Tikkunei Tefilot le-Rav Shlomo ha-Levi Alkabetz." *Sefunot* 6 (1962): 135–182.

Wikan, Unni. "Man becomes Woman: Transsexualism in Oman as a Key to Gender Roles." *Man* (new series) 12 (1977): 304–319.

Wildavsky, Aaron. *The Nursing Father: Moses as Political Leader.* Birmingham: University of Alabama Press, 1984.

Wiley, Tatha. *Original Sin: Origins, Developments, Contemporary Meanings.* New York: Paulist, 2002.

Williams, N. P. *The Ideas of the Fall and of Original Sin.* London: Longmans Green, 1927.

Wirszubski, Chaim. *Pico della Mirandola's Encounter with Jewish Mysticism.* Cambridge: Harvard University Press, 1989.

Wolfson, Elliot R. *Abraham Abulafia—Kabbalist and Prophet.* Los Angeles: Cherub, 2000.

———. "Anthropomorphic Imagery and Letter Symbolism in the Zohar" [Hebrew]. *Jerusalem Studies in Jewish Thought* 8 (1989): 147–181.

———. "Beautiful Maiden without Eyes: *Peshat* and *Drash* in Zohar Hermeneutics." In *The Midrashic Imagination,* ed. Michael Fishbane. Albany, N.Y.: SUNY Press, 1993.

———. "Beyond Good and Evil: Hypernomianism, Transmorality, and Kabbalistic Ethics." In *Crossing Boundaries: Essays on the Ethical Status of Mysticism,* ed. G. W. Barnard and J. J. Kriplal. New York: Seven Bridges, 2001.

———. "The Body in the Text: A Kabbalistic Theory of Embodiment." *The Jewish Quarterly Review* 95, no. 3 (2005): 479–500.

———. *Circle in the Square.* Albany, N.Y.: SUNY Press, 1995.

———. "Circumcision and the Divine Name: A Study in the Transmission of Esoteric Doctrine." *Jewish Quarterly Review* 78 (1987): 77–112.

———. "Circumcision, Vision of God, and Textual Interpretation: From Midrashic Trope to Mystical Symbol." Reprinted in *The Essential Kabbala,* ed. Lawrence Fine. New York: New York University Press, 1995.

———. "Crossing Gender Boundaries in Kabbalistic Myth and Ritual." In *Circle in the Square.* Albany, N.Y.: SUNY Press, 1995.

———. "Divine Suffering and the Hermeneutics of Reading: Philosophical Reflections on Lurianic Mythology." In *Suffering Religion,* ed. R. Gibbs and E. R. Wolfson. London: Routledge, 2002.

———. "The Engenderment of Messianic Politics." In *Toward the Millennium: Messianic Expectations from the Bible to Waco,* Studies in the History of Religions, vol. 77, ed. Peter Schafer and Mark R. Cohen. Leiden: Brill, 1998.

———. "Eunuchs Who Keep the Sabbath: Becoming Male and the Ascetic Ideal in Thirteenth-Century Jewish Mysticism." In *Becoming Male in the Middle Ages,* ed. J. J. Cohen and B. Wheeler. New York: Garland, 1997.

———. "Fore/giveness on the Way: Nesting in the Womb of Response." In *Luminal Darkness.* Madison: University of Wisconsin Press, 2007.

———. "Gender and Heresy in the Study of Kabbala" [Hebrew]. *Kabbala: Journal for the Study of Jewish Mystical Texts* 6 (2001): 231–262.

———. "Iconic Visualization and the Imaginal Body of God: The Role of Intention in the Rabbinic Concept of Prayer." *Modern Theology* 12, no. 2 (1996): 137–162.

———. "The Image of Jacob Engraved upon the Throne: Further Reflections on the Esoteric Doctrine of the German Pietists." In *Along the Path: Studies in Kabbalistic Myth, Symbolism, and Hermeneutics.* Albany, N.Y.: SUNY Press, 1995.

———. "Images of God's Feet: Some Observations on the Divine Body in Judaism." In *People of the Body: Jews and Judaism from an Embodied Perspective,* ed. Howard Eilberg-Schwartz. Albany, N.Y.: SUNY Press, 1992.

———. "The Influence of the ARI on the SHLAH" [Hebrew]. *Jerusalem Studies in Jewish Thought* 10 (1992): 423–449.

———. "Judaism and Incarnation: The Imaginal Body of God." In *Christianity in Jewish Terms,* ed. Tikva Frymer-Kensky, David Novak, Peter Ochs, Sandmel, and Michael A. Signer. Boulder, Colo.: Westview, 2000.

———. *Language, Eros, Being: Kabbalistic Hermeneutics and Poetic Imagination.* New York: Fordham University Press, 2005.

———. "Language, Secrecy and the Mysteries of Law: Theurgy and the Christian Kabbala of Johannes Reuchlin." *Kabbala* 13 (2005).

——. "The Left Contained in the Right: A Study in Zoharic Hermeneutics."
AJS Review 11 (1986): 27–52.
——. "Martyrdom, Eroticism, and Asceticism in Twelfth-Century Ashkenazi
Piety." In *Jews and Christians in Twelfth-Century Europe*, ed. M. A. Signer, J. H.
Van Enger. South Bend, Ind.: University of Notre Dame Press, 2001.
——. "Messianism in the Christian Kabbala of Johann Kemper." In *Millenari-
anism and Messianism in Early Modern European Culture*, ed. M. Goldish and R.
Popkin. Dordrecht, The Netherlands: Kluwer Academic, 2001.
——. "The Mystical Experience of Torah Study in German Pietism." *The Jew-
ish Quarterly Review* 84, no. 1 (July 1993): 43–77.
——. "Ontology, Alterity, and Kabbalistic Anthropology." *Exemplaria* 12
(2000): 129–155.
——. *Pathwings*. Barrytown, N.Y.: Barrytown/Station Hill, 2004.
——. *Through a Speculum that Shines*. Princeton, N.J.: Princeton University
Press, 1995.
——. *Venturing Beyond—Limits of Law and Laws of Limit: Engendering a Kabbalis-
tic Ethos*. New York: Oxford University Press, 2006.
——. "Weeping, Death, and Spiritual Ascent in Sixteenth-Century Jewish
Mysticism." In *Death Ecstasy and Other Worldly Journeys*, ed. John Collins and
Michael Fishbane. Albany, N.Y.: SUNY Press, 1995.
Wright, J. W. "Masculine Allusion and the Structure of Satire." In *Homoeroticism
in Classical Arab Literature*, ed. J. W. Wright and Everett K. Rowson. New York:
Columbia University Press, 1997.
Wyschogrod, Michael. *The Body of Faith: God and the People Israel*. Lanham, Md.:
Rowman & Littlefield, 1996.
——. "Incarnation of God's Indwelling in Israel." In *Abraham's Promise: Jewish
and Jewish-Christian Relations*, ed. R. Kendall Soulen. Grand Rapids, Mich.:
Eerdmans, 2000.
——. "A Jewish Perspective on Incarnation." *Modern Theology* 12, no. 2 (1996):
195–209.
Yeago, David S. "Jesus of Nazareth and Cosmic Redemption: The Relevance of
St. Maximus the Confessor." *Modern Theology* 12 (April 1996): 163–193.
Yerushalmi, Yosef Hayyim. "Assimilation and Racial Anti-Semitism: The Ibe-
rian and the German Models." *Leo Baeck Memorial Lecture* 26 (1982).
——. *From Spanish Court to Italian Ghetto: Isaac Cardoso*. New York: Columbia
University Press, 1971.
——. "The Inquisition and the Jews of France in the Time of Bernard Gui."
Harvard Theological Review 63 (1970): 317–376.
Yosha, Nissim. "The Lurianic Concept of Prophecy in the Writings of Abraham
ha-Cohen Herrera." *Mekherei Yerushalayim* 10 (1992): 389–422.
——. *Myth and Metaphor—Abraham Cohen Herrera's Philosophic Interpretation of
Lurianic Kabbalah*. Jerusalem: Magnes, 1994.
Yovel, Yirmiyahu. "The New Otherness: Marrano Dualities in the First Genera-
tion." In *The 1999 Swig Lecture*, Swig Judaic Studies Program, University of
San Francisco, 1999. http://www.usfca.edu/judaicstudies/yovel.html.
Yuval, Israel Jacob. "Jews and Christians in the Middle Ages: Shared Myths, Com-
mon Language." In *Demonizing the Other: Anti-Semitism, Racism and Xenophobia*,
ed. Robert S. Wistrich. Chur, Switzerland: Harwood Academic, 1999.
——. *"Two Nations in Your Womb": Perception of Jews and Christians in the Middle
Ages*. Berkeley: University of California Press, 2003.
Zizek, Slavoj. *The Puppet and the Dwarf*. Cambridge, Mass.: MIT Press, 2003.

INDEX

SHAUL MAGID is Jay and Jeannie Schottenstein Chair in Jewish Studies and Professor in Religious Studies at Indiana University, Bloomington.